AMERICAN BUSINESS
ABROAD

AMERICAN BUSINESS ABROAD

Ford on Six Continents

Mira Wilkins & Frank Ernest Hill
with an introduction by Allan Nevins

1964
Wayne State University Press
Detroit

Preface

The hero of Jules Verne's *Around the World in Eighty Days* faced momentous obstacles; the authors of *American Business Abroad* recognized from the beginning of their project that they too must encircle the earth and that the task would occupy not a mere eighty but at least eight hundred days. It was a daunting assignment not only in geographical range and the varieties of national conditions to be encountered, but it must also take account of numerous dramatic and even violent changes in government, industry, and business which have marked the last sixty years.

We could not have undertaken the assignment "cold." The chief factor which made its accomplishment a possibility was that both of us had already spent some years studying automotive history, a part of that time on overseas activities. Consequently we started with a rather full background of general and even of particular information and could proceed from that point of vantage.

Important in the initiation of the project was the role of Henry E. Edmunds, Director of Research and Information for the Ford Motor Company and the head of the Ford Archives. Mr. Edmunds encouraged us to lay the project before the Ford Fund, which subsidizes activity it considers in the public interest. The Fund made a generous grant to Columbia University, and we have worked as salaried employees of the university. After two years, the Ford Fund made a supplementary contribution to the university. We have been accountable only to Columbia University. We have also enjoyed the advice and constructive criticism of Allan Nevins, an authority in business, as well as in general history, and co-author with Mr. Hill of the three-volume account of the Ford Motor Company.

Once the project was launched, Ford officials gave us their valuable cooperation. Mr. Edmunds, with Richard Ruddell, Winthrop Sears, and Alice Benn of his staff, were constantly helpful. So were officials of the

Ford International Division, particularly Tom Lilley, W. McKee, M. J. O'Neill, John Mayhew and J. Wilner Sundelson. Miss Charlene Ferrill and Mrs. Ruth Baker were of great aid in locating materials; while such Ford officials as the Secretary Charles J. Fellrath, William J. Mitchel and David C. Duncan extended important assistance. The International Division opened to us the doors of Ford companies throughout the world. (For details of persons interviewed and materials made available, see the Bibliographical Essay.) It would be impossible to thank here the managers, public relations officers, and employees of all the Ford companies abroad. Especially helpful were Sir Patrick Hennessy in England and his associates, R. M. Sale in Canada (Canada controls all Ford companies in British Commonwealth territory outside Britain and the Mediterranean area), and Humberto Monteiro in Brazil; but courtesy and aid were extended everywhere. We are particularly appreciative of the assistance of William Patten and Colin Bray in England (who arranged meetings and provided transportation over a period of months) and of F. G. Batters in Canada, whose advice was of the highest value.

In the preparation of the final manuscript we were fortunate to have had the aid of Miss Elizabeth Rumics, who not only did a superlative job of typing but who noted errors and inconsistencies and helped to set up the more difficult of the appendices.

In writing the book we found ourselves introduced to the methods of transacting business in all parts of the world. While our chief concern was with Ford, we were constantly obliged to consider its competitors. This was true even in the early 1900's and continued to be true as the century advanced. But the types of competition changed drastically, especially with the adoption by most foreign manufacturers of Ford's production methods and with the development of the small economical European cars, such as the Morris and the Austin, the Renault and the Citroën, the Fiat, the Opel and the Volkswagen.

We have sought to paint a true and vivid picture of the chief international automotive activities of the last sixty years. We hope we have been able to marry an exciting story with important information about foreign enterprises. If we have failed to do so, the fault lies in us and not in the available material, which has been colorful, informative, and abundant.

M.W.

F.E.H.

New York, June, 1963.

Contents

Contents

Illustrations

Introduction

by Allan Nevins

It was counted a proud achievement when the first American manufactures—the Singer sewing-machines, the Yale locks, the McCormick reapers and mowers—were exported in quantity to Europe. The planting of American branch factories in foreign lands, a necessary subsequent step for reducing transportation costs, avoiding tariffs or other restrictions on trade and cultivating the good will of peoples, was a much tardier development. It was not until after 1900 that such branches became numerous. Since the Second World War, however, thousands of American firms have created important interests overseas, and more than 3,300 were by 1961 doing business abroad through branches, subsidiaries or other forms of investment.

This expansion deserves far more study than it has received. Most Americans know something about the adventures of individual figures abroad, from Benjamin Franklin and Washington Irving to Dwight D. Eisenhower and T. S. Eliot; but they are ill-informed upon the record of our great economic units.

This book is the first full-length history of the activities of an American company which early became a multi-national enterprise and swiftly grew so successful that its name was (and is) familiar to every child on six continents. The story is of direct importance to the many men and women who, as corporation employees, stockholders, salesmen, or government officers, have a material stake in the way in which our companies are shaping their overseas policies. A representative history of foreign achievements in steel, or oil, or soap, or razor blades, or airplanes can teach many practical lessons. But Ford history abroad is so varied in character and sweeping in scope that it should also be fascinating to the general reader.

At first the Ford Motor Company was a mere exporter of cars. In rapid succession it became the operator of sales branches in foreign lands, the founder of large concerns importing and assembling the American product, the converter of such concerns into manufactories making complete cars, trucks, and tractors on the American model, and finally the owner of still larger factories making (as in Britain, France, and Germany) automotive vehicles completely foreign in design—the Anglia, Prefect, Consul, Vedette, and Taunus—which in time were imported in considerable numbers into the United States.

In the course of its activities the Ford Motor Company has encountered every conceivable obstacle. It has had to conquer alien prejudice and condescension; waves of nationalism expressed in tariff walls, unfair taxes, quota restrictions, and government decrees; special requirements growing out of geography, climate, and unpredictable variations in taste; and all the vicissitudes of both hot war and cold war. In some countries, such as Italy under Mussolini and Japan in the same era, it became virtually or wholly impossible for any foreign automotive company to manufacture at all. Great Britain, on the contrary, permitted the free expansion of the Ford plant near Manchester and, during the 1930's, of the admirably planned and fully-equipped factory at Dagenham and reaped invaluable benefits during both world wars. In the postwar period such ambitious countries as Brazil, Argentina, and Australia allowed foreign-owned automotive plants to operate but only in each case on the condition that any vehicles produced be not merely assembled but manufactured within the nation. This book interestingly shows how Ford experience overseas mirrored a wide variety of national demands and responded to a long gamut of world changes over the years. It is an effective contribution to twentieth century economic history from Denmark to Peru, from the days of Theodore Roosevelt to those of Sir Winston Churchill.

The book also depicts a remarkable panel of foreign industrial leaders who contributed their talents and energy to the growth of Ford enterprise overseas. Chief among them stand two remarkable Britons. Percival L. D. Perry, later Baron Perry of Stock-Harvard, and Sir Patrick Hennessy both possessed the highest business gifts, which were matched by their integrity, public spirit, and personal charm. Perry became a favorite of Henry Ford and other executives in Dearborn, while Hennessy won the confidence of Edsel Ford and C. E. Sorensen and later that of Henry Ford II and his brilliant associates.

Two other executives, Maurice Dollfus in France, a banker turned manufacturer, and Dr. Heinrich Albert in Germany, served ably: Albert in more favorable circumstances might have become a statesman of eminence. Canada, Scandinavia, the Low Countries, and Latin America also gave the Ford enterprises men of ability and of richly interesting personalities. The authors have by no means neglected the human element in their story. They have done full justice to the men in Dearborn who worked with Perry, Dollfus, and the other leaders abroad and who constantly advised and directed them: Edsel Ford, Charles E. Sorensen, and Henry Ford II, Graeme Howard, Tom Lilley, and John Bugas.

Dr. Wilkins and Mr. Hill have travelled widely in Europe, Canada, and Latin America to assemble the materials for their account. They used intensively the huge store of documents in the Ford Archives in Dearborn. All available sources were made accessible to them. They brought to their task the knowledge of Ford methods and policies which they had gained in work upon the three-volume history of the Ford Motor Company published by Mr. Hill and myself from 1954 to 1963.

As the most complete and scholarly account of the foreign activities of a great American industrial corporation yet written, this book claims the careful attention of all economists, historians, and business specialists; as a tale full of dramatic incidents and arresting personalities, and impressive in its narration of multiform achievement which conduced to the closer understanding of nations and the greater welfare of mankind, it merits a wide reading by the general public.

New York, June 1963.

1
First Venture

James Couzens, secretary of the Ford Motor Company, reported to its stockholders at the first annual meeting on October 15, 1903 that in the four months of its existence the company showed a clear profit of $36,957. This was little short of fabulous, for it exceeded the entire cash investment made at and since the launching of the firm. That very day the stockholders urged their directors to "take necessary steps to obtain foreign business."

Couzens had already moved in that direction. As early as July he had appointed a Canadian distributor—the Canada Cycle and Motor Company Ltd. of Toronto—and the sixth Ford car built had been shipped to that agent on August 1. In September Couzens and Henry Ford had selected R. M. Lockwood to handle all other marketing abroad.

These actions and that of the stockholders in October had been taken in the face of grave difficulties. The company leaders—Henry Ford, who had developed the car, John F. and Horace E. Dodge, owners of the factory that produced its chassis, and Alex Y. Malcomson, the coal merchant who had furnished the chief propulsive force for launching the firm—must all have been aware, as Couzens was, that early in July the undertaking had barely tipped the scales from failure to success. They still faced the prospect of a suit by a $70,000,000 corporation which held the Selden patent, and proposed at worst to forbid Ford to manufacture at all, and at best to demand a fee for every car produced!

But the Ford group looked resolutely to the future. They had shipped 195 machines. Production was rising, and an increasing number of dealers were selling their car. Before their company was two months old it had exported. Now, a day before its fourth month of existence, despite the threat of legal strangulation, they had firmly committed themselves to enter their products in the markets of the world.[1]

2

In its first year the Ford Motor Company did not occupy a preëminent position among the automotive concerns of the United States. There were more than a hundred such manufacturers in this country, making steam and electric as well as gasoline vehicles, for it was by no means certain that the latter type would predominate. Among these were a number whose names survive a half century later: the Oldsmobile, the Packard, the Rambler, the Buick, and the Cadillac. The earlier leaders, the Duryea (which in September 1893 became the first American gasoline-propelled vehicle to make a verified run) and the Haynes-Apperson (introduced in 1895) had not fulfilled their first promise, and the Winton, produced since 1896, while still being manufactured, probably depended a great deal on its maker's prominence as a racer. In sales the Olds Motor Company in 1903 was obviously king, marketing about 4000 cars a year, or more than six times the 658 units produced by the Ford firm from June 1903 to April 1904. The Cadillac Automobile Company, founded August 22, 1902, had sold 1895 units in its first year of operation.

The Ford commitment was an act of faith—faith in its capacity to forge ahead in competition but even more faith in the automobile. Henry Ford, particularly, but also Malcomson, the Dodges, and Couzens were aware of participating in a new and expanding industry. They were convinced that the motor car would revolutionize existing methods of transportation. "Horses will be driven from the land," a sanguine Henry Ford had told a reporter as early as February 1900. Probably he and his associates did not see their work as a more dramatic change than those already effected by the steamboat and the railroad, but they were convinced that it would create new conditions and with them new markets. And as men bought automobiles increasingly, those who produced them would surely win rewards (they could not guess that these would rival the fortunes of Croesus or Rockefeller). This implicit faith in the future of the motor car undoubtedly influenced them to plan for a world market.[2]

At the same time the product itself and the men in charge of manufacture gave the stockholders confidence. The first 2-cylinder Model A represented an advance over the Oldsmobile and the Cadillac, both 1-cylinder cars. Its selling price was higher than the Oldsmobile's—$750 at first for the Model A runabout and $850 for the tonneau (with additional rear seat), while the Oldsmobile cost $650. But Ford offered much more than his rivals. His Model A was light, dependable by existing standards, and easy to manufacture; moreover, he and his assistant, C. Harold Wills, were sure that they could improve the quality of their car, simplify it, and lower the price.

Undoubtedly they were also aware of what was happening at the Olds Motor Company. Olds favored continuing the high-volume, cheap model he had developed, which then outsold any other in the world. But S. L. Smith, his principal backer, had two sons who wanted to enter the "good" field, as they put it. "You mean the high-price field," Olds corrected them, and threatened to go. They accepted his resignation and he left the company in 1903. His departure meant that Ford would soon cease to have serious competition from the Oldsmobile, for although it sold 5000 cars in 1904, output then dropped sharply.[3]

As for the Selden patent, Ralzemond A. Parker, one of the best patent attorneys in the United States, assured the Ford group that they could successfully defy it, and by taunting advertisements they had practically forced the holders, the Association of Licensed Automobile Manufacturers, to sue them. Some of them must have had second thoughts later, for the menace of the suit was to hang over the new company for eight long years.[4]

Ford's chief obstacle in developing the car he favored lay in his own company; and to understand the situation we must consider his earlier career and the attitudes of his associates.

Ford had been born in Dearborn township on the outskirts of the rapidly growing town of Detroit on July 30, 1863. Son of an Irish immigrant farmer, he felt as a boy that "considering the results there was always too much work on the place." He showed an early interest in mechanics, and even as a youth dreamed of lightening the drudgery of agricultural work with machinery. After spending some years as an industrial apprentice, and several more as a skilled workman, in 1891 he became night engineer for the Edison Illuminating Company in Detroit. By this time he had a plan for constructing "a horseless carriage."

While he rose to the post of chief engineer for Edison he studied, observed the products of others, and at length on the early morning of June 4, 1896 drove his first completed car about the streets of Detroit. In comparison with many other experimental machines of that day, its outstanding merit was its low weight. Ford had seen an imported Benz

3

in New York in 1895 and felt that it was much too heavy. "I was working for lightness," he later recalled, and his quadricycle, as he termed
the little car, more than met this objective. Indeed, he himself soon perceived that it was not rugged enough, sold it, and built other cars.

His third machine inspired the formation of the Detroit Automobile
Company, and he left Edison Illuminating, declining an offer to become
its superintendent, for the hazardous post of engineer and stockholder
in the motor car concern. It failed.

But Ford then designed a racer and in 1901 achieved notice by driving it himself in competition with Alexander Winton, the foremost
American pilot of speedy automobiles, and besting his rival. Soon backers helped him form the Henry Ford Company, which he left in less
than four months. He then constructed two more successful racing cars.[5]

Now Ford began to build a "family horse" and engaged the interest
of Alex Y. Malcomson, a dynamic coal merchant, who found the money
to complete this "horse" and organize a company. On June 16, 1903, the
Ford Motor Company came into existence, with an authorized capital
of $150,000 of which only 1,000 shares (at a par value of $100 each) were
issued. Ford and Malcomson each received $25,500 worth of stock in
return for the car and some patents; other stock was allotted for services
rendered and goods supplied; and only $29,500 worth was sold for cash.
Of the initial stockholders, John S. Gray was Malcomson's uncle, Vernon
C. Fry, his cousin, John Anderson and Horace H. Rackham, his lawyers.
Charles H. Bennett of the Daisy Air Rifle Company, Charles J. Wood-
all, and Albert Strelow had also been persuaded by Malcomson to invest.
But Malcomson's most important gift to the new company was his assistant, James Couzens, who likewise became a stockholder. Ford seems
to have been responsible for bringing John F. and Horace E. Dodge in
as shareholders—and as the company's main supplier.

The Dodges owned one of the best machine shops in the Middle
West, employing several hundred men and manufacturing bicycles,
steam launches, engines, and various machine parts. When in 1903 Ford
was prepared to produce a car in quantity, he did not consider manufacturing the chief elements himself. Rather he proposed to the Dodge
brothers that they furnish the chassis (including the engine, the axles,
and the transmission). They agreed, and rejected a contract with Olds
in order to undertake the assignment.

Other suppliers contributed wooden bodies, cushions, tires, and
wheels. Thus the Model A, completed at its new plant on Mack Avenue,

was largely an assembly job. This was common practice. The automobile manufacturer, remarked *Motor Age* as early as 1900, could "buy almost everything that goes into a motor vehicle and can assemble it . . . and devote the rest of his time to selling the product." [6]

The president of the new Ford company was Malcomson's uncle, the banker John S. Gray, who lent a stabilizing influence. Henry Ford became vice president, Malcomson, treasurer, and James Couzens, secretary. A passport description of Couzens not long afterward gave his height as five feet, nine inches and noted a high forehead, blue eyes, straight nose, small mouth, and a round chin in an oval face. Born in Canada in 1872, the son of a former English grocer's clerk, Couzens had an insuppressible will to succeed. As a youth he reproached his mother for having permitted him to be born in Canada. "I can never be King of England," he pointed out, "but if I had been born in the United States I could be President." He was a furious worker, exacting but just, and quickly took charge of the Ford Motor Company's business affairs. It was he who would be principally concerned with setting up Ford's overseas operations.

The founding group had only a superficial harmony. Malcomson, like the sons of S. L. Smith at Olds, wanted to produce a luxury car. Henry Ford's goal was a low-priced product of good quality, and this appealed also to Couzens, the Dodge brothers, and Gray. For a time Malcomson had great influence, and in 1904 succeeded in getting the company to offer a large automobile—the Model B, priced at $2000. The low-priced car was also continued. Had Model B sold well, Malcomson could and doubtless would have produced a crisis by insisting that it alone should be pushed. But it sold with difficulty, and while the issue remained unsettled, the company relied on its cheaper automobile both at home and abroad. This would win it a definite advantage in the foreign markets, but not for several precarious years.[7]

3

When the Ford Motor Company offered its cars beyond the borders of the United States, it was a late arrival and an obscure one among American companies selling their products abroad.

Already two distinct modes of foreign selling existed. Manufacturers could send their goods to agents or to customers outside the United States, and have no permanent establishment of their own overseas. Or they could set up sales branches in foreign lands, thus making an investment there. Often these earliest sales branches would undertake the assembly, and then later the manufacture, of the American product. The evolution was from the export of an American-made article, to the exportation of a branch of the business, to augmentation of the investment, to assembly, and then to full foreign manufacture.

Such activities had been intensifying as the character of American production changed. Soon after independence was won in 1783, manufacturing had spread rapidly in the new republic, whereas under colonial rule it had been sharply restricted. Skilled workmen came from England with knowledge of new machine processes, acquired in what was then the center of world industrial activity. American inventors and factory owners made their contributions: Eli Whitney's manufacture of rifles with interchangeable parts was a step forward not only for American but for world manufacturing. Through their production of revolvers, agricultural machinery, sewing machines, and a dozen other native products, Americans developed their own industrial processes. They became steel makers.

Consequently, while throughout the middle years of the nineteenth century exports had been chiefly agricultural or forest items—wheat, corn, cotton, meat and meat products, lumber—after the Civil War the situation began to change. Although by 1900 less than a third (31.65 per cent) of American export trade was in manufactured goods, this represented a sizeable increase over the 12.48 per cent of two decades earlier. Our investment abroad, termed "negligible" by the Department of Commerce when it looked back to 1843, had risen in 1897 to $69,000,000 —not an enormous sum but a beginning.[8]

Among exports of American products, Colt revolvers had found a European market in the 1840's. Yankee locks gained a place in the next decade. Waltham watches were sold through a London agency in 1873. McCormick's reapers were highly esteemed abroad. By the mid and later 1870's several European countries were using American rifles and importing machine tools from the United States for making them. Russia and Turkey, fighting in 1877, were both equipped with American small arms. Several years earlier the Prussian government had furnished its arsenals with Pratt & Whitney machines and machine tools, and in 1875 a report noted that it "could furnish the parts of the gun automatically, and with such precision of finish as to render them fit for the polishing process without hand work." American machinery, other iron and steel products, and also cotton goods found an ever-enlarging market in Europe. While there is no record of the number of agents handling American products there, by 1900 they must have run into the many hundreds.

The Standard Oil Company, the Eastman Kodak Company, the American Radiator Company, the National Cash Register Company, and the Diamond Match Company all operated in Europe before the Ford Motor Company was born. Tiffany had presented wares in its glittering Paris shop as early as 1850; Singer had started to make sewing machines near Glasgow in 1867; Burroughs had established a plant in England in 1896. By 1900 some twenty-eight American-owned manufactories were located on the continent and many more American firms had sales organizations there.[9]

American capital had ventured into Canada and Mexico as well as Europe. Our lumbering and mining enterprises appeared early in the Dominion. "The Canadian iron and steel industry," notes one authority, "was partly founded by American entrepreneurs who had taken root in Canada in the nineteenth century." By 1900 Canada had paper mills, agricultural implement and sewing-machine factories, a distillery, a silk manufactory, and various pharmaceutical companies controlled from the United States. More than a hundred Canadian companies were affiliated with or controlled by American firms. In Mexico, Americans invested mainly in railways and mining enterprises.[10]

Elsewhere in the world American businessmen had fewer permanent interests. In South America European capital far exceeded United States investments. Diamond Match's controlling interest in a factory in Lima, Peru, and Edison's sales company in Buenos Aires, first established in 1889, appear to have been the earliest extensions of American manufacturers into South America. Standard Oil had also ventured into the southern continent. There were a few mining and a number of trading enterprises. But most industries that sold in that large area were not yet ready to set up permanent organizations there.

In Asia there had been more American trade than in Africa, which was the region least explored. China had long known American merchants, and after Commodore Perry's visits to Japan in 1853 and 1854 a market for United States products had opened. Firms such as Frazar & Company, Yokohama, founded in 1867, imported the Edison electrical system, the Baldwin locomotive, and other American products before 1900. Standard Oil had long maintained representatives in the Far East.

The Orient had a lure for the American businessman, although by 1900 only 5 per cent of our foreign trade was with Asia, and with the exception of two American cotton mills in China, American manufacturing was nil.[11]

Yet most American businessmen shared President Theodore Roosevelt's optimism when he declared in April 1903, "as a nation we stand in the very forefront in the giant international competition of the day." [12] Ford officials agreed, and when they turned to foreign markets they joined many others who were pushing beyond the country's frontiers. However, the prospects for the sale of American automobiles abroad were not altogether encouraging.

4

Europe had been the mother of the automobile. There the revolutionary machine had been conceived and created. Siegfried Marcus' crude model of 1875 had never been manufactured because its inventor saw no future for it. "Who would use it?" he shrugged. Nevertheless it was operable. Gottlieb Daimler and Karl Benz in 1885–1886 had developed greatly improved gasoline engines and drove experimental motorboats, motorcycles, and cars. Their patents had been used in France to create the first commercial automobiles, and by 1903 stylish French cars had become toys of the rich: the Panhard-Levassor (using Daimler's patents), the De Dietrich, Darracq, Mors, De Dion-Bouton, Delahaye, Renault, and Peugeot.

European automobile production at this time was certainly greater than American, and the French output may have surpassed that of any other country in the world. Certainly America's preëminent position in this industry had not yet been established.[13] The French cars, expensively and beautifully hand finished, represented the aristocracy of the motor world. They were used in the United States by the Newport group and numerous other wealthy individuals. To make a cheap American car a rival of these fastidious productions seemed to border on *lèse majesté*. France exported the world over and in every market could still look down on American competition.

R. E. Olds had sold the first American car abroad in 1893—a steam-propelled vehicle. The first American car using a gasoline motor, the Duryea (1893), competed against European machines in the rugged Chicago endurance race in 1895 and beat an imported Benz; it then entered the London to Brighton Run (November 14, 1896) and bested the very Panhard-Levassor which had recently triumphed over all the picked cars of Europe.

Other American cars went overseas. The Cadillac, Pope, White, Waltham, and Locomobile appeared with the Oldsmobile and the Duryea in foreign markets. By 1904 the American magazine *Horseless Age* boasted that American automobiles were being marketed in five continents. Actually, the automotive exports for the year ending June 30, 1903 were valued at $1,207,064, which probably meant that about 1,200 cars had been sent abroad! But even this was impressive when compared with the total American production for 1899 of 3,723. The bulk of the exports were in the low-priced range—Cadillac, Oldsmobile, Duryea.[14]

In general the American cars sent to Europe were ill-received. This may have been partly because of national prejudices, but it was also a matter of comfort and performance. Some units had "narrow seats, hard springs, and [they] were simply torture machines." The 1902 Oldsmobile, for example, with its "coughing, spitting, one-cylinder engine that seemed to be suffering the final stages of shaking palsy" (as one automobile pioneer phrased it), was undoubtedly among the number that did not find favor. Likewise, slighting comments were made on the workmanship of the Duryea. Europeans were quick to point out that American imports lacked hand finish and were unattractive; a typical European verdict was that they were "cheap and nasty." Taking note of this reception, *Horseless Age* remarked: "The cars exported were of a low grade and naturally failed to give complete satisfaction in many instances. When the shortcomings of these cars were widely known, the demand for them shrank." [15]

Everywhere for the moment the French cars were in the ascendant, popular not only with wealthy Americans but also with the well-to-do in countries like Mexico and the Argentine. The favored few, taking their holidays in Europe, purchased the expensive French machines and brought them home, creating a desire among others to go and do likewise. While French manufacturers were preëminent in Europe, the building of cars had also begun in Germany, Austria, Italy, Belgium, Spain, the Netherlands, and England.

In Great Britain no incentive to produce motor cars had existed before the passage of the new Highway Act of 1896. This repealed crippling restrictions which had been clamped like a vise in mid-century on all free-moving, self-propelled vehicles. The adverse legislation, passed when the development of English steam cars first became encouraging, was the work of hostile railroad and carriage interests. But for the absurd laws, one of which fixed a speed limit of four miles an hour or less, English inventors would probably have developed excellent steam automobiles long before the gasoline motor car appeared. When finally freed, the native genius quickly asserted itself, although H. T. Lawson, the first to act, established in 1896 the Daimler Motor Car Company, thus using a foreign car.

In several years dozens of British firms had begun to build automobiles. The Lanchester Engine Company, formed in 1899, produced sufficiently to expand in 1903. Herbert Austin, experimenting for the Wolseley Sheep Shearing Company from 1895 onward, drove his first model in the Automobile Club's Thousand Mile Trial, which began on April 23, 1900. Montague S. Napier had built a car in 1898–1899 at his own factory and entered an excellent 2-cylinder machine in several tests. In the 1902 Paris-Innsbruck race it triumphed over all the French entries. By 1904 Napier's company could show a profit for the year of £18,117.[16]

Thus as the Ford Motor Company went abroad late in 1903, it faced not only the existing prejudice against American cars, but varied competition. Nonetheless, certain promising omens were apparent. Production for any European firm was small, as hand labor was used and each unit was a special creation. Foreign automobiles were also expensive. With a few exceptions they ran from $2000 up. As noted, American manufacturers could produce for $650 up, with $1000 the average ceiling for a low-priced car. Ultimately this would give them a great advantage.

Why the difference in cost? Materials and labor were as high in the United States as in Europe—sometimes higher. The answer lay elsewhere and comprised several reasons.

In the first place, American automobile manufacturers used machine tools to a far greater extent than the Europeans. Even as early as 1885 a shrewd visitor in the United States remarked that "the tools and processes we are inclined to consider unusual are the commonplace of American shops." The machine tool reduced the labor bill and quickened the whole process of manufacture for the American car maker.

The automotive producer in the United States was also served by suppliers. He could turn to dozens of shops or plants (all like him employing machine tools) that made tires, wheels, engines, forgings, transmissions, and other parts, and stood ready to supply them in quantity at a low rate. The European car maker could call on few if any such firms. Often he made every part of his car himself. This required much time, labor, and concern, and his costs were appallingly high.

As a result, the Americans could produce in volume far more easily and, if the volume were high, charge much less per unit. Their lower prices increased the number of customers. The market in any case was definitely better in the United States, which had a considerably larger population than France, Britain, or Germany, and a per capita income that was higher than any of them could show.

Some of the disadvantages under which the European manufacturer labored need not have continued to handicap him. For example, he could have procured machine tools and encouraged suppliers to serve him. Unfortunately he was smugly satisfied with his hand-wrought product. He was proud of building an elegant, expensive car and felt that machines and quantity production would destroy individuality in craftsmanship. "If our own makers have serious regard for lasting fame," advised the *Automobile Engineer* (London) with conviction as late as 1911, "they will probably be wise enough to let the cheap trade alone."

A year later Lawrence Moore, an American motor car producer, made a trip to Europe, and on his return told the *Detroit Journal* how amazed he had been "that manufacturers abroad do not use much labor-saving machinery, apparently regarding labor as too cheap to justify costly machines with which to save it." In general Europeans maintained this attitude practically up to World War I. In 1903 it was a religion with them, and as a consequence Americans were bound to build cheaper cars.[17]

The Americans were also bound to build better ones and to reduce service problems. Beautiful as hand-finished parts might be, they were trouble makers in any car compared with accurate machined parts. The Dodges could work to tolerances of $\frac{1}{1000}$th of an inch or less. Also, by 1904 many parts in American automobiles were interchangeable, and the goal was to make all of them so. The more precisely made car was the smoother running and more dependable car. To replace a damaged part in the European car might take weeks, for it had to be handmade. On the other hand, American manufacturers stocked spare parts, and a new one could be provided quickly and at small expense. The life of the American product was longer and its upkeep cheaper.

The Americans, including Ford and his associates, knew the advantages of their methods. Certainly there was a market for their car in the United States. Europeans, however, doubted it could conquer world markets. Nonetheless, as we look back, we can see that the need for a cheap, dependable car was recognized from as far away as Bombay, India, as early as 1896. A prescription from there called for a "perfect type of motor vehicle, which is of simple design and can be operated by untrained labor. It must be strong in all parts and cheaper in working than animal power." This was the car that American manufacturers were trying to produce, but neither the Oldsmobile, nor the Cadillac, nor the Duryea had as yet created it.[18]

Ford executives felt that the Model A was the answer. An advertisement published in 1903 proclaimed: "It is positively the most perfect machine on the market, having overcome all drawbacks such as smell, noise, jolt, etc. common to all other makes of auto carriages. It is so simple that a boy of 15 can run it." The blurb added, "For beauty of finish it is unequalled."

As the sales records of the company reveal, this was an optimist's description, for many complaints had to be dealt with before even the American owners of the car were placated. Yet the Model A, the forerunner of that fabulous creation, the Model T, commanded the support of the stockholders. Henry Ford was sure that he could improve it and reduce its price, was confident that he could make a product that would be competitive the world around.[19]

5

Robert M. Lockwood was an export agent who in 1903 resided in New York and had handled foreign sales for the Daisy Air Rifle Company and other concerns. Charles H. Bennett, a Ford stockholder, headed the rifle company, and when Henry Ford asked him, "Who is your export agent?" Bennett named Lockwood.

"Has he done a good job for you?" asked Ford.

"We think so," Bennett replied.

As a consequence of this recommendation, Lockwood was engaged to manage all Ford Motor Company foreign sales outside of Canada.

He worked entirely on a commission basis and was "to devote his time, energy, and attention" to Ford affairs. He agreed not to handle the export sales of any automobile comparable with the Ford. He would appoint agents and make contracts with them only with the approval of the company.

To assist Lockwood, the company sent him 3000 catalogs "appropriate for introducing to the export trade in foreign countries the [Ford] business." Lockwood was to sell the Model A runabout for $830 FOB New York, and the tonneau for $120 more. These export prices were subject to a trade discount of 20 per cent, and Lockwood got an extra 5 per cent commission "in consideration of his handling the entire export business." The final agreement was made on November 11, 1903.

Clearly Lockwood was a beginning. In appointing him on a commission basis, the company followed usual practice. As volume grew, it might make him an employee, or take over his task itself. The contract with him covered only a three-year period. Other than the expense of 3000 catalogs, the firm invested no cash in its first effort to obtain foreign business.[20]

Thus, the Ford Company entered the world market. It faced a sharp struggle before it could win a place, if indeed it was to do so. Could its model pierce the encrusted hostility to American cars in Europe, and compete against European products in Latin America? Would it appeal to buyers in countries like China and India where horses were expensive and the demand for a sturdy, simple car existed? Logic seemed to say, "Yes," but practice would be the test. And practice would present problems and obstacles quite surprising to the confident Americans who sent their products abroad in the last months of 1903.

2
Probing for Markets

Early in 1904 Henry Ford received a visitor from Canada and a proposal that burst in the area of foreign trade like an explosion. Gordon M. McGregor, a thirty-one year old businessman from Walkerville, Ontario, half an hour's travel across the Detroit River from the Ford company's plant, placed before him a plan to organize a company for the manufacture of the Model A in the Dominion.

For several years McGregor had managed a wagon works and, like the Studebaker brothers and the founders of the Oakland and Pontiac firms in the United States, had become convinced that he should shift from the carriage trade to the production of automobiles. His father, William McGregor, formerly a member of the Canadian Parliament, had done well enough as half owner of the Walkerville Wagon Company; but Gordon, who had taken over as manager not long before his father's death, had found competition devastating. In a year his 102 employees (March 1903) had melted to 28. He concluded that he was in the wrong business. He had noted that in Detroit several motor car firms (Olds, Cadillac, Ford) were thriving. Wagons wouldn't sell, but automobiles would. McGregor headed for the American city with a conviction that salvation lay in the new industry.[1]

The legend is that he first interviewed Henry M. Leland of Cadillac; what we know surely is that he turned to Ford. When he learned that Ford's company had paid in nine months dividends amounting to 32 per cent of its capital, and by the end of its first year would pay more, he was prepared to act. He had a well-matured plan to lay before the shrewd American who had developed the car he wanted to make and sell.[2]

The two men naturally attracted each other. Ford, in his forty-first year, alert and active, was a veteran in the automobile world; Mc-

Gregor, who had worked as a bookkeeper in Detroit for a number of years, knew him by reputation. In an unsigned memorandum which he prepared and circulated not too long after their meeting he termed Ford "one of the most successful and practical men in the business."

It is not difficult to guess what Ford saw in McGregor. Here was a young man in charge of a business who was prepared to labor diligently to change it for another that he (and Ford) believed to be a better one. Ford came to deplore investors who were mere "parasites." "We have no place for the non-working stockholders," he said later. "The working stockholder is more anxious to increase his opportunity to serve than to increase bank dividends." McGregor would obviously be a working stockholder. Ford doubtless classed him with James Couzens and the Dodge brothers, who were putting their full energies as well as their money into the Ford company. His stocky young visitor, although quiet in manner, also gave the impression of being a fighter.[3] *

McGregor's plan was simple and convincing. A 35 per cent tariff on American cars entering Canada exerted an unpleasant leverage on their price: Fords selling for $800 in Detroit were being marketed in Toronto for $1000.** But machines made in Canada would pay no duty whatever. Canadian shops or factories could manufacture parts, and what could not be made in Canada could be supplied from the United States at a far lower rate than that imposed on complete machines. There was an opportunity, McGregor argued, to put on the Canadian market a car for the multitude, a need that was not being met. "The dealers in Canada," he noted, "have been unable to get enough Ford machines to supply the demand, as the factory in Detroit is several hundred machines behind their orders at the present time." Finally, he proposed to find financing in Canada for the new company.[4]

Ford may have had his doubts. Canada could show no automobile industry at this time, and at the end of 1903 only 220 cars were on Canadian roads. Ford may have known that some models had been built in Canada: the Still, the Moss, the Leader, the Austin, and the Queen—none of them successful. An Englishman visiting the Dominion in January 1904 informed a British motor car magazine that all cars in

* Not only was he a fighter in business, but "quite a scrapper" with his fists, according to his brother Don. The latter recalled meeting "a big tough guy" who told him that Gordon had once given him "the best licking ever."

** The tariff was based on wholesale rather than retail price, which explains why the Toronto price is not $800 plus 35 per cent.

active use were American. "Automobile manufacturing in Canada has not attained any volume at present," he added, "although several enterprises are likely to take up the industry." He could not have known of McGregor's plan, but his appraisal indicates that there was hope for some such undertaking.

Ford, impressed by his visitor's quiet confidence, dismissed the discouraging aspects of the Canadian scene and looked to its potentialities. He was soon accompanying McGregor through the Walkerville-Windsor region to appraise the manufacturing resources the latter had described.[5]

2

Together the two visited such plants as the Canadian Bridge Company, the Walkerville Malleable Iron Company, and the Kerr Engine Company. The young promoter undoubtedly painted a picture for Ford of recent developments in the Dominion.

Canada now lay in "the sunshine of success." When in the eighteen-nineties the American frontier had ceased to provide opportunities for emigrants, many had turned to the Canadian Northwest. A rush to take up free or low-cost land had brought eager settlers to that region. Soon "wheat was making the west" as cheap acreage and large crops created new fortunes. Railway lines spurted out, reaching distant points and multiplying areas of settlement.

Rising from a previous state of depression, of disharmony between Protestants and Catholics, and between French- and English-speaking groups, Canada was coming to think of itself as a nation. The eloquent Sir Wilfrid Laurier, fluent in English as well as in his native French, directed the vast territory from Ottawa as the Liberal Prime Minister. One historian writes that when he took office in 1896 he seemed with "a few passes of his enchanter's wand" to bring the nation to unity and prosperity. "It was Canada's Golden Age, an age of economic revival," wrote another. McGregor, son of a Liberal member of Parliament, doubtless pointed out to Ford the prosperity his party had brought the country.[6]

Henry Ford could see it for himself. Walkerville, adjacent to Windsor, symbolized the transformation.* In 1904 it was building new

---

* Walkerville had become a town in 1890 and was incorporated into metropolitan Windsor in 1934.

roads, a new public library, a new public school. For years it had been known as "the jug town," for there in 1858 Hiram Walker had established his distillery and given his name to the community. Parke, Davis & Company already had a laboratory there. Goods of many types were brought thither by the Walkerville & Detroit Ferry Company, which was now adding extra service. During the fiscal year of 1903–1904 the customs officials collected $177,608.01 in revenue, a fact the Windsor *Evening Record* hailed as happy for the Dominion and the town.[7]

The Walkerville Wagon Works, occupying a portion of the river front practically next door to the distillery, had been purchased in the late 1890's by McGregor's father and John Curry, a local banker. McGregor senior had seven children and the family was highly respected in Walkerville and Windsor. Gordon assured Ford that Curry would subscribe to a new Canadian Ford company; C. M. Walker, a wealthy nephew of Hiram, had promised a substantial investment; and he felt confident of support from dozens more within and outside his family. McGregor showed Ford his factory—comprising buildings, engines, a boiler, electrical fixtures, a blacksmith shop, a machine shop (of sorts), a box department, and a print shop. All these facilities could be utilized by a Ford Motor Company of Canada.[8]

Henry Ford brought the idea of a Canadian firm back to his directors, who during June and July 1904 discussed it. Meanwhile McGregor must have been given a conditional approval, for he began to raise funds. C. M. Walker became the largest subscriber, investing in 100 shares for a total of $10,000. John Curry paid for 40 shares in the new firm. Others like J. O. Reaume, a practising physician later Commissioner of Public Works for Ontario, added capital. However, raising the full amount that McGregor wanted was not easy. "Gordon went a-begging," remarked his secretary later. Sidney and Arthur Robinson hunted up the money for 30 shares each. Joseph Maw, whom McGregor asked to support him, at the same time suggesting that he become a Ford dealer, wrote from Winnipeg:

> As you understand we are handling both Olds and Cadillac and have them pretty well advertised here and unless the Ford [Company] turn out a very different machine to what they have at present I would not want to entertain handling it and drop the others. Now I might say this much if the stock is not all subscribed for in order to keep in touch with the company you can book me for $1000.00 worth of stock.

17

Maw thus resembled the ancient Romans who sacrificed to all the gods, including new ones, to make sure they missed nothing. He got his 10 shares. Altogether McGregor enlisted 28 Canadian stockholders, among them two wine merchants, a few lawyers, a bicycle store owner, a carriage builder, and a grocer. C. H. Bennett of the American company had friends in Michigan who also invested. But the cash involved was over 60 per cent Canadian.[9]

McGregor, Henry Ford, and the Detroit stockholders now reached an agreement signed August 10, 1904. The Ford Motor Company of Canada, Ltd., would be capitalized at $125,000.00. Henry Ford and the American company would furnish it with patents, plans, drawings, and specifications needed to build Ford automobiles. Ford would give "such reasonable and sufficient oversight" as was necessary to assure the "proper mechanical construction" of cars, and would be paid a fee for this service. In return the new company got "the sole and exclusive right to manufacture and sell its automobiles" in Canada.

What was potentially more important, it got the same right through-out the then-existing British colonies, possessions, and dependencies. Thus from the outset India, Malaya, South Africa, New Zealand, and Australia came under the authority of the Canadian company. The stock-holders of the Ford Motor Company of Michigan were to receive paid-up shares in the Canadian company equal to $63,750.00 (that is, 51 per cent of the capital) in consideration for the transfer of patents, drawings, and so forth, and for Henry Ford's services. As for the remainder of the $125,000 capital, $5000 was issued in stock to John Curry and the Mc-Gregor estate, in part payment for the assets of the wagon company. This should not be confused with the $5000 in cash invested by Curry. Mc-Gregor himself invested $1000. The total cash subscriptions for stock came to $56,250, almost twice that received by the American Ford company.

Ford-Canada thus became the holder of a vast commercial empire outside the Dominion—an impressive domain; but the stockholders of Ford-US retained control of the entire enterprise, which cost them not a penny in cash, which had no adverse effect on the American balance of payments, but to which Ford-US had to contribute patents, highly valuable designs, "know-how" and technical assistance.[10]

If the tariff had been a motivating factor in the establishment of a Canadian affiliate, it was also the chief consideration in the grant of commercial rights covering the entire British Empire. Sir Wilfrid Laurier's Liberal government had established in 1897 a broad British preferential tariff system, the first to be set up by any colony or dominion. It provided unilateral concessions to British goods, but the Canadians hoped for reciprocity.[11]

In England Joseph Chamberlain in 1904 was waging a campaign for a protective tariff, and seemed on the verge of success; he had endorsed imperial preference. In July 1904, while Ford and McGregor negotiated, Windsor newspapers announced that a preferential tariff had been extended to Canada by the South Africa Customs Union Convention. "With the aid of preference and the direct line of steamers established by the Ottawa Government between the Dominion and South Africa," the Windsor *Evening Record* concluded, "Canada ought to enjoy considerably the best of it in commercial competition with the United States." Other reciprocal tariffs seemed assured.[12]

While the probability of a preferential tariff on automobiles motivated the American company in its assignment of Empire rights to Canada, it could not sell the rights for England and Ireland, previously granted until December 1, 1907 to an English agent. The agreement left open the possibility that after this date Canada might be assigned rights in England and Ireland as well.

As the Ford Motor Company of Canada began to function, McGregor acted as general manager and secretary; the post of president went to John S. Gray (also president of the American Ford company); Henry Ford became vice president, and John Curry, treasurer. The new firm was quietly incorporated on August 17, 1904. Almost seven weeks earlier the Windsor *Evening Record* had carried an item announcing that the Walkerville Wagon Works would be refitted and might produce "devil wagons," but when the plant began production in 1905, the newspapers failed to notice it.[13] Yet the event was momentous, for now the motor industry of Canada for the first time became a reality.

3

"Detroit is without exception the automobile center of the world," McGregor had declared while soliciting subscriptions of stock, "and Walkerville being situated directly across the river is only a half hour's journey to almost any of the Detroit concerns. This firm [the new Ford of Canada] would be in direct touch and would lead in the production of automobiles in this Country."

In early 1905 this assertion had still to be proved. The adaptation of the two-and-a-half story wagon plant to motor car assembly was at first a limping operation. Most of the parts came from Detroit. There were exceptions: William Gray & Sons, of Chatham, supplied the bodies, and the Chaplin Wheel Company of the same town furnished some of the wheels. In all, there were twelve American suppliers (Dodge Brothers, for example, furnished the chassis) and an unknown but certainly smaller number of Canadian firms. With time, these would grow.[14]

As early as February 1905 a consignment of the new company's cars was shipped to the Canada Cycle and Motor Company of Toronto, which will be remembered as Ford-US's first distributor in the Dominion, and now became McGregor's first dealer. By the end of six months the Walkerville plant had delivered 114 cars, 107 of them Model C's (an improvement on the Model A) and 7 more expensive Model B's.

Ford-Canada began operations modestly with an office staff of three, and fewer than two dozen hourly employees. Besides McGregor, there was his secretary, Miss Grace Falconer, and the bookkeeper, H. E. Miller, who could tap dance. "He danced around, taught me a few steps," recalled Miss Falconer. "You can see how busy we were." In September 1905 W. R. Campbell, who had gone to school with one of the McGregors, worked for another, and more recently acted as bookkeeper for a Standard Oil affiliate in Canada, joined the little group.

In its first year, the company's production fell short of the 400 units McGregor had hoped to build, but automotive production everywhere was low outside the United States and France, and an operation could be sustained on a few hundred cars. Moreover, by the end of that year Ford-Canada had begun to export. A Model C had been ordered by Oakes & Company, London, and was shipped to Calcutta.[15]

This seemed a favorable augury, for of all export markets India had at first looked like the most promising. But a dozen years after the first Olds had appeared in Bombay (1893), when the first Model C arrived in the colony, there were only about 150 cars in the entire Indian peninsula, and these in the larger cities. The earlier promise of a brisk market had not been fulfilled. There were three obvious reasons for this condition: the lack of experienced drivers, the absence of knowledgeable mechanics, and the non-existence of repair shops.

Too common were experiences such as that of His Highness the Nijem of Secunderabad, one of the wealthiest princes in India. The prince had heard of the new invention, and had paid 12,000 rupees (about $3800) for an electric carriage which was shipped to him from Paris. One of his grooms undertook to operate it, and burned out the motor in a day. His Highness promptly asserted that the machine was a humbug and ordered it removed from his sight. To avoid catastrophes of this sort, a reliable, sturdy, and simple car was needed, easy to drive and keep in order. There must also be service stations to supply parts, make repairs, and advise the too frequently ignorant owners.[16]

4

The Canadian company in 1906 and 1907 grew slowly, increasing its meagre manufacturing equipment, adding to its staff, and slightly enlarging its shipments in both domestic and export markets. An observer might well have wondered whether it would cling to life or collapse. Up to August 1907 its total sales amounted to only 540 units.

Lacking facilities of its own for the handling of goods abroad, and any experience with such activity, the company engaged R. M. Lockwood as its export agent, and from New York he managed the foreign business of the Canadian company as well as that of Ford-US. As for domestic sales, McGregor dealt with them personally, in addition to managing the office and keeping an eye on manufacture. He was freed to an increasing extent from this last responsibility after October 1906, when George Dickert, an able German-American production expert, arrived to assist with manufacturing and assembly. Dickert had worked for the Ford Manufacturing Company, a subsidiary of the American firm, and had a full knowledge of the latter's products, an apparently infinite resourcefulness, and a driving energy that soon made him a giant in the factory.

Henry Ford later wrote, "I do not believe a man can ever leave his business. He ought to think of it by day and dream of it by night." McGregor in 1906–1907 was seventeen years away from being able to read this statement, but he followed it to the letter. Besides helping to set the policies for the company, presiding over the office and supervising the shop work, he went forth to promote its fortunes in the field. He had appointed a few dealers, but conditions were not yet ripe for an extensive sales organization. He would drive away in a car, sell it, and return to Walkerville by rail. It was a way of increasing sales, and it won McGregor an immediate knowledge of conditions throughout Canada.[17]

In these early days he had some difficulty with his father's former partner, John Curry. The minutes of the meetings show that Curry assumed an important part in the new company's affairs. "It bothered

Gordon once in a while," his brother Don recalled. But Curry, with his somewhat pompous banker's manner, was a non-working stockholder, while McGregor was always pushing the fortunes of his young organization. He had the support of the Americans, who liked what he did and gave him a free rein from the start. His was the firm, persistent hand that in the end would bring growth and prosperity. With time, his father's old partner ceased to be influential in Ford-Canada.[18]

In 1906 the company marketed the Models K and N, both of which were being pushed by Ford-US. The high-priced, 6-cylindered K, a luxurious touring car, sold badly both in the Dominion and in the United States. Model N, cheap and reliable, and well-adapted to the poor Canadian roads, became popular. In 1907 the Ford Models R and S were introduced, both modifications of Model N. The R was a dressed-up, heavier car; S was a "composite" of R and N. In 1907 McGregor's company sold 327 cars in all, of which 241 were marketed in Canada and 86 abroad.

As might be expected, the record in profits was not exciting. A 6 per cent dividend had been declared on October 2, 1905, and in 1906 and 1907 none whatever. In contrast, the American company had paid five large dividends in the first three years of its existence, amounting to $298,000, or almost three times the issued capital of the firm. Rough roads, the higher prices of the cars (because of tariffs on parts and small output), the lower per capita income of Canadians as compared with Americans, and the pioneer nature of the business all helped to check the development of the industry in the Dominion. Yet for these early years Canada showed the largest volume of Ford sales for any foreign market. The fact that it had the only Ford assembly operation outside the United States partly explains the record, and proximity to the parent company helped.[19]

So too did the lack of any well-organized competitors. Rivals existed: there were several firms selling Oldsmobiles, and Robert McLaughlin and his sons in 1907 organized the McLaughlin Motor Car Company, which obtained rights for the Buick. But McGregor had a better plant and a headstart in industrial efficiency.[20]

5

Unlike the Canadian story, for which the documentation is good, the account of the first Ford activities in England is veiled in obscurity and confusion. No contract exists between the first agent there and the Ford Motor Company. We merely know that by 1904 the American Motor Car Agency and Central Motor Car Emporium was being operated in London by a certain Aubrey Blakiston and was selling Ford cars. Apparently it also handled other automobiles.[21]

Had Blakiston gone to the United States, made an arrangement with Lockwood, and brought back the Model A? Was it, as one important witness later inferred, his son? Or had a third party crossed the Atlantic in late 1903, got the right to sell Fords in England until December 1, 1907, to dispose of his rights to Blakiston on arrival in London? Certainly somebody brought the Model A to England, and Blakiston himself seems the best candidate. At any rate, in 1904 he was the British agent for the car.[22]

All the evidence we have indicates that his role was no easy one. It has been noted that American automobiles met with little favor in Europe. Lockwood, touring that continent in the summer of 1904 to discover ways of introducing Model A, noted this prejudice. "There was then," he wrote later, "no foreign car selling at a moderate price, a good low-priced car being looked upon as impossible by foreign manufacturers. The only opening wedge for an American car was a low price, without sacrifice of quality, and this chance had been almost totally eliminated by the failure of the two low-priced American cars which had previously been exported." Lockwood, in other words, encountered the current European opinion that American cars were "cheap and nasty." [23]

Blakiston himself may have collided with this belief; at any rate, before the end of the year he sold his business to a firm he helped to form—the Central Motor Car Company. In other words, he acquired a number of new associates, added funds, and continued his agency under a different name. Percival Perry, soon to become of importance in the English scene, later recalled that a group assembled at the Albemarle Club in London in the summer or fall of 1904. Herbert Stourton (of the well-known Mowbray family), Anthony Hasslacher (a wine merchant), C. W. Russell (a banker), and Blakiston were among those present. Perry was there because Stourton had suggested him as a man who knew motor cars.

Percival L. D. Perry was then twenty-six and already a veteran in the new automobile industry. Vigorous, alert to opportunity, he was a driver of motor cars and probably active in sports (he had formerly played football, and later at least was a golfer). He also had some facility with his pen, both in prose and in verse—within the next two years he was to publish his first volume of poems. Born in Bristol and educated at the King Edward School in the grim industrial city of Birmingham, he had come to London in 1896 in response to a newspaper advertisement to work for the dashing Harry J. Lawson, then rapidly becoming the best known figure in British automotive circles. Soon busy with the futile effort to buy all the rights and patents for the manufacture of motor vehicles in Britain, Lawson, as we have seen, founded the first firm in England to produce cars—the Daimler Motor Car Company.* Perry as one of his employees appeared in the procession that celebrated Queen Victoria's Diamond Jubilee. Dressed as a Pierrot, he sat in a car which he maneuvered back and forth on a float, which carried the sign: "Even a fool can drive a Bollee." [24]

At the Albemarle Club Perry seems to have been accepted as an authority on matters automotive. He recommended the Ford car and may have helped to dissipate any doubts the group had as to its future. The Central Motor Car Company was soon incorporated—November 18, 1904—with a capital of £10,000 (10,000 shares at a pound each). Perry was allotted 500 of these. Blakiston, who had the Ford rights and the shop at 117–119 Longacre with its equipment, received 2400. Directors of the new organization were Blakiston, Stourton, Perry, and Russell (who soon resigned and was replaced by Robert A. Hoghton).

The agency did not prosper. Its sales of Fords and other cars went slowly, and in 1905 and 1906 the company issued debentures to raise new funds. Eric Byrner Schreiber paid in cash for some of them and assisted with the financing of the firm. The Model A and its successor Model C did not prove popular; Perry later recalled that some of these machines were excessively noisy. Blakiston left the dealership, and Schreiber became a director in his stead. At some time in the spring or early summer of 1906 Perry was chosen to operate the firm as managing director. He appears in the Public Record Office files in this capacity as of June 14, but probably took his post somewhat earlier.

Perry seems to have recognized that strong medicine would be needed to bring the now faltering organization back to robust health. He determined to seek financial support from the Ford Motor Com-

* Lawson was credited with the invention of the safety bicycle, was a founder of the first automobile club in England, and set up the first English motor exhibition in the Imperial Institute.

pany in the United States. Taking ship for New York, he dined there with Lockwood, then pushed on to Michigan. In Detroit he called upon John S. Gray, the Ford president, who talked with him briefly and dismissed him with a "Well, I guess you'll have to see Henry."

The young Englishman sought out Henry and was cordially received. For some days he stayed as a guest at the Ford home on Harper Avenue, and discussed conditions in England. But his effort to raise funds failed; Detroit was not yet ready to invest any of its money overseas.[25]

The Central Motor Car Company consequently hugged its debts and lack of business during the summer and early fall of 1906. It seemed to have reached a period of stagnation, and in February 1907 two of its backers with B. M. Thornton planned a new organization, which was incorporated on the 16th as Perry, Thornton & Schreiber. This agency took over the right to sell Ford cars from the now moribund Central Motor Car Company, and for a time even used its premises. The older corporation became a shadow which was expunged the following July 6.

Meanwhile, with the appearance of the Ford Model N in the fall of 1906 the prospects for business began to improve. On November 10 in *Autocar* (London) came the first public listing of any Ford car in England, and the unit was noted in *The Car* for November 21 with an illustration and the remark that the designers had devoted their care "to the actual working parts . . . rather than to the attainment of a fine finish." Both magazines noted the selling price (£152—or about $739), which made Model N the cheapest 4-cylinder car on the English market, and more attractive than the Standard (£195) or the two American 1-cylinder imports, the Cadillac (£195) and the Reo (£165). Only two 1-cylinder English cars, the Starling (£120) and the Horley (£105) undersold the Ford. A few months later Perry drove the 15 h.p. Ford in the Irish Reliability trial and won a gold medal. Model N was the first car, he recalled later, that "I made any money by selling." He was still fighting English prejudice against American products, but between October 1906 and September 1907 he took delivery on 102 units, a number pathetically small by modern standards, but representing at that time larger sales than the Ford could show anywhere else outside the United States except in Canada.[26]

But some time was still to pass before any English Ford company could go forward with assurance.

6

Canada and Britain had made the greatest progress in the sale of Ford cars abroad. Had this success in English-speaking lands been a mere coincidence? The facts speak otherwise. To be sure, the existence of a common language in Windsor, London, and Detroit was no disadvantage. But other and more important elements made for the superiority of Britain and her North American Dominion as marketing areas for the Model A and its successors.

In the first place, both these lands had a high standard of living, lower than the American but higher than any country's in Europe, Asia, or Africa. More people in England and Canada could afford motor cars than in France, for example, or in Germany or Italy.

A second notable factor was the quality of Ford leadership in Windsor and London. McGregor and Perry were forceful personalities. They were happy accidents (they could not be called "finds" because they had come to Ford, not Ford to them). Both were citizens of the countries in which they operated, both were able drivers of cars, both had not only ideas and abounding energy but readiness to give personal attention to the details of their businesses. McGregor had the further advantage of manufacturing in Canada (it was still more assembling than manufacturing, but manufacturing was the goal), and he had adequate financial backing to push this enterprise to success. Perry, less fortunate, lacked even an assembly plant, and could command little in the way of funds; nevertheless he showed resourcefulness and practical ability in managing his difficult task.

Finally, the tariff was a factor as important as either of the other two. It was behind this rampart that McGregor was building Dominion production. On the other hand, England had no tariff; indeed, she was the sole European country without duties on automobiles. Paradoxically, the absence of a customs wall was as favorable to Ford progress in Britain as the presence of one in Canada had been helpful to the company there. For the next nine years Ford cars were to come freely into the English market, their lower prices giving them an advantage in competition with local products.

Elsewhere an armor of protective duties had made Ford sales more difficult. The record of how the cars were marketed is a barren one, to be pieced together from entries in ledger books which tell only the number of units shipped, their destinations, and the agents who handled them.

We know that one Model A was exported to France and delivered to the Automobile Union early in 1904. It had been dispatched direct from Detroit, and was the only model made by the Ford company to be sent there for some years. In 1907 Lockwood appointed a French agent, R. E. Mathot, but he worked against formidable opposition. The French exhibit at Paris late in 1906 was crowded with spectators and won the attention of the president of the republic, "who stopped at the stands of the largest French makers. . . . This official recognition by the French Government is sufficient testimony, if any were needed, of the position which the automobile industry holds in France." Mathot faced a nationalistic prejudice and an array of capable competitors calculated to discourage any dealer.

Elsewhere in Europe results were little better. The ledger shows that Lockwood appointed distributors widely—two in Germany and one in Belgium, Spain, Holland, Italy, Denmark, Sweden, Austria, Poland, and Russia. All were functioning by 1907. But in competition with expensive European cars, still carrying great prestige, the headway they made was negligible. Still, each contributed a few sales to swell the export total. Seven Fords sold in Spain perhaps sowed the seed for a later harvest. As one commentator remarked, "In no well-known country of Europe are the roads generally so bad as they are in that country." The Fords were winning a reputation for their ability to negotiate execrable roads.[27]

The ledgers tell us also that Lockwood was exporting Fords to Australia, Africa, Asia, and Latin America, acting for Canada in the case of British territories, and usually for Detroit in the case of the others. He arranged with various firms to do the shipping—the New York export houses of Crossman & Seilcken for Australia and Latin America, Arkell & Douglas for Africa, Carlonitz & Co. and Frazar & Company for Japan, and Peabody & Company for India. He had an agent in Shanghai as well. The New York house of Melchior, Armstrong, & Dessau shipped cars to Denmark and Cuba. W. R. Grace took charge in Peru.

Lockwood in this manner developed relationships with the largest of export houses in New York, firms that operated in many parts of the world. Some of the connections he made were continued for two decades. All were satisfactory from the point of view of the Ford Motor

Company. It took no chances with what it sold. Some exporters, like the American Trading Company, acted solely as commission houses: they would buy on behalf of a foreign client, and would store, ship, and insure the consignments, taking the financial risks and a commission. Ford would be paid at once on the presentation of the invoice in New York, while the customers of the trading house might have as much as a 120-day draft. There were other firms who handled Ford business as distributors for a specified region. Such was Arkell & Douglas. These would sell in their areas, employing agents of their own and sub-dealers, both of whom would market the Detroit company's products. These exporters also took the financial risks.[28]

By 1907 a routine for preparing cars for overseas shipment had already been established. Each car was packed separately, but because freight rates were levied on bulk as well as weight, its crate was made as compact as possible. It was strong, being made of one inch boards lined with heavy paper and stiffened by diagonal braces. The process of packing was described a few years later by the *Ford Times,* and was doubtless the same in 1907:

> To pack the car, it is run onto the floor of the crate and the water, gasoline and oil drained out. The wheels are then slipped off, the car is lowered to the floor of the crate and the axles fastened in place by wooden blocks bolted to the crate.
>
> The top is then removed and fastened securely to the under side of the crate, and the glass windshield is folded in burlap and secured to the inside of the rear end. . . . After taking off the steering wheel, brake shoes and other small parts, the starting crank and doors are tied so that there will be no loose parts anywhere. Each wheel is bolted (two on each side) to the insides of the sides of the crate, which is then closed up and another Ford is ready for its long journey to a foreign land. The whole operation has taken four men about an hour.[29]

By the seventh year of the decade Lockwood had found for Ford 22 foreign agents. The most active overseas markets at this time were England (103 cars for October 1906 to September 1907, inclusive), Germany (41), Belgium (24), and Mexico (23). Of the eight countries to which Ford-US exported more than 10 units, four had active local industries: England, Germany, Italy, and Belgium. There were, according to one report, 62 Italian automotive manufacturers and numerous builders in Belgium. Canada as already noted had an infant industry which amounted to little. Argentina too had at least one car maker: the engineer Horatio Anasagasti, who started in 1906 to produce a French-designed automobile. In the other areas, Mexico and Java, there were no local plants and the competition was mainly from Europe. The first car in Mexico City had been of European make, but by the time Ford arrived, other American cars had begun to make headway against the French, German, and Belgian models. In both Argentina and Java the dominant influence was European. The earliest Ford successes abroad were in countries highly developed industrially or in those which were in the "take-off" period, that is, one in which old blocks and resistances to steady growth were being overcome. Ford-Canada's largest single foreign market in 1907 was Australia, an example of the second type of country where Ford cars were successful.

By modern sales standards, Lockwood was doing very small business. But the total for that day was enough to give him good returns. He sold 277 cars in 1906–1907 and received a 5 per cent commission on each. Nor was the Ford Motor Company doing badly for that time. Altogether, when the Canadian sales are included, it sold 604 cars in foreign markets in the same period, which was a welcome addition to its domestic sales of 7719 units. It was in fact about 7.1 per cent of total sales, and more than a fifth of the total American exports of 2862 (from July 1, 1906 to June 30, 1907). Ford-Canada found its export trade even more significant. Sending 86 units abroad, it saw its overseas shipments take approximately 26 per cent of its total sales. The Dominion company's exports would for most of its history run relatively high when compared with Detroit's.[30]

The Ford Motor Company's trade had now been soundly based and was growing. However, officials began to perceive that more vigorous action would be necessary if there was to be the expansion that seemed possible. An article in *Horseless Age* late in 1906 on the Automobile Club of America show in New York made some significant comments on European and American exhibits. "The impression . . . is that foreign manufacturers are resting on their laurels and that American makers are rapidly improving their product. Most of the foreign cars exhibited were of high power and high price, and as the native products shown ranged upward in price from $450, a general comparison would not be valuable." The commentator especially noted the superiority of American automobiles in "neatness of outline and symmetrical arrangement of parts." The French were once superior in these matters, now the Italians surpassed them, "and the American product is best of all. American designers have taken the best of French ideas and in many cases have improved upon them." [31]

Here seemed to lie a great opportunity, and the Ford Motor Company was soon to explore it.

7

In mid-June 1907 James Couzens, secretary and treasurer of the Ford company and also its sales head, took ship for Europe to survey conditions both in England and on the continent. The Panic of 1907 had depressed the market in the United States, and Couzens knew that such activity as he left behind him did not require his attention. And while possibilities abroad hardly offered him a field that would compare with domestic production even at its worst, they were more inviting now than during a period of American prosperity.

Couzens visited London, Brussels, Paris, Berlin, Madrid, Copenhagen, Stockholm, Vienna, Rome, Budapest, and even Helsingfors and Moscow. His postcards to Henry Ford's son Edsel, then a youth of thirteen, show that he was not unaware of the scenic attractions of his journey, but his primary purpose was the study of possibilities for the expansion of his company's business.

He could look forward with certainty to the kind of product the Ford Motor Company would bring to Europe in the future. A year earlier he could not have done so. Although his firm was then readying the Model N for manufacture, Alex Y. Malcomson was still one of its important stockholders and still wanted to produce a large luxury car. While Ford, the Dodges, and Couzens had restrained him, conceivably he might be able to reverse company policy and (in the opinion of his associates) wreck the prospects for an increasing export trade. Suppose the low-priced car was burdened with the white elephant (like the Model K) that Malcolmson wanted? Suppose there was no low-priced car, but only an unsaleable monstrosity? Ford and Couzens must have shuddered at such possibilities. But now Malcolmson was out. On July 12, 1906 he had sold his stock to Henry Ford, who then became the holder of 51 per cent of all company shares. A week earlier the company's president, John S. Gray, had died, and Ford was soon elected to fill the vacant place. Later that year he and Couzens had bought 60 more shares from other holders, and with Couzens' own interest and the 10 per cent owned by the Dodges, the four proponents of the cheap car held almost 70 per cent of the firm's stock and had complete control of policy. The Ford of the future would be a low-priced model of high quality, and Couzens could observe and plan accordingly.[32] *

He was encouraged by the European automotive scene. "The prospects for American car manufacturers in Europe," he told a reporter on his return, "would appear to be good if they will meet the conditions and requirements of these various countries, but to attempt to do so on the lines on which business is done in America would make it a fruitless task." (This statement might have been pondered thoughtfully some years later by Henry Ford.) Some American products, he continued, had not been good, and the Europeans "are somewhat unfriendly to American automobiles." It was a difficult but necessary task to convince them "that we have improved our product and that it is now equal to any in the world, besides being cheaper, due to our advanced manufacturing methods." He used a metaphor to drive his point home. "There is no fruit over there ready to pick, as it has to be cultivated, nursed, and one must wait until it ripens; and the manufacturer who can and will do this will surely pick the fruit, as it will eventually ripen without undue delay."

There is no evidence that Couzens thought the Ford car should be adapted to European taste. With McGregor in Canada he was confident that the foreign market could be successfully invaded with a cheap, reliable car. He pointed out that already the export of motor vehicles from the United States exceeded the imports, and indicated that Ford would ride with this trend.[33]

Not long after his return he took a step toward a more vigorous assault on Europe: he appointed a manager for the company's activities there. The man he chose was H. B. White, formerly of the Adams Express Company's French office. The Ford Board of Directors authorized the new appointee to set up a Paris branch and to conduct from there all the business the Ford company might have both on the mainland and in Great Britain. For a brief period (and never thereafter) English activity was supervised from across the channel.

Lockwood remained in New York, at 18 Broadway, his contract being renewed in November 1906 and again in December 1907. The 1907

---

* The remaining stockholders who had been Malcomson supporters disposed of their holdings in 1907. When Couzens returned from Europe, Ford held 585 shares, he 110, and the Dodges 100 out of the 1000 total—79.5 per cent.

agreement stressed that his efforts must be made outside of Great Britain and continental Europe, these areas now being covered by White. Unlike White, who was paid a salary, Lockwood continued on a commission basis. While he had lost Europe, Ford sales everywhere were going up, and his position was still remunerative.

Of rather stocky build, White wore a mustache and had developed a Parisian strut, along with European habits of dress and manner. He appointed a number of new dealers to replace some of Lockwood's agents who seemed inefficient, and aimed to have at least one Ford representative in every European country. He visited both his continental European and his English agents and urged them to greater efforts. "Be forge-like in the heat of your persistency," he told a group of British dealers in November 1908. "When depressed and downhearted—when things don't seem to go as they should—when the favorite you have backed blows up in the stretch and the rank outsider comes home with the money—just take a good cathartic and remember that bad business is frequently merely the result of bad liver." This bombastic speech must have bounced off the dealers, few of whose troubles would be cured by a laxative. But if White failed to recognize the scope of possible European operations, he at least was ready to attack them with vigor.[34]

8

As the new European manager harangued his cohorts, rumors of a new Ford, the Model T, ran briskly about Europe. The first circulars for this machine had appeared in Detroit on March 19, 1908. In October it was available to the American public. The car embodied Henry Ford's long-nursed goal: it was an automobile for the masses, providing cheap, satisfactory transportation. The "Tin Lizzie," as it later came to be known, was superior at its price to anything else on the market. America applauded it at once.

The Model T had four cylinders and developed 20 horsepower. Many of its mechanical features had been tested in previous models. Its high clearance made it adaptable to rough, uneven terrain; its sturdy construction, with vanadium steel, promised reliability; its light weight was designed to keep operating costs low; its simplicity made service easy (the interchangeability of all its parts meant that faulty elements could quickly be replaced); its planetary transmission gave the driver excellent control. Already Ford was aiming at higher volume and lower price, while at the same time he began to emphasize service. The Model T would have facilities everywhere to meet the needs of its owners.

In November the new car appeared at the Olympia Show in England and soon afterwards at the Paris exhibit (on the 13th and the 28th, respectively). *Autocar* described it and *Motor Trader* commented reservedly that "visitors interested in American practice should not fail to see the new Ford." In contrast, the Paris press showered praise upon the Model T. The article in *La Voiturette* could easily have been written by a Ford public relations man: "L'apparition de la voiturette Ford a causé . . . une véritable sensation," it began. The Ford Motor Company was described as "la plus importante fabrique d'automobiles du monde entier," which was quite a concession for the French.[35]

When by the end of 1908 the Model T was shipped to foreign markets, it lifted Ford sales around the world. If the totals were still small, they were rising, and a world pattern of agents had been clearly established. The company was still primarily an exporter. The Paris branch represented its only cash investment, one of $1000.00 "imprest cash" (money advanced). In the Canadian operations, as we have seen, no Ford Motor Company cash had been invested. In England, Ford had only a distributor and its sub-dealers, who of course found local financing.

The Panic of 1907 was but a temporary setback, not seriously affecting the technological and economic development of the United States. The five years from 1903 to 1908, years of peace, had seen a steady and even brilliant industrial growth in the country. The Spanish-American War had been won in 1898, and while the Caribbean simmered with discontent, Roosevelt's big stick policy and American control of both Cuba and Puerto Rico had kept the area relatively quiet. Construction of the Panama Canal had been begun. Abroad, Roosevelt had been instrumental in settling the Russo-Japanese War (1904–1905) and agreed that we would not interfere with the ambitions of the victorious Japanese in Korea so long as the Philippines were recognized as an area of American interest.

Despite Roosevelt's frequent talk of the United States as a world power, this country had kept aloof from the shifting alliances of European nations: the Anglo-French Entente, the German-Russian rapprochement, the Anglo-Japanese alliance, and the Anglo-Russian Entente. England's "splendid isolation" had been broken down; ours had not. We still had no "entangling alliances."

While there was much talk in American financial and industrial circles about foreign affairs, the chief interest centered about what was happening at home. Here there were dramatic signs of growth. The automobile industry had increased its output four-fold; steel production had climbed from 14.5 million long tons in 1903 to 23.7 million in 1907; the chemical industry was showing an amazing growth; and the American machine tool activity, already leading the world in 1900, was pushing on to new and astonishing accomplishments. Still unrecognized as a world leader, the United States was quietly assuming preëminence in industry, and the Model T was one of numerous products that would symbolize spectacularly the growing power of the nation.[36]

3
Model T: Triumph and Fable

The Ford Motor Company had purchased in April 1907 a 57-acre tract of land in Highland Park, a few miles north of Detroit, for $81,225, to expand the manufacture of its car. The act was revolutionary. Its old plant on Piquette Avenue, Detroit, which it proposed to abandon, occupied 2.65 acres; Henry Ford was probably right when he said later: "It was as good as, perhaps a little better than, any automobile factory in the country." He recalled that people were asking, "How soon will Ford blow up?"

Ford officials could smile at that query. They had paid their shareholders fabulous sums on the original capitalization of $100,000, and in 1908 would declare $2,500,000 in regular and stock dividends. During that year they would also produce 10,607 cars, which gave them first place among automobile manufacturers in the United States, and in the next year would almost double this sale, repeating the achievement in 1910–1911 with 34,528 vehicles. Moreover, they stood high in an American industry that in 1910 put out 181,000 cars to 64,000 for France, England, and Germany combined—the outstanding automotive countries of Europe.[1]

In September 1908 William C. Durant united the Olds and Buick firms to form the General Motors Company, to which Oakland and Cadillac were added the following year. Ford lost first place as this powerful combination in 1909 made dollar sales thrice those of Ford. Durant even tried to buy the Ford company, and the story is that Henry Ford was willing to sell it for $8,000,000, but insisted on cash. Durant's bankers told him, "The Ford business is not worth that much money." Events were soon to prove them badly mistaken.[2]

The makers of the Model T had numerous other competitors, but they were aware of superb financial strength and had in their new car a superlative product. In 1908 the company began to erect its Highland Park factory, soon to cover 32 acres. As this structure arose its unique character became apparent. It was providing extensive experimental and testing facilities. It was making most of its own parts, all standardized. "Every part must go into its place without causing a moment's delay in the assembly room," noted a trade journal. Henry Ford pointed out that he and his technical aides had reduced the number used in a car, installed special machinery, designing much of it, quickened production, and kept careful checks on stock that avoided shortages or undue crowding. Finally, a sequence of operations had been developed that in time would become the fabulous moving assembly line.[3]

We have already seen how a network of Ford agents covered the world. Norval Hawkins, who had taken most of the burden of selling from Couzens' shoulders, was improving the dealer system in the United States and assisting in the promotion of activities overseas. Ford printed catalogs in French, Spanish, and German, and placed advertisements abroad in those languages. Appeals to potential customers even appeared in Japanese and Chinese. In addition, steps calculated to win publicity were taken in all foreign countries.

One was the use of the Model T as a taxicab. This helped to advertise the car in England, Russia, Cuba, and Japan; for a taxicab, cruising the streets daily, made the model familiar and often won new purchasers. In similar fashion, Ford agents entered their machine in foreign races, endurance runs, and feats of mountain climbing. Frequently a Ford agent drove his Model T through rough and colorful lands, snapping pictures in the Alps, the Andalusian peninsula, or the Gobi desert. Alexander Lie of the Paris branch took his way through the Balkans, and European manager H. B. White threaded the Simplon Pass.[4]

Dealers from Calcutta to Manchester astutely adapted their vehicles to the tastes of customers. In the Orient, they often replaced the wooden wheels of the Model T with the more popular wire ones. Agents would change the grills on the radiator (sometimes to imitate the Rolls-Royce) and build their own bodies for the Ford chassis. But the product was basically the same (the chassis remained unchanged), stood up to rugged use, and came more and more, at the insistence of Henry Ford, to be backed by excellent service facilities. Overseas dealers were selected because of their ability to furnish skilled mechanics and repair shops as well as for their sales talents and their financial standing.

The Ford Motor Company expanded its business abroad as well as at home through superior engineering, production, marketing, and servicing methods. The company did not seek government aid. In fact, on November 23, 1908, Couzens on behalf of the corporation signed a petition to the chairman of the House Ways and Means Committee protesting a proposal to raise the 45 per cent American tariff then existing, and saying: "We are unalterably opposed to any increase in this tariff. We believe that this so-called infant industry is fully protected . . . and, in fact, *we believe that the present tax is a greater protection than this industry should have."* (Italics ours.) He argued that the levy should be *reduced* so as merely to equalize the difference in labor costs, which he termed "insignificant." American wages while far higher than European were offset by the use of more machinery.*

Many European manufacturers asked not only for tariff protection but for direct government export subsidies, something neither Ford nor any other American automotive producer ever requested. Indeed, industry in the United States gained advantages by independence, for the assistance of some foreign states brought unfortunate results (their manufacturers, lulled into security by subsidies, lacked incentive to reduce costs and as in Germany were urged to make vehicles for military purposes). In general, state intervention meant heavier, higher-priced products, while the American manufacturer pushed ahead to develop lighter, cheaper, more saleable cars.[5] **

2

Early in August 1909 Couzens went to Europe for a second time, with the authority of the Ford Board of Directors to form a branch in England. As he arrived in London Couzens was well aware of the massive strength of the firm he represented. We have seen the dividend record for 1908. Already in 1909 an additional sum of $1,300,000 had gone to the stockholders, and further disbursements would be made, one of $100,000, while Couzens was abroad. Probably no company had ever made such payments on a capitalization of $100,000, of which only $29,500 had been paid up in cash!

* Couzens in asking lower tariffs argued against other representatives of the American automobile industry.

** Lockwood once raised a call for government help, asking a ship subsidy bill, but he seems to have had no support from the Ford company, other than space in the *Ford Times.* (See note 5.)

Ford's European situation greatly resembled that which Couzens had found in 1907, except that White had made modest progress with continental sales, disposing of 251 units in the first eight months of 1909. In England, however, the Ford agency had encountered difficulties. In 1908 two of its Model N's had placed first and second in the All-Comers Handicap Sweepstake, an accomplishment which Perry, Thornton & Schreiber had vigorously publicized. But the partners had begun to quarrel. As a result, Schreiber resigned; then in July Perry decided he could no longer work with B. M. Thornton and Thornton's father, who had acquired some stock and was insisting on a dominant role in the agency's management. Perry departed, leaving B. M. Thornton sole managing director. With the drive of the most enterprising partner gone, the business floundered.

Perry had turned to selling Reo cars (put out by R. E. Olds), but he still retained an admiration for and a deep loyalty to Henry Ford. He heard in the spring of 1909 that the manufacturer was coming to England and promptly wrote him. "I should like to remind you of a promise," he said, "very often repeated by you to me when I was in America . . . that you would look me up when . . . in England, and I trust that although I am not now connected with the representation of the Ford car that you will . . . give me the pleasure of seeing you again and the opportunity of endeavoring to show you some of the interesting features of our country." If Mrs. Ford were coming, he would like to have her meet Mrs. Perry. Ford replied that he did not plan to go abroad that season, "but very likely next year, and you may rest assured that whenever it is my privilege to be in your country I will certainly live up to my promise." [6]

Ford and Couzens had perceived that Perry alone of the English personnel was fitted to head the branch they proposed for Britain. The husk of Perry, Thornton & Schreiber was not equipped to handle a large marketing enterprise, and Detroit was confident that the London establishment would have such a character. Couzens asked Perry if he would like to direct the new undertaking, and the latter promptly agreed.

Thirty-one years of age, rich in automotive experience, full of ideas, energetic, Perry was a happy choice. And for him too the event was fortunate. He was getting all and more than he had sought when he visited the United States in 1906. For several years he had pushed the Ford cars in the face of a dogged English prejudice against them. He had had meagre financial resources and inefficient, bickering partners.

Now he would have full charge of a branch and money to promote it; he would be a part (not just an agent) of the growing Ford company. In the Model T, hailed in both America and Europe, he believed he had a car that people would buy. His own salary of $250.00 a month was merely respectable, but he knew that with success it would become larger. He took charge of the new English enterprise on October 1, 1909.

The London branch had firm financial backing. Its balance sheet in the Detroit records as of September 1909 (its first appearance there) carried these items:

Assets		Liabilities	
Imprest cash	1947.00	Loss & Gain this year	(202.65)
Mdse Automobiles	8802.00	Home Office	11626.00
Sundries	562.00		
Prepaid Accounts	112.35		
	$11423.35		$11423.35

In contrast, the September 1909 assets of the Paris branch were $1413.42, which included $1000.00 in imprest cash, the remainder representing machinery, tools, and other equipment.[7]

Perry started with 9 salaried and 13 hourly employees, a force he would soon enlarge. A point of interest in connection with the birth of the London branch is that on October 5, 1909 Ford-Canada passed a resolution waiving any rights in Great Britain or Ireland that it might have had under the 1904 agreement with Detroit. McGregor's organization renounced "any right . . . to share in any way in any business done or hereafter to be done [in Great Britain and Ireland] by the Ford Motor Company of Detroit." Henry Ford thanked W. R. Campbell, secretary of Ford-Canada, in a letter of November 24, noting that the action "is duly appreciated." Perry accordingly was operating a branch that would be unshadowed by the claim of any outside firm, although from his later correspondence, as we shall see, he did not seem to know the exact arrangement between the Detroit company and the Canadians.[8] *

* Why did the Canadians take such a position? When in 1904 the agreement was made, there was a chance of an English protective tariff with imperial preference. In 1909 this had not yet come into effect. The English Ford business had developed separately from the Canadian, and to inject at this point the Canadian company into it would not only be superfluous but might be destructive. It made far more sense, McGregor recognized, to have the English operation an offshoot of the American Ford Company.

The new London branch strengthened the foreign trade network of the Ford Motor Company, and the fabric became firmer when, about the time of Couzens' trip to Europe, McGregor made a long voyage to Australia and started a comparable sales operation in Melbourne. He had already set up a domestic branch in Toronto; now half way around the world he formed his first one overseas. To head it he appointed a Canadian, R. J. Durance, formerly of the Dunlop Tire Company, who had had experience in both Dominions. Durance opened the new Melbourne unit in October, not long after Perry had taken charge in London.

These were evidences of a growing control of foreign business direct from Detroit and Windsor, and for a time it looked as though this might be extended to Latin America. Shortly after his return from Europe, Couzens took Norval Hawkins to Mexico, intent on establishing a branch there. Nothing came of their excursion. Couzens may have held off because of incipient revolutionary activities against President Porfirio Díaz. At any rate, he took no action, and events proved his decision sound, for Mexico soon lapsed into a prolonged period of violence and political unrest and when it finally emerged took a less important role in automotive activity than other nations farther south. Ford's first Latin American office would soon open, but not in Mexico.

Despite its new overseas branches, Ford in 1909 continued to rely chiefly on export houses and dealers appointed by Lockwood and approved by Detroit. Each of these agencies had the right to sell Fords for limited periods (dealers usually a year). Each agreed to "appoint a subdealer or to establish a properly equipped Branch House or garage for the sale and repair of Ford automobiles in every City or Town within the above-described [a specific] territory as may at any time be designated by the Manufacturer." The distributor also pledged himself to take a certain number of cars each month, an evidence of demand and growing Ford prestige.

From Detroit Couzens directed American sales around the world, while Norval Hawkins in 1909 had authority to execute contracts with "dealers, sub-dealers, limited dealers, and foreign dealers." The branch heads endorsed such agreements as were in areas they supervised.

Lockwood remained as export agent for the company until 1910. From 1903 to that year he had laid a sound basis for Ford expansion abroad. Officials in Detroit now saw that the expanding business could be better managed by salaried employees rather than by one on a commission. Couzens told Lockwood: "We're going to take this agency over," and his contract was not renewed. The position of "foreign department manager" with offices in New York was created and filled at first by men less capable than Lockwood: H. B. Harper (1910–1911) and A. C. Vanderpoel (1911–1912); then by the astute, highly competent and resourceful Ellis Hampton (1912–1913). All these executives were on salary and reported to Couzens and Hawkins in Detroit. The boxing and crating for export continued to be done in Detroit and Walkerville; the New York office allocated orders, processed contracts, handled administrative work, and made collections. It acted for Ford-Canada as well as for the American company in Detroit.[9]

3

"As a rule business institutions in the Dominion do not develop so rapidly as do their American cousins," remarked the *Christian Science Monitor* in 1912, "but this has not applied to the Ford company." The occasion was a review of the progress of Ford-Canada.

That record was remarkable. Up to 1908 the Windsor company had paid only one dividend of 6 per cent in 1905. But with the Model T in 1908, its business soared. That year saw the declaration of a 10 per cent dividend. In 1909 one for 25 per cent followed. In 1910 sales swelled to astonishing dimensions and went on increasing at what seemed a fantastic rate. A 100 per cent dividend was announced; in 1911 this was repeated, with a 500 per cent stock dividend thrown in.* Nineteen twelve saw another stock increase of 33⅓ per cent and a straight 20 per cent dividend out of profits. A man who had bought one share in the company in 1904 for $100, now had eight (worth $500 each), and had received $361.00 in dividends.

Of course, the remark that Ford-Canada was advancing as rapidly as Ford-US showed that the *Monitor*'s writer had never really compared the two. Windsor had made an almost fabulous record, but its production was low compared with Detroit's (11,584 to 168,304 in 1912–1913)

---

* At this time the Ford Motor Company of Canada (an Ontario company) was replaced by a new Dominion company, Ford Motor Company of Canada, with an authorized capital of $1,000,000—a sign of Ford-Canada's growing scope.

and its total dividend payments to date had been less than a tenth of the parent firm's! [10]

Aside from having a superlative car to sell in the Model T, how had McGregor progressed so profitably? In the first place, he had enlarged his manufacturing capacity. From its earliest years, Windsor had steadily acquired machinery and by 1908 was fabricating front axles, spindles, and control parts. In 1910 it had started a program designed to make it an imposing concern. In the next two years it erected a three-story factory, a two-story office building, and a powerhouse. In 1912 it purchased a 52-acre site, planning further expansion there. In 1913 for the first time Ford-Canada built its own motors and made plans for the manufacture of transmissions and all other parts previously purchased from the Dodge brothers. A new six-story building was constructed in 1914, of which the top floor was used for offices and all the others for factory operation.

In short, between 1910 and 1914 the company increased its factory area by almost 600,000 square feet. Sandwich East, Ontario (adjoining Walkerville), where the new property had been purchased in 1912, was renamed "Ford City." Soon a dozen small factories were located there, all supplying the Windsor organization.[11]

While McGregor and his associates developed manufacturing, they had not neglected sales. In addition to the Toronto and Melbourne branches, by August 1913 others were formed in London (Ontario), Montreal, Winnipeg, Hamilton, Vancouver, Saskatoon, and Calgary. In Toronto an assembly plant was soon to rise to expedite distribution in the eastern provinces. All the branches sold Ford cars both retail and wholesale, and helped to penetrate the vast temperate belt of Canada which stretches from east to west north of the American border for three thousand miles.

The growth of the country was no less a factor in the company's success than manufacturing and marketing facilities. In 1901 the population of the Dominion was 5,571,315; in 1911 it stood at 7,206,643, almost 30 per cent greater. New industries had sprung up in Canada, the mileage of good roads had increased, and people had become educated to the usefulness of, and even the necessity for, an automobile. It brought the farmer's products quickly to railhead, lake, or river for further transportation. A. N. Lawrence, Windsor's new sales manager, early in 1914 vividly explained this:

For some time I had reason to suspect that Fords were plentiful and popular in Canada. But I wasn't prepared to find them at every bend in the prairie trail, and see rows of them, from twelve to twenty, lined up on the single street of a town of a few hundred people. . . .

An automobile—a Ford—isn't just a luxury or even a comfort to the pioneers. It is a necessity. They buy a Ford as they buy farm tools. It *is* a tool to them. They must have it to get to the nearest town for supplies. They economize rigidly in their food and clothes to buy a Ford.

In 1913 the *Ford Times* boasted that Walkerville was turning out more cars than any other automobile plant in the British Empire, *including England*. In 1914 more Fords were sold in Canada than the sum of all other automobiles marketed there. The export trade was likewise moving briskly. McGregor's dream in 1904 of a cheap car for the many had come to be a fact.[12]

Ford of Canada with minor modifications built a replica of the Detroit Model T. Its machinery, adjusted to smaller volume, was often the same as that used across the Detroit River. The Toronto assembly plant, both in style and construction, resembled similar buildings in the United States.

Yet the management of the Dominion operation, considering that the main plants of the two companies lay only six miles apart (as the crow flies), showed an independence that seems unusual. McGregor, Campbell (now assistant manager), A. N. Lawrence (who had taken charge of sales in September 1912), George Dickert in production, and P. W. Grandjean (accounting), all helped to give the affiliated company its own individuality. Henry Ford had become president of the Canadian firm on the death of John S. Gray, and Couzens became vice president in 1907. But the participation of these executives in Dominion affairs was nominal. McGregor consulted them, both attended Board meetings, but the stocky manager from Walkerville was creative pilot and complete boss of the corporation he had brought to life.[13]

While Ford-Canada sold more cars in the Dominion in 1914 than all its rivals combined, it leaned heavily on its foreign sales to complement domestic ones. If the mileage of good Canadian highways was increasing, in many areas roads were literally nightmares. Sales Manager Lawrence reported driving his car "down to the hubs in ooze," and such conditions restricted the number of his customers. Many Canadian car owners stored their machines in winter because of deep snow, mud, or extreme cold. Consequently the Walkerville organization regarded itself as fortunate that during 1910–1913, from 38 to 43 per cent of all its production was exported. The total sent overseas amounted to between two and three times the exports of Ford-US, although Canadian production was only one-tenth of the American. Foreign trade also meant the company could have even year-around production, for India had a tropical climate, and South Africa, Australia, and New Zealand, south of the equator, were taking summer in full swing while the Dominion was deep in snow and icicles. As Campbell pointed out, "The peak demand from our foreign territory . . . comes when our domestic demand is at its lowest ebb." [14] *

During these years a department of the large export house of Markt & Hammacher handled the expanding Canadian Ford business in the East. Two brothers, V. A. and Henry T. Dodge, represented this firm. They traveled throughout the Orient, and among other duties set up agencies to sell the Model T. Soon in India, Ceylon, Burma, and Malaya Ford showrooms and garages opened. When George V was crowned Emperor of India at Delhi in December 1911, V. A. Dodge was one of the spectators. "The procession was magnificent," he recalls. "There were elephants, camels, Ford cars, and everything all mingled together" in oriental magnificence, "a beautiful showing."

In the fall of 1911 Dodge had gone to Malaya, hoping to find there an agent for Model T's. He met Australian-born J. B. Wearne, then selling English automobiles in Singapore, and offered him a Ford agency; but the Australian repeated the worn cliché that American cars were not good business. When Dodge returned several months later, he found that Wearne meanwhile had driven a Model T and overnight had become a convert. "Say, V. A.," he said, "I think we could do something. Give us the agency."

Wearne had a well-equipped workshop, a brother who was a mechanic, and considerable automotive experience. "I gave him the agency," Dodge said later, and it became one of his best. Miners, rubber planters, importers, and rubber speculators—all British—made good money in the region. There were also some Chinese who owned small rubber groves and traded in shares and were prosperous. Most persons

* Most Canadian sales were in the British Empire; on a few made in areas served by Ford-US, Ford-Canada paid Detroit a 2½ per cent fee to recompense the American company for sales expenses.

in this motley group were purchasers of Fords, which enabled them to do their business more expeditiously and offered a pleasant means of transportation in a hot climate.

Everywhere in the East the Dodges chose agents who in their opinion would do a good job of marketing. The merchant firm of Kilborn & Company was an old English partnership that had traded in the East for years. This firm had a subsidiary, Russa Engineering, which handled the Ford business along with other products, mostly machinery. The Englishman A. R. (now Sir Rowland) Smith came to India to work for that agency. "When I arrived on July 10, 1912," he later recalled, "I saw natives stripping open cases of K.D. [knocked down] car parts." Russa Engineering used native labor entirely, and Eurasians for supervisors. Both were efficient. "There were no Canadians employed," Smith remembered, although the cars being assembled by the dealer were Dominion Model T's.

In Burma V. A. Dodge chose McKenzie & Company, an organization owned by an English department store, Rowe & Co. In Ceylon he selected Brown & Company Ltd., which had a handsome establishment and was also under English management. All these firms handled other products as well as Fords.

But although his distributors were English-owned, Dodge stipulated that they must follow "American marketing methods." The British had the idea," he remembered, "that everyone should come to them; the American practice was the reverse: we went to our customers." He also stressed the importance of service. Competition was weak on mechanics and repair shops. Dodge made sure that his agents had both and said of their rivals: "You can beat them on service."

In the East, buyers were mostly Europeans, although some wealthy Indians, and as we have noted some Chinese, also bought cars. In India and Ceylon the British had built highways for military purposes, so also in Malaya. The existence of well-paved highways was important: the better the roads, the better the market for cars.[15]

As Markt & Hammacher operated through the Dodges in the East, so Arkell & Douglas handled Ford-Canada trade in South Africa. This New York export house (with its Montreal office) dealt not only in automobiles, but also in machinery, tools, electrical appliances, chemicals, and other products. It had branches in Johannesburg, Port Elizabeth, and Capetown. Its representative, C. B. Wessinger, with headquarters in

Port Elizabeth, appointed Ford dealers for the important South African cities and towns. One was to be selected for Kimberley, where in 1907 H. G. Holmes had set up a shop to repair "any make of Motor Cars, Cycle, or Machinery of any description." He had been called upon to repair a Ford and was so impressed with it that when Wessinger arrived in 1912 to find an agent, Holmes asked for and got the post. His son remembered later "the great decision . . . to order the first six Fords. . . . Father was very worried about the risk he was taking, and six months were required to guarantee delivery." But the cars were sold quickly, and Holmes' sales grew. In 1914 he gave up the British automobiles he had been handling and concentrated on "the Universal Car." * Arkell & Douglas used some dealers like Holmes who financed themselves; others operated businesses owned by the New York firm.[16]

Oceans away, Colonial Motors Ltd. of Wellington took over the distribution of Ford-Canada cars in New Zealand, using 29 sub-dealers and doing a brisk business. For the Australian market, the Windsor company continued to operate its only foreign branch at Melbourne, which R. J. Durance managed well. "When I first tried to sell an American car to them [the Australians] they couldn't see anything but British and Continental makes," he recalled later. "For a time I found the selling rather hard." But he appointed distributors and began to get results. The Ford gained a reputation for reliability and endurance. In 1912, alarmed and impoverished by a period of drought, Australian buyers turned en masse from high-priced English cars to the lower-priced Fords. In his first three years Durance sold almost 2000 Canadian Model T's, which made his island-continent the best outlet McGregor had overseas.[17]

4

Meanwhile, Perry in England was having less trouble combating British car competition. Mounting sales convinced the American directors that it made sense to erect an assembly plant in that country. If parts were sent there knocked down, freight would be lower, for as earlier noted, bulk as well as weight determined the shipping fee. There

---

* He won considerable publicity for an endurance run from Johannesburg to Kimberley, 320 miles, which he did in 11 hours and 57 minutes, 5½ hours faster than the previous record. On the trip he had to open and close 130 gates! Such was motoring in South Africa in 1914.

would of course be no savings in custom duties, for England was still a free trade country.

During 1910 Perry sought a plant site and finally found one in Manchester, forty miles from the west coast of England, but having direct access to the sea through the Manchester Ship Canal. Consignments from Detroit or New York could come directly to this assembly location. He chose a 5½-acre tract managed by Trafford Park Estates, Ltd. In 1897 this firm had acquired some 1200 acres of flat land, much of it covered by virgin forest, which had been owned by the De Trafford family. Here deer had roamed, pheasants had nested, and rabbits scampered about or fed quietly at the edges of the glades. By 1910 nothing remained of the original wooded quiet; Trafford Park, as it was still called, had become an industrial center occupied by numerous manufacturing firms, a few of them of American origin. The Ford assembly plant would help to complete the transformation from the idyllic into the harshly mechanical. Perry was satisfied. Not only would the crated Model T's be delivered at his doorstep, but railway lines ran from Trafford Park to all parts of England. He later (in 1913) called the spot "the very best geographical and economic center for our business." [18]

Detroit accepted the selection, and Perry arranged to transfer activities there. Even as he planned to move, the Scottish Ford dealer Henry Alexander drove a Model T up rough roads and over ravines, boulders, and through bogs to the top of the lofty peak Ben Nevis. The idea had been Perry's, the ruggedness to accomplish the feat Alexander's. The resultant publicity fully met Perry's expectations; British papers were eager to tell the story of the first ascent of a noted mountain by a man in a motor car, and talk about it sped the work of Ford salesmen.

The Manchester plant was ready for operation in October 1911. Meanwhile, Detroit officials perceived their next natural step: to replace their British branch with a company. This gave them certain tax advantages and opened up possibilities of strengthening the firm they proposed to create by making it an English corporation. Its reputation would be greater as an independent unit rather than a branch.

Accordingly on March 8, 1911 the Ford Motor Company (England) Ltd. was incorporated. It was wholly owned by the stockholders of the parent American firm. It had a capital of £1000 ($4860.00), and 200 shares were issued at £5 each. Of these Henry Ford held 117. Although Perry acquired no stock in the new corporation, he was well rewarded. His income in 1912 had risen to $25,000, equal to that of Gaston Plan-

tiff, Ford's New York manager, highest paid of all the branch heads.*
For the year ending September 30, 1914, Perry was paid $15,000 in
salary and an $18,000 bonus. During the two years he had operated the
English enterprise as a branch, it had sold 1023 Model T cars and made
profits of $145,333.04. But as a company it was destined to have even
greater success.[19]

Perry and Henry Ford saw each other when the British manager
came to Detroit on business and maintained a close friendship. On July
13, 1912 Ford with his wife Clara, his son Edsel, and Mrs. Ford's brother,
Marvin Bryant, sailed for Europe, landing at Plymouth on the 20th.
Perry could now hold the industrialist to his early promises and met the
four tourists with a Rolls-Royce. He took them on a guided tour of
England, stopping to inspect the premises of a few Ford dealers, and
leading them through Bath, Exeter, London, and Warwick, where Clara
Ford's mother had been born.

Finally the party arrived at Lymm, twelve miles from Manchester,
where the Americans resided in luxury at Perry's mansion-home. Clara
noted that it had "a fine old garden, orchard, and bowling green." On
this Henry Ford and Perry competed with Marvin Bryant and Edsel.
Edsel, now nineteen, was just entering the company, where he had often
worked during summer vacations. While for several years he would be
moving about the factory, becoming familiar with the operations, he
would soon take an important role in its affairs as an executive.

Perry took the father and son repeatedly to the nearby Ford plant
at Manchester, then to Coventry, the center of English automotive industry, and the home of the Hillman, Rover, Standard, Singer, Riley,
Siddeley-Deasy, Humber, Daimler, and Triumph (then making motorcycles). At Birmingham they inspected the Wolseley works and went on
to Derby to see the Rolls-Royce factory.

The review of English automotive industry well in hand, Henry
Ford and his party embarked for Ireland (August 8), where they visited
Killarney and Dublin as well as Cork. This was the land from which
William Ford, the manufacturer's father, had emigrated, and the indus-
trialist examined it with great interest. The seeds of his later activities
in Ireland were probably sown at this time.

The culmination of the European journey was a whirlwind trip
around France, with visits to H. B. White, the early Ford dealer Henri

---

* Charles E. Sorensen, who would later become the head of Ford production, at this
time earned $10,000 a year, and that too was the salary of F. L. Klingensmith, soon to
replace Couzens as vice president of the American company.

Depasse, and the Renault, Clément-Bayard, and Charron automobile factories. The four returned home on August 25.[20]

Henry Ford's opinion of the Manchester plant on this trip was not recorded. No doubt he found it similar to assembly centers in the United States; we do know, however, from later comments, that he was dissatisfied with its status: he wanted a factory on freehold property and not on leased land (as this one was). Moreover, the operation was cramped.

Ford had seen the English plant in its first year of operation. It was not very large: the Canadian company's capacity was 25,000 cars a year, Detroit's 250,000, Trafford Park's no more than 15,000. While it was still primarily an assembly operation, some local manufacturing was creeping in. As yet the English contribution amounted to little, but as bodies and other elements came to be furnished by local suppliers, and some by the Ford plant itself, the proportion of local content steadily increased.[21]

Not long after Ford returned to the United States, serious labor unrest occurred at the Trafford Park plant. "Manchester is . . . the hot bed of trade unionism," complained Perry. From September 1912 well on into 1913 he had to deal with a series of annoying strikes which seriously curtailed production. On February 13, the sheet metal workers walked out of both the Ford plant and a nearby body works. Perry asserted that the strike at "the outside Body Working Factory is being used by the metal workers as a lever . . . to force us into settling the dispute within our own Works." He was deeply distressed. "The recent labor disputes have almost broken my heart," he wrote Ford in February 1913.

Ford was firmly opposed to labor unions, and Perry refused to bargain with them. A blond champion charged in to deliver him: Danish by birth, but an American since early childhood, Charles E. Sorensen took ship from America, came to Manchester and assessed the situation there. Originally a pattern maker in the Detroit Ford foundry, Sorensen had already assumed some authority in the field of production, had Ford's full trust, and an aggressive, driving, dynamic ability. He was shrewd also. By assuring strategically placed workers of both job security and high wages, he broke the union power at Ford-Manchester and ended the dispute. In April 1914 when Sorensen was again in England, he was pleased to learn that "in the past six months there has been no sign of labor trouble. The unionism which has always been cropping up heretofore has been absolutely broken up."

Sorensen was the more delighted because there was not an employer in the Trafford Park area, he boasted, "who is not obligated in some manner to labor organizations. I can also say that we are the only company in that vicinity who are absolutely free and independent and who are not having controversies any more with their men." The company had acquired the outside body plant that had promoted the original trouble, and Sorensen in the spring of 1914 hailed it as "the best body building plant that I have yet seen." [22]

He reported that the Manchester factory made "an exact replica of the American car." Slowly it edged into manufacturing, under Detroit's careful supervision. It set up a purchasing department to buy parts from English suppliers—lamps, horns, wiring, and soft trim. This new unit worked in complete harmony with the American Ford purchasing organization. With every item available in England, a comparison was made between its price and that for the same article in Detroit; if the quality was good and the cost less than that in Detroit plus transportation across the Atlantic, the local product was bought. Harry Hudson from the Highland Park plant started work at Trafford Park, assisting in production, the first of a number of Americans in that field to join the staff of Ford Ltd.

Ford of England was expected to build exactly to American Ford patterns. However, certain concessions were made to local practice and taste. For example, in 1913 the Manchester product showed a right-hand rather than a left-hand drive, adapting the car to the British custom of driving on the left side of the road. Again, while Trafford Park built the standard Ford body, some English dealers made special bodies for the Ford chassis. But variations at the factory were rare, and Sorensen's assertion that the English cars were reproductions of those produced in America was essentially accurate.[23]

In production and purchasing techniques the resemblance between Manchester and Detroit was also close. Only in the English company's marketing was there any significant divergence from American methods. In setting up a dealer organization Perry had followed the standard British pattern: a dealer was permitted to sell other cars as well as Fords. In contrast, the American practice demanded that every agent deal exclusively in Ford Motor Company units. It would have shocked the father of the Model T to know that Ford Motor Company (England) Ltd. permitted its representatives to offer Austins and Crossleys, for example, as well as the "Universal Car," but this was the fact.

When Norval Hawkins, the American sales manager, made inquiry

1a. Henry Ford in 1904.

1b. Ford with Percival Perry in September 1916.

2. The Old and the New: A South Australian donkey wagon and a Ford car (1916); *below* An overseas shipment of Ford cars being loaded on a vessel of the Ford fleet (1924).

about the matter, Perry briefly explained his method, adding "We beg of you not to interfere therewith, as our organization has been built up with 'maximum terms for Everybody' as the cornerstone. Another enormous factor in our success has been the claim which has never been violated, that we have never gone back on an Agent who served us well." No one from Detroit at this time moved to disrupt the English manager's procedure.[24]

In 1912 Ford of England sold 3187 cars; in 1913, 7310; a year later, 8352. Wolseley was its closest competitor, with an output in 1913 of between two and three thousand. Morris, Austin, Singer, and Rover each produced about a thousand vehicles. Perry declared in April 1914: "Today we have near upon 1,000 agents in our organization. . . . The car is established. Its qualities are known. It is far past the position of numerical domination in the English market. It takes the combined output of five of the next largest car manufacturers in this country to equal Ford sales." English passenger car production for 1913 came to about 25,000, so that the Model T was responsible for almost 29 percent of the total.

While the rapid progress of the ungainly American car shocked British manufacturers, who were soon to seek tariff protection against this alien in their midst (and get it, but not find safety for some years), the British public in contrast continued to be pleased with the Model T.

Perhaps the highest tribute to Ford's success in England was that the enterprising manufacturer, William Richard Morris (later Lord Nuffield), took it with complete seriousness. Setting out to compete with the Model T, he produced his first car, the Morris-Oxford, in April 1913. Like the Detroit manufacturer, he emphasized reliability and used standardized parts. His biographers tell us that he wanted to capture "the market which hitherto had been dominated by Ford." Morris would be a keen competitor in the future. But meanwhile happenings in Detroit were to strengthen the Model T's position all over the world.[25]

5

"Beyond all doubt or question, the Ford Motor Company's plant at Highland Park, Detroit, Michigan, U.S.A. . . . is the most interesting metal-working establishment in the world." This was the verdict of two engineers who had made an exhaustive study of the center—its laboratories, its thousands of machine tools, its economy, its use of power, and above all its merging of such factors into time-saving movement.

For, to cut through a dozen phases of production that had been growing in the United States for years, we may say that American industry was on the verge of achieving mass production, which must be sharply distinguished from quantity production. The latter had been a fact for some years. Mass production had never existed, and its dramatic character lay in bringing to bear, coordinating, and making one process, many elements, among which were power, standardization, machine tools and allied processes, the exact repetition of mechanical performances, and above all in moving all these and other factors by power-driven devices without the least pause to the final assembly of a complicated product.

In 1912–1913 about everything was ready for the achievement of this goal except the means of continuous assembly. "The full realization of mass production . . . hinged on this problem [*i.e.,* moving assembly]," wrote Samuel Reznick. "It was a broad problem of management and control and coordination of production. . . . In supplying the control and coordination the automobile industry became peculiarly important in the evolution of mass production; its history in fact epitomizes the triumph of mass production in the United States."

He might have added, "and in the world"; for nowhere else were men at the point of achieving this miracle. And while various American automobile firms made important contributions to the final achievement, it was at Highland Park, and in the factory of the Ford Motor Company, that the idea of a final moving assembly was realized—a practice which used slides, rollers, and power-driven conveyors to bring the work to the men in the plant, did away with pushing, lifting, and even adjusting for proper height, and enabled a chassis which had taken 14 man-hours to complete to be finished in less than 2! Minor moving assembly lines fed into the final one, and the time required for the production of all automobile parts was similarly reduced. For example, the commutator, a small unit which had taken hours to be produced in 1912, was in 1915 produced in 16 minutes and 27 seconds of one man's time.[26]

The moving assembly line was soon adopted by most automotive firms; it permeated American industry as a whole, infecting factories everywhere with the germ of a new and more abundant life. But its importance to the Ford Motor Company and the Model T should not go unrecognized. It was a magic that transformed both. Ford permitted full observation of his processes, but to reproduce them took years, and the Highland Park factory was constantly improving its methods. Consequently for a decade no company could match Ford production. From an output of 78,440 cars in 1911–1912 the firm leapt to 168,304 in 1912–1913. The succeeding year the total soared to 248,307. At the same time the methods that turned out machines in dizzying quantity made possible startling reductions in prices. On October 1, 1910 the Ford roadster had sold for $680; on October 1, 1912, it was priced at $525, a year later at $500, and in August 1914 at $440. Nowhere else in the world during this period could anything like a comparable car be bought for such prices. The position of the Ford can be seen from the fact that its 1914 production was about 43 per cent of the total American output of 573,039 cars.

In 1913 the sales of the Model T swept past those of General Motors, to hold first place among all automotive firms in the world for the next twelve years. The single Ford model was able to outsell all four GM cars and its truck unit. The mass-produced Model T with fabulously low prices had achieved a superiority and had become a legend in every land where automobiles were driven.[27]

Hard upon its startling successes in production and pricing, the Ford Motor Company on January 5, 1914, announced that it was reducing its work day to eight hours (forty-eight hours a week), and would pay a basic wage of five dollars. This approximately doubled what had been previously paid at Highland Park, and more than doubled what most workmen received elsewhere. The company's chief reason was logical but to most employers outrageous: it was making too much money, and felt that the workers who built the car should share in the golden harvest. Its profits were indeed enormous, for the corporation had paid $11,200,000 in dividends in 1913. (As a matter of fact, it was to pay a million more in 1914 despite its higher wage bill!) Labor leaders and social liberals hailed the act as a step toward a new earthly paradise, but many economists and business leaders felt it would breed trouble. Ford was an angel to the millions, a demon to the powerful few.

Wages were soon raised in England (April 1914) and in Canada (April 1915). In each case the effort was to translate the five-dollar day into British and Canadian equivalents. In all Ford offices around the world employees were beneficiaries of the policy initiated in Detroit.[28] *

---

* In England the first step was to establish a 48-hour (instead of 50-hour) week with no cut in wages, while the company added £50,000 to the total wage payment and termed it a "distribution of profits." The result was a minimum wage of 1s. 3d. an hour

6

Low prices and news of the Ford largess had a quickening effect on the foreign trade of the company everywhere. Even in France, where Renault, Panhard, Lorraine-Dietrich and other makes flourished, the situation for Ford salesmen brightened. Could Fords be sold there? "Difficile, mais pas impossible," crisply answered the French dealer, Henri Depasse. He had started in 1908 on the fashionable Boulevard Haussmann in central Paris but had been forced to move the next year to a humbler location in the suburb of Neuilly. Yet now in 1912 and 1913 his sales zoomed upwards, as did those of other French agents.

H. B. White opened a Bordeaux Ford branch in October 1913, but in its first six months this office did business amounting to only $14, 592. Paris, however, showed cash sales for 1913-1914 of $1,762,584. Both Bordeaux and the capital got cars and parts from Manchester as well as from Detroit, and White allotted some of the English Model T's to his numerous European dealers outside France. He had appointed George Catala and Paul Vandersmissen as distributors for western and eastern Belgium respectively, and in 1913-1914, with the low prices of the Detroit and Manchester models, their sales had risen sharply.[29]

E. C. Gjestvang in Sweden and Norway and F. Bülow in Denmark were also active. Bülow, a Ford agent since 1906, illustrates the growth of business at the time. He had sold only 11 cars in 1907; in 1909, only 32; but in 1913 he disposed of 109 and his volume was rising. A Spanish Ford agency had opened in 1910 and sold 5 cars in its first year; in the next, 190.

In Russia the progress of dealer M. S. Friede, formerly a Detroit journalist, had been phenomenal. With branches in Odessa, St. Petersburg, Libau (Latvia), and Reval (Estonia), his sales ranked second only to the French dealers. He wrote home in the fall of 1913:

> In the dense forests of Siberia twenty Fords are aiding the engineers in the construction of the Amur River Railroad. In the oil fields of Baku the only car to be seen is a Ford.

as compared with a former 10d. In the late spring of 1914 Sorensen went over to England and on June 3 wrote Henry Ford of his efforts "to assist Mr. Perry in arranging a profit-sharing plan on the same basis that is being carried forward in our Detroit plant" (the five-dollar day was called profit sharing). Canada at first established a $4.00 a day minimum, later raised this to $5.00; by 1919 Canadian and American Ford wages were the same.

Ninety per cent of the cars in the far eastern city of Vladivostock are Fords. The Ford is the most popular car in the fertile black earth sections of Central and Southern Russia.

A good number of the regiments of the army . . . have Fords as part of their equipment. Two Grand Dukes and nineteen Princes own Fords. The President of the Duma, Prince Volkonsky, has three Fords . . . and drives them himself.

At the recent maneuvers near Peterhof, the Generals of the Imperial Staff were carried from point to point in eight Fords. Two heavy cars of German make attempted the work but failed . . . in the heavy mud.

The streets of Moscow, Odessa, and St. Petersburg are alive with Fords. Merchants, banks, newspaper offices, the Secret Police, the palace Guards, Government officials—all use the Universal Car.[30]

Germany offered a discouraging contrast. "The use of home products is regarded as a duty almost amounting to a religion," asserted an article in the *Ford Times.* A United States Department of Commerce report noted that "no American manufacturer can hope to have any great success without establishing in Germany at least one depot for supplies and repairs." Early in 1912 Ford did just that, organizing a center for spare parts in Hamburg to supply not only Germany but also the entire European continent. A Belgian dealer in 1912, inquiring about a rear axle, was informed that "the shipment had been made through our Hamburg branch." New York Export Manager A. C. Vanderpoel assumed too much for the German center: he dispatched there cars and parts destined for southern Europe! This meant a delay of weeks and needless wear and tear in transshipment and excessive handling. His naïveté became the object of ridicule in a later Department of Commerce report.

The branch at Hamburg was operated by a German, A. Tuma, who was not a high-ranking official, and in 1914 earned a daily wage of $6.00. The business he did seems to have been proportionate to his pay. Company sales throughout all Germany were modest, amounting to 171 cars in 1912–1913 and 283 in 1913–1914. They compared with 370 and 425 shipped to Russia in these years. Sorensen saw little evidence of Ford activity in the Reich. "The only place I saw any Ford cars was Hamburg," he reported in 1914 to Henry Ford.

It has already been noted that Manchester shipped some cars and parts to continental Europe, and Perry's secretary, Miss Vera Howard, recalled later that White was often in London, consulting with her employer. The two made a contrast in manner: "White very much more vociferous," Perry reserved. At times they disagreed, and on at least one occasion referred their dispute to Detroit. Manchester in 1913 had "definite instructions not to attend to any correspondence with Continental dealers." The latter were under White, but the Englishman was already nursing the idea that some day he would direct Ford operations on the continent from his office in Britain.[31]

7

Ford branches in the United States had multiplied to 31 in 1914; the Canadian company, as we have seen, had also increased its sales outlets in the Dominion and had made a start in Australia; Ford-US now operated a French branch and an English company. Distributors sold the Ford car everywhere else—from Salisbury in Rhodesia to Tientsin in China. The Ford factory at Windsor with sales of $8,796,024 was the largest plant in the British Empire; Manchester did a business of $4,974,091 to lead by a wide margin all the motor car firms in England. Now the parent firm in Detroit began to consider expansion in Latin America.

American trade with neighbors in the Western Hemisphere had doubled from 1903 to 1913, and Ford sales had also increased in these years. The automobile business was limited by the wretchedness of existing roads and their almost complete absence in some countries. Paraguay was considered impossible. In Peru and Venezuela there were only a few miles of roadways in or near the larger cities. The American consul in Chile warned his countrymen in the motor car business that any efforts they made in that republic "would be practically wasted." Mexico was in the throes of revolution.

But Couzens believed that markets could be developed in Argentina, Brazil, and Uruguay. There Ford distributors had proved sales could be made. Roads were better, and all three countries had enterprising populations. In 1913 Couzens urged that Ellis Hampton, the Ford export manager in New York, be sent to Argentina to report on the establishment of a branch there. Hampton took the assignment, and the December 1913 Ford-US Board of Directors minutes record: "It is deemed advisable for the . . . transaction of the business of the Ford Motor

Company that it establish in several South American countries branches for the care and conduct of its business." Argentina was selected for the first experiment, and "Eli. [*sic*] Hampton of Buenos Aires" was appointed "true and lawful agent and attorney" for the Ford Motor Company in that republic.[32]

Without knowing it, the directors had acted with great daring. Although confident of the future, Hampton had not told them all the difficulties that darkened the present. He was to write later that "conditions . . . could not have been more discouraging." Argentina tottered on the verge of a panic, crops had been poor for several seasons, credit was overexpanded, and interest rates in Europe had risen, cutting down investments in the country. Many businesses in Buenos Aires were failing. Nevertheless in February 1914 Hampton rented a store as a show room for automobiles and spare parts. Soon his sales force was out marketing Fords all over the country. The branch did retail business but also operated through dealers, who covered specified territories.

Hampton had full authority on behalf of the company. He needed it: to reach New York from Buenos Aires took twenty-one days. The new manager had to get the fullest information he could and then make his own decisions. He did not confine himself to Argentina, but traveled throughout South America, discovering that conditions were often not so bad as they had been painted. For example, in Chile he signed on an agent who agreed to take 60 cars, although "prior to making this connection, we did not sell more than two cars annually [in that country]." Again, although the United States Department of Commerce pronounced Venezuela a poor risk for marketing automobiles, Hampton signed another contract there calling for 60 cars. In São Paulo, Brazil, Ford distributor William T. Wright promised to accept 325 units, and Juan Shaw of Montevideo, Uruguay, gave an order for 100.

In a few months world events would operate to enlarge enormously the sale of American cars in these countries; but even in a period of economic depression Hampton had shown that they could be marketed successfully.[33]

8

In New York Hampton's enterprising successor, Eber Sherman, pushed the sale of Model T's in areas not served by companies or branches. He executed foreign dealer agreements for areas from the Philippines to Japan, from Mexico to Ecuador, from Portuguese West Africa to Togoland.

As noted earlier, the American Ford company, like the Canadian used the "Asiatic Department" of Markt & Hammacher for its Eastern trade. Under special contract, this agency sold Fords in the Dutch East Indies, Siam, Indo-China, and China. For the year 1913–1914 it agreed to accept not less than 250 cars and promised to represent "almost exclusively Ford Motor Cars in the countries . . . designated, and if he [the commission house] should handle any other make of motor cars it is understood that the selling price of such motor cars will be at least Six Hundred (600) dollars in advance of the list price of Ford Motor Cars." (In effect, Henry T. or V. A. Dodge could sell Rolls-Royces, Pierce-Arrows, or Packards, but nothing to compete in the Model T's low-priced field.) The contract specified that either Dodge "will visit the principal cities of the countries above named, at least once during the life of this Agreement . . . [and] that they will push the sale of Ford cars to every possible extent in all the countries named." In return Markt & Hammacher received a 2½ per cent commission.[34]

Early in 1914 Ford foreign sales everywhere were at a new high. Walkerville was shipping 110 cars a day. McGregor, a frequent visitor at the Highland Park plant, dropped in to see F. L. Klingensmith late in February 1914 to tell him that "conditions were the best there that they have ever been."

Perry felt the same way about the English and European situation. Brilliant and ambitious, he was planning for a dazzling future. He saw Manchester as a temporary location. He was convinced that the English Ford company should own an ample site, build an imposing plant, and supply the European continent as well as Britain. The Manchester plant was repugnant to him because of the labor troubles encountered there, its ugliness, and its grim climate. Ford of England could be a giant, and no giant could be contained in the Trafford Park area. Henry Ford agreed, and suggested that Cork would be a good location for a manufacturing center. Perry rejected this plan as impractical. Ireland, he wrote Henry Ford, was "remote." The great factory should be in England, and his own choice was Southampton, the large port on the south coast of England, directly across the channel from continental Europe, and close to London. Perry was dreaming of a supply post for most of the British Empire. England, he maintained quite justly, was a far better site than any in Canada for shipping to India and South Africa. "Imagine a concern wanting to do business with the Ford Motor Company trying to deal with a branch at Fargo or Dallas!" he exclaimed. "Great Britain to the British Colonies is the Detroit of Ford Motor Company." [35]

Product, price, social reputation—all conspired to give these sentiments force. Offspring of the magic moving assembly line, cheap enough for a skilled workman, built by men paid at a rate that shocked economists and bankers, the Model T was a living legend to which Perry's plans did no more than justice.

Sorensen at least agreed that these were good. But after talking with H. B. White, he also favored assembly plants in Hamburg and France. Perry opposed such continental developments; he wanted all European countries to be fully dependent on his super-British factory.

Henry Ford had not made up his mind. He respected Perry and was fond of him personally. He too was dissatisfied with the Manchester site. Yet he was by no means sure that it made good sense to erect a manufacturing plant at Southampton and give Perry authority over all of Europe. Moreover, he knew what Perry did not: that he and Ford-US had granted an exclusive license giving patent and other rights to the Canadian company in respect to the British colonies and possessions.

Ford reserved decision. Perry had an option on the land at Southampton, but getting no word from Detroit, he procured an extension on July 21, 1914. Then in less than two weeks (on August 4) Britain entered World War I.

No thunderclap changing a clear summer day to a black sky lit by jagged lightning was more startling than this event to the Ford organization everywhere. Earlier international crises had passed and even the assassination of the Austrian Archduke Francis Ferdinand at Sarajevo had left the officials of the company unprepared for a resort to arms. As we shall see, the effects in Europe, North America, Africa, Asia, the Far East, and South America were to be momentous. But the immediate facts were that with the beginning of the conflict both Great Britain and Canada were affected. We can turn now to the English scene, which felt the first brunt of hostilities.[36]

4

The Alchemy of War

The entrance of their nation into the First World War on August 4, 1914 appalled many British citizens. The country had joined with France and Russia in opposing the Central Powers only after the invasion of neutral Belgium by German armies on August 3. Two weeks later Percival Perry himself wrote to Norval Hawkins, sales manager of the American company, that Britain had passed through "a period of panic and paralysis." The English *Ford Times* commented with bitter regret on what had occurred. "There is war," it proclaimed. "The greatest human agent of devastation, swollen and malignant as never before . . . is sweeping across Europe with fire and sword." The little house organ saw the event as maniacal. "There is no brain in a fist. . . . Force is no argument."

These sentiments anticipated those of Henry Ford himself, who some months later was to launch a year and a half of war-against-war. But they represented an emotional outburst and not a declaration of policy, and by August 18th Perry was loyally supporting the British cabinet and working "to secure orders from the Government for our Chassis for war purposes and for ambulance work." He was successful. On September 28 company records show a War Office order for "9 van ambulances," and others followed. The company was also selling Model T touring cars for war use.[1]

Perry quickly perceived that in battle-torn Europe the surge of Ford sales progress would be checked, and in his letter to Hawkins he prophesied that trade there would be "a negligible quantity for years to come." At the same time he recognized that something existed which he and his associates should seek to preserve: "The good will of the Ford name has been established in every country on the continent, and that good will should not be allowed to die. Plans should be made for a permanent and consistent effort." The letter indicates that Perry saw in the situation a special possibility for expanding the area of the English company's control, a policy which, as we have seen, he had already frankly expounded to American officials.[2]

He was soon in Detroit, taking counsel with Ford and Couzens as to his future actions. Ford had not yet begun his pacifist campaign, but Perry knew his sentiments, while he himself indicated Ford of England must be loyal to its government. On this visit he may also have spoken for Manchester employees who had joined the colors. Either then or later he reminded Ford that his (Ford's) workers in Detroit who took part in the Mexican campaign (1913–1914) had been promised their jobs on return and protection for their families in the interim. He asked as much for British workers. "You do it here in America," he recalled arguing, "and it is as fair in England." Ford recognized the soundness of the appeal and permitted the creation of a fund to care for the widows and children of Manchester volunteers. This act was to give Perry a strong charge of ammunition to fire on behalf of his employer when a year and a half later Ford had become highly unpopular in England. Couzens meanwhile had shown himself a firm Allied supporter. "My sympathies are with you in this war," he wrote to an English correspondent that fall.

On this trip Perry probably bid for the right to supervise affairs on the European continent; eventually he won what he wanted. At the same time the Manchester factory had increased its governmental work. Early in 1915 Perry could report selling 150 ambulances, and he was soon to win a standing order for 10 a week; he also undertook a contract (the first of a number) for the manufacture of shell containers for 18-pound guns. The first ambulances which the plant turned out had been rather fantastic creations, but the model was quickly standardized, providing solid walls and bunks for four men. It sold for £125. Ten chassis had also been sent from Manchester to Paris, where tops were provided, and the machines were used to good effect in the Battle of the Marne. A certain amount of civilian production had also been continued.[3]

In 1915 Perry won from Ford permission to spend up to £100 a week for assistance to the Belgian refugees now streaming into England. He and Mrs. Perry, who was also active in managing the enterprise, procured Oughtrington Hall, a mansion on a 30-acre estate only one and a half miles from the Perry home at Lymm. Stables, piggeries, and agricultural equipment were included in the rental of roughly $35 a month. Here a selected group of Belgians was welcomed. Families especially were sought, and soon the colony included a large number of children. The men undertook gardening, the care of the piggeries, and other suitable occupations, and the women teaching and housework. "We have a man who owned his own Restaurant in Liége, cooking the food," wrote Perry to Ford; "another man, who was an engineer at Antwerp, making the fires and attending to the cleaning of fire grates . . . a Barber from Ostend taking care of the haircutting and shaving." Donations were made by many English residents in the vicinity. The Hall finally housed 110 persons. A small wage was paid to each worker, but was held in reserve until the Belgians could return to their own country.[4]

Before the end of 1914 a total of 166 Ford employees from an original work force of 1500 had joined the armed forces. The company soon became a government-controlled establishment.* Perry described the resources of his plant to War Office personnel, offering to supply trained mechanics to service Ford cars and to provide instruction for men assigned by the Army to the plant. He was equally busy seeking permission to export cars to neutral and allied European countries and was able to supply them to Russia, Sweden, unoccupied Belgium, and Denmark. He was also shipping to France. In these activities he cooperated with H. B. White but steadily increased his control of French affairs. By the end of 1915 he was preparing to manufacture light tanks with imported engines. On May 7, 1916 he could write proudly: "We have supplied by direct contract with His Majesty's Government, and otherwise, upwards of 1000 vehicles for military and hospital purposes since the outbreak of the war." For the ten ambulances a week he furnished, he also provided drivers.[5]

Both the Manchester plant and the company's London facilities had expanded to meet the needs of war. Manchester, partly because of the hazards of shipping materials through submarine-infested waters, was making half the parts of the Ford car in England. They were being made there for another very good reason. England in 1915, to gain revenue for wartime purposes, to limit the shipment of luxury and bulky goods, and in a lesser degree to protect British industry, abandoned

* All its stationery was stamped: "This establishment is controlled under Munitions of War Act, 1915."

its former free trade policy and enacted the McKenna duties. These comprised a 33⅓ per cent import levy on motor vehicles and parts from areas outside the Empire, and a 22⅔ per cent impost on cars and trucks from areas within it. A wartime measure, it would be sustained in peacetime and have a profound effect on Ford Ltd. activities.

To take care of the increasing volume of Manchester production, the company had utilized facilities in London, replacing a repair depot on Harper Street established in 1914 with a more extensive one on Ausdell Street, Kensington. In 1915 it set up a large center for the repair and storage of ambulances at Brook Green, Hammersmith, which provided parking space for 250 vehicles under one roof.[6]

2

In the meantime Henry Ford had emerged as a militant apostle of peace. Like many Americans, he had condemned the war from the beginning but had confined himself to private or occasional public expressions up to August 1915. He then burst into print with a fierce arraignment of the conflict. In a long statement on the 22nd he declared: "I hate war, because war is murder, desolation, and destitution," and asserted that if necessary he would devote his fortune and even his life to ending it.* His extreme attitude led to the resignation of James Couzens on October 12 as vice president and treasurer of the company. While noting in a public statement that their different views of the war were chiefly responsible for his act, Couzens wrote to a friend about Ford: "What I objected to was his committing the company to all those [pacifist] views when they were his individual views and not the company's views." [7]

But the climax was to come. As a result of his printed views and professed willingness to work against war, Ford attracted the attention of the professional pacifists. Two of them, Rosika Schwimmer and Louis P. Lochner, met him and at once urged him to channel his activity into the support of a commission which through "continuous

* The roots of Ford's pacifism have never been fully located, but *Ford: Expansion and Challenge,* New York, 1957, 31ff. discusses the influence of his mother, who lost a brother in the American Civil War just before Henry Ford's birth, and the general climate of American opinion in the late nineteenth and early twentieth centuries, which was strongly pacifist.

mediation" would strive to end the conflict. A few days later, he endorsed a plan to dispatch a "Peace Ship" abroad with a representative American delegation which would unite with similar groups in neutral countries to work for peace. The Scandinavian-American liner *Oscar II* was chartered for a voyage on December 4. Henry Ford himself went along. Europe was suddenly confronted with a shipload of peace angels who proposed to invade the war zone crying, "Cease fire!" [8]

In the United States, the venture was regarded with scepticism and growing ridicule. Noble and spectacular as an idea, it became vulnerable because of the haste and inefficiency with which it was developed. In Britain particularly the sheer effrontery of Ford's gesture aroused opposition. As early as November 18, 1915, the London *Daily Mail* had refused to accept advertisements for the Ford car, and in two days it had won the support of eleven other British journals, including the London *Evening Standard,* the *Daily Dispatch,* and the *Daily Sketch.* Some Englishmen took a less serious view of the matter. "I think Mr. Ford deserves a medal for injecting a little comedy into this tragedy we are going through," an unnamed government "authority" was quoted as saying.[9]

Percival L. D. Perry spoke up loyally for Ford. The editor of the English *Pall Mall Gazette,* before taking a Ford advertisement, wanted to know why he would be justified in doing so, and Perry on December 2, 1915, told him. He pointed out that the Ford Motor Company (England) Ltd., "owing to Mr. Ford's mechanical and commercial genius," was employing 2000 British workmen at better wages and in better working conditions than labor knew elsewhere. He described Ford's work with Belgian refugees. He pointed out that the English Ford establishment was a British concern, paying taxes, and training personnel for the Army. Many of its employees had enlisted, and Ford was providing protection for their families and holding jobs for them if they returned. Ford was not pro-German. Finally, Perry pointed out, "Mr. Ford has never at any time taken any action to communicate or impose his political views upon this company," and indicated that with respect to the war, Ford and the Ford Motor Company (England) Ltd. did not see eye to eye and that Ford accepted that fact.

It was a deft and forthright defense, which had some effect. But for the moment contempt for Ford among Englishmen rivaled hate for the Hun.

Difficult as was Perry's position, Ford's executive secretary, E. G. Liebold, in Detroit was doing his best to make it more difficult. On December 2 he had cabled: "Meet Ford Kirkwall Scotland," for the Peace Ship was to be brought to that port and Ford was on it. Perry compliantly responded: "Will Act as Instructed." But on the following day he had new thoughts and information, and wrote Liebold pointing out that the Orkney Islands (where Kirkwall lay) were remote and of strategic military importance and that few civilians were permitted to visit them. He added: "Unfortunately everyone connected with the name of Ford in this country is suffering under considerable disadvantages, and I anticipate that the difficulties of making connection may be impossible."

So they proved; nor could Perry get permission to leave England in order to wait on Ford in Norway. Meanwhile he had written to Ford on December 8 setting forth the English point of view.

> You are probably aware that whilst this country is fighting for peace and desires peace above all other considerations the feeling now current is that a cessation of war at the present moment would not be peace.
>
> At best a termination of the war now would be construed as a Draw, and I know you appreciate that combatants in every walk of life never look upon a draw as a decision.
>
> The prevailing opinion is that if Militarism is to be abolished and lasting peace achieved, it can only come by permitting the present war to continue until a decisive result is attained.

It was a statement that Ford at the time could not accept, but he probably recognized its force. Soon his health and his disillusionment with the Peace Ship caused him to leave the vessel and return to the United States. When the *Oscar II* brought the remaining pilgrims safely to the Hague in mid-January 1916, the world thought Ford's pacifist adventure was ended. It was not; he financed a commission (and later a committee) that worked diligently for peace in Europe for more than a year. Yet with the voyage completed the dramatic flare of the enterprise guttered out. Nobody was excited about the quiet work that Lochner and others carried on. What is more important for us, the image of Ford as a painted devil who was trying to stop a righteous war faded out to the point where it could no longer excite the English. They soon became aware of him again, but this time the image would be angelic rather than satanic.[10]

3

It will be recalled that early in 1913 Henry Ford had contemplated building a plant in southern Ireland. Perry, while noting a good location on the River Lee near Cork, had written on February 25 and 26 to turn Ford's interest to England. Poor steamship service, a lack of skilled labor, and other factors, he argued, made Cork an inferior site to several English cities, notably Southampton. Perry's liking for this city was to grow into love and finally into an obsession, but that is a matter for later consideration.

At any rate, his arguments were sufficiently effective with Ford so that Perry was told to pursue the Southampton project, and in February 1915 he bought the Ridgeway Estate for £5000. But for the continuance of the war Ford might have used it. Perry told one of the lawyers who had helped arrange the purchase that nothing had been done because "Southampton is a closed port at the present time."

Eventually Sorensen took a long look at the Ridgeway property and prepared tentative plans for a development there: with model buildings and tracks in miniature. A group of "Detroit experts" studied the proposed layout, and finally they concluded that the site was unsuitable! A much larger property was promptly discovered by the diligent Perry—the Milbrook Estate, and this was acquired in 1916 for £20,000. Thus Perry's ambition to see a great English factory arise had received the tacit approval of expenditures amounting to $125,000! [11]

Meanwhile, the war operated to further his idea of England as the primary center for European activities. H. B. White, branch manager in Paris and in charge of European sales, had never commanded Perry's admiration and seems to have performed with only routine success so far as Detroit was concerned. In 1914 he had sold 978 cars in France and only 2,113 in the rest of Europe. But White's real problem was that he had put himself in a precarious position with the French financial authorities. Kennerly Hall, a lawyer serving the Ford interests, pointed out that if French tax experts examined White's books they would find that he had been paying taxes on European sales as a *négociant,* which was "not lawful for you," and that the logical thing to do was form a *société anonyme.*[12]

This was in late August 1915. By mid-April of the following year Perry went to France to look the situation over. He decided that an independent French company was an immediate necessity, and on May 15 wrote to Clara Ford that he would "have to return to France to see it completed," and would leave in a few days.* In this reorganization, White returned to the United States—no longer a Ford employee.

Perry formed Automobiles Ford—the new French Ford company —on May 25, 1916, with a capitalization of 500,000 francs represented by 1000 shares held by nine Englishmen. The total amounted to roughly $100,000 at the current value of the franc.** The company's offices were at 61, Rue des Corneilles, Paris.

Actually, the formation of the French *société* from England fitted in with Perry's move to gain control over the entire Ford continental operation. But he had opponents. New York branch manager Gaston Plantiff wrote Liebold from Stockholm in July 1916:

> . . . get Mr. Ford to one side and tell him for Heaven's sake not to tie up Europe to any one man. It is too big a proposition. . . . You know . . . I think the world of him [Perry], and he has a big thing just to take care of England alone after the war is over. . . . But the Englishmen themselves are trying to hog the commercial business of the world. . . . Now do please get to Mr. Ford. . . . When you see Europe it is a tremendous proposition. We do not realize it at home.

Meanwhile, Perry organized the activities of the new French company. He made L. C. Griffin manager. The Bordeaux branch became the center for French Ford activities, being geographically less vulnerable than Paris. The English Ford company regularly shipped knocked-down cars to France; in May 1916, for example, it sent 400 van bodies and 100 for regular cars; the number sent increased, although it met obstacles along the way. In June 1916 Perry wrote Liebold that he had been suddenly prevented from shipping to France by a French government order prohibiting the importation of automobiles! "Meanwhile, I had ordered forward a large quantity of cars for the French market, and Mr. Sherman [Ford-US export manager] advises me that same were alongside of ships, although not actually shipped, at the date of the

---

* In these days, Perry often wrote to Henry Ford's wife when he wanted to be sure information reached Henry's ear.

** At a later date, Detroit inquired of Ford-England how the French company was financed at the time of organization. The then assistant manager replied, "£5000 was paid from Detroit funds at Paris on May 31, 1916, refunded by FMco. (Eng.) Ltd."—See H. E. Hartman to H. A. Bate, Apr. 27, 1920, and handwritten undated reply attached to letter in secty's off., FMC-US.

Prohibition Order." Perry proposed to deal with the matter and did so.

But the French company proved troublesome in other ways. The books were in frightful shape, so Perry dispatched accountants. There was thievery, and the company lost some funds. The personnel in the Bordeaux plant quarreled; Perry sent his assistant manager to investigate.

Nothing could be imported into France without government sanction. "The only legitimate purchaser for our product at the present time in France is the French Government," wrote Perry early in 1918.

Perry had difficulties because the French authorities insisted on purchasing direct from Detroit, which accordingly shipped out the orders. The result was confusion. Automobiles Ford knew the precise routines for handling such shipments. The French government wantonly ignored them but still depended on the Bordeaux branch to assemble imports from Ford-US. Two thousand engines would arrive, and no rear axles; Bordeaux was forced to erect temporary facilities to house these consignments while awaiting the arrival of others to complete the finished unit.

Nevertheless, the new company did well. Its sale of 2,413 vehicles in 1916–1917 was almost double the 1915–1916 figure of 1,267. Ford's continental European sales in 1916–1917 totalled 3,228 (including France), which was a new high. In 1918, with the greater use of motorized vehicles in combat, the figures were still higher. Ford-US filled one order for 8,500 units for the French government and another for 2,500 ambulances. Perry could write Klingensmith in April 1918: "We are today doing a great deal more business in France than ever was done and are making money at it."

Perry had taken charge of Ford interests on the continent. Whether his control would be permanent, as he hoped, or only for the war, at that time was not clear.[13]

4

From the beginning of the war both belligerents had sought by every conceivable means to cut off vital supplies from their opponents. German submarines tried to sink the ships of any nationality bearing munitions (and later all useful items) to England, France, or Russia. The British Navy had blockaded German ports, and even barred ships from neutral countries that might indirectly give aid to the Central Powers. If German factories and households were affected, Britain and France bore growing losses of men, munitions, and, quite as important, food.

In British shipping tonnage, the total sunk grew with ominous rapidity. In 1914 the loss had been 51,000 tons a month; in 1915, 74,000; and in 1916 it rose to 103,000. On February 1, 1917, Germany announced she would wage unrestricted submarine warfare, and the toll for shipping shot up for the next month to 310,868 tons. It reached 526,447 in April and was rising. When Admiral William S. Sims of the United States Navy was shown these statistics in April 1917 he remarked: "It looks as though the Germans were winning the war." Sir John Jellicoe of the British Admiralty replied grimly: "They will unless we can stop these losses—and stop them soon." But for the time he saw no solution.[14]

Outstanding among the products involved in these losses was food. Britain normally depended on imports for two-thirds of what her population consumed. Submarines were sending enough sugar, meat, and grain to the bottom of the sea to threaten her with starvation. It became a highly vital question what could be done in the way of counter measures. One fact shone clear: food raised in England would count immensely; whatever the British earth bore was safe from submarines. Every new acre devoted to crops meant a gain in the battle against want, and cargo space saved for shipment of other vital products.

To meet this challenge, the government resorted to the use of steam tractors, to the employment of skilled farm labor sent back from the front, to the creation of the Women's Land Army as a supplement to the labor supply, to more intensive use of horses and farm resources, and finally to the introduction of gasoline tractors to help with the plowing of the land and the harvesting of crops. The full tale also includes the reappearance of Henry Ford with a new role and a brighter image.

In 1917 there were numerous gasoline tractors in existence, of British, continental European, and American makes. The last showed the greater variety and promise, but up to two years previously no cheap, simple, dependable machine had appeared. However, Henry Ford was perfecting a model low in cost and easy to operate, which promised to be reliable. When first exhibited in 1915 it was hailed for its novel features, and the 1916 model was termed by one expert "a lightning flash from the clear sky of tractor engineering." As it neared final form, 50 units, many of them varying somewhat from each other, were constructed.[15]

Perry had meanwhile been asked by the government to join the Food Production Department, and took a post in the Machinery and Implements Section. In August 1916 and again in late November of the same year he came to the United States, found Ford obsessed with the new tractor, and watched it in operation. He saw the machine as an answer to Britain's food problem. Cheap, easy to operate, it would turn the unused land into cultivated acres and multiply the yield of the soil.

Ford still clung to the idea of an industrial development in Ireland. He liked the idea of a great factory rising in the land of his ancestors like a creative monument to his accomplishments. When Prime Minister David Lloyd George suggested Ireland as a site for producing his tractor, Ford was delighted, and Perry too was agreeable (let the tractors be made near Cork; he had his great English motor car center ready to rise at Southampton). Perry seems to have had an agent active in Ireland as early as November 1916; the New York press reported late that month that Ford was disposed to build there. On his return from Dearborn, Perry himself went to Ireland and reached an understanding with the Irish authorities; he got an Act of Parliament passed so that they could part with municipal property; and finally in April 1917 Henry Ford & Son Ltd. was incorporated—with its headquarters in Cork—a company designed to manufacture the Fordson tractor.*

The selected site was beautiful. A plot of 136 acres, it lay along the southern bank of the River Lee, with 1,642 feet of waterfront. To sacrifice this tract to Ford was no casual act for the inhabitants of Cork, as it contained a large city park and the local race track, the latter especially dear to many citizens. But Irish support for the project was fervent. "Mr. Ford is an Irishman," wrote Thomas O'Donnell, an Irish M. P., defending the project in the London *Times*, "who, by the most scientific methods of business and by the most humane treatment of his employees, has established in America one of the most successful and certainly the most ideal business concerns in that great country." (O'Donnell was wrong as to Ford being an Irishman, of course; he was only half of Irish descent.) The Cork *Examiner* hailed the project as mark-

---

* Henry Ford in developing the tractor in the United States had for some years made use of Ford Motor Company facilities and personnel. In 1916 a settlement was made whereby he paid the Ford company $46,810.76 for materials and time of its employees; he agreed not to call his tractor the Ford; taking instead the name Fordson. On July 27, 1917, a separate company, Henry Ford & Son, Inc., was chosen to manufacture the new machine in the United States. Henry Ford & Son, Inc. and the Irish company, Henry Ford & Son Ltd., were both owned by Henry, Clara, and Edsel Ford.

ing "the true industrial development of Cork City and port, and indeed of the whole of Ireland generally." [16]

Two Fordson tractors had been shipped to England on January 27, 1917, and Perry arranged for them to be tested by the Royal Agricultural Society, which warmly commended the units. Ford Ltd.'s assistant manager, H. A. Bate, wrote Sorensen on March 23 that the two

> tractors . . . are at present working 24 hours per day on the Government's ploughing scheme, causing intense interest and amazement.
> . . . tremendous efforts are now being made in this country to get as much land under cultivation as possible in the short time remaining for spring work.

Up to this point, Perry had worked under the belief that the Fordson tractor could be manufactured at Cork and that production would begin there at an early date. "Cork awaiting details and material from America," he cabled on March 28th. Soon, however, it became apparent that the Irish plant could not be ready to produce for at least another year. Thus the day after America declared war on Germany, Perry cabled Edsel Ford (April 7), "Am requested by high authorities to appeal to Mr. Ford for help."

"Would you be willing," he asked, "to send Sorensen and others with drawings of everything necessary, loaning them to British government so that parts can be manufactured over here and assembled in government factory under Sorensen's guidance?" He added that the government would do the job "for the people with no manufacturing or capitalist interest involved and no profit being made by any interest whatever." Ford's tractor was "considered best and only suitable design." Thus Perry proposed to depend upon English manufacturers for the parts of the machine, with both production and assembly under American direction.

With America in the war there was no question as to Ford's cooperation. He cabled: "In full accord with principle, will work night and day." He asked Perry to gather all possible information that might be useful to Sorensen, and the latter set sail for England with five other American technologists in May.[17]

The group arrived on the 15th of that month, eager to start production of the Fordson—or the M.O.M. (Ministry of Munitions) tractor, as it was called in that country. A number of English suppliers were lined up, and Sorensen cabled Dearborn for nuts, bolts, and screws, because "the English concerns were not fitted up with taps and dies for handling our threads."

As plans got underway, Ford quickly developed a party of admirers in England, and the image of him as an interfering pacifist was replaced by that of a powerful ally in war work. Foremost among his admirers stood Perry himself and the latter's wife, who wrote to Clara Ford in June 1917:

> I should like to express to you my dear Mrs. Ford (yet don't know how) what we feel toward Mr. Ford, for his greatness of heart & greatness of mind, and bigness in every way. I personally believe he will be the saviour of the food situation of the world, . . . he is different from other men, one feels it, when with him, for without knowing it, or trying to, he always encourages & uplifts. It is magnanimous of him to come to the rescue of England with his tractor, & most unselfish and forgiving.

Sorensen and the technicians made a dramatic impression in England, but there (as in Ireland) they found difficulties in getting production underway. At this point, in mid-June 1917, the British cabinet decreed that England's manufacturing facilities must be fully utilized for aircraft engine output. Prime Minister David Lloyd George wrote Perry regretfully on June 28 that it was impossible to proceed with the plan to make the tractors in England and authorized him to make arrangements in the United States for production there.

Perry and Sorensen took ship and arrived in Dearborn with a request that Ford build 6,000 units. He agreed, and Sorensen prepared the Dearborn factory to undertake its first large order. The industrialist had never manufactured his tractor in quantity; indeed, its exact form was still undetermined. Characteristically, he wanted to improve it. Lord Northcliffe, then in the United States, persuasively protested. "We need a tractor," he urged. "Yours is the best we can get. We can't wait for the perfect tractor." Ford yielded. He demonstrated his machine to Northcliffe, who became one of its greatest advocates. "It is literally true that a boy or girl with neither mechanical nor agricultural knowledge can drive it," he reported to the London press. "I mounted the tractor and ploughed a half-mile furrow with ease and accuracy at a speed between three and four miles an hour. . . . It has a strong electric head light, so that it may as easily plough by night as by day." [18]

Meanwhile, Perry intended that by the time the 6,000 tractors from

America had arrived in England, the Cork plant would be ready to make additional units. Christopher Addison, Minister of Munitions, in June 1917 wrote him reassuringly: "In order that the construction of this factory may be expedited . . . I . . . will give instructions that the work . . . shall have suitable priority."

In Dearborn production gathered momentum slowly. By the end of 1917 only 254 machines had been completed, although shipments to Britain had already begun. With 1918, output skyrocketed. When there were delays in shipping the units across the Atlantic, Northcliffe cabled Ford, "Shall not rest until this matter is put right. Am acting vigorously." By March 1918 tractors were being shipped regularly, due, Northcliffe indicated, to the personal intervention of the Prime Minister, Lloyd George.

In England Perry prepared facilities at Manchester for tractor assembly, using two government-owned buildings. Of the 6,000 machines from Detroit, 3,000 were sent knocked down and the balance were completely assembled. By April 1918 the last of the order had been shipped overseas.[19]

According to British production statistics 1500 tractors were in use in November 1917 (few of which could have been Fordsons), 1650 in January, and 2,240 in March. (These rising figures doubtless did reflect the delivery and assembly of American machines.) After completing the British order, Ford supplied American and Canadian farmers with tractors.*

The role of the gasoline tractor in food production should not be exaggerated. It came late. Other forces were already at work to increase production: the Women's Land Army, steam farm machinery, the pullback of numerous soldiers with farm skills. To cite an instance, in 1918 the steam-driven tractors plowed 1,200,000 acres, or three times their normal quota, while from October 1917 to the end of the war the gasoline tractors plowed only 480,000. This acreage may have been crucial, but one imagines that H. C. B. Underdown was rather generous

---

* Ford-Canada did not have the patent and other rights to build the tractor, but became the sales agency in the Dominion for Henry Ford & Son, Inc. In 1917 Charles A. Dunning, Director of Food Production in Ottawa, visited the Dearborn tractor plant and arranged on behalf of his government to purchase several thousand tractors for the Canadian Food Board. Ford-Canada leaflets pointed out that "a terrific responsibility rests upon Canada. Only an increased exportable surplus of wheat from this country will save the Allies from actual starvation and impotence. Food will win the War, and Canada's capacity for producing foodstuffs is limitless." The Fordson would do its part. (See note 20.)

when he wrote Henry Ford in February 1919 that "but for your co-operation the country's needs as regards its food production campaign would not have been met, and the food crisis would in all probability not have been surmounted." What was true was that all elements had been important in meeting the crisis. Perry, first in the Food Production Department and then as Director of the Agricultural Machinery Department, Ministry of Munitions, had exerted himself to the utmost, working "days, nights, and Sundays." The crisis had been met to the extent that food or fodder produced in Britain would if imported have required 4,000,000 tons of shipping space at a time when every ton of such space was desperately needed by the Allies.[20]

Meanwhile the products of Ford ingenuity had been writing an exciting record in other areas of the conflict besides England.

5

We must return for a moment to the first days of the war and understand what the role of the motor vehicle had been at that time and what it rapidly became as hostilities spread from continent to continent.

The existence of the automobile, the motor truck, and the tractor had not escaped the attention of military strategists in the first decade of the twentieth century. British, French, Russian, Italian, and German commanders had tested these units from 1901 onwards. By the beginning of World War I the military potential of automobiles was recognized. Motor cars and motorcycles for the use of officers were commonplace. The British Red Cross had recommended a motorized ambulance. Trucks for the quick transportation of men and materials were seen as valuable, and tractors were being utilized for the transportation of heavy artillery. The Germans had evolved the armored car.[21]

If any tendency to minimize the importance of motorization had existed, with the beginnings of hostilities it disappeared; the Canadian *Ford Times* described this vigorously and well:

> Various newspapers and periodicals have referred to the present conflict as the "Gasoline War." What they mean is that the motor car is playing a most important part in the European drama.
>
> Bodies of troops are moved distances heretofore impossible in a day. Ammunition and supply trains are many times as mobile as in former wars. Generals and staff officers are dashing from one end of a two hundred mile battle line to the other at express train speed. But, best

of all, the wounded are receiving prompt and efficient surgical attention, due to the rapidity with which they may be transferred from the
scene of the battle to a comfortable hospital cot many miles behind the
firing line.

Unfortunately, although there was no question as to the accomplishments of the motor vehicle, it got astonishingly scant recognition
from either battle historians or government agencies. One might have
assumed that horses, mules, and railroads were the chief if not the sole
means of transport available. To take one example, although the British
Ministry of Munitions recognized every element of supply from fuses to
machine tools, and although it coyly listed in an appendix "Mechanical
Transport" ("requirements and allocation of motor transport vehicles")
as one of its twelve major activities, and in another place listed "Motor
Vehicles" as fifth of eight urgently needed items, nowhere in its eight
volume history does it give numbers and types of automotive units employed (except tanks), their performance or their suppliers—facts set
forth freely for all other elements from mules to shells and ships.

Nevertheless the use of motor vehicles, general from the start, grew
to be spectacular. This was true of both parties to the conflict. The Germans, regarded as weak in automotive resources, could command the
Adler, Mercedes, and Opel passenger cars, all efficient, and the Büssing,
Mercedes, Opel, and Krupp trucks. German production for 1913 was
for 12,400 cars and 9,521 trucks. In the war years it was unquestionably
increased for military purposes. The Germans used staff cars, armored
cars, and trucks. The Allies had a much wider range of models: the
Ford, Wolseley, Morris, Austin, Singer, Rover, Vulcan, and Rolls-
Royce in England, and in France the Renault, Panhard & Levassor,
Charron, Delahaye, Clément-Bayard, and Peugeot. The total Allied
production was much higher than the German, but nevertheless low:
England in 1913 produced only 25,000 cars and 9,000 trucks. French
output was less. Canada's production was mounting rapidly (by 1917 it
equalled 93,810 vehicles), while Britain and France could and did increasingly draw upon the United States, where production reached
what seemed astronomical figures (969,000 in 1915).[22]

From the first the Allies employed motor vehicles to supplement
and in some cases to replace rail facilities. Mechanical transport for the
original six divisions of the British army consisted, "besides motor-cars
and motor-bicycles," of about 1,200 trucks, or 200 per division. By
September 1916 the Fourth Army had 235 lorries (trucks) per divi-

sion, besides 1,000 motor cars and 2,000 motorcycles. Many of the lorries were buses and others could be fitted with seats, so that the Army could transport 13,250 men with dispatch.

Not all Empire armies were so well served. The first Australian divisions sent to Egypt seem to have had little motorized transport. The Fifth Australian Division had only two trucks out of 40 vehicles for a Divisional Signal Company, and 7 motorized ambulances out of 20. However, the use of cars and trucks increased as the war went on.

Meanwhile on the European front the motor vehicle became all but indispensable. Joffre in 1914 rushed his troops to the Marne by Parisian taxis; in 1916 troops were sent by motorized units to plug a gap in the English lines; and in the same year at Verdun the French maintained an entire army "almost entirely by motor transport over a single road." [23]

In Europe the terrain close to the trenches was pitted by shell fire, cut by ditches, and blocked by posts and barbed wire. Usually no wheeled vehicle could negotiate it. But vehicles did come to the forward areas. It was the boast of Ford officials that most of the cars used for such work were Fords. As one of them put it:

> The Ford, by virtue of its constructional strength, its lightness, its power, and its suspension, can go where no other motor ambulance can travel; it can cover the rough ground of a battlefield in which heavier vehicles are hopelessly bogged; it can maneuvre in spaces where larger vehicles do not venture; it can travel on the shell-scarred roads with greater comfort; it is quick in picking up and getting away; it can live where other cars die; it can immediately be repaired if damaged; and it can be supplied and kept running at a cost infinitesimal by comparison with the cost of other vehicles.

If this statement sounds rhapsodic, it was nevertheless echoed with innumerable variations by drivers, officers, nurses, and doctors from Belgium to Southwest Africa. Dozens of reports and books of reminiscences attest to the amazing role of the ungainly Ford. Individuals in high places also praised it. Perry cited more than half a dozen eminent Englishmen who spoke of its heroic feats with awe—amused or otherwise. He sent Edsel a rhyme composed by an ambulance driver which parodied Kipling's "Gunga Din," observing that

> It's mighty good to feel
> When you're sitting at the wheel
> She'll be running when the bigger cars are broke,

and ending with a jangling stanza that caught the Model T to the life:

> Yes, Tin, tin, tin,
> You exasperating puzzle Hunka Tin,
> I've abused you and I've flayed you,
> But by Henry Ford who made you
> You are better than a big car
>
> HUNKA TIN!

Perhaps the soberer type of comment came from a Canadian captain who in civil life drove a Simplex, Packard, or Pierce: "I have been on this job since August [he spoke in the summer of 1915 and referred to August of the year before], but I have yet to see a Ford that failed to get there." Other cars were in service; with solid ground to work on the Rolls-Royce gave comparable satisfaction, but apparently no others. The Ford did not essay the heavier hauling jobs. It was "the light cavalry of transport." But one officer in charge of 98 lorries affirmed that even for carrying the Model T should be supplied instead of heavier cars "which . . . are costing the British government a great deal of money." [24]

As we have seen, the English company supplied thousands of ambulances. Others came directly from the United States and an indeterminate number from Canada. That country at first did not seem to grasp the possibilities for the military uses of motor vehicles, and the Ford company there apparently regarded the European conflict as remote. It advised its officials and dealers to "go calmly and honestly about your business" (and by implication to let the war take care of itself). Sales in 1914 at 15,567 were larger than those of the year before, 11,584. This represented to some extent the growth of the country, but there is also indirect evidence that the government was buying Fords for military purposes. They had been functional in training the Canadian troops, and the Canadian *Ford Times* asserts that they were used in France. Thus although the Canadian government took no official note of motor vehicles by the time its overseas contingent numbered 112,000 men, a force "larger than the armies of Napoleon, Wellington, Mead [*sic*], or Lee," common practice would have forced the use of staff cars and motor trucks, and the employment of motor ambulances. The Canadian *Ford Times* asserted late in 1917 that 300,000 motor vehicles had been used in the war, and that "the Model T Ford car predominates every other make or kind of car." [25]

Ford-Canada—which never ceased to advertise "The Ford is 'made in Canada' by Canadian workmen—and serves more Canadians than any other car"—stated in June 1915: "Like all British subjects, we regret that war was thrust upon us. But now that there is war we are glad we can do our share to mitigate its hardships and sufferings." Gordon McGregor, like Perry, recognized that any British Ford company would have to participate in the war effort.

Most of the Canadian Ford contribution went through its export activity. In British East Africa all cars were commandeered as soon as war was declared, and plans promptly were laid for the conquest of adjacent German East Africa. Clement Hirtzel, the Ford dealer in Nairobi, who sold Canadian-built Fords, volunteered with his entire sales and office force and used intensively all the cars he had on hand. He constructed trucks by removing the regular bodies and substituting flats made of the sturdy Ford packing cases. These reconverted vehicles carried from 600 to 900 lbs. of *matériel*, and proved far superior to the oxen the Army at first employed in part, not only because they were five times faster but also because they were immune to the dread tzetze fly. Eventually so dependable was the Model T, according to the *Ford News*, that "all other cars had now [July 1918] been discarded in favor of the Ford." These vehicles were supplied by Arkell & Douglas through the Canadian Ford company.[26]

British troops in Egypt, and finally the Australian division also, were motorized, and the ill-fated attempt on Gallipoli in 1915 saw five or six Ford cars landed on the beach. Since there was never a penetration of more than seven miles, the cars were used for transport jobs, running from unit to unit parallel with the shore line. H. A. Denne, later to have charge of Ford Motor Company Ltd.'s Export Department, drove one of these. "We blew them up when we had to abandon the expedition," he recalled.

All during the war Dodge & Seymour was very active in supplying Canadian Ford cars for the Middle Eastern campaign. A. R. Smith was at that time in charge of Russa Engineering, which sold Fords throughout the greater part of India. "We supplied a large number of cars for the Army and the government service," he recalled later. "At that time the Army was almost mechanized with the Ford Model T. They were the only cars that would go across the desert. There were some Rolls [Rolls-Royce] used. Ninety per cent were Fords. The desert war was won with Fords." (It should be noted that the German and Turkish forces in Mesopotamia used motorized trucks. Any good car was usable on a good road. But the ungainly Fords were also reliable in rough terrain where there were no roads.) Gordon McGregor told the Ford-Canada shareholders that in the last months of the war alone, "we executed orders from the British Government for 2,790 cars for shipment to India and Mesopotamia."

The chief theatre of Middle Eastern war was the area that later became Palestine and the territories contiguous with it. Here the brilliant T. E. Lawrence manipulated a revolt of Arabian tribes and with his aid General Edmund Allenby was able to break the Turkish hold on the region. Lawrence saw clearly the value of both aircraft and motor vehicles. "Lawrence was at least a generation ahead of the military world," says Liddell Hart, "in perceiving the strategic implications of mechanized warfare." Allenby had complete faith in him, but neither had the power to assure their forces of an adequate supply of motorized vehicles. At first Lawrence had used camels; but soon Allenby and he were able to find an increasing amount of motorized units for the army. The official report on the Near East campaign states that during it the number of motor vehicles in use doubled, and lists 617 touring cars, 586 motor ambulances, 1,579 motor lorries, 670 vans, and 873 tractors as being available just before the Armistice. With 37 motorboats there were 5,905 motorized units for a force of about 100,000 men. In addition, 1,523 motorcycles were available. General Allenby later told the newscaster Lowell Thomas that "he believed in giving credit where credit is due, and therefore, was bound to express his admiration of the Ford; it had decidedly helped to defeat the Turks." The official record concludes, "In fact, without the extensive employment of mechanized transport, it is difficult to see how the services of maintenance could have been carried out in the operations which resulted in the capture of Jerusalem in 1917, Damascus and Aleppo in 1918." [27]

By the time America entered the war in April 1917, Henry Ford had placed his factory "at the disposal of the United States government," a fact which pleased Perry and McGregor as well as many Americans who had wondered about their leader's pacifist declarations. The Ford factory in Detroit produced Liberty motors (aircraft engines), Eagle boats (a submarine patrol vessel), caissons, helmets, submarine detectors, shells, armour plate, and developed two tank models.

The Ford-US variety of war production far exceeded that of Ford-England or Ford-Canada. The latter got into the Eagle boat venture. "We built the stacks for those Eagle boats and the boiler castings," Ford-Canada's production manager George Dickert recalls. The Canadian company also manufactured some parts for the Ford tank. But in general Ford-England and Ford-Canada concentrated their productive efforts on "standard" units: cars, trucks, and ambulances.[28] *

Actually, reconversion to peacetime activities was easier for Ford-Canada and Ford-England because they had never made the wartime changeover.

It is impossible to say how many Ford units took part in the war, but we have certain figures which may be considered. During the war years Ford-Canada shipped abroad 41,288 cars, almost all of which went to battle. Fords for Canadian troops would have been supplied from domestic production, which was roughly about twice the volume of exports. Probably not more than a third of that output was taken by the government. Even so, Ford-Canada must have supplied more than 60,000 cars. European Ford production (that is, cars sent from Dearborn and assembled in England or France) amounted to 12,000 units in 1914, 14,000 in 1915, 18,000 in 1916, and 17,000 for the first ten months of 1917. For 1918 we have only the English output, which was 9,000. This total of 70,000 cars was partly for civilian use. European sales outside France—from 1,200 to 1,500 a year—were almost entirely to civilians. Some of the English production, although very little, and a like proportion of the French were not noted for military purposes. But of the total, at least 50,000 were. Even before April 1917 the United States was filling some orders for Europe, and after that it poured a flood of Ford ambulances and staff cars into the Western Front. Altogether there must have been 125,000 Fords in the war.[29]

6

The war had important effects upon the automotive industry of the world and upon Ford activities overseas.

First of all it built up the public confidence in the motor car and in particular spread the reputation of the Model T for fabulous performance. Like a person who even in the prime of life is a subject for tall tales, the Ford car grew in the imagination of men. Henry Ford

---

* McGregor in October 1918 told the Canadian shareholders that Windsor's contribution was "very limited . . . our equipment is not suitable for war business." (See note 28.)

was meanwhile improving its quality and lowering its price, so that the machine continued to live up to the fable.

In the second place, the performance of motor vehicles on all fronts, and the rapid improvement in machine tools, metallurgy, and factory routines under war pressures promoted an interest in improved automobiles on the part of manufacturers. This was to develop quickly in the succeeding years. As we shall see, sturdier cars, cheaper cars, and more beautiful and more comfortable cars were to appear. A number of them would become rivals of the Model T.

The war brought about changes in markets and marketing. We have already seen that Perry had enlarged the British sphere of activity and won a pledge from Ford to establish a great manufacturing center in England. A significant change had taken place in Latin America. Up to 1914 European cars had dominated the market there, although American firms had been working with determination for a share of it. With the war, European shipments to the Western Hemisphere ceased, and the Americans rushed in to fill the vacuum—Ford foremost among them. They continued in first place, doubtless because the values they could offer were far superior to those of the few German, French, and English models that were their only competitors. But the story of Latin-American development will be told later.

More organic than any of the changes noted above were the political and social alterations in the world which came with the war and, by affecting nations, affected motor cars. What happened was in the deepest sense revolutionary. In 1914 the greater part of the world was controlled by empires: the British, Russian, French, Portuguese, Dutch, Belgian, German, and Austrian. These ruled with authority lands that were often alien. But beneath the surface there were active currents and hidden rocks. Some of these became manifest even before the peace of Versailles. For example, the vast Russian realm expunged the Romanoff dynasty and converted the greatest land mass of the world into a communist republic. As it heaved through successive convulsions to an uneasy order, the Czechs were already breaking away from Austria, the Finns from Russia, and the Poles from that country, Germany, and Austria. The actual peace pact of 1919 saw an independent Latvia, Lithuania, and Estonia, a free Hungary, a larger Greece, and mandates covering African and Arab territories, and Palestine. New nations would soon be carved from some of these areas.

But the conflict made possible further changes. The first to be apparent was the shift in primary world power from ruined Germany and shaken France and Britain to the wealthy and unravaged United States.

In 1919 few recognized the scope of the changes or the difficulties the postwar world faced. The moment seemed propitious for trade rather than inimical to it.

7

As for Ford of England, we have seen that the war brought the Fordson tractor to Europe, and while the machines were shipped knocked down from a Dearborn factory and only assembled in Manchester, and while Dearborn manufactured more tractors for the American and Canadian farmers, Henry Ford had never forgotten his idea of a factory at Cork, Ireland. Progress had been made with construction during the war—one building had been completed by October 1918. Now he resolved to finish the plant there.

On October 22, 1918, with the existing capital stock of £100,000 plus loans from Henry Ford & Son, Inc. and Henry Ford himself, the Irish company had £200,000 (roughly $1,000,000) to finance its development. A manager was appointed (Perry had been elected managing director and continued to hold that post), tractor dealers were selected for various areas, and with peace the remainder of the plant would rise on the River Lee.[30]

The light of these events played happily on the Cork project, and for a time it seemed destined to fulfill the sentimental hopes of Henry Ford and the large expectations of the Irish. It was significant as the site of the first Ford tractor production in Europe.

The second effect of the war related to the head of the English company. In 1918 Percival L. D. Perry had been knighted for his services in the war, in the Food Production Department and the Agricultural Machinery Department of the Ministry of Munitions. Later he became deputy controller, the Mechanical Warfare Department, and director of traction, Ministry of Munitions, 1918–1919. Meanwhile he had continued to direct the Ford company and Henry Ford & Son Ltd., while also watching over Ford activities in France. The multiple responsibilities involved long hours of work and a continuing nervous strain, but both Britain and the three firms profited from his originality, judgment, and energy.

3. Men identified with Ford overseas activities: *above* James Couzens, Edsel Ford; *below* Percival, Lord Perry and C. E. Sorensen; Sir Patrick Hennessy.

4. A portion of the Ford plant at Dagenham, Essex, England; *center* Model Y, the first small English car; *below* The assembly plant of the Ford Canadian Company at Oakville, Ontario; the Central Office Building of the company appears at the upper left of the picture.

However, as early as March 1918 officials in Detroit had become dissatisfied with his work. Frank L. Klingensmith, who had replaced Couzens as vice president and treasurer of the Ford Motor Company, wrote to him on the 22nd in a critical vein. Reviewing conditions both in France and England, he felt that Perry had not done the best possible job and had spent time on government affairs which he owed to the business.

Perry answered on April 10, 1918, expressing "grave concern" about Klingensmith's charges. He reviewed conditions in France, where it had been difficult to procure able officials, explained what he had done and why, and pointed out that the business there was bigger than ever, and profitable. He defended his administration in England. At first *persona non grata* because of Ford's pacifist activities, he had persevered, procured orders, and again prospered. He conceded that his assistant manager, H. A. Bate, was not of high ability but indicated that superior officials were difficult to find in wartime.

As to the government, he had been able to protect Ford and the company by establishing relations with members of the war cabinet. "I have been more successful than I could have expected or hoped." True, he had not been constantly in Manchester, but had never ceased to be in close touch with plant and company affairs. His governmental posts had been "of material assistance in enabling me to carry on the Company business." He asserted that "at no time had any interest, either personal or otherwise, been allowed to intrude itself to the detriment of the Company's interests." Perry suggested that someone come over from Detroit to see the situation and get firsthand impressions. He felt that he "ought to receive commendation rather than criticism."

Perry sent a copy of this letter to Edsel Ford, saying that Klingensmith's communication "has considerably upset me," and pleading for trust, "and as far as possible not allow gossip and mischief making to intrude. . . . As you know, my heart is in the Ford business." [31]

Apparently the matter rested there, and Perry's defense was accepted. At the end of 1918 he was full of plans for the company and seemed to feel that the Fords had full confidence in him. However, early in 1919 criticism was revived, stemming from charges made by Bate. Klingensmith telegraphed Edsel Ford about them on February 3, and on the 5th wired: "matter is subordination of funds organization and product to personal interest by individual named." Klingensmith volunteered: "I don't personally believe Mr. Perry could be guilty of this charge." However, he sent Albert Byrns of the Auditing Department and William S. Knudsen to England to investigate. Sorensen cabled Perry that Knudsen was coming: "Don't leave until you have seen him." Knudsen was at this time in charge of production in Detroit.*

By the beginning of March Knudsen and Byrns were in Manchester. There they found Perry "in poor shape physically." He was tired after his intensive war effort, and his health had broken down. He was subject to fainting fits and was consulting specialists.[32]

Yet despite his precarious health, Perry was eager to discuss with Knudsen the future of the English Ford company, the manufacturing plant at Southampton, the re-establishment of business on the continent, and his own proposal that in financing the English Ford expansion, the company invite English capital to the extent of 40 per cent. He told Knudsen that the future policy of Great Britain would include protection of local industry "in more or less virulent form and that most taxation would be directed against foreign-owned corporations." But he felt that with a manufacturing plant with local stockholders and with "his present influence in political circles," Ford would have little difficulty.

Knudsen listened to the enthusiastic, although physically exhausted, Perry, and the American was awed by the rush of ideas, writing Klingensmith of the "sweeping changes" Perry intended and recommending that Henry Ford be consulted first.

Knudsen was dubious of Perry's using political influence in peacetime. ("While I am frank to admit the way in which Mg. [*sic*] Director helped to win the war, I am just as sure that political aspirations as being necessary to conduct of our company's business after the war is pure buncombe . . . in the long run bound to hamper us it being logical that our Co. will not be given advantages which other foreign company's [*sic*] could not have.")

As to the "distasteful" Bate charges, Knudsen tended to reject them. "I am reasonably sure in my own mind that when he [Bate] questions the personal integrity of our Mg. Director, he is unable to prove it. . . ." However, Knudsen himself cast a severely critical eye on Perry's administration. "There is no doubt," he wrote Klingensmith, "that a coterie of men have untill [*sic*] recently received substantial

---

* Sorensen was working mainly on tractor production in 1919, but he still kept in touch with Perry on English problems. He retained along with Knudsen a certain authority in the foreign field.

preference in their business the directorates of which interlock to a great extent, and that these men have possibly obtained such advantage by assisting the Mg. Director's political aspirations which are frank and undisguised." One venture, authorized by Perry, in truck distribution, Knudsen labeled "dead wrong." Another, dealing with selling government-owned new tractors, he harshly condemned. Later, he would add to his list of matters to be cleared up the method of hire-purchase (installment buying) and insurance arrangements made by Perry which Knudsen felt were contrary to company policy. Similarly Knudsen criticized "the way our business here is run [in] . . . that it consists of a head and a tail and no body. The organization is run on a kindergarden plan with different men getting overlapping charges. . . . An enormous amount of business radiates direct from the office on Shaftesbury Avenue [in London] where business, politics, personal matters, and policies are being worked at with feverish haste and in a hopeless tangle." [33]

Knudsen's report did not cast a good light on Perry. In April Perry arrived in Detroit, bringing with him Noel Mobbs, one of the "coterie" to whom Knudsen had referred. On this trip, Perry's illness took a sharp turn for the worse, and the April 24, 1919 annual meeting of Ford Ltd. to be held in Detroit was postponed because of his condition.

Then on April 29, 1919, Perry met with Edsel and Henry Ford, who questioned him sharply about financial dealings, the administration of the business, and the future. At this fateful session, Henry Ford seems to have expressed disapproval of Perry's business practices, announced his unreadiness to build at Southampton, and rejected the idea of introducing English shareholders into Ford Ltd. to the extent of 40 per cent. In fact, he wanted no English shareholders at all; * Ford Ltd. was to be wholly owned by and run from Detroit.

At this time Henry Ford offered Perry a *salaried* position with Henry Ford & Son Ltd., *i.e.,* Perry would continue as managing director of *that* company, but retire from the English firm. After all, Perry had done more than any single individual to start the Cork plant, to intro-

---

* Prior to the war, at a Ford Ltd. shareholders' meeting attended by Henry Ford, the English company's capital had been increased to £200,000 by the creation of 39,800 new shares at £5 each. These shares remained unissued until on June 5, 1915 "pursuant to a recommendation made by Messrs [Henry] Ford and Couzens," 400 shares were allotted to key English employees. Perry got 200, which made his holdings in the English company greater than Henry Ford's (Ford had only 117 shares). Ford would in August 1919 buy back all the shares allotted to the English employees for $62,324.40. (See note 34.)

duce the Fordson into England, and to promote Henry Ford's ideas in the British Isles.

Accordingly, on May 5, 1919, the shareholders of Ford Motor Company (England) Ltd. were called to a special meeting (to be held May 13) to accept Perry's resignation as managing director of their organization.

Perry's tenure with Henry Ford & Son Ltd. was shortlived. Illness forbade his living in Ireland. Ford's secretary, E. G. Liebold, indicated that he must reside in Cork to manage the company; Perry replied that this was impossible, but asked to remain on the Board of Directors. This was refused, and on September 29, 1919, Perry resigned from the tractor organization.[34]

8

He soon took steps to get the rest and quiet which his doctors had long advised. A wealthy man now, with no harrowing office routines to follow, he quickly found himself in improved health. He had been aware that with peace there would be huge surpluses of motor vehicles, English and American, and in 1919–1920 he headed a group which purchased the American cars and parts in France and later acquired the Slough Motor Company Repair Depot in the south of England, comprising 15,000 cars and a great quantity of spares, with some 30 buildings and 600 acres of land, for £7,000,000. The Slough Trading Company, later reorganized as the Slough Estates Ltd., disposed of its cars, trucks, and spares, and then improved the property and buildings, put in roads and provided utilities, and rented portions of the area to manufacturing concerns. Perry served as chairman and managing director until March 1922, when Noel Mobbs took over these offices. He continued to act as a director of the highly profitable enterprise.[35]

In August 1921 Perry, cruising on his own yacht through the Channel Islands area, took an option from the novelist Compton Mackenzie on the little island of Herm, east of Guernsey. It was a magic spot of a few cultivated fields, "warm-colored rock shores and golden sands, moorland, and a mansion amid pines and deciduous trees." In 1922 Perry took over Mackenzie's lease and established himself on a 300-acre paradise. The beaches held great varieties of shells; the meadows showed rockroses, horned poppies, thyme, and innumerable common flowers;

peregrine falcons, pheasants, song birds and rabbits abounded, and in the summer gaudy butterflies made riot in the sunshine.

Here the Perrys lived yearlong and in 1926 celebrated their home in a little book, *The Island of Enchantment.* Partly in prose, partly in verse, it achieves scant literary quality but reflects the enthusiasm of the authors who, far from the complexities and pressures of the motor trade, found their little refuge an isle of the blest:

Happy little Island   And upon those people
Born to give delight,   Dwelling on your shore
Blessings fall upon you   May love, hope, and gladness
Morning, noon, and night.   Rest forever more.[36]

Before Perry retired to his island he received a letter from Henry Ford about his resignation. Ford wrote of "the disagreement of ideas that has existed between yourself and our organization for the past year or so," and approved Perry's departure. "I want you to feel, please," he went on, "that I will continue to have an interest in your future that I have always had and will appreciate it very much if I know that you still have the best of feelings at heart for the institution that you grew up with and for the success of which, I feel, due credit should be given to yourself." He ended with the prediction that if Perry worked "in the same conscientious manner" he did for the Ford Motor Company, he would surely be successful in whatever he undertook.[37]

It was a rather guarded letter, and Perry must have been saddened by it. He had worked with Ford over a period of fourteen years, had built up a company with his heart as well as his administrative skill, and now there were these few cool if friendly words that severed him from the past like the stroke of a knife. The parting seemed to be final.

5

Steps in Expansion

Early in 1919 the Big Four framed a treaty in Paris to end the war and usher in a new era. President Woodrow Wilson for the United States, Georges Clemenceau for France, and David Lloyd George for Great Britain were really the architects, the submissive Italian Prime Minister Vittorio Orlando acquiescing in their decisions. Wilson had sailed for Europe with the hope of building a better world, but found himself too often borne down by the adroit Lloyd George and the witty, savage ("the Tiger") Clemenceau, the latter especially dedicated to the destruction of German power. The result, in the words of the economist John Maynard Keynes, was "a Carthaginian peace." The Germans on June 28, 1919, signed the Treaty of Versailles, admitting "war guilt," surrendering large sections of German territory, agreeing to what would become impossible reparations, and submitting to disarmament.

As a sop Wilson had been tossed the League of Nations, through which he felt that many wrongs could be righted and world peace assured. Ironically, it was the Senate's opposition to the League that led it to reject the entire treaty. Ford had staunchly supported both the League and the Treaty. "President Wilson has done a great work worthy of the endorsement of every citizen," his magazine, the *Dearborn Independent,* had proclaimed while the two were under debate, and after their rejection asserted: "The time must come when the League will be set forth in such terms as will demand the assent of the American treaty-making body. We have arrived at a side-track, not a terminus."

Congress did not agree, and politically for years to come America remained isolationist. Meanwhile its economic power had multiplied. Before the war, despite its immense resources, the United States had been an international debtor. Now Germany was crushed, France exhausted, and Britain had been cut down financially to a secondary role. With small war losses, human and economic, the United States suddenly loomed as the world's greatest creditor nation. Herbert Hoover and his Relief Commission during the first half of 1919 gave Europe "extraordinary assistance," alleviating human suffering and according to one perceptive observer averting "a widespread breakdown of the European system." In the plans for recovery, American goods and financing were the chief recourse of every nation in need.[1]

By the summer of 1919 the new giant saw expanding trade possibilities, and turned to their exploration with an eagerness quite as great as had been its aversion to political entanglements. Earlier legislation by Congress had made American participation in foreign commerce easier, and when in 1920 our exports reached a total of $8 billion, they stood at an all-time high which was not attained again until 1943.

American investments abroad mounted with the swelling volume of exports. Such firms as Standard Oil, Eastman Kodak, United Shoe Machinery, and International Business Machines enlarged their overseas facilities along with the skyrocketing sales.[2]

In the forefront of such vigorous corporations stood the Ford Motor Company, with increasing foreign shipments and plans for new factories around the world. It became a vigorous proponent of greater international commerce. "It is of the utmost importance," ran an editorial in the *Dearborn Independent,* "that Congress shall take early action in the direction of removing . . . existing obstacles and hindrances to . . . our foreign trade." Ford bought some raw materials and manufactured parts abroad, but the company's chief interest was in selling its own products there. At the same time, its leader recognized that other nations needed dollars to buy American cars (his among others) and must sell their products in the United States. He consistently urged his country to take the lead in expanding trade by lowering the tariff. Of course, he needed no protection. In the early 1920's no European automobile could challenge Ford in America, nor could any American machine. As a later government report put it, this was the "Ford era." [3] *

During 1919 Ford's foreign and domestic sales rose to more than a million units, a feat never before achieved by any motorcar manu-

---

* Couzens' earlier opposition to high tariffs, as indicated in Chap. 3, represented Ford's viewpoint in the 1920's. The *Dearborn Independent* denounced "the chemical-dye trust, the sugar trust, the lumber trust and the oil trust" for lobbying to set higher duties on imports. Of the Fordney high tariff, Ford's journal declared: "Plainly the few big beneficiaries of such a tariff bill have been considered more than the people."—*Dearborn Independent,* XXIV, July 30, 1921, 4.

facturer. On the outskirts of Dearborn, Michigan, about twelve miles from Detroit, on more than a thousand acres of land, Henry Ford was building the Rouge, soon to be the greatest industrial plant in the world. In July the newspapers announced that he had options on the holdings of all the minority stockholders in his company, a fact which meant that he and his family would own completely the more than half-billion dollar firm. As Nevins and Hill put it, "never had one man controlled completely an organization the size of the Ford Motor Company. John D. Rockefeller never held more than two-sevenths of the Standard Oil certificates, and J. P. Morgan, who presided over the birth of the United States Steel Corporation, owned a much smaller percentage of the shares. Ford wielded industrial power such as no man had ever possessed."

Ford went further. In August 1919, as we have seen, he purchased the 400 shares of English Ford stock that had been issued to employees of Ford Motor Company (England) Ltd. Hard upon this acquisition he bought the shares of that company held by the Dodge brothers, D. Gray, J. W. Anderson, H. H. Rackham, and James Couzens. Through these transactions the Ford family obtained complete ownership of the British firm as well as of the American corporation.

Previously, on the last day of 1918, Edsel Ford, now twenty-five and for several years the American company's secretary, had been made its president, although the final power remained with his father.[4]

All new company operations at home and abroad Ford decided were to be owned by his family, his American firm, or would be branches of wholly-owned Ford subsidiaries. With the exception of Ford-Canada (which had public ownership of its stock and the status of which remained unaltered), everything in the foreign empire of the Detroit-Dearborn concern was to be fully controlled by the man whose name it bore and who had been chiefly responsible for its success. The era later designated as "the American Period" in Ford's foreign ventures had begun.

In 1919 the Ford Motor Company offered the public only two products. The more important of these was the universally accepted Model T; the other was a 1-ton truck, Model TT, introduced in 1918 to fill a popular demand.

A separate but allied company, Henry Ford & Son, Inc. (completely owned by the Fords and soon to be integrated with the automobile company) manufactured the Fordson tractor. We have seen how quantity production of this machine began in 1917 to meet British wartime needs; in the postwar period Henry Ford's personal interest in this unit never lessened. ."Farming in the old style," he declared, "is rapidly fading into a picturesque memory." He gave close attention to plans for marketing his tractor both at home and abroad.

As 1919 advanced, he was in a sanguine and expansive mood. Power was his, and the tides of trade ran high. As a result, two ambitious programs developed in separate continents where the Model T had prepared a path for development.[5]

2

In February 1919 Ellis Hampton, branch manager in Buenos Aires and supervisor of Ford activities in Latin America, was conferring in Detroit with William S. Knudsen. Hampton, describing in vivid detail the growth of Ford business on the southern continent, proposed a large new assembly plant in Argentina and also new branches at other points where the volume of sales was swelling.

A long and dramatic story lay back of this conference. We have seen in Chapter III that Hampton had launched Ford's first South American branch early in 1914. In that year, despite adverse economic conditions and competition from both Europe and the United States, he had placed with dealers throughout the continent almost 800 cars. With the outbreak of World War I, like irrigation waters shut off at their source by the closing of a dam, most automotive exports from Europe to Latin America ceased. Hampton had quickly enlarged his staff and dealer organization and proceeded to fill the gap. In 1915 he sold 1,455 units in Argentina alone.

In Detroit in 1916, he had argued that rapidly mounting business warranted the establishment of an Argentine assembly plant, and he got authority to set one up. Assembly meant (as it had in England) cheaper freight rates on knockdown units.* With the aid of a technician (H. H. Schultz) from Detroit, he launched his operation in a rented former cigarette factory on Calle Peru in Buenos Aires. He hired a staff locally, among whom were Kristian Orberg, a Dane; Chilean-born Jorge Matray; the American H. S. Jenkins; E. A. Evans, of English birth; Benjamin Kopf, an Argentine citizen of German background;

---

* Initially no tariff advantage was foreseen.

the Anglo-Argentine Arthur Lloyd Davies; and Guillermo Boxer and Raul P. Monteverde, both Argentine-born. S. T. Westray and B. L. Sheppard came from Detroit to serve as chief clerk and sales manager. But most important were the staff hired in Buenos Aires. They would play crucial roles in Ford's foreign operations.[6]

The first automotive assembly plant in all Latin America—this former cigarette factory—quickly proved inadequate, and an assembly plant for bodies was installed in a rented building six blocks distant. When the combined operation became awkward and time-wasting, Hampton urgently advised Detroit to let him purchase land and erect an adequate plant. "The demand for Ford cars has never been so great in the South American republics," he asserted. Indeed, statistics bore him out. Juan Shaw in little Uruguay signed up for 400 units for 1916–1917, while in Valparaiso, Chile, where four years earlier, the American consul had proclaimed that time spent marketing cars would be "practically wasted," Gibbs & Company were taking 500!

But the biggest call for Model T's came from Argentina, where in the single month of December 1917 the branch sold 1,280 units! (Sales in that country for the year totalled 6,957, more than double those of Ford-France!) European competition in South America had disappeared, and against the pack of assorted American imports, the Model T ran a victorious course.[7]

Meanwhile, the Argentine economy was developing. President Hipólito Irigoyen had announced his nation's neutrality in the war, and under his guidance Argentina attracted foreign investors. Hampton, when suggesting that Ford buy land and build there, indicated that Smithfield and Argentine Meat Co., Armour, United Shoe Machinery, West India Oil, and other foreign concerns had purchased property in the republic.

Hampton won agreement from Detroit, and on May 1, 1917 the directors of the parent company approved $240,000 for the new plant. When Hampton's elderly wife wrote secretly to Henry Ford in September, begging him to transfer her husband, since she could not endure "this *uncivilized* country," Ford told his son, "nothing doing for the present." He knew that his South American deputy was needed in Buenos Aires. However, with full American involvement in World War I, construction of the new factory was postponed.[8]

Because of the war, Ford shipments to South America were delayed; business suffered; but the decline in sales did not mirror public demand. This was unabated. Thus, when Hampton came to Detroit early in 1919, he pressed more strongly than ever for expansion. By now he was operating in four leased locations, with two assembly plants, a garage, and a retail salesroom (for the branch still sold direct to customers as well as to dealers). Undoubtedly he painted a vivid picture of the Model T in Argentine cities, on the pampas, in the estancias and far to the west along the lower slopes of the Andes. Knudsen was convinced, and re-endorsed the plant. But Hampton made it clear that if Ford wanted to ride the boom of postwar expansion, it would also have to establish sales and assembly branches elsewhere in South America.

The Ford Board of Directors, as noted earlier, had already provided funds for the Argentine factory; on April 24, 1919, it approved a new branch in Brazil, and Hampton dispatched from Buenos Aires E. A. Evans and Benjamin Kopf to establish it in São Paulo. The Brazilian distributor, William T. Wright, was replaced, and Evans set up headquarters in a small store on Rua Florencio in May and in January 1920 rented a large skating rink, converting it into an assembly unit. The two chief officials for Brazil had been trained in the Argentine branch, and the new firm began to do business with a capital of $25,000, transferred from Buenos Aires to São Paulo.[9]

Meanwhile Kristian Orberg of the Argentine staff had visited the Ford distributor in Uruguay and reported that this agent was complaining of not getting sufficient cars from New York. Orberg stated bluntly: "He is getting cars in proportion to his contract and possibly more; it seems the whole trouble is this: that he made a contract for only 1000 cars a year, when his territory, according to my estimate, should easily be able to take 2000 cars or even more."

With such a volume in prospect, Hampton promptly recommended that a sales branch be opened in Uruguay. Edsel Ford, now assuming an important role in foreign activities, endorsed the step, and the South American supervisor, then in Detroit, was able to cable Orberg: "Prepare open Montevideo branch." Orberg soon became its manager, bringing in as his assistant another Buenos Aires official, Guillermo Boxer. Like Ford-Brazil, the new unit was staffed from Argentina.[10]

As he planned these projects, Hampton had not been idle with respect to the construction of the assembly plant in Buenos Aires, for which he had to procure a site and a building permit and select a local architect. In authorizing the project, Knudsen had written him: "We expect to furnish you with such material as you cannot buy locally, [which] will mean that we will furnish you with everything except sand and gravel and wood work." Hampton was to feel "absolutely independent of our department as far as the execution of this work goes, and our desire is simply to supply information." Actually, he supplied more, arranging with Albert Kahn to design the factory and with B. R. Brown to supervise its construction.

Hampton had chosen Chambers & Thomas as his local architects, but had some difficulty with the site, and it was not until February 14, 1920 that he was able to get the deed for some land at La Boca, on the Rio de la Plata. It is legend in Buenos Aires that when, before purchasing it, he sent to Detroit for an authorization, some official there cabled back: "Land too expensive; try other side of river." The authors have not found such a dispatch, but it seems typical of the ignorance in the home office of local conditions some six thousand miles away; for at this point, as a glance at any map would have shown, the Rio Plata is forty miles across, and the other side is in Uruguay!

Hampton bought the land, price notwithstanding, and a month later Brown, who had supervised the construction of the Highland Park factory, arrived in Buenos Aires to start building operations. So backward was the Argentine economy that Brown at times was desperate. Not only could the country supply little that he wanted, but in addition it exasperated him with needless delays after materials reached the very port where he awaited them. "The steel . . . which arrived here on the 'Helenas,'" he wrote Detroit in a typical letter, "was not passed through customs and delivered to us until four weeks after its arrival, so . . . you will see what I am up against in making the desired progress on this building." An entire steel structure was shipped from Youngstown, Ohio, to Buenos Aires, while more steel for re-enforcement was sent from Chicago. Knudsen rated Argentina too high in assuming that it could supply wood; Brown could not get enough, or the quality he wanted, and was even receiving shipments of lumber from the States!

In June 1920 Hampton was again in Detroit, proposing the construction of a new assembly plant for Ford-Brazil. Knudsen approved this, and soon Brown was busy with two plants, shuttling back and forth across the almost thousand miles that separated his two projects. The new Brazilian factory at São Paulo rose on Rua Solon, in the center of the town. It had no waterfront, for the harbor of São Paulo is Santos, almost fifty miles away. Both the Argentine and Brazilian plants were three stories high, and eventually each added a fourth. They were miniatures of the Ford Detroit center at Highland Park.

In most respects the Latin American branches were treated like domestic branches of the Ford company. However, since the distances involved were so great (and communications so irregular), Detroit could not follow their activities too closely. Henry Ford never went to South America, nor did Edsel Ford, Knudsen, or Sorensen, although the home office sent auditors there about every two years. The result was that managers in Buenos Aires, São Paulo, and Montevideo acted with far more independence than those in Kansas City or Los Angeles.

Since Latin America had no indigenous automobile industry, Ford enterprises there encountered no local competition or government discrimination on behalf of native manufacturers.* The offering of a typically American car—the Ford or any other—met with commendation, for imports were inevitable and cars made in the United States were regarded with enthusiasm by buyers. Such conditions were in contrast to those encountered in industrial Europe, where there was a traditional pride in national products and procedures.

As the year 1920 closed, Hampton's accomplishments verged on the miraculous. Due chiefly to his vision and energy, Ford had risen above its competitors—Cadillac, Willys-Overland, Studebaker, Dodge, Buick—like a mighty mountain above foothills. Hampton had established the first automobile assembly plant in Latin America, had appointed dealers around the continent, had developed a group of associates with managerial talent, had created three branches, and seen two assembly centers rise. October 1920 found him starting a trip up the West Coast of South America which would take him as far north as Panama. He had instructions to find the site for Ford branch on the Pacific side of the continent. Detroit had suggested Guayaquil in Ecuador as a possible location.[11]

3

Knudsen had endorsed Hampton's plans without seeing more of Latin America than a map. Almost at the same time he approved the Argentine plant, the company had faced the necessity of expansion in

---

* The early Argentine attempt at manufacture, mentioned in Chap. II, had failed.

Europe. To carry out this complicated enterprise, Knudsen himself made two visits to observe postwar conditions across the Atlantic and to make decisions as to the sites and character of Ford activity on a continent recovering from war.

He found a confused situation that was slowly working toward order. Private car sales, production, and development work throughout Europe had been suspended during hostilities. As to Germany, the Detroit officials had contemplated a continuance of the prewar Hamburg branch, and Knudsen found that the company's investment there "remains practically intact." However, he advised that on account of the unfavorable exchange rate "no parts or monies be taken out of Germany at present." The company Board of Directors, while authorizing a German subsidy in 1919, followed Knudsen's recommendation that nothing be done at present. In the ensuing inflation, the Ford funds in Germany practically disappeared. In 1921 Ford sold only 3 Model T cars and trucks and 6 tractors in the entire country! Because of economic and political restrictions and general instability the whole development of the German automotive industry was thwarted in the immediate postwar years.[12]

However, in England and France automotive capacity had increased under the pressure of military necessity; these countries prepared to manufacture in larger volume to meet growing public demand, and in England new cars were appearing—forty entered the market in 1919–1920. The French industry showed great vitality. The Model T had shaken the chief manufacturers out of the handmade conception of the motor car, and André Citroën was readying his factory at Javel to produce in the American style. He proposed to imitate Ford in turning out cheap, reliable cars in volume; his competitor Renault prepared to do likewise. Meanwhile in Italy the Fiat was making headway under governmental protection.[13]

Knudsen does not seem to have been concerned with these occurrences (and indeed the English, French, and Italian producers were far from being able to match Detroit techniques); his idea was to re-establish and increase Ford facilities in all areas where expansion was possible. Fortunately for the Americans the European industries were now in a period of transition, and firms in the United States could capitalize upon their unreadiness to offer stiff competition.

As we have seen in Chapter 4, Knudsen had appraised the English firm under Perry, then had made plans for it, and the summer of

1919 saw them activated. The American, Warren G. ("Fuzzy") Anderson, took charge in England immediately after Perry's resignation. Nicknamed for his fuzzy hair, he had had a commendable record in the United States as the head of the St. Louis assembly branch. We have seen that Perry during the war had supervised Ford activities on the continent; after about a year Anderson was also given authority over them. Meanwhile, in August 1919, before assuming his larger role, he announced, with Knudsen's support, his policies for England. These comprised (1) an immediate reduction in car prices, (2) the establishment of exclusive Ford agencies after the American pattern of marketing, and (3) the expenditure of $5 million to remodel the Trafford Park plant at Manchester where, he declared, the company would build 25,000 cars in the ensuing year. (Since no action had been taken at Southampton, Manchester would have to be enlarged and modernized.)

With the Ford French company Knudsen was dissatisfied. It needed, he asserted, a new managing director who would be "a big man." At this very time, in June 1919, Sorensen received an appeal by cable from no less a person than André Citroën, who was "willing to accept any financial cooperation . . . either partnership . . . or formation of a limited company." Here was an opportunity to procure the most enterprising of the French car makers. But any arrangement with Citroën would mean a joint venture, and the maker of the Model T at this time was above any such alliance. As Ford's private secretary, E. G. Liebold, wrote in another connection:

> I do not think there is any object in making inquiries or investigations in regard to other industrial corporations or companies as we are seldom if ever interested in such projects, preferring at all times to build our business from the bottom up and be able to expand as its success justifies and warrants.

Accordingly, Sorensen cabled Citroën, "Impossible to secure Mr. Ford's aid in financing your company." * Knudsen meanwhile found no "big man," and Ford-France with its assembly facilities in Bordeaux pursued its undistinguished course.[14]

Much more promising were Ford activities in Denmark and Spain, which Knudsen selected as areas where trade could be enlarged. As

---

* When in 1920 Sir Herbert Austin in England suggested an alliance of Ford's interests with his, Ford rejected the idea, as he had Citroën's plea.—Austin to HF, July 9, 1920 and Liebold to Austin, Aug. 16, 1920, Acc. 284, Bx. 2.

early as May 1919 the Board of Directors gave him authority to establish companies there. He chose as locations for the new firms Copenhagen and Cadiz, respectively. In both places assembly would start in leased premises. If their business thrived, Ford would buy land from their profits and erect plants. If they failed, little would be lost, as the investment would be modest.*

The Danish Ford company was incorporated on June 25, 1919 with a capital of Kr. 500,000 (about $120,000).** Knudsen chose as its manager the attractive young American James J. Harrington, a former branch manager for the American company at Cincinnati, Ohio, and Cambridge, Massachusetts. Harrington was only thirty. As his assistant, Knudsen selected an even younger man, George Carlson, from the sales department of the branch at Portland, Oregon. The manager there, like all domestic branch heads, had received a telegram from Detroit: "How many employees have you who are capable of taking jobs as assistant manager, superintendent, chief clerk in foreign branches?" Because Carlson had a Swedish mother, his superior sent in his name. Knudsen soon called him to Detroit, where he himself, Klingensmith, and W. A. Ryan (appointed sales manager for the American company on December 31, 1918), interviewed him, a rather dazed candidate. Carlson tells the story:

> First Knudsen saw me. He started to speak Danish very slowly. I understood him. Thus, I passed the first test. He took me in to see Ryan. I was slapped on the back and went to see Klingensmith. "You're of Swedish origin," Klingensmith said. He noted the jealousy of the Danes and Swedes. I agreed . . . and said it didn't bother me. That ended the interview.

Carlson was soon sailing for Copenhagen.

He arrived in the closing days of 1919 as the new company was

---

* The scope of Knudsen's plans is indicated by his hope to handle European sales through six divisions: the Northern, with headquarters at Copenhagen; the Central, controlled from Paris; the Southern, with headquarters at Cadiz; the British, directed from Manchester; the Adriatic, operating from Fiume; and the Black Sea, centered at Odessa. While Ford plants in the 1920's would function in four of these six territories, the six as Knudsen envisaged them never came into operation.

** Copenhagen rather than Stockholm was chosen as Ford's Scandinavian assembly point because Denmark gave a duty reduction on the importation of knocked down vehicles and offered a far bigger market than Sweden. This was partly the result of the splendid work done by dealer Bülow. So successful had he been that the country was now ready for an assembly plant.

assembling its first 700 cars. Even in January 1920 Harrington and he agreed that their plant was too small. Harrington quickly imported a steel building from the United States to stand behind the existing factory and then rented additional quarters. By the end of the year 6000 units had been assembled, and it was clear that the two young Americans were operating one of Ford's most profitable foreign plants.[15]

In Spain Knudsen was impressed by the beautiful harbor of Cadiz, its excellent geographical location, and the potential supply of employees it offered. (He rejected Barcelona because it was a well-known seat of labor difficulties.) He rented a former brewery and chose as manager Arthur Lloyd Davies, who had assisted Hampton in Buenos Aires and knew Spanish. There were delays in forming the firm, but early in 1920 the Ford Motor Company SAE was incorporated, with a capital of 500,000 pesetas (about $100,000 at the time). Production began in April.

Knudsen had scheduled the unit to assemble 2000 cars in its first year of operation, and 5000 in the second. Unfortunately it was the victim of strikes and a prohibitive tariff (levied in reprisal against the French because of their import tax on Spanish wines but raising all automotive duties, so that the Ford touring car soared to a price 438 per cent of what it cost in Detroit). As a result, activities at the Cadiz factory were suspended until July 1921, when Ford cars were exempted from paying the vindictive duties. While no figures exist for the first year of the Spanish operation, between January 1 and November 1, 1921, Lloyd Davies received for assembly 1132 cars. Thus in its second year the new firm did not even achieve what Knudsen had set it as a goal for its first.[16]

4

A severe policy was now being pursued with the Danish, Spanish, French, and English Ford enterprises. Although all four were *companies,* they were operated as *branches.* To have a company made for the prestige of the unit, protected the home office from certain tax liabilities overseas, and gave it privacy from foreign scrutiny. But there was to be no nonsense as to independence of action. "We do not understand," wrote the secretary of the Detroit company, B. J. Craig, to Arthur Lloyd Davies in a scolding letter, "why it should be necessary for us to call your attention to the fact that the Spanish Company is owned by the Ford interests and subject to instructions from the home office the same as any branch house."

And as branch houses they were treated, despite their European locations and problems. They received the same general letters of instruction, the same communications about accounting, sales, production, and purchasing as did the domestic assembly plants. Each company had binders into which these missives went, their rules and policies to be followed implicitly. These came to be known among employees abroad as "the Ford Bible."

For example, the investment certificate plan was to be followed overseas as at home. "We have been advised," ran a letter to all company heads, "that the Investment Plan . . . has been formally approved by your attorney and is in operation. . . . You will of course pay the same rate of interest on the investment certificates . . . issued to employees of your company as paid by this company [the Detroit corporation]."

Auditors from Detroit regularly appeared in Europe to inspect operations. They checked books, management, and plants to see that American policy was followed throughout. Any European prejudice against routines imported from the United States was brushed aside as unimportant. Americanization extended to the management. In the early 1920's, every Ford operation in Europe but the Spanish company had an American directing its activities, and Lloyd Davies was not a native of Spain.* [17]

Likewise marketing had to be done according to Detroit scripture. In England, as we have seen, Ford dealers under Perry had been permitted to sell other cars as well as those they received from Manchester. Now they were commanded to deal in Ford products exclusively. This change violated what was an unwritten law in England and came as a shock. "Ford Knifes Bunch of British Agents," ran a headline in the English *Automobile Topics* of September 1919. The new all-Ford policy, declared the journal, "has proved a surprise to the British motor trade. . . . The previous Ford policy [Perry's] had contributed so much to making the Ford car such a good selling proposition that what constitutes almost a reversal of its policy has compelled the Company to dissociate itself from nearly a thousand agents."

Actually, the dealer force had not been cut so drastically, but it was reduced, and Perry, aware of what was occurring, felt that "the whole organization is disrupted;" many agreed with him. English dealers

* He was Argentine-born of British parentage.

cabled Henry Ford that the policy was "against the best interest of the public, the trade, and the Ford Motor Company." But their remonstrances had no effect whatever.

What was even more unfortunate, while in prewar days the English Ford company had built a car with a right-hand drive (since the English drive on the left side of the road), in the postwar period, in conformity with American practice, the Model T was now put out in England with left-hand drive! Articles in the British automotive press pronounced this change a positive danger, and enterprising English firms sold "converters" to transform the new Model T's into vehicles that their owners could operate with safety.

In Spain where dealers would "doll a car up" so as to "make a Ford look like a Locomobile or a Packard limousine in order to sell it at a price around 9000 pesetas [then about $1800]," Knudsen made it "plain to them that they have either got to quit it or quit selling Fords." (In England where dealers often followed such practice Anderson seems to have been unable to combat it successfully). A plea from Lloyd Davies that the Spanish Ford company should assume a Spanish guise was ignored in Detroit.

Although workers in Europe were demanding unionization, all employees there in Model T assembly plants were strictly denied the right to negotiate with Ford management. In Denmark, when employees sought to organize, the orders from Detroit were "that in case of labor troubles they should be met strictly on our American plan [the open shop] regardless of whether the plant keeps operating or not."

All kept operating, and that they did so was due to two other American features: the investment certificate plan already noted and, most important, the higher wages paid in Ford factories. Everywhere the Ford policy was to pay from 10 to 25 per cent more than the going rate, and with better wages the workers did not insist upon unionization.[18]

For a time Ford rode over a certain amount of prejudice in Europe with relative impunity. There was resentment against some of the American practices which he imposed, but the Ford name had a magic and Henry Ford a high reputation. Moreover, Detroit offered a desired product, low-priced and durable, with dependable service facilities. To be sure, European manufacturers were preparing to offer competition. But as yet the Model T, a dozen years after its first appearance, was in 1920 still a far better buy than any car in its class or price range.

The future was a different matter. Morris, Austin, Renault, Citroën, and Fiat would soon begin to produce in quantity. General Motors in

1920 would sell 30,000 units overseas. Furthermore, it was clear that the wartime McKenna duties in Great Britain, which set a 33⅓ per cent duty on car imports into that country, would be retained. Klingensmith, Sorensen, and Anderson met this hurdle with a declaration in January 1920 that "in the near future Ford Cars sold in the UK will be entirely of local manufacture." (Ford-England had already made progress toward this goal during the war years.) This policy of manufacture at Trafford Park would give Ford the protection of the duty and save freight costs. It remained to be seen if Anderson, with rigid adherence to American policies, could make a success of manufacturing in England.[19]

5

On the River Lee at Cork, Ireland, the tractor plant that Perry had begun for Henry Ford in 1917 was rapidly being completed. It would be a formidable center, with a machine shop, a foundry, a power house, and an assembly unit, and would make the identical Fordson manufactured at Dearborn. Its products were to be sold throughout Europe, in Asia Minor, and in parts of Africa.

Sorensen, who had always supervised tractor production, now sent American technicians over to Cork to get the factory equipped and running. These included Peter McGregor, Ben Mulligan, C. Waldron, and the man who was destined to manage the Irish project, Edward Grace. The latter had formerly been a superintendent at the Dearborn Fordson factory and arrived in July. While Perry at this time was still in charge of Henry Ford & Son Ltd., he resigned on September 30, 1919, and Grace was appointed to succeed him on November 29.

Although parts of the plant were still incomplete at that time, the first tractor came off the Cork assembly line on July 4, 1919, and by the end of the year 303 machines had been assembled (Dearborn in 1919 built 56,987). By the first days of 1920 production was mounting, and tractor manufacturing as well as assembly had begun. Hopes for the future ran high, and Dearborn invested additional funds in the operation which, it seemed, would revolutionize farming throughout Europe.[20]

For at least thirteen years, and perhaps for thirty-three or more,* Henry Ford had seen the tractor as the magic chariot which would de-

---

* Ford had begun experiments with the gasoline tractor about 1907 but always claimed to have perceived the great potentialities for a mechanical horse on the farm in the

liver the farmer from servitude to the ox and horse. In June 1918 when President Wilson had told a delegation of Mexican journalists of his hopes for friendship with their country, Henry Ford had promptly announced to the same newsmen that he would aid Mexico by building a tractor factory there to provide work for their people. He offered to train a number of young men from their nation in Detroit. A little later he declared: "We will build tractors in as close cooperation with the Mexican government as possible. We will sell [in Mexico] virtually at cost, and if profits accumulate, put them right back into the business." He sent Liebold to arrange for students and examine factory sites. The training program was established with the approval of Mexican President Venustiano Carranza, and more young men applied for the course than the Ford staff could accommodate. However, while these students received valuable training, Liebold could not find a suitable site at the right price for the Mexican tractor factory, and it was never started.[21]

Meanwhile, before the year 1920 was three months old, the venture in Ireland faced grave obstacles. In March the Cork sales manager wrote to Sorensen that "owing to the unsettled state of our sales organization in the British Isles . . . [and because] the plowing season is over . . . the demand for tractors has dropped considerably and we are faced with the situation where our production is in danger of overtaking British demands." On April 21, 1920, the Ford Motor Company in Detroit acquired the shares of Henry Ford & Son Ltd. from the Ford family and the entire selling operation was complicated by a shift of responsibility for the Fordson from special tractor dealers to the regular agents who were handling cars and trucks and were unfamiliar with it. In England, Anderson's dealers, as noted, were low in morale and not prepared to do well with a product they did not understand.* Economic conditions also made for a poor market.[22]

By June 1920 the Cork plant was almost fully completed. The machine shop was practically finished, the foundry well advanced, and plans had been made for the power house. (The foundry was the first

1880's, when he employed a steam-driven vehicle in farm work—*Ford: Expansion and Challenge*, 158–59 (gasoline tractors) and *Ford: the Times, the Man, the Company*, 106 (steam power on the farm).

* The shift was made not only in England but around the world. For example, Sherman & Sheppard (a New York firm of which Eber Sherman, former export manager of Ford in New York, was one partner, and B. L. Sheppard, the former Argentine sales manager, the other) had sold Fordsons in Latin America up to January 1, 1921, when the regular Ford branches took over their work. (See note 22.)

that Ford had built abroad.) The sales of the Fordson continued to be poor, while the costs of Irish manufacture were very high. To some extent this was attributable to the fact that the plant was just starting, for most factories make rather poor records at such a time. (Cork also had a problem in the form of a large labor force with practically no previous industrial experience.) But the chief cause undoubtedly lay in the low output, for the total expense of manufacture divided by the number of vehicles produced resulted in an excessive cost per unit. Sorensen wrote Grace in June 1920: "As it stands today European distributors are able to buy a tractor in New York and ship the same into their territory, cheaper than they can through the Cork transaction." This, he pointed out, "is not a very pleasant matter to face," and enjoined Grace and his assistant, E. L. Clarke, to study the problem. However, it was decided that although the Europeans could buy from Dearborn at a lower price, they should nevertheless buy from Cork (which presumably would soon reduce its costs).

But there was no evading the fact that sales were declining. By mid-1920 the promise of prosperity that had danced before Knudsen in early 1919, and encouraged Detroit officials to support the Cork venture, had begun to fade into the darkness of a world-wide depression. It was clear that Cork could not live by tractors alone, for the market was dissolving. Grace recognized this, and in August 1920 wrote to Sorensen: "We are starting to erect machinery on the Model T work."

For, with the depression already an impending fact in the United States, Knudsen had agreed that Grace could supplement his tractor revenue by supplying Manchester with parts for the Model T. This would avoid increasing production facilities in England. Cork had the essentials for manufacture: machine shop and foundry—why not use them? Admittedly the cost of such parts would be higher at Cork than at Dearborn, but freight would be less, and since Ireland was a part of the United Kingdom, there would be no import duty. (Even parts manufactured in Canada would have had to pay a 22⅔ per cent levy and a higher freight.) [23]

At this time Ireland was not the pleasantest place in which to transact business. The Sinn Fein (the Irish revolutionists) and the Black and Tans (British emergency police) were locked in savage hostilities, and one Cork Ford employee reported, "It is a nightly occurrence to see Armoured cars running around the streets and to hear machine guns fire all night; the next morning the show windows in the main street can be seen full of bullet holes."

How the Ford employees answered a call to midday Mass, supporting the Lord Mayor of Cork, imprisoned and on a hunger strike; how Grace in anger (he had forbidden them to go) shut down the plant and threatened to hire a new work force, how he relented and reopened the factory, and how Sorensen warned him, "Be careful. . . . Politics and politicians particularly are things you must be absolutely free and clear of!" are all part of the Irish story. Sorensen had meanwhile temporarily shut down production in the United States for want of a market, but this did not stop him from sending Grace harsh messages urging a better performance. Grace went to London and talked with Anderson. "I left him very much discouraged." At the same time Grace discovered that practically all European countries were closed to tractor imports and moreover that no one was permitted to transmit money abroad (and therefore could not buy machines in any case). "It seems," Grace concluded, "that the only solution we have is a speedy production of Model T parts, which we are working on as fast as possible."

This seems however to have been only a partial answer to a dismal situation. For although the Irish plant began to work for Manchester, Grace had not been told to stop producing tractors. "We are tied on the heels of the sales chariot," Grace's assistant, E. L. Clarke, remarked, "and are waiting for it to break into a gallop." (It didn't.) Meanwhile commitments were piling up for the completion of the plant, especially in connection with the power house.

"If you have no business prospects ahead of you," cabled Sorensen with what seems like sadistic persistence, "how do you propose to carry out your obligations?" Grace replied that the power house construction might be suspended and that he would concentrate on making Model T parts. "Our tractor business will be so small that we could not expect to maintain a plant of this size on such small production," he wrote in December 1920.[24]

That year went out in the gloom of a serious depression, hostilities in Ireland continued, and on December 11 a large part of the business section of Cork went up in flames. Martial law was proclaimed. The Ford factory was not affected; Grace believed that its being an American property made it fairly safe and cabled, "We are not in danger."

Tractor production continued to fall steadily in 1921. In June came what was really the *coup de grâce* for the long suffering Cork tractor activity. The Fordson distributor for Poland insisted on getting prices from both Cork and New York for 100 machines he was purchasing. Grace protested that all European distributors knew they must order from Ireland: "We thought this matter was properly squelched." His letter was referred to Edsel Ford, who discussed it with his father, and reported their joint decision that the Polish order should be supplied from New York. "We further wish to state," Edsel wrote to Sorensen, "that we are accepting orders today for ten tractors for Tunis on the same basis. . . . The writer feels that the only excuse for a foreign plant is the ability to serve the people surrounding it with our products at a reduction from the price at Detroit, plus freight and duty. We have thus far been unable to accomplish this at Cork."

Edsel's decision sounded the knell for Fordson production in Ireland. Sorensen soon instructed Grace to dispose of his remaining stock. He considered sending the Cork equipment to Germany and starting a tractor operation there, but lack of a suitable plant and inflation in the Reich caused Henry Ford to veto this idea. The equipment remained in Ireland. In 1920 Cork built 3,626 tractors; in 1921, 1,433; and in 1922, clearing out its stock, 2,233. The last machine was completed in December 1922 and Grace then assembled all his manufacturing equipment, machines and machine tools, and shipped the entire lot back to Dearborn. It would be years before the Irish plant would resume production of the Fordson.[25]

Meanwhile the plant on the River Lee concentrated on the production of Model T parts. By August 1921 it was producing the complete engine and everything of cast iron that Manchester required. In administering these activities, which required a smaller work force than had tractor manufacture at its peak, Grace was now employing only 1,600 men.

Aware of this fact, in February 1922 the Cork City Council demanded that the terms of the lease arranged by Perry in 1918, which guaranteed work for 2,000, should be complied with. Henry Ford flatly refused.

> Make no changes in your plans and operations whatever [he cabled Grace]. We stand ready to go and will do so immediately on their order without protest. . . . Further we will go no further under any restrictions of this lease. If this lease is not removed at once will proceed to move to other localities where we are not handicapped.

For a brief period the two parties faced each other defiantly; then the Cork City Council withdrew its demand, and by July the matter had been settled to Ford's satisfaction. He had been ready to leave. His investment in Ireland now amounted to more than $5 million, and he knew that barring miracles he would never realize an adequate return on this expenditure. The abandonment of his Mexican tractor plans, if partly the result of a failure to find a suitable site, was surely influenced by the Irish venture. Meanwhile the making of Model T parts in Cork at a considerable distance from Manchester was not an efficient arrangement. Soon it would become an impossible one.[26]

6

If the recession of 1920–1921 had played a role in the Irish debacle, it affected the entire Ford organization from Dearborn to Buenos Aires to Bordeaux. In Detroit Henry Ford had been hard-pressed to meet important commitments and slashed his factory force, his office workers and their equipment, and eliminated or merged departments in an effort to reduce expenditures. At this time a number of executives were discharged or left the company, some because of their ineptitude and the financial crisis, but the most prominent because they had advocated policies that Ford rejected or because they were in his opinion too independent. The most notable among the latter were F. L. Klingensmith and William S. Knudsen.

Comparable changes affected management in Europe. On December 31, 1920, Liebold cabled Anderson, "Secure passage on earliest date possible and report to Detroit immediately on arrival." Anderson queried in reply: "How long do you expect me to remain in Detroit?" and was told, "Arrange matters so you will not be inconvenienced if you do not return to England." He did not return. His tenure had been unhappy. He had not shown stature as the manager of a manufacturing plant, and, following orders, had badly disrupted the English dealer organization. Sorensen condemned "his attempts in managing financial as well as sales affairs."

Nevertheless under his authority, Anderson had operated at the highest profit in Ford-England's history (£852,652 or approximately $3,138,000 for the fifteen months from October 1919 to December 1920) and had sold 46,000 cars and trucks, more than keeping his earlier promise to produce and dispose of 25,000 in his first year! But his success was due to a strong demand for cars and the absence of effective competition, and the unhappy effects of his policies (most of which were dictated to him from Detroit) would only become apparent in ensuing years.

Anderson's successor, H. A. Bate, lasted less than seven months. When he left, the British company was operating at a loss for the first time in its history.[27]

Detroit officials were also dissatisfied with the managers in Spain and France, and these were replaced. In France the "big man" had never appeared, and Ford remained a small factor in the nation's industry as Citroën and Renault gathered strength.

Of all the managers Knudsen had appointed in 1919 only one remained—James J. Harrington of Ford-Denmark. His firm had not been greatly affected by the economic storm of 1920–1921; there was a Danish bank crisis, but it did not dampen sales. As a matter of fact, the depression worked well for Ford, since to cope with its mild unemployment the Danish government undertook a large road-building program, and as the highways were improved, the demand for cars mounted. Harrington was rewarded for his accomplishments by being promoted to the post of general European manager, while his assistant, George Carlson, took over the direction of business in Copenhagen. The two had undoubtedly done good work but owed their promotions partly to the prosperity of the country in which they had worked.[28]

The depression had been felt in Latin America no less than in the United States and Europe. Plans for starting a plant in Guayaquil, Ecuador, had lapsed, and in 1920–1921 there was no thought of enlarging operations anywhere else on the western coast of South America. But the full impact of the economic crisis was received in April 1921, when Charles T. Lathers, branch manager at Detroit, and George Brubaker, brother-in-law of Henry Ford (he had married one of Clara's sisters) landed in South America with full authority to make changes for economy and to review the management of Ford branches there.

"A tornado struck us!" one Ford official later recalled, and so clean a sweep of alleged extravagance and inefficiency did the two visitors make that their work is still vivid today in the minds of those who watched them. The two angry emissaries threw out typewriters, desks, file cabinets and other office equipment at the Buenos Aires, São Paulo, and Montevideo branches, discharged "superfluous" employees, and evicted managers from plush offices (Ford of course had done no less in

Detroit). The Uruguay branch, for example, maintained a fine office in the center of Montevideo, from which it made its retail sales, and also used a former cowshed for the assembly of semi-knockdown cars. Overnight it found itself banished from its elegant city quarters and operating in the cowshed, which Guillermo Boxer remembers as "simply terrible." Similarly, Lathers and Brubaker shut up the show rooms and sales centers of Ford-Argentina and Ford-Brazil. No longer would retail sales be made by the branches. In Buenos Aires all branch activities and employees were centralized at the new La Boca assembly plant, which began to operate on June 9. In São Paulo, where the new Rua Solon plant neared completion, a force of 104 hourly employees shrank to 80 between April and June.

The heads of managers were sent rolling in the course of the cyclonic incursion. "Hampton thru with all Ford business," Lathers and Brubaker cabled Detroit on April 17. They had discovered that he was holding an interest in a dealership while acting as branch manager for Argentina. This was the reason for a dismissal that shocked his friends and admirers. It was a severe sentence on a man who had done more than either of his executioners could even have dreamed of attempting.

In Brazil, E. A. Evans, presiding over a sagging operation (as were not all of them?) was likewise discharged, and Kristian Orberg, the Uruguayan manager, was put in his place. Benjamin Kopf, formerly assistant manager in Brazil, was appointed to direct operations in Montevideo.

All the South American branches now had new managers. Lathers and Brubaker had made as clean a sweep in that continent as Ford, Liebold, and Sorensen acting from Michigan had made in Europe.[29]

As the year advanced, economic conditions improved and, with new and fearful managers pushing sales and promoting economies, business was brisk again.

Altogether in 1922 the branches and companies directed by Detroit in England, Spain, France, Denmark, Argentina, and Brazil assembled 68,858 Ford cars, with England's 27,000 the largest single item in this total.* American production meanwhile had also mounted from 530,780 in 1920 to 1,373,331 two years later.[30]

The Ford foreign operations, if relatively small, were important to the Detroit company. Henry Ford himself watched them; Sorensen,

---

* Montevideo was a sales and not an assembly branch (it only set up semi-knocked down vehicles).

Edsel Ford, and Edsel's capable brother-in-law, Ernest C. Kanzler, all took a keen interest in overseas activities, although all had other and more important responsibilities.

In general, guidance for those in charge of branches and companies abroad was supplied by the most responsible men in the Detroit company. W. A. Ryan was consulted on sales matters of crucial importance, Fred Diehl on purchasing, B. J. Craig on corporate finance, B. R. Brown on building projects.

The Export Department in New York, later called the Foreign Department, over which Harper, Hampton, and Eber Sherman had presided, was a branch of the American sales activity, and on July 1, 1920 R. I. Roberge had become its head. He had already worked there for a number of years, and was familiar with Ford overseas trade. Not long afterward, he was brought to Detroit in order to be available for information that the policy-makers Henry Ford, Sorensen, Edsel, Kanzler, or Ryan might want. Roberge's whole time was devoted to matters international, and he was the only Detroit official solely concerned with them. His position in the company was not that of a top-ranking executive, but he acted as a coordinating agent and a source of detailed information.

It can be seen that there was no foreign division in the American Ford Motor Company. This condition was in contrast to that at General Motors, which as early as 1911 had formed the General Motors Export Company, a unit which, once it had weathered the 1921 recession, became an active force under the skilful leadership of GM's vice president, James D. Mooney. In 1922 Mooney started an aggressive invasion of foreign markets. He had far to go to catch up with Ford. The keen interest of the highest Ford executives, Roberge's constant activity, and above all the superlative Model T, gave Ford overseas ventures a great advantage.[31]

7

In 1922 the Ford Motor Company (England) Ltd. had held first place in the British automotive industry for more than a decade. But despite improving economic conditions, mounting Ford sales elsewhere abroad, and an upsurge of English production as a whole, Manchester sales for the year showed a drop from 1921 figures. The fact sounded an alarm, and Sorensen perceived that concessions to the British market would have to be made. In November 1922 he cabled Grace at Cork: "We have decided to put in right-hand control. Get your tools ready also patterns." Here was the first confession by Detroit that it erred in sending an American product overseas unchanged when conditions warranted modifications. The action was belated, but English Ford sales rose in 1923.

The Manchester company was now managed by C. L. Gould, who had followed Bate in the summer of 1921. Like Anderson, he had headed an American assembly branch (Omaha, Nebraska) and had an aggressive sales personality with little experience in manufacturing. To aid him, Sorensen dispatched W. E. Davis, who had supervised machining at Highland Park. Davis was to improve Ford-England's manufacturing facilities, installing tools, dies, and presses, and making the plant ready to manufacture any parts not made in Cork. At this time the English company was buying parts from Detroit, Cork, and suppliers in the Manchester area, and also making many of its own. The contemplated changes would eventually eliminate American imports and restrict manufacture to England and Ireland, thus reducing freight costs and entirely eliminating import duties.[32]

Soon it was apparent that an even more extensive operation would be required, for on December 6, 1921 the British signed a treaty giving Ireland dominion status as the Irish Free State; a year later to the day the new state was proclaimed. Manchester would have to pay a 22% per cent duty (ad valorem) on any parts it received from the new Irish dominion. Grace had queried Sorensen if he should protest and launch a campaign to bring about a cancellation of the duty. Sorensen was horrified. He cabled Grace promptly: "Have nothing to do with any publicity or propaganda against ruling of the Irish government."

When on April 1, 1923 the duties went into effect, there was no longer any justification for producing Model T parts in Ireland. They raised costs to a point where the Ford car was not competitive in the English market. Austin and Morris had both introduced small, low-priced units which were popular and furnished severe competition.[33]

Everywhere in Europe competition had increased. Others had adopted Ford's techniques. Citroën in his factory at Javel was mass-producing a car, "like Ford, a vehicle responding exactly to the needs of the moment; simple, economical, but also with a great capacity for endurance at a low cost." He had introduced his "first popular" car on June 14, 1919, and other compatriots had followed his lead. The Paris automobile show in 1922 presented light cars by Delahaye, Mathis, Panhard & Levassor, and Peugeot, as well as by Citroën and Renault. Mathis in 1922 launched his slogan, *"Le poids, voilà l'ennemi!"*

The government-protected Fiat in Italy by 1922 had become the largest Italian manufacturer. While German industry had not yet achieved postwar production and in Spain and Belgium the high-priced, luxury cars represented the national industries (the Hispano-Suiza in Spain, the F.N. and Minerva in Belgium were best-known), the English, French, and Italian automotive firms with mass production plants provided stiff competition for the Ford Motor Company. They and not any American manufacturers were the Model T's rivals in Europe.

In Latin America in 1923 Ford reigned supreme and New York export houses and dealers abroad handled company business in Asia and Africa with great success. The Model T, despite threats and competition, still held a secure first place in world markets, and a general optimism pervaded the Detroit organization. The great new plant on the River Rouge was now adding its output to that of Highland Park. With its foundry, power plant, tractor operation, blast furnaces, coke ovens, by-products section, and its networks of railways and conveyors, the Rouge would become the hub of the Ford empire. Construction of further facilities was in the offing: a stamping plant, glass and steel units, and a motor assembly factory.

But the vital place for overseas activity seemed to be England. Here the Ford organization showed some signs of decay. Could a small Rouge be built there? Could the triumph in this market be continued? When the new Irish duties were announced, W. E. Davis wrote Sorensen: "This I believe should open up the Southampton proposition again as we have plenty of room for a foundry there if you allow [us] to buy the mud lands that we wrote you about some time ago." [34]

Should Henry Ford build a formidable manufacturing plant in England—Perry's dream—that would produce the Model T at a cost low enough for it to outsell Morris and Austin and perhaps compete with Citroën, Renault, and Fiat on the continent? This was a question that he would have to answer.

6

The Sun Never Sets

"Moved by Henry Ford, seconded by W. R. Campbell, that the Directors on behalf of the Ford Motor Company of Canada, Limited, desire to place on record their deep sense of loss which this company has sustained by the death on March 11, 1922 of Gordon M. McGregor, its Vice-President, Treasurer, and General Manager." So read the Board minutes five days later. The statement continued, "by his faithful, intelligent, and untiring services and by the loyalty and confidence which he was able to inspire in its officers and employees, he contributed immensely to its [the Company's] success."

This tribute of his associates had for the most part been rendered previously in Dominion newspapers, where his death had been front-page news. The founder of the Windsor company was hailed by the *Border Cities Star* as "the most distinguished citizen" of the Windsor-Walkerville area, and there and elsewhere had been lauded for his public services, his contributions to social welfare, and above all for his achievement in building a notable Canadian industry. The termination of his life by cancer in a Montreal hospital marked the end of an epoch for the Ford Motor Company of Canada. The formative years of that organization had ended.[1]

2

It was indeed an impressive heritage that McGregor left behind him. The Canadian Ford plant was a giant, with a capacity of 60,000 motor vehicles a year. It was still the largest automobile factory in the entire British Empire (including England). It commanded assets of $25.7 million, of which the plant investment alone represented $9.8 million. Ford-Canada operated five assembly plants and four sales and service centers in the Dominion. Its dealers could be found in almost every latitude and longitude suitable for settlement around the world, for they served throughout the British Empire (excluding Great Britain and Ireland). The company now employed in Walkerville-Windsor about 3,400 men. Every other car on Canadian roads was a Ford. Competition was slight: Chevrolet, already the Model T's strongest rival, could claim only 15 per cent of the cars operating in the country (as opposed to Ford's 49 per cent). McGregor had enlarged the manufacturing capacity of his firm and encouraged suppliers to produce in Canada, so that by 1920 more than 75 per cent of the parts of each Dominion Model T were built in that country.[2]

As yet the company had no foundry, body-making plant, or engineering department. But these limitations had worked to its advantage, for no capital was tied up in these activities, and the result thus far had been higher dividends.

Any reluctant investor who had bought stock in the Canadian Ford Company in 1904 now regretted that he had not bought more. For every share he had purchased eighteen years earlier for $100, at the time of McGregor's death he possessed 56 and had received cash dividends of $6,361.

McGregor, although never given the title of president, had in fact presided over Ford operations in Canada. Henry Ford did not attend a Board meeting from mid-1915 to March 1922. There is a story that during the Tariff Commission hearings of 1920 a reporter had asked Ford his views on Canadian imposts. Ford referred his questioner to "my Canadian management."

"Aren't you president of the Canadian company?" countered the reporter.

"I don't know," was the equivocal reply.

Ford was indeed president, but he had complete confidence in his Dominion deputies, left all policy decisions to them, and held office as a formality. The story may be apocryphal, but it has an authentic ring.[3]

When in 1919 and 1920 Ford had needed funds to finance Rouge construction, he had not hesitated to sell 4,305 shares of his Canadian stock, reducing the total holdings of all Ford interests in the affiliated company to about 20 per cent of its shares. He felt that he could still control Canadian operations through engineering and this smaller fraction of the stock.* If Ford himself had not watched carefully over the Dominion developments, other officials in Detroit always did so. No Board meeting of McGregor's company was ever held without an American director present. F. L. Klingensmith had attended regularly until 1921, after which E. C. Kanzler, quite as punctilious, had replaced him. When in 1919 Edsel Ford became a director, he showed a keen interest in the work of Ford-Canada.

McGregor welcomed American participation in its affairs and wanted more rather than less of it. In 1921 he wrote Edsel that "we [that is, you and I] have had many informal talks regarding the general conditions of the company, but . . . I feel we should get together more frequently." He added: "If there isn't any business to be transacted we could even arrange for you and Mr. Kanzler to have luncheon with us and then we could retire to the Golf Links for the afternoon." Edsel had replied that it would be of "mutual benefit for us to get together as often as possible." [4]

Between 1919 and 1922 McGregor in most of his policies had followed the American company's lead. W. R. Campbell, as assistant manager, might tell the Tariff Inquiry Commission in 1920 that "we saw fit to alter the design of the Canadian touring car about a year ago to properly cater to the popular Canadian demand." Other company officials might emphasize the Dominion character of the firm's operations. Nevertheless the basic product it sold was the American Ford Model T; Canadian car parts were interchangeable with those of the vehicle built in Detroit; the labor policy was that of the Highland Park plant; and the expansion plans and sales policies reflected those of the American company. For example, just as in 1919 Knudsen and Hampton had extended Ford operations in Europe and South America, so McGregor in June of that year had sent his flamboyant sales manager, A. N. Lawrence, to explore new trade possibilities in the British Empire. And just as Ford had planned and begun the erection of the Rouge plant, McGregor considered how to expand his manufacturing capacity, and in time he would do so.

---

* The stock he sold consisted of the shares assigned to him as part of the original contract between the American and the Dominion companies (see p. 18 above) and their increase through successive stock splits and stock dividends. He sold these 4,305 shares for as much as $553 each, although for the most part he received from $400 to $500 for them. Altogether, they certainly brought him more than $2,000,000.

It is nevertheless important to recognize that no directives went from Detroit to Windsor. Ford-Canada personnel (unlike the European and Latin American managers) never received general letters in sales, accounting, traffic, and service. Instead, the relationship between the two companies was always informal and cordial. In brief, McGregor consulted frequently with Detroit officials, followed the American policies in all important respects, but also used his own judgment.[5]

The efforts of Hampton in Latin America, of Knudsen in Europe, and of Henry Ford himself in America in 1919–1920 had, as we have seen, brought new assembly plants into being abroad and had also launched the great new manufacturing center on the Rouge. McGregor in contrast had felt his way cautiously during the immediate postwar period. Following Lawrence's exploratory trip, he had taken no action to expand in any part of the Empire. As for Canada, he told his shareholders in October 1919 that "the motor car business seems to be in a very flourishing condition," but because of the Business Profits Tax Act he felt that "it hardly seems advisable to make plant extensions where we can only realize one dollar of every extra four dollars earned."

Nevertheless, he indicated that he was considering an enlargement of his domestic manufacturing facilities, and several days after the annual meeting, the Canadian Board of Directors approved his purchase of properties from the Dominion Forge & Stamping Company, consisting of a sheet metal plant, a power plant, and a frame plant, together with machine equipment, tools, dies, and so forth. By July 1920, when prosperity seemed destined to continue, the Board had authorized a Canadian expansion program of $2.5 million.[6]

Then the economic outlook altered for the worse, and by October McGregor had concluded that the expenditure voted in July should "be deferred on account of the slackening of business." When in December 1920 he lay in the hospital recovering from an operation for cancer the recession had become serious (Detroit at this time was feeling its full and dismal impact). The export business was all but prostrate and during the first half of 1921 fell off even further, for dealers were unable to establish lines of credit.

Yet despite the grim economic conditions that gripped most of the world, the company faced no prospect of disaster. In October 1921 the Ford-Canada directors had taken "considerable pride in submitting . . . the financial statement" to the stockholders. The company continued to pay dividends. While its expansion had been curtailed and sales declined, McGregor stated that the company had "improved its financial position" and could "face the future with confidence."

The manager had steered his firm through this difficult period in a statesmanlike manner. The depression had struck Canada about a month earlier than it had descended upon Detroit, but the effect upon Highland Park was more devastating, for on December 24th the plant there had closed, not to reopen for more than a month. However, the American firm recovered much more quickly. Already in February its sales were rising sharply and by April were practically normal. The sales of Ford-Canada were lower for the year ending July 1922 than they had been for the preceding twelve months, although they had held up pretty well in both years (sinking from 55,616 in 1919–1920 to 46,832 in 1920–1921, and to 45,000 in 1921–1922). But early in 1922 they were showing signs of recovery; McGregor did not live to see the sharp upturn, which occurred soon after his death in March 1922. The recession had only postponed his expansion plans.[7]

3

There had been no extensive changes in the staff of the Dominion Ford firm during the depression period, although some lesser officials left, and the brilliant A. N. Lawrence parted from the company because of a clash of personalities. McGregor's passing resulted in no struggle for leadership. Wallace R. Campbell, as assistant manager, had been acting for him during his illness and had been closely associated with him for seventeen years. He had married into the McGregor family and knew company policy at top level. Now at forty years of age he was the natural heir apparent and quietly took the position of power for which he was well prepared.

On March 16, 1922 the Ford-Canada Board of Directors appointed him vice president and treasurer of their organization. Henry Ford still held the title of president, Edsel Ford became second vice president, and the accountant P. W. Grandjean was elected to the post of secretary and assistant treasurer, becoming Campbell's right-hand man. Henry Ford attended this meeting but did not sit in on another gathering of Dominion directors for twenty years. Campbell was now in charge and from the first as much or more so than McGregor had been.

The new manager had free access to the Detroit and Dearborn plants and held a pass to the latter area, which he treasured with some amusement. It was written and signed by Henry Ford and gave "W. R. Campbell and fiend [*sic*]" the range of the entire Rouge development!

While he had always worked smoothly with the founder of the Canadian company, in personality Campbell bore little resemblance to his predecessor. Everyone testified to McGregor's kindliness, friendliness, and consideration for others. Campbell, in contrast, seemed austere and unapproachable. One employee remembered that for most of the workers he was "pretty near to God." Actually, his closer associates explained, this demeanor was misleading. "He appeared as an autocrat, looked rather dour," remarked one of them later, "but he was not so at all. Rather, he was a deeply thoughtful individual." At the same time, he had no patience with indecision or cloudy thinking. He saw clearly what was to be done, was energetic and "never equivocated." Where McGregor might feel his way cautiously, postponing action, Campbell studied situations, determined what course was required, and took it boldly and promptly. He was far the more venturesome of the two.[8]

By the summer of 1922 all signs pointed to a strong revival of business, and Campbell acted to take advantage of the situation. With the approval of his American associates, he embarked upon the most ambitious expansion program the Canadian company had ever undertaken. His first step was the purchase of 137.12 acres of land in the Windsor area for approximately a million dollars. This tripled the space available for company operations. This purchase he explained at the October 1922 annual meeting. "For a number of years past," he stated, ". . . the Ford Motor Company of Detroit had been very intensively developing a policy of controlling its own sources for raw material, and the development has come to such a point (as evidenced by the Rouge River development) that it is now in a position to produce and sell cars at prices which in effect are keener competition to us than any other make of car." The Canadian company too must save money for its customers, he asserted, and "our present facilities are entirely inadequate" for this, despite the fact that "the prices of our product . . . are by far the lowest in the history of the company." Consequently Ford-Canada must expand its manufacturing potential. The greater facilities would reduce the cost of car construction "and at the same time will enable us to increase production to meet the demand which we believe can now be expected from this territory."

His plan was bold. Construction began in November 1922 and Campbell announced that the scope of the undertaking would involve

$10 million. On the newly acquired land rose a machine shop, covering about fifteen acres, a heat-treat plant, a power plant (with a capacity of 15,000 KW), and a by-products building. In 1923 the company added all told 927,575 square feet of floor area. All structures and equipment were of the most modern design. By 1924 it was possible to transfer operations from the old river factory to the new one; the former was not abandoned but converted into a body-making unit. (Bodies had heretofore been manufactured by a supplier.) With greater capacity came increasing volume, and the company was soon marketing more vehicles than ever before in its history and, with soaring production, at lower prices. The Canadian Ford touring car in October 1922 had sold for $495; now, a year later, it could be bought for $445. (The Detroit Model T touring car was priced at $348 until October 17, 1922, and then at $298; and in 1923 at $295.)

The enlarged facilities permitted Ford-Canada to turn out 500 cars in eight hours. In 1923 the firm replaced its old assembly plant at Toronto with a new one. Assembly was discontinued at London, Ontario, leaving Windsor, Toronto, Winnipeg, and Montreal as the sites where vehicles were put together. George Dickert continued in charge of production. Campbell took account of it for purposes of policy, but left the details to Dickert, a highly competent manufacturing head.[9]

Campbell, Grandjean, and Dickert formed the trio in charge of company management. In the sales field the plump H. S. Pritchard, trained to be a lawyer, had succeeded Lawrence. "He set a pace that had people striving rather desperately to keep up with him," recalled an executive in his department; his whirlwind tactics got him into a variety of troubles, but the end result was always an impressive performance which won the admiration of both dealers and distributors.[10]

4

Quite as important as Campbell's enlargement of manufacturing facilities was his decision to take direct charge of overseas markets and vigorously expand in them. McGregor may have considered developing those areas, but had held off. Campbell did not. "I think he's the man who's entitled to the credit for originating the overseas activities," said an official who had been one of his lieutenants at this time; that is, Campbell was responsible for organizing permanent establishments abroad, with immense increases in sales volume.

The situation throughout the British Empire in 1922 was much what it had been before the war, except that the Melbourne branch McGregor had started in 1909 had been discontinued in 1918. Export houses and local distributors handled all Ford-Canada's foreign business. But several facts had meanwhile become significant. One was that New Zealand and Australia were in third and fourth places, following the United States and Canada, in per capita ownership of automobiles. Another was that the South African, Indian, and Malayan markets, while not impressive for the number of cars per person, nevertheless provided good sales outlets. Furthermore, these territories were vital to the Canadian Ford company. A third or more of all its production continued to be shipped to them, and as previously pointed out, their demand came primarily in the slowest period for Ford-Canada sales. There was the final consideration that the manufacturing potential of Ford-Canada had been decisively raised and that a vigorous development of every foreign area would enable this greater capacity to be used and perhaps further enlarged.

Could export houses and distributors be relied on to provide such a development? Certainly they were not as dependable as a branch or company directly under the control of Windsor. Furthermore, the various agencies Ford-Canada employed were taking profits which might as well come direct to Ford-Canada. Earlier it had not been prepared to establish companies abroad. Now, thought Campbell, it was. But his chief feeling must have been that his organization could not afford to leave the expansion of overseas trade in any hands but its own. Thus, he determined to form foreign corporations and set up assembly plants abroad.

He reported his decision at the shareholders' meeting of October 22, 1923, stating that "conditions now warrant closer connections with our customers in foreign territories." He proposed to make South Africa the first project in expansion but "to develop other portions of our export territory along similar lines as conditions warrant, and our experience in South Africa will very largely govern our future policy."

By this time he had planned and staffed this first overseas venture. Earlier—probably in the fall of 1922—he had received three visitors from Africa and told them of his plans. These guests were Harold George Holmes, who as noted in Chapter III had been selling Ford cars in Kimberley since 1912; his son, and William Atkinson of Bloemfontein, who held a franchise as Ford distributor in that part of the Orange Free State. An employee of Ford-Canada joined in the conference—a

Dane, Hans Ferdinand Axel Stockelbach. Campbell had known him for some time and had selected him to help set up and manage the South African enterprise.

South Africa had been selected for the initial venture rather than Australia, India, New Zealand, or Malaya, because of Campbell's increasing dissatisfaction with the handling of business there by Arkell & Douglas, who had been agent for the Canadian company since 1906.

Arkell & Douglas had a large organization in the African Dominion with many dealers, and it had assembly facilities for Ford cars at four coastal ports as well as Johannesburg. Such activity in itself was acceptable (except for the questionable efficiency of operating five assembly plants), but Campbell knew that it was being used in an objectionable manner. Ford-Canada sold its cars to the export house and then had no further control over merchandising. It now learned that the vehicles were being marketed at excessive prices, thus cutting down the volume of sales without the slightest benefit to the home company. The high prices were doubtless the responsibility of the dealers (who thus made more profit per unit), but Arkell & Douglas had done nothing to control the practice, and Ford-Canada was helpless. Later Campbell learned that the export house was using the same organization that marketed Fords to sell Maxwell, Columbia, and Clydesdale cars. Apparently Arkell & Douglas had come to regard Ford as merely one of a number of *its* manufacturers.[11]

Campbell acted to change the situation completely. On July 30, 1923, Stockelbach and Charles Holmes (no relation to the Kimberley dealer) landed in Cape Town, set up temporary offices, and engaged a law firm to form a company. Arkell & Douglas were notified that this new corporation would take over distribution in South Africa.

The man whom Campbell had selected to manage his first overseas company had shrewd business sense, great industry, and a likeable personality. However, he had had little previous knowledge of automobile production or marketing. Campbell had brought him into the Windsor organization to supply this deficiency. He had learned rapidly, availed himself of the knowledge his associates commanded, and there was never any suggestion that he did not understand the complicated business he dealt with. He promptly took responsibility for forming a company in Africa rather than a branch, pointing out that the latter would make it legally possible "to tax in South Africa the capital of the Canadian Company in Canada."

Soon after arriving in Cape Town Stockelbach and Holmes also decided that the headquarters for the new firm could not be in that city, as it was at the southwestern corner of the continent. Were assembly to be established there (and they concluded that one and not five points was the logical and economic solution for that process), the freight rates to most of the dealers would be excessive. More centrally located, Port Elizabeth was chosen as a better place for all activities. By September an office was rented there, along with a vacant warehouse that could be remodeled for assembly operations. From that point cars would be distributed through all Africa south of the equator, including Kenya and the Gold Coast.

As to the dealer situation, Stockelbach decided that "wherever possible the old dealers should be kept as a nucleus to start with." (He meant to enlarge the dealer force in order to increase sales.) But many of the "old dealers" were not appreciative of this policy. They awaited word from C. D. Wessinger, the Arkell & Douglas representative. (A number of the dealers, as noted earlier, were owned or controlled by that company.) When Holmes and Stockelbach first arrived Wessinger was en route to South Africa from the United States. He reached Cape Town late in August, but showed no disposition to cooperate with the Windsor emissaries. He was the villain of the story. As a report prepared by Stockelbach put it: "As the time passed it was more and more apparent that his intention was to hold up any decisions and then at the last moment cut loose from the Ford Motor Company."

As soon as Stockelbach perceived this he canceled the existing dealerships in Cape Town, Port Elizabeth, East London, Durban, and Johannesburg, replacing them with new agents and lining up an organization that was fairly complete by mid-November. Stockelbach was able to keep a number of the older dealers: Holmes and Atkinson, of course, Duly & Company in Rhodesia (which had sold Fords since 1911), and others.

On December 29, 1923, the company of Ford–South Africa was incorporated, with a capitalization of £200,000 ($960,000). It already had 10 main dealers by this time, and would have 42 the following June. (Arkell & Douglas had used only 10.) Meanwhile, Ford–South Africa had bought the cars remaining in the hands of dealers who had been replaced, the new firm paying Arkell & Douglas £76,467 (or roughly $325,000) for the lot.

The South African company was wholly owned by Ford-Canada.

Campbell and Grandjean became directors, Stockelbach was also on the Board, as were two other Canadians employed by the new corporation. Also serving on it was a member of the law firm which had acted for the subsidiary when it was incorporated. He was expected "to most carefully safeguard our interests from a legal point of view." Meanwhile Stockelbach was very active. There was some hostility on the part of Arkell & Douglas' former agents which he found annoying, and there was difficulty in disposing of the 1923 cars acquired from the export house, "as it had become known that new models were coming out in the near future." Assembly at Port Elizabeth was accordingly not begun on trucks until February, and on passenger cars until April 15, when the crop of older models had all been sold.[12]

Ford–South Africa prospered from that time forward. By early 1925 there were 36 main dealers (a few of the 42 had fallen out), and the number of sub-dealers had been increased from 120 to 180. As Stockelbach explained to the Canadian Ford officials, "the sub-dealer has been found to be a necessity in this country; he cannot become a Main Dealer as he is in most cases without finances. . . . He cannot be done away with entirely on account of the service he renders and because the distances are too great to be covered by salesmen."

The work force of the Port Elizabeth company was entirely white, since there was a reservoir of labor available which was forming a "poor-white" class and giving the government grave concern. Some local purchasing had begun, and the management tried to increase this whenever possible.

In October 1924 Campbell reported to the Canadian shareholders that their firm had spent $1,010,205.79 for subscription to the entire capital stock of the Ford Motor Company of South Africa Ltd. and for certain materials "on hand, in transit, or in process of manufacture in South Africa." He was well satisfied with Stockelbach's performance. In the first year Stockelbach had sold 3,260 cars and trucks and 74 tractors, done a business of $2,578,556, and made a profit of $252,741 before taxes. Already the African activity had been expanded, the prices of cars and trucks reduced, and in Stockelbach's words the new firm was following Ford Motor Company policy of selling products "to the great masses, at the cheapest possible price consistent with a high quality product." Campbell wrote to Edsel in the fall of 1924 that "the result of our operation there [in South Africa] has proven to us the advisability of further developments along similar lines in our other export territories." [13]

5

In October 1924 a group of six men sailed from Canada for Australia. They included H. C. French, who had made a survey of that country in 1923, and P. W. Grandjean, secretary of Ford-Canada. They went to set up a Canadian-controlled unit to direct all Ford activities on that continent. "A great number of considerations," Campbell had written Edsel Ford on September 10, 1924, "have led us to the conclusion that the time is now ripe to carry on business in Australia with our own organization." He pointed out that this market had operated under a number of distributors for twenty years and that it now deserved "a more adequate and economical system for serving the Australian public." Edsel had agreed.[14] *

A little smaller than continental United States and supporting a population (5,436,794) somewhat less than that of New York City, Australia was chiefly engaged in the production of wheat and wool, and as earlier noted showed a high per capita ownership of automobiles, which were essential because of the great distances to be traversed by the many farmers and sheep-raisers in connection with their business.

During World War I the Australian government had considered banning all imports of automobiles to save vital shipping space, but had accepted a compromise which prohibited the admission of car bodies. Chassis could still enter. As a result, the country had developed a body-building industry, and with peace this was protected by so high a tariff as to make it practically impervious to foreign competition. All five Ford distributors there manufactured the bodies for their vehicles; these differed widely from one another in design, and largely determined the prices of the complete automobile. Although the prices varied from state to state, compared with those of Canada they were astonishingly high. This condition infuriated Campbell who, like Henry Ford, wanted conformity in the appearance of the motor cars he sponsored, and aimed to market his output at the lowest possible figures.** With a single body

---

* Edsel Ford at Campbell's request had made $3,000,000 available for Australian expansion if the sum were needed. It never was. (See note 14.)

** The bodies for a number of cars in Australia were made by the Holden's Motor Body Builders, Ltd. of Adelaide. Becoming highly efficient, this firm had rapidly increased its output and in 1923–1924 turned out 18,107 units. Its costs were considerably lower than those of the separate Ford plants. Holden's served Dodge, Chevrolet, Overland, and Star,

plant serving the entire market, he hoped to produce consistency of appearance at low cost.

Campbell also felt that the gains his agents made were excessive, and as he wrote Edsel, he wanted the Ford organization to get "a portion of the merchandising profit at present accruing to our distributors." Again, he learned that the sub-dealers were receiving inadequate commissions; in fact, he concluded that the existing system made "practically no effort to develop sub-dealers." [15]

French and Grandjean were to establish headquarters in Geelong, Victoria, a seaport of 15,000 population, and also to start body-building and assembly plants. Bodies built in Geelong would be used on all Ford products marketed throughout Australia, while separate assembly units would be set up in each of the several states.

French was to become manager of the entire operation (Grandjean's role was simply to assist in the formative period). Born in Michigan, educated in Detroit, French had studied in the college of law in that city for three years. Then in 1904, when twenty-two years of age, he had moved to Canada, working in the construction business for eleven years (an experience that would shortly be most serviceable to him); in 1919 he had joined the sales department of the Ford-Canada. Now at forty-two, seasoned, with great personal charm, he was an indefatigable worker and well equipped for the difficult task he faced.

Altogether Campbell sent about 16 men, almost all Canadians, to help French start the new enterprise. Two companies were formed, the Ford Manufacturing Company of Australia, which would operate only in Victoria, constructing bodies, and the Ford Motor Company of Australia, Proprietary, Ltd., which would manage the assembly plants and the marketing of Ford products throughout the entire country. Each firm had a capitalization of £1,500,000 (a total of approximately $7,270,000). Actually, while there was a distinction between the two units, incorporated separately for tax purposes, they worked together as complementary parts of one business. They were incorporated on the same day, March 31, 1925.[16]

Before this event, Grandjean had secured from the Geelong Harbour Trust Commissioners about 100 acres of land near Cowie's Creek,

and had sought Ford business. Campbell believed the firm was subsidized or controlled by General Motors and had refused. (Actually it was not until 1931 that GM acquired the enterprise.) Campbell felt that with a single body plant Ford costs could be brought down to Holden's. (See note 15.)

Geelong. Here would be the center for Ford of Australia. The site fronted deep water and had a good harbor both for handling imports and for shipping materials to the projected assembly factories in other states. The labor situation there was more settled than in other areas, the cost of property was low and tax rates equitable. There were good power sources at hand, and inland transportation facilities were available (a railroad crossed the property). Finally, the subsoil presented no problem so far as the sinking of foundations was concerned.

The news that the town had been selected, reported the *Geelong Advertiser,* "caused the utmost gratification to all classes of the community." The paper noted the enormous scope of Ford projects and printed a statement from Grandjean beginning, "The growing importance of Australia as a market for our cars was primarily the reason for serious consideration by our company during the past few years of the necessity to establish ourselves in a direct way in this country." But if the populace of Geelong was happy, in other parts of the country the chief distributors were not.[17]

While the companies had been in process of formation, Grandjean and French had located sites for assembly plants in other states than Victoria. Because of poor inland transportation, the dispersion of assembly operations was essential, and it was also mandatory that the factories be located on the coast so that bodies could be supplied from Geelong by steamer. Chassis would go direct from Canada to each separate factory. Grandjean obtained 165 acres of land at Granville near Sydney, New South Wales, on which stood buildings that could be remodeled for automotive purposes. In Brisbane (Queensland) and Adelaide (South Australia) he and French acquired other sites. In Fremantle (Western Australia) French rented a building where assembly could begin. The new Ford enterprise thus would have a single body-making factory and five assembly units.

Ford officials wasted no time. "We astounded the Australians by the speed with which we started," recalled Basil Stevenson, who was among the first arrivals. Under French's experienced eye the buildings went up lightning fast. The government assured Grandjean that it would be impossible to get a railroad siding for two years, but he had it operating in as many months. The first assembly began at a wool warehouse at Geelong. Australian engineers, architects, and labor were all capable, the Canadian supervision was expert, and the attitude of the government was "wonderful." The new controller of Ford-Australia,

Rhys M. Sale, later recalled, "We moved through red-tape with the greatest of ease. . . . This was the ideal climate to attract investment capital." Australia wanted industry. If there was a difficulty to be discussed, "*They listened,*" and acted.[18]

There was now the question of replacing the five distributors. The Ford Motor Company agreed to take over the stocks of these agencies on July 1, 1925. They were Queensland Motors (Brisbane), Davies & Davies (Sydney), Tarrant Motors (Melbourne), Duncan Motors (Adelaide), and Grave & Dwyer (Perth). "Our dealer organization, with the exception of the distributors . . . will continue exactly the same as at present," the company announced.

This was more than satisfactory to those who had been sub-dealers, who now received a higher status and a better commission. New agents were added to the force, looking toward increasing sales. But the situation was resented by several of the old distributors, who wanted to continue taking profits as in the past and who objected to the company's gathering what hitherto had been *their* harvest.

The distributors had a case. They felt *they* had established Ford in Australia. Evidence exists that they had helped to do so. A London Department of Overseas Trade bulletin in 1922 complained that British motor vehicles in the island continent then held a position "unsatisfactory to the extreme." By way of contrast it noted the superior service offered by American (including Canadian) agencies, and indicated that roughly 30 per cent of the cars imported into Australia that year were Fords. In 1923 the distributors had enjoyed an especially profitable year, handling more than 20,000 Ford chassis (approximately $9 million worth of business).

Rhys Sale thought that the distributors showed "no anger" at the formation of a company that deprived them of their special opportunities and profits. "We negotiated a fair deal and they were satisfied. They had been expecting it for some time." Two of the five, Duncan Motors and Tarrant Motors (under the name of Overseas Motors) continued as Ford dealers, and the Tasmanian distributor also accepted an agency. But according to a British source, "some of the biggest distributors . . . saw a possibility that their capital might suddenly be made idle, and turned to investigate agencies for British cars," with the result that "contracts were made which had not been dreamed of." That several of the distributors were indeed bitter against Ford-Australia is indicated by the behavior of one of them who was talking rather expansively about his wealth to Basil Stevenson. "Well, George," the latter remarked, "I guess the Ford Motor Company didn't do you any harm." The distributor "shut up tight," and never mentioned his financial status or the Ford car again.[19]

At any rate, one effect of the establishment of the new company was that when it began its sales campaign in 1925–1926 it found some of its former agents busily promoting British vehicles. The market was thus more competitive than it had been in 1922 or 1923. Without the aid of three of its former distributors, and in some cases with their active hostility, Ford sales declined. Imports of motor chassis from Canada into Australia in 1922–1923 had totaled 22,951 (practically all of these were Model T's); in 1925–1926 they came to 12,251, a loss of 10,700 units. On the other hand, in the same interval, annual imports of non-Ford chassis from the United Kingdom increased by 10,800 units and those from the United States by over 17,000 (none of the latter were Fords).

The Model T had held first place in Australia in 1922–1923, but in 1925 General Motors was getting 16.9 per cent of the passenger car registrations with Ford holding only 14.7 per cent. The next year, when GM established its own assembly and distribution organization, the contrast was sharper: 21.1 per cent (GM) as against 11.9 per cent (Ford). British imports also increased, although they soon fell off abruptly (the distributors by 1927 found themselves overstocked with English units that they could not sell). Ford in Australia had to recognize General Motors as its chief source of competition.

Ford in Australia made the same Model T that was produced in the United States and Canada; special equipment such as wire wheels, balloon tires, and Ruckstell axles had first to be authorized by Ford-Canada. While the dealers improved upon the standard model by using colors and altering the body to make a "Ford De Luxe," Geelong and the assembly plants followed the Detroit and Windsor procedure. The parent firm in Canada set prices and dividends to be declared by its Australian subsidiaries, but otherwise local management was independent.

Ford in Australia was building the car that was still in 1925 and 1926 outselling any other automobile in the world (despite its poor showing in that country). Its international reputation was high. But French, who had expected to manufacture 30,000 bodies and assemble 30,000 annually was not able to realize this goal in either year.[20]

6

Dodge & Seymour, a firm affiliated with Markt & Hammacher, had for some years been selling Fords in India, Malaya, Ceylon, Burma, and the East Indies. They had continued the work of the larger organization, being organized in 1916 to take over a part of its business. There had been no question of the admirable work done by Dodge & Seymour, but in 1926 Ford-Canada felt that the time had come to take over direct control of activities in the East.

Dodge & Seymour sold many other products besides Ford cars—pumps, machine tools, canned milk, and toothpaste, for example. While automobiles represented no small part of its work, they comprised merely one large item, and when Ford-Canada proposed to take over in the East, Dodge & Seymour was philosophical about relinquishing the business. It cooperated in effecting the transfer of authority, and many of its employees accepted positions with the Canadian company's new enterprises and fell in with the expansion plans.

Campbell sent R. S. Milliken, his export manager, to the East to make the arrangements that would be essential. In India first, Milliken selected the American John Chidsey, Dodge & Seymour's manager there, to head a new Ford of India. H. A. Denne, who represented a subsidiary of Russa Engineering, which handled Ford automobiles in India on behalf of Dodge & Seymour, later recalled that Milliken told him, "As soon as I'm finished here, I'm going to Malaya." Denne set out for London (possibly at Milliken's suggestion) and met Campbell who was visiting there. After some discussion the latter told him to go out and get Malaya started. Denne began with a staff of six men, which Basil Stevenson, coming up from Australia, soon joined. In Singapore they assembled Model T's in a leased building. Denne sold these units in Siam, Malaya, and all the East Indies, a considerable portion of it not within the British Empire.[21]

Denne had made some inquiries of Ford-Canada with respect to this domain, but was told in effect, "Go and find out." Actually from Siam to the farthest island of the Indies was a bigger stretch than from Dublin to the Urals. To cover this, there were available only a few short railways and some irregular steamship service. Of course, the distance from Canada was awesome. W. R. Campbell never visited these far areas.

Early in Denne's management of Ford-Malaya the Canadian office had suggested that he didn't seem to be getting around enough. He retorted: "Do you know how big this blasted territory is?" and told them, but had the feeling that he had made no impression.

Besides dealers like Wearne & Company (Australians), Denne used Dutch and English firms but found that he still did not have the force he needed and proselyted among various British companies of standing to take agencies. He would say to these people, "Business is going to change. This is your opportunity to become modern. You will start with motor cars, but you'll find that the entire character of trade will alter. You'll have such volume as you never dreamed of. And if *you* don't get into the business, the Chinese will. They're well aware of what is going on." Usually he got his dealers.

Ford-India was incorporated July 31, 1926 and Ford-Malaya on November 19, 1926. John Chidsey had his headquarters in Bombay, and began assembling there. He also operated assembly units in Calcutta, Madras, and in Colombo, Ceylon. Denne's only factory was in Singapore.

By the end of 1926, Campbell had set up five overseas companies, and they comprised an empire. In 1923 Ford-Canada had no assembly factories abroad (although exporters and distributors operated some); now its balance sheet showed $5,985,534.59 invested in the capital stock (fully paid) of its foreign companies, which maintained assembly plants in twelve cities (in Africa, India, Malaya, and Australia). It owned five companies in these lands (two in Australia). Campbell had carried out his promise to establish "closer connections with our customers in foreign territories." [22]

7

The end of 1924 and the beginning of 1925 saw a depressed condition in the agricultural areas of Canada which affected the industrial sections of the country. Campbell told his shareholders in October 1924 that business "has not been brisk." In 1925 sales were lower than in 1924, but the corporation's profit was higher than it had ever been before. Campbell explained that this proved the "benefit of . . . our expansion program": production costs had been lowered. Minor body changes had been made in the Model T in September 1925, increasing the saleability of the car. Campbell reported on the "wonderful spirit of cooperation" shown by Detroit: "They have enabled us to keep absolutely abreast of themselves in the matter of design so that on the very day that the new models were announced in the United States we were able to get into production on new models in Canada."

Both Kanzler and Edsel Ford had shown an increasing interest in the Canadian company. When in July 1924 H. H. Rackham and his wife asked Edsel if he would like to buy their Canadian Ford stock, Edsel replied, "Yes," and added that he was "picking up some of this stock at odd times lately." On October 9, 1924, the Detroit Trust Company acquired 4,334 shares of the Dominion company's stock, 2,030 of which came from Mr. and Mrs. Rackham. In November 1924 Edsel Ford, in signing an agreement with an agent, indicated that the Ford Company and the family proposed "to purchase all the outstanding shares of the Ford Motor Company of Canada Ltd." On October 15, 1926, Charles S. Mott sold him 2,765 shares, and on the same date the Detroit Trust Company transferred 4,334 which it had been holding for him to his account. Henry Ford, despite his stock sales in 1919–1920, still held 12,484 shares. Edsel Ford's holdings at the end of 1926 totaled 7,359. A block of 2,000 shares stood in his wife's name as trustee for his sons Benson and Henry Ford II. The American Ford company had no Ford-Canada stock. But the total family interest represented 31.20 per cent of the 70,000 Canadian shares outstanding. While far from a majority, this holding was enough to insure control.[23]

In 1926 the sales of the Dominion company reached an all-time peak. There were several reasons for this. The chief one was that the economy of Canada had recovered from the depressed years of 1924–1925. Crops were good. People were buying cars as never before. During the year 204,727 vehicles were produced in the country by eleven manufacturing and assembly plants. It was the highest production the Dominion had ever attained, and of the total the output of Ford-Canada was 100,614.[24]

Of all the models offered for sale the Ford touring car at $440 was the lowest in price. Increased efficiency in manufacturing was partly responsible. But the low figure was also essential to meet competition, for on April 16, 1926, under the Liberal government of W. L. Mackenzie King, the tariff on motor vehicles was reduced from 35 to 20 per cent. Ford-Canada was forced to cut its prices to compete with American imports. The tariff slash had stunned the personnel of the company, who held to the position taken by Campbell in 1920, before the reduction: "We do believe . . . that the present margin of protection should be continued for the welfare of the industry and for the good of the country in general." [25]

Henry Ford, always an advocate of a lower tariff for American automobiles, was quoted by the *Ottawa Evening Citizen* in April 1926 as opposing all import duties, and congratulating the Canadians: "You people are just waking up. You ought to rub the other eye, now, too, and clean out the Tariff." The Ford Dominion management ignored this statement, and soon, probably in deference to their position, Ford executed a *volte-face* and according to the *New York Times* told the reporters:

> Though I am not a tariff advocate in the United States the situation of the two countries is quite different. . . . The United States has attained industrial maturity and should be able to stand on her own feet in competition with the world, but Canada is still in the formative stage industrially, and if a higher tariff will foster industry there, who can object to that?

There is no evidence that Ford ever insisted on his Canadian officials favoring lower tariffs; he let them do what they thought best for their company.

Campbell expressed their feeling in 1926 when he protested, with others in Canadian industry, that it was cheaper to import the built-up car (duty 20 per cent) than to assemble or manufacture in Canada, since the tariffs on motor vehicle parts ranged from $27\frac{1}{2}$ to 35 per cent. To compensate for the drastic cut in protection, the government made certain parts of "a class or kind not made in Canada" duty free when they were used in constructing automobiles. In addition, it provided a drawback, by which the Canadian manufacturer got a 25 per cent rebate on any duty paid on vehicle parts for his car, if the finished product contained a specified per cent of Canadian content.

Ford-Canada could easily meet the "Canadian content" requirements, and with the April 1926 tariff changes it gained free entry on parts not made in Canada and rebates on others imported. Consequently it could lower its prices. This, with the prosperity of 1926, was responsible for the record sales of that year.[26]

The demand for Model T's remained high during that season. But in the Dominion as in the United States Ford began to feel the pressure of competition, particularly in the passenger car field. Nonetheless at the close of 1926, of all the cars on Canadian roads, 45 per cent were Fords. In the truck field Ford-Canada was even more successful, supplying 66.8 per cent of all such vehicles in use.

Ford-Canada was an imposing organization. By December 31, 1926 its assets stood at $46,110,916.49, of which plant investment comprised $20,594,990. Its home office employees numbered 6,411. Its dealer force in the Dominion amounted to 698. It was still the largest automotive manufacturer in Canada *and* in the British Empire. Campbell, Grandjean, and Dickert continued to lead the company, with Campbell shaping policy. He was daily proving his value to the American management across the Detroit River.[27]

7

Prosperity and Frustration

Edward Grace, manager of the Cork plant, came to Detroit in May 1923 to discuss the situation created by the English tariff on Irish products. As already noted, this had made the manufacture in Cork of car parts for Manchester economically impossible and posed a double dilemma. There would have to be a new future for the Irish plant, and Manchester must get duty free the engines and castings it had been receiving from the factory. The decision was "for the time being motors and axle assemblies will be manufactured at Cork." But it was understood that "Cork is to stop manufacturing as soon as it is possible to secure a suitable site in England and erect buildings necessary to accommodate our Cork equipment." Edsel Ford and Sorensen deputized Grace to scour England and find a location for the new manufacturing center.

It will be recalled that Henry Ford owned land at Southampton, but was not inclined to build there. Grace, with C. L. Gould, manager of the English company, now looked for a better site and soon reported that "after having thoroughly investigated England . . . the most suitable place for the future plant is in the London district—somewhere in the neighborhood of Dagenham." For the first time, on July 10, 1923, that name was laid before Ford officials in the United States.[1]

Grace probably knew that this expanse of Essex marshland had been used generations earlier by smugglers as a repository for cargoes of lace and brandy which they intended to slip past customs officials and sell at enormous profits. (A few who were caught with their forbidden merchandise dangled from gallows at Dagenham.) Probably Grace did not know that the area had a history dating back to A.D. 692 when Holderod, father of Sebbi, King of the East Saxons, had endowed an abbey at Barking. If he were acquainted with such details, he did not mention them in his report, nor note that the land was now being used as a rubbish dump!

Very properly, Grace was concerned with the potentialities of the site for manufacturing purposes and wrote only about them. He explained that Dagenham was located on the north side of the Thames River, twelve miles southeast of London (that is, toward the sea), that it had excellent railway connections with "the Midland Railway, which serves that portion of England where nearly all our inland raw material comes from, as well as the district where most of our cars are shipped out to." It had abundant deep water frontage, permitting ships to come in or leave at all tides and in all seasons. There were of course many scheduled freight sailings to and from London and all the chief ports of the world. Furthermore, Grace pointed out, "from the standpoint of 'driveaways' the situation at Dagenham is the best possible. . . . You have good roads directly into London and good roads to the North without going through London." For these reasons he and Gould considered "the locality at Dagenham to be the best in England."

In the summer of 1923 Henry Ford dispatched Ernest C. Kanzler to Europe to verify this judgment. Spending but one day in the English capital—August 5—Kanzler drove with Gould and Harrington out to look over the marshy tract of Essex countryside. He at once called it an ideal location for the new Ford plant. As he put it later, "our big plant could not be in Southampton, it had to be near London." He recalled his visit to the site as determinative. "I chose Dagenham," he said.

Besides the many advantages that Grace had described, the proposed location had others. For example, a factory there could draw on the immense London labor supply and use nearby manufacturers as the makers of car parts. Moreover, Dagenham was no Trafford Park, where plots containing only a few acres were doled out; it offered abundant land for expansion. However, neither Kanzler, Grace, nor Gould had sought technical advice as to subsoil, water supply, and drainage. Was there a bottom to the marsh? Was adequate water available? Could the area be drained by ditching or pumping? These questions were never asked. Like the site for a city emporium, the spot was selected because of its perfect location. When Kanzler left London he had fully decided on Dagenham. Here, he felt, should rise the walls and chimneys of the plant that would produce Model T's in massive volume.[2]

Thus at about the same time that Campbell was preparing his overseas branches, the American Ford company was planning further expansion in Europe.

2

Such plans soon transcended England when a conference of foreign managers was convened in Detroit late that October. Kanzler attended it after a two-and-a-half-month survey of Europe (England had been his first stop). He was convinced that the time had come to increase the tempo and scope of Ford activity overseas.

To this conference also came J. J. Harrington, European general manager; the heads of seven European companies,* the men directing the three South American branches (Argentina, Brazil, Uruguay), and the manager of a new Cuban branch organized in 1922. No representative appeared from the Orient, for as yet no company-owned agency operated there. Of all the officials present, with the exception of the leader of the French company, not one was a native of the country in which he was representing Ford. Practically all were Americans, although there was one Dane (Orberg, Brazil), one Argentine (Kopf, Uruguay), and one Norwegian (Lie, Italy).

The theme of the conference was expansion. All the managers were instructed "not [to] allow themselves to become overburdened with details." They were to delegate authority. The great possibilities for growth were dangled before them, and it was stressed that more dealers should be appointed, more salesmen hired, more service provided. "The prompt selection of agents is more important than finding the right man," they were told. "More dealers mean more sales." Already Ford had almost 2200 foreign agents, but "if every dealer employed one additional salesman it would mean 2,174 more salesmen!"

W. A. Ryan, the American sales manager, impressed upon the overseas captains that they should give their dealers constant and persistent supervision, with practical advice on selling and servicing. As for those who were non-exclusive (that is, handled other cars as well as Fords), "you should instruct your roadmen to point out to them the advantages of devoting their entire time to our product." This was very different from the Anderson policy in England; persuasion was now

* New companies had been formed in Italy and Belgium in 1922 to add to those in England, France, Spain, Denmark, and Ireland.

to replace coercion, and there was no talk of expunging recalcitrant agents!

At the conclusion of the meetings Harrington felt elated. He was returning to Europe, he wrote Edsel Ford, "brim full of enthusiasm." His salary had been raised. He observed that "as a result of many of your decisions during the Convention, now [I] believe that the European division of our business is no longer looked upon as an orphan, but rather as a favored child." Edsel replied cordially, "We are all very enthusiastic about the future of Europe." [3]

In late 1923, of the European Ford establishments, Manchester towered above the others with assets of $14.8 million and a work force of 2580. Cork with $7.3 million assets and 1850 employees ranked second. Next came Denmark, with resources of $6.8 million and 390 workers, and there followed France, Spain, and the new companies in Belgium and Italy, all with smaller capital, property, and number of workers. Kanzler felt that Detroit should have a much larger representation. Europe supplied more than half of the 8 per cent of the American Ford company's export business. Leaving Latin America for later consideration, we shall now follow his thoughts and acts as to the European area.

On his recent trip he had visited most of the countries there. He had written to Detroit about the heads of the existing Ford companies. While in France he had visited the Citroën plant and drawn from Edsel an alarmed cablegram: "Don't think advisable to purchase Citroën" (an echo from Henry Ford's refusal to do so in 1919). As a result of this survey and his consultations with Harrington, by 1924 he was ready to act.[4]

It should be remembered that much of Europe at this time bore little resemblance to the continent that had existed before World War I. Russia was a mammoth socialist state. Latvia, Estonia, Lithuania, and Finland were proud if diminutive nations. From centuries of subjection Poland had erupted as a republic with a territory larger than Italy's and a population greater than Spain's. Hungary, Austria, Yugoslavia, and Czechoslovakia had risen as independent countries from the shell of the shattered Austro-Hungarian state. Far to the south Turkey was ruggedly discovering modern life under Kemal Atatürk. Mussolini in Italy (1922) and Primo de Rivera in Spain (1923) had imposed fascistic governments on their restless populations.

Ford could expect little success in most of the new nations. Russia had immense possibilities, which will be considered later. Many of the peoples in the other new republics and kingdoms were in the midst of political and social changes and in any case lacked money to buy motor cars. In Italy the government was backing Fiat, a firm which utilized American methods, including the moving assembly line; still, the Ford branch did profitable business there in 1925, but mostly from tractor sales, at that time the largest for any country in Europe. Spain showed high profits in 1923, with almost 10,000 cars and trucks and 500 tractors sold; but under Rivera's dictatorship, which imposed a high tariff, the results were relatively poor.[5] *

In contrast France, the Low Countries, and Scandinavia afforded far better hunting grounds. Kanzler in 1924 organized new companies in Holland and Sweden, both of which were destined to prosper. Meanwhile he and his associates had been watching Germany and by 1925 felt that conditions there warranted action.

As noted in Chapter V, Germany after the war had been in political and economic turmoil. Carlson in Denmark, as manager of a contiguous territory, had nevertheless watched it as an area which might show a demand for Model T's and Fordsons. E. F. Posekel, a Ford representative in Germany, won the Ministry of Agriculture's approval of the tractor, and soon imported a number of machines. The events that led toward a normalization of the country were first of all the stabilizing of the mark in November 1923, then the adoption of the Dawes Plan (April 1924) and then the return of the Ruhr to the Reich (November 1924). All these steps fortified German prestige and credit, and the Dawes Plan marked the first step toward the nullification of the Treaty of Versailles.

In 1924 the largest German automotive manufacturer, Adam Opel, A. G. (*Aktien Gesellschaft,* meaning a joint stock company) installed methods of production that adapted the best American practice, just as Citroën and Renault had already done in France and Fiat in Italy. The German industrial output grew rapidly, and at this time about 150 makes of automobiles competed in the market.[6]

Admission of foreign units was by license, and Ford first obtained permission to bring in tractors, selling 1,019 of these between March and

---

* In March 1923 the Spanish branch was moved from Cadiz to Barcelona. Apparently Detroit executives were no longer worried about the labor situation there.

November 1924. A lifting of the ban on cars now seemed assured, and W. A. Ryan, then in Berlin with the Detroit production expert Frank Hadas, cabled Edsel Ford on November 21 that there was a "heavy demand for our products in Germany." They planned to seek permits "for finished and unfinished products to facilitate our working towards complete manufacturing basis thereby placing our request on different basis from any other foreign automobile manufacturer." Assured that restrictions would be removed in January, they proposed to bring Carlson from Copenhagen to Berlin "to remain and handle details connection licenses and formulation of company." They suggested a capitalization of 10 million marks, which would maintain an office in Berlin until the new tariff was set, and then consider changing location and operating as "service plant assembly plant or work toward manufacturing."

Edsel cabled on November 24, 1924: "Agreeable to organization of German company capital ten million marks." Carlson was promptly brought down to Berlin, and after some changes, including the reduction of the capitalization to 5 million marks, the Ford Motor Company A.G. was incorporated on January 5, 1925. Carlson staffed the new company with men from Copenhagen, Erhard Vitger, his chief clerk, and W. Schmidt, in production, being two of them. As assistant manager, E. C. Heine, who had served in Spain and won Kanzler's praise, came to Germany to assume the same position there. Carlson became head of the new company. He had previously sent some of his assistants down from Copenhagen, who had appointed 15 or 20 agents late in 1924; and by July 1925 the number had increased to 85.[7]

The outlook for the new company was promising. Carlson called on the German Minister of Labor, who welcomed the prospect of an American firm assembling cars in Germany. "We need some fresh air," he remarked. Carlson explained that the manager, foremen, and superintendents would be foreigners. The minister waved this detail aside. "All I insist upon is that the common labor on the conveyor line is German." Carlson assured him that it would be.

Cars for a time were shipped from Denmark. By October 1, 1925 the company was in business, and three months later Carlson rented a warehouse at West Harbor, Berlin-Plotzensee, where assembly on trucks was begun in April and on Model T's in June 1926. The offices of Ford Motor Company A.G. were moved from the heart of Berlin to the factory location. At about this time both General Motors and Chrysler also started assembly of cars and trucks in the Berlin area. But despite the American invasion the German Opel car remained the best-seller in the country.[8]

Ford had meanwhile added a new company in Finland, and a branch in Egypt (both in 1926). Altogether Detroit had provided four new outlets in Europe and one in northern Africa, those for the former continent representing an increase of almost 60 per cent in the number of its directly controlled companies. All the new firms were owned by the Ford family. Only one of them, the German corporation, had undertaken assembly; the others existed for sales and service only.

As the 1920's advanced, along with the new operating corporations, Ford also had or soon would establish credit companies: in France (1925), Germany (1926), Belgium (1926), Italy (1927), and England (1927). These were all wholly-owned subsidiaries of Ford-Detroit and handled both retail and wholesale financing.[9]

Ford-US had extended its activities just as European conditions seemed to be on the ascendant economically. International trade had expanded, and some nations were returning to the gold standard. The period seemed to promise a restoration of the "normal" trade relations that had existed before the war.

3

We have already seen that Ford policy was to start foreign operations in rented properties. If the venture did not thrive, the location could easily be changed or the entire project abandoned. If it succeeded, the practice was to buy land (from the profits realized) and build plants, establishing permanent bases of operations. In the early and mid-1920's four European Ford companies had prospered and took steps to buy land for their own factories: in Copenhagen (1922), Dagenham (1924), Hoboken (near Antwerp, 1924), and Asnières (near Paris, 1925).

All these properties were located near the largest markets in their respective countries; all fronted deep water. Two companies already by 1926 had erected assembly plants: Denmark (1924) and France (1926), and at the third, Belgium, assembly had also begun (1926) in remodeled buildings on the Hoboken site. Planning for Dagenham, however, offered a challenge to Detroit. Here was to rise no mere assembly unit but a great manufacturing complex. The site embraced 310 acres; the price had been £167,695 ($776,366). In this plant Ford expected to manufacture 500 cars a day, approximately three times the output of any Ford plant in Europe.[10] *

But about the time of the purchase of Dagenham the errors of five years of mismanagement and misdirection in England began to show in a glaring manner. "A bunch of clowns ran the English company!" was Kanzler's derisive comment as he looked back later on what had happened. This was essentially true, but high Ford-US officials tended to forget that *they* had chosen Anderson, Bate, and Gould, and had laid down sternly the policies that the three had followed toward disaster. The clowns were clowns because they had been assigned jobs for which they were unfitted and had been shackled by Detroit. Managers and home office had alike been at fault, and Perry's judgment was true of both—that "it is no use burying one's head in the sand and going ahead applying policies over here, no matter how successful they may have been in America, because conditions here are different." This had not been understood by Ford's representatives in England or by Ford officials in Detroit.

In the case of Gould, who still presided in Manchester in early 1924, the British dealer organization, which had clashed with him from the first, was now seething with resentment. Gould, who ironically had been praised by both Sorensen and Kanzler,** was according to the later opinion of one official serving under him, "a real bad egg." He had tried to force sales, dumping cars and trucks upon dealers who had not requested them. Dealers refused to accept delivery, and the machines, shunted onto unused switches, rusted at the stations. Gould would then expunge the stubborn dealers. "When the dealers complained," recalled an employee, "Gould canceled out more of them." This choleric guillotining of sales representatives won the attention of an English motor magazine, which published an article by a Ford agent entitled "Sacrificed Again."[11]

These difficulties were, theoretically at least, susceptible to psychological treatment and cure. The cure did not come and the clash between

---

* Of the Ford plants, Manchester had the greatest productive capacity, from 150 to 200 cars per day; the others, from 100 to 150.

** At first Sorensen was greatly pleased with Gould: "impossible . . . to describe improvement in every way over previous managers," he had written Edsel. "Unquestionably qualified to carry on . . . work," was Kanzler's surprising verdict in September 1923. These opinions would be decisively changed.—CES to EBF, Dec. 3, 1921, Select File, and Kanzler to EBF, Sept. 26, 1923, Acc. 6, Bx. 47.

company and dealer hurt sales. But a more inflexible obstacle—the English Finance Act—was already worsening the position of the Model T on the market. Effective January 1, 1921, this act introduced a tax of one pound (£1) per horse power on all passenger cars. The precise levy was determined by a formula, $\dfrac{ND^2}{2.5}$. N equaled the number of cylinders, D their diameter. The fewer the cylinders and the smaller their width, the lower the resultant horse power. The depth of the cylinder was not considered, so that a long narrow one might and often did give as much power as one that was broader and shorter, although by law it was rated much lower and the tax was smaller.

English car makers at once began to adapt their engines to the provisions of the act. Thus in 1923 Austin was selling a 7 h.p. car (by the formula) and Morris one of 12, while the Model T by the same standard was rated at 23 h.p. Its buyer thus paid in taxes about $73 per car more than the owner of a new Austin. Moreover, as an American production expert noted of the English models: "These small-bore, high-speed motors would do thirty miles per gallon on gasoline, whereas our Model T at best would give twenty." Nevertheless in 1923 Ford still held first place in England.[12]

After the October conference on foreign trade in Detroit, the American company sent to England a number of experts to improve the manufacture of the Model T in that country. They included Theodore Gehle (Kanzler's assistant), William Klann (production head at Detroit), Victor Perini, and Ed Harper. All came direct from the Highland Park plant and were "all old-timers who knew the car inside and out." In addition to improving Ford-England's manufacturing, they were to make some modifications in the Ford car which would help it in the English market and were to prepare plans for the Dagenham center. They were also to make such changes in personnel as they considered to be essential.

The group from Detroit were shocked at the conditions they found. Gould and Davis, the production head, were not speaking to each other. Klann had the greatest difficulty in seeing Gould, and finally, "I just busted the door open and there he was with his feet on the top of the desk, drinking tea and reading the morning paper." Klann reported this to Kanzler, querying: "What shall I do—fire him?" Kanzler advised waiting. Finally they let Davis go, stood over the new factory head while he learned his job (protesting that he couldn't do it!) and set about putting a new "English body" on the car Manchester was producing.

The revised Model T, according to *Autocar,* was not new at all; the "most striking change in the vehicle was that it was no longer black" but was painted gray, with upholstery to match. Some minor modifications such as a lowered chassis and altered cowl received scant attention. The new Ford proved to be of little help in the worsening sales situation.

Two other events promised to give greater aid. One was the forced resignation on April 15, 1924 of C. L. Gould. The second was that by mid-1924 the Model T had become a British product. As early as March *Autocar* had proclaimed it to be "almost entirely of British material," and in August the company announced that it was 92 per cent of that character. The word "British" was significant, for many parts of the car were still coming from the Cork factory.[13]

"Have selected you for manager of Ford Motor Company of England," cabled the American company president, Edsel Ford, to H. S. Jenkins in Argentina on March 24, 1924. "When can you arrange to leave Buenos Aires stopping off at Detroit on your way to England?" This was Edsel's redemption of a promise made to a Manchester official who revealed to him in full the chaos Gould had created. "I will choose a very good man to send over," he had said. Jenkins soon confirmed his promise. Even-tempered, with a keen sense of justice, and a tact that made him liked at once as he took effective command, the new manager quickly converted the exasperations and confusion of the company into a memory. On July 10, 1924, almost at the start of his administration, he announced Ford's intention to build a large new plant at Dagenham. He predicted that production would be tripled and 10,000 men employed. "LATE EXTRA—GREAT FORD FACTORY FOR LONDON," stridently called the news venders of the city that evening.

Aware that the horsepower tax was costing the company many buyers, Jenkins, following Edsel Ford's injunction, added to his announcement a reservation that the new factory depended upon "the trend of legislation"—that only when a fairer type of levy was in force would the factory near London be erected. On September 25, 1924 Edsel cabled Jenkins: "Intend commencing Dagenham plant construction immediately when horsepower tax is placed on equitable basis."

The year 1924 came to an end with no change in the tax, but with statistics that were disturbing to Ford officials. Manchester production for the year had declined to 27,505 units (from 30,698 in 1923). This left the English firm still the largest of Ford overseas operations, but little greater than Antwerp (25,206 Model T's) or Buenos Aires (23,210 units). Furthermore, economic conditions in England had improved from 1923 to 1924, automobile production as a whole had increased, and, most alarming, Morris Motors had disposed of 32,918 cars and chassis in England. Ford had lost the first place in the English market, which it had held for more than a dozen years.

The 250,000th Ford produced in England left the Manchester factory in April 1925. That August a Ford assembly line operated at the British Empire Exhibition at Wembley. The king and queen were visitors, and watched the car grow from rear-axle to finished product. "Wonderful," exclaimed George V as the finished Model T was driven off the line. But it was scant comfort that the car attracted interest, while sales sank and while the company sold more Model TT trucks than cars, and would for years to come.[14]

Since no change seemed likely in the horsepower tax, Jenkins began to press Detroit for a car with a new engine. "The entire Manchester organization are hoping that the Company will give them a redesigned motor so that they can overcome the well-nigh impregnable sales resistance they now encounter," W. E. Carnegie of the Ford accounting staff reported after a visit to England in June 1925. Kanzler's assistant, Theodore Gehle, returned from Trafford Park in that year and dined with Henry Ford. Edsel and Kanzler asked him, even at the risk of discharge, to paint a true picture of the English situation. Henry Ford, says Gehle,

> wanted to know what kind of a car, to my mind, we needed there. . . . I gave him my idea of what I had in mind. Then he burned up. He said, "You are trying to tell me how to design an automobile for the English market?" I said, "No, Mr. Ford . . . I am giving you . . . what I think the Ford Motor Company will have to do to retrieve their share of the English market, or they will continue to go down hill." . . . Henry Ford didn't reply at all. He just walked out.

Because of Henry Ford's confidence in the Model T, the English company got neither a new motor nor a new plant. The land at Dagenham remained idle. On December 25, 1925, Edsel Ford cabled Perini: "Do not see developments in Great Britain in the near future. Think full development at least two years away."[15]

By now General Motors had entered the British market, starting in 1924 with a Chevrolet assembly plant in London. Because of the horsepower tax, it met the same sales resistance as Ford. But GM, more adaptable, used the British system of marketing rather than the American; then in 1925 they purchased the Vauxhall Company of Luton, an old established firm (1903) with a fine plant and range of cars. The smallest Vauxhall had a horsepower rating of 13.9. The Luton plant had a capacity for only 1,700 cars a year. GM officials thought it could be expanded to 2,500 units annually. GM was still far from being a competitor, but it was busily planning to be one.

Toward the end of 1925, Ford-England encountered rivalry from many light cars with low horsepower ratings: Singer, Clyno, Standard, and the Italian Fiat. The Austin 7 was selling faster than Austin could build them. Morris propaganda mounted. These small car competitors relentlessly harried the Ford.

Consolingly, in the rest of Europe Ford sales were increasing. Model T and Model TT deliveries from the continental plants totaled 65,479 in 1923, 74,924 in 1924, and 98,114 in 1925. At the same time competition was mounting on the continent. The challenge from the European-produced light cars was far greater than that from General Motors or from Chrysler or other smaller American manufactures.* However, although their competition was less in Europe, it had grown in the United States, where the price gap between Ford and its rivals had lessened and GM's Chevrolet particularly was presenting increasingly attractive features at a cost not far in excess of the Model T. But of all cars, European or American, Ford still stood supreme in total sales around the world, and in the breadth of its operations.

It ranked high among the many American businesses now entering European markets for the first time or expanding existing operations. Shredded Wheat and Palmolive soap were two typical American products first manufactured in Europe in this decade. Tariffs had made production or licensing agreements desirable. Many American firms entered into such arrangements. Some companies, such as Liggett, purchased the entire share capital of firms in their lines of business. Ford preferred to follow its established and successful policy of "going it alone." [16]

4

In 1926 more Model T passenger cars were sold in Latin America and the Far East than in Europe. This fact is a measure of the importance of those markets to Detroit. To be sure, the total sales of vehicles

---

* The Hudson-Essex Company, Willys-Overland, Durant Motors, Studebaker, and Graham-Paige all had European subsidiaries.

were never higher there than in Europe, chiefly because of the much smaller truck demand there. But without question, these two areas provided a rich market for the Ford Motor Company.

Of all the Ford company's ventures south of the Mexican border, the Argentine branch gave the most impressive performance. Ford assets in that country in 1923 totaled $8.9 million, an amount second only to that represented by the Manchester company's $14.8 million. Ford in Brazil in that year already had assets of $1.4 million, and these were destined to grow; Ford-Uruguay commanded resources amounting to $800,000.

Everywhere throughout Latin America the Ford branches developed their dealer networks. "Sell service above all things," was the first injunction drummed into these agents. A sale did not end with a customer driving away; the dealer had an obligation to provide help as often as it was needed.

The Latin American branches adapted their methods of doing business to their customers; they arranged caravans, celebrations, contests, to advertise the Model T. Each branch had a "Ford Semana," or Annual Ford Week, with banquets for the dealers and special activities to publicize the vehicles. Ford claimed to have the largest sales organization among all industries in Brazil; it probably stood first in Argentina as well.

Ford roadmen (sales representatives) traveled the length and breadth of the continent. "We had to teach the dealers," recalls Pedro Zinkgräf, then sales manager of Ford-Argentina. Many of the agents came from rural areas; some were butchers or grocers, some cowboys. Often they could not read or write, but they sold Fords. Orberg in Brazil used farmers, doctors, and mechanics. Such men, distributing the Model T in the far interiors of these countries, literally opened them up.

The years 1922 to 1925 saw stable economic development (along with social reform) in Argentina, Uruguay, and Chile. In Brazil, a revolt in July 1924 found the rebel general Isidor Lopes marching on São Paulo, but Orberg was able to report in August that the Ford branch there had suffered only minor damage. The government restored order, and Ford-Brazil managed to build 14,861 units that year, only a little less than the Ford-France production of 16,161.[17]

Up to this year the Detroit company's branch operations had been confined to the eastern coast of South America. Individual dealers had handled sales in countries fronting the Pacific, getting built-up cars direct from Detroit, in some cases knocking them down and packing them in bundles to be carried over the Andes by mules. One animal could carry 120 pounds of Model T parts; and such shipments to a sub-agent in Cuenca, Ecuador, took two days to reach their destination.

When Benjamin Kopf was appointed manager for Uruguay in 1921, Detroit gave him supervision also over dealers in Chile, Bolivia, and Peru. He visited these dealers and soon reported to Ryan that business in Chile warranted an assembly plant. "I agree," came Ryan's reply, "and you will be its first manager."

Thus at Santiago, Chile, in 1924 Ford opened its first branch in Latin America west of the Andes. It had an assembly plant and was to supervise the Bolivian and Peruvian markets as well. With large, poor, and illiterate Indian populations and with roads for the llama and mule and not for automobiles, these last two countries, especially Bolivia, were meager automobile markets.

In 1925 Ford sales in Latin America rose to an all-time high. As at Wembley in England, so at the Grand Exposition of Automobiles in Rio de Janeiro that year a Ford assembly line was installed for demonstration purposes. Workers from the company's São Paulo plant operated it, and the awed Brazilian public watched the cars come into being.[18]

Ford also started a new enterprise in Mexico in 1925, planning its first assembly operation there. Supervised up to this time by the Houston and Los Angeles branches in the United States, Model T sales in Mexico now far exceeded those of any of Detroit's forty competitors in the northernmost Latin American republic.* As manager of the new company, A. R. Lajous, a Mexican of aristocratic parentage, who had served Ford in Buenos Aires, Detroit, Houston, and Havana, took charge of the new project. He knew Mexican President Plutarco Elías Calles personally, and was able to negotiate important concessions of railway freight rates, customs duties, and taxes. Lajous found the labor situation "unsettled," but cabled Ryan: "President [Calles] emphatic we will have no trouble." As to wages, which averaged a dollar and a quarter per day, he suggested that Ford should pay no more than three. (In Mexico as elsewhere Ford workers were to receive more than the "going rate.") In 1926 assembly began in a rented warehouse in Mexico City.[19]

From Brazil came a protest from Orberg that the sales in his territory, larger than all continental United States, could no longer depend

---

* In April 1925, when the first steps were taken to establish a Ford company in Mexico, of 299 new cars registered in the capital, 111 were Fords. Buick ranked second with 57 units, Dodge next with 20, and Chevrolet had only 8. (See note 19.)

on a single assembly unit in São Paulo. As a result, new plants were soon opened in Recife (1925), Pôrto Alegre (1926) and Rio de Janeiro (1927). There seemed to be justification also for a new sales branch in Peru, and Kanzler suggested to Jorge Matray, the new Chilean manager, then in Detroit, that he start it. "No," the latter replied in effect, "I am Chilean born and every time I have gone to Peru I have been arrested, so bad are the relations between our two nations." Detroit found another manager and opened a sales branch there in 1926.

Ford branches were also started in San Juan, Puerto Rico, and Caracas, Venezuela (sales and service operations with no assembly). When Roberge came to San Juan a year later the manager there, W. W. Townsend, told him that communications in the Caribbean area were poor, and that his business was low. The manager in Caracas, George Jenkins (no relation to H. S. Jenkins), also reported that his location was unsatisfactory. These two branches were accordingly closed, and a single one opened in Cristobal in the Canal Zone, with Jenkins as manager and Townsend as his assistant. Formed in 1927, this office had responsibility for Ford sales in the entire Caribbean area, excluding Cuba, all Central America, and Ecuador, Colombia, Venezuela, and the three Guianas. This area comprised the territory that up to 1926 had been supervised by the American foreign trade operation at Kearny, N.J., and then for a single year by the San Juan and Caracas branches.[20]

By 1927 there were eleven Ford companies and branches throughout Latin America, a formidable network, and in January of that year they used 1,172 dealers. (This compared with the European Ford companies' selling through 2,189 agents.) General Motors, with assembly plants only in São Paulo, Montevideo, and Buenos Aires, had begun to provide competition in those territories. But Ford was a leader in all industry. One study of American business in Argentina, Brazil, Uruguay, and Chile found that although in the 1920's a number of companies—Armour, General Motors, International Cement, I.T.&T., RCA Victor, and others —had operations in three out of four of these countries, only Ford had invaded them all! [21]

The profits from Ford's Latin American activities were not negligible. In 1925–1926 the earnings of the Argentine branch alone amounted to more than $6 million, and those of Brazil to $4 million. In the last half of the 1920's Argentina, Canada excepted, was Detroit's largest foreign market, ranking from 1925 through 1929 above England in car and truck sales. Argentina and Brazil furnished the great bulk of profits, for the rest of South America still had too few roads and its populations had incomes too low to provide for a large automotive business.

As indicated in Chapter V, neither Henry Ford nor any other top-level American executive ever visited South America to appraise its possibilities for business and help develop them. The highest Ford officials to travel there in the 1920's were C. Lathers (who came every two years), B. R. Brown (for construction work), W. E. Carnegie (accounting), and R. I. Roberge. Ford auditors also made regular trips. Contrary to some present-day impressions, Detroit sent representatives to visit the southern plants, but they were few, stayed briefly, and lacked high management status. In contrast, the South American executives—managers, assistant managers, production and sales managers—visited Detroit often, and all later attested that they learned more from these expeditions than they did from their American visitors.[22]

5

A guest of Henry Ford, Joseph Bailie of Peking University, had urged Ford in June 1920 to establish a plant in China. That vast land seemed a fitting place to begin intensive work in the Far East, an undertaking that Ford was prepared to assume. A year and a half later Liebold wrote to Bailie that "Mr. Ford had expressed considerable interest in the affairs of China, and I believe has in mind some tangible means whereby our business may be expanded." What information was available on water power sites and sources of raw materials? Bailie responded with a flood of suggestions, adding: "China is the field where the big heart of your chief can find responsive hearts among a nation that is just hungering for that leadership which Mr. Ford's ideality, ability, and disinterestedness, qualify him as no other man to take advantage of."

Ford made a beginning by offering to train Chinese students at the Rouge, and by 1923 had 100 of them studying and working in Detroit. But his plans for action in China developed slowly.

He did not lack encouragement. No less a person than Sun Yat-sen, the founder of modern China, begged him to come to China. "I know and I have read of your remarkable work in America," he wrote to Ford.

> I think you can do similar work in China on a much vaster and more significant scale [he continued in this 1924 letter] . . . here in China

you would have the opportunity to express and embody your mind and ideals in the enduring form of a new industrial system.

I am of the view that China may be the cause of the next World War if she remains economically undeveloped and thus becomes an object of exploitation and international strife on the part of the Great Powers. For this reason I began, as soon as the Armistice was signed in Europe, to think out a plan for the international development of China with a view to its consideration by the Powers at the Peace Conference in 1919. This plan has since been worked out in my book, "THE INTERNATIONAL DEVELOPMENT OF CHINA," which was published in Shanghai in 1921 and in New York in 1922 by Messrs. Putnam's Sons.

I now realize that it is more or less hopeless to expect much from the present Governments of the Powers. There is much more to hope, in my opinion, from a dynamic worker like yourself; and this is why I invite you to visit us in South China in order to study, at first hand, what is undoubtedly one of the greatest problems of the Twentieth Century.

It was an opportunity which might have meant much to the Ford Motor Company, which perhaps could have aided in the industrial development of the new-born Chinese Republic, and thus changed its future. But Ford probably did not know who Sun Yat-sen was; the letter, on modest stationery, did not indicate the writer's importance. Dr. Sun received a routine reply from Detroit to the effect that Ford had no plans for visiting his country.[23]

Instead, it was Japan that engaged Ford's attention. The Model T had become well known there through the activity of the export-import house of Sale & Frazar, which had handled the business of the Ford company in Nippon for many years. But when Roberge visited that country in 1924, one year after the devastating Tokyo earthquake, he concluded that the Ford Motor Company was not being well served by its agents. "Dealers as we know them do not exist," he wrote to Edsel Ford. "We must start from the very beginning to develop a real organization. Very little effort is being made to sell cars at present as Sale & Frazar do not allow sufficient commission and the dealers are most interested in selling parts."

With Edsel's approval, Roberge formed a Japanese Ford company which was incorporated on February 17, 1925. It was to have an assembly operation in addition to managing sales and service. Roberge arranged with the Yokohama Dock Company, then building warships for the government, to erect some sheds of corrugated iron with cement floors. These, on the Dock company's waterfront property, were to be rented and used for Ford assembly.

Meanwhile Kopf in Chile, who had only started the branch three months earlier, was told by Ryan he must go to Japan. He left for Tokyo via Detroit, where he learned that he was to be manager of the company Roberge had incorporated. The latter, now returned from the Orient, gave the new appointee a U.S. Department of Commerce report (probably that of 1922) on the automobile industry in Nippon. Kopf read the bulletin on the long sea trip across the Pacific, found it very pessimistic about the possibilities of selling cars in his new territory, and wondered, as he recalled later, what Ford wanted "with a plant in Japan under such circumstances." With him went a formidable shipment of vehicles, and he must have shaken his head as he thought of them. Nevertheless upon landing he quickly readied the sheds for assembly, and began to put the knockdown cars together.

He very soon discovered that Roberge had been right and the Department of Commerce completely wrong. Business possibilities in Japan were splendid, and the new enterprise flourished from the start. In 1925 and 1926 a total of 16,909 American and Canadian cars were exported to Japan, and of these 16,689 were Fords.* In his first two years Kopf was able to report profits of $1.9 million.

Before he returned to Detroit, Roberge had visited China, where he found Ford "representation . . . was practically nil." He appointed new dealers but decided that the time was not ripe for a new plant; low standards of living and bad roads constricted the automotive market. A Department of Commerce report in 1923 indicated that it would amount to 2,000 units annually; pessimism in this case was confirmed, for Ford delivered only 1,090 vehicles in 1925 and 1,918 in the following year.[24]

6

The year 1925 marked the peak of Ford prestige throughout the world. During it the Ford foreign plants delivered 195,087 cars and trucks and 28,652 tractors to their dealers. Ford's name and methods were themes in dozens of tongues around the world. A professor at the

---

* The Department of Commerce report had estimated that the market would take a maximum of 3500 units annually.

University of Berlin lectured on "Fordismus"; in Japan a business man translated Ford's *My Life and Work* into his language. A Dutch rendition appeared in Java, and book stalls in most European countries offered it to their customers. In Lenin's private library reposed a film of the Highland Park factory. Children in the Caribbean chanted the jingle

> Tin and Board
> Make a Ford.

In some countries the word "Ford" was practically synonymous with "automobile."

Fame had a golden lining. If the profits of the Ford Motor Company had astounded most financiers before World War I, they all but burst the imagination in the 1920's. From 1920 through 1926 the company's net income after taxes reached an incredible $619.2 million (this included the relatively modest but by no means negligible profits from foreign trade). The Model T seemed to be the goose of the fairy tale blown to giant proportions and laying its golden eggs abundantly.[25]

Like a flourish after a distinguished signature, in the middle 1920's came the use of company ships for the carrying of exports. The SS. *Onondaga* (1924), the SS. *Oneida* (1925), the SS. *East Indian* (1926) and others bore shipments to such ports as Copenhagen, Yokohama, Buenos Aires, and Antwerp. The process of packing was an elaborate one, the engines in one box, rear axles in another, body parts in a third. The components were shipped from Detroit to Kearny, N.J., and prepared there, the metal elements being oiled to prevent rusting. Each shipment had a lot number, with numbered boxes—an essential regulation, for "we were always losing a box," and then confusion resulted overseas.*

Eventually the company, which had continued to patronize outside shipping lines, discovered that it was generally more economical to use these almost entirely (no return cargo need be sought, and a shipment did not have to fill the vessel). The Ford fleet was then mainly employed for intra-United States shipments.[26]

In the late 1920's, as earlier in the decade, the basic principle of

---

* If a certain box failed to arrive at Buenos Aires the whole assembly line might have to be shut down, as parts could not be purchased locally. If the same thing happened at Antwerp the crisis was not so great, as the assembly branch could probably make local purchases.

directing foreign operations from Detroit and in accordance with American practice continued to be followed, but Knudsen's insistence on rigid conformity had mellowed with the years. The heads of Ford establishments abroad were now a more sophisticated group, and were no longer recruited from the executives of the thirty-odd American branches. Yet there was no concerted effort to find local managers. H. C. Møller in the Danish company (after 1925), E. L. Clarke at Cork (1926), and Jorge Matray, the Chilean manager, were exceptions to the general practice.

Later, when once again the pendulum would swing to what can best be called the "American direction," there would be not only managers from the United States but American *finance* managers as well. In the 1920's no such officials had existed; the chief clerks discharged all financial duties and were generally natives of their respective countries. The Ford-US auditors, and Craig, Kanzler, and Roberge saw to it that they served the interests of the Ford family.

Most overseas operations paid their own way, Detroit making virtually no investment in them. Cash was furnished for the first pay rolls and for customs duties on the initial consignment; credit was also extended for these vehicles. Then the foreign branches and companies, as they sold cars, would pay their debts, and from their profits invest in new equipment and plant facilities. Within a few months most overseas ventures did not need any added assistance from Detroit. The managers of each operation noted the exchange rates, purchased units from the United States, set their selling prices,* and remitted according to instructions from the home office. Funds were dispatched rapidly where there was inflation and where no immediate expansion was planned. But in the 1920's, most Ford companies and branches planned expansion. Ford approved. He stated emphatically:

> We ought to wish for every nation as large a degree of self-support as possible. Instead of wishing to keep them dependent upon us for what we manufacture, we should wish them to learn to manufacture themselves and build up a solidly founded civilization.

Ford unsparingly condemned "foreign exploiters" and asserted that in his own overseas operations he was reinvesting earnings to help build up the economics of foreign countries and training workers and officials abroad in the methods that had made him a success.[27]

* Based on Detroit quotations, plus boxing, freight, insurance, and customs duties.

7

After eighteen years of continuous triumphs the Model T by 1926 was facing a difficult situation. With the notable exception of Canada, Australia, and the Orient, the sales of the car were fewer than they had been in earlier years. As they sank, so did those of the truck, Model TT. The decline was both in number of buyers and in percentage of the market held.

That this situation might develop had been recognized for many months by certain Ford officials. The causes were varied. For several years competition had been steadily increasing; suddenly it had become effective. Price was a factor: once the Model T had cost but half what its nearest competitors had asked; the gap had slowly, then more rapidly, narrowed; while Ford still had the cheapest car on the market, it was so by a much smaller margin. Again, in 1920, only two makes of cars sold for less than $1000 in the United States; in 1926, there were five. Roads were a consideration, particularly in America, where the need for a tough car, no matter how unattractive, had now ceased to be vital. Still further, people had more money to spend on their automobiles than in earlier years and wanted better products. Although higher in price than the Ford, the Chevrolet was more attractive; it did not overheat so quickly on hills, was faster to start, more comfortable to ride in, easier to steer, and quieter. Moreover, it had a pedal accelerator, while the Ford retained the old-fashioned hand throttle. Once a superior feature, the planetary transmission of the Model T was now also *passé*, for competitors used the sliding gear transmission, which gave better speed, acceleration, and overall performance. Toward the middle of 1925 Edsel Ford and Kanzler had recognized the trend in consumer taste, saw that prompt action was required, and had begun to press for a new car. Henry Ford perceived that eventually one must be designed, but he wanted to evolve something as novel and dramatic as the Model T had been in 1908 and felt no urgency. In 1926 as the trend away from his car became more pronounced he still held proudly to the "Tin Lizzie." [28]

In September 1926 Orberg reported declining sales in Brazil, and early in 1927 wrote Edsel Ford that "extremely adverse conditions over a long period of time have gradually discouraged our dealers and coupled with a completely wild competition, it has made our work in every respect very hard." He explained that there "has appeared a hunger on the part of the public for trying something else than a Ford which in many places has been their only car for years." From 25,000 units in 1925, Brazilian Ford sales declined to 15,500 in 1926. The Ford car met less competition from General Motors in Argentina, chiefly because of poor management by its rival. Although the situation was better there than in Brazil, the number of cars marketed in 1926 and 1927 showed a continuous decline.[29]

Of all foreign countries, England represented the low point in Ford accomplishment. "We have been defeated and licked in England," moaned Kanzler early in 1926. A "Don't-Buy-American-Products" campaign mounted at this time, and the Model T was now vulnerable to such a slogan as it had not been to comparable pressure in 1912.

When Edsel embarked for Europe in April 1926 on his second trip abroad—the first having been with his father in 1912—he knew that in England he would find Jenkins full of complaints about the situation of the dealers, of the need for a light Ford car, of the effect of the horsepower tax on sales, and of the uncertainty as to when Detroit would offer a new product. Edsel was on holiday; he didn't want to be badgered with these problems to which he had no answer. Both he and Kanzler had pushed very strongly for a radical change since early in 1926, and Kanzler would be discharged in July for urging it. Meanwhile Henry Ford was adamant, and Edsel could do nothing.

Jenkins as English Ford head was instructed in advance not to meet Edsel at Southampton or in London, but to wait for him at Manchester. There Edsel tried to listen patiently to Jenkins' account of his troubles and to be optimistic about a replacement for Model T. Continuing on his way to France, he received there through his secretary a letter from Jenkins asking if he should purchase for him (to take back to America) a 7 h.p. Peugeot and two Austin 7's. Obviously Jenkins was trying desperately to engage Edsel's interest in low horsepower cars, the only hope for sales progress in the English market. Jenkins must have been disappointed with the reply: "Mr. Ford has requested me to tell you to never mind about buying either the Peugeot or the Austin 7's at this time."

To a representative of the *New York Herald* Edsel "flatly denied rumors" that the company intended to place a smaller and cheaper car on the market to compete with well-known French makes. The first Model T's were then coming off the line at Ford's new Asnières plant, and Edsel declared: "There is our product, and Europe seems pretty well satisfied with it."

It was the statement of a proper salesman. It countered Jenkins' complaints and those of Carlson, now manager of the German plant and "District Supervisor" for Northern Europe, who had written that "the writer has been analyzing the competitive situation in Northern Europe" and that it was "becoming serious." [30]

The picture was not a pleasant one. In November 1926 a letter from Sir Herbert Austin had brought to Henry Ford the humiliating news that "the sale of the Ford in this country has dropped to a very low point." (This was a guess, as no registration figures by make were published in England, but it was an accurate one.) Austin now once more posed the idea of collaboration with Ford in the British market, and Liebold replied that Ford would be "glad to again have the pleasure of meeting you when you are . . . in the states." Ford may actually have come to the point of considering Austin seriously.

A little earlier Jenkins had written Edsel that company prestige was steadily falling. "People cannot understand why we stand back without combating in a more emphatic way the competition with which we are faced." To Ryan he wailed even louder. The General Strike of 1926, while not affecting the Ford plant, had jeopardized its sources of raw material such as coal; and the London *Daily Mail* had begun "a direct battle against everything American." He expatiated on this, taxes, car design. "The odds against us are severe," was his conclusion.

Jenkins may well have exaggerated the effect of the *Mail*'s campaign; if Ford was unpopular in the kitchen, he was a favorite in the parlor. The London *Spectator* in October 1926 invited him to England at its expense because of "a very great admiration for your outlook and constructive ability." The paper wanted to get and publish Ford's "fresh impressions and advice." Ford courteously declined, adding that when he next went to England it would be as a private individual.[31]

Ford was a very busy man at home. At this point he had just begun work on the successor to the Model T, for even he now conceded that the fabulous "Lizzie" must go. Finally in May 1927 he discontinued its production. On the 25th of that month, extolling the famous vehicle as running "before there were good roads to run on," breaking down rural isolation, and placing "education within the reach of everyone," he promised only a short period of inaction before a new and better Ford would be pouring from many factories.

In anticipation of these events and in response to poor sales Jenkins had begun cutting down his work force, discharging in August 1926 approximately 500 workers and taking 102 names off the salaried roll. On the continent, Ford companies were similarly busy, but on November 15, 1926, Sorensen informed Jenkins (and presumably the others) of the impending arrival of George Brubaker, Fred Hoffman, and J. J. Harrington. Brubaker was general representative for the company, Hoffman had charge of American branch assemblies; Harrington had left his post as general European manager to become assistant sales manager at Dearborn under Ryan.

Perhaps when Brubaker sent Sorensen a message from the mid-Atlantic that "a storm raged all day yesterday," the elements were firing a fitting salute for the task the trio would soon accomplish in Europe. Known variously as the "Three Horsemen," the "Yougos," the "Firing Squad," and the "Commission of Murderers," they were empowered to check on quality of operations, the functioning of plants, and the elimination of useless paper work; but their primary task was to disgorge personnel. The mission resembled the Latin American assignment of Brubaker and Lathers in 1921. Now, five and a half years later, they dismissed 250 factory employees at Manchester, turned 145 men out of their jobs at Cork, discharged 60 in Berlin, 38 in Antwerp, 32 in Trieste, and so on. Their name "Yougos" was derived from the fact that the three were constantly saying: "YOU GO." The method can be illustrated from the case in Holland where the three arrived, dined, summoned the chief clerk and his assistant, and bade them select in one hour twelve men for sacrifice. "The next morning," the chief clerk recalled later, "the people were called in and we handed them their checks. In one minute we fired just like that." *

The dismissals were hailed in Detroit-Dearborn. P. E. Martin and Sorensen cabled the executioners Christmas greetings, and announced: "You are all cooperating in a way that is pleasing to us." In Rotterdam, Antwerp, Manchester, Cork, and Asnières the season could not have been merry for hundreds of former Ford employees.[32]

With the announcement of May 25, 1927, the American and Cana-

---

* It is an interesting sidelight that the three cabled home about the Cork plant, "Hennesy [*sic*] service manager appears most likely candidate for development should visit Detroit January first." Earlier H. S. Jenkins had called twenty-seven-year-old Patrick Hennessy "a promising young man . . . very well informed . . . of good personality and one that I would say would have good prospects with the Company." Hennessy would more than live up to these favorable comments. (See note 32.)

dian Ford factories suspended operations. Around the world, Ford assembly plants put together what cars they could, and dealers assembled
complete vehicles from available spares. Chevrolet, which heretofore had
never approached Ford in sales (although its rise had been the chief
factor in the decision to abandon the Model T), now moved into the
vacuum created by the idle plants of its rival. In 1926 the Chevrolet
showed only 486,392 passenger vehicle registrations to 1,129,548 for the
Ford product, but in 1927 it achieved 647,810 to 393,424, while the total
sales in that year for all GM products were 1,472,721 units.

Many Ford dealers in the United States went over to the rival company; in Europe and Latin America they had more loyalty and the loss
was smaller. Ford officials promised often that the new car was just
around the corner, but only hope and dogged faith kept the agents together during this difficult year.[33]

On December 2, 1927 the Model A appeared. According to Ford
sources 10.5 million people saw the car on the first day it was exhibited
in the United States.* A Model A was taken to the Melbourne Town
Hall for display secretly at two in the morning, but word about it got
out, and thousands of people crowded the streets at that early hour to
catch a glimpse of it. In three days 100,000 people in Australia saw the
car, and souvenir hunters almost wrecked it.

Halfway around the world at the Holland Park Show in London,
the Model A was "eagerly examined by dense crowds, which had to be
marshalled by the police."

The American company radiated confidence in its new automobile.
"All that engineers have learned, all that millions of owners have experienced in nearly a quarter of a century, have made possible this car
which is today as far ahead of its time as was the famous Model T in
1908," boasted a Ford advertisement. The company claimed that the
model had "niceties of mechanical design, lavish use of the finer metals,
precision in delicate machining processes," together with "a new standard of acceleration, speed, power and smoothness that heretofore has
marked only expensive cars."

To adapt his product to the European sales situation Henry Ford
had prepared a special engine, the AF, which was the same as the regular one, but with a smaller bore. It had a taxable horsepower of 14.9 in-

---

* The Model A was assembled at the Rouge plant at Dearborn, and from this time forward Detroit ceased to be the headquarters for the company. Dearborn had however
been of increasing importance since the early 1920's.

stead of 24 for the A engine. With the exception of the right-hand drive and minor alterations in body design made on earlier British vehicles, this was the first concession by the home office to specialized needs in foreign markets.[34] *

Throughout the world Ford made preparations to produce his new 4-cylinder cars. In most locations his existing plants could deal adequately with them. In Japan, however, the factory was too small, and sales prospects seemed to warrant constructing a new one. Moreover, Chevrolet in 1927 had set up a large assembly operation in Osaka, and Ford meant to meet its challenge. The new Ford plant would be "earthquake proof," would produce 100 cars a day, and would open in 1929.

About the time Ford's Japanese plant was planned Kopf, its manager, had been empowered to organize a branch in China. He set up a sales and service branch in Shanghai during March 1928, which was managed by J. V. Crowe, an American, and covered China, French Indo-China, and the Philippine Islands. Crowe remained in charge of this unit until World War II. Similarly, in Turkey William G. Collins (also an American) was authorized to "locate, organize, and manage" a branch there, for which $150,000 was allocated.

In Latin America the existing facilities could be converted to Model A assembly, and business improved as knockdown models became available. During 1928 these arrived slowly, as Detroit was still not producing in volume.

Ford-Canada went to great expense for the changeover to Model A. Canadian suppliers were not equipped to furnish many special items for the new car, and temporarily these had to be imported from the United States. In 1927–1928 the Ford-Canada spent more than $3 million for machinery and fixtures needed in the production of Model A and Model AA cars and trucks. Campbell, however, was highly enthusiastic about the new vehicles.[35]

In England the outlook was more doubtful. Jenkins had greeted the prospect of the cars with high optimism, writing Sorensen in July 1927 that "the entire public here is very much interested in what we are going to bring out." In November when he could see and touch the actual cars he reported: "They are certainly wonderful looking. . . . I can foresee a very outstanding success in this country." From the Holland Park Show in London a little later he cabled Henry and Edsel Ford

---

* As noted, foreign dealers had often altered cars in superficial ways to change their appearance; the reference here is to factory changes.

the dealers' "enthusiastic congratulation and appreciation." The Cork manager, E. L. Clarke, also testified: "Our very best anticipations have been more than fulfilled. The design of the Engine, Transmission and Axle is so clean-cut, robust, and practical that it cannot fail to appeal." The British motor press was favorable. "The new Ford is . . . distinctly pleasing to the eye," pronounced *Autocar*.

Like a beauty queen who dazzles the eye but proves a failure in the kitchen, the models on closer scrutiny were regarded as not so satisfactory. As the *New York Times* reported it, English feeling "is that far from justifying the prediction that they would have small high-efficiency engines, and be built along European light car lines, they are typical American automobiles." And the prices, while low, were higher than those of the Morris and Austin cars.

In France there was a similar reaction. While Citroën, Renault, and Peugeot stood dominant with their light cars, they watched uneasily the threat that Ford posed and were prepared to urge a higher tariff if the old master should offer a serious challenge. But when the new models appeared "sighs of relief went up from the French automobile manufacturers." The cheapest Ford sold in Paris for $900, and against that price the native producers could operate with complete confidence.

In Germany in mid-December 1927, the Reichstag debated a measure to raise the tariff, which affected all automobiles and parts. The bill was passed on December 16, 1927, and sounded the death-knell for American assembly plants there.[36]

Meanwhile exports to Europe, because of low production in Detroit, did not begin until May 1928 and then set a slow pace. However, the American public liked the car and it seemed destined for success, if not in 1928, then assuredly in 1929. Meanwhile the Chevrolet continued to outsell the Ford in the United States and Canada.

The Australian picture was not too bright either. There the Chevrolet with the Holden-made body was making tremendous headway. In 1927 General Motors garnered 35.1 per cent of the Australian registrations, Ford, a meagre 9.6 per cent. H. C. French, still managing the two Ford companies, looked hopefully to the new unit.

But the most serious situation was that in Europe. The slow changeover at Manchester, the tariff in Germany, the tepid reception of the Model A in France and elsewhere, together with the fact that not until October 1, 1928 were all the European Ford factories producing the new car, meant that the sales of Models A and AF were dangerously low.

In England, for example, Ford had sold more cars in every year since 1913 than it disposed of in 1928. In the peak postwar year and a quarter from September 1919 to December 1920 Ford-England had marketed 46,372 vehicles. Now with the Models A and AF the English sales dropped to 6,224 cars and trucks. Yet the total automotive production for the country was at its highest—211,877 machines. Obviously something was catastrophically wrong. A glance at the facts revealed the trouble. Morris now dominated the British market, with Austin in second place. Their light cars were lower in horsepower than the Model AF, cheaper, and more economical to operate. The 1920's had seen Ford fall from a comfortable first place in the English industry to a position below the top three, for even Singer was outselling Ford. On the continent, because of low-priced, low-powered rivals, Ford was not in first, second, or third place in France or Germany, the most important markets.[37]

Certainly 1929 would be a better year, with full instead of limited production. Henry Ford had his mind on a dozen projects: in Brazil he was starting a rubber plantation, and he had plans for the Model A in Russia. Nevertheless he perceived the dismal situation in Europe and was already considering the problem that confronted him there.

8

The Missionary Spirit

On February 17, 1923 Harvey Firestone of the Firestone Tire and Rubber Company invited Henry Ford to attend a conference in Washington "on the British Rubber Restriction Act which became effective November 1, 1922." This act, popularly known as the Stevenson Rubber Scheme, had been designed to aid British planters of rubber in Ceylon and Malaya by restricting output and raising prices. Already, Firestone noted, rubber had risen 22 cents a pound in three-and-a-half months. "This means an increase of $150,000,000 in the crude rubber bill of the United States for 1923," he pointed out. He wanted Ford, other American industrialists, and the American government to assist him in publicizing the improper features of the scheme, and to help devise means of combating it, perhaps by establishing rubber culture under American control.[1]

In responding to this appeal, Ford undertook to further a crusade which might reduce the cost of one of his raw materials, but which he also considered a patriotic duty.

2

When Columbus on his second voyage to the mainland of South America landed at the mouth of the Amazon near what is now Belém, Brazil, he saw the natives throwing about a ball that bounced as if alive. This was the first encounter of white men with the product of *Hevea brasiliensis,* a native American tree which yields in its sap the purest raw material for the making of rubber.*

---

* The balls Columbus and his companions saw were probably made from *Hevea brasiliensis* sap but could have been made from other Brazilian trees which yielded inferior rubber. *Ceara* is such a product. In Central America the *Castilloa elastica* supplied the

For several hundred years rubber was regarded as more of an odd-ity than a usable product. Even when articles were manufactured from it in the early nineteenth century (shoes, raincoats, and so forth) they proved unsatisfactory because they became soft in summer and brittle in winter. But with the vulcanization of the material by Charles Good-year (patented by him in 1844) rubber retained its basic quality in any temperature and soon came widely into use. The Amazon Valley, home and sole producer of the precious sap, entered upon a period of prosper-ity as wild as California's in its gold-producing era, and seemingly more permanent, for the rubber tree yielded latex every season with no lessen-ing of quality.

Growing in the jungle, and usually at least 100 meters apart, the *Hevea* demanded considerable attention—the maintenance of paths from tree to tree and the services of skilled workers who knew when and how to gather the sap. As early as 1834 Thomas Hancock in England had suggested plantations as a means of cheapening the cost of the raw material. Quite independent of him a few attempts had been made in Brazil to establish them. They were not successful. The planted trees seemed to yield less than the wild ones, and in any case both the owners of tracts of rubber trees and the collectors of latex preferred their elab-orate but independent activity to the tame routines of a plantation. And since the *Hevea* existed only in the Amazon Valley, why should they change? With the river town of Manaos as the rubber capital, the whole region basked in growing prosperity.[2]

It was not to endure. In 1870 H. A. Wickham, one of those roving Englishmen who used to turn up with disconcerting regularity at the beginning of crucial activities, completed a tour of central Brazil and in a book, *Rough Notes on a Journey Through the Wilderness* (1871) dared to assert that the systematic cultivation of the *Hevea* was practica-ble. Most of his readers found this opinion fantastic, but Sir Joseph Hooker, director of Kew Gardens, and a proponent for new products that might suit the varying lands of the British Empire, had confidence in the proposal. He believed that rubber could be grown in India and Malaya and proposed to Wickham that he procure seeds of the best type of *Hevea* and bring them to England. Wickham was "left quite

---

Maya and other Indians with rubber. The output of the *Funtumia elastica* of Africa, the *Dyera costulata* of the East Indies, and the guayule rubber of Northern Mexico were all resinous. None of these bore as large a quantity or as pure a latex as the best *Hevea brasiliensis* or responded so well to tapping.

unhampered by instructions as to ways or means. A straight offer to do it: pay to follow the results."

By this time Wickham was gathering rubber above Santarém, Brazil, below Manaos. By good fortune he found that a ship, the *Amazonas,* had come up the great river and had then been abandoned by those who had chartered it. Its home port was Liverpool, and the captain, a Scot, was ready to charter his vessel for carrying the seeds. "I determined to plunge for it," said Wickham. Engaging the ship, he dived into the jungle with a crew of Indians and gathered a tremendous quantity of seeds "from large-grown trees in the forest covering the broad plateaux dividing the Tapajos from the Madeira Rivers."

The captain sailed the laden vessel down the Amazon toward the Atlantic. With every mile Wickham's fear of Brazilian officials increased. "I was perfectly certain in my own mind," he recalled later, "that if the authorities guessed the purpose of what I had on board we should be detained under plea for instructions from the central Government at Rio, if not interdicted altogether." He approached the exit port of Pará in something like a panic. But the British consul there saved him. Suavely the diplomat informed the customs official in charge that Wickham had "a botanical cargo of delicate specimens . . . for delivery to Her Britannic Majesty's own Royal Gardens of Kew" (a completely true statement!) and the gallant tax collector, as a courtesy to the Queen, waved the vessel on without examination.

The ship brought her cargo safely to Liverpool; a special train was waiting, and soon some 7,000 young plants were being successfully raised at Kew (1876–1879). These were duly transported to the Far East, and after an experimental period a number of trees began to yield, especially in Malaya and Ceylon.[3]

The *Hevea* had been catapulted halfway around the globe to find a new home. But the results were slow to appear. By 1900 only a trickle of Far Eastern latex was produced. However, the development of the motor car industry now greatly increased the demand for rubber and encouraged new planting. By 1910, 12,916 long tons of it came from Far Eastern sources. Brazil, to be sure, delivered 37,938 tons, and the Far Eastern output was only 8.52 per cent of the total. But by 1914 it had surged upward to 52.17 per cent, while Brazilian production declined. In 1926 it was only 24,298 long tons, while the British output stood at 367,647. Other Far Eastern sources, chiefly the Dutch East Indies, contributed 216,083 tons more.[4]

The production of rubber had thus soared with man's need for it, and Asia had supplanted South America as the chief producer. The event had been tragic for Brazil. From 1890 to 1912 the country had rioted in rubber prosperity. Manaos, in the jungle 900 miles up the Amazon, had become a golden city with palatial residences, an opera house, and ships going and coming at its piers. Then the bubble had burst, and those who had been a part of its iridescence were aware of competitors who could outgrow and undersell them. Far Eastern labor was far cheaper than the independent latex collectors, and the plantation required not half the trouble that jungle trees demanded. The perpetual gold rush had collapsed like a punctured tire, and there was no super-human mechanic who could mend the inefficiency and stubborn in-dividualism that had caused its deflation.[5]

Meanwhile the Far Eastern planters had prospered beyond calcula-tion, earning dividends alleged to have equaled from 50 to 250 per cent annually of their shareholders' investment. World War I maintained the demand for rubber, with prices for fine Pará fixed by the American government in 1917–1918 at 68 cents a pound. Then with 1920 and the depression of that year demand lessened, prices fell, and the opulent planters sought some means of curtailing the supply in order to main-tain their income. The Stevenson scheme of October 1922 was the result —an agreement enacted by the colonial governments of Malaya and Ceylon and approved by the British colonial office.

Allegedly the scheme merely sought to stabilize the price of rubber, and some color was given to it by the fact that 1922 prices had sunk to 14 cents a pound. The law curtailed production to 60 per cent of the previous output, but permitted a quarterly increase of 5 per cent if the market averaged 30 cents during the previous three months and a cut-back of 5 per cent if it went lower. The joker in the situation was that while the market was momentarily flat, the impending increase in motor vehicle output would promote a dramatic rise in price.[6]

Harvey Firestone perceived the potentially devastating effect of the scheme on American buyers of rubber. He investigated the events lead-ing up to it, found that the British Rubber Growers Association was largely responsible, that British industry did not want its enactment, that British economists frowned upon it, and that it would increase the cost of producing rubber. He laid these facts before President Warren G. Harding, Secretary of Commerce Herbert C. Hoover, and members of Congress. This had been done previous to the conference he called for early 1923.

All approved his position, but the federal government felt that it could not protest to Britain. However, it did propose an expenditure of $500,000 to study the production of rubber (and possibly locate sites for it on the American continents), which Hoover called "essential to our national welfare." The War and Agriculture departments supported him; the requested money was appropriated, and investigations of rubber growing were undertaken. Unfortunately Firestone's own group, the Rubber Association of America, listened to representatives of the British planters, who argued that only stability was sought by the scheme, and refused to cooperate with Firestone. He continued his fight.[7]

Henry Ford and Harvey Firestone were friends of long standing, having enjoyed annual vacation trips together and exchanged visits as families. They were also closely associated in business, for Firestone supplied upwards of 65 per cent of all the tires for Ford cars. Ford was thus conditioned to respond favorably to his associate's appeal, and early in 1923 the two were planning a two-pronged attack upon the British planters. One activity was to encourage their friend, Thomas A. Edison, to experiment with rubber-producing plants or shrubs that might be grown in the United States. The other was to find sites abroad for producing rubber that would be under American control.

Probably by agreement Firestone turned to sources outside the Americas: the East Indies, the Philippines (which for a time looked very promising), and Africa. In December 1923 a Firestone emissary arrived in Liberia, who found conditions there highly propitious. Negotiations were begun at once with Liberia; these were completed in November 1926, when the Liberian Congress ratified an agreement which permitted the establishment of Firestone plantations. Meanwhile the price of rubber in 1925 had soared to $1.23 a pound. Firestone seems never to have considered Latin America, possibly because he knew that Ford was interested in doing something there. W. D. Hines, a Firestone executive, early in April 1923 was corresponding with Ford about the possibilities of Panama, Central America, Mexico, and Brazil.

Meanwhile the voice of Brazil itself was heard in Detroit and Dearborn. J. C. Alves de Lima, the consul for that country in New York, wrote Ford on April 9, 1923 to tell him of the favorable terms the Brazilian Department of Agriculture was prepared to grant American capitalists who would "cultivate rubber plantations in the state of Pará."[8]

Even aside from his relationship with Firestone, Ford would have acted out of character, once he was aware of the situation, had he not shown an interest in rubber. This was the period when he was concentrating on raw materials: coal, iron, glass, lumber. "We have got to protect our supply of raw materials," he told Norman Beasley early in 1924. And again, in one of his own books, "If those who sell to us will not manufacture at the prices which, upon investigation, we believe to be right, then we make the article ourselves." Rubber was a raw material —a highly important one. Furthermore, it offered Ford an opportunity to demonstrate the efficiency of his organization, which had already improved coal mines, operated a railroad with signal success, and introduced revolutionary techniques in glass-making. Rubber was a new challenge, and undoubtedly he hoped to improve existing methods of production. This was a matter of pride and public service with him.

To the Brazilians it was no less a challenge. If they could harness Henry Ford's genius, they might turn the tables on the Far East by developing plantations in the very home of the *Hevea*. A new Manaos would rise in splendor with a golden future before it. Had not Ford created the moving assembly line and a motor car for the working man? Would not his genius produce miracles in rubber culture? They must have hoped so, and de Lima continued to dangle the Brazilian plantation before Ford's eyes. The consul came to Michigan early in 1925, and later forwarded from Dionisio Bentes, governor of Pará, a proposal with favorable conditions for the experiment.

Liebold, as Ford's administrative assistant, wrote Bentes on August 26, 1925 asking for a map and the "most desirable location for the establishment of a plantation which would be contiguous to deep water." Meanwhile a few weeks earlier Ford had heard from W. L. Schurz, who had headed an expedition into the Amazon Valley for the Department of Commerce in 1923-1924, now spoke favorably of it, and offered advice.[9]

Still, Ford wanted further information before he launched a great project in the tropical wilderness. For one thing, Edison was still experimenting, and Ford wished to make certain that the culture of rubber-bearing plants in the United States was or was not feasible. By 1925 the prospects were discouraging but not final. Ford and Firestone were both financing Edison. Ford now sent Hudson McCarroll, a capable young chemical engineer, on a trip to the Far East to report on conditions there and commissioned Dr. Carl La Rue, an American scientist with experience in the Dutch rubber plantations, to visit the

Amazon Valley and consider the prospects for rubber culture there. From his and McCarroll's reports it was evident that a South American rubber production center would have disadvantages in its remoteness (river as well as ocean travel for shipments) and of higher-paid labor; also, that because of the location and climate sanitary measures would have to be taken and medical service provided to deal with diseases promptly.

However, other factors seemed favorable. La Rue proposed a site in the Tapajos River area, a natural home of the rubber tree. Land would be provided at minimal cost, labor seemed to be plentiful, and a deep-water site available from which the product could be carried by river, ocean, canal, the Great Lakes, and the sluggish Rouge to the great new plant Ford was creating in Dearborn. As a final precaution Ford sent out an expedition headed by W. L. Reeves Blakeley to locate the final site and conclude a bargain with the state of Pará.

Tacitly Ford was committed. As Blakeley disappeared into the Amazon jungle, he wore the aura of an explorer dispatched to locate and gain possession of a modern El Dorado.[10]

3

On October 26, 1927, Edsel Ford, as president of the Ford Motor Company, announced that his organization had completed arrangements with the Brazilian state of Pará for a gigantic rubber plantation on the Tapajos River. "The details have been closed, the company organized, and work will begin at once," he declared. By this time the Stevenson Rubber Scheme was tottering to extinction. The Dutch planters had refused to join it and were contributing half the world's rubber supply. In November 1928 the British government removed all restrictions on planting. Nevertheless Ford planned to proceed with his Brazilian project, and Edsel's statement followed a pact which Blakeley, with the aid of O. Z. Ide, a Detroit attorney representing the Fords, had made with Dionisio Bentes, the governor of the state, and with Jorge Dumont Villares, who owned the concession.

Ide had gone down in the summer of 1927 to supervise the closing of the contract. He eventually procured a tract of about 2,500,000 acres on the eastern bank of the Tapajos, with a frontage of twelve miles on the water. Its 3,906 square miles were about 82 per cent the size of the state of Connecticut. It lay across the river from the area where Wickham had gathered seeds some fifty years earlier. In all these plans, the manager of Ford's Brazilian automotive activity had not been consulted. Then, out of the blue in October 1927, the company office in São Paulo received a cable from Detroit to pay $125,000 to Villares for the land.

Ford's contract with the state provided that the company could import machinery and all other materials needed on the plantation duty free, that it was to pay no export duty on its rubber, but that after twelve years it would give the state of Pará 7 per cent of the profits. The Ford organization was authorized to operate railroads, airports, banks, stores, schools, and a hospital, and could deal in "skins and hides, oil-seeds, timbers, and other products and articles of any nature." Ford promised to plant 1000 acres of rubber trees during the first two years of his occupancy and a larger number in the two succeeding ones. The Companhia Ford Industrial do Brasil was formed on October 10, 1927 to manage the great undertaking.[11]

Ford engineers immediately made plans for the next seven years of operation, during which an area of 84 square miles was to be cleared and planted. The Detroit company had acquired 199 ships from the federal government; two of these were reconditioned for the expedition: the *Lake Farge* and the *Lake Ormoc*. These boats were loaded with building materials, hardware, a power house, a sawmill, and railroad equipment, as well as a diesel-powered tug and motor launches. The *Lake Ormoc* was also provided with an electric light plant, a small hospital, a machine shop, refrigeration, and food for the American personnel of the expedition. It was well-ventilated. Its passengers included a doctor (from the Ford Hospital), an accountant, a research scientist, a power engineer, and a number of good mechanics. The two vessels were under the command of Captain Einar Oxholm. The *Lake Farge* left the Rouge slip July 11, the *Lake Ormoc* July 26, 1928.[12]

For a time, at the Companhia's direction, W. L. Reeves Blakeley became managing director of operations at the site. While he and Ide had been negotiating the contract, on his own he had planted a million seedlings on the opposite side of the Tapajos (in the state of Amazonas). Now in early summer, Blakeley with a small crew of men began to clear some of the land Ford had acquired, looking toward the arrival of the two ships.

The new center was named Fordlandia. At first glance its location seemed beautiful and even romantic. It lay far enough up the river and on sufficiently elevated land to make a vivid contrast to the average

American's idea of a tropical lowland. The water of the river, in contrast with the yellow Amazon a beautiful blue, spread out at this point for a distance of from five to seven miles before touching the far shore. On the Fordlandia side the land rose "abruptly to a height of 50 feet within 100 yards of the water's edge, and . . . continued gradually to rise as one goes inland." The area was covered with tall and graceful trees—the Spanish cedar, amargose, uxy, castanheira or Brazil nut, the itauba, and others. Many of these could be used for building at Boa Vista, as the headquarters town was called. As a picture, the site was attractive, but the expedition would find it not pleasant to live with.

Because of a misunderstanding as to his part in the completion of the contract, Blakeley was discharged in August 1928. B. J. Craig promptly appointed (August 2) Kristian Orberg as managing director. As we have already seen, Orberg was supervising the company's assembly plants and offices in Brazil, with headquarters in São Paulo, south of Rio de Janeiro and several thousand miles from Fordlandia. He made the long trip to the Amazon and then 450 miles up the river to Santarém and 110 miles further by boat to the plantation.

He did not remain for any length of time but was there when the *Lake Ormoc* and the *Lake Farge* arrived, "chock full of materials." No documents covered the goods, and the new managing director had trouble getting them approved for landing. "Detroit thought they could fill the boats and send them down just like that. You can't do it," Orberg explained. He negotiated with the governor, who was sympathetic, and eventually got everything cleared. The Companhia minutes note that Orberg remained in charge of the plantation but that Captain Oxholm would represent him "in his absence." Orberg quickly departed; he remarked years later: "Since 1928 I have never had occasion to visit the plantation again." Unprepared to manage a rubber plantation, Oxholm found himself facing a welter of problems. After two years he remarked, "This is the hardest proposition I ever tackled in my life." [13]

4

Boa Vista indeed lived up to its name as far as the view was concerned; beyond that it was a grim abode of heat, rain, discomfort, and disease. The climate in itself was not unbearable. Temperatures were high, but no worse than those of New York or Detroit in a summer hot spell. The humidity was unpleasant, but the nights were cool. But malaria and typhoid raged rampant in the region, and the inhabitants suffered from tuberculosis and the yaws, an affliction related to syphilis. There were also numerous local ailments—ulcers, ringworm, filariasis (leading to elephantiasis), and several unpleasant parasite afflictions. Malaria and typhoid, however, were the worst maladies. What with these, the heat, the lack of comfortable habitations, and the confusion of launching the enterprise, the region for a time won the local designation of *"inferno verde."*

The settlement's hospital, now under construction, was not stocked with medicines for many of the local maladies, and the Ford doctor was unacquainted with them. For a time a considerable number of the technicians and workers were unfit for duty.[14]

One of Oxholm's first discoveries had been that the Tapajos was navigable for his loaded ships only during the season of high water. For the remainder of the year their cargoes and many other needed supplies often had to be brought in by small craft.

The ship was not a satisfactory hot weather home, and the construction of offices and residences had to be pushed. Flies and mosquitos swarmed. For a time there were only makeshift shelters for the native workers. One difficulty soon encountered was that the clearing of the land had scarcely begun when the rainy season started. Huge piles of green wood that could not be burned in the wet weather prevented the rapid development of the plantation area. Nevertheless, 972 acres were cleared in 1928. Other work was also advanced. The Companhia minutes of March 24, 1929, show that progress had been made with the "construction of buildings intended for workshops, warehouses, offices, and other dependencies, also for the lodgment of the staff and the workmen of the company." The cleared acreage had been prepared for seeds and seedlings from the state of Matto Grosso, "which are of the best quality, and were duly given clearance by the respective local authorities." But the state of Amazonas refused to let them pass. It also forbade the removal of Blakeley's seedlings from within its own borders (Wickham had gathered his supply there). It tried to persuade the company to acquire land and start a plantation across the river. Instead, the Ford Companhia commenced unsuccessful lawsuits to establish its right to acquire and transport seeds and seedlings from one state to another. Meanwhile, seeds of an inferior quality were planted. It was a discouraging situation. Up to January 1929 $1,578,627 had been spent, and there was little to show for it.[15]

A further source of trouble developed when in February 1929 the benignant Bentes was succeeded as governor of Pará by Enrico Valles. The new executive showed a disposition to review afresh every point of the contract and at once clapped import taxes on all materials brought in that did not contribute to the growing of rubber and export taxes on all non-rubber materials sent out—*e.g.* lumber. Ford had planned to export wood cleared from the estate.[16]

But it was not the Ford way to let an expensive operation die in its birth throes. Sorensen on July 5, 1929 exhorted Oxholm to carry on in the company tradition and overcome the obstacles that impeded him. The able William C. Cowling was sent down to deal with the federal and state duties and took the Ford case to President Washington Luis and other officials in Rio. "I showed them how we had come down there to help Brazil and improve it," he recounted later, and he got some of the troublesome imposts canceled. Yet the question of federal duties on materials for the plantation was not resolved—and would continue to plague the Companhia.[17]

Meanwhile, the discharge of West Indian workers who were objected to by the Brazilians and who had stirred up considerable trouble, improvements in food, and progress in developing the site produced some betterment of the situation although the labor turnover remained very high. On August 28, 1929, J. S. Kennedy, in charge of the rubber company's Pará office, reviewed developments on the plantation in a cable to Sorensen. He reported the clearing of 1,440 acres, the completion of the $65,000 hospital and other buildings, and the enrolling of 1,360 employees, of whom 82 were in the hospital with minor ailments.[18]

This was progress, but Sorensen was dissatisfied with the pace of the work and sent W. E. Carnegie of the Accounting Department to report on the situation. On October 7 he cabled Dearborn: "Present head unqualified by inexperience past personal conduct and lack of respect of staff." This seems to have been a wholly realistic appraisal. Oxholm, whom one of his subordinates called "a big man with a weak mind," as a plantation manager was a good sea captain. Yet Sorensen aggressively supported his fumbling fellow-Dane. "We want Oxholm retained," he insisted. "You must lend all aid to show him where he is wrong. Neither Rogge [John Rogge, in charge of the plantation] nor Kennedy can be encouraged to take his place." Carnegie presumably carried out instructions, but left in November, and Sorensen tried to incite and guide Oxholm by cable and mail. He got little response, and the captain finally left Fordlandia on the *Lake Ormoc* May 18, 1930. Kennedy temporarily took charge.[19]

On October 5, 1930, Carnegie again arrived at Boa Vista, and after a thorough examination of affairs, made a 26-page typed report. Evidently Kennedy had used the intervening time well. "He is conscientiously and energetically trying to do what he believes the company expects of him, . . . is setting a fast pace, and so far has been able to carry the organization along with him." Kennedy had served the project from the start, knew the Brazilians and the country. Carnegie reported that the work force now amounted to 3,009 men, that there was modern housing for some and a "straw village" (native huts) for the remainder. Labor turnover had been reduced. Americans were in charge of all the chief activities (logging, seeds, planting and cultivating, transportation, etc.). A total of 2,117 acres had now been cleared, and 1,996 of them planted. There were 139,016 seedlings. Lumber was being produced at a rate of 16,319 board feet a day and was used for construction. River transportation was bad, the water supply not fully developed, a school was being built, sports were encouraged, and Carnegie suggested a motion picture house. "At present the employees have practically no diversion, and get extremely tired of seeing the same faces at all times and places."

In other words, Boa Vista was rapidly maturing as a town but lacked essential transportation because it must be supplied during the dry season by small river craft. Also, a fact that Carnegie did not note, because of the hilly nature of the terrain it faced planting difficulties. Neither did Carnegie report on the condition of the trees, which was discouraging.

If Boa Vista was a "green hell" for its human inhabitants, it was quite as infernal a habitat for the *Hevea*. This tree was subject to root diseases, leaf maladies, fruit and flower blights, injuries caused by phanerogamic plants, brown bast, abnormal nodule structure, cortex nodules, abnormal exudations of rubber pad, chlorosis of the leaves, and numerous other hazards. Many of these seem to have been less lethal when the trees grew wild, usually standing a considerable distance apart from each other, and had the protection of the surrounding jungle.

Set out in the open in rows, all specimens quickly acquired any disease which attacked one of them, and the burning tropical sun seemed to retard the growth of the tender seedlings, and by weakening them, to intensify the effects of pests and blights. An American government pamphlet on all these afflictions was available after 1926 but was probably unknown to Rogge and his assistants.[20]

At this time the labor situation was still tempestuous, and on December 22, 1930, a riot broke out when the company started to serve its employees on a cafeteria line. Considerable damage was done, and state troops were flown in to quell the disturbance. Thereafter, a Ford restaurant replaced the mess hall and a place was set up for movies, a pool room, and a dining room. The school, where only Portuguese was taught, opened for the employees' children, and a night session was held for adults.

Although Kennedy had finally brought order from the chaos Oxholm had left, he was not retained as manager. Archibald Johnston succeeded him in the fall of 1931. With a keen mind, executive ability, and a realization of why the Ford center had been established, he moved quickly to take positive action. On November 17, 1931 he outlined for Sorensen a plan of operation:

> Everyone agrees that a great amount of work has been done at Boa Vista, and a great deal of money has been spent, but it is very noticeable to the writer, after studying the situation closely, that very little has been done, along the lines of what we came here to do, "namely, plant rubber," so that we could at a later date refine and manufacture rubber articles.

In the same letter Johnston also pointed out that while the Ford plantation had cleared 3,335 acres and set out seedlings on 3,251 in three years and seven months, in the Far East it was customary to start from 15,000 to 18,000 acres a year. The cause of the slow Ford pace had been the effort to save marketable timber. He proposed to burn 100,000 acres and plant quickly. On December 17 Sorensen approved this idea but asked for further details.[21]

Meanwhile, Johnston met some of the same type of frustration as Oxholm had encountered. Dr. Getulio Vargas became president of Brazil in October 1930, and all agreements made with President Washington Luis had to be renegotiated. Johnston wrote Harry Braunstein, Ford manager in Rio, on December 10, 1931: "We have just received letters from Detroit which give me lots of heart and believe me, we will go, if you get what we want in Rio, and, of course, you know what we want, namely, exemption of all duties on all materials now at Boa Vista, exemption of road tax, right to use our radio as we are doing, etc. etc."

But Braunstein found himself caught in a swirl of political eddies. Brazilian visitors to the plantation, among them Minister of Labor Lindolfo Collor and Major Magalhães Barata, the federal "interventor" for the state of Pará,* all thought the installations "splendid"; yet to get action on the issues of duties, taxes, and licenses seemed increasingly difficult. Braunstein wrote Johnston in February with a burst of impractical bravura, "What we want is a new decree or law which will clean up for us all pending questions!"

He talked with the federal Minister of Finance, Dr. Oswaldo Aranha, who, he reported, gave a lengthy "tirade against foreign capital." Braunstein replied stoutly that the Ford rubber enterprise, unlike other foreign companies, was "pouring gold into this country and . . . without the investment of foreign capital in projects such as ours the tremendous untapped natural resources of this country would remain dormant, because there is no capital here to develop them." Dr. Aranha then "hastened to assure us that he agreed with our thoughts and that he had always considered the Companhia Ford Industrial as being unique in its program and unselfish development of what had been nothing but wilderness."

Braunstein next saw Dr. Lindolfo Collor. Collor explained that "he had begun to hear already that he had been subsidized by us, and that if he kept on insisting with the President and the Minister of Finance, they too might be suspicious of his possible selfish interests in our case." Collor accordingly refused to do anything "for the imaginary reasons indicated," and Braunstein despairingly remarked of the ministers: "They all agree that we should enjoy exemptions on *everything,* but they do nothing."

At this point Johnston replied confidentially to Braunstein, "We are not now going ahead this year on the large scale that had been approved, this has been changed to a minimum, 'cause'? Well, the Company enthusiasm sometimes gets dampened and we cannot wonder at it." [22]

Complications continued, but eventually decrees in 1933 gave Ford

---

* Under Vargas, state governors were replaced by "interventors," appointed by the President and acting as official representatives of the federal government.

exemption of all duties on what it imported for the plantation. It was victory, but the struggle had been so long and exasperating that all the Ford personnel who had taken part in it were exhausted and disillusioned.

5

In July 1932 Johnston had written to A. M. Wibel in Dearborn that lumber export "seems the only possible means of income so far discovered at Boa Vista." At Fordlandia had been installed the most modern sawmill in all Brazil. Roberge took samples of wood from the plantation to possible customers in the United States. He found some buyers, but American mills were reluctant to handle the hardwoods, which dulled their tools and which in steam-heated interiors showed a tendency to crack. After a thorough investigation, in April 1933 Roberge calculated that on an exportation of 4 million feet per year "based on current costs of production and selling prices," there would be a loss of $11,988 per month. Few expenses could be reduced by increasing production and he recommended that sawmill operations at Boa Vista (except of course for local purposes) be discontinued. This suggestion was followed, and the one immediate source of revenue turned out to be no source at all.

To make matters worse, Johnston also grew increasingly dissatisfied with the rubber trees at Boa Vista, all of which had been grown from seeds of inferior stock (see p. 172 above). On the basis of his reports, the Ford company for the first time turned its attention to the real *problem* of rubber production. Wibel in July 1932 had exchanged information with Harvey Firestone on the use of "proven clones" developed in Sumatra. Firestone indicated that the trees on which these were grafted produced excellently. He had grafted all the Sumatra plantings for the past two years and had markedly increased the yield. A United States Rubber Company representative, writing from his firm's long experience in the Far East, also assured Wibel that his corporation approved this procedure.[23]

If the Ford Motor Company was going to procure specimens of high-yielding clones in quantity from the Far East, obviously it needed an expert to get them. It was equally in need of an expert at Fordlandia, where most of its seedlings were dying from one or more of the innumerable diseases that preyed on the rubber tree. The firm now employed a scientist, James R. Weir, who had acted as plant pathologist in the investigation of crude rubber possibilities in the Amazon Valley conducted in 1925 by an expedition of the U.S. Agriculture and Commerce departments. Weir had served both before and after this survey as pathologist in charge of collections for the Bureau of Plant Industry. He was the author of a formidable pamphlet, "A Pathological Survey of the Pará Rubber Tree (*Hevea Brasiliensis*) in the Amazon Valley." He began active work for the Companhia on February 6, 1933, and presented a preliminary statement on rubber tree culture and bud-grafting on March 31. Edsel Ford asked him to visit the Brazilian plantation "and then proceed to the East for the collection of clones."

At last the Brazilian company had employed a specialist in rubber culture. Almost five years had passed since work had begun at Fordlandia, and during that period all arboricultural activity had been conducted by men with only "practical" knowledge of the complex problems they faced. It was almost as bad as putting a hospital orderly in charge of an operating room. Weir was soon off to Sumatra and Malaya to seek high-yielding stock and obtained 2,046 stumped buddings.

These were carefully boxed in sterilized sawdust and shipped from Singapore on December 15, 1933. They traversed the Indian Ocean, threaded the Suez Canal and went through the Mediterranean and across the Atlantic and up the Amazon to arrive at Fordlandia on February 15, 1934. One day later they were planted in prepared nursery beds, within a few miles of the area where sixty years earlier their ancestors had flourished.

In 1934 the British, Dutch, and French colonies formed a committee to prohibit the export of rubber tree seeds, seedlings, and clones, but by that time the stumps were successfully growing at Fordlandia. By 1934 Johnston had planted 8,300 acres with 1,390,000 trees (nothing near his original intention), and he and the Dearborn officials both felt a new optimism. In July 1934 Wibel wrote him:

I certainly believe you will make a go of the rubber plantation, and personally I am very anxious to promote all possibilities of the bud grafting system. I am thoroughly convinced that this is the only procedure to use. . . . I am certain Dr. Weir has laid the foundation for some good work along these lines. . . . The writer believes that it was a mistake to have started as we did, concentrating on seedlings, but that is past history, and we certainly should profit by our experience along these lines.[24]

In Dearborn there was talk of building a tire plant in Brazil to use the rubber that would be produced on the plantation; this dream was indicative of the new hope that better methods had inspired.[25]

However, a drastic change was now made with respect to the location of the project. Everyone on the Boa Vista staff had come to feel that much of the land at Fordlandia was unsuitable for a large rubber plantation, both because the hilly terrain made cultivating and spraying difficult and because the soil itself was not the best for the growth of seedlings. The tapping of trees on the hills (as compared with the same work on level land) was furthermore a difficult process. The situation of Boa Vista, which made transportation unsatisfactory during the dry season, was also a factor.

A new location had been found on the Tapajos about eighty miles from Boa Vista and thirty from Santarém which had rich, level soil and could be reached at any time of the year by large vessels. A tract of about 700,000 acres at Fordlandia was traded to the state of Pará for an equal acreage at the new site, Belterra. Here another Ford town arose in the wilderness. Roads were built, the area cleared, dwellings erected, a modern water system installed, a hospital constructed, and the jungle tamed to the ways of orderly cultivation. Here as at Fordlandia a golf course was laid out and other recreational facilities provided.

Soon at Belterra the stumps began to grow and Johnston was once more encouraged. By March 1936 1100 acres had been planted with 500,000 rubber trees, and in spite of the difficulties with dry weather and insects, progress was made. A year later the number of rubber trees set out and growing at the new plantation had risen to 700,000; and many thousands of these had been successfully bud-grafted from known high-yielding trees. Ford was doing the first bud-grafting ever done in Latin America. A nursery with 3,250,000 young rubber trees had been set up and was making satisfactory progress.

Belterra soon eclipsed Fordlandia. The first intention had been to continue operating the latter plantation, but in 1935 a bug attacked the trees there; they lost all their leaves, and an entomologist, Dr. C. H. T. Townsend (an American who had been in Brazil eighteen years) was called in to diagnose the problem and prescribe treatment. He did so, but the difficulties proved mountainous. As a result of this experience Ford by 1937 had decided to use Fordlandia as a large experimental station, although still trying to maintain the planted area and develop it for commercial production. There a new department of scientific rubber research was created, directed by Weir and his assistants. "It is hoped to develop a strain of rubber trees that will be entirely free of the South American Leaf Disease that destroys the rubber trees for only after these diseases are successfully controlled can cultivated rubber trees produce in competition with cultivated rubber in other places in the world," concluded Johnston.[26]

Yet as the progress went forward (with still no profit, and continuous investment on the part of the American Ford company), the manager of the plantations encountered more baffling political complications. There was the difficulty, for example, of a law that forbade foreign doctors from practicing in Brazil; there was also a matter of radio licenses that defied easy solution. (Ford had employed both American and Brazilian doctors and operated its own radio station.) The Brazilian government officials seemed to wax hot and cold on the plantation, giving and denying help to the point of frustration.

The later 1930's saw the armor of Ford enthusiasm pierced numerous times. "The plantation got off on the wrong foot," one Brazilian later remarked. It was an uphill fight all the way to tame the forest and mold it to modern needs. The federal interventor Major Barata was helpful, but only a few other Brazilian officials supported him. There was constant carping criticism, some of it warranted but most of it irrelevant and destructive. In April 1936 Dr. Weir wrote Dearborn a disturbing report. Fordlandia would have trees ready for tapping soon but too few to realize a profit. As for Belterra, this plantation would not become a productive enterprise for some time. Weir thought progress there was "possible" if the company were to increase its investment.

> From a strictly dollar and cents point of view [he continued], it is not recommended. As a contribution to science and to the world's rubber plantation industry and from the point of view that nothing would be left undone to test a rubber plantation in Brazil, it is recommended. The alternative is abandonment.*

Johnston did not agree that the plantation would never be profitable, and neither apparently did Henry Ford. At any rate, he showed no inclination to abandon the project. Accordingly, more acres were

---

* Dr. Weir later came to modify his opinion. "Whatever the economic returns to the company may be and we think in the long run it will be of the best," he wrote in September 1936, ". . . a successful rubber culture from our combined efforts will be in itself a great achievement for the company." (See note 27.)

cleared and planted at Belterra. Budding with the high-yielding clones from the Far East was carried on. More houses were built, more offices and schools. The Research Department at Fordlandia undertook extensive work "with a view to developing a Brazilian clone with immunity to South American leaf disease and with a yield superior to anything yet developed in the Far East." [27]

Health conditions improved as the mosquito was vanquished. By 1940 the progress at Belterra became heartening, but the expenditures had been enormous. The total investment in the plantation as of February 1940 stood at $9,535,000, and there was no prospect of a quick return on that immense sum.

In October 1940 President Getulio Vargas made his first visit to the plantation. Vargas had long known of its activities. Early in his regime he had his federal interventors cancel all concessions in the states of Pará and Amazonas, except those of Henry Ford and one other concessionaire. Coming north from his post at Rio, Braunstein conducted the President around Belterra. Johnston was not there, for he had returned to Dearborn because of his health, and Howard C. Deckard had taken his place. The latter was to remain as manager for two years.

Touring the plantation, Vargas remarked on the excellence of the roads and the overall cleanliness and order. General Edgard Faco, who was the acting chief of the President's military staff and one of the party, added that although he had been born and spent most of his life in the northern part of Brazil, he had never seen such a healthy group of men as those on the plantation.

A contest was held to find a single house fly, and no one won. Not a single specimen could be produced, so effective had been the efforts to rid the region of all insect pests.

The President praised the experimental work, particularly the budgrafting. Speaking to those gathered, he said that if there were more men like Henry Ford in this world, no social legislation would be necessary. Moreover, he told the Ford representatives "that anything we ask for, provided it is just—and he has never as yet found us asking anything unjust—he would be very glad to listen to us and requested that we come to him whenever we feel the need of it." The next night in a broadcast from Manaos, Vargas declared "the only place he found in the interior with proper sanitation and healthy people was at Mr. Ford's Plantation." [28]

6

By this time Europe was at war, the seas were filled with submarines, and the American government was becoming aware that the United States might become involved and that Japan might become a combatant cutting off rubber imports from the Far East. In 1940 the United States paid $318,000,000 for imported crude rubber, but less than 3 per cent of this sum went to Latin America. Nevertheless, with war threatening, officials in the United States turned their attention southward. On June 22, 1940 Congress authorized a plan for establishing an efficient and self-sustaining rubber-growing industry in Latin America.

There was a new interest in the Ford venture, and at Belém a team of Department of Agriculture workers from the United States cooperated with the new Northern Agricultural Institute, a part of the Brazilian national Department of Agriculture. The staff of the Institute for the most part was being trained at the pioneer plantation set up by Ford; as one writer put it, "to the corps of investigators now at the Institute such an example [that of Ford] provides a powerful stimulus and abiding faith in the nearly unlimited possibilities of this immense region."

The Americans found that Ford had developed resistant strains of *Hevea,* which represented the only practicable solution to the leaf blight problem, and that the company had discovered how to combine excellent resistance with high-yield trees. Belterra's and Fordlandia's best clones were made available for general distribution, not only in Brazil but to the Department of Agriculture also for widespread intergovernmental cooperative programs.[29]

The Ford plantations had now begun production. Belterra had 3,651,000 trees at the end of 1941, and a yield of 750 tons of latex was claimed. Fordlandia's 839,000 trees yielded 216 tons. This accomplishment may be compared with Firestone's record in Liberia. Beginning in 1926, he had trees ready to tap in 1930, produced 1,030 tons of latex in 1936 (because of the depression and the collapse of the Stevenson scheme he had not developed his plantations in the early 1930's), and shipped nearly 7,000 tons in 1940.

While in the war years Firestone's rubber production climbed rapidly (it showed an output of 20,000 tons in 1945), Ford's did not.

Despite all encouragement from United States government agencies and officials, the yield of the Ford plantations remained practically stationary. In October 1942 Johnston visited Brazil* and reported that Belterra had been attacked by the greatest multitude of caterpillars ever seen in the area—they came "in swarms like locusts and laid their eggs only on the new shoots at the top of the trees. At that height they cannot be seen until it is too late, then they swarm down the tree eating all before them." The trees were completely defoliated, but soon they put out new shoots which in turn were besieged by the most severe attack of leaf disease in the history of the plantation. This too stripped them of leaves, and "in many cases they had not strength to put out a third flush of foliate. With the excessive dry weather the trees started to die back. Some have died half way down the trunk and may die completely."

Johnston had suggestions to make on the leaf disease and the caterpillars, but there was also the lace bug, the yellow scale and the red mite to be combated. In addition, a shortage of labor had developed.

However, Johnston in 1942 reported that while, for the present, rubber prices were guaranteed at a high level by the Rubber Reserve Company in Belém, this applied only until 1946, and he and Charles Townsend (son of the expert C. H. T. Townsend, and now running Fordlandia) were of the opinion that "when rubber finds its normal price level" the volume tapped would not be sufficient to cover the heavy overhead."

A point not mentioned by Johnston but rapidly becoming of crucial importance was the great development in the field of synthetic rubber, which might one day replace the natural substance or at least control its price.[30]

Indeed, by now Dearborn officials had reached a point of saturation. The expensive plantations had long been sources of frustration and exasperation. Their accomplishments, while great in the experimental sphere, had been negligible in that of production. An occurrence of some influence was the sale in the fall of 1942 of the Ford Rouge tire plant to the Russians (see Chapter XIV). Shortly thereafter Johnston telephoned J. W. Thomas, chairman of the Board of the Firestone Tire & Rubber Company, telling him that since the Ford com-

---

* By this time Deckard had returned to the States, and D. H. Stallard was acting manager of both plantations. Stallard would soon become manager. Of course when Johnston visited, he was the man in authority.

pany might never again make tires, it occurred to E. F. Wait (the former manager of the tire plant) and Johnston that "we may not require our plantations in Brazil." Johnston wanted to discuss with Thomas the possibility of Firestone's buying the plantations. The telephone conversation had been authorized by Edsel Ford, but when Harvey Firestone wanted to see Edsel about it, the latter demurred, penning on an inter-office memo of November 24, 1942, "If Mr. Johnston can work up any interest with Mr. Thomas or Mr. Firestone OK. I personally dont [*sic*] care to get into the matter at this time." Apparently the effort to make a sale was dropped.

In 1943 Dearborn again considered disposing of the plantations; Kristian Orberg recalls that Henry and Edsel Ford "called me to Dearborn [in that year]. We took out a globe, and discussed where the plantation was. I was afraid to explain to them that the project wasn't feasible. I did explain however that no profits could be expected from the venture for years." Johnston had told them the same story. Now Henry Ford said, "Well, Edsel, I guess we better let it go."

Then came Edsel's death in May 1943, and once more the matter hung in abeyance. In Brazil, Orberg says, political conditions made it impossible to sell the plantation.

On September 21, 1945, Henry Ford II, son of Edsel, became president of the Ford Motor Company; his first aim was to cut costs and turn the company into an efficient, profitable operation. Very early he realized that the rubber plantations must be sold, and one of the first decisions of his General Planning Committee, made on November 5, 1945, was to do this. Before the close of the year, the plantations were conveyed to the Brazilian government for the nominal sum of $244,200. The company's net loss on the sale of the assets was $7,840,171.50.[31]

The Northern Agricultural Institute of Belém took over the administration of the plantations, with an eagerness of youth and enterprise. It believed that it could make a go of the venture where the big American company had not. Indeed, in 1944 the director of the Institute had spoken of Ford's rubber plantation "as the cornerstone of the economic advancement of the Amazon Valley" and had declared that the solutions of plant disease problems would aid "future rubber plantations in the Amazon Valley." This contribution, he continued, "takes on the character of a social work of great merit and the future generations of the new world will pay tribute to the memory of Henry Ford."

Ford had built homes, two hospitals, roads, and modern water systems in the backward Amazon region. He had cleared the jungle, introduced towns with schools, nurseries, and churches. The two rubber plantations were model communities in a wilderness.

The Brazilians took them over, but their interest in the properties soon waned as it became apparent that the plantations would not become profitable. Fordlandia is now (1962) used for cattle raising. Belterra maintains some rubber production and operates a small experimental plot. The *Hevea* trees lift their fronds skyward, but walking beneath them the visitor makes his way through knee-high weeds. The great development that Ford had envisaged has withered to a mere trace of what he planned, and Brazil today uses more imported and synthetic rubber than it does the product of its own trees.

But if Ford failed to develop the plantation as a source of crude rubber, he set an example of efficiency and social progress that the Amazon Valley still remembers. His hospital at Belterra still serves the surrounding area. Tragically, the modern water system he installed has broken down and remains unrepaired, and the neat, well-organized community he created is slowly being devoured again by the jungle. Still, the name of the great industrialist is a magic one, and the people seem dazed that he is gone and his achievements are literally disintegrating. "Why did Ford leave Brazil?" a member of that country's Congress asked one of the authors at the slowly crumbling plantation.[32]

The answer of course is simple. After eighteen years of conflict with the tropical forest, eighteen years of fighting human and tree diseases, eighteen years of often needless friction with Brazilian authorities, and eighteen years of pouring funds into an enterprise that still promised no sure return, there came a moment of recognition. Henry Ford II perceived that if he were to transform the then-faltering Ford Motor Company into a modern, efficient business, he would have to rid his corporation of this devouring incubus.

Thus in December 1945 Ford's sole attempt to establish an important source of raw materials abroad, and to create at the same time a great rubber industry in the Western Hemisphere, ground to an unhappy end. It was an expensive failure, but it left a shining example of how the Amazon Valley could be transformed into a healthy region and the vast jungle conquered if man had the courage and persistence to remake the great "heart of Brazil."

9

The Best-Laid Plans

For the public of two continents the arrival of Henry Ford at Southampton on April 6, 1928, was a momentous occasion. The creator of the Model A was now ready to resume the leadership of the world automotive industry that had been his up to the death of the Model T. He took the honors of a Caesar modestly, even affably. Sixty-five years of age, with a keen blue eye and the color of health in his cheeks, he fenced in friendly fashion with the reporters who boarded his ship in the harbor. "The Model A," he prophesied, "will last as long as the Model T." The very heavens seemed to approve, for the English Easter season that year was clear, warm, and sunny.

Rumors had run across the Atlantic in advance of Ford's arrival. One proclaimed that he had come to Europe to establish a great automobile center. Mrs. Foster Welch, the woman mayor of Southampton, was on hand to urge the advantages of her city as the hub of Ford operations. Despite the announcement in 1924 that Dagenham would be the site of the new plant, nothing had been done about it, and the location of the great factory seemed to be again a matter of uncertainty. Mrs. Welch begged Ford to examine the land he already held in her city, and the potentialities of the port. But Ford deftly pushed this request aside. "I have no intention just now of looking at any factory sites," he said.* He had come to meet people and to study the tariff situation.

Yet that very day he accompanied H. S. Jenkins, manager of the Ford Motor Company (England) Ltd. on a tour of the Dagenham

---

* Mrs. Welch appealed to Mrs. Ford to persuade her husband to look favorably upon Southampton. "We women must stand together, Mrs. Ford." "We certainly must," Clara Ford replied, "but Mr. Ford himself must decide about the site. I have nothing to do with that."

area. The truth was that his faith in the Model A had revived and strengthened his determination to build a European manufacturing center. "I must not have the whole of my resources in America," he told an English official not long afterward. "I must expand elsewhere. I want an English company that will be the Detroit of Europe." Already all his energies were bent on launching this center in an appropriate way and in selecting the right person to administer the great undertaking.

As to location, he had considered and dismissed Ireland because of the tariff and also probably because of lack of skilled labor, raw materials, and central location. Perry, as previously noted, had been a passionate advocate of Southampton, but Ford was convinced that if a good site had been available on deep water near London, it would be superior. Dagenham satisfied him. On April 10 he even noted the burning garbage dump maintained there by the City of London and considered how the fires might be usefully employed in his manufacturing activity.[1]

Ford felt his way cautiously toward the action he contemplated. He was well aware that his English and European ventures of the last eight years had been ineptly handled. He was convinced that with the Model A he could capture leadership in the great potential car market that Europe offered: production there, compared with American output, was clearly in its childhood. But he also knew that General Motors and various European manufacturers stood ready to challenge him. Accordingly he gave the clamoring reporters little satisfaction. He took tea at Lady Astor's with the King and Queen, dined with representatives of the English automobile industry and with the American Society, and sharply announced that he would not visit Ireland until the Irish-English customs duties were removed. "I don't believe in anything else than free trade all around," he declared. "I don't know what a tariff means, except that it means giving one crowd an advantage over another. Free trade is competition, and nothing can get large enough if you don't have competition."

But meanwhile he was gathering information for his guidance both as to Ireland and England. He conferred with Dulanty, the trade representative of the Irish High Commissioner in London. The manufacture of the Fordson had been suspended in the United States in January, and Ford indicated that he might resume production of a new tractor at Cork under favorable conditions. Dulanty assured him that tariff adjustments could be made. There for the time being the matter seems to have rested.

As for England, Ford made it his business to get further advice from Sir William Letts, head of Crossley Motors. Some eight months earlier the two had conferred in Detroit on the unsatisfactory state of Ford (England) affairs; and Ford had suggested offering shares in that company to the English public. Sir William had discussed the idea in British financial circles and had written in November 1927 that "as a purely American owned company, with so much British propaganda against it, it [Ford of England] would never have the same chance for its merchandise as a company of which the British public were part and parcel." He suggested "floating your British company, retaining control, but letting in the public, not in big blocks of shares, but spread over into as many hands as possible." Sir William added that "if you wish to go further, and secure a British name, I know you could not do better than to get a name like Austin."

As we have seen, Austin himself had earlier proposed a union, although he had meanwhile also vainly sought to make an agreement with General Motors. Beyond polite acknowledgements of Sir Herbert's letters there is no evidence that Ford, who had previously ignored offers from Citroën to unite with him in France, had pursued the matter further. Perhaps he had thought of Sir William Letts as a possible head for his European ventures rather than Austin.[2]

However, during this period Ford had undoubtedly considered another possibility—the return of Sir Percival Perry. While after 1919 there had been no direct communication between either Henry or Edsel Ford and Perry, the three had been aware of each other and to an extent had maintained contact through a correspondence between Perry and Sorensen. This had been continuous from 1922 to 1926, and shows that Sorensen, who had now assumed control of American production and managed the great Rouge plant, had several times been invited to Herm, where Perry lived from 1921 on. (At this time Perry was a director of the Slough Estates and was drawing an adequate income from it.) He was however frankly eager to return to the company he had helped to build. Late in 1922 he wrote to Sorensen: "I expect I shall always have the FMC more at heart than anything else because the best years of my life were spent working with you all. I hope that you and Mr. Ford don't feel that I am so entirely separated that you wouldn't call upon me in case there is anything I can do to help your interests on this side." A little later he even ventured to suggest an association with the English company. On July 24, 1923, Sorensen had written about this, and what he says is highly significant:

> I had refrained from replying to your last letter, in which you wrote of doing something for the Company again, because I had hoped that Mr. Ford, himself, would be making a trip to Europe, and thought perhaps you would have a good opportunity to renew acquaintances again, but from present indications, I do not think he will be going over this season. I had a good chance to show your letter to Mr. Ford, and while he did not comment on it in one way or the other, I felt that you would have no trouble in having a pleasant meeting when you met again, and perhaps you prefer to leave this matter as it is until you have an opportunity to talk to Mr. Ford.

Sorensen's final sentence is especially important, because it indicates clearly that Ford could not have been set against Perry. Sorensen, who took policy directly from his chief, would otherwise never have suggested the possibility of a "pleasant meeting." * Perry was well aware of this and so must have judged that he was not *persona non grata*. There the matter rested. Perry did not visit the United States, rightly sensing that this would have been a mistaken move, and Ford did not arrive in England until 1928.** Immediately the Perrys extended an invitation to the Fords to visit them in Herm, and Perry went to London to press the matter personally. He was unable to see Ford. On April 21 Lady Perry wrote to Clara Ford:

> Perry has just returned home. He went to London last Tuesday, hoping to see you, and has tried to get in touch with Mr. Ford each day since, without success; and as he heard you were going North, he has come back again. When you come to England for a longer visit, I hope you will spare part of it to come here.

---

* Sorensen always claimed to have approved of Perry, and in 1923 drafted a letter to Roland Philip, a high Ford of England official, which read: "I, of course, feel that we never had a manager who was understood by the agents as well as Perry." W. A. Ryan, the Ford (Dearborn) sales manager, read the letter and suggested omitting the reference to Perry, which Sorensen did. See draft of first letter, Apr. 9, 1923, and memo Ryan to Sorensen, Apr. 10, 1923, Select File, Dearborn. The episode plainly shows Sorensen's feeling.

** Edsel Ford had come to England in 1926, but Perry's concern was with his father, who had brought him into the company and who held the real power.

By this time Ford was in Manchester; either there or on the return to London Clara received the letter and doubtless read it to him. It may well be that Ford had deliberately avoided Perry while he was making decisions about the industrial center that would produce the Model A for Europe.[3]

He had already decided that the site of the new center would be Dagenham. He must now choose its managing director, for only with the right director could the venture take form. Ford quickly recognized that Jenkins, an able sales executive, lacked the vision and resourcefulness to guide the new project. If he had considered Austin or Sir William Letts he must have felt that they too were unsatisfactory. More and more it was borne in upon him that Perry alone had the qualities he wanted. Perry had outlined the very English company Ford now wanted to create. Perry had been devoted to the Ford name and fame, had kept English goodwill, had made money. The men who had been responsible for his resignation, Klingensmith and Knudsen, were no longer with the Ford organization. Liebold, who had sided with them, was now without influence. Sorensen, Ford's right-hand man, admired Perry. On May 1, the day before he was to leave England, Ford wired Perry to meet him on the boat at Southampton before he sailed for America.

The telegram came to Perry "out of the blue." He had not even been able to see Ford. But without hesitation he hastened to Southampton, prepared to put his full talents at the service of the company and its master. Ford asked him to take charge of England again, to bring the Ford organization there back to its old preëminence, to launch it on a new and larger career with the Model A as its basic unit. As Perry's secretary put it years later, "The expansion that Perry had wanted to undertake in 1919 was now being offered to him."

He accepted the opportunity at once and with enthusiasm. Ford returned to Dearborn announcing, "I've rehired Perry." Sorensen applauded the act, but Clifford Longley, the company's legal adviser, got out the records dealing with Perry's resignation. Ford snapped: "Never mind those papers. I made a big mistake."[4]

Thus in the late spring of 1928 the conception of the new British company began to take shape; it had a habitation (at Dagenham) and a leader. It was to alter the automotive map of Europe.

2

"Father has advised me of his conversation with you at Southampton," cabled Edsel Ford to Perry on May 23, 1928. "Can you come to Detroit for further discussion?"

This was obviously a necessity, for Henry Ford and Perry had only spoken briefly of the reorganization the former proposed to make in Europe. Sailing from England on June 9, Perry spent about two weeks in the United States, leaving Dearborn on the 30th. Sorensen later recalled that he was "bubbling over with ideas for the reorganization of Europe." With Henry Ford, Edsel, and Sorensen he considered chiefly the projected factory at Dagenham and the English company. Ford himself had selected the site for his European plant, had proposed that the English public become shareholders in the English company* (an idea which was soon extended to all companies on the continent), and had thought of returning tractor manufacture to Ireland. But Perry was to supply the imagination, skill, and dynamic force that would give these activities final form and creative growth. The brief June trip had left some important matters undecided. "You will recall," wrote Perry to Edsel on August 8, "that during our discussions in Detroit the inclusion of Continental Branches was omitted." Perry wanted a clear understanding on the relationship of the English company to these. "It is necessary to include the Continental Branches," he wrote, "because the European demand for Ford products must be filled from Dagenham (to justify the plant), and in my judgment it is advisable, therefore, that not only the manufacturing for, but the assembling and selling in, that territory should be in the same hands."

This was an extreme doctrine but a logical one, and while we do not know what the Fords had expected the exact role of the English company to be, nothing appears in their letters which indicates that they questioned Perry's conception.

They in fact went even farther and agreed that the newly reorganized English company would also own the controlling interest in the continental Ford companies. Now Perry could see his road ahead. He could make plans for the transformation of the English company and

* See Chapter 4. Perry had suggested the arrangement in 1919 and Ford in 1927, before his 1928 meeting with Perry, had adopted it.

give thought to other aspects of reorganization. One of his immediate needs was to enlist certain men as his lieutenants.[5]

Jenkins ceased to be head of the Ford Motor Company Ltd. and left England early in August of 1928. He had been capable and well-liked and was disappointed at being dismissed, but unquestionably he was not equipped for the task Perry was undertaking. "Jenkins was good as manager of a sales branch," remarked one English official later, "but Perry was ten times as high in stature."

Perry's first move was to engage the man he had chosen as second in command. This was A. R. Smith, engineer, production expert, administrator, whom Jenkins had unreservedly recommended. Perry may have known of Smith when the latter was handling Ford affairs for Russa Engineering Company in India. What is certain is that Perry had heard of his work in England after 1923, when Smith had made a fine record under Gould and Jenkins. He had aspired to become assistant manager, but Jenkins in 1927 had refused him this advancement, explaining that it would cause jealousy in the company. Soon afterward the Standard Motor Company had tendered Smith the post of works manager; he accepted the offer, and in 1928 when Perry turned to him he was a Standard employee.

Sir Percival telephoned and asked Smith to come to see him, and the two arranged a meeting for Sunday. It was their first face-to-face encounter.

Smith later recalled that Sir Percival, now fifty, had the look of a benign clergyman. But he went right to the heart of the matter with a directness that belied his mild appearance.

"How would you like to come back to Ford?" he asked.

"No," said Smith and proceeded to tell him forcefully what had been and still was wrong with the Ford organization.

"How would you like to change and improve all that?" persisted Perry.

"What have you to do with it?" Smith demanded.

"I have a lot to do with it," replied Perry with the ghost of a smile.

He then told Smith of his return to the company, of the plans for an English Ford organization that would manufacture cars for all Europe, and of his hope that Smith would take charge of manufacturing, immediately at Manchester, and later at Dagenham. To the latter it was an astounding statement, setting up a new image of the English

Ford company, and offering him a high post in a great enterprise. At once he agreed to return, and Perry had secured his first important recruit.

In a similar fashion he recaptured a few other workers who had strayed from the company, such as Anthony Hall (sales) and Roland Philip (purchasing), who had held important posts in the 1909–1919 period. From the Slough Estates he brought the able construction engineer J. H. Boyd. These men and a few others were called "the Perry group." They were important, but no more so than certain officials already in the company, like H. S. Cooper and F. S. Thornhill Cooper (the two were quite unrelated), both of whom were soon to occupy influential positions.[6]

Perry's return was not a matter for rejoicing among company personnel. Many who had known him were gone. To others the event was just another jolt—like a glass of water suddenly flung in the face. "There was an atmosphere of wonder," recalled Sir Stanford (formerly H. S.) Cooper later. "We had gone through company earthquakes—Anderson, Bate, Davis, Gould, Jenkins. The organization was on edge. They said, 'What next?'" But it was not long before Perry made it clear that he was ushering in a new era. Then confidence in him grew, and with it approval.[7]

In October Perry was in Dearborn again, working with Henry and Edsel Ford and Sorensen to mature what was eventually called "The 1928 Plan."

The time seemed appropriate for Ford expansion and for American overseas activity in general. Model A production in the United States, which had reached only 140 units per day in January 1928, had soared to 4300 by June, and in the fall it was mounting toward the impressive figure of 10,000. Already it was clear that 1929 would be the biggest year to date in American automotive history.

General Motors, as well as Ford, was expanding abroad. GM in 1927–1928 had invested an additional $3.6 million in its English operation, Vauxhall. Its executives were in the process of negotiating a $26 million purchase of 80 per cent of the German firm, Adam Opel, A.G., a purchase that would be consummated in 1929. GM also acquired, in 1929, McKinnon Industries, Ltd., a firm engaged in manufacturing automobile parts and located in St. Catharines, Ontario.

Ford's and GM's moves were in consonance with a surge of American investment abroad. From $7 billion in 1919, U.S. investments overseas had risen in 1929 to $17.5 billion. "Perhaps the outstanding change in foreign commerce in recent years has been the exportation of American industries themselves," remarked a contemporary commentator. One estimate indicated that in 1929 there were more than 1300 companies or organizations in Europe either owned by American corporations or under their influence. In Latin America, Canada, and the Orient the acceleration of American investment was comparable.[8]

What was the Ford design for production in Europe at this promising moment? By November 1928 the plan had emerged clearly.

A new English corporation would be created, called simply Ford Motor Company Limited. This would replace the Ford Motor Company (England) Ltd., and would acquire all the latter's assets including Henry Ford & Son Ltd. in Ireland.* It would be the central element in Ford's European activities.

It would have a capitalization of £7,000,000 as compared with the former company's authorized capital of £200,000. The plant of the new enterprise, at Dagenham, would be the largest automobile factory in the world outside the United States, producing 200,000 Ford cars a year. These would be shipped within the "United Kingdom . . . Irish Free State, the Channel Islands and the Isle of Man, the Continent of Europe (with the exception of European Russia . . .), Asia Minor, including Palestine, Syria, Arabia (except Aden), Iraq, Persia, Afghanistan, Egypt, and certain other parts of Africa."

It will be recalled that Perry had insisted, and the others had agreed, that to justify the building of the enormous Dagenham plant, the new English company must have wide markets. It obtained the "sole and exclusive right of manufacturing, assembling, distributing and marketing Ford and Lincoln Motor Cars, and Fordson Tractors and other Ford products" in these areas. The future was expanding, trade was following an ascending line on the charts, and it never seems to have occurred to Henry Ford or to Perry that Dagenham could not produce the Model A for these extensive markets both cheaply and at a profit.[9]

Under the plan, the new Ford of England would acquire the shares of the nine Ford operations on the European continent, which at that time were owned either by the American Ford company or the Ford

---

* Until 1927 the Ford family owned Henry Ford & Son Ltd. In that year the family sold the stock to FMC (England) Ltd., because (according to Sir Stanford Cooper) the Cork and English plants were working so closely together.

family. Ford of America would own 60 per cent of the English company's stock and thus control its policy. The other 40 per cent would be offered to the British public in small lots so as to get the widest possible distribution. In a similar fashion, the English firm would hold 60 per cent of the shares of each of the European affiliates, and would offer the public in each country the remaining 40 per cent. As we have seen, Ford had hopes that with national participation in ownership would come the feeling that the Ford company in any country was not a foreign corporation.

Each European Ford company would take on a national character. In Holland, for example, not only would shares be owned by Dutch citizens, but among the directors would be eminent Dutchmen. There would be a Dutch manager, increasing purchases of parts in Holland, and the employment of Dutch workmen. Arrangements would be the same in France, Denmark, Sweden, Germany. As Sorensen put it, "The entire organization must be developed from the other side." In certain countries there would be new assembly plants; in many there would be new companies.

However, there was still no thought of providing a national product, built for any particular country's needs. The Model A and the Model AF (with the smaller bore engine) would be sold everywhere. After all, the entire plan had been one for promoting the widest possible use of the Model A. Neither in Dearborn nor in Manchester was it yet recognized that the best machine in America might possibly not be the best for France, Denmark, or Finland.

While under the 1928 plan the big manufacturing plant would be at Dagenham, the factory at Manchester would be used for assembly purposes and the Cork plant would build the tractor; at the three locations 20,000 men would be employed. Dagenham would be completed without any further issue of capital. Finally, Perry predicted that in 1929 120,000 Ford cars and trucks and 30,000 tractors would be sold in England and on the continent.

In planning for Dagenham, Henry Ford did almost exactly what he had done twenty-five years earlier in Canada: there would be local management and direction, and the public would hold a substantial proportion of the shares. Detroit would engineer the product. As Windsor provided leadership for Ford activities in India, Malaya, Australia, and South Africa, so Dagenham was to direct Ford affairs in Europe, Asia Minor, and parts of Africa. The Canadian Ford company had the benefit of the American Ford company patents and inventions, so had the Ford Motor Company Ltd. in 1928. As Ford of Canada had wholly-owned subsidiaries in its territories, so Ford of England would own the majority of stock in the continental companies.*

In short, there would be three manufacturing centers for the Model A: Windsor, Dagenham, and Dearborn, and each would have a group of foreign assembly plants and marketing companies.[10]

The prospectus for the Ford Motor Company Ltd. stock flotation was issued on December 7, 1928. "It was the quickest big flotation that I've ever heard of," remarked Sir Stanford Cooper at a later date. The other continental issues soon followed. In all countries the demand for the 40 per cent which most companies offered to the public was astounding. Brokers had to ration the shares. No one could buy any stock of the American Ford Motor Company, but here was Ford stock they *could* buy. Everyone wanted to partake of the profits of the fabulous business. To be sure the distribution was not always as general as Ford had envisaged, nor did the nationals of a given country always acquire the shares. In England a good many Americans managed to displace British investors; in Germany, as will soon appear, there was no popular distribution. But in general Ford was credited with good intentions, and the effect upon the public was encouraging.

For the new companies in England and on the continent Perry found a galaxy of wealthy, distinguished directors: bankers, lawyers, businessmen, former government officials, and even one farmer. He seemed to collect celebrities as easily as a television star collects autograph seekers. In England, he procured for his board Lord Illingworth, director of the National Provincial Bank; Sir Roland Kitson, Director of the Bank of England; and Sir John T. Davies, Director of the Suez Canal Company. In France, Maurice Dollfus, a banker and Hispano-Suiza director, and Jean Charles Charpentier, director of the Crédit Mobilier Français, decorated the Board.

For Germany, Henry Ford asked Perry to find "the best lawyer, the best farmer, and the best industrialist" in the country. For the lawyer, Perry chose Dr. Heinrich Albert, who had acted as counsel for

---

* There was no sign at this time that the public would be permitted to buy any stock of Canadian subsidiaries in India, Australia, South Africa and Malaya. The 40 per cent participation in European countries was strictly a feature of the reorganization on that continent.

195

the Ford Motor Company and other American concerns in Germany. Dr. Albert had visited the United States on a mission during World War I; he had also served in the cabinet of Wilhelm Cuno when the latter headed the Weimar Republic. The farmer Perry found was Alwin Schurig. However, most notable of the German board members was Dr. Karl Bosch, general manager of IG Farbenindustrie. Ford in Germany was the merest midget compared with this powerful firm. Bosch agreed to serve on the Ford directorate only if Edsel Ford would join the Board of the new American subsidiary of IG Farben. In Germany no public issue of Ford stock was made. IG Farben took a block of 15 per cent, and 25 per cent went to Ford dealers, personnel, and other selected individuals.*

Among the notable directors for Ford companies were August Philips in Holland, a prominent industrialist; in Belgium, Camille Gutt, later to head the International Monetary Fund; and Count Carl Moltke, former Danish Minister of Foreign Affairs, in Denmark. Perry himself became chairman of every board except the Swedish, while Sorensen and Edsel Ford became directors of all the companies. (Henry Ford sat on the English Board only.)

By the time of the first annual meeting of the Ford Motor Company Ltd. on March 7, 1930, Perry could report that "the continental companies (with the exception of the Italian company) have been reorganized . . . and 40 per cent of each Company's interest has been disposed of in the country where it is incorporated." [11]

From the start the direction of the subordinate companies and the handling of dividends from them promised to make difficulties. To separate the extensive undertakings of the English company from the administration of those in other countries, Perry late in 1929 set up the "Office of Sir Percival Perry" to deal with the latter. Likewise, taxes threatened to devour the profits rolling into England, for each continental nation taxed the Ford affiliate, and England proposed to tax again the profits which were transmitted to Dagenham. Accordingly on January 2, 1930, Perry formed a holding company in the little state of Liechtenstein. It would receive the dividends of the various European

---

* Some writers on Ford have eyed with suspicion the Ford–IG Farben link and have suggested a "strange working agreement." No evidence of this exists. Ford knew that Bosch could give helpful advice and valuable prestige and apparently sought his cooperation for this reason.

companies and protect the English company from double taxation. An immediate saving of $13,200 was made on the Dutch dividend. However, five months later the Société d'Investissements Ford was set up in Luxembourg and replaced the Liechtenstein unit. This new holding company acquired Dagenham's stock in six of the continental subsidiaries and accumulated dividends, which they declared.[12]

3

Before the end of 1928 Perry with Sorensen's cooperation was giving vigorous direction to the reorganization—the re-establishment of the Cork plant as a tractor producing center, the building of Dagenham, and the revitalization of the continental European companies.

As to tractors, when manufacture of the Fordson was stopped at the Rouge plant early in 1928, both Henry and Edsel expected to resume later with an improved design.* This was undoubtedly the "new" tractor that Ford discussed with Dulanty, the Irish trade representative, in London. By summer it was apparent that no such machine would materialize in the foreseeable future, but Perry surveyed the Cork plant, and reported on its advantages. Particularly, it had a good foundry, which could be used in the production of tractors. (No longer would this be needed for car parts, for under the new plan the parts would be made in England. If tractors were not to be made at Cork, the foundry would stand idle.)

These facts were borne in on Henry and Edsel and Sorensen. Perry, who had found the Fordson so useful in 1917–1918, was still a believer in the machine. It was popular in Europe. It had already been produced in Cork from 1919–1922. He favored resuming production there. Henry Ford, always hopeful of establishing an industrial center in Ireland, approved. Thus, Cork was chosen to make Fordsons for world markets (though certainly the Irish factory could not have turned out tractors as cheaply as could Dearborn). Perry and Sorensen assembled the manufacturing machinery and dispatched it to Ireland, where the first shipment arrived on November 7, 1928. In late 1928 and early 1929 Sorensen also sent over a dozen American experts to work with E. L.

---

* The reason generally given for stopping production was to make room for the Model A. New facilities would thus be needed for the new tractor.

Clarke, manager of the Cork plant. It was a strong team, and Clarke needed it.

A deluge of orders, especially for spare parts, awaited fulfillment, and he lacked knowledgeable workmen to man the factory. His was a stiff race against time. In January 1929 he reported to Perry that "we have made our first small shipment of tractor service parts." By March the Irish company was "making service shipments to all European branches, South America, one large shipment to the United States, another one being packed, and have started on the Russian order." (The largest tractor orders were from Russia for service parts.) So great was the pressure on the plant that production began without a roof over a number of the machines. The men worked in the rain. One employee recalls that "over the machines, we built 'dog houses' of tarred felt to keep the water out." By the end of 1929, a total of 9,686 tractors had been produced and shipped to twenty-five countries, among them Morocco, Canada, China, and Chile. To the United States Clarke had sent a total of 1,502 units.[13]

Ireland was a sideshow, although an important one, in comparison with Dagenham. The building of this plant loomed up as a great height the English company would have to climb before it could begin its new life. From the start the project was a joint Anglo-American venture, for it had been agreed that that center would be a smaller Rouge. Sorensen took an active but advisory part in the work, with H. B. Hanson as his representative at the site. Hanson had been responsible for the construction and layout of the Rouge buildings, to which Albert Kahn had given final architectural form. For the British A. R. Smith supervised the entire operation, with Charles Heathcote & Sons as architects and J. H. Boyd as construction engineer; the American William Squire, a specialist in layout and machine tools, soon joined the group. As Smith put it, Squire quickly became "my right hand man," taking on numerous additional duties. A number of other Americans were helpful at Dagenham: A. M. Wibel, Archibald Johnston, Mead Bricker, and D. L. Newkirk among them.

Smith remarked concerning the international team work: "Boyd worked in collaboration with Hanson [who] played a very great part in the general structure of the buildings but had nothing to do with the equipment used in them. . . . He was an ideal man to work with; he knew his stuff; he would very soon see that anything we wanted to make as a deviation from the American plan was justified." But as to equipment, the Rouge was a 2,000,000 car a year factory and Dagenham a 200,000 one. "If you make millions of things you want different equipment than if you are making thousands." Here Squire was invaluable, for he knew the entire range of machine tools and other factory equipment and could select unerringly what Dagenham needed. "I could not pay a great enough compliment to Squire," recalled Smith. "To me he always stands mountain high in what this company achieved." [14]

Obviously the great center would not rise in a day, nor easily. "Even if we commenced right away," wrote Perry to Sorensen on August 7, 1928, "it will be at least two years before we are in production there." Several weeks later (August 24) he complained that the property had been acquired "without taking any competent technical advice as to its suitability, e.g., foundations, water supply, drainage, levels, etc." Perry employed experts to check on such matters, and they sank holes, drove piles, and took soil samples with discouraging results. "The land is way below the level of the adjoining River Thames, and the dumped portion contains enormous holes such as you might expect in any rubbish heap." (To his dying day Perry lamented the defects of the Dagenham terrain and sighed for lost Southampton like a man who mourns a beautiful fiancée who died before he could marry her.) Nevertheless he worked diligently. His fears as to the character of the subsoil were fully justified. At enormous expense Ford had to sink 22,000 piles for the foundation, most of them 47 feet long by 14 inches square and reinforced with steel. Concrete was then poured on the upper surface. The factory was finally built on a kind of concrete raft, anchored by the piles.

Construction at Dagenham began on May 16, 1929, after Edsel Ford had cut the turf of the site with a silver spade. (The spade bent, but Edsel straightened it and lifted the sod.) From that time forward the complex of factory buildings began to rise impressively. The plant included coke ovens, a power house, a blast furnace, a foundry, a high line for the reception and distribution of raw materials, factory units for the making of parts, and an assembly building. Sorensen was frequently at the site, speeding the work, and responding to calls for help. Perry followed the construction closely and took pleasure in bringing his house guests out at five or six in the morning to appraise progress—the best time, he declared, for observation. The whole work force was aware of the importance of its task and was prepared to push ahead briskly. "It was easier to build Dagenham than to get my house painted," recalled A. R. Smith. "Everyone was keen and eager." [15]

In the summer of 1929, while piles were still being driven, Sorensen and Perry made a tour of Europe, considering sites for new assembly operations, and discussing their layouts and capacities. They made tentative plans for such factories in Rotterdam, Antwerp, Cologne, Gydnia, and Livorno. They also planned a new headquarters building for the Swedish Ford Company. This was the trip that eventually led the two to Russia (see Chapter X) but the time spent in the rest of Europe was much greater, and the results were momentous. Everywhere Sorensen saw a promise of big things to come. Volume shipments of Model A were coming in or were being awaited with eagerness. "The car has a great reputation everywhere," he wrote to Edsel on August 16.[16]

4

"While this Company has had its Head Office in the Dominion of Canada for approximately twenty-five years," ran a letter from W. R. Campbell to his shareholders on March 15, 1929, "and derives all its revenues from business in Canada and in the British Overseas Dominions, only a comparatively small per cent of the Company's shares are actually held within the Dominion of Canada." Campbell deplored this fact as "a serious handicap in many ways" and now announced a startling remedial action. (During March he himself assumed the office of president, an evidence of growing Canadian influence in the company. It was a post McGregor had never held.)

The plan Campbell put into action provided for a twenty to one stock split and an increase in company shares from 70,000 at $100 par value to 2,000,000 (1,900,000 Class A non-voting and 100,000 Class B voting). These new shares would have no par value. Any stockholder at the time of the split would receive 19 Class A shares and 1 Class B share for every original share he held, and could also buy two additional Class A shares at $20.00 each. In addition, the public would be offered 100,000 Class A shares at $30.00 each. Prospective purchasers were reminded that since 1904 Ford-US had assisted the Canadian company in every possible way and that "production at the present time averages in excess of 600 motor units per day, which constitutes a record in the history of the Company's operations." [17]

No less in Canada than in the United States was this the era of stock booms. Doctors, small shopkeepers, office workers, teachers, and all persons who had any savings, were investing them in securities. Ford-Canada's March 1929 offering was among the last made by big Canadian companies. The stock was snapped up as fast as it was put out; optimism soared unfettered. Unlike many issues offered that year, this was a sound investment, but it too would be affected by the events of the coming months and years.

The split, the increase in and the reclassification of shares, and the offer of an additional block to the public were in part devices to get more Canadian shareholders. They also provided the company with extra capital. Finally, they were designed to secure control of Canadian operations by Dearborn. Edsel Ford in the spring of 1930 would propose to trade Class A stock for Class B on a basis of three shares for two, and as a result American Ford interests by summer held almost half of the voting stock.[18] *

While Model A sales were mounting north of the United States, they were also rising in Latin America and the Far East.

Although in 1928 the volume of Model A deliveries to these regions combined had been only a little less than those made to the Western world, Ford executives made no broad plan for their increase such as was being evolved for England and Europe. Latin America with its jungles, its high peaks, its cattle ranges, and its coastal cities was not like Europe an easy region to organize for production and trade. Perry, manufacturing cars in England, had at hand coal, iron, and steel, skilled labor, subsidiary industries—in fact, a developed economy. Nothing comparable existed in Latin America. "Argentina is the most important automotive market in South America," stated a United States Department of Commerce Report in 1929. Ford recognized this, for its branch in that

---

* F. G. Batters, who assisted with the reclassification, split, and offerings stated to one of the authors that to get more Canadian stockholders was the chief reason for the action. However, W. R. Campbell wrote E. G. Liebold (Henry Ford's secretary) on June 21, 1929 that the alterations in the capital structure were made because "from a strictly financial view the Canadian Company passed out of the status of what was intended under the original agreement of 1904. . . . . The intention is, without any financial benefit accruing to the Ford family, to return to them the voting control originally contemplated in the agreement of 1904."

country sold 26,207 units for that year. Yet this volume did not warrant a manufacturing venture, since none of the main prerequisites for production existed.[19]

Again, communications between London and Antwerp, London and Copenhagen, or even London and Barcelona were relatively easy. In contrast, distances in Latin America were appalling. Although all were in Brazil, Rio de Janeiro, Recife, and Manaos were isolated from one another not only by thousands of miles but by poor transportation. And as to exporting from one nation to another, high tariff barriers and the absence of respectable roads and good rail service made this impossible. In time and convenience, Lima in Peru was closer to New York than to Buenos Aires, and Rio de Janeiro to Paris than to Valparaiso.

Each South American branch reported directly to Detroit, and each manager received instructions for his work. The São Paulo,* Santiago, Montevideo, and Buenos Aires branches all acted autonomously. In Detroit R. I. Roberge, thoroughly familiar with the company's operations abroad, received their monthly reports, their complaints, commentaries, and problems, and gave them an aloof but capable guidance. Roberge circulated the more important correspondence throughout the offices of Edsel Ford, John Crawford (his assistant), B. J. Craig (in finance), and Max Wiesmyer (who assisted with production problems).

Yet if they lacked a Dagenham, the Latin American branches shared fully in the spirit of expansion that characterized 1929. Everywhere plans developed for new ventures. W. C. Cowling, visiting the Argentine in 1929, endorsed F. F. Griffith's plan for a new factory there. Kristian Orberg got a similar authorization for a plant in São Paulo. Edsel Ford and Crawford approved Adrian Lajous' proposal for an assembly operation in Mexico. Meanwhile the sales of Model A in all the American countries were sensational. In no area in 1929 or 1930 did General Motors lead Ford. In 1930 in the Argentine Ford held 54.1 per cent of the car and truck registrations while its rival captured only 17.9 per cent. In Chile, where General Motors had established no branches, the figures were crushing: Ford 70.1 per cent of the market and its competitor 1.5 per cent. In Brazil, Ford had 58.4 per cent of the market, GM 17.1; in Uruguay, 66.1 per cent, GM, but 13.1.

The new Ford assembly plant in Japan (opened in 1929) sold 9,005

---

* The Brazilian branches at Rio, Pôrto Alegre, and Recife were coordinated from São Paulo.

vehicles in that year, practically an all-time high for the company and an evidence of the dynamic situation in the Far East. Since Japanese manufacturers were developing various types of local industry, Ford found itself able to purchase an increasing number of parts from native suppliers. There as in Latin America Ford sales surpassed those of General Motors. To the Orient in 1930 Henry Ford sent Cowling to investigate another avenue for expansion—he was to select if possible an assembly plant site in China.

Thus, mounting sales and enticing projects marked the Canadian, Latin American, and Far Eastern activities; in Near Eastern, African, and Australian areas the mood was also exuberant, for Ford opened a new assembly plant in Turkey in 1929, and would launch others in Port Elizabeth, South Africa, and Fremantle, Australia, during 1930. Had all the plans materialized, Ford would have had 36 assembly plants around the world, of which 15 would have been built in the years 1928–1931.* The Model A was to have every possible outlet. Actually, the car was selling better in many of these territories than in parts of Europe. Everywhere the future seemed full of promise; the new plants were the evidence of confidence in it.[20]

5

The stock market crash on Wall Street in October 1929 was the first rumble of a grim and continuing storm, but for more than a year it did not darken the skies of Dearborn. Henry Ford refused to believe in the oncoming depression, and in November and December of 1929 he, along with the chairman of Bethlehem Steel, the vice president of the National City Bank, and the president of the National Association of Manufacturers, issued statements expressing confidence in future prosperity. Ford did not curb his manifold activities, but raised wages and launched new construction programs. "The immediate cure for depression," he said a little later, "and by depression I mean a period when

---

* The following locations would have new plants, replacing former assembly plants: Buenos Aires, Mexico City, São Paulo, Yokohama, Cologne (also manufacturing), Rotterdam, Antwerp, Livorno, Port Elizabeth, Dagenham (also manufacturing), Shanghai, Gydnia, Istanbul. These new plants would be added to existing assembly operations at Recife, Rio, Pôrto Alegre, Santiago, Cork, Copenhagen, Barcelona, Manchester, Asnières, Windsor, Toronto, Winnipeg, Bombay, Calcutta, Madras, Colombo, Singapore, Geelong, Queensland, Granville, Adelaide.

men are out of work . . . is told in one word, 'quantity'—quantities of goods pushed out into the world."

All foreign expansion plans went forward. Dagenham rose day by day. Late in 1929 and early in 1930 the English company purchased 191 more acres of land, enlarging its Thames property to 501 acres. The Ford Motor Company Ltd. was at this time planning to occupy only 71 acres, and Perry felt that the Ford operations could not possibly require more than an additional 41 acres, which it had reserved. He favored turning the remainder over to an estate which would justify the building of roads and railways "on a larger and more adequate scale than we should feel was warranted were our own company requirements only to be considered." Eventually the English company itself set up the Industrial Estate of Dagenham and encouraged outside companies to lease and build upon the land. Thus the Briggs Manufacturing Company, which had for years supplied Ford-Dearborn with bodies, was persuaded to launch an English subsidiary there. Similarly the American firm of Kelsey-Hayes set up a plant on the estate to manufacture wheels. Other tenants, like the National Provincial Bank, moved in. As this industrial growth went forward, the London County Council was constructing in the town of Dagenham the largest housing project in England, providing 25,000 homes.[21]

Meanwhile the plans of Perry and Sorensen for continental factories were being expedited. In the fall of 1929 the Italian Ford company purchased 14 acres of land in Livorno, Italy, for an assembly plant. Late in 1929 and in 1930 it opened sales and service stations at Genoa, Naples, and Bologna. Land was acquired at Rotterdam for a Dutch plant. On October 18, 1929, Mayor Konrad Adenauer of Cologne offered favorable tax terms for six years "in case you purchase the property offered by the city of Cologne . . . for the purpose of assembling or manufacturing automobiles, trucks, and also tractors." He noted that the Ford company would agree "to take your workmen and office employees, as far as possible, from the district of the city of Cologne." E. C. Heine, the new German manager, wrote Perry: "I accepted the above offer." By this transaction Ford acquired 52 acres on the Rhine River.*

In Antwerp land for a new assembly plant had meanwhile been purchased, while in Sweden the construction of a headquarters building

---

* E. C. Heine had been appointed manager of the German Ford company in 1929, replacing George Carlson, who was promoted to general European manager. Carlson held the latter position for only a few months.

had been begun. In Poland there was no comparable activity, for the Polish government had refused to grant a permit for the erection of a plant.

As 1929 came to an end, prospects for the Ford business had never looked brighter. The best year to date in American automotive history, 1929, saw the industry producing almost 5.4 million units. Ford sales nearly equaled the combined sales of all of GM's U.S. products: the Chevrolet, Oldsmobile, Buick, Oakland, Pontiac, Cadillac, and La Salle. The Model A easily surpassed the Chevrolet, capturing 34 per cent of the American market while Chevrolet took 20 per cent.

American automobile production equaled 85.31 per cent of the world automotive output. To fill the demand abroad, the United States was exporting so many vehicles that the motor car ranked third among our exports, following raw cotton and machinery.

In England and on the continent, 107,113 Model A and Model AF cars and trucks and 3,954 tractors had been sold (note that the full total of 9,686 sold by Cork represented the world as against the European sale). These figures did not fulfill Perry's predicted 120,000 cars and trucks and 30,000 tractors, but at least in the car-and-truck category they almost matched his hopes. Ford-England still lagged behind Morris, Austin, and Singer, but when Dagenham came into production, Perry expected to turn the tables on his rivals. In Latin America and Asia, Ford sold 84,952 Model A cars and trucks during the year, and the Canadian company disposed of 85,135, a figure which included business done in South Africa, India, Australia, and other overseas countries.[22]

The early months of 1930 seemed to proclaim that the boom would continue indefinitely. At Cork the tractor plant had more orders than it could fill and in February alone assembled 3,026 machines. The foundry hummed with full-time activity making Fordson parts and castings for Ford-England. The plant now employed 7,000 men (Manchester used only 2,600) and was the largest employer of labor throughout the Ford overseas empire. Aside from the railroads, it used more workers than any other company in the Irish Free State.

But the tractor situation was soon to take a turn for the worse, to be described in Chapter XI. Meanwhile the American Congress had been debating the tariff question, and in June 1930 passed the notorious Smoot-Hawley bill which erected a high wall against imports. Ford had vigorously opposed it from the start. He feared no competition from abroad. Furthermore, the bill promised to affect his business adversely in three ways. First, since he bought some parts abroad, it would force him to increase the selling price of the American Ford car. Second, he recognized that in order to buy American products foreign enterprises should be able to sell in the United States and get dollar exchange. The bill would make this difficult, and the foreign ability to buy Ford cars was therefore greatly reduced. Finally, and most important, foreign countries were almost sure to retaliate, and the high tariff barriers they would erect would make the task of selling the Model A abroad an all but impossible operation.

By the time Ford sailed for Europe on September 6, 1930 to survey progress there, the tractor operation had sadly altered in character, and the effects of the Smoot-Hawley bill were beginning to be felt in various ways that will be noted later. A blind man would have sensed danger, but Ford ignored all unpleasant occurrences and gave his full attention to his growing European domain. On September 13 he surveyed progress at Dagenham and according to Perry seemed "very pleased." The great plant was no longer foundations, but roads, walls, and half-completed buildings, and as Perry wrote Wibel, "the transformation is wonderful." Ford later told some of the British contractors: "You do not need to send to America to learn how to do good work," which was high praise from him.

From England he crossed to France and went on to Germany, and on October 2 laid the cornerstone of the new Cologne factory. By this time it was clear that Ford would have to manufacture in Germany, but this necessity harmonized with his idea that America should aid all nations industrially. Asked if he thought that hard times would diminish the buying power of the Germans, he retorted stubbornly:

> I don't see any hard times. The people look well fed and busy. Everywhere I have been I have seen people working, even little children. . . . But what Europe needs is leaders. What is a leader, anyhow? It is a man who visualizes what the people want and goes ahead and produces it.

This comment, which might have been interpreted as praise of Hitler, was ominous in view of events to come. In recent elections the National Socialist party had emerged as the strongest single party in the Reichstag. Also ominous, and quite ignored by Ford, was the competition which his company faced in Germany, particularly from General

Motors, which in 1929 had purchased Opel AG, the largest producer of automobiles in the country. Making a Chinese copy of the 4 h.p. Citroën, this company, as in earlier years, led German sales in 1930 with 24,000 units. Ford was second (11,150), but hoped to forge ahead once its Cologne plant was ready to produce.[23] Ford's operation in Germany was far smaller than in England, while GM had its main investment in Opel rather than Vauxhall.

From Cologne Ford took his way to Rotterdam to lay the cornerstone of the new Dutch plant. Here town officials in tall hats and tails assembled for the ceremony on October 3. G. J. J. Both, manager of Ford-Holland, drove his eminent guest around before the ceremony. As they circled the square they could see the crowd gathering and the foundations of the new Ford building.

"Where is the water?" Ford asked.

Both explained that there was water half a mile away, and that Ford had the best of facilities.

"No water, no plant," Ford replied. "Drive on."

He would not participate in the ceremony, and Both had to tell the crowd to go home. Ford-Holland abandoned its Rotterdam project, and eventually the city of Amsterdam offered a splendid location on the waterfront, where in 1932 a new Dutch plant was opened. Ford had decreed some time earlier that all plants must be on the water for the easy reception of parts and the dispatch of their products; in this unhappy episode he showed that he meant what he said.

From Rotterdam Ford went to the Hague, then back to England. Here his "Detroit of Europe" was daily growing toward completion. At Dagenham, reviewing his European travels and the reports of activity in the Scandinavian countries, Ford could see the pattern of the European project. Changes had already begun that were likely to alter the pattern—in Italy the future looked dark, and in France and Germany conditions would be very different from what Ford and Perry had imagined. Yet to Ford, impatient of depressions and unwilling to recognize "impossible" situations, the outlook seemed good. As a matter of fact, in 1930 his company was once more ahead of GM in total sales.[24]

Around the world the Model A still rode the wave of success. Ford had underwritten that success with a bold construction program, which would soon appear in tangible plants linked together by shrewd financial commitments.

10
Marriage of Convenience

The Communist regime in Russia had made a decision to enter the field of motor car production and proposed to erect a plant "for the manufacture of 100,000 automobiles annually," as their representative in the United States, Valery I. Meshlauk, wrote to Edsel Ford on May 6, 1929. "Owing to the high standard of your machine," he stated in the same letter, "and the popularity it enjoys at the present time in Soviet Russia, we are considering the manufacture at such a plant of your Model A automobile, with such improvements as may be introduced in the future."

He asked for the Ford Motor Company's assistance, and got it. On May 31 a contract was signed between the Supreme Council of National Economy of the USSR and the Amtorg Trading Corporation on the one hand and the Ford Motor Company on the other. It provided for a Model A plant in Russia and the sale to the Union of Soviet Socialist Republics of 72,000 Ford vehicles in the next four years. It was an extension of Ford activity abroad that confirmed Henry Ford's expectations as to the possibilities of his car in foreign trade.[1]

2

The richest capitalist in the world had made a compact with a government as yet unrecognized by the United States, which was also the proclaimed arch foe of capitalism and dedicated to its destruction. To understand this action it is necessary to consider briefly the relationship of the Ford company with Russia, beginning almost a decade prior to the communist revolution.

Before World War I the Ford company, as previously noted, had maintained a distributor in the Czar's European territory. This distributor had built up an expanding business for the Model T, so that by the start of the war, the Russians were quite familiar with the insuppressible Lizzie.[2] In July 1916 Gaston Plantiff, the New York branch manager, wrote from Stockholm to Henry Ford's administrative secretary in Detroit, "In Russia alone, Liebold, in ten years, once we get our factories started there, in automobiles . . . we will do nearly as much as we are doing in America today." The ledger books of Ford-England gave support to Plantiff's prediction, for of all European markets the Russian had shown the most rapid growth.[3]

Then in March 1917 came the revolution. From November of that year, when the Bolsheviks seized power, until the spring of 1920 the Red and White armies were locked in a convulsive civil war in which the motor car had no significant role. From the time they came to power, the Soviet leaders had controlled the heart of the country. For a while they lost most of Siberia to Kolchak, but eventually captured and shot him. Meanwhile, neither Denikin, striking toward Moscow from the Crimea, nor Yudenich, moving toward St. Petersburg from Estonia, ever won more than minor victories. Even by early 1919 Soviet agents were active in Western Europe and the United States, seeking trade and credit. While some of the Allies were still maintaining troops on Russian soil as well as assisting the Whites, the representatives of the USSR tried to tempt private firms in these lands to sell to them.

A Russian commercial bureau was established in New York, and in the spring of 1919 approached such business leaders as Henry Ford and Frank Vanderlip. The Lusk Committee, then trying to ferret out American communist activity, raided this "embassy" (it had no diplomatic status since the United States had not recognized Red Russia), and found some interesting correspondence. On April 9 the Russians had asked for a meeting with Henry Ford. They stated, "We believe we could make you understand that Soviet Russia is inaugurating methods of industrial efficiency compatible with the interests of humanity." Frank Campsall, Ford's assistant secretary, had agreed to make an appointment for E. G. Liebold to see the secretary of the mission.

If the Lusk Committee had had access to Ford Motor Company correspondence it would have uncovered more startling evidence of the company's relationship to Russia. On March 14, 1919 a contract was drawn up between a Petrograd firm, Ivan Stacheeff & Co., and the Ford company, by which 400 Ford touring cars were to be bought on terms by the Stacheeff organization, with further purchases contemplated.

Edsel Ford on March 31 advised R. S. Neely, manager of Ford's foreign department in New York, "to keep in as close touch with Russia through various channels in New York as is possible." Actually, during the two years covered by this contract only 238 cars were purchased, and Ford was left as creditor to the amount of $4,851.11.[4] *

In pursuing such activity the Ford company hoped to re-establish itself in what had been a most promising territory. With a striking disregard for politics and an incredible naïveté, the company sought trade where it existed. To be sure, the Bolsheviks announced their hostility to capitalism, had expropriated foreign property during the Revolution, but they had no automobile factories and no means of establishing any. For a time they must buy from others, and Ford stood ready to sell.

If the company had ever been disposed to advertise its Russian activities, the actions of the Lusk Committee served warning that it should be discreet. It was.** But in Henry Ford's magazine, the *Dearborn Independent,* Russia in 1919 received considerable attention. Two articles by a Communist in defense of the Soviet regime were published; one "White" denunciation of it appeared. The magazine itself never praised Red rule or doctrine. However on April 26, 1919 it printed an account of "Russian Trade and Industrial Opportunities," which assumed that private firms could sell to one or both warring factions, and declared in conclusion: "What Russia really wants is small mobile tractors . . . together with new modern agricultural machinery and implements on a large scale, sent with the necessary number of instructors who could show [that country] . . . how to use and operate these agricultural tractors, machines, and implements." Any concern which meets this need "would immediately conquer the Russian market." The opportunities, the author concluded, were boundless. Meanwhile, according to L. A. Martens, a Soviet representative in New York, E. G. Liebold was carrying on conversations with the Communists along these very lines.

During this period, the American press followed events in the war-torn nation with keen interest, but these articles in the *Dearborn Inde-*

---

* It seems that the Ivan Stacheeff & Co. contract was with a private party, and was not a government-sponsored contract. Later, toward the end of 1920, correspondence relating to this agreement was handled through the Communist Peoples Industrial Trading Corporation in New York. (See data in Acc. 49, Bx. 1.)

** As early as March 31, 1919 Edsel Ford instructed R. S. Neely that the agreement with Ivan Stacheeff & Co. was to be kept confidential "for the present." (See note 5.)

pendent clearly indicate that Ford was similarly alert to what was happening and, more important, was seeking with an open mind for the best way of making a profitable contact with that nation—if necessary through the Soviet regime. This opportunism becomes more comprehensible when certain utterances of Henry Ford himself are noted.

In each issue of the *Dearborn Independent* Ford was the nominal author of "Mr. Ford's Page," a contribution put into final form by W. J. Cameron, but always composed either after talks with Ford or read and approved by him. Direct references to Russia and Bolshevism appearing in this department took for granted the complete absurdity of Red theory and practice. But on March 8, 1919, appeared several sentences which could be applied to Russia (although that country was not mentioned) and were to describe Ford Motor Company policy with respect to it for the next fifteen years. They referred to lands that were undeveloped industrially and ran:

> We ought to wish for every nation as large a degree of self-support as possible. Instead of wishing to keep them dependent on us for what we manufacture, we should wish them to learn the arts themselves, to clothe and feed and house themselves and build up a solidly founded civilization.

> When every nation learns to produce things which every nation can produce, then we shall be able to get down to a basis of serving each other along those special lines in which there is no competition.

Eleven years later Ford was to apply this philosophy specifically to Russia. In 1919 it was not an expedient and might even have been a dangerous thing to say. But if we accept that statement as applying to the Soviet Union, we can see that something larger than immediate profit (although undoubtedly that was important) motivated Ford in his attitude toward Russia.[5]

Ford was to make another significant comment that ties in with his attitude toward undeveloped nations. A number of years later he wrote that the old patterns of world life were breaking up and that new ones were replacing them. "Well, it need not alarm anyone. . . . You can sit and look at the fading out of all that made the old era, and you can wail about the calamity to come, or you can stand up and watch the new era come in, looking for your place in its ranks." This was no implied praise or acceptance of Bolshevism; Ford was convinced that in the end it would go under. But his remarks show that, always a believer in change, he recognized it now as a ferment in the life of mankind which must be accepted.[6]

After the expiration of the Ford-Stacheeff contract in 1921, which was not renewed, the company continued to trade with Russia. For a time the Allied American Corporation of New York acted as an agent, it appears in the correspondence for 1923. This firm, working amid difficulties, made some progress. Its Moscow office dealt with cars, trucks, and tractors, and translated Ford manuals into Russian. However, it seems to have ceased its representation of the Ford Motor Company in 1924. The Amtorg Trading Corporation, incorporated on May 27 of that year, took over the business. It became the official commercial arm of the Russian government.

In 1922 Ford shipped 585 units to Russia: 261 cars, 56 trucks, and 268 tractors; in 1923, 624: 30 cars, 192 trucks, 402 tractors. Then as private agencies faded out and the USSR dealt directly with Ford, the total leapt to 3,323 for 1924: 61 cars, 154 trucks, and 3,108 tractors. The increase probably reflected the greater confidence of the Russians in dealing directly with Ford but also a decision to mechanize their farms and use the tractor as an instrument of propaganda. The peak year of 1925 would see a total of 11,140 units bought: 162 cars, 463 trucks, and 10,515 tractors. In the first two months of 1926, Ford sold to Russia 5,432 tractors, and for the rest of the year another 30 units.[7]

3

The Ford hesitation about publicity as to the company's dealing with the Russians in 1919 did not exist in the mid-1920's, even though the United States government still looked askance at such trade and America still did not recognize the USSR. "Russia Orders 900 Tractors for Farm Use" ran a box head on the first page of the *Ford News* for August 15, 1924. Subsequent orders received equally flourishing announcements. The popularity of the Fordson tractor in Russia had mounted in the 1920's, and in the fall of 1923 a Fordson had gone on its own power from Rostov in the Ukraine to an agricultural exhibition in Moscow. In village after village excited Russian peasants had clustered about the "little iron horse." The early part of the decade had seen the Fordson outselling all other tractors in Russia at a rate of two to one.

The Russians, however, were not content to continue to import and became eager to build their own factories. Accordingly in 1923 they established in Leningrad a plant to produce a replica of the Fordson tractor. This was the old Putilov works, and they blandly called the product a Red Putilov. They claimed to have centers for tractor distribution at Vladivostok, Odessa, Moscow, and Leningrad. Similarly, they listed various schools for tractor and implement operation and for maintenance.

The façade of accomplishment was imposing on paper, and the Russians were evidently determined to enlarge their activity and hoped for assistance from the Ford Motor Company. As a means of exploring the general situation, they invited a Ford delegation to visit the USSR in 1926.

The company now had 20,000 tractors in Russia and was eager to see how the machines were performing, how the Russian Fordson schools were organized and conducted, what the prospects might be for a further expansion of automotive activity in the vast Soviet territories, and what the social and political conditions might be under which work could be conducted. Five executives were chosen to represent the company interest; they sailed from New York on April 3, 1926, accompanied by a contingent of workmen to assist in the assembly of machines and the setting up of exhibits.[8]

In the Archives at Dearborn, Michigan, there exists a 266-page report made by this delegation. A foreword headed "SPECIAL ATTENTION" indicates the difficulties under which the trip was made. This foreword urges that the report itself be kept under lock and key and be examined "only by responsible and interested officials within the Company." The reasons advanced for this exhortation are that if the main document fell into the hands of Russian agents its frankness might well result in making the delegation members *personae non gratae* and perhaps subject them to "prison terms and even violence" if they again visited Russia. In addition "the Company's business relationships might be seriously affected in a market which today shows so much promise of future development."

These dangers no longer exist, and the delegation's account may be fully examined. The five men traveled 6,000 miles within Russia, visited factories and tractor centers, held exhibits, wrote a frank but tactful letter-report to the Soviet government, and brought back a rather astounding picture of Russia's first faltering steps in industry.

They found a nation eager to accord them honor as emissaries of

Henry Ford, now regarded as the man best fitted to guide the Russians on the great industrial adventure to which they were passionately dedicated. The people everywhere, and particularly all officials, were converts to the religion of planning. The delegation found that they "have gone mad entirely on the subject of charts, diagrams, mathematical tables, etc." which they seemed to regard as carrying them more than half way toward accomplishment. Charts for tractor repair shops, schools, and inspections per month by region were triumphantly exhibited at Moscow to the Americans, who began to wonder for what purpose they had come to Russia!

They were quickly disabused. As they traveled they looked in vain for the schools and shops that matched what they had seen on paper. In the Ukraine, where the tractor was most in use, they "were unable to find a single Fordson repair shop worthy of the name." The same situation existed in other districts, although "one fair repair shop" was operating at Rostov. The delegation set up a successful exhibit of Ford tractors, trucks, and cars at Tiflis, which pleased the Russian authorities, then returned to Moscow and made excursions to various industrial centers, and helped to improve schools and tractor repair stations.

They saw the Putilov works at Leningrad, where a copy of the Fordson was produced (at a cost of $2200 a unit and an alleged rate of 2 a day, which was actually 20 a month!). They visited Russia's single truck factory, the AMO-Fiat plant in Moscow, where the management claimed to have produced 35 trucks during the preceding month—a record. They also saw plants manufacturing such products as tires, electric fixtures, agricultural implements, and locomotives. The machine tools often seemed to be modern, the layout logical, but production lagged in an atmosphere of dirt, workers' committees, laziness, and poor supervision. Many of the employees had had experience in the United States, but only in subordinate positions. The delegation was shocked at the poor performance, lack of organization, and dominance of the political in the factory.*

---

* It was little wonder, for Stalin's speech of May 1925 before the 14th Congress of the Russian Communist Party shows what was most important to him. "In Ford's factories," he declared, "all the work is done with great precision, and there is perhaps less peculation than in some of our State factories; but Ford's factories are working for the capitalists, are working for Ford, whereas our enterprises, where there is a good deal of peculation sometimes, and where the technique of the enterprise is often far from satisfactory, are none the less working for the proletariat." (See note 9.)

The Americans wrote an honest but tactful letter to the government stressing the dangers of poor driver instruction, the lack of well-run repair shops, the failure to procure spare parts, the careless unloading of tractors (resulting in crucial damage), the failure to use proper oils, and in general the absence of system in tractor maintenance. They advocated that instead of using motorcycles, officials visiting repair stations use Ford cars, which could carry repair equipment. They tried to get this report translated and distributed; finally it was translated, but the Russians prevented its dissemination, as it reflected upon their official handling of the tractor.

The delegation fully realized the hazards of doing business with Russia. They advised against credit or a Ford factory (at Ford expense), for it might eventually be seized by the government. But they advocated Ford representation in Russia—perhaps a service plant or parts depot and a mechanics' instruction school. There was a poor prospect for car sales, although the Model T performed best of any vehicle on the bad Russian roads, and the Ford reputation was high. Tractor prospects were bright. Of 25,000 in Russia, more than 20,000 were Fordsons.[9]

4

The visit of the delegation provided an occasion for further Russian effort to procure American aid. Even while the Ford representatives were in Russia Paul J. Ziev, president of Amtorg, the Russian trading organization, was planning a trip to the United States for the purpose of getting better credit terms and persuading Dearborn to set up a service depot in the Black Sea area. The delegation reported his intentions, warning the company that even if he made acceptable proposals "we should not labor under the impression that all will be smooth sailing." For example, impossible credit terms would probably be asked.

Even before the Ford officials had left for Russia the Ford Motor Company had agreed to accept 50 Russian students at the Henry Ford Trade School to study tractor manufacture, maintenance, and repair. They were due to arrive in June. This seems to have been the first group from the USSR to come to work in Dearborn, and they joined 360 other students of fourteen nationalities. These Russians were followed by many others, and doubtless several hundred persons in this manner gained intimate familiarity with Ford methods and helped to improve tractor manufacturing and servicing in the Soviet Union.

There is no evidence that Ziev achieved any results in 1927, but in February of that year Amtorg placed an order for an additional 3,500 tractors, raising the total of Fordsons sent to Russia to more than 24,000. Meanwhile reports came to the United States of the terrific influence Henry Ford was exerting on Russian industry. If his capitalist point of view was deplored, he had inspired a spontaneous enthusiasm close to a religious cult. In the engine shop at Kharkov, the work was "fordized," and quickly production was reported to be leaping upward. A bell factory introduced Ford routines, and at once raised its output sharply, while "substantial results" were achieved in the same manner in metallurgical factories in Leningrad. These events were reported by various people; but Maurice Hindus, a Russian-speaking expert on the Soviet system and author of several books about the USSR and the revolution, retailed them with pungent vigor in a magazine article, "Henry Ford Conquers Russia." He quoted the Russians as saying, "Do it the Ford way because it is the best way," and told how foremen, clerks, managers, and even chairmen of "trusts" were studying Ford "with as much zeal as Communists study Lenin." Communes adopted the name of Fordson, and Hindus found that ignorant peasants who had never heard of Stalin or Bukharin knew of the man who made the "iron horse." For a brief time Ford the arch-capitalist stood by the side of Marx and Lenin as one of the demigods of the revolution.[10]

Meanwhile, discussions on credit and on Ford's building a factory in Russia had apparently gone forward, but the report of the American delegation, backed by conversations with some of its members, killed progress in both these matters. Sorensen learned that commissars would police any plant Ford might build and told Bredo Berghoff of the delegation, "Well, that settles that," dismissing it as a possibility. Russian ideas of credit must also have seemed fantastic to Ford officials. The company was expected to build a factory and then await payment for its products over a period of years!

In 1928, the reader will recall, Fordson production stopped in Dearborn and in November of that year the machinery for its manufacture was sent to Cork, Ireland. The Irish Ford plant took over the Russian account, and when in 1929 it got into production it received large Soviet orders for both tractors and spare parts.

Eventually Henry Ford did offer to aid the Russians in building a tractor factory there. According to Liebold, Ford suggested to Amtorg representatives that they see Albert Kahn, Inc. (the Ford architects) and have that firm design a building for tractor production in Russia.

Kahn agreed to comply with Amtorg's request, and not long thereafter, on May 8, 1929, Henry Ford called in the architect. Sorensen, who was present, wrote Perry the next day that Ford had told Kahn that "he wants to help them [the Russians] in every way to see that this plant is properly laid out, and will give them everything they need." Sorensen continued:

> Mr. Ford's point is that the sooner we can get started in Russia industrially, the better it will be for us as well as for England, because they will draw on us for supplies of all kinds. The exchange of business is all he cares for. He doesn't care what is done to get this under way. His picture is that the quickest way to cure your feelings toward anybody is to fill them full of industry.

"This is certainly good logic," he added. He advised Perry: "This is a cue to us that we must pitch in and help them all we can."

Russians visited Cork to see tractor production methods there, but Perry had more hesitancy than Sorensen about this cooperation with alien ideologies. "It is the political aspect that worries me," he wrote Sorensen. "The Russians deliberately use every means in their power to sow dissension amongst the British working class," and he didn't want the seeds of Bolshevism planted in Cork. However, he would do the best he could to follow Dearborn instructions, and the Irish plant would certainly fill the Russian orders.[11]

5

On October 1, 1928 the First Five Year Plan of the Soviet Union was announced, which provided for heavy industry, increased coal and oil output, more electrical energy, and automobile, tractor, and machining plants. It heralded an industrialized Russia. The Soviets, however, recognized that they could not make these major strides forward on their own, and thus they entered into a large number of "technical assistance" agreements with American corporations and engineers. These agreements were all made at a time when the American government had not granted the Soviet government diplomatic recognition.

By the end of 1930, such large firms as Radio Corporation of America, Du Pont, Bethlehem Steel, General Electric, and Westinghouse had entered into contracts with the Russians. By the time Henry Ford was advising Albert Kahn to give the Soviets all possible help, he too had been negotiating to aid the Russians in building an automobile as well as a tractor industry.

The contract of May 31, 1929 referred to at the beginning of this chapter set forth the terms of the joint venture in the manufacture of motor vehicles. The contract is in the Ford Archives. It indicates that the Russians wanted to erect an automobile plant or plants for the manufacture in the USSR of passenger cars and trucks similar to the Ford Models A and AA. For the period of the agreement (nine years) Ford granted to the Soviets "an exclusive license to manufacture, use and sell in the USSR, as now constituted, under all present patents and future patents and inventions owned or controlled by the Company or its subsidiaries covering all materials and component parts or units of the Company's Model A cars and Model AA trucks." The Russians would have access to information and patents on equipment, tools, processes, and methods for producing these units.

The Ford company also agreed to supervise the building of plants and make detailed layouts for their equipment so as to provide a capacity of 100,000 units annually. Ford would furnish plans for the Models A and AA, and the Soviets were allowed (with prior consent of the company) to make modifications of the original designs to meet the needs of the Russian market.*

Technical personnel from Detroit were to advise and assist the Russians in preparing for manufacture, and it was agreed that up to 50 Russians per year could come to the Rouge plant to learn the "methods and practice of manufacture and assembly."

In return for all this, the Russians contracted to pay (1) the costs incurred by the company in preparing and furnishing the drawings, designs, models, and plans; (2) the salaries and expenses of company personnel working in Russia and Russians working in the Rouge; and (3) the actual cost of service (labor and overhead) rendered by company engineers. More important, as already noted, the Russians signed up to purchase from the company through Amtorg, within the next four years, the equivalent of 72,000 knockdown Ford cars and trucks, exclusive of tires (6,000 in the first year, 18,000 in the second, and 24,000 in the two subsequent years). They agreed that all parts purchased for repair or for assembly purposes outside the USSR in the next

* Only changes in chassis design required Dearborn assent, while changes in body design were to be sent to Dearborn for information purposes.

nine years would be procured from the Ford Motor Company. The price for the 72,000 units was to be factory cost plus 15 per cent, and the payment was to be made in cash.[12]

For the Russians the proposed automobile plants represented a giant industrial step forward. The USSR had no capacity for motor car production. The 1926 Ford delegation stated: "Only one truck and no automobiles are being manufactured in the Soviet Union at the present time." Stalin himself confessed in 1933 that prior to the First Five Year Plan (1928) "we had no automobile industry." Now, however, thanks to the cooperation of Ford, the nation could anticipate having facilities for producing cars in quantity. With the improvement in the Russian roads, the transportation system of the country would be immensely strengthened.

After the signing of the agreement, Meshlauk, as head of the Russian delegation, urged Sorensen, who found him likeable, cooperative, and knowledgeable, to come to Russia at once, see the chosen sites for the factories, and become familiar with industrial conditions in that country. Sorensen agreed to make the trip and, accompanied by Perry, reached Russia August 3 and arrived in Moscow on the 8th. The two saw the site for the main production plant—one that would be comparable to Dagenham—prepared at Nizhni Novgorod, some 300 miles east of Moscow on the Volga River. They viewed another location in Moscow where an assembly plant was planned. They also visited Leningrad and toured the Putilov tractor factory. Forgetting the report of the Ford delegation to Russia in 1926, Sorensen was astonished to see that the factory was building Fordson tractors.

"Where did you get hold of the design for this tractor?" he asked his host.

"We engaged some of the engineers that had worked in your tractor plant," was the reply he got. Actually the Communists had not only hired some Highland Park employees but had dismantled a Fordson, made drawings of the disassembled parts, and proceeded from that point forward. As Sorensen put it, "They had stolen everything they could of the tractor." Nonetheless the result was not very successful, and when Meshlauk called together the technical staff of the plant, Sorensen "gave them a thorough going over." He reports, "I really heaped coals of fire on their heads over the poor quality work they were doing," and he "offered to help them clear up the whole matter by sending them one of our experts." He arranged to have Peter McGregor, a tractor specialist, then at the Cork plant, lent to the Russian government.

On this trip Sorensen's main concern was to scrutinize the plans for the automobile factories. The Russians had resolved to model the chief one at Nizhni Novgorod on that in Dearborn. They would also have a small assembly operation in that city that could get into production rapidly. In addition, the Soviets also wanted an assembly plant for the Models A and AA in Moscow.

Sorensen recalls in his autobiography that he suggested to Meshlauk that the Russians produce the V-8, then in the early stages of development at Dearborn. But Meshlauk firmly insisted on using Model A, as being simpler. "[He] was right in rejecting my suggestion," Sorensen conceded later, after noting the difficulties the Russians encountered in producing the 4-cylinder, less complicated car. Perhaps also the Communist government was eager to get started and did not want to wait for the V-8.

One question that haunted Sorensen was the location of the raw materials that would be required for car production in the Soviet Union. "Where are these coming from?" he asked time and again. Finally he got an answer. "I learned that the iron ore came from the Ural mountains . . . a long way from Nijni Novgorod. . . . The coal that they proposed to use was just as far off in the opposite direction. . . . Other required materials like copper, lead, and manganese were likewise widely scattered." He could not help contrasting this condition with the position of American automotive plants, which had easy access to their iron ore, copper, coal, etc., and cheap transportation by water.[13]

Leaving the Soviet Union on August 14 after a wildly exciting week during which he and Perry were treated like emperors, Sorensen returned to Dearborn and attacked the really great problems discovered during the Russian adventure.

While he had been away, Ford had arranged to have Albert Kahn proceed with the designing of the factories. In mid-August Kahn mailed detailed drawings to Russia "so [they] can start before the cold weather." He sent drawings for an 80-car-per-day Moscow assembly plant, and in Dearborn Ford officials began placing orders for equipment for the 20-car assembly plant at Nizhni Novgorod. By this time there were already 30 Russians at the Rouge, giving their OK to the plans.

Amtorg had contracted with the Austin Company of Cleveland to supervise the construction of the giant Nizhni Novgorod production plant, and the Ford executives maintained contact with Austin officials.

In Dearborn, the Russian engineers occupied offices on the second story of a building on Miller Road. The structure was within the Rouge complex, and they had access to all the developments taking place there during the next six years (until 1935). So much a part of the Ford organization had they become that they actually had stationery printed with the Ford Motor Company address. In 1932 in the midst of the depression when Communist hunger marchers stormed the Rouge plant, the Russians blandly watched the demonstration from the capitalist citadel. The mob flung rocks at the Gate Four office building, and Harry Bennett wisecracked, "You're stoning your own fellows up there." But the Russian engineers—indifferent to the political implications—stayed on to continue their study of Ford methods at first hand. Their indoctrination in American technology undoubtedly had a profound influence, which spread beyond automotive practice to affect many other aspects of Soviet industrial performance.[14]

One of the American technicians who worked with the Russians at the Rouge and prepared for the shipment of jigs and tools to the Russian factories was Frank Bennett (no relation to Harry). He went to Russia, arriving New Year's Day, 1930, to work at Nizhni Novgorod, aiding in the plant construction.

Bennett had left Dearborn with a high sense of his mission. Henry Ford had said to him on his departure: "Mr. Bennett, when the first car comes off the assembly line, would you send us a cable? It means very much to this company."

Bennett soon discovered that he had a long task ahead of him. He arrived to find much of the machinery set up in the temporary factory. But it wasn't running. "It couldn't—only a short survey showed me that it wouldn't run." He worked diligently and with full authority, but he and his associates had to teach Russian workmen how to operate the unfamiliar and often complicated American machine tools. Some of the plant's officers who had worked in Detroit or Dearborn assisted him. Still, it was an exacting assignment, for if one small operation misfunctioned, the entire line was affected. The Russians had difficulty in understanding this. "They would put cars on and then they'd miss a part here and there."[15]

Before Bennett had come to Nizhni Novgorod, McGregor had arrived in the Soviet Union to study the Fordson operation. He was horrified at the conditions he found there and made a blunt report to the government. "If my boss owned or had charge of these works tomorrow," he stated roundly, "he would immediately call it to attention by shutting off power . . . until everybody in the plant . . . cleaned out everything from their office or department that is not used in the manufacture of the product of the factory. . . . You have enough cast iron and steel lying around the shop to build at least ten years' production of tractors." He advocated abolishing piece work, raising wages, and clearing out the bureaucratic confusion that paralyzed the factory like a disease. "I have met only one [official] in the place that seemed to have any initiative, and he cannot go ahead because the general system of getting work done is so bad that no speed can be put into it. For instance, . . . it takes from one to four weeks to get a blueprint made for the tracing. . . . In our American or Irish plants you can get a blueprint made and dried in less than five minutes."

If McGregor did not succeed in improving tractor production, it was not for want of the scope of his recommendations or their telling force, for they hit the target like so many successive bullets.[16]

At Nizhni Novgorod Bennett finally achieved steady operation and found himself a hero. The first car came off the small assembly line there in February 1930. Droves of Russians visited the plant to watch the miracle of continuous production. However, they regarded the accomplishment as mainly their own and made dazzling predictions for the future. A jubilant banquet was held, and Bennett was tossed in a blanket by his Russian associates. He still found it necessary to continue to supervise the operation, as the Russians were careless about details.

After completing his task at Nizhni Novgorod, he went on to Moscow and by September 1930 had the larger assembly line in that plant running smoothly. He was now eager to return home, but the Russians insisted on his taking a two-month vacation in Russia. Returning from the Crimea to Moscow, it dawned upon him why he had been detained. "They didn't want to let me go until they were sure the factory would run without my presence." When Bennett left Russia in February 1931 the two assembly plants were busy making cars from imported parts. The production plant of Nizhni Novgorod was still to be finished.

At this stage Ford had every reason to feel pleased with the arrangement he had made with the Russians. The latter had fully met their obligations in the first year, ordering more rather than less of the specified number of units.

"As to Russia's meeting of its financial obligations, we have neither complaint nor misgiving," Albert Kahn declared in December 1930 before a Cleveland engineering group. He continued:

> Our own attitude has been this—that we are not interested in their politics. . . . We feel as Mr. Ford so well expressed it, that that which makes for the upbuilding of Russia is bound to prove of benefit to all nations, America included. With this in mind, we believe it only right to help in whatever manner we can.

Ford was now preparing to supply the Russians with large quantities of tools, dies, jigs, fixtures, etc. for the new Nizhni Novgorod plant. Since the company was going to substitute the Model V-8 for the Model A, it could send the Soviets much of the used equipment that otherwise would have been discarded. H. L. Moekle in a memorandum dated April 3, 1931 noted that "it is believed that the value of equipment to be supplied by the Ford Motor Company may be as much as Three Million ($3,000,000) Dollars."

By this time the Russians had begun to feel the pinch of the depression and the contraction of international trade. They wanted to discuss credit terms, to which Roberge replied bluntly, "We would not be interested."

By the end of the second year of the contract (May 1931), it was clear that the Russians could not meet their obligations. They had not purchased the 34,000 units that they were to have bought by that date.[17]

Nonetheless their factory construction at Nizhni Novgorod continued. Ford's manager in Japan, Benjamin Kopf, visited the new plant on his return from Dearborn to the Far East in October 1931. He also had a chance to see the assembly unit in Moscow. Kopf found the Nizhni complex of buildings an "important undertaking" and noted that the Russians claimed it would have an annual capacity of 140,000 units (the initial plans had been for a potential of 100,000).

Kopf found the structures nearly completed and learned that the Russians thought they would be able to begin manufacture by the end of the year. "I should not be at all surprised if it takes them still longer," was his private appraisal. He saw a large number of men in Russia who had studied in Detroit, and he reported that the Nizhni plant manager "expressed his great appreciation of the valuable aid rendered by the

Ford Motor Company." Here also were many other foreigners, among them a group of German engineers. Kopf heard it rumored that 700 ex-Ford employees were being brought from the United States.

He noted with some amusement, "Where pure communism does not work successfully, it is discarded, and the Soviets have no compunction about approaching nearer and nearer to the capitalist system. . . . the Government is now enforcing piece work in all its factories. . . . The consequences sometimes are peculiar. For instance, the Moscow assembly plant is on piece work. As a result, there is no proper timing of operations. . . . I saw piles of frames with rear and front axles assembled, because the group working on frames, front and rear axles were able to do their work much quicker than the succeeding groups."

As for the quality of the Russian products, Kopf found it "simply awful." The paint was poor, "the enamel dirty and Phaeton tops, awful. However, as all units are supplied to Government departments or State enterprise, they do not have to worry about quality." [18]

At the end of January 1932, the big Soviet plant at Nizhni Novgorod turned out its first all-Russian Model AA unit. No Ford officials were on hand for the occasion. They learned the news from Amtorg personnel. The plant was shortly renamed the Gorky Automobile Works.

The depression had limited the Russians' ability to buy abroad. Kopf had noted that the Soviet Union would be one of the world's most important markets, were it not for the fact that they were unable to establish foreign currency credits to pay for cars and trucks.[19]

Despite the fact that the Russians were failing to live up to their 1929 contract with Dearborn, Sorensen still hoped that they might do better. He tried to sell to Russia the surplus inventories of the Model A's of Ford-Germany, urging upon Perry the need to expedite this matter. "We consider Russia one of our best customers," he wrote Perry in June 1932. "To date they have purchased 27,808 units from us." Then he added in a postscript, "Please help us keep this business." [20]

To do so proved to be impossible, for the Russians had no money to pay for the cars, and moreover they now had their own production plant, not an efficiently operated one, nor one large enough to meet all Russian needs, but at least a local source of vehicles.

As for the tractor, Ford had lost the market for it completely. When Fordson production moved to Cork, there was a time during which the

Ford organization could not fill any orders, for there was no output. International Harvester met the immediate demand. When Cork was prepared to produce, it had Russian orders but no satisfactory credit arrangements.

International Harvester was ready to give far better credit terms than Ford. Sorensen wrote Perry on July 13, 1931,

> We think you should let the Soviets understand very definitely that they cannot expect any assistance from you in securing credit. Do not let anyone around consider the question for a moment. If you will do this, we think that in time they will come around. If they need tractors so badly they can economize in other directions.

Sorensen was mistaken, and the Russians turned elsewhere. By this time, in addition to the Putilov plant in Leningrad that had turned out almost 10,000 Fordsons in 1929–1930, they had the Stalingrad tractor plant that started production June 16, 1930 (designed by Albert Kahn and supplied with equipment from 80 American companies), the Kharkov tractor plant, and had started on a giant tractor factory at Cheliabinsk. There was no further market for the foreign-built Fordson in Russia.[21]

By the time Ford's 1929 contract with the Russians had run four years—*i.e.,* to May 1933, the Russians had purchased only 7,142 cars, 21,050 trucks, and 159 Lincolns, along with a quantity of spare parts. This was less than half the quantity of vehicles they were obligated to take and represented a value of only $17,067,155.14 as against $33,600,900 worth of units originally promised.

On July 15, 1933 Roberge pointed out this failure to comply with the contract and asked in a later letter, "What may be expected from you in order to carry out the performance of the agreement?" He received no satisfaction. On November 16, 1933, President Franklin Delano Roosevelt recognized the government of Russia. By this date, however, Ford's adventure in cooperation with the Soviets had just about ended. Eventually, in the spring of 1935, his 1929 contract was canceled. The Russians continued to buy in small quantities and to demand better terms. Since the Ford Motor Company had counted on the sale of 72,000 cars, it was left considerably out of pocket as a result. By the end of 1935, the relationship between the company and Amtorg seems to have shrunk to a negligible one, and the Russian engineers had been asked to leave the Rouge plant.[22]

6

Ford had never wavered in his determination to assist the Russians. True, he had realistically refused to invest in a plant in Russia and had denied Amtorg the long-term credit it desired. But he had generously helped the Soviets to help themselves. He had made available his patents and methods of work, furnished supervisory personnel, and had paid no attention to remonstrances that in providing the USSR with American-designed factories, machine tools, and expert direction, and in giving their engineers full opportunity to become acquainted with the Rouge and its techniques he was supplying a future enemy with important resources.

In an interview in the *Nation's Business* with William A. McGarry he defended his policy.

> Russia is beginning to build. It makes little difference what theory is back of the real work, for in the long run facts will control. I believe it is my duty to help any people who want to go back to work and become self-supporting. . . .

> This system of keeping certain nations dependent on others economically must disappear. It is going to disappear. Then, when we know just what every nation can do, we will be in sight, for the first time, of a civilized economic practice. . . .

> When Russia and China and India and South America come into consuming power, what are you going to do? Surely you don't think that Britain and America will be able to supply them! Surely you don't visualize Britain and America as nothing but vast factories to supply the world! A moment's thought will make clear why the future must see nation after nation taking over its own work of supply. And we ought to be glad to help the work along.

It was a bold course, typical of Ford in the earlier days of his maturity. What he had to say was to become increasingly true in a changing world. Today it is the accepted policy of many "have" nations toward the "have nots."

Ford was convinced that what he was doing would alter for the better the attitude of the Russians toward the Western nations. In this he was mistaken. They learned much from Ford, but his aid did not alter in the least their resolve to bring capitalism to an early end. The instruction they received in Dearborn, Nizhni Novgorod, and Moscow assisted them to improve their industry at a faster pace, and today they are more formidable enemies of Ford's way of life because of the pains he took to teach them. Of course they would have learned in any case, but Ford hastened the process.

At first they credited Ford with contributing toward their progress, but later they conceded little beyond the grudging admission that "the Soviet automobile industry was oriented in the advanced technological experience of the United States." They have given their Communistic energy and understanding the ribbons for what was achieved. Incidentally, it has not been unduly impressive. After almost thirty years of automotive activity, Soviet production of trucks, buses, and cars reached an annual figure of 524,000 units in 1960. It is about a third of present production in Great Britain, although Russia is roughly eighty times the area of the United Kingdom and has about four times the population.[23]

However, even had Ford fully foreseen the course of events it is doubtful if he would have changed his policy. He would consider the gain in industrial experience an asset not only for Russia but for the world. In the end, he would have argued, it would justify itself. In aiding the Russians, Ford may have sustained a loss. The financial data of the Ford company in the 1930's are so bad that this is hard to determine. The company's treasurer's office gives the total sales under the 1929 contract from its start to 1935 as $18,116,000; the cost of materials to Ford as $15,928,000; the commercial expenses as $2,766,000; and the final loss as $578,000.* But these figures do not include the sale to the Soviets of a large quantity of Model A machinery and equipment— perhaps totaling $3 million—equipment which might otherwise have been scrapped. Likewise, the figures do not acknowledge that the added output brought about by the Russian car and truck orders reduced the cost of other Ford units.[24]

Meanwhile, as the depression sharply curtailed Russian orders from Dearborn, it had an even more devastating and crucial impact on the entire Ford overseas activities. It is a matter of doubt whether, even if there had been no depression, the Russians would have fulfilled the contract. There is no doubt of the completely disastrous effects of worldwide economic conditions on other facets of the Ford business.

---

* These figures are hard to reconcile with the billing under the agreement, which according to Craig was current cost plus 15% profit plus 12% freight, boxing, and delivery FAS NY. (See note 23.) Also, the figures of the treasurer's office omit labor and overhead, which are probably included in cost of materials.

11

Time of Desperation

By the late spring of 1930 the prospects for the tractor plant in Cork, Ireland, already looked grim. E. L. Clarke, the manager, wrote to Perry on May 14 that he was discussing an order for 4,000 tractors with the Russians but saw no agreement ahead on credit arrangements. And if no agreement were reached, "We shall be forced to shut down practically all departments." Negotiations proceeded, but work at the factory did not. "We have had to lay off almost 6,000 men during the past three weeks," wrote Clarke to H. S. Cooper on June 5, "which is a very serious consequence in a city of this size. . . . Naturally these men are all on the dole." By August the Cork factory was a ghost plant.

What had caused this sudden collapse? Six months earlier Clarke could not get enough men or pour out tractors enough. To be sure, Russian orders had helped to swell the volume of business, but they had been only the largest among others from many parts of the globe. The truth was that the automotive business was running head on into the growing economic depression which Henry Ford had been refusing to recognize. Spreading out from the United States, where it had affected American capital and government, like a collapsing house of cards it had now wrecked their European counterparts. For during the 1920's the nations most affected by World War I had looked to America as they had rebuilt their shattered economies. (Great Britain was an exception.) By 1930 America had invested (apart from war debts) $15,170,000,000 abroad. No small amount of this had gone to Germany, which between 1924 and 1931 had borrowed more than $5,000,000,000 through short-term and long-term loans.[1]

Once America curtailed her loans, private and governmental, in order to deal with her own economic situation, the stream of dollars that had previously flowed steadily to Europe diminished to a trickle.

There was then no money for tractors. Indeed, the condition extended far beyond Fordsons, and Perry, struggling to establish a greater automobile empery for Henry Ford, had to meet and deal with it as best he could.

2

Perry had prepared for expansion with a care that commanded admiration. He had available competent men in every branch of the business whom as need arose he could dispatch to troubled areas. He had selected as his assistant for continental activity F. S. Thornhill Cooper. "I propose to attach him to the coordination of Europe generally," he wrote Sorensen on October 14, 1929, "and to rely upon him as my deputy throughout Europe in respect of keeping everybody and everything up to the mark." He felt that Cooper was especially qualified because of his knowledge of a number of languages.

F. S. Thornhill Cooper was energetic, coolly audacious, and inclined to be autocratic. He admired Sorensen and, according to his British associates, modeled himself upon the dynamic American. Nothing could disconcert him. The tale goes that he took Sorensen on his first tour of Dagenham and characteristically played up the sensational aspects of the factory. "Look," he said at one point, "by pushing a button I can stop the entire assembly operations." He pressed the button, and all the windows of the plant flew open! Thornhill was undaunted. He laughed and pushed the right button. The episode showed his ability to carry things off with an air, for if abashed by anyone, it would have been by Sorensen. In many parts of Europe Cooper was feared by Ford employees. But everywhere he knew the officials in power, or how to reach them, and was widely respected by those in command.[2]

Perry needed all of Cooper's abilities as the depression settled on Europe and all of his own. During 1929 everything went well. Indeed, through the fall of 1930, except for Ireland and one other major disappointment, the general situation wore an encouraging aspect. It continued to be fairly satisfactory in Belgium, Holland, and the Scandinavian countries, but elsewhere in varying degrees it worsened.

The major disappointment was Italy. The land purchased at Livorno in 1929 as the site for an assembly plant, together with the new sales offices established in Genoa, Naples, and Bologna had marked that country as an important field for Ford expansion. The Italian company announced its plans in early November 1929. At once Giovanni Agnelli, president of Fiat, protested to Mussolini. Thornhill Cooper visited *Il Duce,* and found him friendly. Mussolini suggested that Ford reach an agreement with Fiat. Negotiations began but were soon suspended. Then on November 18, 1929, a royal decree forbade the construction of any unit such as the Ford assembly plant without permission of the government (which clearly never meant to give it). Shortly after this Mussolini sent for Cooper and told him that "it was not the desire of the Italian Government to permit any big volume of imported automobiles, but rather to foster a 100 per cent Italian manufacture thereof."

Ford officials concluded that a union with an Italian automobile company was imperative. In the manufacturer Isotta Fraschini they discovered a receptive firm. But the government frowned upon this alliance, and after again vainly seeking an agreement with Fiat, Sorensen and Perry reluctantly abandoned both the assembly plant and the hope of a merger. (Incidentally, the negotiations in Italy showed Ford for the first time ready to consider a combination with a foreign company.)

Italy had now raised a high tariff wall as a reply to the Smoot-Hawley law, and a Ford car in that country cost more than two-and-a-half times what it did in the United States. Sales quickly became nominal. Perry summed up the Italian government's attitude in a paraphrase of Brutus' declaration about Caesar: "Not that I love Ford less, but that I love Rome more."

Italy became the only country where Perry did not remake the financial structure of the existing Ford company; with prospects so gloomy, such action seemed unnecessary. In 1930 Ford held only 6.6 per cent of total Italian registrations, Fiat 60.6 per cent. Furthermore, Ford's share would shrink while that of the Italian company continued to rise.[3]

By 1930–1931 a discouraging situation had developed in Spain from the depression and the Smoot-Hawley tariff, although abetted by two revolutions. When the new American protective rates were announced in June 1930, the Spanish government at once raised its duties on cars. Ford in Barcelona closed in protest, and the manager, George Jenkins, asserted that he would not reopen until "the unfair tariff discrimination is ended." Madrid was not impressed. "Tell your objections to the President of the United States," a government official snapped. Eventually Jenkins had to eat his words and reopen, with a smaller work force.

Spain encountered its first revolution when Rivera fell from power and the King tried to establish an autocracy; the second one, soon afterward, brought in a republican government. Yet Jenkins dealt skilfully with the changing situation, and while profits dipped sharply, they remained. In contrast to its position in Italy, Ford in Spain was still a factor on the market.[4]

Meanwhile, France too had erected high tariff barriers. Before they were imposed on April 18, 1930, Maurice Dollfus—one of the French Ford company directors—recalls, he had protested to the government and to the French manufacturers Renault and Citroën, who had urged their enactment. Finding all three immovable, he telephoned Detroit to dispatch a large number of automobile parts at once, for if shipped immediately they would not be affected by the proposed legislation. The official at the other end of the wire felt that he could not take responsibility for this act. "Who can tell you to do it?" demanded Dollfus. "Edsel Ford could," was the reply. Dollfus promptly got hold of Edsel, and won his assent for the shipment of a nine-month supply of cars, thus outwitting the French manufacturers and the government. This was Dollfus' second shrewd move. Earlier, at the time Perry engaged him, his advice had saved Ford-France a large sum in taxes.

Consequently the Fords felt very friendly toward this tall man "with the physique of a Rugby player," whose brilliant mind worked so well in their behalf. Henry Ford had told Perry he wanted a Frenchman to lead the company in that country, and on November 14, 1930 Dollfus was made managing director. Perry, however, wrote Sorensen that he sought a man for general manager who was a seasoned Ford employee, "because he [Dollfus] is untrained in Ford policies, and has been put in from the top, a practice which I know you disapprove of." If the depression increased the difficulties of French business, including Ford's, the difficulty of finding managerial talent made the situation worse. From mid-1928 to 1932, Perry tried a series of general managers. Alexander Lie, a Norwegian who had long been a Ford executive in France, had not satisfied him. A Frenchman, W. K. Hyslop, failed to meet the test. He installed Louis Carle. "He was a washout." Hopefully, Perry finally brought William G. Collins from Istanbul, but by early 1932 was ready to call him worthless.

By now Dollfus had been learning the business, had formed a friendship with Edsel Ford, and was moving toward greater power and responsibility. When in 1932 Perry sent his personal assistant, Maurice

Buckmaster, to France as assistant manager, it was clear that there would be no general manager; Dollfus would do that official's work.

Dollfus had his own ideas about France, which did not tally with Perry's. From the day he was appointed managing director, he had argued that Ford should manufacture in France. He believed that to be competitive Ford must get inside the tariff wall. On the other hand, Perry held that Dagenham must supply the European companies, France included, in order to achieve the volume necessary to make its operation economical. Already, Perry had discovered that customs duties made manufacture in Germany essential and that this market would be cut off. Now he persuaded Dollfus "to keep quiet about manufacturing motors in France until we had a fair go at Cologne."

In France, as in Italy and Germany, the role of the imported car was fast becoming an empty one. Although the French Ford company increased its use of locally made parts, this was not a sufficient answer to the situation. For 1931 its profits were less than half of what they had been in 1930, and in 1932 Dollfus would report a deficit. Meanwhile, conditions in Germany grew even more complicated and discouraging.[5]

3

We have noted that when Henry Ford laid the foundation stone for the Cologne plant in early October 1930, it had been decided that this was to be a manufacturing rather than an assembly plant.

Reviewing the tariff situation with Dr. Heinrich Albert in Berlin in July 1930, Perry had agreed with Albert that since additional duties were certain to be imposed "notwithstanding all efforts we are making and will still continue to make," it was imperative to make the Model A in Germany. Otherwise the Ford product would be priced out of the market. They decided that an extension to the Cologne plant would be necessary for the manufacture of engines. Other parts not made in the Cologne plant would be purchased locally, "so as to enable us to maintain the existing retail prices." Sorensen had agreed, endorsing the proposed addition to the plant, and sent Joseph Lawry and C. Duncan from Dearborn to Germany to aid in establishing the new manufacturing plant.

Perry indicated that Ford Ltd. might finance the German plant at the start, but he added in a letter to Sorensen, "you very kindly promised that America would lend monies to the German company to finance this extension and for other purposes if it were found to be necessary." The projected tariff was forcing the Ford organization to spend an unanticipated $1,680,000 (the estimate was $280,000 for the building extension plus $1,400,000 for machinery).

As already noted, Ford-Cologne was now under the management of E. C. Heine, a German-born American citizen. Under him was Erhard Vitger, as chief clerk; R. H. Schmidt in charge of purchasing, and Roslof Sorensen as works manager. While the 1928 plan had stressed the use of nationals, Heine was a naturalized American, Vitger and Sorensen Danes, and Schmidt the only German citizen among the chief officials of the firm.

Dr. Heinrich Albert was a director—an important one. In Germany the Board of Directors does not manage, but checks on management. It can appoint and dismiss chief officials, but technically it can take no part in their work. Dr. Albert, however, played a fundamental role in the development of Ford-Germany. If he seldom visited the Cologne plant, and if his letters to Dearborn and Dagenham were written from Berlin, he kept himself fully informed on all activities, and participated in negotiations with the representatives of German government and industry. Dollfus in France may have had a day-to-day contact with operations that Albert never knew, but in fundamental matters affecting company policy Albert came to have as much influence on Ford AG as Dollfus had on Ford SAF.

In the spring of 1931 Heine and his associates should have been entering a happy era. The new plant at Cologne was practically completed, and would be open to the public on June 12. Then, the management hoped, Ford would press Opel closely for leadership in the German industry.

The new plant was small but impressive. It overlooked the Rhine River, and the Ford-Germany *Annual Report* for 1930 stated: "Our own quay wall permits steamers and barges to come alongside. When completed we will have 33,000 sq. m. [meters] of covered floor space. Concrete roads will be constructed all around the plant, and four railroad tracks with a total of about two kilometers own track [*sic*] will take care of incoming and outgoing traffic."

Neither Perry nor Sorensen could be present for the June 12 celebration, which seems to have been a success. Heine wrote that people came from Sicily and Constantinople, from Gibraltar and Finland— more than 100,000 of them including Germans, and "we were in continuous touch with 2,200 newspapers." Mayor Konrad Adenauer of Cologne hailed the new factory as "an enrichment of Germany industry." There had been criticism of Model A as a foreign car, but Heine declared in his welcoming speech that rear axles, motors, transmissions, and many minor parts were made within the Cologne plant or in other German factories. Thus the car, he asserted, was no mere assembly job. He conceded that America had contributed the Ford name and design, but concluded: "Our work, however, our efforts are German, and this is not an assertion, but a fact." [6]

Unfortunately, on May 11, 1931, a month before the opening at Cologne, the largest commercial bank in Austria, the Vienna Creditanstalt, failed; and this worsened the already precarious economic situation in Germany. A memorandum issued by the government on June 5 indicated its financial insecurity. Immediately the banks began to close. Perry exhorted Heine not to give up. On June 10 he wrote that many papers and persons were asserting the existence of a world depression. "I do not wish to enter into a discussion of the authenticity . . . of this statement, but I do wish to exercise every effort possible, and ask you, as Manager of your Company, to do the same, to ensure that your staff and your Dealers' Organization do not throw up their hands in despair and use this so-called 'World Wide Depression' as an alibi for reduced efforts."

Heine claimed that he tilted gallantly with the panic. He reported that on June 15, the Monday after the opening, the dealers had met, and while "two of our most intelligent dealers rose to talk about the economic crisis, and . . . found plenty of sympathy, I am happy to report that the spirited reply which absolutely denied any existence of depression was received with so much enthusiasm that all our dealers rose and voluntarily brought out three cheers 'for the Ford Motor Company A/G and its administration,' promising us that they would go back, take off their coats, put their shoulders to the wheels, and make things move."

This was encouraging news. On June 25 Perry was able to call Heine's attention to President Hoover's proposal of the 21st for a moratorium on all reparation and war debt payments, which he felt would soon reduce unemployment "with a consequent revival of industry . . . and a very much stimulated demand for our product." But Heine was already telling Perry of further attacks on the Ford car as a mixture of English and American materials.

The difficulties of the German government put a temporary end to Heine's worries. It declared a bank holiday, and the Cologne plant, operating at only 13 per cent of capacity, closed on July 13. "Everything is at a standstill in Germany," wrote Perry to Sorensen. "Our business is completely stopped." [7]

Ford-Germany soon resumed work and increased the number of German-made parts in its cars. The factory work force and the number of dealers had been reduced, and the company gave its attention only to "definite orders in hand." Throughout the country clashes between the National Socialists and the Communists became frequent, and to some persons it seemed that the nation would have to choose between these two authoritarian parties. Rumor had it that Henry Ford was supporting Hitler; Ford officials denied this, and there exists no evidence in company records to support the charge.

It was a difficult time, but Heine did not respond creatively to the challenge it presented. Later his chief associates agreed that his appointment as manager had been a mistake. He had permitted his office to get into a state of confusion. J. T. Riordan, an accountant sent over by Perry in September to examine the company's books, sent in a devastating report of waste and inefficiency. On October 16 Perry wrote Heine a blistering comment. "Most childish and elementary errors have been committed which are inexcusable. . . . It will be a long time before I will feel any confidence in your organization." However, on October 30 Perry asked Riordan, now reorganizing Ford-Germany's business practices, not to rub salt into the wounds of the guilty officials. "Do all you can to assist them to get matters right. . . . Now that we have inflicted the pain, let us try to restore good feeling and efficiency." [8]

Heine had been the victim of hard times, but so had all his competitors. His record was worse than theirs. In 1932 Ford in May and June commanded only 1.9 and 1.3 per cent of the market and had fallen from second to ninth place among German manufacturers, while Opel continued to hold first place with 20.2 and 18.6 per cent respectively. Ford's German operation was a wasteland. It was an expensive manufacturing plant with no market for its products. Soon it was to encounter difficulties of a new and even more extreme character.

Thus the European operation outside Britain, while fairly encouraging in the northern countries, was temporarily darkening in Spain, had blacked out in Italy, was becoming a deficit operation in France and a catastrophic performance in Germany. It may be added that the assembly plant established at Constantinople in 1929 operated from the first at a loss. Perry staunchly clung to hope for a better day, but all the economic weather signs seemed to promise a worse one.[9]

4

"Towering above the Essex marsh," wrote an observer of the works at Dagenham in January 1931, "are the huge stoves and chimneys of the biggest blast furnace in England. Endless vistas of steelwork, under glass roofs so wide that they scarcely intercept the view of the sky, and standing on acre after acre of concrete, are the main shops of the factory, soon to resound to the hum and clang of giant Ford machines producing two vehicles every minute."

It was as if at the muttered words of an incantation the north bank of the lower Thames had been incredibly remade. Embankments that had confined black farmland and tracts of reeds now bristled with geometric factory buildings, and where only a few boys or a stray. farmer had wandered, an army of workmen would soon crowd into foundry, engine, and assembly units. Dagenham rose royally, commanding the awe of visitors. And the impression it made was justifiable, for when completed it would stand as the largest automotive plant in Europe. It would give Ford-England an immense advantage over rivals that in recent years had sped by her in the race for production supremacy.

The great complex was not yet ready for operation early in 1931. It represented a £2,000,000 investment, on which the Ford Motor Company Ltd. was getting no return. Some buildings were completed for functional purposes as the year advanced and could receive machine equipment. By late summer a considerable part of that had been installed, and finally on October 1 A. R. Smith could cable Sorensen: "First truck came off assembly line at Dagenham today 2 P.M. Production continuing." This was a token rather than a volume output. *Automotive Industries* stated in January 1932 that the plant was "gradually coming into production," and in June the chemical laboratory, the river wall, the roads, the hot-metal building, the blast furnaces, and the power house all had work to be done on them, and interiors and exteriors for the most part still had to be painted. Not until the end of the summer of 1932 was Dagenham a massive, working, indisputable reality, and the Ford Ltd. *Annual Report* of that year announced proudly: "The

Company is now independent of supplies from the U.S.A. Over five thousand new employees have been absorbed into the Dagenham factory, principally from the immediate neighborhood." The work force at the end of 1932 was 7,024, some two thousand men and officials having been brought in from Ford plants in Ireland or Manchester.[10]

As Dagenham grew, Manchester diminished. By the end of 1931 all its chief buildings had been vacated. This had not been the original intention; the older center had been scheduled to become an assembly plant. However, with the depression the demand for cars had so fallen off, and Dagenham's capacity was so much greater than the company required, that Manchester, if retained, seemed likely to be an incubus. The transfer from the old to the new location was made smoothly. Squire, who managed the operation, went back and forth between Manchester and London. "We would load a train of tools one night," he recalled later, "it would arrive at Dagenham the following day, and be installed in the factory before night." Meanwhile the workers would have come down, and production would be resumed at the new site.

Dagenham had been more expensive than expected, and so had other Ford factories in Europe. For example, the erection of a manufacturing instead of an assembly plant at Cologne had been especially costly. (Perry pointed out that this and all other departures from the original scheme had been ordered and approved by Dearborn.) In addition, the depression and the higher tariffs of most European countries had cut down Ford sales. To meet the situation Perry proposed an increase in Ford-England capitalization, which was raised from £7,000,000 to £9,000,000. Dearborn paid its share of the increase (60 per cent), but the general public, which had been told in 1928 that Dagenham would be completed with the capital the company then commanded, did not. As a result, the offering of shares in March 1931 did not bring in the money required, and Ford-England was obliged to borrow from Ford affiliates on the continent.[11]

As if the firm did not have enough problems at Dagenham and elsewhere, it found the tractor operation at Cork hanging about its neck like the ancient mariner's albatross. Conditions there had not improved. As early as March 1931 Perry told his shareholders that the Irish factory was "going through bad times owing to the intense and world wide depression in Agriculture. Farmers cannot afford to buy." Five months later he reported to Sorensen that Ireland "is only doing a negligible turnover in tractors," and on April 15, 1932, he suggested to Edsel Ford that tractor production should be transferred to Dagenham. Clarke, the Cork plant manager, resigned a week later because his salary had been reduced. Cork in 1932 built only 3,088 Fordsons. This marked the end to tractor production in Cork. The plant was then converted into a small car and truck assembly unit for English Fords.

The tractor machinery was shipped to Dagenham in 1932 and Howard Simpson was called from America to help improve the design of the model. Perry had always believed in the Fordson. Through it, he had rendered his most signal service to his country in World War I. During the year 1932 several articles in the English *Ford Times* show that he was busy with the new tractor. The firm of Sherman & Sheppard planned to market the Fordson in America when Simpson finished his work. With Simpson's aid an improved model emerged and the first Dagenham-built tractor rolled off assembly on February 19, 1933.[12]

By the time that truck production began at Dagenham (and the 1931 output was all commercial vehicles except for five passenger cars), the Models A and AF had been offered in England for three years. It will be recalled that Perry's 1930 sales had been less than anticipated; those for 1931 were still lower—less than 23,000, including 4,000 tractors. All producers in this period suffered, but Perry more than his rivals, the Morris, the Austin, the Standard, and the Singer.

These competitors had several advantages over Ford. All put out cheaper cars than Dagenham. Again, at a time when Europeans were considering not only the purchase price, but the cost of operation (gasoline was much higher in Europe than in America), all the leading English cars cost less to operate than the Ford. Moreover, the Ford AF, with the small bore engine, lacked the power required for a Model A car; if the regular engine were installed, the price was forbidding because of the higher tax (on 24 as against 14.9 h.p.).

As early as 1925, as we have seen, before Perry's return, Jenkins had asked for a small, low-powered automobile to compete with the Morris and the Austin. Perry had accepted the AF as this car. Henry Ford, however, realized that such a vehicle would not do, and in 1928 he showed Perry drawings and designs for a new small car.

When Ford was in Europe in 1930 he stated to Perry that he intended to build such a small car. Perry, fearing extra expense, was not very enthusiastic. Nonetheless, at Ford's request he shipped to Dearborn fifteen small cars, both French and British models. "Fifteen cars sound an awful lot," he wrote Liebold. ". . . But if he [Ford] wishes to make comparisons, I think he should see everything." [13]

By mid-1931 Perry had changed his mind. He discovered that the market for bantam units in England was increasing at a rapid rate, and the 14.9 h.p. Ford was no success. For the first five months of 1931 (compared with those of 1930) sales of cars under 10 h.p. had increased by over 2,000 units, while the sales of those over 10 h.p. had declined by more than 10,000.

"Everyone in this country is agreed," Perry wrote to Edsel Ford in July 1931, "that the only path out of the present intense industrial depression is one of economy, and as this reacts upon the motor industry, it means that the tendency everywhere is to buy smaller and cheaper motor cars."

Meanwhile the financial situation of Ford-England was calculated to drive home Perry's new conviction. The cash on hand which the 1929 *Annual Report* set at £2,204,226 had shrunk in 1930 to £894,000 and was only raised slightly in 1931 with the increase in capitalization. As fast as Ford-England got funds it spent them on construction.

In October 1931 A. R. Smith as general manager reported to the Board of Directors that "owing to heavy withdrawals to meet commitments on Dagenham contracts our books show an overdraft at the bank." He also pointed out that "our line of passenger cars shows no price advantage compared with the popular type of British cars of equal or lower horsepower."

In the same month Perry was protesting to Dearborn that Dagenham faced financial disaster unless it could have a bantam unit. Henry Ford agreed. His engineers went to work at once, and in December they summoned A. R. Smith to the United States to inspect their plans and assist them with further work.

"This job was done pretty darn quick," recalled Dearborn's chief engineer, Laurence Sheldrick, in what was unquestionably an understatement. He and his associates worked unremittingly on the task, even devoting New Year's Day to it. Sir Rowland (then A. R.) Smith remembers lying beneath the model one Sunday in January, adjusting the brakes. "Who's under the car?" came a voice from above, and Smith peered out and up to see Henry Ford looming above him. "Move over," commanded Henry, then sixty-seven years old, and joined the English Smith as an emergency worker.[14]

By mid-February 1932 the car was ready for exhibition but not yet for production. Ford's earlier studies and plans had undoubtedly helped him to cut corners, but from formal approval of the project in October to exhibition in February was nevertheless a miracle.

The new car promised to better the position of the British company in its rivalry with Morris and Austin and also in its overseas sales. By February 1932 Ford-England's sales of American-type cars in Europe had fallen off sharply. Ford of Germany was manufacturing, and Perry recognized that "we shall probably have to face the promotion of similar manufacturing facilities in other countries in our territory." Undoubtedly he had France in mind.

Dagenham still built the Models A and AF and by August would offer the new Ford V-8. It also made 6 commercial vehicles, weighing from 10 to 30 hundredweight. But chiefly because of its low volume, the English plant could not meet Dearborn prices with these models. Perry himself wrote in July 1932: "I am satisfied that Dagenham can never produce at dollars and cents costs which can match Detroit." * Some of the European companies had already recognized this fact and appealed to Edsel Ford for the right to purchase in the United States. He ruled that they could buy in the cheapest market, and some promptly ordered from Dearborn. In this situation the new "baby" Ford appeared as a deliverer. It was made only in England and was sold only by Ford Ltd. It could be offered in the markets of the world. It was thus a special product with which Detroit would not compete. Dagenham would continue to sell English-made American-type cars, and with its new unit would build up the total of its production.[15]

The small car soon after its debut in England was christened the Model Y. It had been engineered and styled in America, by American engineers, aided by A. R. Smith. It was first shown at the Ford Exhibition at Royal Albert Hall, London, February 19–27, 1932. The unit had

---

* The reasons why Ford-England could not produce at Detroit costs were explained by Perry as lack of volume and the heavy expense of the new facilities. An additional factor in costs was the slower pace of the British workmen as compared with the American. W. J. Squire later contrasted Dearborn and Dagenham: "I was as mild a young man as you would want to see when I went to work in Dearborn, but two weeks after I arrived I saw that it was either get tough or get out, and I got tough. Henry Ford paid a high wage, but he wanted a hard day's work. You did a son-of-a-bitch of a day's work at the Rouge. It was a lot more of a day's work than the English ever thought of doing." The Ford-England *Annual Report* of 1932 referred to the problems of untrained personnel at Dagenham. This also added to costs.

a 4-cylinder engine and a 90-inch wheel base; its motor was rated at 8 h.p. but really delivered something like 22 h.p. by American standards. It sold for £120, a price lower than that of the Morris or the Austin.

The presentation was wholly a success. "Nothing like it has ever occurred in the motor industry in this country," reported Perry happily to Edsel Ford. A. R. Smith cabled to Sorensen: "Have never seen Ford dealers so enthusiastic. . . . Public opinion and press everywhere proclaim 8 h.p. car just what is wanted here. . . . Anticipate that many months will elapse before we can overtake the demand."

The next problem was production. Fourteen models had been built in the United States, but nothing had been done preparatory to turning out cars in quantity. Ford-England now worked on this while at the same time it dealt as best it could with its increasingly dreary financial condition. Construction on the big plant was still in progress, and there was little income from the great industrial complex. Effective April 1, 1932, all wages and salaries were reduced 10 per cent. Patrick Hennessy, who had become purchase manager for the English firm in 1931, recalled later: "No one outside really knew how bad the situation was. We would pay off one supplier, and then another, keeping the secret successfully." The Model Y was a hope, but it lay in the future, and meanwhile the company staggered from one financial crisis to another.

By September, output of the new car was assured in growing volume. In eleven months the model had leapt from inception to quantity production—a fantastic accomplishment. By the end of 1932, 8,260 of these cars had been built; the total would soon mount. At last the company had a promising candidate in the popular field.* It was the first vehicle Ford had ever designed to meet foreign laws, needs, and preferences.[16]

5

The *Annual Report* of the Canadian company for 1929 showed a profit of $5,461,000; two years later the firm reported a loss on its operations of $1,668,630. It had paid a dividend of 60 cents per share in June, but made this statement for the rest of 1931: "Inasmuch as the operations of the Company were adversely affected as a result of prevailing

---

* This did not mean that the Model Y had no faults. As was the case with most new cars, it had a number, one of the chief complaints relating to the rear axle, which was not sturdy enough for hilly country.—See Perry-Sorensen Corresp. 1933–1934, Select File.

world conditions, it was not considered advisable to make a further dividend distribution during the year."

Ford-Canada lost $5,206,736 in 1932 and $1,174,991 in 1933. In three years it had dropped almost a third of the cash resources it held in 1930. Its sales had declined from 70,259 in 1930 to 26,371 in 1933, while the industry in the Dominion, hitherto second to the United States in the production of automobiles, had dropped to fifth behind England, France, and Germany.[17]

As Ford-Canada, so its offspring. Year after depression year, Ford sales in South Africa, Australia, Malaya, New Zealand, and India fell. In Australia, for example, the Ford company had sold 13,980 Model A's in 1929; in 1930, 1031, and 1932 the totals were 6,383, 1,607, and 2,599. A new assembly plant at Fremantle, in Australia, opened in March 1930; for the month of April its total sales were three units! By 1933, the Australian company suspended assembly at Adelaide and Sydney. The omnipresent depression held the automotive industry as if in an enormous fist, constricting its activity and paralyzing its will to accomplishment.[18]

Ford-Japan, wholly owned by Ford-US, had built an assembly plant and had done comparatively well in 1930. It showed 6,551 new registrations compared with General Motors' 4,445. Benjamin Kopf, in charge there, was an able and astute manager. In 1931 he foresaw an abandonment of the gold standard. He cabled in October: "Recommend making forward exchange contracts to cover present stocks. Cannot lose and may gain." Actually, Japan went off the gold standard in December 1931.

In 1930 Henry Ford sent W. C. Cowling to China, and early in 1931 Frank Riecks and Max Wiesmyer followed him to help appraise Ford prospects. Ford had a small sales and service branch in Shanghai, and J. V. Crowe, who managed this operation, joined the three visitors in seeking a suitable assembly site and in negotiating with the Chinese government. At first they met with little enthusiasm from the Chinese, but by 1932 government officials were expressing considerable interest. T. V. Soong, vice chairman of the National Economic Council, wrote to Henry Ford: "We are hoping that you could turn your attention to China and assist us . . . to solve some of our problems—the construction of simple, rugged, and inexpensive cars, trucks, and tractors, in a country of tremendous distances and very low economic standards."

5. Belterra, the second development for the growing of rubber trees in Brazil; *below* Sorensen and Sir Percival Perry in Poland, 1929, about to visit the Soviet Union. Sorensen stands at the extreme right; Sir Percival, with light suit and cane, foreground center. Between them stands Fred L. Rockelman.

6. Three chief executives of the Ford international activity; *above, left,* Graeme K. Howard and Tom Lilley; *below,* John Bugas, the present head, and Ernest R. Breech, executive vice president of the Ford Motor Company.

Soong hoped Ford would at least establish an assembly plant and possibly one for manufacturing.

Edsel Ford replied encouragingly. But Cowling had reported that "China will not progress very rapidly until she gets more settled in her government affairs." Riecks and Wiesmyer saw "no market for any kind of automobiles in any volume," since China was still a prisoner of her past with low incomes and wretched roads. They advised against any plant. Edsel, however, wrote Soong that as soon as a daily demand for at least 25 vehicles existed, Ford would start assembly in China. In 1930 China had received only 1,289 cars from Ford Motor Company, or about 4 a day; so that Edsel was not likely to be called upon to fulfill this promise.

Meanwhile the Japanese occupation of Manchuria and her landing of troops at Shanghai (which defeated Chinese contingents) made the prospect for automobile sales, or for any regular commercial activity, most doubtful. In February 1932 Crowe wrote that while the Chinese branch was doing its best, "with the bombardment of Woosung and Nanking and trouble at Swatow and Hankow, our business is almost at a standstill." The market did not grow. Wiesmyer later recalled that plans for China "just died a natural death." [19]

Conditions in Latin America were temporarily worse than those in the Far East, for the depression came there earlier. Even in 1929 Brazil had been shaken economically by the overproduction of coffee. With the price of this crucial commodity falling, the prostration of business extended into 1930. The Latin American economic depression was compounded in that year by revolutions that toppled the presidents of Argentina, Bolivia, Brazil, and Peru; and in 1931 revolutions shook Peru, Venezuela, Chile, Ecuador, and Paraguay.[20]

The effect on Ford business was catastrophic; in Brazil Roberge reported "no indication of improvement for a long period," and proposed to eliminate Rio de Janeiro as an assembly point. In Getulio Vargas' rise to power, both he and his opponents seized Ford trucks and cars. In Argentina, the overthrow of President Hipólito Irigoyen wrecked the Ford company's business. "Our sales are greatly affected," reported F. F. Griffith sadly in 1931.[21]

All the new governments felt the force of world depression, and in 1931 most of them imposed foreign exchange controls (regulating the payment of monies to persons or firms beyond their borders). Ford branches could not import cars or parts except under licenses provided by each nation.

Money everywhere was scarce, and a great outcry arose from all Latin American Ford operations for credit facilities; B. J. Craig in Dearborn finally provided these through arrangements with the National City Bank in New York. Ford-Brazil and Ford-Argentina set up credit departments. Ford founded Crédito Centrale, SA, to finance Mexican sales. These credit agencies continued to operate through the 1930's even after Ford-US sold its interest in its own credit company. They were vital to the increase of business in Latin America.[22] *

Meanwhile the economic and political storms flattened most building plans in Latin America. Albert Kahn had designed a factory for Ford-Brazil and billed Dearborn for $40,612, but the structure did not rise. In Argentina Griffith did not buy the site for his approved plant until 1934. Assembly operations were snuffed out at Rio de Janeiro (1930), Recife (1930), and Pôrto Alegre (1933), and only at São Paulo was Ford-Brazil putting vehicles together. In Chile, Peru, and Uruguay Ford business ceased or was negligible. Only Mexico saw a new assembly plant rise. Ford and government officials attended a gala opening on September 14, 1932. The factory had a capacity of 100 units a day, and the press, perhaps with sly humor, congratulated Ford on foreseeing a time when such production would be warranted.**

Despite new credit plans and the Mexican plant, 1932 was a grim year for Ford in Latin America. With a second revolution in Brazil, sales there sank to 1,464 as against 18,274 in 1929 and for all Latin America were only 12,728 as compared with 72,205 three years earlier.[23]

With the beginning of 1933 there was a further collapse (the nadir, as it happened). In April Ford-Argentina sold 3 Model A's, 2 Ford V-8's, and 6 Model Y's. There and in Brazil the new English car had been imported, and the São Paulo journal, *O Mundo Ford,* saluted it bravely: "The new small Ford is a car destined to conquer in our markets, as it has conquered in the old world, the unanimous applause of the public." Alas, it was the voice of a false prophet. In 1933 only 149 Model Y's were delivered in Brazil, and in the next three years only

---

* In Europe and Japan, Ford also continued credit operations.

** The new building was located on Calzada de Guadelupe, near the famous shrine of that name. Every day pilgrims made their way by the plant with bouquets of flowers, musical instruments, lanterns, balloons, lighted candles, to pay their tribute to the Virgin. Workers from the Ford plant would make an annual pilgrimage to the nearby shrine.

24 more were sold. The car was neither cheap nor sturdy enough to succeed in South America, where the V-8 was now coming in and giving satisfaction.

This successor to Model A, a unit with an 8-cylinder motor which more than answered the challenge of Chevrolet's new Six, provided speed and dependability but in the United States ran second in the low price field. It was deficient in finish and comfort although not in durability and power, and Latin America had a terrain suited to its best qualities. General Motors outsold Ford in 1932 both with trucks and automobiles, but the V-8 was not yet in volume production; and when this was achieved in 1933 Ford again led its rival throughout Latin America. Unfortunately total Ford sales there for that year amounted to only 13,284 units.[24]

6

During the fall of 1932 the wheels of Dagenham were turning fast, and production mounted. A goal of 400 vehicles a day (120,000 a year) hung alluringly before the company, and on September 28 the directors voted £20,000 for machinery to equip the plant for such production.*

Perry and his associates were already aware of the high cost of the vehicles they were producing, and to save money held up a number of contracts not vital to Dagenham operations. He also begged the American company to modify its bill of $535,360 for the Model Y, and Dearborn reduced it to $210,000. Ford-Holland made the English firm a loan of £1,000,000. Yet despite such savings and borrowings the company reported for the year a loss of £681,828.[25]

Early in 1933 a controversy developed on whether or not to operate Ford-England's coke ovens, blast furnace, and by-products plant. To complete these units would require additional capital, surpluses would have to be sold, and English demand for pig iron and coke was practically non-existent. Sorensen, however, insisted "that it was essential in the interests of economy and manufacturing efficiency to make and control the quality of the iron used in the factory and that he and his U.S.A. colleagues were convinced as to the wisdom of operating Power House, Blast Furnace, and Coke Ovens as early as possible." He suggested economies which would take care of the financing and added

---

* This was a reduction from the 200,000 output initially planned.

that if necessary the associated companies in Europe be called upon to advance additional funds. The directors voted to complete all the projects, which were finished in June 1934.*

Before the end of 1933 the Danish, Dutch, Belgian, and Spanish Ford companies reduced their capitalization by 40 per cent, returning the funds to the shareholders. Ford-England could use this cash for the completion of Dagenham manufacturing facilities. In 1933 it paid no dividends. Yet a credit balance of £388,170 in December testified that at last the company was on the way to recovery.

During 1933 Dagenham built 32,958 Model Y's and achieved a total vehicle production of 55,339 units. It was now one of the Big Three in the British automobile industry. It still lagged behind Austin and Morris in sales (28.8 per cent and 27.2 per cent, respectively, of the Big Six passenger car market as against Ford's 18.9 per cent). But the Model Y had given Ford-England standing, for the low-powered cars now dominated the market. In 1928, 25 per cent of the motor vehicles sold in Britain had less than 10 h.p.; now in 1933, 60 per cent were in that category. The "baby" Ford thus made it possible for Dagenham to compete successfully in the area where customer demand was greatest.

Notwithstanding the trade restrictions imposed by many foreign countries and increasing competition from United States products, the exports of Ford-England rose in 1933.[26] Perry had developed new sales outlets in Portugal, Egypt, Roumania, and Greece. Meanwhile, he encountered further difficulties in Germany and France.

7

The Model Y had been received with applause by officials both at Cologne and Asnières. Heine thought he could sell 10,000 units in 1933, and Dollfus placed an order for the same number.

Heine desperately needed a car that he could dispose of in quantity.

---

* The company faced the discouraging problem of selling its surplus product, particularly pig iron. A flood of this had come in from India and made sales seem all but impossible. Nevertheless Sorensen insisted on their being effected, and deputized Ford-England's able young purchasing agent, Patrick Hennessy, to do the job. He brushed aside all objections, saying: "I think you can do it. Get cracking." Hennessy sold a large order, and although he had to cut prices, this one was soon followed by more and manufacture became profitable. Sorensen was delighted, and Dagenham was established as a producer of pig iron. It even sold to its competitors, including Lord Austin; "We could show them that we were able to deliver a better product at the same or a lower price than they could get elsewhere."

With a capitalization of $3,567,182, Ford-Germany owed Ford-US "a frozen debt of $4,157,857 in addition to a debt arranged by the Luxembourg company." Perry brought this out in an August 2, 1932 letter to Edsel Ford, and added that during the first six months of 1932 Heine had lost $501,780 more.

When Heine urged that the Model Y be made in Germany, Perry pointed out to Edsel that to convert the Cologne plant to Model Y manufacture would cost $400,000 and was therefore "out of the question, *quite apart from the handicap which Dagenham would suffer from the loss of business.*" (Our italics.)

There was, however, no choice. Dagenham would have to lose this market, for it was impossible to sell a foreign car in Germany because of government restrictions on importation and mounting nationalistic pressures demanding a national product. Thus, Heine reported to his directors in October that "it was decided to start with the production of the Model Y car here in Cologne on January 2, 1933." [27]

By January 1933 the Nazis constituted the largest single group in the Reichstag; early in March, although still lacking a majority of votes in that body, they seized power. The state of the country and of the motor industry were reported by Heine on March 24 in a long letter to Thornhill Cooper. Heine named the date when the Ford car must be entirely German. "After May 20 the Cologne organization must manufacture or procure motors, transmissions, front and rear axles locally, if we are to be considered a national German product, and if our business is not to be jeopardized by arbitrary taxation." [28]

This necessity was a severe blow to Dagenham. Up to this time the English company had manufactured a considerable portion of the Model Y as sold in Germany. Now this market would be blanked out, and Germany as a source of profit to Dagenham would disappear, except that the British through its 60 per cent ownership might one day share in Ford AG profits, if Hitler should ever permit any money to leave Germany. That possibility was a remote one, as the foreseeable future seemed to promise nothing but losses for Heine and his associates.

In 1934 Ford-Germany was financially reorganized; the greater part of its indebtedness became new stock, mostly held by the American Ford company. Ford-England readily relinquished its 60 per cent holding, which was reduced to 45.8 per cent. Ford-US, which previously had held no German stock, now owned 34.2 per cent, IG Farben's holding dropped to 7.5 per cent, and the public's share to 12.5 per cent. In subsequent financial adjustments, Ford-US's holdings increased while the percentages of the other three groups declined. It was Ford-US that assumed the brunt of the Ford-German financing.[29]

Meanwhile, in France the government continued to discourage the importation of foreign cars. Dollfus had to sell the Model A at the equivalent of $1,020, the highest price in any of the northern European countries; the V-8 (which sold in the United States for $550) had a French price tag of $1,484, while the little Model Y sold in France for about $920. Dollfus could not get anywhere near his 10,000 Model Y estimate, and in 1932 and 1933 together he managed to dispose of only 2,839 small cars. The French did not like the unit, which was definitely English in appearance, and the V-8 with its greater power and size was a better buy.

Ford in France was not among the big three: Citroën, Renault, and Peugeot. General Motors had decided that its French operations were not profitable and maintained little activity in France. But Ford did not give up, despite the fact that in 1932 Dollfus lost $257,000; and as 1933 advanced it became certain that the deficit for that year would be catastrophic (actually, it came to $1,269,000).

Dollfus continued to press for manufacture in France. Perry remained dubious:

> I have my doubts as to whether the small production [in France] will be profitable [he wrote to Sorensen in December 1933] even having regard to the enormous duties which are imposed on imports into France at the present time. In this regard I spent last weekend in Germany . . . the problem is much the same in both countries, viz: can a manufacturing plant be made to pay when output is confined within the limited areas which national tariffs are building up?

Dollfus, on the other hand, declared, "There is no other future for Ford S.A.F. than the one that can be found in local manufacturing." [30]

Dollfus took the matter direct to Dearborn. In the last days of November 1933 he came to the United States with E. E. C. Mathis, an old established French automobile manufacturer. In that year Mathis was selling in France more units than Ford. His firm held fourth place in the French industry. But it was a small company, and the depression had gone far to wreck it financially; without substantial aid, apparently it was doomed. Dollfus proposed a merger with Mathis. Ford would put up most of the capital and would gain manifold advantages: in the first place it would take on a French appearance. Mathis had a complete factory at Strasbourg—with a foundry included. If Ford kept its Asnières plant, near Paris, and also utilized the Mathis factory, it would have both manufacturing and assembling facilities. It could build an American-designed car of French character that should gain a substantial place in the national market.

Mathis saw the merger as the rescue of his company. Actually, Dollfus and he mixed like oil and vinegar, but he needed aid. Edsel Ford and Sorensen listened to the two Frenchmen, especially to Dollfus' dramatic presentation of his plans. The latter envisaged no difficulties; he saw only a rosy future; he cast aside Perry's doubts: "I am more optimistic than you are. . . . I believe that there is no question that the French market is sufficiently wide to justify the investment we are proposing to make."

In April a group of Ford officials from Dearborn went to France to investigate. They found Mathis' plant "in fair condition." "They have about 2,000 machine tools of which we estimate 75% to be in fair condition," reported H. C. Kellogg. Later, Sorensen, with Perry, inspected the Strasbourg factory, and the former approved its neat appearance and its capable Alsatian workmen.

Accordingly, Sorensen, Edsel and Henry Ford sanctioned the merger, and Perry reluctantly helped with the details. Dearborn rather than Dagenham, it was agreed, would take over the manufacturing control of the new enterprise and put up the money for it. Thus in 1934 Ford-US, and Henry and Edsel Ford, purchased 442,000 shares of Ford SAF from Ford-England's holding company. The price, insisted upon by Perry, was $4.582 per share—a highly inflated figure. The transaction gave American Ford interests 34 per cent of the outstanding stock in the French unit.*

Then on September 27, 1934 a new company was incorporated which was called Matford. It was owned by the Mathis group (40 per cent) and by Ford interests (60 per cent). It had no property but rented the Strasbourg plant from Mathis, SA and the Asnières factory from Ford SAF. The lease on the Strasbourg factory was for nine years, but

---

* Forty per cent was of course owned by the French public, and 26 per cent was retained by the Luxembourg holding company.

could be terminated by Matford after four, the actual cancellation to take place eighteen months later. The new company had 300 Ford dealers to sell its products and 200 Mathis agents.*

Mathis was quite aware that Ford interests had control of the joint enterprise. Although apparently distrustful of Dollfus, who made it clear that he expected to dictate policy, the Strasbourg manufacturer counted on a more generous attitude from the Fords. "I would take this opportunity of drawing your attention to the fact that by agreeing to place in your hands the majority [stock] of the Société Matford, I have shown clearly my intention of identifying myself with the fortunes of Ford in France," he wrote to Edsel just before the merger. Mathis pointed out that production on his car might be stopped. "Even my name might be obscured."

Edsel replied, "I fully realize and appreciate the extent to which you are cooperating with us . . . and I sincerely hope there will be nothing in our contacts which will be disappointing in the long run." Later both men would have cause to remember this interchange of sentiment.[31]

8

Five-and-a-half years had passed since the launching of the 1928 plan. What had happened to this once promising scheme?

First of all, it developed in a period of economic adversity. When Henry Ford, Perry, Edsel, and Sorensen had brought it to life in Dearborn, the world was riding on a wave of prosperity, and the fathers of the plan had assumed that this happy condition would continue. That a devastating depression had come instead was both disastrous and unexpected; much of the world of 1929–1934 was molded by that merciless experience, and the plan of necessity was affected by it. How the scheme might have fared in a happier economic climate can only be guessed; we do know that it suffered much from this financial and industrial tragedy.

Yet in certain ways the plan was realized.

For example, it was expected to draw the nationals of Europe into the Ford enterprises; it was to develop "from the other side." This it

---

* Perry remained chairman of the Board of Ford SAF but he did not join the Board of Matford, now the operating company in France. He had disapproved of it before its birth and as it took its first steps continued to regard it with suspicion.

successfully did. In 1933, of the fourteen European and North African Ford companies, only two had American managers. In almost every country there was local participation in ownership through the holding of Ford shares in their respective companies by Danes, Dutch, English, French, Belgians, and Germans. All the new Ford factories in continental Europe and Britain had been built by local labor, and by May 1931 not one of the European assembly plants used more than 50 per cent American material (in value) in making a standard Tudor unit.* All factories were manned by local workers and local officials. In the case of Model Y in England, and Ford manufacturing activities in Germany and France, the company's enterprises in Europe forged far beyond what Henry Ford and Perry had expected in the way of putting the stamp of national character upon their activities. In this area practice surpassed planning. It was the only one in which that held true.

The 1928 plan had been deftly tailored to promote the sale of one product, the Model A. It was not permitted to do so; the car itself was quickly modified, then replaced by the V-8. The appearance of the Model Y further confused the original undertaking.

Central in the 1928 plan had been a plant that was to create a "Detroit of Europe." Dagenham was to rise as the largest automotive complex in the Eastern Hemisphere and was to produce for all Europe from Norway to Italy. As we have seen, the great group of factories was completed, although scaled down from a planned capacity of 200,000 vehicles a year to one for 120,000. This was still an impressive manufacturing potential. Unfortunately the rapidly falling market for cars and the high tariff walls erected in many countries cut down the demand for its products. We have noted that with loss of volume costs arose. In 1934 Dagenham built only 57,195 vehicles, working at less than half capacity. Its management despaired of ever meeting Dearborn costs.[32]

Particularly galling to Perry as master of Dagenham had been the change from assembly to manufacturing in both Germany and France. "Perry didn't like the change one bit," said Dollfus. "He thought there

---

* Percentage of cost per two-door unit in American and local expenditures, May 1931.

Country	Total Cost	Amer. materials	Local duty, labor, overhead	European materials
Belgium	$547.10	43 per cent	34 per cent	23 per cent
France	663.28	42 " "	41 " "	17 " "
Spain	947.79	37 " "	62 " "	1 " "
Germany	617.49	33 " "	34 " "	33 " "
Denmark	487.85	49 " "	23 " "	28 " "

was no place for a manufacturing plant in France. Perry was 200 per cent British." No more did he warm to Ford manufacturing in Germany. But he had to accept the inevitable in both countries and after seeing to it that Dearborn financed the expansion, reconciled himself to no longer directing developments in either. However, the remaining European nations in which Ford had plants—Belgium, Holland, Spain, Turkey, Ireland, and the Scandinavian countries, as well as sales companies in Portugal, Roumania, Greece, Italy, and Egypt—continued to take guidance from Ford-England and bought some of its cars.

Fortunately into the rather bleak scene of diminishing and lost markets had come the Model Y, which could be sold in England and elsewhere. It helped Dagenham to maintain itself and grow despite the hammer blows of adversity it had received. Ford-England was thus somewhat like a man who has lost a leg, or even two, but has retrained himself to manage despite his handicaps. The Model Y carried the promise of a happier future.

So the plan had readjusted itself to realities, and if it had been somewhat mangled, nevertheless retained most of the basic bone structure it had known at birth. Meanwhile, how had the companies fared in profit-making?

In 1929 and 1930 they had shown overall gains. Germany, Italy, and Finland reported losses in 1931, but the entire group of associated countries showed a favorable balance of more than $3,500,000. In 1932, however, came small losses in France, Egypt, Roumania, and Greece, plus large ones in Great Britain and Germany; while certain countries like Belgium (which up to World War II was never to show a deficit), Holland, and Denmark made money; but the entire operation was in the red by more than $4,000,000. The following year saw recovery, with Britain again profitable and the total of all European ventures returning a small gain.[33]

Nonetheless, the future still looked black. "Just at the present time international business is awful and no-one can tell from one day to the other what is likely to happen," Perry wrote Sorensen in December 1933. This was a just comment upon a world that had seen automotive production shrink by more than 50 per cent, the gold standard suspended or inoperative in more than forty countries, and the volume of world trade lessened by 40 per cent from its total in 1928.[34]

12
A World Disturbed

"The urge to industrialize this country has gathered such an impetus that it is incredible that it can be permanently checked," wrote Benjamin Kopf, manager of the Japanese company, early in 1935. The people "have become so proficient and efficient that today Japan is one of the serious rivals in world commerce." The motor car and the truck had become necessities. The next step, predicted Kopf, would be manufacture by the Japanese, with measures against imported cars. As the operator of an assembly plant, Ford would be penalized. "The only way for us to retain this important market is to take timely steps to manufacture locally." Dearborn agreed with him, and Kopf, Frank Riecks, and H. R. Hesser sought a desirable site for a factory in the Yokohama district.[1]

They had been matching stride for stride the Japanese efforts to control the manufacture of motor vehicles in their islands. This urge was one aspect of the sense of national destiny that had been mounting in Japan for a generation. Already victors in wars with China (1895) and Russia (1905), the Japanese had been exhilarated by a sense of achievement and prepared to push along the road to power. As an important step, in September 1931 they seized Manchuria.

This was the first aggression since World War I by a nation that felt itself entitled to larger territories and greater prestige. The act launched Japan upon a career of empire building—a dangerous course from birth, for the Chinese were determined to regain the lost area, the Russians were suspicious, and the United States denounced the conquest as a violation of international agreements. The League of Nations also looked askance at it and appointed a committee to investigate. However, the conquerors rapidly converted the area into the "independent" state of Manchukuo, with Henry Pu-yi, former Emperor of China, as its puppet-ruler.

For the time nobody was prepared to use force against the aggressor. Russia was fully occupied in forging her new socialistic order. Europe was sick of war and depression-ridden, and the United States, despite its disapproval, was in the most serious economic collapse of its history, and unready for a war 7,000 miles from its western shores.[2] Japan, however, knew that she must acquire resources to match her new status and worked desperately to develop industrial strength. She had a steel industry and various manufacturing activities. The capacity to make her own motor vehicles would be a large contribution to her growing economic power.

In 1930 this capacity had been wholly lacking. Only 458 motor vehicles had been built in Japan that year, while imported cars and trucks assembled there had numbered 18,663. But by 1934 the home-made machines had risen to 2,701 (613 had been exported) and a year later they amounted to 5355.* This was microscopic by American standards, but the Japanese had faith that their industry would soon become gigantic and supply not only their own needs but also those of most of the Far East. The Manchurian adventure had underscored the need for modern transportation; and although the conquerors had constructed 2,650 miles of railroad by 1936, doubling what had previously existed, they had also built 5,000 miles of highways.

A number of Japanese firms were attempting vehicle manufacture, but those with the greatest potential were the Nissan Jidosha Kaisha and the Toyoda Motor Car Manufacturing Company. However, their growth was still so negligible that Kopf felt a Ford manufacturing company in Japan would be welcomed as raising the total capacity of the country's plants. It was in this belief that he and his associates were searching for a factory site. Dearborn beamed upon their efforts.[3]

They found 91.5 acres on the Yokohama waterfront, purchased them, and in June 1936 applied for two permits, one to erect manufacturing and assembly buildings and the other to operate them. Prospects for Japanese business were now excellent. From a sale in 1932 of 6,505 vehicles, Ford by 1935 had made a recovery to 13,744 units. With Japan busy in Manchuria and speeding up modern transportation at home, the future held a promise of dazzling expansion.

* The Japanese used more trucks than cars (51 to 60 per cent of the total). According to Kopf, this was because the average Japanese lacked space for a garage, and because the truck had become a profitable unit of business. Ford truck production in the USA had increased during the 1920's by 200 per cent, but was less than a fourth of total American output (355,453 to 1,870,257 for all vehicles). (See note 3.)

In 1936 the Japanese home industry produced 9,632 trucks and cars, and Kopf's two applications were refused. "Sorry, we can't allow you to build. We want to protect Japanese industry." Kopf thought that Yoshiyuki Aikawa, the head of Nissan, was responsible for the refusal. "He had convinced the government that he could build a car." On July 11, 1936, the official attitude was firmly embodied in a motor car manufacture law the operation of which limited the making of cars in Japan to the Nissan and the Toyoda firms.[4]

Ford as a manufacturer thus seemed to be shut out. However, the Japanese encouraged the company to maintain its assembly activity. In September 1936 Ford was assigned a quota of 12,360 units annually (while General Motors with smaller sales was restricted to 9,470). Kopf concluded that there might be ways in which Ford could enter manufacturing. "I am not sure of this but believe it to be so." He conferred frequently with officials of the Ministry of Commerce and Industry in Tokyo, and when they continued to tell him Ford could not expand, he favored an association with a Japanese company. Dearborn agreed, and considered a union with the Furukawa and Mitsubishi interests. Kopf meanwhile reported that 1937 was a fabulous year. "We are just coining money." He sold 18,379 cars and trucks (was the quota suspended?), many doubtless used in Chinese operations, which had begun in July 1937.

The prospects for a merger with a Japanese group seemed good, but Kopf found negotiations "discouragingly slow." When in 1937 a new cabinet came in, he grimly reported that the country was "tending definitely toward planned and controlled economy, and private enterprise will have little freedom from now on."

Ford officials, who earlier had demanded a majority interest in any Japanese enterprise, were now willing to take as little as a third * if this could be managed. The change in company policy since 1928 had been drastic. Up to that time Dearborn refused to merge with any national company anywhere. Then in 1929 they had accepted the idea of an Italian merger (which failed), and in 1934 actually effected a union with Mathis in France. Later still, as we shall see, they were willing to unite with a German firm. In all these arrangements Ford had insisted on holding a majority of the stock in any company formed. Now they

---

* Under the July 1936 motor car law, licenses to manufacture in Japan went only to firms that had more than 50 per cent Japanese shareholders, directors, and capital. The law was designed to keep control of new industry in Japan. (See note 4.)

were ready to join a Japanese firm, and for the first time to accept a minority interest.

Nissan now wanted to buy Ford out, and even this was acceptable to Dearborn, but Kopf did not "think they can get permission to remit such a large sum of money as would be involved in this case." Such proved to be the fact. Meanwhile the land for a Ford manufacturing plant at Yokohama was left unused.

After 1938 the Japanese government gradually reduced Ford's exchange and import permits. In 1939, while discussions about a merger with Nissan dragged on, Ford-Japan assembled only 7,894 vehicles (7,004 of them trucks). In 1940–1941 its operations practically ceased, while the native activity flourished. There was no future for Ford in a country where industry was being pushed toward a regimentation as complete as that of the Japanese army or navy.[5]

2

A Japanese stepping off a steamer in Brazil or Peru during the middle 1930's would have found a certain similarity in the condition of either country and his own. Practically everywhere in South America dictators held power. They varied from the gentlemanly Augustín P. Justo of Argentina, whose opponents were "neither murdered, jailed, nor exiled, were even permitted . . . in some instances to sit in Congress" to the harsh Juan V. Gómez of Venezuela, who preferred expulsion, prison, or the firing squad. All these rulers faced desperate economic problems and, like the Japanese, sought solutions benefiting their countries. Everywhere they spoke passionately against the domination of foreign capital. But beyond these points, similarity disappeared.

In 1933 no Latin American nation was close to industrial self-sufficiency. Significant coal and steel industries did not exist.* Manufacturing was so rudimentary that it might be called decorative. In the automobile business a few batteries, springs, wooden car bodies, and tires were made, but little more. The cars on the many new roads were either imported complete from foreign factories, or assembled at plants in the Latin American nations.[6]

The great depression had disrupted business in all these lands. Europe, for generations a chief customer, had suddenly begun to buy

* Only Mexico had a single large steel works.

sparingly and to erect high tariff walls. In self-defense, most of the Latin American republics adopted retaliatory measures: control of exchange, greater tariffs, quotas for imports. Accordingly, while none of them promoted native automotive industries, they created interferences with normal trade which, even as the depression lessened, curtailed activity everywhere.

After 1933 Ford sales gradually rose throughout South America and by 1937 reached a peak for the decade—52,887 cars and trucks (compared with 72,205 in 1929). Throughout the 1930's Argentina remained the largest market for motor cars in Latin America.[7]

Competition had increased everywhere, and General Motors firmly moved in to what had been Ford's preserve; to a lesser extent Chrysler was also a factor. While Ford in the 1930's led GM in Latin America, its margin of superiority was narrow.[8]

In no nation in South America did the heavy hand of the state become a factor, as in Japan. When in 1927 Ford-Brazil began to manufacture truck bodies, it was not responding to governmental pressure. The American-built bodies had not performed well on the country's poor roads. Ford officials knew that Brazilian hardwoods were reasonably priced. They began to construct stake (or simply frame) bodies, then later manufactured panel and cab types. They could thus meet local customer demands and speed deliveries. "We used to make the program for the next month in advance, rather than the three months that would be required were the bodies imported," recalled Humberto Monteiro. In 1937 the Ford-Brazil body factory delivered 1,850 locally made bodies and 2,811 locally made cabs. This activity harmonized with Getulio Vargas' nationalistic sentiments, although undertaken for purely business reasons. It sowed the seeds of vehicle manufacturing in South America.[9]

In Mexico there were no restrictions on foreign exchange, and Ford prospered. (Until the mid-thirties it operated the only assembly plant in the country.) Lázaro Cardenas (president 1934–1940) caused some alarm by his expropriation of the properties of British and American oil companies in 1938, but it soon became apparent that he was interested only in natural resources and that the automobile industry had nothing to fear from him. Cardenas, however, created a difficult situation for the Ford-Mexico management when in that year he permitted a strike against the company. Sorensen and Harry Bennett advised A. R. Lajous, in charge of the Mexican unit, to stand firm: "Don't give them a damn thing." Following orders, Lajous even talked of abandoning Mexico, and soon the Federal Labor Board ruled that the strike was illegal. Unfortunately, Ford sales had meanwhile been cut down to half of those for the previous year (1937: 8,000 vehicles; 1938, 4,000).[10]

After the V-8 cars from Dearborn appeared in Latin America, the older Model A's and Model T's continued in circulation. They passed from owner to owner; their highness off the ground and their rugged construction sustained them. In 1935 a young Argentine, Miguel Divo, drove a Model T from Buenos Aires over the Andes to Santiago, Chile, and up the coast of western South America on to Mexico and New York—a 22,000 mile trip, one-third of which was over high mountains or deserts and through tropical forests. It took him thirty-three months. Two companions who started with him died on the journey. This was only one of the dramatic feats of the legendary Model T, which helped to keep the Ford name alive. The newer products, the V-8, the Lincoln-Zephyr (1936) and the Mercury (1939) never matched the glory of the earlier Fords in South America.[11]

In the 1930's deliveries from the Latin American branches did not achieve a volume comparable with that of European or Canadian Ford factories. Nevertheless in terms of profits and percentages of the markets which they held, the companies in the southern republics did better than Ford-Dearborn. In the ten years 1930–1939, while the parent company showed a *loss* of $62,764,000, net *profits* from Latin American assembly plants amounted to $30,965,668. This startling difference was largely due to the fact that the branches spent virtually nothing on new plants, nothing on automobile design, and nothing on manufacturing. Since they were all wholly owned by the Ford organization, all the profits came back to Dearborn. On no other continent did the American company earn so much.[12]

3

For the year 1935 Ford-Egypt showed profits of $724,000, higher than those of any European Ford company except Dagenham. In the three previous years it had begun with a deficit and then recorded modest gains. Why this pyramid rising suddenly where hitherto no more than a hillock had arrested the eye?

The Ford Motor Company (Egypt) SAE had been founded in 1932 by Ford-England. Operating from Alexandria merely for sales and service, with no assembly plant, it conducted Ford business in Iraq, Ethiopia, Saudi Arabia, Cyprus, Rhodes, Italian Somaliland, Oman, Muscat, Bahrein, Malta, Sudan, Syria, Iran, Eritrea, Yemen, Albania, Sinkiang, Mongolia, Transjordania, Hadramaut, and Kuwait as well as in Egypt.

In 1934 an official from Alexandria was traveling in these lands setting up a dealer network. He was about to return to headquarters when he remembered that he had not vitited Mogadiscio in Italian Somaliland. It was out of the way, but he decided he had better go there.[13]

In Mogadiscio the most promising candidate for a dealer was the owner of a grocery store, an Italian of some local standing. He approached his prospect.

"How would you like to become a Ford dealer?"

The other countered: "What do I do to become one?"

"It's simple. You buy one car and £25 worth of parts, and sign yourself on."

The grocer reflected. "Well, I can use the car myself," he concluded, "and I can afford £25 worth of parts. All right: I'll sign."

The man from Alexandria returned home. Meanwhile Mussolini was planning to invade Ethiopia, and General Rodolfo Graziani came to Italian Somaliland to prepare for the operation. He wanted trucks and was referred to the grocer. "No difficulty at all," the latter told him. "I'm a Ford dealer."

Soon Ford officials in Alexandria goggled when they received an order for 750 trucks from an area that previously had taken none whatever. Ford-Egypt put the order through to Dearborn and followed it with another for 1,100. The American company agreed to furnish these vehicles, and a credit of $1,160,000 was to be established by the Italians in New York. Ford-England guaranteed to provide shipping arrangements for the total number to arrive at Mogadiscio by September 5, 1935.

As a result, Ford-Egypt in 1935 sold 4,767 trucks—422.8 per cent more than in 1934. The manager told his directors in mid-year, "Recent political events in Italian territories along the Red Sea littoral have caused a sharp rise in truck sales." Three months later he recorded "considerable business . . . with the Italian colonies."[14] In October 1935 the *New York Times* reported that Ford-Dearborn had sent about 2,200 half-ton trucks to Italian Africa. The number may have been larger.

With the appearance of this news shipments stopped. Unquestionably Henry Ford's opposition to the sale of vehicles for use in war was responsible. He may well have been ignorant of Ford-Egypt's activities, but the *Times* article made his course clear. The League of Nations soon (November 18) voted sanctions against Italy, which proved to be ineffective. In contrast, Ford's veto had a sharp impact. General Graziani declared in December 1935 that but for Ford, he would have been well on his way to Addis Ababa. "We paid for 800 Fords in advance, but the sale was canceled when Henry Ford began his private sanctions." Had Ford known about and acted to forbid the orders from the start, and had the League dealt as effectively with other commodities, Mussolini's venture into Ethiopia would have been deep in trouble.

Ford-Egypt sales were lower in 1936; in 1937 and 1938 the company paid 200 and 150 per cent dividends, but these were in anticipation of the Egyptian profits tax of 1938. For several years afterward dividends were modest but rose sharply again with World War II.[15]

Ford-Egypt had been exceptional among Dearborn's foreign units in that it had profited rather than suffered from a dictator's policy. Nevertheless, its activity showed that authoritarian government was expanding. Italy, like Japan, was building an empire. What effect this would have on automotive activity was still a question.

4

Elsewhere in southern Europe the sale of Ford vehicles seldom ran smoothly. In Italy tariff barriers all but excluded the V-8 there. By June 1936 Perry admitted that "our experience in Italy has been disastrous." Yet because of Italian government restrictions, Ford Ltd. could not liquidate its large investment. It had to retain its small Italian company, and from 1934 to 1939 suffered a loss of $31,000, which was negligible compared with the 1931–1932 deficit ($699,000).

Perry also fared ill in Greece, where the Ford management fled the country because of a government investigation; in Roumania, where there were vexing lawsuits; and in Turkey where the actions of employees brought on a litigation that drained all the cash reserves of the branch, although finally the Ford management was vindicated of wrongdoing. The Turkish assembly plant—the only such factory in the Near East—was never a profitable operation.

In 1935 the Roumanian government assured Ford-England that if it undertook assembly there, Ford-Romana would encounter no dis-crimination because of its foreign ownership. Accordingly it purchased land and erected Ford's first Eastern European automotive assembly plant, which began to operate in May 1936. For some years it put out about 2,500 cars annually, a modestly profitable enterprise financed en-tirely from its own earnings.[16]

Across the continent Ford-Iberica (Spain) made a 1935 report that showed a net profit of $624,000, the highest in five years. Edsel Ford sent manager George D. Jenkins congratulations on the "splendid results." Jenkins commanded 30 per cent of the automotive business in Spain, and showed the greatest profits of any European Ford company but Dagenham. (Ford-Egypt, with a better record, was in Africa.)

Ford-Iberica assembled its vehicles in a leased factory in Barcelona; about 50 per cent of each unit comprised local parts. As in France and Germany, the government was urging that the proportion of nationally-made parts be increased. Accordingly on May 5, 1936, the Ford-Iberica directors voted to establish a manufacturing operation. They took an option on land for a factory, and Dearborn engineers and architects prepared plans for the building. Then like a convulsive earthquake, on July 18, 1936 the Spanish civil war broke out.[17]

The ensuing hostilities saw the Loyalists (pro-government) achieve control of Madrid and Barcelona, while the rebels, led by General Francisco Franco, held Cadiz, Seville, Córdoba, and Granada. In Bar-celona the Loyalists seized both the Ford and General Motors plants. Jenkins on July 30 fled with his family to France, leaving Juan Ubach, the assistant manager and a Spaniard, in charge of the Ford works. Ubach soon became *persona grata* with the Leftists, who requested him to come to the factory and "be around." They assured him that company property would be protected and expressed their apprecia-tion that in contrast with General Motors, which had closed down, Ford had remained open and was "paying wages and salaries decreed." They promised that when the war ended, "their control will also cease," and Ford "will be the master of the market as it deserves." *

Ubach maintained a precarious but sound position. The workers

---

* Ubach, in thanking the workers, "took advantage of the moment to remember [*sic*] them that Mr. Henry Ford was the only industrialist in the United States who opposed Government orders at the time of the NRA, and that certain impositions might not hold good with the Ford organization." This was a warning against too much control of Ford production by the workers. (See note 18.)

were in control; he was there to protect Ford property and advise about production. He was acting under duress. Ford-Iberica resumed activities, and at the end of August presented 20 armored trucks to the Loyalists, as well as 1,133 new cars and trucks for military transportation.[18]

Meanwhile Jenkins, who had gone on to England and then to Lisbon, had become an avowed Franco partisan and directed all Ford dealers in rebel-held territory to sell cars and trucks to the insurgents. In London Perry objected vehemently, believing that Ford should sell to neither side. He was alarmed when Dollfus proposed to provide ambulances for Franco.

But Jenkins pointed out that if Ford refused to sell to Franco, who he thought was winning, the company would incur the enmity of the new regime. Perry was shaken. Then Ubach with two Barcelona workers came to London; the latter presented the Loyalist case, and while Perry seems never to have supplied them with parts, he recognized that they controlled the works.

Perry's chief concern was for the preservation of Ford assets in Spain. Yet he conceded to Jenkins: "It is admittedly the duty of everyone to do the maximum amount of business." Finally he agreed that Ford-Portugal dealers could sell in Franco territory, but only for prepayment in sterling or dollars. Ubach, who worked under a strain and asked to be relieved, for a time saw production sink to less than 50 units per month, but finally brought it back to 150. Altogether the Franco forces received from Ford-Portugal 5,978 vehicles with spare parts; the number Franco received from Ford-Germany or Ford-France is not known; nor is the production of the Barcelona factory for the Loyalists, although it must have been less than half of what was sold to the opposition. Ford-France made sales to the Loyalists as well as to Franco, but again the number of vehicles involved is unknown.

Franco's army captured Barcelona in July 1939: Ubach was imprisoned, then soon released to help the victorious officials at the Ford plant. When Madrid and Valencia surrendered in March 1940 the civil war ended.

It had been a disastrous conflict for Ford, even though sales had been made to both sides. Its Spanish losses for the 1936–1939 period came to $1,085,000. The plans for manufacturing in Spain were indefinitely deferred.[19]

5

As the head of Matford (the union of Ford-France and Mathis launched in later September 1934), Dollfus in October sent his works manager, G. A. Panier, to Strasbourg to ready the Mathis works for Ford production.*

Dollfus faced a situation bristling with difficulties. The state of Europe was precarious politically, with thunderclouds on the horizon that might mean war. The government of France was changing regulations for business, and imposing tariffs and quotas on imports. The financial outlook was uneasy, and labor a matter of concern to all employers. Competition from Citroën, Renault, and Peugeot was severe. Furthermore, Matford already suffered from internal friction, for the doubts of Mathis had grown with the consummation of the merger, while more and more Dollfus regarded his new partner as an obstacle to progress. Finally, the Strasbourg plant was no prize. "I was unhappy about it," recalled Panier later, for he knew that in comparison with the shining new establishments of Ford-England and Ford-Germany it was a derelict.

However, there were positive factors. The Ford assembly plant at Asnières provided an efficient operation, Dollfus' surging optimism gave the enterprise momentum; and the French government became increasingly friendly as Ford took on a French guise and was much less literal than German authorities in its insistence on what made a national product. Finally, there were the American technicians.

No sooner had the merger become assured than Dearborn specialists in layout, tool design, axles, cylinder blocks, etc. appeared in Strasbourg, ready to help modernize the factory and the foundry. By January 1935 they numbered 17, with Lester Mix in charge. New machine tools were introduced, and the Alsatian workmen taught to use them. With such assistance, Panier rapidly built up an organization and prepared to manufacture two separate automobiles—the regular V-8 with a French-designed body, and a similar car (which came into production

---

* From its formation, Matford was the active agent for both Ford SAF and Mathis. While the latter maintained some independent activity, the French Ford company assigned to Matford all manufacturing, assembly, sales, and service operations. Ford SAF controlled the new company, owning 60 per cent of Matford stock, but in function was merely a holding company.

later) built around a smaller V-8 engine. These two were called the "Alsace" automobiles. As to the second unit, Dollfus on a visit to Dearborn had seen the small motor, identical except for size with the larger one. "I want it!" he had exclaimed at once. "You can have it," he was told. The French supplier Chausson agreed to furnish a body for the car with this engine.[20]

Meanwhile the 4-cylinder Mathis automobile was being produced but without the benefit of Ford machinery and know-how. Dollfus seems to have tried to improve the engine, but a cable from Sorensen in August 1934: "Impossible to interest Mr. Ford in redesign," ended such thoughts. Dollfus, according to one observer, now proceeded to "push Mathis out." The latter protested, got no satisfaction, and soon became a chronic annoyance to Ford SAF.

Visiting Dearborn in the summer of 1935, Panier laid the problem before Sorensen and got some brutal advice. "Why doesn't Mr. Dollfus let him [Mathis] understand for good that the Matford organization is to be ruled by Ford methods?" Sorensen demanded. "Let him be rough once, then he can afford to deal with Mathis in a nice way. . . . Is he afraid I would double-cross him? He can rely entirely on me." Mathis had worried about profits. "Hell, did you expect to make money the first year?" Sorensen demanded. "Build your organization, have your factory equipped 100 per cent and . . . you'll make money after two or three years. If you think too much about money now, [it] may injure you in the future."[21]

Before Panier had left for America, he and the American experts had re-equipped the Strasbourg plant to produce the larger V-8. In February they began manufacturing the engine and completed 43 units that month. On May 29, 1935, on the maiden voyage of the French superliner *Normandie,* Dollfus sailed to the United States to present Henry Ford with a French-made V-8 automobile. "We were the first European Ford company to start building the V-8," recalled Panier later.

The French automobile journals applauded the Alsace, noting that it had been built by Frenchmen with French steel. Dollfus could tell the annual meeting of Ford SAF shareholders on June 28, 1935 that "the aim of our general policy during the past few years, which has been to make a French national work, is fulfilled." By the year's end, 6,709 V-8's had been made at Strasbourg.

Plans meanwhile went forward for the smaller V-8 engine and car, which Mathis wanted to market under his name. Dollfus objected, for there were no Mathis elements in the vehicle, and at his urging the Board in September approved its name as "Matford." [22]

Soon Panier returned from America with a design for the chassis of this smaller car, which he and Sheldrick, the chief engineer at Dearborn, had developed. In France this so-called "Alsace 62" was to become more popular than the larger V-8 model. By the early summer of 1936 the two vehicles with large and small engines were both in production.[23]

Sorensen had correctly prophesied that manufacturing would at first move slowly. A rise in sales for 1935 reflected in part world economic recovery, but there was a loss of $401,000. However, in 1936, with an output of 9,438 vehicles, Matford showed a profit of $138,000.

During 1935 Mathis produced his car but at a loss which mounted to millions of francs.* Dollfus may have expected such a development. Later he said, "It was cruelly underlined from the start to Mathis that we might drop his car." In the fall of 1935 he proposed such action, which, bitterly opposed by the Alsatian manufacturer, was duly taken. In November the last Mathis car was produced (2,983 had been built by Matford). Dollfus had gone beyond Sorensen's advice to "treat Mr. Mathis rough for once"; he had acted to extinguish him.

But Mathis would not be extinguished. The exact right and wrong of all that occurred is not clear; still, as noted, Mathis had never got what he had hoped for from the merger—Ford financial and technological aid to improve *his* car. On the other hand, his factory methods were inefficient and he did not contribute financially to the joint venture. Ford SAF had put in 35 million francs; Mathis, supposed to pay proportionately to his stockholdings, nothing. Dollfus proposed a redistribution of shares to take account of the Ford payment; such action required Mathis' assent, and he refused it. Eventually bonds were issued to cover the Ford payment.

There was now war—open on the part of Dollfus and a guerilla action of petty harassment by Mathis. He sniped at Dollfus' management, even carping at the production of V-8's—a success in contrast with his own failure. Dollfus wrathfully exclaimed to Sorensen in June 1936,

---

* Dollfus put the loss at 9 million francs, enough to more than cover Matford's 1935 deficit.

"Needless to say I am taking no notice of what Mr. Mathis does or says."
Nevertheless the latter had become a running sore on the Matford body
which the organization could not ignore indefinitely.[24]

The international situation was now disintegrating in a manner to
cause alarm. From its first days of power the Nazi regime in Germany
had adopted an almost arrogant attitude toward the victorious European powers of 1918. In March 1935 Hitler denounced the Treaty of
Versailles and re-established general military conscription for his nation. The implications were sinister. A year later the sudden reoccupa-
tion of the Rhineland by German troops, violating the treaties of Versailles and Locarno, alerted all Europe. Lester Mix at Strasbourg wrote
to Sorensen that German forces were taking their positions and the
French were quickly moving up trainloads of soldiers and heavy
artillery. "Just about all the prewar moves were made," he ended.

He, his fellow Americans, and the French were all nervous, but
Sorensen in Dearborn, accepting Henry Ford's assertion that "they
don't dare to start another war," nonchalantly cabled Dollfus, "No
sense in our boys leaving Strasbourg." Of course they didn't; nevertheless the international situation worsened. The Italians occupied
Ethiopia; the failure of the League to enforce sanctions against them
dealt a sickening blow to its prestige; the Belgians abandoned their
military alliance with France and proclaimed their neutrality; and the
Spanish civil war saw Left and Right in fiery conflict. All these events
promoted a sense of calamity in France that shook the business world.
The "Popular Front" government under Léon Blum, which came to
power in June 1936, intensified its apprehensions.[25]

French labor chose this time for a menacing test of power. It began
numerous strikes for better wages and hours, long overdue. So far as
Matford was concerned, these measures posed no serious threat. Ford
wages were higher, the workday shorter than with Renault, Citroën,
and Peugeot. At Asnières the men went out for a token seven-hour
strike, then returned to their jobs. Strasbourg was unaffected. The only
injury to Ford was felt at Asnières because of strikes against suppliers.
As Dollfus stated: "Most of the workmen's demands had already been
met by Mr. Henry Ford, in the past of his own free will."

In fact, Ford temporarily throve, for the plants of its competitors
were closed for weeks. Its sales, which normally could not approach
those of Renault, Citroën, or Peugeot, now surpassed them. In the settlement that was soon made Matford had to make only slight wage in-

creases, while those of the other companies were large. In particular the 40-hour week, imposed by the new government, meant no pay raise whatever for Ford, since it already operated on that schedule. Its rivals, previously working 48 hours, saw their wage bills rise 20 per cent because of that item alone. Matford, in short, had fared well. It felt no slackening of plant performance after the disturbances ended. In contrast, Renault was operating at only 45 to 50 per cent of its previous production.[26]

Dollfus and the Ford directors had now to deal with Mathis, and as 1937 advanced they became convinced that to get rid of him was the only path to company peace. They considered buying the Strasbourg plant, but its owner set impossible conditions. They proposed to purchase his 40 per cent interest in Matford and renew the lease on the Strasbourg factory. Mathis agreed but asked an exorbitant price. However, the escape clause in the original lease permitted Matford to give notice of cancellation in 1938 and abandon the Alsatian plant in 1940, and this acted as a lever to bring their tormentor to a more reasonable attitude. He finally agreed to sell his Matford interest for 142,000,000 francs and settled in the end for 30,000,000 francs in cash and 6,000,000 in Ford SAF stock. This was in July 1938. Early in 1942, after arbitration, Mathis received an additional 5,500,000 francs. The total amounted to more than $1,150,000, not a bad recompense for five years of quarreling.[27]

Since Mathis would keep his factory, Ford SAF was forced to buy or build a manufacturing establishment of its own. This would require extensive financing to cover the cost of land, buildings, and machinery for the complete production of cars. "It would be impossible to find fresh capital in France," sighed Dollfus, for in 1937–1938 the value of the franc was falling and money was fleeing the country.

Nevertheless he had plans for raising the necessary funds, and Sorensen and Edsel Ford agreed with him that capital for the project could be found. On October 26, 1937, the Board of Ford SAF authorized their manager to seek a suitable site and prepare plans for a center that would be ready to operate in 1940, when the Strasbourg lease expired. Dollfus soon discovered a 60-acre property on the Seine near Poissy, only fifteen miles from Paris. It could be bought for $170,000. Dearborn approved, and Dollfus proposed to inform the French Ministry of Labor that Ford would construct a new factory. "In these days I believe this news will be well received by them."[28]

At the same time he proposed an ambitious step: a new small car for the French market. Sorensen was receptive and suggested adapting the latest German Ford. Dollfus agreed, but stipulated that the car must be French in materials and appearance. Such a model would challenge the leading French firms in the low-price field, while Ford SAF would continue to manufacture the two types of the V-8. Dollfus thought that an extra million dollars would provide facilities for making the new car. Roberge later remarked that for a banker Dollfus was unexpectedly prodigal in laying out capital. "He forgot his banking background when he got around to spending Ford money." However, on May 2, 1938 the Board of Ford SAF approved the construction of a plant near Poissy for the manufacture of both the V-8's and the proposed 4-cylinder car.

Financing included (1) the use of available Matford and Ford SAF funds, (2) a loan from Ford-Belgium of 30 million Belgian francs (about $1,000,000) at 5 per cent interest, (3) machinery procured from Ford-US and other Ford firms (eventually bought with borrowed money), and (4) proceeds from the sale of the Asnières assembly plant. The total estimated cost amounted to about $4,000,000.[29]

Thus Ford-France as well as Dagenham and Cologne was to have a modern new plant, one larger than Ford-Germany's. Work upon it began in the fall of 1938, but the time was not auspicious. Matford's 1937 record had been satisfactory considering the state of France and Europe, showing a profit of $127,000. Now, however, with more strikes early in the year and the Czechoslovakian crisis (including Munich and Hitler's seizure of the Sudetenland) sales fell, and some technicians, including the architect of the Poissy project, joined the army. Nevertheless by the end of 1938 Frank Riecks, who had come from Dearborn to supervise construction, could report that contracts had been awarded and construction begun. Happily, a loss which Dollfus had set in December at 13 million francs came to about a fifth of that, or $76,000.

After Munich, a Rightist government came to power in France, and the attitude toward business was favorable. Its officials advised Dollfus that as Strasbourg lay in a danger zone, he would do well to prepare for "a wholesome contribution to the national defense." He began to look for a plant in a "safe" area to which machinery could be transferred from Strasbourg until the Poissy factory was ready.

He concluded that the manufacture of aircraft motors would constitute a needed defense project. Hispano-Suiza and Gnome were the only firms producing them "and in very small quantities indeed."

Dollfus went to Dearborn and won the assent of Edsel and Sorensen to the manufacture of aircraft engines by Ford SAF. A Rolls-Royce contract was contemplated. Dollfus and Panier visited England to study factory equipment and methods and concluded that Ford-France could produce the engine. Later, American Ford technicians came over to help them. The government was now urging haste and almost daily increasing the size of the order it proposed to give.

As a result, on June 23, 1939, Fordair was organized. The government would pay for a plant and its equipment. The new company was owned almost entirely by Ford SAF. About the time of its formation the Ford-France directors authorized the purchase of a factory at Bordeaux. It was a large structure in good condition, with some useful equipment. Dollfus was soon in a position to undertake special war orders and received several contracts for trucks. In August he assumed Lord Perry's place as chairman of the Board for Ford SAF. Meanwhile he was pushing the work at Poissy, preparing the Bordeaux plant for more extensive operations, and continuing to manufacture at Strasbourg. Including the Asnières assembly unit, he thus directed four centers of activity.

In the midst of these defense efforts Dollfus never relaxed his efforts to get the new small car into production. He cabled Edsel in May 1939: SMALL FOUR CYLINDERS IS NOW VITAL TO THE COMPANY. . . . MUST DRAW YOUR ATTENTION TO SERIOUS CONSEQUENCES TO OUR DEALERS AND TO OURSELVES IF PRODUCTION THIS CAR POSTPONED.

Edsel cabled in reply that work on the model was proceeding rapidly. As later correspondence shows, machinery for the vehicle had been assembled in August and was about to be shipped when on September 1 Hitler sent his tanks crashing into Poland and began World War II. The consignment was then held at Dearborn.[30]

13

Extreme of Nationalism

On February 11, 1933, the new chancellor of the Reich, Adolph Hitler, spoke at the International Automobile Exposition in Berlin. His remarks electrified the representatives of automotive firms gathered there. Hailing their activity as "this most important industry," he proposed measures to encourage automobile manufacture, chief among them a gradual reduction of taxes and an extensive road-building program. "If in former days the standard of life for peoples was measured by the mileage of railroads, in the future it must be measured by the mileage of roads for motor vehicles." There was no doubt as to the vigor and importance of Hitler's words, and they came like a strong breeze to a ship lying becalmed with drooping sails.

Hitler looked to American methods as a model for German activity. "You can tell Herr Ford that I am a great admirer of his," he told Prince Louis Ferdinand, grandson of Kaiser Wilhelm II, when that young man talked with him a few months later, just before taking ship for America and the Rouge. But Hitler's aim was to create a wholly German industry, quite independent of the United States or any other country, and in April he had taken his first step by exempting from taxation all new passenger cars. This measure affected the vehicles of the Ford-Cologne factory; but that factory was a stumbling midget, and any admiration Hitler felt for Henry Ford did not extend to his German factory. Under E. C. Heine's clumsy manipulation the Ford operation had sunk in March 1933 to sixth place in car production, with only 5.5 per cent of the new registrations. Opel held 37.7 per cent. In trucks Ford AG had done better: third place and 12 per cent of the total market. The overall accomplishment was unimpressive, and the German automotive firms were determined to keep the "foreign plant" in its obscure position or thrust it further downward.[1] *

* Opel, owned by General Motors, with a long history of activity as a German firm, was not regarded as foreign.

As already noted in Chapter XI, 1933 ushered in a period of great political and industrial uncertainty for Ford-Germany. An overview of its situation, both as to personnel and company problems, will be useful.

2

Unquestionably the dominant personality in Ford AG affairs was Dr. Heinrich F. Albert, its outstanding director, now sixty years of age. Writing and speaking English with ease, widely traveled in Europe and the United States, learned in the law, familiar with the automobile industry, he had unusual talents for shaping company policy. "Albert was not a very strong individual," said the French leader Dollfus later, "but he was a very clever individual." The statement is true insofar as it emphasizes Albert's resourcefulness. It is untrue as to his lack of strength, for the German possessed that too. He could not match Dollfus' pyrotechnic eloquence, but he could assess situations sagaciously and press a point boldly when convinced of its soundness. In 1933 Dr. Albert had not yet assumed the active role he would play later.

In 1933-1934 Heine continued to act as manager, for although his faults were recognized, both Karl Bosch and Albert as directors felt that "we have no German substitute to put in his place." Erhard Vitger in accounting or R. H. Schmidt in purchasing could have handled the company better than Heine, but they were still in their thirties and seemed to lack the experience the position called for.

At this time Prince Louis Ferdinand gave promise of exerting an important influence on Ford activity. He had worked at the Rouge,* was an ardent admirer of Ford, wore the glamor of a high title, and felt that he was in tune with the revolutionary regime over which Hitler was presiding. Although the control of the German company was shifting from British to American hands, Sir Percival Perry continued to guide it. (He remained until June 11, 1937 as Chairman of the Board, when Albert succeeded him.) Sorensen now began to take a fuller role in German operations, and soon other Americans would render valuable service in building up the feeble company.[2]

While Ford AG was now becoming a manufacturing unit, it came slowly to this status and, as noted, had the reputation, maliciously

---

* Prince Louis Ferdinand had visited Dearborn, and at his request Henry Ford had let him work at the Rouge.—(See *The Rebel Prince*, cited in note 1.)

fostered by its competitors, of being "foreign." Through the Society of German Automobile Manufacturers its rivals kept up a drumfire of slander which turned many customers from its dealers' salesrooms. The National Socialist Party looked coldly on the American firm. It issued "Certificates of German Origin," but although by mid-1933 Ford-Cologne merited one, it had not received that precious document.[3]

At the 1934 Berlin automobile show Hitler produced an even greater sensation than in 1933. He declared categorically that "The Government of the Reich will give all support to the development of the motor car industry." The problem of supplying German-manufactured fuel (gasoline and oil) would be solved. He promised the completion "of the enormous network of automobile roads," which had already been built in part. Above all, he proposed the creation of a *"volkswagen,"* a cheap but dependable vehicle for the masses.

"If the German Government wants the German people to take lively interest in the motor car," he pronounced, "then German economic policy must produce an appropriate vehicle for them." He set this as the first task of the automotive industry, for it would open "the market . . . to millions of new purchasers. If we can only succeed in winning the masses to adopt this means of transportation, the economic as well as the social profit will be undeniable."

Scathingly referring to the annual German automotive production of 500,000 units, he called for 3,000,000. He summoned the industry to work toward standardization; that is, that *all the chief parts of any manufacturer's car should be interchangeable with those of all other makes.* All motor car producers in the country but Ford at once approved this step in principle. Ford-Cologne temporized, and while the company was now making an all-German 4-cylinder model and was preparing to produce a German V-8, its attitude as to standardization was to prove an obstacle to the full acceptance of its products.[4]

Perry, surveying the situation, was worried. "The real problem," he wrote Sorensen, "is whether to take action to line up with political conditions now existing, or struggle with them under the belief that they will be only temporary and that reconstruction when it comes will be influenced by old industrialists such as Bosch and Albert." As to the campaign against the Ford car, the situation seemed to him to be desperate. Cologne wanted to court popularity by calling its small car the "Volkswagen," but German automobile industry representatives sternly forbade this. "You know how important this name is to us, after the

Fuehrer's speech." Ford's all-German cars would have to find other names.[5]

The shift to all-German manufacture might have daunted an abler man than Heine. His letters to England reflect constant confusion, now pleading for the cancellation of orders that he could fill in Germany, now begging for parts that a German supplier had failed to produce on time or that were defective. However, most German parts were incredibly expensive because of the need to pay for new machine tools essential to their manufacture, the unfamiliarity of the supplier with his task, and the smallness of the Ford orders.

The limitations of the Cologne plant also made great difficulties. It had a small, meagrely equipped manufacturing department but no foundry. It could finish engines, transmissions, and rear axles, but was forced to draw on suppliers for about 80 per cent of car elements. These included bodies, chassis frames, axles, crankshafts, camshafts, engine blocks, cylinders, storage batteries, magnetos, carburetors, wheels, and many other elements. Of course Ford-Dearborn also used suppliers, but for a much smaller percentage of parts, which it procured in a competitive market at low prices. Ford AG had a desperate time meeting competition from firms like Opel, who made a far larger proportion of their cars in their own factories. In 1933 Ford AG was a deficit operation and in 1934 was still floundering. Letters from Perry comparing the prices of the German Ford with competing makes, and anguished sales conferences which left the products still too costly, both testify to the welter of difficulties.[6]

The state of affairs was known in Dearborn. Sorensen noted it in a crackling letter to Perry, in which he pointed out that Bosch and Dr. Albert must be *personae non gratae* with the German authorities, or "there would not be the opportunities to kick our business to pieces." Not long afterward Prince Louis Ferdinand visited Cologne and on April 26, 1934 aimed a blast from Stettin at the Ford organization. "The ways things are now in Cologne we will be out of business in a year," he declared. "It is absolutely beneath the dignity of the Ford Motor Company to be satisfied with 5 per cent of the German business, whereas Opel-General Motors sell 50% of all cars made in Germany." He called the chief officials "unfit for their jobs." The plant situation was "chaotic," and the dealers uneasy. "Mr. Ford," he announced, "has only two ways to choose with his German plant: to close down or to go ahead in a real Ford way, which means a big way." The prince wanted to accept Hitler's program. He wrote later: "The present system might do [*sic*] its blunders but at large it has saved the German nation from chaos." Of Dr. Albert he wrote that the director "belongs to the passed regime," and that "his system will certainly not return."

Sorensen replied on July 12 explaining the financial problems of the company. He concluded with a sharp comment on the German government, "which will regulate makers and give quotas to each manufacturer. . . . Prices will be determined by them, and they are even talking about design. *I am not sure that Mr. Ford would accept this plan anywhere in the world.*" (Italics ours.)[7]

Dr. Albert had been busy during this period with the refinancing of the company, described in Chapter XI. He was fully aware of the deplorable state of affairs. In a memorandum of June 14, 1934 on the new distribution of stock, he also dealt with the political situation and now indicated that cooperation with the government was desirable. He also seems to have been considering a merger with a German firm, for in August two of his letters mentioned this possibility. On the 16th of that month he wrote to Sorensen about standardization, which he favored.

Dearborn officials meanwhile took measures to deal with Cologne's manufacturing difficulties. In March 1934 A. M. Wibel had protested the high costs in Germany; in July he wrote from Dearborn to Albert expressing anew his amazement at the payments to some suppliers. "We cannot see any justification for prices in Germany being in many instances from 200 to 500 per cent in excess of prices paid here." After making some suggestions, he ended: "Mr. T. F. Gehle of our Purchasing Department is arranging to sail for Germany August 4, and will be with you until such time as the purchasing problem is well under way." Wibel promised to come over later himself.[8]

Gehle duly arrived and found another American already there: V. Y. Tallberg, by birth a Swede, who had been at Cologne since 1929 and had risen from the post of chief inspector to that of chief engineer. The two formed a nucleus for an American group that would soon revolutionize Ford AG's manufacturing methods.

By this time Dr. Albert had visited Dearborn and fully established himself there as the leader of the German company. He was disturbed about the activities of Prince Louis Ferdinand, who had convinced the Nazis that Ford would erect a new plant at Hamburg (they considered Cologne too near the western frontier). He need not have worried.

Two modern Ford European cars: *above,* the Consul Cortina, 1962; *below,* the 1961 aunus.

8. Henry Ford II.

Sorensen had brushed the idea aside. "I believe Ferdinand is very sincere in trying to help us," he wrote Perry, "and that he has not been able to help us as yet. . . . He has no job of any kind in Germany or here, and whether he is ever going to settle down to one, I do not know." He added that "Dr. Albert is still the highly esteemed gentleman we have looked upon him as being."

Albert had been quietly active in making contacts with economic authorities. As he wrote Perry in September 1934, he and Bosch were "members of important institutions of official character by appointment of Mr. Hitler himself. . . . We cultivate this [economic] relationship. But we refrain from approaching the *political* authorities . . . and avoid dragging them into our business." Perry replied that this course was correct and would be approved by "Mr. Henry Ford, Mr. Edsel Ford, Mr. Sorensen, and everyone in authority in America."

In November a third Dearborn expert arrived in Cologne, Fred Young, who began to deal with suppliers handling engines, heat treatment, glass, and enamel work. Wibel himself came early in December and spent a week getting a firsthand sense of the situation. He conferred with Wilhelm Keppler, Hitler's representative, and explained why a new location for Ford AG's factory was for the time at least impossible. On his return to America he wrote Gehle emphasizing the need to strengthen the purchasing department, which really meant strengthening production.[9]

By this time it was apparent to everyone that Heine was a failure, and late in January 1935 he was called back to Dearborn and discharged. To replace him, Dr. Erich Diestel was brought in on probation. He had worked for Albert when the latter had been general manager of the North German Lloyd Steamship Company. Now in his late forties, Diestel held a law degree, had served on the board of the Hamburg Electricity Works, and more recently had been mayor of Altona, a city near Hamburg. Highly recommended by Albert, he was described by Prince Louis Ferdinand as "a very capable man." Tallberg later disagreed. "I have never seen anybody know less about the automobile or automobile business," he said. "He couldn't drive a car; he never even owned one. . . . He wouldn't know a blueprint from a plate of steel." Diestel was undoubtedly a babe in the motor car woods. Auditor A. L. Byrns, reporting on Cologne in April, remarked: "The present intended Manager may make the best Manager in Europe, but the gap between now and that particular time . . . is bound to be expensive for the company." He added that Diestel had never been a Ford employee and was ignorant of company policies. Nevertheless, after less than four months he was elected manager on May 28.[10]

By now Ford AG had produced a 4-cylinder car, the Köln, which was soon to give way to a new model, the Eifel, with greater engine efficiency and a more modern body, which appeared in June. In March the company also offered a V-8, but while the Eifel was entirely of Germany materials, the V-8 was still in process of being shifted from American to German manufacture (the task would be completed late that year). Model BB, a 4-cylinder truck, was soon to be supplemented by Model 51, an 8-cylinder vehicle. As compared with 1934, the sales of all products were rising, and for the year the company was to claim 8 per cent of all passenger car registrations in Germany, and fifth place, while in truck production its sales were creditable, and would win second place for it in 1936.

3

The upward curve of Ford accomplishment reflected the steady effort by the American experts to increase purchasing and manufacturing efficiency. Gehle's earlier efforts were now bearing fruit. He had visited practically all Ford AG suppliers, had made numerous suggestions for economies, and had put strong pressure on them to lower their prices. In February 1935 E. G. Budd, an American owner in Ambi-Budd, the chief body supplier, had promised "a better understanding" as to bodies. W. R. Loughran of Dearborn Purchasing, Harry Ford, expert in heat treatment, Ernest T. Sellman and several other specialists came to aid Gehle. These with Fred Young were all at work by May. Later George Fenske, George Moss, and Rudy Herklotz arrived. They were experts, respectively, in machine-shop layout, machinery, and stock and floor layout.

These Americans waged a comprehensive campaign on dozens of fronts, ferreting out faulty organization, the use of poor materials, inept shop practices, and instructing the firms they visited how to achieve better, quicker, and cheaper production. Supplier after supplier took program from them. The whole German potential for automotive production went up, and prices of parts for Cologne came down.[11]

Albert and Diestel in September 1935, and also in January 1936, petitioned the Economics Minister for a recognition of "equal rights" for Ford AG and an end to discrimination against Ford cars. Because Cologne's products were known as "foreign cars," Albert wrote Sorensen:

No one who is in the public service or on the staff of a Party Department or any semi-official department . . . no officer in the Army, Navy, or Air Force, no member of any undertaking financed by the Government or any of the industries with which Government orders are placed would dare to buy a Ford car.

Albert urged cooperation with the authorities, and the company reduced the amount of "foreign materials" in the Eifel and the V-8 to 0.4 per cent. Meanwhile it sought to meet the wishes of the regime by exporting. Up to 1936 German Ford sales outside the Reich had been negligible. Byrns had described the unit in charge of this work as an "Export Department of two [men] with nothing to export." He proposed to expunge it. But Dagenham learned late in 1935 that an export subsidy was procurable (although to mention it was sternly forbidden), and as a result Perry authorized the Spanish Ford company to buy some cars from Cologne.* This was the entering wedge for a highly essential activity.

At the same time Albert noted that the question of standardization operated against the company in "a purely psychological way," and suggested a merger with some German firm to overcome this final obstacle. We have seen that Ford was willing to consider mergers elsewhere. Early in 1936 the economic delegate of the chancellor, Wilhelm Keppler, urged a union with the Stoewer-Werke, Stettin, and Albert and Prince Louis Ferdinand promised to take the matter up with Dearborn. Ferdinand, now in the Lufthansa, was granted a leave of absence to go with Albert to America and convince Ford officials there that the step would be a wise one. The Nazi regime favored it because Stoewer had government orders but lacked financial backing to fulfill its contracts.[12]

As the merger became a probability, Ford prospects improved. Hitler visited the company's display at the International Automobile Exposition in Berlin in February 1936 and posed for pictures with Diestel. Goering purchased a new Ford car, an Eifel cabrio-limousine. In his

---

* This was before the civil war; after the war broke out, as we have seen, Ford-Germany continued to export to Spain; but now the vehicles went to dealers in Franco territory and not to Ford-Iberica and the Loyalists.

opening speech at the show Hitler spoke of Ford as a pioneer in automotive industry whose principles German motor car firms should follow. As a result of this governmental favor, Ford dealers took orders for 2000 units in March 1936, a new record for the company.

Thus all seemed to be going along more than well when Dr. Albert discovered that Diestel, applying for admission to the Nazi Party, was found to have Jewish ancestors, a fact he had concealed. Although once an opponent of Nazism, Albert now insisted that his former protégé resign, since his continuance as manager would be inconsistent with his heading an all-German organization.*

Sorensen and Edsel Ford were not impressed by this demand. They were much more interested in the merger plea presented by Prince Ferdinand and Dr. Albert. Stoewer was an established German company. Moreover, it possessed a body factory, which when developed would make Ford AG less dependent on its supplier Ambi-Budd. In addition, the manager of the Stettin factory, Frederich Hoyler, seemed well qualified to direct the joint enterprise. Then there was the important fact that Stoewer had government contracts. So tentatively the Americans agreed; Hoyler was to come to Dearborn, and Ford AG was to investigate his company. Ford-Dearborn made it a loan of 500,000 marks for the expansion of its factory.

Unfortunately the investigation by Erhard Vitger of Ford-Germany, completed in July 1936, disclosed that the impressive façade of Stoewer-Werke hid a company that was all but bankrupt. For years it had operated at a loss, and Hoyler had misrepresented its condition. It had large debts, and the loan of 500,000 marks had already been almost exhausted. Vitger and Albert nevertheless felt that a new loan of 800,000 marks would put the crippled firm in a position to make money.

Perry and the American directors firmly refused to pour this sum into a perhaps bottomless hole. Albert, while bitterly disappointed, had to accept their decision. He admitted that Ford-Dearborn might become involved with creditors. "So I cut the Gordian knot and walked out," he reported.[13]

Although the merger had fallen through, Ford had profited from the negotiations. Sales had improved, particularly those of trucks, which had doubled. Prejudice against Ford AG had all but disappeared; it stood firmly in second place in truck registrations and maintained a strong fifth place in the passenger field. Already the Cologne factory

---

* There had also developed personal antagonism between Albert and Diestel.

was being enlarged, particularly by the addition of a new machine-shop building, planned and equipped by Fenske and Herklotz. George Moss had effected a reduction of standing stock, a better use of floor space, and a smoother flow of work through the plant. The suppliers were furnishing parts of higher quality at lower prices. Finally, under Sales Manager E. Haas, with assistance from the Dearborn company, the sales force had been greatly improved.*

But Albert pressed for an even more fully German company. Ford, he argued, had suffered because, unlike General Motors, it had not appeared "on the scene in a German cloak from the start." It should quickly don that mantle. Antagonism had "only receded into the background" during the Stoewer negotiations; it might revive. Ford should standardize all its vehicles, seek government orders, increase its export business, and change its management, *i.e.,* get rid of Diestel.

He considered standardization essential. Actually, no German firm applied it fully; the important thing was to accept it in principle and practise it within reason. Sorensen agreed and approved the conversion of the V-8 engine to a standard motor. Many car parts could be made to the German pattern, but, he pointed out, the interchangeability of *Ford* parts must be assured. If Ford-Cologne wished to export, her cars must have parts usable in Ford cars anywhere. This argument was effective, for Germany needed to export badly; and eventually a limited conformity was worked out which left Ford fairly free.

As to government orders, nobody disdained them, although Henry Ford had specified that they could not be war orders (tanks, for instance). Of course Hitler wanted an automotive industry that he could use effectively in war. Cars and trucks had carried soldiers into the Rhineland. But there was as yet no war, and Cologne, already making a few sales to government officials, hoped for truck contracts.[14]

4

Sorensen's words about export were soon matched with deeds. He encouraged Dagenham to purchase German products, particularly magnetos for its tractors. He also had Dearborn buy German parts.

---

* In 1936 the German industry disposed of 244,289 passenger cars and 71,043 trucks, a 315,332 total. Opel (106,260), DKW (46,020), Mercedes (22,810), Adler (21,480), all surpassed Ford (13,029) in automobile sales, but Ford (7,814) ranked second to Opel (18,280) in truck sales, with Mercedes (6,500) third. It would go on to do better. —Figs. from FMC-Ger., based on industry statistics.

But he went beyond this and urged England to open the markets of northern Europe to Cologne. Perry suggested that the Germans develop markets in Hungary, Czechoslovakia, and Austria, but agreed to their promoting their products in areas principally served by Dagenham. The manager of Ford-Germany reported to his stockholders on May 13, 1936 an export business in "cars, parts, and spare parts" in Denmark, Spain, Roumania, and Bulgaria, and expressed appreciation to Dagenham which "assisted us in obtaining it." During 1936 Ford AG's foreign sales rose 283.25 per cent over the previous year, although the total was only 1,048 vehicles.[15]

During this period Dr. Albert was diligently trying to cast off Diestel. He proposed Vitger and R. H. Schmidt as joint managers, and Perry was receptive. Sorensen, in contrast, opposed the plan. "It looks now that he [Albert] is going to spoil something that is really functioning," he wrote Perry. "Everyone here has been watching Diestel's management and they are pleased." In vain Albert protested that the company had prospered *in spite of Diestel* and not because of him. The man who had never driven a motor car and had been set in the driver's seat by Albert himself continued to pilot Ford AG and was able to report continuing progress.[16] *

While the battle over Diestel was waged by letter, a new crisis arose to confront the Cologne company. "Tire situation catastrophic," cabled Albert and Vitger to Dearborn on August 30, 1936. Tires, in short supply, had been allotted by the government by quota. Now they could not be procured at all unless Ford AG could arrange to buy abroad the rubber for their manufacture. If this were impossible, the company would have to shut down on October 1.

By the German 1936 Four Year Plan all German manufacturers had to export, in order to get exchange to purchase raw materials; not only Ford but Opel and other automobile firms were affected. General Motors assisted its German company to increase its foreign trade; other firms formed an export association. Ford AG looked hopefully to Dearborn. With aid from America, Diestel declared, "We shall not only hold our own but even continue the favorable development of this year."

Vitger and the Ford AG export manager soon sailed for America to present the German case at Dearborn. In conference with American officials they worked out an agreement by which Ford-US would supply

---

* Albert did finally succeed in forming a managerial trio of Vitger, Schmidt, and Diestel. But the latter was *"vorsitzender"* (chairman) and wielded final power.

$60,000 worth of rubber monthly, and Cologne would pay for this with various exported items. While complicated, the pact promised to work, and in several months, despite initial difficulties, the scheme was operating well.[17]

In the course of these negotiations Sorensen came to recognize the vulnerable condition of Ford AG. He again urged Dagenham to permit Cologne to sell increasingly in northern Europe. "This would cut into your market considerably," he conceded, but argued that the very life of Cologne was at stake, and England should make a sacrifice. Perry finally agreed, but warned Sorensen that he would not "keep off the grass entirely with the Dagenham product, so as to permit Germany to build up a monopoly for Cologne cars of the small type." [18]

The further arrangements by which Cologne procured raw materials involved complicated financing as well as trade agreements. Under the latter, Ford-Germany exported a variety of goods to Dearborn (truck transmissions, axles, speedometers, etc.), which Dearborn placed in large part in Japan or South America. But Cologne relied chiefly on car exports to provide foreign exchange for purchasing abroad. For 1937 it hoped to dispose of 8,000 vehicles in outside markets, and, conditional on doing so, was permitted by the government to sell 24,000 cars and trucks in Germany. Technically it met this schedule, producing 24,629 vehicles for Germany and, including parts, exporting 7,688 (more than 700 per cent of the 1936 level). It was granted the right to make up the rest of the 8,000 in 1938.[19]

5

With its factory improved, its suppliers delivering cheap parts of high quality, and the raw material situation under control, Cologne now held a sound position. Its status as a German firm had improved in 1936 and became impeccable when in January 1937 the propaganda office of the Reich Ministry of Economics published a statement of recognition; one was issued by the Army on June 18 and another by the Traffic Ministry on September 1.

Ford-Germany now manufactured the 4-cylinder Eifel and the V-8 and had edged into fourth place for 1937, beating out Adler and pressing Mercedes closely for third. It held second place in truck sales. "Our new Model C car (Eifel) is designated by friends and enemies as the best sales object in the German automobile market," boasted Diestel to Sorensen in the spring of 1937. Roberge, who several years earlier had the worst to say of German sales, found in May that "all units are disposed of to dealers as soon as they are available." [20]

As the year advanced, Albert hoped for large government orders. Sorensen approved. Albert suggested a special 3-ton truck to be designed by a government engineer, clearly for military use. The regime would supply the motor, and assembly would take place in Berlin, where Ambi-Budd was ready to rent Ford a portion of its premises. A. M. Wibel questioned if the vehicle were not "war munitions," but Sorensen eventually vetoed it because he thought Cologne was not technically capable of its production. He said, "Let us make a product that our organization is trained to produce"; but added, "In principle we have no objection to the plan." Albert was delighted, feeling that the way was now open for constructive action. Sorensen had no qualms about working for the government. He scoffed at the danger of war, and felt that orders from the regime would simply help the company.

As a result, on April 20, 1938 the Board of Directors of Ford AG voted to construct an assembly plant in Berlin. Both trucks and passenger cars would be finished there. It was known that the government stood ready to place orders for V-8 chassis, the bodies to be supplied by Ambi-Budd.[21]

In June 1938 the Ford company was promised an order for 3,150 V-8 trucks, and Albert, pleased, wrote to Sorensen: "This is one of the results of your approval to erect an assembly plant near Ambi-Budd at Berlin-Johannisthal." Diestel in July reported that "orders from new [government] sources indicate that we shall benefit thereby." The new building was to be in operation by December 1. Albert wrote that "a satisfactory basis for our production in 1939 seems to be fully assured."

Hitler was taking cognizance of the new Ford organization in Germany, and it may have been responsible for the award to Henry Ford on his seventy-fifth birthday, July 30, 1938, of the Grand Cross of the German Eagle, which he accepted in Dearborn from Fritz Hailer, the German vice consul. A storm of disapproval in America distressed Ford, and he maintained stoutly that he had accepted the decoration from the German people. He was still firmly convinced at this time that there would be no war in Europe. Others did not share his faith: Germany had taken Austria, and there was growing unrest when conditions in Czechoslovakia led to the capitulation of Chamberlain at Munich in September.

Cologne offered an impressive 1939 program, which R. H. Schmidt in September 1938 brought to Dearborn for approval. As to cars, the Eifel was to be continued along with the 85 h.p. V-8. In addition, a new model, the Taunus, would be launched. Tallberg, with Sorensen's encouragement, had been working on this since 1936. It used the Eifel motor but offered a new body with a larger wheel base and attractive lines: it was expected to be "more competitive" than the Eifel. Sorensen called it "the nicest small car that I have ever seen."

In trucks Ford AG had been offering two 3-ton vehicles—the 4-cylinder BB with a 50-60 h.p. engine and the 85 h.p. V-8—and now planned a unit that could use either of these engines. The company also proposed to introduce a 1½-ton truck with a 60 h.p. V-8 engine. It had tooled up for the production of this model.[22]

The Ford truck program interested the government, and on November 24, 1938 Diestel was invited to a meeting at the Air Forces Ministry in Berlin. Representatives of other automobile concerns, suppliers, and various government officials were present. Field Marshall Hermann Goering and Colonel von Schell, newly appointed commissioner for the automobile industry, both addressed the gathering. Goering announced that the Army needed 100,000 trucks, and that the performance of German firms on a voluntary basis had been wretched. "It will now be necessary for me to interfere." Von Schell explained the program. The government would designate certain types of trucks. These the companies would produce. That ended the meeting. Later Diestel learned that both Goering and von Schell had Ford and Opel trucks in mind. Albert wrote Sorensen confidently that he could convince the authorities "to leave us alone as much as possible." The event proved him to have been right.[23]

Not long after this Diestel was asked to resign. Edsel Ford, Sorensen, and Perry, all perhaps worn down by Albert, now agreed that he must go. Diestel had become difficult to work with, and Albert attributed the resignation in September 1938 of Rosloff Sorensen (the company's production head) to his inept administration. Schmidt and Vitger were to manage the company jointly. By December 15 the *"vorsitzender"* was no longer in power at Cologne.

Judged by the results, Diestel's management had been strikingly successful. In 1934 the company had sold 10,008 vehicles; in 1938, 36,748. It stood in fourth place in the sale of passenger vehicles, with 23,969 units, with Opel (114,020), DKW (50,340) and Mercedes (25,330) ahead of it and held second in trucks, its 12,613 being surpassed only by Opel's 22,430. The employees had risen in number from 1,139 to 4,262. While Cologne for Heine's final year (1934) had shown a profit of $2,000, it could now point to one of $487,000. For the first time in its history Ford AG paid a dividend in 1938. Its exports were soaring to a new high.

Had this progress been made in spite of Diestel? He does not seem to have been unpopular with the Nazis,* and one is persuaded that he had contributed strongly to keep the company on its upward course. He got little cooperation from Albert. Albert himself deserves much credit for outlining and pushing the policies that brought the company success.

6

After Diestel's departure the Berlin plant was completed, and the manufacture of vehicles for the government went forward briskly. Planning a domestic sale of 33,000 units, with 9000 cars and trucks for export, Cologne counted on government contracts for more than a quarter of its home production. Ford AG was now cooperating closely with Hitler's regime and, as the summer drew to a close, would become serviceable to him in war. As a symbol of its wholly German identity, the company changed its name in July 1939 from the Ford Motor Company, AG to Ford-Werke, AG.

The policy of Cologne during the preceding four years had paved the way to its present status. Despite some brave remarks by Perry and Sorensen in 1933 and 1934, the only road it could take to success after the political revolution of the former year was one of teaming up with the National Socialists. Albert, a former anti-Nazi, perceived this, and his English and American associates soon swallowed any qualms they may have had and joined him in a bid for prosperity.

The Nazis made them pay dearly for it. They forced the company to manufacture in Germany of German materials practically all the cars it sold there, they compelled no small degree of standardization, set up an export policy that required galling accommodations from both Dagenham and Dearborn, blocked remittances of profits earned in Germany, and imposed truck developments that served their military purposes.[24]

---

* Diestel's Jewish ancestry does not seem to have alienated the Nazi hierarchy, either while he was the manager of the Ford enterprise or afterward. His managerial talents were used by the German government throughout the war.

The iron hand gripped Cologne firmly, although the velvet glove of approbation and profits (which eventually might be taken) made it fairly acceptable. Both Italy and Japan could have learned from Hitler. He did not expel the alien company which his German automotive firms would have liked him to banish. Rather he permitted it to grow and thrive but in the process tamed it thoroughly. In the end it became a favored unit and, when the tocsin of war sounded, was a convenient instrument in his hands for the prosecution of his ruthless policies.

14

The British Empery

"I thought this car really a wonderful production, as exhibited, as unveiled; just as it was, without one plea," declared an English Ford dealer on first seeing the Model Y, in the spring of 1932. "And when I learned that it would (as a production job, coming through the mill at Dagenham, in hundreds, thousands, tens of thousands) be all of twice that job—better-looking, roomier internally, with its fuel tank aft, I decided that it might not be so bad a thing to be a Ford man, and would certainly be roses, roses, all the way, to be a Ford dealer."

The intoxication of this observer with Ford-England's first 8 h.p. unit, designed to meet specific national needs—the first Ford to be manufactured exclusively in Britain—was not atypical. "The fact of the matter was, the little car saved us from going under," and "The Model Y was our only salvation," were the later recollections of higher company officials.

The baby car was supplemented in 1934 by a 10 h.p. Model C for the buyer wanting additional power. These two vehicles—the Popular and the De Luxe as they came to be called—transformed the British company from a deficit to a profitable enterprise. With them, Ford in England was again in a position to challenge the leaders of the British automotive industry, the Morris and the Austin. In that year and the next Dagenham captured between 13 and 16 per cent of the passenger car market, not a giant slice but a substantial share and a promise for the future.

The V-8 car, offered by Henry Ford in 1932, provided exceptional value in the low-priced field to buyers in the United States. Campbell in Canada considered it suited to his market and had promptly begun to manufacture it; but Perry, seeking to avoid extra expense and to concentrate on the new small cars, at first did not want to produce the car at

Dagenham. Instead, in 1932 he began to import a certain number of Canadian-made V-8's, and later assemblies and parts, while Campbell in turn agreed to market the English-made Model Y in Canada and other lands of the British Commonwealth.[1] *

Although successful in England, the small car did not appeal to the Canadians, for with shipping costs it was little cheaper than the V-8. The horsepower tax, which had turned the English buyer to the low horsepower cars, did not exist in the Dominion, and few baby British cars were sold there.** In certain other British territories, however, the Popular created a moderate interest.

Later, Perry altered his opinion of the V-8. It performed brilliantly in British competitions, winning the Gloucester Cup in January 1934 and sweeping the Royal Scottish A.C. Rally in July. For a high-powered car it was relatively cheap and apparently appealed to a limited group of buyers. At the meeting of the English company's Board on November 28, 1934 Perry announced that on July 1, 1935 the company would produce the V-8 car, although the expenditure for machinery, tools, and fixtures would amount to $1,282,400. Thus, shortly after Matford began to manufacture this unit, Dagenham commenced to build it for the British market, ending importations from Canada. The company was now offering the Popular (8 h.p.), the De Luxe (10 h.p.), and the V-8 —all three entirely made at Dagenham. It also imported the Lincoln car and in 1936 formed a subsidiary, Lincoln Cars Ltd., to market it.[2]

In 1933–1934 the British motor industry took remarkable strides toward full recovery from the depression. Unlike the American, Canadian, and French automobile producers, whose output stayed well below their 1929 level, the British manufacturers moved far beyond their former production. They had made 238,805 cars and trucks in the last peak year of the 1920's, but in 1934 turned out 342,499. Ford rode with this surge of sales.

The Model Y had an exceptional year in 1934, selling 54 per cent of all vehicles of 8 h.p. or less. This was an achievement, but late in the year Morris introduced a new 8 h.p. model. Ford itself had offered its

* By importing from Canada rather than from the United States, Ford-England paid 22⅖ per cent *ad valorem* duty rather than 33⅓ per cent; it could also get the right-hand drive, which Canadians made for their overseas markets.

** There was no duty on British imports of automobiles into Canada, but even without protection, the American type car manufactured in the Dominion triumphed, for Canadians demanded power and endurance not yet available in the smaller unit.

10 h.p. Model C that year, which took sales from the Popular, and in 1935 the new Morris also began to lure customers from the company's smaller unit.

Perry and general manager A. R. Smith watched with growing alarm as the percentage of the market held by the Popular steadily declined. Dagenham had made a good profit in 1934 (£508,663 or $2,512,797). Still the company investment at Dagenham in buildings, machinery, tools, and other equipment including blast furnaces, coke ovens, and foundry amounted to more than $39,000,000. The last three units "were white elephants in those days of small production," Sir Patrick Hennessy recalled later. He believed it would have been better to have built a body plant rather than such facilities. Dagenham, the best integrated automobile plant in Europe, needed volume if its size were to be an advantage, and now the sales of its most promising product were falling off.

Perry's response to the challenge of the new Morris Eight and the decline in demand for the Model Y must be considered in the light of these facts. He and Smith desperately wanted to meet the new competition, but without adding to their already formidable investment. When Perry had taken over the leadership of Ford-England, he had expected to deal with only one car, the Model A and its variant AF. The following years had brought Model B, a unit with a new body and the 4-cylinder Model A engine; * then the Model Y (Popular), the Model C (De Luxe), and the V-8 would soon appear. Here were five models, where only one had been anticipated. They could put out a new car in answer to Morris, but this was a costly and doubtful measure and could not be effective for two years at least. Their financial obligations could be met only by big volume production, and that production was needed at once.[3]

Perry knew well the story of the fabulous Model T and how by reducing its price and increasing output, Henry Ford had sold millions of cars and made a billion dollars. The Model Y was a Ford-designed car; could not the story be repeated? Would a sharp reduction in price create a surging demand for the now-faltering English unit?

With Smith he studied the multitudinous aspects of manufacturing with possible economies in mind and felt that the required reduction in cost might be possible. Under pressure from him, all Dagenham be-

* The Model B was built by Ford-England in 1932–1934 in small quantities.

came "cost conscious." He also asked Hennessy, as purchasing manager, to hammer down the prices of suppliers. Up to this point Hennessy had been a rather junior executive, far overshadowed by A. R. Smith, H. S. Cooper, Thornhill Cooper, and Roland Philip (who handled purchasing for the European installations and who left the Ford organization in December 1934). But Hennessy, by getting pig-iron orders for the Dagenham works, had recently shown he could accomplish the impossible in selling; perhaps he could do as well or better at buying.

It was his task to visit suppliers, evaluate their equipment and procedures, help them to improve their methods, and thus enable them to lower costs. A. M. Wibel, William Loughran, Joe Stanton, Charles Carroll, and Claude Nelles from Dearborn all gave him advice, and Hennessy applied American techniques in purchasing, the first time they had been used in England.

Hennessy explains that "whereas previously buying had been haphazard and the supplier—after bargaining—generally got his way; now things were different." Dagenham officials assessed the cost of every part, and used this information to evaluate suppliers' prices. Helping the supplier to lower his costs, they requested of him information on his expenses. Repeated time and again, these methods effected a revolution. Meanwhile, Smith was fostering hundreds of economies in the Dagenham departments.

There was no lowering of wages, but costs on the innumerable purchased items and on those manufactured in the Ford plant were lowered. "It was a splendid combined effort," later recalled Sir Stanford Cooper, who had himself played a part in it.

Perry was now prepared to follow Henry Ford's example. Thornhill Cooper suggested the dramatic form of the final act: the offering to the public of a £100 car. The impact of the event was modified by a gradual lowering of the price, from £120 to £115 on December 31, 1934, and then to £110 on September 25, 1935. But after perceiving that with a slight cutting of dealer profits a further reduction was possible, Perry on October 17, 1935 at the Royal Albert Hall exhibition announced that Ford would offer a £100 Popular car ($493.00)—"a saloon [sedan] car at £100, not only roomy and comfortable, but exceptionally economical."

The news was sensational. "For the first time in motoring history," wrote Dagenham to its dealers, "a saloon car is available to the public at the price of £100. . . . *There has been no reduction in quality, the only reduction is in price. . . .* You may wonder how this feat of economies has been performed. It is an act of trust—we have anticipated the increased sales volume which our dealers should secure and have laid our production plans accordingly. We have done our part of the bargain. It is now for you to do yours."

The public was somewhat bewildered; many thought Ford was offering a new model. The company denied this at once:

> This is a complete misconception, for the really important fact about the £100 Ford—and one of the reasons why it has attracted such remarkable attention—is that it is *not* new, or even a "cheapened" model, but is a car of thoroughly proved design.

> The £100 Ford is, in fact, simply the well-known "Popular" Ford, which has been on the market for nearly four years, and has won a splendid reputation. The price-reduction has not affected the design or manufacturing quality in any way.

A car buyer could purchase a fully-equipped 4-seater Popular Ford for £2 10s. cheaper than the lowest priced 2-seater Austin and for £18 less than the lowest priced 2-seater Morris. Customers flocked to Ford as they would to a bargain counter. Dagenham's share of the "8 h.p. and under" market, which in 1935 had dropped to 22 per cent, in the next year soared to 41 per cent. And not Morris, not Austin, nor any other British rival had the audacity to meet Ford prices. Fords were the talk of automotive circles, and with the renewed popularity of Ford Ltd.'s cheapest car the company's percentage of "Big Six" car production in Britain * rose in 1936 to 22.1 per cent, and in 1937 to 22.3 per cent. It was still some 5 to 7 percentage points behind Morris, but its production of 78,000 cars in 1937 compared favorably with Austin's 80,000. That year was the best twelve-month period in Ford-England's history to date.[4]

2

"The Ford organisation in England has now come to be considered entirely British," stated Perry in 1936. With its British directors, management, and shareholders, with British labor, facilities, and final prod-

---

* The production of the six leading companies, which by 1938 amounted to more than 90 per cent of all British cars. The Big Six, which changed in order but not in identity, were Morris, Austin, Ford, Rootes, Standard, and Vauxhall.

ucts it was indeed a national company. Its executives took counsel with Dearborn specialists on production and purchasing, but they rarely requested or received advice as to sales, finance, or labor relations. In these areas they were on their own. Perry had reorganized the selling practices of his company to follow those of British industry. The injunction of the 1919–1928 period that Ford dealers must sell Ford products only had been completely relaxed, and the smaller dealers were permitted to offer other makes as well as the Popular, De Luxe, and V-8.

In engineering Dearborn continued to insist upon a close control of design. Nevertheless even in this field Dagenham personnel were showing an independent spirit. High executives in the English company later gave credit for this development to Smith, himself an engineer and the overall manager of the great plant. He later summarized what happened:

> We had to take risks. . . . We had to do things in defiance of the gods. There were occasions when we just had to find our own way simply because the Americans were so busy with their own problems that they could not pay much attention to what we were doing. The generation of engineering competence was a very gradual thing covering a long period and I would say that it extended back to about 1932. You can't draw a sharp line and say: "After such and such a date independent English engineering began."

By 1935 British engineers had contributed to the re-design of the Fordson tractor (in which Dearborn was little interested), and were offering important suggestions as to car design, although the Americans still made the final decisions.[5]

To carry the story further and indicate the character of the change, in that year Dagenham planned two cars which later became the Anglia and the Prefect. The English directors were delighted with the accomplishment, but realized that their engineers had violated a sacred canon of procedure, and that Dearborn would have to approve the proposed vehicles.

Perry decided to send Patrick Hennessy to America with the mock-ups and see what he could do. It was a formidable assignment, but Hennessy took it, although he had recently returned from the United States. When he arrived again at the Rouge Sorensen demanded: "What the hell are you doing here? I thought you'd gone home." Hennessy then had to tell him about the new cars.

Sorensen blew up, stormed up and down about British audacity, flatly refused to look at the vehicles, and told his visitor to head for England immediately. Hennessy decided to have another try at it, borrowed a company car and spent a week in northern Michigan, and then returned and sought out Sorensen again. Sorensen, in a better mood, invited him to a world series baseball game, and Hennessy asked him once more to examine the cars, arguing that they supplied definite needs in the English market. Sorensen exploded again but finally simmered down and agreed to see the two models. However, after looking them over he snapped: "Take an ax and chop them up. You're fired." Then he added with a grin: "Now we can go to the ball game." After that, like a man who has protested loudly but has finally taken a bitter dose of medicine and is glad to have it over with, he was very affable. Detroit won the game and the series, and he was in still better humor.

The next day after lunch Hennessy found himself with Sorensen and Edsel Ford. Sorensen's amiable mood still held. Hennessy determined to make a plunge for his objective, and said: "Mr. Ford, have you some time?" "I always have time for you, Pat," was the response. Hennessy explained that he wanted Edsel to look at some cars and led him to the mockups. He was "keyed up to do a wonderful selling job," but to his amazement Sorensen took the ball from him and began praising the English vehicles. "Aren't they two nice jobs?" he demanded and repeated to Edsel all the arguments Hennessy had used the day before. The cars were accepted and in 1937 were put out by Dagenham. While they were modifications of the Popular and the De Luxe, they were the first notable contributions of English Ford engineers to automobile design.

They marked an exception to and not a reversal of policy. English activity in car design was still "sternly forbidden," recalled Hennessy later. At the same time, the British felt an advance had been made, and it was to affect future practice.[6]

Meanwhile the £100 car had advertised Ford Ltd. into a position of importance, and Dagenham production had more than doubled that of Ford-Canada, so that the English company stood as the leader in all Ford operations abroad.

This position had not been obtained without some sacrifice in the field of employer-employee relationship. Dagenham had been called a little Rouge, and it now began to resemble the Rouge, which American workers called "a place of fear," in spirit as well as in appearance. Like

Henry Ford, Perry believed in high wages and paid them; and he took pride in a clean factory, which he maintained. He was consistently considerate of his employees. Yet Dagenham did not win the plaudits of its workers. There had been only one short strike in 1932, and it was to be the only strike of the decade for the plant. The hours of labor were not long. Dagenham employees earned more than English workers in comparable jobs; they bought cars, radios, and other conveniences their parents had never known. Yet the drive for lower costs and higher volume brought with it a pressure and monotony which most factory employees grimly felt. A biased novel of the 1930's about Dagenham by Cresswell Curtis (pseudonym for John Watson) describes the typical foreman's attitude as "I'll get costs down" and tells how in pursuing this aim he pushed and badgered his work force and "saw in the men and the ranked figures on the cost sheet a resemblance." While the picture was not so black as Curtis painted it, there is no doubt that it was a dreary gray and was so chiefly because of the unrelenting effort to increase the man-hour product.[7]

Indeed, with 8,605 employees in 1935, and a constant pressure for greater efficiency, Dagenham saw personal relationship between management and labor dissolve in the size and routines of the factory operation. Nevertheless, Perry continued to be mindful of his employees, and in that very year he began to expand social welfare benefits. (It will be recalled that in his drive on costs he had not lowered wages.) In 1934 Ford Ltd. paid the absurdly small sum of £19 for employee welfare (£4 for a Sports Club and £15 for gardens). By 1937 the total had been enormously raised, and came to more than £136,000. The largest single item of £125,000 included a pension plan for salaried employees and a special scheme for hourly workers, by which every individual on leaving the company would get £5 for every year of employment after January 1, 1935. Dearborn officials complained that one plan of Perry's, for holidays with pay, put "a rather heavy handicap upon your business." Nevertheless in 1938 the English company also put this feature, costing more than £90,000, into operation. In general the policy at Dagenham was no union, a clean factory, high wages (for the time), and enlightened welfare plans.[8]

As the British operation expanded, Perry recognized that it could not be governed well by a single individual, and shared responsibility at the highest level with A. R. Smith, H. S. Cooper, Thornhill Cooper, and increasingly with the brilliant and energetic Patrick Hennessy. A decision by any of these men came to be recognized as authoritative, while Perry himself kept well informed on what they did and was always available for consultation.[9]

Dagenham in the early 1930's had not given special attention to the export problem, for Perry and Ford in 1928 had assumed that once Dagenham achieved volume production, it would automatically supply all the nations of Europe. When the factory output rose to a substantial level in 1932 and 1933, conditions, as noted earlier, had changed. The Model A was going out and the V-8 coming in, and it had become apparent that Dearborn could supply either car to the continental markets at a lower price than Ford-England. In Britain the Model Y and the Model C saved the situation, but demand for these cars was slack in Europe, where customers could obtain the V-8 at a slightly higher price. "Foreigners, including our own colonists," Perry himself stated regretfully, "do not like these cars and will not buy them in any considerable quantities."

In addition, as we have seen, these vehicles when sent abroad were too English in appearance, and encountered high tariffs, as in France, Italy, and Spain. Ford-Germany adopted the English small car, but produced it in its own factory at Cologne. Moreover, Denmark, Greece, Hungary, Italy, Portugal, Roumania, Spain, Turkey, and Yugoslavia all had established government exchange controls, which limited the number of cars that could be purchased. Belgium, France, Holland, Ireland, Sweden, and Switzerland imposed no exchange restrictions, and in these countries the imported V-8 sold best (although British-made V-8's took only a minor portion of the market). In Denmark, despite restrictions, sales could be made in limited quantity, although never in volume comparable with the 1923–1926 or even the 1929–1931 periods.

Nevertheless, Dagenham always wanted to develop its exports. In 1933 H. A. Denne, manager of the Malayan subsidiary for Ford-Canada, decided to return to England, and Campbell, who reluctantly agreed to his leaving, sent him word that there was something for him at Dagenham. When he went there A. R. Smith offered him the post of export manager for the Ford Motor Company Ltd.

Denne accepted it. He found that he was filling a vacuum: no one had given attention to organizing the exportation of company products. "I didn't even have a desk at first," he recalled. But he did have ideas as to what might be done. He found a man or two with experience in the field, trained a few others—"It was a catch-as-catch-can activity"—and in two years had a staff. By 1935 he exported 23,436 vehicles, about 30.9 per cent of the Dagenham total output (75,746). Tractors were a large part of what was sold abroad (82.4 per cent in 1938), and the chief customers were, in order, Ireland, Australia, Sweden, New Zealand, the United States, and South Africa.

The new department was operating in a period of growing tensions so far as Europe was concerned. In many countries on the continent where Ford had companies, these could purchase parts locally far more cheaply than from Dagenham. This applied particularly to the Belgium, Dutch, Danish, and allied companies (Sweden, Finland), and contributed to lower British Ford exports.[10]

Perry complained grimly at a meeting of Ford Ltd. stockholders in early 1939 of the "tragic degeneration of international trade" during the last decade and took the experiences of his own company as an example. It was on economic nationalism that he put the chief blame. Nevertheless if the European associated companies did not meet expectations in absorbing Dagenham exports, those in Denmark, Holland, Belgium, Finland, and Ireland (after 1935) showed profits, and Ford Ltd. benefited from the good returns. The gains in these nations far offset the European associated companies' losses in Turkey, Greece, Italy, and after 1936 in Spain.

Perry's "Office of Sir Percival Perry" in London, with H. S. Cooper, Thornhill Cooper, and their staff, kept in close touch with all the companies. Perry himself traveled in Europe regularly, and Sorensen often joined him. Other Americans, among them Roberge (foreign sales), H. L. Moekle (accounting), Al Byrns (auditing), Tom Naubert (service), William Loughran (purchasing), and Laurence Sheldrick (engineering) also appeared on the continent.

All instructions came from the London office. But some of the European managers preferred to look to Dearborn for guidance. When the Dutch manager deviated from routines, Perry protested to Sorensen:

> I believe . . . you do not intend that other Companies in Europe [that is, other than those in Germany and France] shall make direct contact, either with the French and German Companies, or with America and other Ford organizations, independent of this office and established procedure.

Sorensen agreed. His instructions to Perry on how to deal with the Dutch manager were forthright: "Stop him. That is the only thing I can say." [11]

Perry's relationship with the European managers was in general harmonious. That these companies had local directors, in many cases national managers, and large blocks of stock publicly owned in their respective countries rarely interfered with their working together. Only once in the decade did the directors of an associated company threaten to resign on a question of policy. The profitable Belgian company had been lending money to Ford-England; toward the end of the 1930's Perry asked it to assist Ford-France. But Camille Gutt for the Belgian directors insisted that the terms of the proposed loan would "detrimentally affect the moral and perhaps the material position of the Ford Motor Company of Belgium." He argued: "No first class Belgian company would accept such a practice." The question was referred to Edsel Ford in Dearborn, and the matter was resolved by changing the terms of the loan. The Belgian directors did not resign. This was the sole crisis in a sea of decision-making, discussing, and organizing that embraced the Ford relationships throughout Europe.

Perry held annual dinners in Paris for the managers and directors of the associated companies, and it was a brilliant group that he assembled on each occasion. They represented the cream of European industrial leadership. With the exception of Leroy Wood, the Belgian manager, and George Jenkins of Spain (whose role as we have seen was diminished because of the civil war), those gathered were of entirely European background: Danes, Englishmen, Dutchmen, Frenchmen, Germans, Spaniards, and Belgians.

In the 1930's all these executives had fought an uphill fight against numerous obstacles, often formidable, to expand Ford business. Perry had backed them and participated in their battles. He was a very active director of all the companies. Yet his real achievement had been in England, and to that story we shall return after taking account of the other great British activity across the Atlantic.[12]

3

For twenty-eight years Ford-Canada had produced more cars than any of Dearborn's foreign companies. When Dagenham in 1932–1933 began to manufacture in quantity and took the high place the Dominion had occupied, the Windsor organization still remained impressive in size, output, and profits. At the end of 1934 it could show total assets of $56,490,254, of which $25,619,523 was represented by land, buildings, and equipment. Its net gains for the year amounted to $1,878,112. In April 1936 its president, W. R. Campbell, announced that the company counted 20,875 shareholders, of whom 14,027 were resident in Canada. He himself and all the company's chief executives except production manager George Dickert were Canadians.[13]

Unlike Ford-England, the Dominion company did not introduce special products for its home market. As in McGregor's days, and the earlier years of Campbell's leadership, it felt that Americans and Canadians were sufficiently similar in their tastes to be offered essentially the same vehicles.

Sorensen on one occasion wrote Perry of Campbell, "He is so close to us that his men who contact our engineering as well as manufacturing end sometimes sense changes that are coming along before even the drawings are completed." When Perry complained about Dearborn charges levied on Dagenham, Sorensen noted, "We have never had any argument with Ford of Canada on the cost of engineering charges" and recommended that Perry talk with Campbell to learn how Dearborn and Windsor got on so well together. The Canadians dealt with the American officials on a topmost but informal level. Rhys Sale later recalled that Campbell was across the river "almost once a week," and on these occasions would lunch with Henry Ford.

So great was the confidence of Dearborn in the Dominion management that although Edsel, P. E. Martin, and Henry Ford were directors of Ford-Canada, they did not attend its Board meetings. Correspondence between the two companies was scant; minutes of Dominion Board meetings were kept in Windsor, not in Dearborn. Campbell frequented the Ford Engineering Building when the V-8 was being designed, and watched, inquired, prodded, and even advised on its construction. As noted earlier, he became an enthusiastic proponent of the car. When in 1935 Ford-Canada built its own foundry, Dearborn executives helped with its construction.[14]

Campbell and Perry knew each other only casually. They had discussed the marketing of the Model Y and the Canadian V-8 in their respective countries, but in general had few business dealings. The Ford empire was of such a character that both men looked to Dearborn for guidance, and both tried to model their industrial policies after that of their common hero, Henry Ford. Both also shared a respectful confidence in Edsel Ford, who discussed their policies with them and showed a keen interest in the operation of their companies. Campbell and Perry were both brilliant executives, both were self-made men, and both combined a certain idealism in their attitude toward their workers with a resolute antipathy to trade unions.

We have seen that Perry tried to provide high wages, a clean factory, and definite benefits for his employees. Campbell's attitude was in the early 1930's in some ways even more pro-labor. Addressing the Canadian Chamber of Commerce in September 1934, he declared that in this time of depression, "until every man in this country capable of working is able to find gainful employment, the prime responsibility of industry is to the worker. The employee's interest must not be subordinated to the interest of the stockholder." Workers, he asserted, "ask employment at a reasonable living wage, under proper working conditions. They ask the continuity of their employment be reasonably assured, and they ask these things rightfully. . . . Labor is entitled to a greater return for its production than has generally been accorded."

His statement continued: "What we must do is start the ball rolling upwards, injecting more money into our economic structure at the bottom through wages of these industrial workers and profit by the steadily increasing circulation of this money upward through our whole business fabric. . . . Our first objective, therefore, is to improve the conditions of our industrial workers." Campbell argued that conditions "which breed discontent . . . upon which radicals and malcontents fatten . . . must be rooted out and replaced by conditions which foster a contented employed class."

Not five months before this speech (March 13, 1934) wages at Windsor had been raised from a minimum of 50 to 62½ cents an hour; in May 1935 they again went up, and the 75 cents minimum restored the rate of $6.00 for an eight-hour day, which had been Ford practice in the 1920's. The wage was identical with that paid by the American Ford company and was good for the era.

Campbell saw himself as a benevolent employer. Like his mentor Henry Ford and like Perry he saw no reason for labor unions or labor-management negotiations. He felt that he would do well for his workers. As the 1930's waned and the spirit of trade unionism permeated labor in the Detroit area, an older Campbell shifted from benevolence to intransigence. Workers at Ford-Canada, although well paid by current

298

standards, wanted a voice in the setting of work conditions, and Campbell couldn't understand their feeling. The result was the growth of an explosive labor-management relationship which was destined to erupt later. However, for the time it was ignored. "I don't recall any labor problems in the thirties," remarked one executive later.[15]

Ford-Canada in this decade was not a growing operation: at no time did its output equal the 1929 level. It was also marked by a concentration of power. Perry had broadened the base of management; Campbell contracted it. He shared high authority with no one, but rather hugged it to himself, becoming an autocrat and making decisions unilaterally. He was of course experienced and highly capable, and the smaller size of the Canadian operation made his course practicable, although unhappy for the future.

Perry and Campbell each had extensive areas abroad to supervise: as we have seen, Perry kept in touch with most of his territories by personal visits; Campbell in contrast never once called upon any of the wholly-owned Canadian subsidiaries overseas. (However, Perry could easily go to nearby European cities, while the distances from Windsor to Singapore, Port Elizabeth, or Melbourne were fabulous. Campbell often visited the United States and on occasion was in London.) No top rank Canadian officials went to Africa, India, or Australia in the 1930's, although as we have seen P. W. Grandjean, Ford-Canada's secretary, had helped to establish H. C. French in the latter continent in 1924–1925, and the Windsor export manager, R. S. Milliken, had also traveled in the 1920's. Actually, it was an exceptional trip when Ford-Canada's assistant secretary, G. G. Kew, went in the early 1930's to South Africa to make an audit there. This was an almost 8,000 mile journey, and India, Malaya, and Australia were much more distant.

However, the managers of these Ford-Canada subsidiaries made regular pilgrimages to the home office. H. F. A. Stockelbach from South Africa; H. C. French from Australia; J. L. Chidsey and, after 1936, Basil Stevenson from India (where Ford operated three assembly plants); Stevenson and then C. J. R. Michels from Malaya—all these came to Windsor to report to Campbell and to discuss future policy with him. On these occasions, the officials would stop at the administration building in Dearborn for lunch and a social call on the American officials. Because of their remoteness from Canada the overseas managers had of necessity a large amount of independence, and Campbell expected them to exercise it; at the same time, he watched their activities carefully and they had to get approval from him on prices of vehicles, dividends declared, and leases or purchases of property.[16]

Only rarely were Dearborn officials consulted on problems in South Africa, India, Malaya, or Australia. There is no evidence, for example, that Dearborn was a party to the decision in 1936 to set up a wholly-owned Ford-Canada subsidiary in New Zealand. When in 1935 Indian government officials in Bombay considered erecting a car manufacturing plant, they immediately thought of Henry Ford and asked him to help them "as he has helped Russia and so many other countries." Having made their appeal, they did not press it for several years, but in 1939 renewed their request. The Indians wanted the Ford company to make an arrangement for the "manufacture in India of Ford cars and trucks on a royalty basis." They wanted permission to sell the units they built.

Campbell went to Dearborn and participated in all the discussions. Sorensen proposed to leave the matter to Campbell's judgment, but the Indians continued negotiations with Edsel Ford. Eventually, Henry Ford stated that it was impossible to help them, and his refusal appears to have been based on Campbell's conviction that their plans would be disruptive to the Ford organization in India. The attitude of the Indian leaders bore a resemblance to movements for industrial self-sufficiency in other developing nations like Russia, Japan, and Spain, but in this case the call for help fell on deaf ears.[17]

The 1930's saw the maturation of the Australian Ford enterprise. Facilities at Geelong for body manufacture and assembly were enlarged in 1934, 1935, and 1937, and new branch assembly plants were authorized. Ford made bodies for the V-8 cars, and after 1935 produced them for the 10 h.p. English Ford De Luxe. This model achieved some popularity in Australia. However, the V-8 continued to lead all Ford cars in the Commonwealth throughout this decade. Never in the 1930's did H. C. French achieve the 30,000 vehicle goal he had set in 1924. In 1939 Ford-Australia did dispose of 17,808 cars and trucks, an all-time high, and achieved the largest market penetration of its history—22.6 per cent of registrations compared with 37.1 per cent for General Motors.

It was the dividends of the distant subsidiaries of Ford-Canada that made the Windsor organization a profitable enterprise in the 1930's. During the decade, between 30 and 61 per cent of Ford-Canada's output each year was sent abroad, most of it to the wholly-owned companies. Without such export opportunities, Ford of Canada could never have maintained its position as the largest automotive firm in the country. In 1935 it produced 46.4 per cent of the total Canadian output and of this production, it exported almost 48,000 units, or 59.54 per cent of its factory sales.

In most of Ford-Canada's foreign markets it outsold General Motors. (Australia was the exception, chiefly because General Motors in 1931 had purchased the Holden Motor Body Builders Ltd., which, as noted in Chapter VI, had served a number of firms, and gave General Motors a strong position in the country.[18] By buying the Australian company, GM assured itself first place in the Dominion.)

At home the Windsor record for the 1930's was not a happy one.* The company sold 24,216 cars in 1935, 24,066 in 1937, suffered a decline with the recession of 1938, and in 1939 marketed only 19,260 vehicles. In no year of the decade did its performance approach the 37,503 record of 1929. Moreover, by 1935 Windsor stood in second place in Canadian sales behind its great rival, and for the rest of the period ranked in third place, its sales falling behind those of Chrysler as well as those of General Motors.

Chrysler was a pioneer among American companies in introducing a special Canadian-type car. The small Dodge, as it was called, was first offered in 1933. It got 6.4 per cent of the low-priced field that year, and increased this share until after 1937 Chrysler's two cheap cars, the Plymouth and the small Dodge, together outsold the Ford, while the large Dodge, the De Soto, and the Chrysler models added to Chrysler's totals. General Motors in 1937 offered its second low-priced Canadian car, the "small Pontiac." Ford made no response to this new competition; not until the postwar period would Ford introduce special "Canadian cars." However, in 1938 Ford-Canada did offer the Mercury (in the medium-price range), which in 1939 took 3.78 per cent of the market.

In trucks the company did better, taking first place in Canada in

---

* To a large extent, the decline in the Canadian market reflected a comparable and in certain years a more serious loss of position of the American Ford company in its domestic sales. The latter company lost first place in the passenger car market to General Motors in 1931. In 1933 and in every year for the remainder of a period of ten years following 1936 Ford sales followed those of Chrysler as well as GM.—See Nevins & Hill, II, Chaps. 3 and 5.

1935, 1937, and 1938; GM led in 1936 and 1939, while Chrysler lagged behind. But it was the passenger car market that was important, and here Ford-Canada had been defeated.

During the 1930's the Windsor and Dearborn companies turned out models at exactly the same time. "Just as soon as they issued the engineering [information] we'd make the change," recalled R. M. Sale. "There was no delay." But toward the end of the decade, when the 6-cylinder engine was being introduced in Dearborn, first in trucks and then in the cars, Ford-Canada did not follow. Sale and others were eager to get a 6-cylinder car for Canada, but Campbell "was smitten on the V-8," and did not start producing the new motor.

In the mid-thirties Windsor realized that its 1922–1924 facilities were inadequate for the production of V-8 cars, and began a program of expansion and modernization. In 1935 came its new foundry. The company also increased its power-house facilities, enlarged its machine shop, and erected a new building for bodies and final assembly. Furthermore, it built new branch plants at Vancouver, B.C., and Saint John, N.B. The cost of the program, completed in 1939, ran to $10 million. The company now had relatively modern facilities, but they failed to help the sagging domestic sales situation.[19]

4

The dynamism that Windsor lacked was evident in Dagenham. Yet the Popular with its £100 price, which was the vital element in the situation, had won Dagenham prestige at the sacrifice of a small financial loss. In addition the dealers were restive: they sent a deputation to the company, which protested that with the cut in their margins that Perry had made, their earnings were too small. Nevertheless the Popular aided in raising Ford Ltd.'s production to the high point of 112,863 in 1937. Moreover, on all its other Ford products the firm could show respectable profits, even aside from the gains that came to it through its affiliated European companies.

In terms of the world-wide Ford organization, Ford-England's sales were better than those of other foreign Ford companies. Ford in most markets sold more cars in the 1920's than in the ensuing decade, but in Europe it did much better in the mid-1930's. Appendix 5, Chart III explains this. The introduction of the special European-type car (in the main the English car) made the difference, and accounted for the Ford success.

Perry had had the support of Dearborn in bringing out the low-priced Popular, and Sorensen kept urging him to ignore immediate financial results and keep the price down. Sorensen drummed this into Thornhill Cooper, then visiting Dearborn. Sorensen explained that the purpose of bringing Cooper over was "to see how he could help from a sales standpoint the production angle and its costs." By the end of 1936 Thornhill Cooper had become the key man in the Sales Department at Dagenham.[20]

More important was the introduction by Dagenham in the fall of 1936 of a new English-made V-8, and much more important, the offering in the fall of 1937 of two new cars, one a Ford Eight (8 h.p.) and the other a Ten (10 h.p.). These were the models Hennessy had taken to Dearborn with trepidation two years earlier. Henry Ford was now playing no part in selecting Ford-England's cars. Hennessy remembered having lunch with him when he visited Dearborn but recalled that "I never talked business with Henry Ford." It was with Sorensen and Edsel that he discussed his work.[21]

The new cars won a good press in Britain, and they marked a point of departure for Perry. By this time he recognized that he could not continue to sell the Popular at £100. The matter had been considered fully at the June 1937 Board meeting; the car carried a price far below competition yet was being outsold. Perry now declared that a policy of reliance upon low retail prices could "obviously be carried too far." Accordingly, when the new models were introduced in September 1937 their prices were raised, as were the discounts to the protesting dealers.

The new cars did not sell as well as expected, for just as they were introduced the market took a turn for the worse. They were still priced below competition, and Ford boasted of the lowest prices, roomiest bodies, and the best all-around performance. In October 1938 the Prefect car was introduced (the Ford 10 h.p.), and on January 1, 1940 the Anglia (8 h.p.). It was these small cars rather than the V-8 that accounted for most of Ford-England's volume.

The decade closed unhappily for Ford Ltd. The company's percentage of Big Six production fell in 1938 and 1939 (to 19.0 and 14.7 per cent). Dagenham still ranked as one of the Big Three, but the competition of Vauxhall, Standard, and Rootes for its place had become severe.

The English market was now suffering from the 1938 economic recession and the unstable political situation in Europe, as well as from a flood of German vehicles which provided a new and serious rivalry to the English small cars. Although Ford passenger automobiles never outsold Morris or Austin in this decade, Dagenham's recovery in the low-priced field had been sensational.[22] On the other hand, it had more difficulty with trucks. The V-8 power plant, which it used, was not economical, and Vauxhall's Bedford (a British edition of the American Chevrolet truck) far outsold the Ford model. Ford dealers demanded a 4-cylinder engine, and the English company began to import from Ford-Germany the old BB engine that was still being made there. By September 1937 "in deference to persistent requests from our dealer organization," Ford of England resumed production of a 4-cylinder truck engine. This soothed the sales organization and somewhat improved the situation. But the company still had an uphill fight and stood in third place in trucks after Morris and Vauxhall.[23]

5

Of all Dagenham's products, the Fordson tractor was the most successful. In England this machine had no rival whatever.

We have seen that in 1933 tractor production had been moved from Cork to Dagenham. Here it started slowly, 2,778 units in 1933, 3,582 in 1934, 9,141 in 1935, 12,675 in 1936, and a culminating 18,698 in 1937. These figures correspond closely with those for *total* English agricultural tractor production as given in the statistical summations of the Society of Motor Manufacturers and Traders. Ford thus had a virtual monopoly of the English tractor market. The mounting volume of Fordsons produced at Dagenham was a welcome addition to that factory, for it helped notably to carry the heavy overhead of the plant.

In most of this decade, Ford-England was the only Ford enterprise in the world to build a tractor, and it sold this unit in numerous countries, including the United States. With the recession of 1938 and the market uncertainties caused by the tense political situation in Europe, the Fordson output declined in that year to 10,647. But about this time it became a factor in the international situation.

To Dagenham officials many signs in 1938 pointed to war. Perry knew his way in high government circles; in January 1938 he had been created a baron in recognition of his contributions to automotive progress and his stature as a business leader. From his contacts in the political arena he had become sharply aware of the explosive condition of Europe.*

So too had the perceptive Patrick Hennessy, who in the late thirties had come into greater prominence in the English Ford organization. As manager of purchasing, Hennessy had continued to reduce the cost of parts and materials. From May to October 1938, for example, he had lowered the average of costs about $16 a unit. "We think this is good, . . . but we are still continuing our efforts," he wrote to A. M. Wibel, the American purchasing manager in Dearborn.

Perry thought Hennessy's work much more than good and in January 1939 promoted him to general manager. A. R. Smith and H. S. Cooper became directors of the firm (later they were called managing directors). Thornhill Cooper not long before had been made Ford manager in Egypt. The trio of Hennessy, Smith, and H. S. Cooper, under Perry, formed the ruling junta at Dagenham.[24]

In Dearborn, no company executive recognized the significance of the political happenings in Europe. But to high Ford Ltd. officials the rearmament of Germany, Hitler's invasion of Austria, the move to the brink of war temporarily halted by the Munich pact of September 1938, and the menacing reports of the Fuehrer's further intentions, all meant that war was imminent. Nevertheless while Dagenham had won an increasing independence of Dearborn, Perry felt that so far as manufacturing for defense was concerned, his hands were tied. Henry Ford hated war with a passion that the English leader had known well since World War I. Ford would never permit Ford Ltd. to produce for military purposes, at least not while Britain was still at peace.

To be sure, as yet Chamberlain's limping government was lax in seeking the assistance of industry. But Perry at this point recalled Ford's role in tractor production during World War I. Tractors were not used on battlefields. Thus early in 1939 he and Hennessy approached officials of the Ministry of Agriculture and Fisheries. They proposed to increase the number of tractors available for food produc-

---

* Perry became Percival Lea Dewhurst Perry, Baron of Stock Harvard. When Sir Rowland (A.R.) Smith was asked why Sir Percival became a baron, he replied: "Perry was tight in government circles and with high people. It would have been peculiar had he *not* become one. It was quite an obvious thing."

tion in case of war. A reserve of 3,000 machines would be set up, sold to the government at list price less 27½ per cent, and stored for the Ministry by Fordson dealers, who would keep the units in condition for use. Should a national emergency arise, the Ministry would have these stocks immediately available. Should there be no war, Dagenham would buy back the tractors.

The British government took great interest in this plan. It recognized that if war came, England would need all the food her own soil could produce, and would profit immensely by Perry's scheme. No other British firm was capable of making the machines in quantity; the price was reasonable, and if they were not needed the buy-back provision guaranteed the government against loss.

But just as the arrangement was being consummated the minister of Agriculture and Fisheries (Sir Reginald Hugh Dorman-Smith) received a letter from Harry Ferguson in America, stating that he had an agreement with Ford-US for producing tractors in that country and suggesting that the minister might consider their manufacture in England.

In alarm Sir Reginald telephoned Perry asking if the Fordson would be abandoned and if Dagenham might shift to another model. The minister was concerned lest the government should be buying an obsolete product. Perry knew little of what had just taken place in Dearborn to warrant Ferguson's letter. But because of the long-range importance of events in America on the Ford story these may be detailed here.

What had happened in the United States was that on an October day in 1938, a flamboyant Ulsterman named Harry Ferguson had demonstrated his tractor at Dearborn to a receptive Henry Ford. Ferguson's machine utilized an hydraulic lift mechanism and a three-point linkage device which he asserted would "revolutionize agriculture." Ford had wanted to develop a new tractor and manufacture it at the Rouge ever since he had sent the Fordson equipment to Ireland in 1928. His concern with the V-8 cars had temporarily deflected him, but ever since 1933 he and his engineers had been trying to design a satisfactory model for farm use. When Ferguson appeared with his machine Ford was responsive, and the two made a "gentleman's agreement"—"no contract nor even the scratch of a pen."

Ferguson had presented highly useful devices but not a satisfactory tractor, and Ford engineers at Dearborn worked with him and his experts to produce what came to be called the "Ford tractor–Ferguson system." On June 29, 1939, this model would make its debut in Dearborn. Manufactured at the Rouge, it was distributed by a company run by Ferguson and Eber Sherman (formerly of Sherman & Sheppard, the English Fordson distributors in the United States). Needless to say, the implications of this activity would in time be felt by the Dagenham organization.

But in early 1939 the new product was still to be produced and tested, and in May Perry was able to tell the Ministry of Agriculture that he had no intention of making any changes in the Fordson in the near future. With this assurance, Sir Reginald backed Dagenham's tractor proposal, and well past midnight on May 18, 1939, Parliament made the appropriation to cover the arrangement Perry and Hennessy had advanced.[25]

6

On June 30, 1939 Ford Ltd. signed the contract with the government to establish a stock of 3,000 tractors. By this time Perry, Hennessy, H. S. Cooper, and A. R. Smith were fully aware that war was as close as a thunderclap in a seething black sky. In January 1939 they had proposed to spend £28,834 on tools, sandbags, air raid shelters, fire engines, and ambulances. Perry had transferred the assets of the Luxembourg company to a new holding unit (Ford Investment Company) incorporated March 11, 1939, in Guernsey, where it was thought they would be less exposed to enemy action.

Nonetheless, in June Perry had spoken warily at the dinner he held for the managers and directors of the associated companies in Paris, where both German and French officials were present. As he wrote Sorensen:

> I tried to make use of the occasion to emphasize the vastness of the Ford organization and the inevitability of Ford having a foot in both camps in case the present tension culminated in war. I used this to underline the outstanding features of Mr. Ford's love of peace and hatred of war and to emphasize how necessary it was that everyone connected with the organization should refrain from taking sides or showing bias in any way.

Perry was in an awkward position. The day after writing this letter, he attended a Board meeting of the English Ford company at which H. S.

Cooper reported its difficulties in getting British government contracts, because of the official view that Dagenham was highly vulnerable to enemy attack. Perry and his associates were avid patriots and regardless of Henry Ford were now ready to put their plant to work for the defense of England. They knew of Dollfus' plans for the manufacture of parts for the Rolls-Royce engine in France. They were resolved to serve *their* country's needs.

However, they trod carefully in deference to Dearborn thinking, for they perceived that neither Henry Ford nor Sorensen recognized the storm signals in Europe. Ford's acceptance of the German cross in July 1938 had distressed them, and charges in the United States that he was pro-German had been picked up in England. Perry found himself again walking a tightrope, as he had in World War I. Talk against Ford may well have helped to depress Dagenham sales in England in 1938 and 1939.[26]

H. L. Moekle from Dearborn visited Cologne in the summer of 1939 and endorsed the recommendation of Erhard Vitger (joint manager), who favored expansion of Ford facilities there. The possibility of war was not considered. Roberge also visited Europe that summer and went with Moekle to Spain to assist in the re-establishment of Ford activities there. Now that the civil war was over, the new Spanish government was urging Ford to manufacture in that country and negotiations for this project went forward.

Roberge traveled to Paris, Cologne, and Dagenham, and there in August talked with Hennessy. The Ford Ltd. general manager assured him that war would break out any day; Roberge recalls: "I was just as certain that it was not imminent. I had been through Germany. . . . all over the place. . . . I saw no military activity." Roberge says that Sorensen had access to "the same type of evidence as I had, and probably was equally mistaken." From current correspondence it is clear that Sorensen ridiculed the idea that Hitler had plans for conquest; he was responsive to Henry Ford's attitude, and Ford had had an almost fanatical confidence that there would be no war.

As noted earlier, Ford liked the German people: their cleanliness, thrift, technical aptitude, and discipline. He seems even to have admired certain traits of Adolph Hitler: his capacity for leadership, his successful war against unemployment, his urge to build an automobile industry in the Reich, and perhaps his anti-Semitism, although Ford had no sympathy whatever with the Fuehrer's ruthlessness, violence, or plans for conquest. Ford had no comprehension of the extremes to which Hitler's anti-Jewish policy had brought him, and refused to listen when told.

> Mr. Ford was convinced that once Hitler got the Polish corridor, he would seek no further territorial gain, but would turn to building up Germany. When, however, Hitler went right ahead with his conquests, Mr. Ford changed.

> He said to me then [writes Harry Bennett, who was close to Ford], "Well, by God, we're through with him. He's just power-drunk, like all the rest of them."

But in the summer of 1939 as Dollfus, with Edsel Ford's encouragement, prepared Ford-France to fill the defense needs of the French government, as Perry started full production under the tractor contract and tried to get other government orders, as Schmidt and Vitger increased the output of the Cologne plant and the Berlin assembly factory to higher and higher peaks, and as Hitler ominously threatened the Poles, Henry Ford still scoffed at the possibility of war, and those around him accepted his faith in continuing peace. Ford was aging; he had suffered a slight stroke in 1938, and while almost no physical evidences of it appeared, and he continued to make the chief decisions in company affairs, a certain erratic quality marked his conduct.

Within the company some decline in his health was recognized and it was evident that with increasing years he had become more rigid and static; he vetoed some important engineering proposals, and his eccentricities on occasion dominated his reason. He assigned to the opportunistic Harry Bennett the handling of many vital matters, including the simmering labor situation. For decades Ford had been a blend of Dr. Jekyll and Mr. Hyde, an idealistic strain warring with meanness and sadism, and although for years Dr. Jekyll had been dominant, now Mr. Hyde was increasingly in the ascendant.[27]

In Dearborn in the 1930's the Ford officials with their hopes for peace and their world-wide business relationships had watched the march of world events: they had seen the growth of militarism in Japan; Mussolini's drive against Ethiopia (when Ford had invoked his sanctions too late); they had received reports from Lester Mix and others in France of the mounting tension along the Franco-German border, and its causes; they had beheld with deep uneasiness Hitler's successive steps in his career of aggression. But if in the summer of 1939 some of them sensed the probability of war, they knew that Henry Ford fiercely denied the possibility of strife and dared not speak.

When at dawn on September 1, 1939, German tanks rumbled across the frontier into Poland and German planes showered bombs on Polish cities, railroads, and bridges, when England and France on September 3 declared war on the Reich, none of the Ford European leaders was surprised, and even Campbell in Canada quickly accepted the grim reality. Sorensen and Henry Ford, on the other hand, were wholly unprepared for the cataclysm.

15
On Both Sides of World War II

Britain and France responded to Hitler's invasion of Poland by declarations of war against Germany; yet with the width of the Reich and the submarine and mine-infested Baltic between them and the conflict, it might as well have taken place on the planet Mars. The French could have surged out to assail the Siegfried Line ("I could go through it in four days," the French Chief of Staff General Maurice Gamelin had asserted) but they stayed warily behind the Maginot ramparts they had erected against a German attack. With his blitzkrieg of tanks and airplanes, Hitler completed the conquest of the Polish republic in a few weeks. He was assisted by the Russians who began to occupy the eastern section of the country on September 17. On the 29th the two victors partitioned the prostrate nation between them.

Only U-boat attacks on British merchant vessels and preparations for future hostilities reminded the English that a state of war existed. Both they and the French worked to improve their armed potential. The English were developing their fighter and bomber aircraft and bringing radar to a practicable status; the French too were seeking to improve their air force, but the two nations groped to war preparedness with the slowness of sleepwalkers.

Dagenham moved toward war footing with a pace that Chamberlain's government never achieved. Soon after the outbreak of hostilities the Ford Investment Company had been transferred to London from Guernsey, which the Germans soon occupied. Government ministries had been dubious about giving military contracts to Ford of England, for its plant on the lower Thames seemed to be a perfect target for enemy bombers. It was the first factory they would pass on the way to London; its location was well known (and as developed later was photographed by the *Luftwaffe*); and at night its chimneys and blast furnaces made it a glowing target. Its personnel had been instructed how to destroy it in case of invasion.

But Ford officials meant to use Dagenham, and during the fall of 1939 they worked desperately at what seemed an impossible conjuror's trick: *to make a teeming factory complex of more than 60 acres completely disappear!* Air Force experts were called in, and the entire works overlaid with metal sheeting, including the dumping ground of red-hot slag from the blast furnaces. No lights were permitted to show. On the vast roof masking the entire center a picture was painted which made the area seem from the air to be an expanse of marshland with roads running across it. A German pilot hunting for the factory would look in vain, and wonder if his maps were wrong.[1]

Meanwhile within the plant the production of tractors under the contract described in Chapter 14 went forward. Already by September 1, 500 had been produced for stockpiling, and the full government order for 3,000, with 300 additional machines later requested, was soon met; Dagenham daily lifted its output, building between July 1, 1939 and the last of April 1940 more than 15,000 Fordsons. This was crucial, for in 1939 the tilled land in Britain comprised only 8,813,000 acres, 2,000,000 less than had existed in 1914. But with a subsidy of £2 per acre for plowing up grassland for crops, the farmers were rapidly extending the cultivated area, and tractors were in demand. In the next two years the acreage of planted farmland would grow by 50 per cent.

As early as September 8, 1939 Perry received a cable from Sorensen about the new Ford tractor–Ferguson system. "Shipping 50 per day by December 1," ran the message. "Your tractor production should finish December first and our new tractor come into the market on a fixed schedule." Four days later he persisted, "It just does not seem possible that you could go on with the old tractor, the way this new one is coming into the picture. . . . [It] will so outperform the latter [the Fordson] that it is almost pitiful."

Perry was amazed at Sorensen's expectations. He explained patiently that in wartime the government would not permit conversion to the Ferguson model. Authorities "consider the present time is inopportune for either importing them [the new tractors] or sanctioning the import or local construction of machine tools necessary for their manufacture." In addition, plows and other implements required for the Ferguson machine were not obtainable in England.

But Ferguson, backed by Sorensen, blindly insisted that production on his model should begin at Dagenham immediately. Encountering Perry's refusal, he was furious. He demanded to be made a director of Ford Ltd., a prospect that Perry and all the English Board members regarded with deep distaste. Lord Illingworth was particularly emphatic. "He would be an infernal pest." A new tractor could not be introduced while "an efficient one is already on the market. It has been explained to him why it is impossible during the war, and neither he nor Henry Ford nor Jesus Christ can alter it."

Edsel Ford moved to quiet the turmoil, voicing his confidence in both Perry and the Ford-Ferguson tractor, and the English company kept turning out Fordsons in increasing quantity (100 a day by April 1940) and did not alter its program.[2]

Meanwhile Dagenham was busy with several other developments. German magnetic mines had been sown in English harbors, and the V-8 engine came into demand as an auxiliary power plant to supply current for Wellington bombers that were destroying these devices; they were also employed for the degaussing* apparatus of merchant vessels. In October the English company undertook a £500,000 contract with Roumania to supply ambulances and specially equipped Fordson trucks. The ambulances were powered by the 10 h.p. Dagenham motor, and accommodated four recumbent patients. The company also had some contracts for long wheel-base 5-ton trucks and was completing another agreement with the Air Ministry, placed before September, to supply the Balloon Command with six-wheeler trucks and winches used in its work.

Perry in the fall was appointed adviser to the Ministry of Food and devised a plan for wartime milk distribution.

In October the Ford Motor Company Ltd. was asked by the Air Ministry to build, equip, and operate a factory to produce Rolls-Royce Merlin aircraft engines. This plant, like other similar ones, was called a "shadow factory," because it supplemented the production of a main plant elsewhere. The government's request had an interesting background. Sir Wilfred Freeman, head of the Staff College of the Air Force, had visited Dagenham in 1937 or 1938 and later had sounded out A. R. Smith on the manufacture of Merlins. Embarrassed because of Henry Ford's opposition to production for war, Smith had suggested: "You *order* me to make Merlin engines." "No," said Freeman quickly,

---

* A process of establishing a magnetic field that protected a vessel from magnetic mines.

"I can't do that." Smith then summoned his courage and said, "Very well, we will make them." This led to the formal request by the government, which came after the commencement of hostilities.

In the fall and winter of 1939 Smith, with William J. Squire of Ford Ltd., and government and Rolls-Royce officials, prepared the design of the factory, to be located near Manchester. Squire rendered invaluable service in planning layout and machine tool equipment. He spent nine months at the Rolls-Royce plant at Derby (while his Manchester factory was being constructed), studying the production there in order to adapt it to Ford practice. "We could never have made the engines with Rolls-Royce methods," he recalled later, as these involved much handwork by expert craftsmen, for which Ford, having few such men, had to substitute machine tools and mass production. The winter of 1939–1940 saw only the early construction phases of the undertaking.

On January 1, 1940, the Anglia appeared—a new British Ford 8 h.p. car, which the company produced in limited quantities until November 1941.* Meanwhile Ford Ltd. persistently sought more government contracts, although it encountered resistance from War Office officials, who still felt that Dagenham was vulnerable.[3]

2

During the "phony war," as the winter of 1939–1940 and the ensuing spring were called, combat went on in eastern Europe and on the high seas. In November, after its demand for drastic territorial adjustments had been rejected, Russia attacked the little republic of Finland, which after an amazing resistance made a humiliating peace in March 1940.

It had been no fault of Hitler's that the chief opposing nations had not come to grips. "I shall attack France and England at the earliest possible moment," he told his generals in November and would have moved at once to fulfill his promise but for bad weather and the *Reichswehr,* which insisted on further time to prepare. The Germans used the interval to far better advantage than did their opponents.

---

* Civilian vehicle production ceased April 30, 1940.—Hall to dealers, Apr. 27, 1940, FMC-Eng. files. The Anglia may have been built afterwards, in small quantities for the armed forces. Production Sheets, FMC-Eng., give November as the terminal date for its manufacture.

Finally on April 9, 1940, the Fuehrer struck, and the bloodless occupation of Denmark and the conquest of Norway merged into the attack on Holland on May 10, followed by the sweep through the
Ardennes (to the north of the Maginot Line), and across Belgium. It
is now common knowledge how Hitler's war of lightning mechanized
movement (massed tanks and planes) baffled the Allied commanders,
tore a gap between the French and British, and with the surrender of
the Belgians forced the British army back toward the seacoast.

On the very day that Holland was invaded Chamberlain in England had been forced from power and Winston Churchill had taken his
place. The new prime minister had immediately begun to marshal
talent and resources for a greater effort, although he had neither the aircraft nor the troops to reverse the outcome in France. But under his
leadership the British, French, and a few Belgian forces that had pushed
toward the seacoast were dramatically rescued. With the aid of British
warships and the Royal Air Force, 222 naval craft and 665 privately
operated vessels of various types took 338,226 men, 139,911 of them
French and Belgians, from the beaches at Dunkirk. The British nation was elated by an operation carried out "in defiance of time, circumstances, of death itself." Churchill had to remind his countrymen
grimly "that wars are not won by evacuations." [4]

This was a cruelly true statement with respect to equipment: of
2,794 guns and 64,618 motor vehicles with the British forces in France,
only 322 cannon and 4,739 vehicles were brought away. In a few weeks
the broken French army surrendered and Britain stood alone and
practically disarmed, except for her navy and air force. [5]

The situation was a bugle call to her factories around the world.
As we shall see, it was widely answered abroad, while in Great Britain
the industrial power of the nation was now exerted to the utmost.
Dagenham had emerged from the limbo of neglected works, and Hennessy reported on May 10 that "our total production is perhaps the
highest ever. . . . Our Foundry, for the first time, is at full capacity and
this applies to other parts of the factory also." [6]

Well before Dunkirk Churchill had appointed the Canadian-born,
dynamic Lord Beaverbrook as Minister of Aircraft Production (a new
ministry). Seeking a much greater volume of plane production. Beaverbrook was looking for assistants, and Arthur Greenwood, Labour
member of the war cabinet, recommended Patrick Hennessy to deal
with materials. When the minister approached Hennessy, he at first de-

clined the appointment. He told Beaverbrook: "You already have A. R. Smith [at the Merlin shadow factory]. It is quite impossible for me to leave my business."

But Perry recommended that he take the position, and Hennessy entered the Air Ministry, thus bringing Ford into the very heart of the "Battle for Britain," as the air conflict that began on August 12 was soon termed. After Dunkirk Hitler had expected England to sue for peace; when she did not, he proposed to invade her. Had he been prepared to undertake this task at once, he might have become the first enemy since William the Conqueror to establish himself on the island, for England was in wretched condition to fight a land battle, having practically no equipment and few experienced soldiers. (The evacuees from Dunkirk were in no condition to go into combat immediately.) But "Operation Sea Lion," as the proposed invasion was termed, required landing craft (as yet unassembled and readied for use), trained crews, and synchronization between the German army, navy, and *Luftwaffe*. Above all, the Germans must have control of the air. Their planes could then protect the invasion flotillas from British destroyers and other naval craft. Accordingly, Hitler early in August ordered Goering to attack and destroy the Royal Air Force.

Aircraft and more aircraft were the immediate need of the British. They had to have them or else, as Hennessy said later, "You'd have the Germans eating breakfast with us." A miracle of production was needed and Beaverbrook brought "all the fire and energy— I've never known anyone in England or America who could match him in energy—" to the production of planes and engines. "He never slept, or let anyone else sleep," recalled Hennessy. "You'd work until two A.M., and be at it again at seven." If there were bottlenecks, Beaverbrook at once pounced upon them and eliminated them. He and Hennessy "used to fight like tigers," but the results they and their associates achieved were superlative.[7]

Just before the Battle of Britain began the Ford Motor Company in the United States accepted a contract for the production of Rolls-Royce engines. The American government was to take 3,000, and Washington officials thought they had made it clear that the British would receive twice that number. Henry Ford did not so interpret the agreement, and when on June 18 Lord Beaverbrook announced that Ford would make 6,000 engines for England, Ford at once canceled the entire arrangement. "We are not doing business with the British government or any other foreign government," he asserted. "If we make 6,000 Rolls-Royce engines it will be on an order from the United States government." He added that no offer of such a contract had been received.

The fury of the Canadian and English press, and of millions of pro-Ally Americans was immediate and loud. It was somewhat mitigated when Ford's executive secretary cabled to the London *Daily Mail* on June 26 as follows:

> Mr. Ford has authorized the following statement: "Preliminary work we are doing will proceed without interruption in order that we may be ready for our government when needed and orders for production are given. Ford Motor Canada and England are using their facilities to the utmost for production military equipment for defense of British Empire and will continue to serve their countries as they should do. While I am against war nevertheless I believe our facilities in America should be preserved for American defense when and if so required."

With this statement the excitement began to die down, but the English Ford officials had been embarrassed and Henry Ford's position was doubtless disappointing to both Sorensen and Edsel Ford, who had negotiated the Rolls-Royce agreement. Needless to say, the engines Ford was expected to manufacture would not have been available for more than a year, nor would the Rolls-Royce shadow plant at Manchester come into production before that time. For the present, the problem of supply for the Air Force devolved entirely upon Beaverbrook, who increased the number of fighter planes from 782 in mid-August to 1,228 by the end of September. As Hennessy later remarked: "Toward the end we were *not* running out of airplanes; we were running out of pilots."

Meanwhile the British ground forces rapidly increased, as did adequate equipment for them. Factories turned out guns, munitions, and vehicles, and American aid appeared. At no time had the common people been fearful of invasion. "Don't worry," the workers in the Dagenham plant would say. "Let them come over. This won't be like France. They'll have to fight all of us. We'll fight them with clubs and pitchforks if we haven't guns."

Hitler had hoped at first for a clear-cut victory in the air; when he shifted to bombing he expected that his attacks would bring terror and demoralization. While he continued to bomb, he at length perceived that his task was hopeless, and in mid-September turned his attention and his chief power to other projects.[8]

3

"Bordeaux will be functioning in a month," Dollfus had cabled Sorensen on September 9, 1939. "Have substantial orders our commercial line, but I am discontinuing production of passenger models." Though many of his employees had been mobilized, he had been able to hold 600 workmen at Strasbourg and was shifting the pick of his foremen to Bordeaux.

Thus Ford-France was continuing to function, although at this time it lost its works manager, Panier, whom Dollfus after a quarrel discharged. "Better if Dollfus had gone," scrawled Sorensen on a letter he had received from Panier. At about this time, at the government's request, Dollfus shifted from the manufacture of Rolls-Royce engines to that of Hispano-Suiza. The latter were easier to make, and the sanguine Frenchman laid out a schedule calling for the production of 550 a month by the end of 1941. At Poissy, in his incompleted plant, he planned in late 1939 to assemble trucks. He believed the factory, operating at 10 per cent of capacity, could be raised in two months to 50 per cent; but after three months he was utilizing Bordeaux for trucks and planning to make Poissy his assembly plant and the center for Fordair activity.

In other European Ford companies, business during these months continued. Dearborn was shipping parts to the Low Countries and Denmark, and Sorensen's assistant Russell Gnau reported to Edsel Ford that Spain was "clearing up." Trade with Portugal posed few difficulties. In Germany, Erhard Vitger had been pushed aside, and R. H. Schmidt became the sole general manager. Dr. Albert wrote that "you can rely on our handling all matters . . . in the spirit of the Ford tradition." Cologne was producing trucks chiefly, and although the government had suggested that it manufacture "war material," Albert and Schmidt had thus far avoided such activity.[9]

With the invasion of Denmark and Norway the situation sharply changed. The Danish Ford plant, operated by H. C. Møller, was soon visited by Nazi officials. They insisted that the factory produce for German needs. The Danes pointed out that they were equipped for automotive assembly only, and still had a quantity of parts on hand for this work. For the present they were permitted to continue.

The Danes thus preserved a certain independence but nevertheless served the Germans. They kept their employees busy, which was a chief objective, and their plant remained intact.

In Holland and Belgium the conquerors took hold of the situation with a firmer hand. Dutch resistance had ended on May 15, 1940; on June 13 the commander-in-chief of the invading army told Ford-Holland's directors that he was appointing "Robert H. Schmidt, General Manager of [Ford] Cologne, as the Directing Manager of your company, until further notice." Schmidt soon took over the management of the Belgian Ford company as well. While he was the agent of the Reich, and bound to see that the plants operated for the good of their new masters, he was also a Ford employee and, along with certain arbitrary actions (the increase of capitalization and the setting of dividends), showed such loyalty to Ford interests as his official role permitted. He and Albert cabled Edsel Ford on June 28: "Trying with approval of authorities to safeguard your interests for plants in occupied territory. Antwerp, Amsterdam both working." They were able to report that the Dutch manager, C. G. F. Stenger, was in charge of his works and soon made James Van Luppen head of the Belgian factory. "Both plants produce commercial vehicles only," they advised, "with stock to be completed from local sources and Cologne." There had been no injury to Ford property. By this time Paris had been taken by the Germans, and the two Cologne officials informed Edsel that the company plants near that city were deserted.[10]

In France Schmidt was also given overall charge of Ford properties. He and Albert soon arranged for Dollfus and his staff to return to Poissy. "Trying to reestablish them," cabled Schmidt on July 9. According to Dollfus the relationship between him and the German was not pleasant. "He behaved like a pig," the Frenchman declared later. Under pressure to produce war materials, Dollfus refused (he had ended Fordair operations); later he claimed that Schmidt tried to have him jailed. The head of Ford SAF then went to Berlin, argued his case, and was permitted by Nazi military authorities to manufacture trucks! These he quickly turned out in quantity, and by August 1941 reported to Edsel that his output of parts and complete vehicles had risen to 1,000 a month. Needless to say, Hitler could use this production to advantage.

It must be remembered that throughout 1940 and 1941 the United States was technically neutral, and although Lend-Lease had become a factor on March 11, 1941, Hitler was probably satisfied with the industrial support he was receiving from the occupied territories and had every reason to protect the Ford factories as useful to him. At Schmidt's request V. Y. Tallberg returned to Germany for some months to assist Cologne in the engineering field. He found a situation that aroused his suspicions, and justly so, for Albert and Schmidt seem to have been secretly engaged in the production of war materials.* (They were of course doing no more for their country than Perry, Hennessy, and A. R. Smith were doing for Britain.) Roberge in June–July 1940 made a survey of Ford factories, reporting to Perry. The Americans, he noted, were shipping some materials to Petsamo, Finland, for the use of the Ford company there. The Mediterranean was blocked off by the British and Italians, and a shipment for Roumania at Dearborn could not be sent and was turned over to the agents of that nation in the United States. However, the American Ford company was able to ship via the Cape of Good Hope and the Red Sea to Alexandria, Egypt, where Ford materials were being used by the British in their wars against Italian armies in Libya, Eritrea, and Ethiopia.[11]

It was a weird situation, with Ford production in Europe serving the two opposing camps. The British were fiercely active, with Ford output rapidly rising. Cologne, with greatly inferior resources, was working for Hitler, but its vehicle production of from 14,000 to 16,000 a year was not more than a quarter of Dagenham's. Indeed, while the Germans commanded Ford establishments in seven countries,** and would soon have an eighth, for in November 1940 Roumania was drawn into the Axis, the great English plant contributed more to its cause than all these and Cologne combined did to Hitler's.

After June 1941 the Fuehrer's attention and resources were increasingly engaged in the invasion of Russia. At the same time the Ford contribution to the Allies was being augmented for the British by the dynamic role of Canada and its factories throughout the Commonwealth, to which we must now turn our attention.[12]

---

* Tallberg could not find out what was going on, and during the war years Ford-US never knew. Apparently Schmidt and Dr. Albert had invested in a supplier called the Arendt Company. This firm used Ford equipment and labor and worked on a contract for the German government. In a plant near the Cologne factory it manufactured parts the purpose of which neither the workers nor their officials understood, since they saw only the parts and not the whole. It seems, however, that the production was for the turbine of the V-2. (See note 11.)

** France, Belgium, Holland, Denmark, Finland, Italy, and Hungary.

4

The United Kingdom in 1940 covered an area of only 94,000 square miles and its population was about 46,500,000, but the British Commonwealth of Nations occupied almost 13,000,000 square miles and contained 500,000,000 people. Practically all its members had declared war on Germany (and later on Italy) and offered a reservoir of men and resources that was potentially formidable.

Of all the countries of the Commonwealth, Canada promised most as a source of men, food, and equipment. Much of its territory (almost as great as all Europe including western Russia) lay in barren northern latitudes, but a great southern belt along the American border consisted of rich farmland and woodland, a capacious bread-and-meat basket for Britain. The population of 11,500,000 was eager to supply combat personnel, and the land was dotted with industries surprising in variety and development and able to expand quickly.

Unfortunately the beginning of the war found Canada, like other units of the Commonwealth, lacking in military and naval strength. The Dominion declared war on Germany September 10, but it possessed at that time an army of only 4,500 men (and a militia of 65,000) and a navy of 15 small war vessels and 1,774 personnel in active service. The Royal Canadian Air Force was somewhat better developed, containing about 3000 men with some hundreds of experienced flyers.

However, Canada plunged into the conflict as if it already had the arms and men it needed. The navy expanded rapidly, and only six days after the declaration of war undertook its first convoy service. Immediate plans for enlarging the army resulted in the training and equipping of two divisions, which arrived in Europe in the spring of 1940. Late in 1939 the British Air Ministry ordered "that a Canadian squadron should be formed from Canadian personnel" already serving in its forces, and Fighter Squadron 243 came into being, with a leader who had served with the RCAF, and pilots, gunners, observers, and navigators representing every province in the Dominion. A second group from Canada appeared in February 1940 and two more before the Battle of Britain got under way.[13] *

* In addition to the Canadian squadrons, one of which was a reserve unit, there came into being a Polish group and another composed of Americans in the RAF. Thus at least five of the 60-odd squadrons of the Royal Air Force were non-English in composition. (See note 13.)

These events had occurred while extensive planning was under way in Ottawa. The Dominion had already developed with the United States plans for common defense. As the industrial resources of Canada were expanded, W. R. Campbell, president of the Ford Motor Company of Canada, was called to the capital as an industrial adviser and spent some months there, giving particular attention to motorized equipment. He returned to Windsor in April 1940.

In contrast with the fumbling efforts toward the use of motor vehicles in World War I, preparations on both sides in World War II were made with a full recognition of the importance of gasoline-driven equipment. Ford of Canada promptly devoted its facilities, as needed, to military uses. It adapted trucks for the use of Canadian land forces, supplying these to the first two Canadian divisions "as soon as they were required." Late in 1939 the company joined with the Department of National Defense "in the development and engineering of a series of mechanical transport ranging from eight cwt. to three ton capacities, with four-wheel drive on vehicles exceeding fifteen cwt. capacity." (Deliveries on these were not made until 1940.) Campbell was very "war-minded." He held conferences with his staff on war work, eventually almost every day. At the beginning of the conflict the chief men in the company were Campbell, Dickert (production), Douglas B. Greig (finance), and Rhys M. Sale (domestic sales). It was already apparent that the company would have to make recommendations to the government and design vehicles, which the American company, then neutral, could not develop for it. (Ford-Canada, as often noted earlier, had hitherto always depended on Dearborn for its designs.) Consequently it needed an engineering department and set one up, with E. L. Simpson in charge.

In 1939 Windsor produced 61,015 of the 155,316 Canadian output of cars and trucks, or 39.3 per cent. Both the production and the percentage of Canadian output were slightly less than in 1938. It sold altogether 62,544 units (some 1938 vehicles), 26,511 in Canada and 36,033 abroad. Some of the latter were utilized for the equipment of armed forces in Commonwealth countries overseas. The war still showed little effect on overall production, but Campbell knew that it soon would. The conflict not only affected Canada, "the country in which our principal operations are carried on," he told his stockholders in April 1940, "but also the countries which are the export markets for our products." [14]

With the fall of France and the almost complete destruction of the

British army's equipment, Dominion industry bent to an extremity of effort. "The incredible happenings in Europe . . . in the spring of 1940," said Campbell half a year later, "left the British Empire standing almost alone as a defender of . . . freedom, and the United Kingdom the besieged citadel of democracy." Throughout all Canadian industry production sights were lifted. The Ford Motor Company was asked to double its output of 4-wheel drive vehicles by 1941 and spent $3,122,000 for new machine tools and $3,477,000 for additional plant facilities. Just previous to the war it had devoted $10,000,000 to the enlargement of its factories, and the need for expansion was less than otherwise would have been the case.

In May 1940 the company received its first contract (600 units) for the universal carrier, a large armored vehicle sometimes called a tank. Six Canadian firms were soon producing this machine, and by July Windsor had assumed responsibility for the final assembly of all carriers made in the Dominion. A special factory was constructed for this purpose. During the year Ford-Canada produced 96,449 vehicles,* 43.2 per cent of the national production of 222,984. It had been importing Ford-Ferguson tractors from the United States, and in 1940 sold 3,729 of these, the highest tractor sale since 1927. Canada was shipping large quantities of wheat to Britain, as well as bacon, poultry, eggs, and other foodstuffs, and the nation needed the tractors.[15]

With the Italians active in Greece and Egypt, 1941 was an important year for the British, and particularly so for Canada. "Canada has become the most important source of mechanical transportation in the empire," Campbell announced in April. To streamline the performance of Canadian Ford vehicles, A. S. Ellis was sent over to England with a group of technicians. Formerly service manager of the Windsor organization, he set up headquarters in Southampton and supervised the assembly of the company's vehicles and also cooperated with the Canadian army in repairing or altering motorized transport. In 1943 Rhys Sale took up the same task with the British army. Meanwhile Canadian-made Fords continued to be assembled in South Africa and India. The South African company readied 17,290 units for service in 1940, and 8,619 in 1941. For these two years India put together 15,000. General A. P. Wavell, in routing the Italians in Egypt and Libya and occupying Eritrea and freeing Ethiopia, used Canadian Ford vehicles

* These included universal carriers, field artillery tractors, ambulances, 3-ton load carriers, reconnaissance cars, and numerous types of lorries.—See Address to Shareholders of Apr. 28, 1941, which contains pictures of 12 types of military vehicles.

sent from assembly points at Port Elizabeth and Bombay. They performed superbly, whether in the rugged uplands of Abyssinia or in the deserts of Egypt or Libya. Said a Canadian driver: "I have ridden them across deserts and along mountain passes where it didn't look as though a mule could get through, let alone a truck." "I know of one Ford we have had which has done more than 30,000 miles across country and is still in use." When Field Marshal Erwin Rommel was sent to Africa by Hitler in 1941, Canadian-built trucks and carriers, along with British-built Ford units, were the mainstay of the African army defending Egypt.

"Canadian motor transport is acknowledged to be the best that has been produced in this war," said the Dominion Minister of Supply C. D. Howe. Dagenham claimed as much for its machines. The two were both superior. Rommel wrote an order on December 15, 1941, which fell into British hands: "For desert reconnaissance only captured English trucks are to be employed, since German trucks stick in the sand too often." That was praise for both Dagenham and Windsor, and must have been deserved, considering the source.[16]

The British in Africa opposed Rommel with diminished forces, for Wavell had had to send a portion of his army to Greece. The Germans swept on toward the Nile, and Rommel seemed to be on the verge of an Egyptian conquest; but while awaiting men and transport for the final lunge, he found the British gathering men and weapons on an extensive scale. Mostly coming around the Cape of Good Hope and up the Red Sea from Britain, Canada, and the United States, new matériel and combat troops were fed into the army of General Bernard L. Montgomery. Divisions from New Zealand and Australia contributed magnificently to his strength; he commanded Indian and South African units, and many British infantry, tank, and air forces. The Indian company meanwhile increased its output, assembling 14,693 vehicles in 1942 and 32,706 in 1943; most of this went to the Near East and Africa. With 1942 had come an increasing production from Britain and the United States, while Canada was pouring out larger and larger quantities of arms, ordnance, aircraft, and vehicles.

5

In mid-1941 George Dickert retired as head of Windsor production, and was succeeded by J. E. Porter, and after his death in June 1942, by Floyd Millmun. At this time the Canadian company encountered difficulties in the labor field. On May 21, 1941, the UAW-CIO had won an election at the Rouge plant in Dearborn which empowered it to negotiate for the workers there, and late in June Henry Ford signed a contract giving his employees a union shop, that is, compelling all of them to join the union. His company also accepted a "checkoff," *i.e.*, agreed to deduct union fees from its workers' pay envelopes.

Canadian and American labor leaders began to demand a sharply improved status for Ford workers in the Dominion. Late in September a mass meeting of employees at Windsor voted to affiliate with UAW-CIO. Resolutions were passed by them calling for "democratic liberties, [higher] wages, [shorter] hours, decent working conditions, health standards and union rights." The meeting had drawn only 1,400 persons, and the work force at the central plant numbered 12,000. Recognizing that they lacked a mandate from the majority, union officials appealed for support from all workers, and backed up their appeal with diligent proselyting. One militant leader, George Burt, declared: "Every man in the plant who does not sign up with the UAW-CIO is a menace to those who are signed, and . . . to the successful termination of the war." The feeling of company officials was equally bitter. "We had a tough and dirty union in Windsor," one of them said years later.

On November 6 Campbell rejected the UAW and proposed a company union. He also suggested that pay, seniority, grievance procedure, medical protection, and any other matters in dispute be negotiated under the Canadian Department of Labor. As a result, the minister of labor on November 13, 1941, called an election at which all employees could vote to accept the company's offer or choose the union as their representative. In this test the UAW-CIO was victorious by 6833 to 4455 votes. On January 15, 1942 the union and the company signed an agreement which Burt called the best "we have ever signed with a major Canadian plant." It set a basic hiring wage of 75 cents an hour and gave the union various fringe benefits, such as time-and-a-half pay for work beyond eight hours per day or forty per week.

Soon afterward the Ministry of Labor took over the regulation of employee status in war plants, and further adjustments between the company and the workers were made under its supervision. The union had established its power, and now became increasingly resolved that the Windsor Ford workers should receive comparable treatment to that accorded employees in Dearborn (an objective which despite the election and the contract was still far from being realized). The resentment of the UAW-CIO would erupt in grim action when the war ended several years later.[17] Ford-Canada was the first foreign Ford plant to be unionized.

6

Let us go back to Dagenham and late September of 1940. Up to that time there had been no bomber raids on the camouflaged works. The first near hit by the enemy did not come until July 26, when a high explosive bomb fell near the factory. On September 18, 1940, the first Ford worker was killed, and on the 21st 284 incendiaries fell on the plant, starting 40 fires. "The Works Fire Brigade," runs an account of Dagenham's ordeal, "assisted by enthusiastic volunteers in the factory, tackled these outbreaks . . . so successfully that not one . . . reached serious dimensions."

The plant by this time was fully organized to deal with enemy attacks. An Air Raid Precautions Group had been formed. The Ford Fire Brigade had been enlarged from its peacetime strength of a single pump to a five-pump unit, with a proportionate increase in personnel and new apparatus. In addition, a band of 500 workers (mostly maintenance and service men) had been drilled in anti-gas, fire prevention, first aid, and other emergency skills. As the German aircraft had become more active, the company had established a three-shift system of roof-spotters, who could warn the factory of approaching enemy planes.

When these began to appear in numbers, Dagenham operated under a round of alarms that was to last pretty steadily for years. The company had provided shelters which the workers would seek on a signal from the spotters. At first these were beyond the factory, but many were soon provided beneath the floors of the buildings: a series of steel-sheathed rooms to which the employees could retire quickly and on signal be back at work in a minute.

Operating the Dagenham complex under constant attack was much like running a factory in an infernal region. Enemy bombing attacks on London were continuous for months at a time. "We could feel the shock of bombs falling a mile away," one Air Raid Precautions official recalled. Another said, "The noise was terrific. Gunfire commenced at dusk and ended at dawn. . . . On the outer fringes of London, there was no escaping the noise. No deep tubes, no shelter, nor rest from it. Yet we slept, or most of us did."

The entire factory worked under this thunder of sound. At first there were frequent excursions to the shelters, for the spotters sounded an alarm every time enemy aircraft appeared. In 1940 the factory was idle for 630.54 hours, or more than twenty-six days. This was a great loss of time when the nation needed vehicles and implements as badly as a hospital patient in extreme jeopardy needs blood transfusions. A way out was soon found. It was recognized that the spotters, with the aid of information relayed from government lookouts elsewhere, could distinguish the destinations of German bombers, and most of them were not headed for the Ford plant. This permitted the workers to stay on their jobs. The great time-saver was "the Alarm within the Alert," adopted January 20, 1941. This restricted alarms to occasions on which the factory itself was menaced, and the workers agreed to remain at their posts except when immediate danger threatened. In 1941 only 86.56 hours (less than four days' time) was lost, and in 1942 only 1.04 hours. When the flying bombs came in 1944, the time away from the job rose from 15.07 hours in 1943 to 114.59, but the power to paralyze production had been sharply controlled.[18]

During 1940, 1941, and 1942 Dagenham was busy producing motorized vehicles, tractors, and engines, particularly the V-8. The output of Fordson marched steadily upward (22,210 in 1941 and 27,650 in 1942), and thousands of wheeled and tracked vehicles were being made for military uses. By 1941 these were being turned out at a rate of 130 a day. They included the Bren carrier, of which more will be said shortly. As to V-8's, they were being manufactured to neutralize magnetic mines, power ship-to-shore landing craft, serve winches that controlled balloons, activate the flails with which tanks destroyed enemy land-mine fields, and provide the power plant for Bren carriers. They also drove the thousands of trucks that Dagenham produced. The factory had begun the production of tracks for tanks and other vehicles, of which all told it was to make 6 million. Along with the V-8, the Ford 8 and 10 h.p. engines were being fashioned for various military uses. Altogether, 75,000 V-8's were manufactured in excess of those used in vehicles.

The work force at Dagenham steadily increased, even though workers left to join the armed forces. A total of 4,259 were to enlist before the conflict ended (144 did not return). However, increasing production demanded more men and, since men were not easily procurable, women. Never before employed at Dagenham, these numbered 1,100 in September 1941, helping to swell a work force that had risen from less than 12,000 in 1939 and would total 34,163 in the spring of 1945.

The Bren carrier mentioned above was the design of Sir John Cardon of Cardon & Lloyd. It was an armored vehicle using tracks instead of wheels. It quickly proved to be successful, and soon six British firms, including Ford Ltd., were engaged in its manufacture. Ford supplied not only the engine (Sir John had chosen the V-8 after extended observation), but the axles, chassis, frame, and tracks for the machine. The government soon asked the company to establish a separate plant wholly devoted to its manufacture. An old factory was found at Leamington in Warwickshire, ninety-nine miles from Dagenham, and this was taken over for modernization on October 1, 1940. Here a foundry was built, and the first tracks produced on March 5, 1941. The first completed job came off the assembly line in February 1942, and altogether 13,942 were made before the war ended.[19]

Meanwhile the Ford shadow factory for Rolls-Royce engines, near Manchester, came into production. Squire had planned a layout and an array of jigs and machine tools to make possible the mass production of a unit which in the past had required a large amount of handwork by highly skilled mechanics. "He did a magnificent job," said Sir Rowland Smith later. "Squire was the pivotal man." But Smith also leaned heavily on H. A. Denne, who was his assistant controller and administrative deputy and had "to battle to get our steel and other raw materials. It was a constant job of trouble shooting." G. A. Phillips was general manager of the factory.

The site covered 118 acres of ground, and the plant, partly because of a German hit sustained in the early stages of construction, was "dispersed" in three units, which when completed occupied a total of 44.75 acres. Squire's layout and battery of machine tools permitted the employment of unskilled workers. "In half an hour," he stated years later, "we could teach a girl or a tradesman to operate a machine." The machines did most of the work. A good example of the difference between Rolls-Royce and Ford practice was the making of the cylinder blocks, crank case, and cylinder head. "For these Ford used a multiple-spindle and multiple-way tool," said Squire, "where Rolls-Royce had employed a single-spindle radial arm drilling machine [and much hand work].

The multiple-spindle bored all the holes [in these units] at the same time it was performing several other jobs, but the Rolls-Royce method required each of some forty holes to be bored individually." Rolls-Royce and Ford got along beautifully. At first some Derby officials were sceptical as to the achievement of mass production. But later at a shadow factory near Glasgow the Rolls-Royce engineers adopted some Ford practices.

A work force of 17,000 was eventually required, at least 7000 of which were women. The Manchester factory lived by precision. Gauges were constantly used to check accuracy; one, for example, showed the amount of sag in a steel bar, although it amounted to only one ten-millionth of an inch. On November 28, 1941 A. R. Smith wrote Sorensen that the factory had completed 160 engines to date and needed some 300 machines and 3,000 additional employees before going into quantity production. "Apparently we rather set up a record over here," he reported, "by the fact that the first two engines we produced went right through the completion of the flying test without any adjustment being necessary." Squire too was proud of the plant and its work. "It was the most advanced of any aircraft factory in the world," he asserted later. The scheduled production of 400 engines a month was reached early in 1942, and by 1943 had risen to 900. Altogether, more than 30,000 Ford Merlin engines were made.[20]

7

For some time before Pearl Harbor, the Ford Motor Company in the United States had already been engaged in the manufacture of defense materials. It had participated in the development of the jeep, had undertaken the production of the Pratt & Whitney R-2800 18-cylinder aircraft motor, had helped redesign the American medium tank and provided the armor and engine for this unit (soon to be employed by the British in North Africa), had turned out a reconnaissance car in quantity, a "swamp buggy," had begun to make aircraft detectors, and finally had started the great factory at Willow Run for the output of Liberator bombers. With American entry into the war on December 7, 1941, it pushed ahead with all these projects, soon became the largest producer of gliders in the United States, and undertook contracts for other war material, including magnesium and magnesium castings, gun mounts, and universal carriers (for the British). It was to employ more than 200,000 workers and expend $371,000,000 for war manufacturing facilities.[21]

Once America was at war the Ford companies on the European continent, of which fitful intelligence had previously come to Dearborn, were blanked out almost as completely as a stage set by the dropping of a fire curtain. Only scanty information by way of Vichy-France and the reports of British and American flyers trying to bomb out Ford factories as assets to the enemy threw quick flashes of uncertain light on Poissy, Cologne, and other sites of company activity.

The Germans had entered Athens late in April 1941 and taken possession of the Greek Ford sales headquarters there. Hitler now controlled Ford activities from Norway to the Bosphorus, and evidence available after V-E Day shows that the control was fairly effective. As earlier noted, R. H. Schmidt was the German supervisor for numerous factories, and after the United States became a belligerent he was made custodian of Ford-Werke at Cologne (now "enemy property"). Ford factories in Roumania and Hungary, like those in Belgium, Holland, Denmark, and France, produced according to agreements with Nazi authorities.

"You have a choice to work or not to work," Schmidt told factory managers. "Trucks are just a vehicle. If you don't cooperate, the premises will be used without you or me." That is, the plants would be put under military control, or the machinery (and perhaps the workers) moved to a site in Germany. It was a bitter alternative, and all officials preferred to cooperate. They could thus keep their workers employed, protect their properties, and in general enjoy a pleasanter existence than if they were regimented by the Nazis. So Ford-France manufactured trucks and Ford-Holland assembled them. They were always in demand by a modern mobile army. In Belgium the Ford company undertook manufacture as well as assembly. The Antwerp management in fact soon supervised an array of plants: a foundry, a forge, and machine shops, along with the assembly operation as it had existed previously.

Ford-Werke produced trucks and, for a time, some passenger cars for army use. In 1940 at its Berlin plant it built in addition the SPKW, an army unit for rough terrain, turning out 1,072 of these vehicles that year. Later the SPKW was discontinued and Cologne made the "Maultier," a truck with tracks at the rear instead of wheels. In 1943, with the enforced assistance of Ford-Holland, it assembled 10,000 Maultiers. Cologne reached an output of 16,500 units in 1940, 14,330 in 1941, 14,672 in 1942, 17,202 in 1943, and 12,915 in 1944. The total of 75,619 was little more than a fifth of the Dagenham vehicle total, and much less than Cologne had produced in the five years preceding the war.

Like Ford, Opel was manufacturing for Hitler. "In Germany," reads a General Motors account of its Overseas Division during the conflict, "the plants . . . at Russelsheim and Brandenburg were seized by the Nazi Government and integrated with the German war economy under German management." Similarly, GM factories in Belgium, Denmark, and France operated under Nazi commissars. The Fuehrer used all the industrial resources at his command. In Denmark, as the war progressed, the Ford factory manufactured generators and, later, filters and coolers.

Dollfus in France for a time kept in touch with Dearborn. "We are manufacturing trucks for the occupants [*i.e.,* the Germans]," he wrote Edsel Ford in January 1942, "but notwithstanding the fact that we are encountering big difficulties, we are still maintaining our schedule." British Ford officials bitterly resented his willingness to serve the Nazis. "Dollfus does not appear to have enhanced his reputation," drily remarked Sir Patrick Hennessy (he had been knighted after his service with Beaverbrook, which he completed in 1941).

American bomber pilots held Dollfus in no higher estimation, and on March 8, 1942, they attacked the Poissy plant, which had to close for three months as a result. In April it was again bombed; new buildings were smashed and machinery wrecked. Dollfus then proposed a "scattered production" plan which the Germans approved. But on April 29, before dispersal could be effected, Poissy was again assailed. "Poissy certainly got a good hammering," wrote A. M. Wibel to Hennessy as the result of information trickling through to him from the State Department. Actually, the entire western portion of the machine shop was destroyed, the roofing blown away, and part of the assembly building demolished.

French Ford activity was now dispersed to five new locations (with Poissy still functioning), and by August 1942 was operating fairly smoothly. In May 1943 the Bordeaux plant was bombed and so effectively that the Ford SAF directors concluded that "no reconstruction would be undertaken under present conditions."

Meanwhile Dollfus saw a steady deterioration of his relations with the Germans. Dr. Albert was appointed administrator of the French company, with Major Hans Tannen as his assistant. German supervision became closer, and the French protested. A Lieutenant Colonel Herbert Beckers took charge but could not calm the conflict, and French Ford production declined sharply. It fell from 4,693 units in 1940 to 1,591 units in 1943. "It should strike you now," wrote a high German official to Beckers, "with what carelessness people have been working at Ford SAF." This carelessness increasingly became a deliberate activity of French patriots.

In Dearborn, Ford officials were convinced that the Cologne plant had been hit and was probably "a sieve." Such was not the case; the factory had never been injured, only a store of spare parts beside it having been destroyed. It produced throughout the war. However, when the American Third Army entered Germany early in 1945 it shelled the Cologne works with somewhat disastrous results. Meanwhile dispersal had been effected, an assembly plant having been set up on the right bank of the Rhine to turn out trucks. Dr. Albert was arrested by the Nazis for alleged implications in the July 1944 uprising against Hitler but finally was released. His old antagonism to the National Socialists seems to have reappeared late in the war.

In Denmark the Ford plant was forced toward the end of the war to undertake the manufacture of M-Boats (tugs), but the first boat was destroyed by saboteurs, no progress with the work was made, and the German police occupied the premises.

To the south and east, as the German forces were pushed back by the Russians, Ford-Werke officials managed to transfer the machinery in the Hungarian assembly plant to Austria, where a German-controlled operation was established at Salzburg. As the Allies came in after D-Day, the French, Dutch, Belgian, and German plants fell into their hands; all operable facilities were at once devoted to Allied uses.[22]

8

Throughout the war the English Ford Company had been mindful of both its plant employees and its dealers. As to the former, early in the conflict Dagenham had made provision for those workers who had joined the armed forces and for their dependents. The employees were supposedly guaranteed by the government the right to organize and bargain with their employers. Those at the Manchester-Merlin factory came under the supervision of the Labour Ministry and were unionized. "We had to recognize the union," recalled Denne, and he further explained that no labor problems existed there since "what instigated union action is private profit, and there was none involved here."

In contrast, at Leamington and Dagenham (where the unions had pressed for recognition since 1937) a formal relationship between the company and its workers was not established until 1944. Austin, Morris, and Standard had all been organized before the war. However, Ford now made an agreement for the period 1944–1946. Perry at first represented the company, then transferred the leading role to Sir Patrick Hennessy. Sir Rowland Smith and Sir Stanford Cooper (both knighted for their war services), participated in the Joint Managing Committee which was set up, and of which Sir Patrick acted as chairman. He termed the relationship between Ford Ltd. and its workers "reasonably good." Labor felt differently. A Dagenham industrial relations official who joined the company in 1952 found that "the atmosphere was bad," and laid the ill-feeling to the 1944–1946 period. As we shall see, in the latter year a second contract was made.[23]

As to the dealers, the war had very quickly cut off the business of those who dealt only in cars and trucks. As earlier noted, deliveries of passenger vehicles ceased on June 30, 1940 and those of trucks were curtailed. Dealers who handled tractors found the situation different. They were called upon to teach many farmer-buyers how to operate Fordsons and how to service them and, in addition, supplied new parts as these were needed and installed them. The company made prompt deliveries of spares, which continued to be manufactured at Dagenham.

Other dealers found themselves working for the government. As early as November 1, 1940 they provided aid in assembly and driver instruction, and in June 1941 the Ministry of Supply expressed a readiness to use the facilities and skills of Ford sales representatives, who from that time forward participated regularly in the assembly and repair of vehicles and in instruction to army drivers. Dagenham provided spares for trucks and military wheeled and tracked units and distributed the work according to the facilities and the prewar activities of the dealers.

A special Ford center for the rebuilding and repair of models and engines was located at the Lincoln Car Depot on the road from London to Bath. Here 26,200 overhauls were completed up to October 1944.

Dealers participated in the assembly of knockdowns from Canada and the United States. Part of a training shed at Wigan in Lancashire was devoted to such work, and the first jeep put together in England was driven from there in June 1942. By 1944 10,000 vehicles had been assembled at and shipped from this point. Facilities at Cramlington and Barking were used for similar purposes. In addition to assemblies, they repaired 18,000 wheeled vehicles.[24]

In March 1941 Edsel Ford wrote to Perry that he and his father were willing to "have you spend 50 per cent of the dividend due us" for the provision of food cars or vans, which enabled the head of Ford Ltd. to provide 350 fully-equipped emergency vans "to feed practically every section of the populace that has had difficulties because of war conditions." Ford companies throughout the Commonwealth and Empire provided 23 additional vans, and other donors brought the total of these vehicles up to 450 by the end of the first year of service. In that period, more than 6,000,000 meals were served. Dagenham provided hot meals for its more than 30,000 workers during most of the war.[25]

Ford enterprises during the war were profitable. Dagenham distributed a dividend of $1,356,750 for 1939 (£337,500) and $1,084,750 (£270,000) for each of the remaining years except 1945, when $1,494,361 (£371,250) was paid.* Canada surpassed this accomplishment by distributing to its shareholders $1,658,960 in 1939, $2,558,960 and $4,591,089 for 1940 and 1941 respectively; $1,658,960 for each of the three succeeding years, and $1,244,220 for 1945. The Canadian dividends covered the profits of the Dominion's wholly-owned companies throughout the Commonwealth and for a brief period the subsidiary in Malaya.

The European companies operated at a handsome profit in all years except 1943, when they showed a loss of $1,780,000, chiefly due to the impending collapse of Germany.** Their blocked dividends did not come to Dagenham or to Ford-US, or to the Ford family, which had a

---

* These dividends were declared despite extraordinarily heavy taxes. In 1940, for example, a reserve for an excess profits tax of £920,000 was set aside, and the income tax on the remaining net profit of £1,125,179 brought the gain after taxes down to £390,179, from which the dividend of £270,000 was deducted. For some time the payment of dividends to persons or firms outside the United Kingdom was blocked.

** Germany also showed a loss for 1944, but it was not sufficient to create a deficit for total European operations.

share in them, until after the war. The net paper profit for the war years was $10,978,000.[26]

The Latin American companies also operated at a profit, although complete figures for them are not available. The flow of parts from the United States was cut to a trickle early in 1942, but up to the end of 1940 deliveries had been practically normal,* and with the entrance of America into the war the dealers turned to selling spares, gasoline, and oil, and doing repair work. The sales organizations of the various companies were maintained practically intact. In the Argentine, Brazil, and Mexico there was a limited production for war, in which the Ford companies joined, and suppliers began to appear, making an increasing number of automotive parts. They laid the basis for independent automotive manufacture. The Mexican company made a profit every year, ranging from $112,000 in 1939 to $851,000 in 1945.[27]

The war exerted a compensatory influence on the foreign companies in the long run, creating bases for independent industries where nothing had existed but assemblies and, with companies already developed, plowing the field of activity for a larger postwar harvest.

9

The Ford companies of the British Commonwealth produced a prodigious number of military vehicles, trucks, and cars, besides manufacturing tractors, automobile engines of various types, aircraft motors, and some arms and ammunition.

Ford-England delivered 144,495 vehicles to the government for military use and built 136,811 tractors and other wheeled-machines that raised the total to 355,202. It also made 93,810 V-8's and other engines for non-vehicular use. It built more than 30,000 Merlin aircraft motors, assisted continuously in the assembly of knockdowns from overseas, taught farmers to use and service their tractors, trained army vehicle drivers, and overhauled and repaired an immense number of engines, trucks, cars, and carriers.

Considering her limited population, Canada proved to be a giant in war production. "Your company," D. B. Greig told the Canadian

---

* As compared to the 30,166 vehicles delivered to seven Latin American Ford centers in 1938, 25,861 were sent in 1939 and 25,142 in 1940. By 1941 the American government had already curtailed the manufacture of automobiles.

stockholders on April 29, 1946, "was the largest single producer in the British Empire of motor vehicles for military purposes." * Ford-Canada, he stated, contributed 45 per cent of all such equipment produced in the Dominion. It furnished 381,530 military vehicles, including 33,993 universal carriers, supplied many additional cars and trucks for civilian and military use, and made castings for arms and aircraft. The sales value of her vehicles alone amounted to $690,510,262.[28]

The task of the other Commonwealth Ford companies and branches had been mainly one of assembly. Altogether, they completed as vehicles 197,836 knockdowns sent from Canada: Ford–South Africa 35,510 units, Australia 35,146, India 119,873, New Zealand 15,199, and Malaya (soon overrun by the Japanese), 2,114. All the companies except the latter also rendered additional services, Basil Stevenson in India working closely with the army and putting his facilities at its disposal for the assembly of products of other companies, for repair, maintenance, etc. As already noted, Australia was seeking to develop an independent automotive industry, and the Ford company there worked toward this end. It cooperated with the Americans in manufacturing equipment to use against the Japanese, making boats, mines, aircraft patrol petrol tanks, pontoons, ammunition, and parts for Bofors and 25-pound howitzers. Ford New Zealand undertook a variety of similar tasks.[29]

As the sound and smoke of battle cleared away, a changing world began to result from the six-year-long conflict, for like World War I, this second struggle had altered many conditions of life on the planet. Power would shift more to the United States than ever and also to the Communist regimes of Russia and China. Colonialism would crumble. Dozens of new countries and a number of old ones which had not been industrialized now began to plan for manufacturing that would vary and enrich their economy. All these conditions affected Ford companies abroad, which marched forward into new patterns of operation.

* Greig was then president of FMC-Canada. For Campbell's death, see Chap. 16.

16

The Crippled Phoenix

In all the automobile plants of the Ford empire from Dearborn to Geelong V-J Day, September 2, 1945, was one of rejoicing. For three years no civilian cars had been produced, and millions of buyers now clamored for them. With a few exceptions, those units in use were relics, many with rusted bodies and patched tires. It was a magnificent seller's market, but for the moment no Ford company had anything to sell. Each was feverishly working on new designs, meanwhile beginning manufacture of prewar models with "cosmetic" changes.

Some automobile executives, recalling the boom after World War I and the searing depression that followed it, advocated caution; the majority wanted to get into the fullest civilian production. These were hampered in England by "a ceiling on car and commercial vehicle production for the home market" (although output for exports was encouraged) and by production that was "limited from day to day by unbalanced and short deliveries from suppliers." In the United States the prices set by the Office of Price Administration on both automotive parts and complete cars, along with coal and steel strikes and a succession of difficulties with automotive workers, impeded the flow of cars. Similar conditions crippled the Canadian output. The golden day of a free market hung enticingly beyond reach, like the treasure at the end of the rainbow.[1]

2

In Dearborn on September 20, 1945 a feeble, eighty-two-year-old Henry Ford tendered his resignation to the Board of Directors of the Ford Motor Company. "May I recommend to the board that it consider the appointment of my grandson, Henry Ford II, as my successor," ran his letter. On the following day his retirement was approved, and Edsel Ford's twenty-eight-year-old son became president of the company. Less than three weeks after V-J Day the young man found the tasks of postwar reconstruction for the company challenging all his energy and resourcefulness.

When Henry Ford II took command, he perceived clearly that to make his business competitive in the domestic market, which would affect all Ford interests overseas, he must reorganize the administration of the firm, prepare new car models, wage a difficult war with the OPA, settle labor strife, close out wartime contracts, and solve his impossible relationship with Harry Ferguson. Actually the Ford Motor Company was tottering. It had fought increasingly effective competition from General Motors and Chrysler and operated at a deficit in the 1930's, and it had lost a series of highly valuable—almost invaluable—men. Edsel Ford had died in 1943; C. E. Sorensen had resigned in 1944; and earlier H. C. Doss (sales manager), the brilliant A. M. Wibel (purchasing), and Laurence Sheldrick (chief engineer) had left the organization. It needed new executives who could set its finances to rights and reduce costs.[2]

Edsel Ford, Sorensen, and Henry Ford, Sr., the chief architects of overseas policy, were now gone. As early as mid-May 1945 Henry Ford II turned to R. I. Roberge, who, as we have seen, had worked intensively in the foreign field, and asked him to coordinate affairs abroad. But Henry II never elevated Roberge to the company's General Planning Committee, the first governing agency of the new regime.* Few officials in Dearborn recognized the importance of the field over which the former foreign sales manager held command.

Seeking an official with General Motors experience to head the domestic company, Henry II in 1946 found the man he wanted in Ernest R. Breech, who became executive vice president; and, largely through Breech, Lewis Crusoe was brought in to handle finance and Delmar Harder to supervise manufacturing.** The young president did not see

---

* The first General Planning Committee was composed of the company's chief executives: HF II, Mead Bricker, John Bugas, B. J. Craig, C. H. Carroll, J. R. Davis, R. H. McCarroll, and H. L. Moekle. In the past, to be sure, Moekle and Craig had played important roles in dealing with the financial and auditing facets of Ford operations abroad.

** Breech as president of Bendix was no longer technically a General Motors man, although Bendix was considered part of the "GM family." Crusoe, who had been one,

any immediate need to go outside the company for an officer to manage foreign business, and Roberge remained in charge of it. When in September 1946 an International Division of the Ford Motor Company was formed, Henry II appointed him as its first head.[3]

In the early months of his administration, Henry II made two crucial decisions respecting foreign operations. The first involved, as we have noted, the disposal of the Brazilian rubber plantation for the nominal sum of $244,200. The realistic grandson meant to end this drain on company resources and confine the Ford Motor Company to automobile production. With economy also in mind, he and his associates disposed of the ocean vessels of the Ford fleet. Henceforth, all Ford exports would be carried by commercial shipping. Both actions were part of a process of rebuilding the Dearborn corporation as a modern business.[4]

3

With the end of the war Ford-England at once began conversion to peacetime production. Perry still led the company, holding the title of Chairman of the Board. He had three lieutenants, all of whom had been knighted for achievements in World War II: Sir Rowland Smith, Sir Stanford Cooper, and Sir Patrick Hennessy. The first two were "managing directors"; the third, also a director, was general manager. Perry, now sixty-seven years old, leaned heavily on Sir Rowland, fifty-eight, Sir Stanford, fifty-seven, and Sir Patrick, forty-seven.

After V-E and V-J days, government war contracts had been canceled; employees were returning from the service to their jobs at Dagenham; and the shadow factory at Manchester closed its doors. The English company in the spring of 1945 had introduced the Fordson Major, a new tractor replacing the Fordson. Before the end of 1945 Ford Ltd. had built 10,412 units of this machine, which should not be confused with the Ford tractor–Ferguson system, produced at Dearborn. The Fordson Major was a distinctive British-engineered, British-made product. Perry had seen to it that neither Ferguson nor the tractor he had worked on in Dearborn would play any role in Ford Ltd. history.

had assisted Breech; and Harder, also formerly with GM, came from the presidency of the E. W. Bliss Company. Henry II's reasoning with respect to GM was that since that firm had been the most successful of American automotive companies, men with GM training could best remake the Ford Motor Company.

Passenger car production was resumed at Dagenham on May 26, 1945, with the Anglia, while a month later the prewar Prefect reappeared, both 4-cylinder cars. The difficulties of converting to peacetime manufacturing proved formidable, and by the end of the year only 2,324 passenger cars had been built. The bulk of the English Ford output consisted of commercial units (26,266 in 1945). In addition, the company did an impressive business in building new engines (57,044) and in reconditioning those in use (43,536).[5] (Trucks, engines, and tractors had been war products, and the plant was geared to produce them.)

During the war the British had needed the dynamic Winston Churchill as a leader; when peace came they chose the colorless Labourite Clement Attlee as prime minister. Under his regime, the company found itself fettered by controls. The government requested all automotive firms to export half of their passenger car output, and allocated materials according to their success in exporting and their prewar rank in automotive output. Sharp restraints were placed upon plant expansion. Shortages abounded, the worst scarcity being that of steel.

As a further impediment to company progress, labor, under trade union leadership, made a succession of new demands. A restlessness characteristic of workers in postwar United States, Canada, France, and Germany had its counterpart in England. Under the 1944 Dagenham-Union Agreement friction had developed between labor and management which in March 1946 erupted in an "unauthorized" strike at the plant—the first there in more than a dozen years and a prelude to poor postwar labor relations. Dagenham was shut down for a week. (Workers at Austin and Humber were also out on strike.) However, the men soon returned to their jobs, and the company and the unions (a number were involved) negotiated a new labor agreement. During 1946 Ford production was not disrupted by further labor difficulties.[6]

Far more serious was the general situation in Britain, for the winter of 1946–1947 proved one of the most bitter in years. Zero temperatures and heavy snows crippled transportation. Sir Rowland Smith wrote Roberge in February 1947:

> It's bad enough to have the country frozen up, but the chaotic situation brought about by coal shortages, closing everybody down, is too serious for words. Despite Government regulations on the uses of coal and electricity, we are managing to work a shortened week.

"We are," he stoutly declared, "bloody but unbowed." Finally, with shortages in power, supplies, fuel, and transportation facilities, the company was temporarily forced to shut down.

All during 1947 both shortages and government controls continued. Since the firm was not permitted to build new plants or additions, it purchased existing ones, buying the Kelsey-Hayes factory (which for years had supplied Ford Ltd. with wheels) and also a building at Walthamstow (a stopgap measure to obtain extra space). In 1947 Dagenham introduced the Pilot (a modified prewar V-8 car with the new name). Despite adversities, the production of Anglias, Prefects, and Pilots rose in 1947 to 44,125 units, and the company made in addition 35,832 trucks and 34,915 tractors.[7]

4

While Perry, Smith, and Hennessy administered affairs at Dagenham, Perry and 'Cooper supervised the activities of the continental European associated companies. In September 1945 Cooper wrote Roberge: "As a matter of principle, Lord Perry and I would very much prefer it if you and your office would write to The Office of Lord Perry [rather than directly to the European Ford companies], and if we cannot give you all the information you want, we will obtain it. Lord Perry is most desirous that the coordination of the various European companies should be via his office."

Dearborn officials were not however inclined to work through Dagenham. Already American Ford executives in government service had brought firsthand reports back to Dearborn, and the new American officials wanted more such reports. However, for a time matters were permitted to go through The Office of Lord Perry.

The first American visitors to war-torn Europe had been Frank Cort and Jules Gutzeit, who arrived in France on a United States Army mission early in January 1945. French-born Gutzeit had worked many years for Matford SA, while Cort, an American, had served in France as a Ford technical adviser in the 1930's. The two found Ford of France building trucks and reconditioning tank engines for the American army. Cort reported that the company was disrupted and lacked "supervisory and trained personnel." Yet the Poissy plant was operating, and by January 1945 all five shadow plants established during German occupation had been liquidated and their machines returned to Poissy.

Cort believed that sufficient Ford-trained personnel should again be sent to France; he concluded: "The future of the French factory, if properly managed, seems to be very bright." [8]

Ford SAF remained under the leadership of Dollfus. He had been accused of collaboration with the Germans and arrested by the Allies; but his detention was brief, and the company was not deprived of his guidance. Under his direction it reconditioned 864 tank engines, continued truck production, rebuilt the damaged Poissy factory, and made plans for the future.

As usual, Dollfus radiated optimism. He had the new plant at Poissy. Renault, the largest French automobile concern, had been nationalized. Peugeot was physically destroyed; only Citroën seemed formidable. Roberge, visiting France on a War Department assignment in June 1945, found that all the French automobile factories, except the Simca, still small, and Ford, had poor equipment and antiquated machinery. He too had high hopes for Ford-France. Dollfus talked with him of building a foundry at Poissy; he wanted Hispano-Suiza to manufacture a diesel engine for the French Ford truck. Soon Dollfus made a visit to Dearborn and saw a car designed for the American Light Car Division in the styling laboratories. He decided that it would be a good model for the French market, and suggested that Ford SAF could equip it with a 60 h.p. V-8 engine. As for a 4-cylinder car, which the reader will recall Dollfus had passionately wanted in 1939, and which Ford-Dearborn had helped him adapt from the German Taunus, Dollfus now rejected it. He told Roberge that the small car market in France was "extremely competitive," and thought it doubtful if anyone made any money in this field. He asserted: "The companies which made these small cars, for example, Renault and Citroën, also have larger models, from which they derive their profits." Dollfus late in 1945 authorized the scrapping of the machinery assembled in Dearborn for the prewar model. He would have the new car he wanted and call it the Vedette.[9] *

In May 1945 the French government adopted a Five Year Plan designed to revive the country's automobile industry. Manufacturers were divided into six groups, each to build a limited number of models. Dollfus arranged for Ford to constitute one of the six and to build a 3.5-ton truck and the V-8 passenger car.

---

* The Vedette was a medium-sized car, smaller than the Ford of that year but a good deal larger than the Renault.

By January 1946 Ford's monthly production at Poissy had risen to 900 units. Citroën was turning out 1,600, while the government-operated Renault manufactured 1,250. Ford held third place in the French industry. Dollfus had fully repaired the Poissy plant and had new buildings under construction. His passenger car production had begun with an improved version of the prewar V-8 (a stopgap until the appearance of the new Vedette).[10]

Dollfus developed his plans with little advice from Dagenham or Dearborn. No experts from either of these plants came to France to assist him with reconstruction. He asked, however, for financial aid, pressing both the English and American companies to provide it. Perry and Cooper demurred. "Regarding Mr. Dollfus's proposals in respect to the funds which we have so carefully accumulated in England for European reconstruction," they wrote, "we should be most unwilling to invest any substantial part thereof in an adventure in France." Knowing of their reluctance, Dollfus was up in arms and wrote Henry Ford II: "I will certainly make every endeavor . . . to get Perry to see things as they are, but he must really stop seeing them on [from] an exclusively English point of view. After all these are Ford Enterprises, financed . . . with the purpose of developing Ford interests and not handicapping them."

As in prewar years, Dollfus preferred to deal directly with Dearborn rather than with Perry and Cooper. He believed that Dearborn officials would be more amenable to his suggestions. In this he was right.

In considering Dollfus' request for financial aid, the American executives sought information about the profits and losses of Ford SAF, and as in the past found it difficult to obtain it. Finally they assembled some data and in 1946 for the first time in eighteen years reviewed the history of their French investments. What they saw gave them pause. Up to 1929 the Ford family had spent only $49,193 in France. It then held 100 per cent of the stock in Ford SAF. In 1929 it sold its interest to Dagenham for $3,517,598. Later, it had repurchased some French company shares, and between 1933 and June 1946 had invested $4,002,834 in the Asnières-Strasbourg-Poissy venture; yet with the decline of the franc the net worth of its equity had shrunk to $1,829,362. The sole return to Dearborn since 1929 had been one dividend of $24,055. And now Dollfus clamored for more funds to increase the capitalization of his company.

Yet just as he had enchanted Edsel, he now beguiled Henry Ford

II, and Perry's warnings were ignored. E. R. Breech studied French Ford finances as one of his early assignments, and in October 1946 he and Henry Ford II met Dollfus' hopes for the recapitalization of Ford SAF, which was completed in 1947.

But the future of the company remained doubtful. Like Dagenham, it found itself short of supplies; unlike the English company it lacked gifted personnel. Dearborn needed all its talent to expand and reorganize its own operations and could send no men to France, where Dollfus had no equivalent of Perry's three knights. A further matter of concern in 1947 was the possibility that France might go Communist.[11]

5

Cologne offered even more problems than Poissy. Cort and Gutzeit visited the Ford plant there in April 1945, before V-E Day. "Everything was down and smoking," Gutzeit recalled; while Cort's first inspection "left me with the impression that the plant was badly destroyed." Soon, however, he realized that the Ford-Werke had suffered little damage "by actual bombing or shelling." The greatest injury, he reported, "was being done by rain and weather, because nearly all of the windows in both roof and sides were shattered." The factory, on the outskirts of the city and not near any major bridges, had survived almost intact the tons of bombs that had pounded central Cologne.

Ford-Werke personnel had moved materials and machinery to the right bank of the Rhine for the alternate assembly plant,* but Cort found the "assembly line and second floor sub-assembly [of the main plant] were in such condition that they could be placed almost immediately in operation." He discovered abundant rough and finished materials, although critical parts were lacking, as suppliers had been bombed out.

Cort met R. H. Schmidt and works-manager Hans Grandi, both "very anxious and humble in their manner." Since he was on an army mission, he did nothing toward reopening the plant. But just as the German surrender began, on May 4, 1945, a team of Ford executives from Dagenham arrived, led by Charles Thacker, former stock superintendent of Ford-England. Thacker concluded, as Cort had, that the Cologne factory could resume production at once. And sure enough,

* See Chap. 15.

despite the protests of Schmidt, by May 8 the Englishman had begun to produce trucks. It was a notable achievement, for raw materials were in short supply; steel and tires were at a premium and semi-finished goods were frequently unavailable because suppliers had not resumed production. Erhard Vitger later remembered, "We got parts out of barges that had been sunk in the Rhine." Machinery was brought back from across the river. In the last days of the war German officials had ordered the Ford-Werke staff to destroy the equipment, but these instructions had been ignored, so that all the physical assets could be put in order. But workers were short of food, and absenteeism ran high because of illness and lack of transportation. Nonetheless, by the end of 1945 Ford had built 2,443 trucks, almost half the total German output of 5,512 units. Never before had Ford-Germany produced so high a percentage of the industry. Opel, which had held the key role in Germany, had far more trouble getting started. Its factory had been destroyed.[12]

For a time Thacker worked with Schmidt, but at the end of June 1945 American authorities arrested Schmidt, imprisoned, and interrogated him for three months. In the end he was cleared and returned to Cologne, now in the British zone of occupation. Here on November 8, 1945, the military authorities forbade him to resume his position at the Ford plant. During the war he had held the title of *Wehrwirtschaftsfuehrer,* and by military law this automatically made him unemployable.

Soon afterward Dr. Albert applied for the custodianship of the Ford-Cologne plant, but the occupying authorities refused his request; for although he had been implicated in the July uprising against Hitler and imprisoned by the Germans, the British were suspicious of his wartime record, which showed his association with the Arendt undertaking.* He became the custodian of the small Ford office in Berlin.

The Americans first, and then the British occupation officials, questioned Erhard Vitger. The reader will recall that he had been joint manager of the company with Schmidt before the war and during it Schmidt relegated his former colleague to a subordinate position. Now the Allies cleared Vitger of any pro-Nazi acts, and in September 1945 the Military Government appointed him "custodian" of the Ford plant.

Thacker left Germany in December 1945, and others from Dagenham came to help Vitger keep the company in production, make repairs,

---

* See Chap. 15.

and promote more efficient operations. Broken windows let the winter air into the factory, machines froze because there was no proper heat, employees were ill-fed, ill-clad, and ill-housed. Rubble lay everywhere. When on February 15, 1946 an employee accidentally left a welding instrument exposed, a fire broke out, destroying four-fifths of the Ford administration building and causing greater destruction than had been sustained throughout the entire war.[13]

As if these difficulties were not sufficient, steel became so scarce that early in 1946 the company built truck cabs with pressed boards and was unable to resume the making of steel cabs for more than a year. To cope with the general shortage of parts, the German Ford company imported Bren carriers from the United Kingdom, dismantled them, and used the major assemblies for its own products. It built a variety of vehicles for the armies of occupation and also reconditioned engines. Its products were distributed in the three Western German zones according to instructions from the authorities.

Thanks to the small damage suffered by the plant and its machinery, and to the initiative of Thacker and Vitger, Ford-Werke had got a headstart in the industry.* However, under the threat of being dismantled or taken over for reparations, Volkswagen soon started up in the British zone. In the American sector both the badly destroyed Opel and Daimler-Benz also resumed operations. During 1946 Ford-Werke built 4,550 trucks out of 13,916 commercial vehicles produced that year in West Germany. After severe losses in 1944 and 1945, in 1946 its operation was not only once more in the black but reached a new all-time peak of profits. This was attributable to the reduction of overhead and operating costs and to the fair prices set by control authorities.[14]

As 1947 began, most Germans still lived in basements and buildings without window panes. Because of poor diets and lack of food, sickness raged. With materials and parts still difficult to get, Cologne operations did not approach normal. Nor had the factory resumed passenger car production, although other manufacturers in West Germany had begun this activity and in 1946 turned out 9,962 units. The Ford management found its task complicated by a Works Council dominated by Communists, which suggested that it inspect company data on operations and participate in the management.

Anyone familiar with the German scene early in 1947 might well

---

* Its Berlin factory, in the Russian zone of Berlin, never resumed output after the war.

have wondered if the stricken country could ever recover. Children scampered through rubble-strewn streets and the tattered ghosts of houses, stealing food and clothing. Normality seemed a dream. Because of the lack of materials and the steady deterioration of the workers' health through malnutrition, Ford production actually declined. Absenteeism and shortages of steel and iron haunted the management. Many German plants had strikes, but Ford managed to avoid them and settle its labor problems by conference. The company served hot meals to improve the pathetic physical condition of its employees.[15]

On December 31, 1947, Ford closed its Berlin office, and Dr. Albert was left with no position in the company. When the Ford-Werke Board of Directors had been reconstituted earlier in that year Albert, then seventy-three, was not made a member. Dearborn officials felt that younger men should lead the company.* Of the Big Three in the European Ford organizations of the 1930's (Albert, Dollfus, and Perry), Albert was the first to retire. Dr. C. W. Hauss, his law partner, replaced him as chairman of the Board but would never play the same dramatic role.

Vitger, first as custodian and then as manager, assumed control. He tried to convince Dearborn and Dagenham that the German company should invest its large cash resources (36.5 million marks by March 31, 1947) in fixed assets. Dagenham officials did not listen. In June 1947 Vitger went to Dearborn and talked with Breech, Crusoe, and Roberge. He pointed out that before and during the war Germany had printed quantities of bank notes to pay for military supplies. Consequently when a new government was established the war claims against it would be enormous. "Such a state will be broke before it starts to exist," he told them. Remembering the inflation and ensuing currency reform after World War I, he predicted similar events in the closing 1940's.

Breech, Crusoe, and Roberge accepted his appraisal, and the latter cabled C. B. Lonsdale, Dagenham representative at Cologne: "Buy immediately land on which we have option south and north of the factory. . . . Buy and pay soonest all necessary equipment for foundry and forge." Vitger wanted 28 acres south of the Cologne works and 52 to the north of them. He hoped to spend 15,564,431 marks at once. Had

---

* No one was left in the Ford organization to remind Dearborn of Dr. Albert's contribution. Vitger and Dollfus disliked him; Roberge seems to have been uninterested; and Perry, who now carried less weight at Dearborn, was not disposed to back Albert strongly. R. H. Schmidt, loyal to Albert, was of course no longer with the German company.

all his intentions been consummated, the German Ford company would have faced the future in a very strong competitive position. Unfortunately, as we shall see, he met with unexpected obstacles.[16]

6

Meanwhile in September 1945 the manager of the Dutch Ford company and three other of its high executives had been arrested for alleged wartime collaboration with the Germans. In April 1946 the charges were dropped, and on the 8th of that month C. G. F. Stenger was reinstated as Ford manager. Equipment that had been removed to Germany in wartime was brought back to the Netherlands and peacetime assembly operations were resumed.

Likewise in Belgium the plant manager was arrested. The company was deprived of his leadership for quite an interval. When that country was liberated, the United States Army requested the Ford company to assemble army trucks, and on November 30, 1944, the company began an order which when completed on May 29, 1945 came to 35,000 units, three times its entire wartime production. On April 14, 1945, the Belgian company got a contract from the army to disassemble, process, and pack American vehicles for the Far East. The work, involving 4,060 units, was completed in September. As these orders were filled, the Belgian plant, 60 per cent destroyed, was reconstructed, and under orders from Dagenham Ford-Belgium divested itself of many enterprises it had undertaken during the war. The foundry, forge, and machine shops that it had operated during the conflict were dismantled, the premises returned to their prewar owners, and the machines sent back to their former locations. From a manufacturing company, Ford-Belgium resumed its old character as simply an assembly plant. In December 1945 Charles Thacker came from Cologne, and for the next two years managed the company. Ford-Belgium resumed the assembly of passenger cars as well as of trucks.[17]

As we have noted, the machinery from the Ford plant in Hungary had been removed by the Germans and stored at the Salzburg branch of a new Austrian Ford company.* The Roumanian government at the

---

* The Hungarian Ford company had been owned by Ford-Werke. After the war the Russians seized the stock of the firm and gave Ford-US a 57 per cent interest (equivalent to Ford-US interest in Ford-Germany) while the Russian government held 43 per cent. Ford-US could not liquidate its interest because a stockholders' meeting could be held

war's end used the Bucharest Ford assembly factory to work on vehicles, which went to the Russians to help meet Roumanian reparations. Dagenham sent no vehicles or parts into Roumania, and in the fall of 1946 Perry decided to liquidate Ford-Romana SAR. Before his decision could be implemented the Roumanian state in June 1948 nationalized the assets of the company; from that point on Ford had no connection with the organization, which operated as the Auto Independents.

With the nationalization of the Roumanian and Hungarian companies, Ford's only Eastern European assembly operations ceased. Its Greek sales and service company, geographically in Eastern Europe, likewise never resumed peacetime activities.[18]

In Spain the government sharply limited passenger car imports, and Ford assembled only trucks. In the fall of 1945 that country asked for cooperation in building a 100 per cent locally made truck (Ford already used 75 per cent national materials), but a feasible basis for the project was never developed. Temporarily, Ford-Spain continued its existing program, and it did not undertake full manufacturing.

Actually by July 1946 every West European Ford assembly unit had resumed the output of trucks, and all but the German and Spanish companies had begun assembling prewar passenger cars. Perry and Cooper watched the construction of a new truck assembly plant in Finland (completed in 1946), another new plant in Sweden, and considered proposals for the first assembly plant in Egypt (not completed until 1950).[19]

7

In 1945 Ford-Canada decided to build a larger assembly plant for its South African company. Thirty-nine acres were purchased in Port Elizabeth, and the plant—said to be the largest in Africa under one roof—was completed in 1948. It replaced the previous Ford–South Africa works, which had been operating since 1930 and were inadequate for the postwar program.

Ford-France had formed a subsidiary in Algeria during the war, but Dollfus was more concerned about his domestic operations than

only in Hungary, and Ford was not in a position to send representatives there. In 1948 the Hungarian government nationalized the firm, but since Ford was unable to dispose of its share, the corporate structure remains. The government company, Mogurt, moved into the premises.—Interv. R. M. Campbell, Dearborn, May 12, 1960 and data in Hungarian-Historical Data File, FI.

with the previously planned assembly in Africa. The French Ford company sold to distributors there.

There was not now (and never had been) a coordinator of African Ford activities. Ford-South Africa handled trade in an immense area. The remainder of British Africa was covered by distributors who received units direct from Ford-Canada. Ford-France sold through agents in French territories like Algeria, Tunis, and Morocco; Ford-Egypt covered such areas as Ethiopia, French and Italian Somaliland, and the Sudan; in the Congo Ford-Belgium had distributors. American Ford units went to other parts of the continent. In much of Africa American Ford vehicles in 1945–1947 were sent to distributors and their sub-dealers. In these areas the export pattern was virtually what it had been in England prior to 1909.[20]

F. J. Dover, assistant manager of Ford-Argentina, reported to Dearborn in April 1946: "It will be easy to sell any quantity of cars and trucks that you are able to ship." F. F. Griffith, manager there, announced: "There are ten buyers for every unit!" The demand was so great that Griffith with Roberge's consent prepared to enlarge plant facilities in Buenos Aires.

In similar fashion Kristian Orberg reported from Brazil: "Our chief concern at the present moment is to enlarge our present plant capacity to take care of the great demand expected." In Mexico City the Ford manager urged additional factory facilities to meet the demand for cars. Throughout Latin America customers called for more vehicles.[21]

E. A. Richards, prewar Ford representative in the Philippines, opened a new Ford sales and service branch in Manila and reopened the company's Shanghai branch in November 1945. As for the Ford assembly plant in Japan, it had been occupied by the United States Army. An Ordnance Department officer wrote to Dearborn in September 1945 that the properties had suffered little damage. Since the army was well entrenched on Ford land, it seemed unlikely that the company's operations there would be resumed in the near future.

The Japanese had interned several Ford-Malaya employees, and when released these officials visited the Ford plant in Singapore. One of them reported:

> We found the plant occupied by Ghurkas. . . . We were brutally denied admittance and marched off to their sentry post. Here we spoke with a British officer . . . and were conducted through the plant. It had

been used by Japanese Army ordnance. There was not a stick of our brand new furniture within it. There was, however, furniture that came from we know not where. The plant was full of lathes and other fine machinery from other Singapore concerns. . . . A veritable swimming pool with sides twelve feet high had been erected in front of our crane bay. I think . . . for fire protection in case of bombing. . . . One odd thing, in walking through the plant, I casually opened the door of a paint oven. There sitting in it, as it had been three years and seven months before, was a metal car body painted in prime. No one had found a use for it.

A little later an American State Department official reported that Ford's property in Malaya "was in very good condition, and 80 per cent of the assembly intact." By January 1946 the manager of Ford-Malaya had returned, attached to a government unit, to assist in re-establishing industry in that country.[22]

Of all the Ford Asian assembly operations, only the Indian presented no problems with occupying authorities. A potential difficulty was that the new Indian government might demand local manufacture. For the present, however, manager Basil Stevenson in 1946 quickly resumed peacetime output, and in the following year the civilian sales of Ford-Canada cars and trucks by his company reached an all-time high of 5,099 units.[23]

8

The Indian and Spanish governments might talk of local manufacture; the Australian authorities insisted upon it. Canberra officials realized that the country's industrial output would have been only a token shield had the Japanese pushed invasion plans for Australia. The Commonwealth must develop industrial power. Since World War I its own companies had made car bodies, importing only chassis. Now the government wanted the entire vehicle made nationally, and requested "all interested parties" to submit proposals. If none was satisfactory, the state would introduce its own production policy.

In response Ford-Australia's manager, H. C. French, in October 1944 journeyed to Windsor to consult with Campbell and, on April 4, 1945, reported to his firm's directors that he had "submitted to the Chairman of the Secondary Industries Commission of the Ministry of Post War Reconstruction a proposal to manufacture a range of motor vehicles in Australia."

The proposal was for the production of V-8 cars and trucks. It included a request for a government subsidy and other assistance, which the authorities rejected. Ford was asked to revise its plans. Meanwhile General Motors submitted a program for a 6-cylinder car, and this was accepted. Ford-Australia continued negotiations, and in June 1946 its manufacturing program (still based on V-8 units) was approved. At an estimated cost of $1,755,000 French agreed to make some 288 parts of chassis components that had hitherto been imported. Compared with the activity of GM's Holden, the Ford effort was modest. Chrysler and International Harvester also developed manufacturing programs in accord with government wishes.[24]

9

The Australian Ford program was directed from Windsor, which also continued to control Ford companies in New Zealand, Malaya, South Africa, and India. At home, the Canadian company reconverted to peacetime production, with the sixty-three-year-old Wallace R. Campbell still maintaining his one-man rule of this company with assets of $93,809,325. He had been its leader for twenty-two years (and had served the organization for forty). During the war he had labored prodigiously, and peacetime found him a tired man, ill-equipped to handle the first obstacles that blocked the path of his giant corporation.

On September 12, 1945 some 10,000 Ford workers at Windsor began one of the most bitter and protracted strikes in Canadian history. They demanded a checkoff of union dues and a union shop. Violence and confusion ensued. "Mob rule has taken the place of law and order," declared the Windsor *Star*. Intransigence on the part of both management and labor prolonged the dispute for ninety-nine days; finally in a compromise settlement the union was granted the checkoff but no union shop, that is, no employee was compelled to join the union but all would have union dues deducted from their pay.[25]

A month after the strike began Campbell was partially paralyzed by a stroke. He subsequently played no part in the negotiations and never resumed his leadership of the company. In April 1946 former treasurer D. B. Greig became the new president. He formed a ten-man management committee which met twice a week for about two hours. "I used to feel that I had had stolen from me too much of my productive day," recalled one member. But all were "thrilled and inspired by

Ford-USA" under Henry Ford II and wanted to follow his method of reaching important decisions through committees.

In March 1946 the 1946 Model Ford with a V-8 engine was revealed to the Canadian public. It was a modified prewar automobile. Windsor, unlike Dearborn, still did not offer a 6-cylinder car. However, a Monarch (a Mercury with special Canadian trim), a Mercury, and a small Mercury (a Ford with special trim) were also presented, all basically prewar models.

Ford-US after the war had set up separate dealer networks to handle the Ford and Mercury lines. Windsor wanted to do the same but feared that the Mercury dealers with a low volume of sales would encounter financial difficulties. Accordingly, Canadian officials worked out a "dual line" merchandising plan by which their Ford dealers marketed the Ford and the Monarch, and the Mercury dealers the Mercury and the small Mercury (later named the Meteor). Thus each group of dealers had two cars to sell. In contrast with the American company, which merely offered the Ford and the Mercury, the Dominion sales force could present the Ford, Monarch, Mercury, and Meteor. Such Lincolns as were marketed in Canada were imported by the Mercury dealers.[26]

Rhys Sale, who was appointed Canadian sales manager in 1939, had long considered that self-distinctive cars for Canada were desirable (he had discussed the idea with Edsel Ford, and won his approval of it). With the new units, his purpose was effected. These could compete with GM's and Chrysler's wide range of cars. To handle the four models and the dual line of dealers, the company increased its number of agents from 703 to 1,113. Since the 1920's the Canadian marketing organization had comprised about 700 dealers, so that this was a major development, giving 410 more sales outlets for Ford products, and expanding Windsor service facilities. Immediately the Ford-Canada organization became more competitive.

It was Sale who had planned the merchandising, worked on the styling of the new Canadian cars, and increasingly took a larger role in the company. He had joined the firm in 1915, had served in the cashier's office, gone to Australia in the employ of the Ford company there, and then returned to Ford-Canada to serve in various capacities and finally to take charge of sales. When in April 1946 Greig became president of Ford-Canada, Sale was elected vice president. Two months later Greig announced that "due to the demands on his [Greig's] time permitting only intermittent participation in direct management . . . Mr. Sale is to be responsible for direct management, effective immediately." Accordingly, Sale took leadership in the Canadian company.

During 1946 the company staggered on its way, thwarted first by its own strike, then by labor disputes in steel, coal, and in suppliers' plants. These interferences, the difficulties of reconversion, and rising costs put a severe financial strain on the company. In June, Greig reported to his management committee that current operations showed a loss of $12,000 a day, and for the first half year would amount to $2¼ million. "We can wait no longer for cost-reducing actions," he asserted.

In the second half of 1946 the losses were checked, so that for the entire twelve months the firm showed a deficit of $2,322,830 (only a little more than what had been forecast for the first six months). This sum was almost offset by dividends from Windsor's overseas subsidiaries, profit on the sale of certain fixed assets, and recoverable income tax, reducing the total loss to $239,448.[27]

In 1946 Ford-Canada built 80,267 cars and trucks, more than in any peacetime year since 1929. Total Canadian automotive production was 175,500; the country ranked second only to England as the largest producer of motor vehicles outside the United States. Ford at Windsor stood first in truck sales (36.78 per cent of the total) and took second place in passenger car sales (23.27 per cent to GM's 40.08 per cent). But because of its high exports, it retained its historic position as the largest automobile producer in the Dominion.

As 1946 ended, practically all Ford prewar plants except those in Roumania, Hungary, Japan, and Malaya were back in civilian production. Some of the larger units, the Canadian and American, for example, operated that year at a loss; others, the French, German, and English, for example, made profits. Recovery from the disruption of war was by no means complete at the beginning of 1947.[28]

10

During the new year two men died who had helped to make the automobile industry a world-wide agent of revolutionary change. In April 1947 at the age of eighty-three Henry Ford ended a long life, and in August, at sixty-five, Wallace R. Campbell followed him.

When the two giants bowed out, many observers were quick to recall the intransigence of both in labor relations, their stubbornness, and their autocratic direction of great industrial corporations. But seen in perspective these undoubted faults were of small importance in comparison with their great achievements, particularly those of Henry Ford. "For most purposes," Ford had said, "a man with a machine is better than a man without a machine." He early set himself the goal of making an automobile that a mechanic, a clerk, or a factory worker could buy. By the use of low-priced, but high-quality materials and the evolution of the moving assembly line he had attained that goal. By doing so he had created the strong position that American automotive production has held throughout the world. He had furnished the impetus for volume output in Europe: Renault, Citroën, Morris, Austin, Agnelli of Fiat, and Hitler with his plans for the Volkswagen, all had acknowledged their great debt to Ford. Campbell as his disciple had spread his methods throughout the British Empire, and even more than his predecessor, McGregor, had proved they were effective in many lands and climates. Ford and his followers had put the world on wheels, ending the social and economic isolation of many population groups throughout the planet and stimulating patterns of life startlingly different from those of 1900.[29]

In 1947 the immense size of the automotive market remained, but the tastes of car buyers had changed. "Time was," wrote a commentator as early as the late 1920's, "when we asked no more of an automobile than the ability to 'get there.' Now it must please the eye as well." Even then to an extent, and much more later, buyers were also willing to pay more for extra power and comfort. In the year of Henry Ford's death his successors in Dearborn proposed to provide such improvements. The company also set up a Light Car Division to produce a small, cheap unit. But soon (when surveys indicated that the American buyer preferred a standard-sized unit) this effort was dropped; as noted, the division's product, having been admired by Dollfus, went overseas to become the French Vedette.

In the United States marketing studies showed that the public wanted a roomy well-equipped product. "When we begin to ask about accessories," remarked the American sales manager, J. R. Davis, "comments from all areas show conclusively that radios, heaters, lighters, clocks, sun-visors and ash trays are now widely regarded as necessities." Moreover, with the high demand for vehicles, the company could sell all the larger models it could manufacture. The margin of profit was greater on big cars than on smaller ones. So temporarily the vision of a "light car" in the United States faded, and the larger one only was made.[30]

The more powerful, comfortable, stylish car of greater dimensions was the right choice at the time for the American market. Interestingly enough, it was also the choice of Ford's foreign companies. Dollfus, in France, rejecting the 4-cylinder car as having a lower margin of profit than an 8-cylinder unit, was applying the basic philosophy of Dearborn to his market. H. C. French in Australia chose the V-8 for that Commonwealth, arguing that his customers wanted a powerful engine. Even the English executives later decided that their first postwar cars would be the more expensive Consul and Zephyr rather than the cheaper Anglia and Prefect. Ford-Canada clung to the V-8. In no case were such selections made at the command of Dearborn. In England the decision was a desirable one, for Ford Ltd. soon revived its small cars. In other instances, as we shall see, it was not.

Thus in 1947 the Ford company had so far departed from Henry Ford's original concept that nowhere in the world except in England and in the markets to which the Anglia was exported, were Ford cars the lowest-priced vehicles offered for sale.[31] *

In the first postwar years prices of all American cars rose steadily as labor, raw materials, and overhead became more expensive. In 1947, the year of Henry Ford's death, there were no "cheap" cars in America. Also, throughout the world taxes and license fees added to cost, while tariff duties pushed up the already high price of imported vehicles.

When Henry Ford first sold his Model T abroad there had been few restrictions on dollar transactions; high tariffs existed in only a few markets. American-built "Lizzies" could for years be priced under all competition the world around. In 1947 that situation was only a happy memory, and many obstacles blocked and clearly would continue to hinder the sale of Fords built in the United States and Canada. Ford-Dearborn exported more units in 1947 than in 1946, but the ratio of exports to production was lower. Windsor exported 54 per cent of its output in 1946, but only 40 per cent in 1947.

From that year forward, Ford-Canada found that its car prices

---

* The English company consistently kept its prices low. The Anglia sold for considerably less than the Morris Minor, the Austin A30 and A35, and the Standard Eight. In the summer of 1946 when these firms raised their prices, Ford Ltd. kept its prices the same throughout 1947.—Maxcy & Silberston, *The Motor Industry*, London, 1959, 113.

were too high for world markets, that exchange controls cut its export trade, that such political events as the departure of the British from India adversely affected its foreign sales, and that the insistence of the Australians on local manufacture further reduced Dominion shipments abroad.

Likewise, the American Ford company discovered that import and exchange permits and quotas by European and Latin American governments reduced its overseas sales. The shortage of dollars in these countries meant the marketing of fewer cars. The Ford plant in Japan remained under army control; few orders were taken there; shipments to Shanghai were spasmodic because import permits were unavailable. In 1947 for the first time Mexico imposed quotas and for a time forbade the importation of any foreign automobile! Brazil restricted foreign exchange in the second quarter of 1947, and Ford was forced to suspend shipments to that country from late June to mid-August. Argentina, once one of the American company's largest markets, overnight became no market whatsoever. The Perón government required exchange permits for all imports, and on June 12, 1947 the Argentine Central Bank refused to issue any new permits for trucks, and on the 14th extended the ban to cars. Manager F. F. Griffith could get no more materials, and so Ford assembly operations in the country ground to a stop on January 16, 1948.

To be sure, European-built vehicles as yet provided little competition in world markets. American automotive production in 1947 was eight times that of France, England, and Germany combined. Nevertheless, the American cars with their large size, great power (which meant forbidding gasoline bills), and high prices were luxury models abroad and would be difficult to market even when and if the dollar shortage eased.

The Ford company had one important means of coping with the situation. In England, Germany, and France it owned manufacturing plants, and another was being planned in Australia. If American and Canadian exports were doomed to decline, why not use the overseas factories to supply world markets? In consonance with such a policy, the governments in England, Germany, and France were or soon would be encouraging the export of automotive as well as other products.

The English balance of trade had caused the British government to urge its automobile industry to export widely. The industry was apprehensive of action by the Labour cabinet in the face of fuel and power shortages in 1947. "All sorts of wild schemes are being hatched by Government departments," reported Smith to Roberge early in 1947.

> Everything depends on whether the motor industry is treated as an unnecessary luxury to be shelved in favor of absolute necessities, or whether its export value will keep it in the front line. I think the latter position is our trump card, as I am certain that but for this the present Government would discourage the manufacture of motor cars by every possible means.

In accord with government wishes Ford exported in quantity. It sent units to markets where in the past its products had sold little. In 1946 it shipped to 125 ports. In South America its sales in 1938 had totaled well under 1,000 vehicles; in 1947 they were ten times that number. Dagenham was exporting prewar models, for as yet no new ones had been designed.[32]

Ford-France also began to ship abroad, and Ford dealers in South America arranged to sell its cars along with the British. As yet the consignments were small. The German Ford company was still not prepared to send cars overseas, but would be eventually.

When Henry Ford II, Breech, and their associates looked at their companies' activities in many lands, they anticipated a confused situation with all three of their European plants exporting different products in large quantities. They also perceived other possibilities for disorder in their international empery. They began to wonder if European operations were being satisfactorily administered from England, and if in fact the American company ought not to direct all the foreign plants. To Ford and Breech it seemed a financial whirligig that Ford-US owned 59 per cent of Ford-England, which in turn owned 60 per cent of Ford-Denmark, which owned 60 per cent of Ford-Sweden, which owned 60 per cent of Ford-Finland! This weird complex of relationships was a tax collector's paradise, for Ford profits were being tapped at practically all stages of the crazy pyramid.

As a result, in November 1947 Lord Perry learned that "the distinct inclination in America is to acquire shareholding control" of the European companies. This step by now had been approved in principle and Roberge was "giving the matter close and constant attention." * As

---

* The genesis of this approval is not clear. Probably it developed from the comments of Ford-US financial experts, who indicated that American Ford interests were not being served by England's control over the European Ford companies. It may also have been

Henry Ford II later testified, "I felt it [that is, control] should rest in the United States and not in England and their direction and their policies [the European companies'] should be laid down by America and not by Britain." [33]

To the new leaders in Dearborn it seemed equally bizarre that their company did not have clear voting control in the Canadian company. As of July 1947 Ford-US had but 42.20 per cent of the voting stock and only 17.23 per cent of the total shares of its Windsor subsidiary. Remedial action seemed mandatory.

At about this time Henry Ford II and Breech also questioned whether Roberge was the right man to supervise their complicated multi-national business. There was no question of his familiarity with the field. But already in 1947 it was clear that the 292,770 trucks and cars which were either exported by the United States or produced by Ford in Canada, England, France, and Germany represented a dynamic element. The total was roughly one-third of Ford production for the United States market and might increase, perhaps explosively. The man in charge of this rapidly growing field must have imagination. Roberge in their opinion lacked it.

Even before Henry Ford's death, with his grandson's accession to power in September 1945 had come a new regime for the Ford Motor Company. For two years reorganization had been in process and was still going forward. But now the overseas activities of the company had come to the attention of the higher executives in Dearborn as an important part of their work. The company's new leadership: Breech, Crusoe, Harder, Harold Youngren (the new head of engineering) and William Gossett (the new general counsel) had been trained in the General Motors organization.* Perhaps an important figure from General Motors with experience in the foreign field could best preside over Ford's business abroad and develop its immense possibilities. Henry Ford II and Breech began to look for such a man.[34]

derived from the desire of Dearborn officials for closer control over overseas operations and, possibly, from the comments of Dollfus, who as early as September 1945 was writing HF II about divesting Ford-England's holding company of its shares of Ford-France stock.—Dollfus to HF II, Sept. 22, 1945, Acc. 713, Bx. 30.

* Gossett had been general counsel for Bendix (which was partially owned by GM). He was never an employee of Bendix or GM, but knew their personnel and procedures.

17

The New Company

"We have come to the International Division late in the problems of the Ford Motor Company," declared Henry Ford II in 1948, "so you haven't seen anything yet of the changes we want to accomplish." From 1945 to 1948 the young president had miraculously transformed the company. Shrewd modern management had replaced the disorganization of 1945. Costs of production had been steadily lowered, improved manufacturing techniques introduced, and a range of new products engineered and styled. After suffering a loss in 1946, in 1947 the company showed a profit before taxes of $108.5 million. The wholly unsatisfactory relationship with Harry Ferguson had been severed.* If the company still ranked third in the American automobile industry, following General Motors and Chrysler, its rapid rise to second place seemed inevitable.[1] Henry Ford II was now prepared to consider the vast overseas operations of his firm, and turned first to Europe, where operations were largest in volume and most profitable.

Early in 1948 Europe had yet to recover from the shock and ravages of war. Reconstruction dragged along, quickly absorbing funds without seeming to gain much strength; and after extensive appropriations by the United States, Secretary of State George C. Marshall in June 1947 had outlined a European Recovery Plan directed "against hunger, poverty, desperation, and chaos." The early months of 1948 found the American Congress debating this plan and other possibilities for foreign aid.

Since World War II the shift in European and Asian feeling had been startlingly toward the left. A socialist government held the reins in

---

* Neither party could agree on a mutually satisfactory program, and Ford in 1946 set up an independent company to distribute the tractor. Ferguson soon sued the Ford Motor Company. (See Nevins & Hill, III, Chap. 14.)

England. France and Italy showed radical tendencies, and although control still remained with democratic parties, Communist forces clamored for power. Russian influence cast a shadow of varying strength in most countries from Finland to Greece.

When the Allied armies met in Hitler's ravaged land two separate Germanies arose, a Russian-controlled East and a democratic West. The division between the two was hardening almost daily. Unfortunately the Western Allies (England, France, Canada, the United States) were slow to agree upon what they wanted Germany to be. They had asked themselves if the country should be developed as an impotent agricultural state (the Morgenthau plan) or encouraged to move like England, Belgium, and Holland along the paths of industrial efficiency and democratic government. By 1948 a strong industrial democracy had become the accepted image of what they wanted Germany to become.

The character of European political life and the poverty or prosperity in Europe influenced Ford's business activity. After World War I until 1929, American firms had operated in most of Europe with a minimum of foreign governmental interference. There were taxes and tariffs, but these were relatively low and the period was a golden age for American exporters and overseas establishments. But as we have seen, in the 1930's many states had increasingly bent industrial activity to their political purposes. After the Second World War governments were exerting even greater power, often in unprecedented ways. Some set production levels, prescribed what should be done with the output (what part would be exported, what used domestically), and controlled materials and distribution of profits. They regulated dollar exchange, set quotas for manufacturers and importers, made numerous miscellaneous regulations, and of course used with new vigor the long-standing instruments of taxes and tariffs.

Americans in business faced a succession of jungles, all carefully prescribed as to character, but all promoting intense competition and baffling restrictions. The companies selling Ford products would have to operate in these jungles, conforming to numerous, exacting, and sometimes confusing laws.[2]

2

In February 1948 Henry Ford II set out for Europe to appraise the markets and review political and economic conditions. He had as a companion and adviser a man he was already considering for the future head of his International Division, Graeme K. Howard, tall, lean, enthusiastic. Howard possessed the imagination that Ford and Breech considered mandatory for that post, and he nursed high ambitions and had visions with sweep, force, and originality. He was no neophyte in overseas matters. "Nobody in Ford had Howard's experience in foreign affairs," one of his assistants later remarked.

After studying at the Harvard Business School, Howard had joined General Motors in 1920. Throughout the ensuing decade he had worked under the able and distinguished James Mooney, then in charge of the corporation's export activities. Howard had successively taken charge of General Motors operations in India (1923–1924), Denmark (1924–1925), and London (1925–1926). With his office in Singapore from 1926 to 1929, he had acted as regional director for the Eastern ventures of the General Motors Export Company, and then from 1929 to 1930 (when GM purchased Opel) served in the same capacity for Europe. In 1931 he became general manager of GM's Export Division in New York, and in 1939 a GM vice president. After serving the government during the war, he returned to GM and from 1945 to 1947 had been vice president in charge of Europe. Ford's choice of the fifty-one-year-old Howard as a consultant on overseas matters would seem on the record to have been excellent.[3]

The two travelers proposed to visit the headquarters of the various European operations and to formulate policies for Ford overseas activity in the decade to come. Their bold project involved an appraisal of all Ford had done in Europe, decisions on essential changes, and a program for expansion. That Henry Ford II was personally involved seemed to promise that the originality he had shown in the United States would invigorate and transform the company's work abroad.

The first stop was England. The visitors found the Ford Motor Company Ltd. performing brilliantly in a highly competitive market. The variety of English automotive products in 1948 was much greater than in the United States. As the London *Times* put it, "The motor cars offered . . . by the British motor industry are . . . more diverse in size, style, and price than the products of any other manufacturing country. The smallest British cars are among the cheapest in the world, and at the opposite pole the most expensive British cars are the most luxurious motor vehicles anywhere." Some twenty-three different manufacturers presented sports models (Healy, Jaguar, MG, and Aston

Martin among them), luxury automobiles (notably Rolls-Royce and Bentley), and economy cars (Ford-Anglia, Morris, and Austin leading). But if there was a medley of products, the concentration of ownership in the industry was also significant. More than 90 per cent of the motor vehicles built in Britain were made by the Big Six: Nuffield (Morris, MG, Riley, and Wolseley), Ford (Anglia, Prefect, and Pilot), Austin, Rootes (Hillman, Sunbeam-Talbot, and Humber), Standard (Standard and Triumph), and Vauxhall.[4]

The Ford plant at Dagenham had an all-English management and in 1948 held first place in British automobile production. Howard must have compared Dagenham with Luton, the English Fords with the Vauxhall, and seen clearly why GM in England could not hold a candle to the Ford Motor Company.

Perry, representing the older generation of Ford management, would retire as chairman of the Board in April 1948,* but Ford and Howard found younger men prepared to assume leadership. Their "hope of the future" lay in Sir Patrick Hennessy, the charming and dynamic Irishman who had begun work in the Ford Cork plant as a laborer in 1919, risen to general manager of Ford Ltd. in 1939, distinguished himself in wartime, and promised to show his energy and genius in peace. At fifty years of age he would become managing director (in 1948); Sir Rowland Smith, ten years his senior, would become deputy chairman of the Dagenham Board of Directors. Sir Stanford Cooper was to have the post of vice chairman of the Board; Ford and Howard felt that he "had a particular contribution to make in the financial, legal, and export areas." Lord Airedale (formerly Sir Rowland Kitson), a director of the Bank of England who had been on the Ford Board since 1928, would succeed Perry as chairman for "the next twelve to eighteen months"; ** the Americans noted that "he has the attributes and character of those men which [*sic*] made English history."[5]

These distinguished British executives were leading their company in a period when capitalism was under severe challenge. In England the railways, coal, and steel had been nationalized. The automobile industry operated under stringent controls. The extent of government supervision can be perceived from the fact that when in April 1948

* Perry remained as a director of Ford-England until his death on June 17, 1956.

** At sixty-five Lord Airedale did not expect to serve long.

the company reduced its prices, Sir Rowland Smith reported to his associates that the Chancellor of the Exchequer, the President of the Board of Trade, the Minister of Supply, and the Minister of Agriculture and Fisheries had all been informed!

Sir Patrick Hennessy told a Detroit management group in June 1948:

> They [the government officials] tell us what to do, what to make, when to make it, and what to do with it when we have made it. . . . If we do not do what they want, we do not get the material. Let me describe how we are affected. They allocate material to us telling us what we are going to get every three months. Those of you, who like myself, have had to do a certain amount of production planning will be surprised to know that Government Socialist Planning means this:—on the 1st of January they tell us what sheet metal we are going to get for January, February, and March. In some cases we *fabricated* the steel for January, February, and March six months before the beginning of the period. In some cases we have to start on things a year or fifteen months ahead of production. They tell us the *day* before, and they call that planning.[6]

Despite these obstacles, the English company prepared carefully for the coming years. The two Americans participated in the process, and they and the Ford Ltd. management decided that as to future products the Anglia and the Prefect would be continued, the Pilot (V-8) dropped and that the English company would introduce more "new name products," possessing possibilities for worldwide sales. The Americans agreed that Dearborn would help engineer these models. In the decision to drop the V-8 passenger car, Ford Ltd. was taking a course entirely separate from that of the parent company.

Worldwide sales were the theme for many discussions which Howard and Ford held with the English executives. While at first the British government had set an export quota of one-half the cars and one-third the commercial vehicles produced in the country, when this was met it promptly raised its sights and suggested that *three-quarters of the cars and two-thirds of the trucks and tractors* manufactured should be disposed of abroad. At the same time, a warning was served that steel for production would be allocated in accordance with success in the export field.

Ford and Howard understood that Ford Ltd. needed assistance to meet British government goals. On February 11 Henry Ford II drove the 250,000th car built at Dagenham in the postwar period off the

assembly line. He then announced that the machine, a Prefect, would
be the first British automobile of a large consignment to be sent to
America. For the first time in its history, Dearborn was officially welcoming English products into the United States.[7]

Perry in 1928, as the reader will recall, had argued that Dagenham
would never be successful without large markets outside England. The
great plant was to manufacture for all the Ford European companies,
and because of this role the older Ford had agreed to sell to the English organization Dearborn's interest in the stock of those companies.
But Dagenham had lost the big French and German markets and
achieved success in large part only by increasing domestic sales. Facing
this situation, Henry Ford had never permitted the English to broaden
their outlets by shipping cars to America.*

The new Dearborn administration sharply changed this policy.
Ford Ltd. was to be encouraged to export around the world, including
the United States. However, Henry Ford II and Howard saw no point
in Dagenham's continuing its control of the European companies and
reiterated what Perry had been told in November, that the American
firm should own the stock of those corporations. Lord Airedale and his
associates agreed "upon the mutual advantage and necessity of Ford
Motor Company Ltd. (Dagenham) completely divesting itself" of its
continental holdings. All recognized that the British firm could apply
the funds it received from this sale to much-needed expansion at home.
The transactions involved were intricate and would require time.

The executives also agreed upon the necessity for a complete revi-
sion of existing agreements to ensure that the products of all Ford
manufacturing companies would be "available in all markets, the
consumer making the decision." This change was based in part on a
recognition that Dagenham must export throughout the world; it also
met new attitudes of the United States Department of Justice.** The

---

* H. S. Cooper had once ventured to suggest it in 1932, but the idea was not appreciated
in Dearborn. In any case the English Ford would not have been competitive in America
during the lean years of the 1930's.

** Once not interested in American business abroad, the Department of Justice now was
showing concern. In the case of *U.S.* v. *National Lead Company,* agreements which
explicitly governed U.S. exports and imports were seen as "vulnerable even if imports or
domestic production were not proved to be seriously curbed or extortionately priced." In
the just-initiated Timken Roller Bearing Case, the Justice Department sought to prove
that Timken's agreements not to compete with its French and British affiliates, nor to let
them compete with it, were illegal. (See note 8 for further information.)

various plans also marked the first step in Dearborn's resumption of control over its foreign operations.

In the course of the fruitful meetings, Ford and Howard recognized the desirability of important engineering activities at Dagenham. "The introduction of a Chief Engineer is required as well as a Body and Styling Engineer. . . . Action is necessary." In other words, in contrast with past policy, Dearborn executives now perceived the importance of Ford Ltd.'s sharing in the development of new cars. At first American aid was to play a dominant part in such activity. Both Ford-US Harold Youngren, vice president of engineering, and John Oswald of his division were to spend time in Dagenham. However, soon the English role became larger. When the American company had too much engineering work of its own, Henry Ford II told Hennessy: "Look here, Pat, you'd better take care of your own problems." This by no means indicated the complete withdrawal of American talent. Constant advice was sought by Dagenham from Dearborn and was always given. But a considerable independence and initiative on the part of the British became the norm.

Henry Ford II and Howard left London with a feeling of confidence in the English company. It was reciprocated. "Mr. Henry Ford II," wrote Hennessy later, "believed in what we were trying to do and gave us constant support. During his visits we exposed the good and the bad to him, and he knew the organisation and personnel very well." This mutual trust was a sound basis for future action.[8]

3

The Ford manufacturing companies in France and Germany did not present so heartening a picture. In Paris the vital Maurice Dollfus greeted Ford and Howard with his habitual graciousness. He spoke of his work with animation and conviction, and impressed them with having "made great accomplishments under most difficult conditions." The beautiful Poissy plant, in an attractive suburb and showing no signs of the wartime damage it had sustained, seemed a promise for the future. Yet the Americans were not deceived. They recognized that the French company was weak in personnel, for although near the retirement age, Dollfus had not yet found an able successor to take up his tasks. They also perceived that to trust his exuberance fully would be folly. "Because of his extraordinary imagination we believe that his ideas and proposals should be screened." Furthermore, it was soon apparent that the organization was even weaker in finances than in staff, despite the generous recapitalization of 1946–1947. Inflation had already largely devoured its resources. Again, production was poor. The Monnet Plan of 1945 had set a goal of 396,800 vehicles for the nation's automobile industry in 1947; actual output had been less than a third of that figure, and Ford SAF was among the laggards.

The political situation may have worried the visitors, but they were assured that France would never go Communist and they had seen that the English company despite its difficulties could operate under a socialist government. Of more impact on Howard was the fact that General Motors now maintained no automobile plant in France. While he never referred to that organization, he was unquestionably influenced by his long association with it, and his associates say he tended to think: "If GM doesn't think France a good risk, why should Ford?" At any rate, the Americans considered the possibility of a merger of Ford SAF with some French company. However, it was an idea that at this time seemed unlikely to be realized.[9]

Howard had more knowledge of German than French conditions, a greater sympathy for the nation, and a stronger desire to develop a significant operation there. He and Ford found themselves in a ravaged land amid a population suffering hunger and want and the "utter hopelessness of despair." Ford-Werke was still manufacturing only trucks, of which it had made 10,000 since the war. Vitger repeated to Ford and Howard his forebodings as to a currency inflation and again urged the need to acquire more fixed assets, especially land. The Americans were not impressed, partly no doubt because Vitger's repeated efforts to buy new acreage had thus far been blocked by the military authorities.

Early in March, at a Ford-Werke board meeting in Cologne, Henry Ford II discussed with the directors a plan for a new small passenger car "which would *possess individual characteristics sufficient to distinguish it from any other Ford product.* [Our italics.] As the same principle is being followed by Ford Motor Company, Dearborn; by Ford Motor Company Limited, Dagenham; and by Ford SAF, Paris, the Ford organization would at a later date be able to market a large range of cars without having several factories building the same kind of car."

Ford and Howard conferred with General Lucius Clay, then commander in chief of American forces in Germany. They found him in

367

"good spirits" and reassured because the Morgenthau Plan had been abandoned for a policy that recognized the necessity of German economic recovery. The inclusion of Germany in certain projects of the Committee for European Economic Cooperation was encouraging. Wartime disaster might yet blossom into prosperity, although at the moment that flowering seemed remote.

Of more than passing interest was the possibility of a purchase by the American Ford interests of the Volkswagen. This idea won the approval of Ford and Howard. But it died in its cradle when investigation showed that ownership of the German firm was both complex and seemingly undeterminable; furthermore, certain Dearborn executives regarded with contempt the small beetle-shaped model. "You call that a car!" one of them was reported to have exclaimed derisively.[10]

The other Ford companies that Ford and Howard visited were of course smaller than the English, French, and German plants. In Belgium, Holland, and Denmark they saw assembly factories and met company personnel. As for Spain, they agreed that the position of the Ford firm was untenable, for the government continued to insist on the manufacture of passenger cars and trucks, and the Americans felt that such an operation was economically infeasible.[11]

From their study they recognized that European consumers demanded small cars with low operating costs. They also felt the introduction of the diesel engine was important. In the United States the Ford Motor Company had never considered making a diesel, for it had won little popularity here. Its initial cost was much higher than that of a gasoline engine, and in America gasoline was relatively inexpensive. However, European Ford executives forecast the diesel's popularity on their continent, especially if initial costs could be lowered.

Since 1944, under Sir Patrick Hennessy's supervision, English Ford engineers had been working on such an engine (in fact, on a multiple type engine that with modification or accessories would be suitable for use with gasoline, crude oil, or kerosene). Hennessy's engineers assured him that it was possible to design such a product and manufacture it cheaply. However, Dagenham had adopted a truck and tractor program with which Hennessy's diesel plans would clash. He and Sir Rowland Smith, who was doubtful about the engine, argued the matter at length, and finally Sir Rowland said: "I'm going to back you. You haven't been wrong in my time." So the existing program was scrapped. However, when Breech and Howard arrived somewhat later, the matter was taken up again, and Howard asserted that Hennessy's program "would wreck the company." * A group assembled in the London office and argued with Hennessy. He stood firm. "I wouldn't change. They either had to let me have my way or fire me. For some extraordinary reason they didn't fire me." The engine was completed and was an immense success. In the interim Dagenham had used the Perkins diesel, both for its tractor and for trucks. The French and German companies made arrangements to use diesel engines in some of their vehicles.[12]

Meanwhile the English engineers were hard at work on designs for small cars, and the German engineers had authority to go forward in this area (see Henry Ford II's encouragement above). Ford SAF already had its new postwar product in the Vedette, to be introduced later in 1948. Other new products for France were not pushed, because the entire situation there was under review in Dearborn.

The exploratory trip of Ford and Howard had appraised facilities, management, and products throughout Europe. Howard returned to proclaim that Ford potentialities abroad were unequaled. "They are far superior to those of General Motors, or any other competitor," he asserted.

At this time Congress, which had been considering the foreign aid bill, was spurred to action by the Communist seizure of power in Czechoslovakia. On April 2, 1948, it authorized $6 billion for economic and military assistance to Europe and China. The next day President Truman signed the bill, announcing: "This is the answer to the challenge facing the free world."

Twelve days later the Ford Motor Company, which had faced its own smaller but highly important problems in the foreign field, made a decision which would be vital in that area. It appointed Graeme K. Howard vice president in charge of international activities.[13]

4

Howard began his work with great zest. He employed new men. He visited Latin America, and in the fall of 1948 went with Breech and Gossett to Europe. He laid plans for a complete reorganization of

---

* Sir Patrick Hennessy writes of the British program that was scrapped in order to develop his diesel: "I wanted a wider variety of diesel, gasoline, and kerosene 4-cylinder engines for tractors and trucks and 6-cylinder engines to be made on the same machinery for bigger trucks. . . . We knew that if the idea worked we could make the cheapest diesel engine in the world."

foreign activities, which, considering the new Ford outlook on affairs abroad, was essential. Nothing was sacrosanct. The capable R. I. Roberge was virtually ignored in the enthusiastic ferment of reorganization. In time, he left the company. In international activities Howard saw himself as king of an expanding domain. For Breech and Gossett their trip to Europe was an eye-opener; they as well as Ford and Howard soon came to take an active part in overseas developments.

In June 1948 Ford managers converged on Dearborn from all over the world—Singapore, Lower Hutt, Bombay, Buenos Aires, as well as from European locations—28 managers and 3 assistant managers. They were to see the new company and know its policies at firsthand. They met the new Ford vice presidents and took cognizance of the great renovation in the American company. They viewed the new 1949 Ford, the first wholly new postwar unit. But perhaps the new American leaders who were behind the Henry Ford II regime most filled them with confidence: the dynamic Breech, the shrewd Lewis Crusoe, J. R. Davis (sales manager), Delmar S. Harder (head of production), Harold Youngren (engineering), John Dykstra (in charge of new factory expansion), John S. Bugas (then of industrial relations but later to deal with international matters), and the brilliant "Whiz Kids," among them Robert S. McNamara,* as well as Henry II's younger brothers, Benson and William Clay Ford.[14]

As they listened to Dearborn executives who explained sound organization, "teamwork," management by committee, profit centers, and financial technique, they became aware that the reorganized Ford company was sharply distinct from that of the 1930's and 1940's. Henry Ford II told them bluntly that in Dearborn "the chaos had to be cleaned up and order made of it," and that a comparable change would alter overseas activities. This, he said, would take place under a new Ford International Division. The former state of affairs abroad, he declared, had been preposterous and would be replaced. "We are going to have one principal office for the International Division. . . . We are going to formulate the over-all policies right here. . . . This is an American company and it's going to be run from America."

Many of his listeners were older men. Most of them took pride in the changing company, for they saw the new president working with a vigor reminiscent of Model T and Model A days to carry the company

* The Whiz Kids were a group of ten young men who joined the Ford company as a team in 1946; six of them became Ford vice presidents and two of these later rose to the presidency of the Ford Motor Company.

to the top of the industry. Some managers, on the other hand, wondered if this youthful enthusiasm would come to anything; the Dearborn slogan, "Beat Chevrolet!" meant little to them, for many had been outselling that car for years in their local markets while the parent company lagged behind.

Yet the meeting of 1948, like that of 1923, undoubtedly raised the morale of most men who attended it. They felt, as Harrington had a quarter of a century earlier, that overseas activity was "no longer looked upon as an orphan." It had won a high place in Dearborn policy.[15]

In December 1948 Howard presented specific plans to the Ford Policy Committee. "The Ford Motor Company is engaged, whether we like it or not," he stated, "on a large scale in the business of foreign trade." Dollar sales overseas for the year had reached $655 million—more than those of all Woolworth branches in the United States, or of the Firestone Tire and Rubber Company at home and abroad. Howard suggested that the Ford Motor Company, like General Motors, should operate this mammoth business through a New York firm, which he proposed to call the "Ford International Company." It would be a non-profit, wholly-owned subsidiary of the Dearborn corporation and would offer "coordination, advice, and assistance to all Ford international activities." Over this powerful unit Howard himself would preside.

He also planned an "Overseas Distributors Branch," located at Harborside, New Jersey, to distribute "products to those markets not handled by assembly plants and where as a consequence shipments are made on a direct factory-to-distributor basis." Thus for such areas as the Caribbean, the South Sea Islands, and most of Central America, which lacked Ford assembly plants, Harborside would act as a middleman.

Still a third Howard proposal was for an export division of the Ford Motor Company. It would supply all overseas selling organizations, including the Overseas Distributors Branch, with American Ford products. Since Ford-England, Ford-Canada, Ford-France, and Ford-Germany were now exporting, or would in the future, they too would have export divisions.[16]

Howard's proposals were accepted by the Policy Committee in December and all were put into effect. Four months later, on April 25, 1949, Henry Ford II wrote Sir Stanford Cooper that Ford International, Inc., with offices at 455 Park Avenue, New York, "was formally activated today." From all parts of the United States Howard hired a staff —215 persons in all. (Roberge had run the old International Division with 10 men or less.) In April, with his large staff, new offices, and plush furnishings, Howard's aspirations bubbled over. Surveying the foreign scene, he envisaged immense expansion. Already new assembly plants in South Africa and Argentina (for trucks only) had been opened in 1948.* Another would soon follow in Sweden in 1949 and still another would be completed in Egypt in 1950. Ford's Foreign Operations Committee had approved in principle new plant facilities for Brazil. Five days before Ford International had been incorporated, the Dearborn company's news bureau announced that a $2 million building and expansion program would be launched in Mexico, where the company would increase its capacity by 50 per cent.

Howard removed the able Benjamin Kopf from the post of manager in Mexico and substituted a GM-trained man, Fraine B. Rhuberry; he sent J. R. Roda to Argentina to replace F. F. Griffith, in charge there since 1924. In dispatching Roda, Howard wrote that in the next two or three years "fundamental decisions as to plant site, design, and capacity of the new plant, and the rebuilding of the organization, which . . . has grown old in service, must take place."

Everywhere the head of Ford International saw the need for reorganization and "rebuilding." At a later date Sir Patrick Hennessy referred to Howard as having "an idea every five minutes and making empires overnight." [17]

5

Meanwhile on April 19, 1948 came the first imports of British Ford cars to the United States, accompanied by H. A. Denne and Harold Mortimore of Dagenham, who would try to interest American Ford dealers in marketing these products. The Englishmen, Mortimore recalls, "fought tooth and nail to get their warranty established and to get the price right." At first they encountered trademark difficulties which seemed insuperable. "We'll catch the next boat back," said Denne at one point, for the entire project seemed to be doomed because of this problem. It was solved at last, but Denne and Mortimore then faced what seemed an even more difficult task: to convince Ameri-

---

* The Argentine plant was dormant as no import licenses for trucks could be obtained.

can Ford dealers that they should stock English cars that they had never handled before. The Dagenham products were prewar models, and even though automobiles were still as scarce as the one-hoss shay and far more precious, these specimens took a lot of selling. All dealers were accustomed to larger cars and were soon seeing the first postwar samples of Fords, Buicks, and Chevrolets. Yet Mortimore pushed his vehicles everywhere in the United States. "I never worked so hard in my life." In Corpus Christi, Texas, where he made his pitch one evening, a group of Ford dealers bluntly told him his wares were impossible. Then one of them noticed him taking snuff from a little silver box.

"What's that?" the American demanded.

Mortimore told him. Placing some snuff on the back of his hand, he sniffed it with a flourish, declaring, "This is the way Churchill takes snuff."

One dealer asked to try it, did so, and burst into a fit of sneezes. Others attempted the feat, and likewise sneezed. But the experienced Mortimore demonstrated again, as smoothly as ever. One dealer decided that the Englishman was "all right."

"I'm taking 12 units," he volunteered, "if you will," addressing the others. Amused, they agreed, and the Dagenham representative took orders for more than 200 cars! By the end of 1948, 12,250 British Ford cars and trucks had been sold in America.

But with 1949 the competition from new postwar American models checked this promising start. Americans wanted the new, attractive homemade product, and not the prewar importations. Moreover, Ford-US interest in helping Dagenham market its cars here had slackened. "We shall give you every reasonable assistance," said Breech, "but the Ford Motor Company has its hands full with a little outfit called the Chevrolet. . . . We have too much at stake in this competitive market . . . to jeopardize our program which is rolling along so satisfactorily at present." In 1949, sales of British Fords fell off sharply, amounting to only 391 units.[18]

In other foreign markets, particularly Australia, Ford-England did well. Dagenham's shipments abroad in 1948 reached a new high of 97,690 cars, trucks, and tractors (63.8 per cent of production) and even in 1949 amounted to 92,866 (61.1 per cent). This was more than the total of vehicles exported in that year by all other Ford companies. The English products went to markets that had previously been served chiefly by American and Canadian units. A shortage of dollars and the demand for a cheap car with low operating costs accounted for the shift. Dearborn car and truck exports dropped from 88,559 in 1947 to 75,111 in 1948, and to 53,700 in 1949, the year when the dollar shortage around the world became truly desperate. Similarly the Canadian Ford company sent 41,141 units abroad in 1947, 34,835 in 1948, and only 17,415 in 1949. The English automobile industry had as yet no serious competition from continental Europe and consequently filled most of the world demand for small, cheap units. Ford-Werke began to build the prewar Taunus car in 1948 but did not yet export in any quantity; Ford SAF with its new Vedette (introduced in 1948) sold the car primarily in France and French colonial markets.[19]

6

The decline in American Ford exports and the collapse of the dollar market abroad were both well under way as Howard set up his Ford International, Inc. office in New York. Other factors were also prompting Dearborn officials to economize just at the time when Howard wanted to launch ambitious plans, employ more men, and spend more money.

With the spring of 1949 Breech, Ford, and their associates were inclined to forecast a recession. They believed that the pent-up demand of the American public for cars would soon be fully met. Automobile sales seemed likely to falter. Again, in May 1949 a strike broke out in the Ford plants, and Dearborn management, focusing its attention on labor, now had little interest in Howard's activities. Indeed, it looked with mounting annoyance at the extravagance of the Ford International president. "Howard had drawers full of organization charts, with slots to be filled by new executives," recalled one young man who with others had been tantalized by job offers from the head of Ford overseas enterprises.

Abroad, the tensions over blockaded Berlin did not make for peace of mind at home. Dearborn officials concluded that this was not a time to expand in Germany. Furthermore the plan for Ford-US to acquire the chief holdings in the continental Ford companies had met with unexpected technical difficulties, and an important step in the company's progress abroad was consequently held in abeyance.

In other parts of the world events were occurring which could not have encouraged the American management with respect to their

374

foreign investments. In December 1948 the Shanghai branch closed because of "adverse local conditions." Soon Mao Tse-tung and his Communist forces would be taking over the mainland of China. To be sure, that vast territory had never offered a large market for Ford. Japan on the other hand had once been a good field. Perhaps Dearborn had hoped for a postwar renaissance of Japanese trade. If so, that hope was now dashed; the United States Army still camped in the Ford plant, and the Japanese made plans to continue domestic manufacture and export of automobiles, which, since the revival of the Japanese economy was highly desired by Washington, were looked upon benignly there.[20]

Argentina had proved another trouble spot for Ford International. Perón's dictatorship had wholly destroyed the Ford business in that country. While Howard had high hopes for future activity there, and Roda purchased 157 acres of land for a new plant, he was still unable to get import licenses for assembly materials and could do nothing. In Buenos Aires the branch subsisted on the sale of spare parts. Other Latin American nations offered no heartening prospects: Brazil, Uruguay, and Chile had tightened their exchange controls. And Mexico had reduced her import quotas on American products.[21]

Howard, sitting in his Park Avenue offices in New York, could not of course control these numerous obstacles to international trade, but they contributed to a feeling in Dearborn that foreign operations carried unusual risks. Furthermore, Howard had antagonized the Canadian Ford executives. At the 1948 conference of overseas managers, he had spoken of "this ripe plum" (the Canadian empery) which should be plucked by the Dearborn company. He wanted to abolish the traditional relationship between Ford-Canada and the parent company and coordinate Canadian and other "foreign" activities under Ford International in New York. Henry Ford II and Breech approved. Even before Howard took his post the American company had attempted to win clearer control over the neighboring operation. On January 30, 1948 the Ford-US Board of Directors had authorized the purchase of additional shares of Ford-Canada, and in August 1948 for the first time in its entire history the American company acquired clear voting control (51.85 per cent) of that firm. Early in 1949 a draft had been made of a new agreement between the two corporations which provided for wider obligations by Dearborn toward its affiliated company in "commercial assistance, the supply of materials, and furnishing technical and other information." This agreement would remove restrictions in effect since 1904 on the sale of Canadian products outside the British Commonwealth. If Ford International were to be effective, logically it should exercise authority over Canada as well as other foreign lands.[22]

But Dominion executives opposed the idea of working with Howard in New York. After all, they were only forty minutes by car from Dearborn, and why, they submitted, disrupt the top level communications that had been so successful in the past? Some of the higher Ford executives in the United States thought the Canadians had a point.

In fact, during the spring and summer of 1949 high American Ford officials came to feel that Howard was assuming powers unwarranted by his position and the state of the market. As a result, they ordered a halt to recruitments for Ford International. In July 1949 the Export Division and the Overseas Distributors Branch were consolidated. On the 15th of that month, a special meeting of the Board of Directors of Ford International was convened, and Howard reported, doubtless with chagrin, that "it appeared that certain economies might be effected as a result of operating Ford International, Inc. as a Division of the Ford Motor Company," rather than as a separate organization. The directors authorized the liquidation of the International Company (after only three months of glory); Howard's staff was cut from 215 to 26.

Moderation had triumphed. Howard's unit was once more called "the International Division of the Ford Motor Company." It kept its headquarters in New York until 1956 and slowly increased its staff. Although it retained most of the functions Howard had prescribed for it, with its limited personnel it was unable for some time to extend its influence in the manner he had envisaged.[23]

The late summer and fall of 1949 saw a decided improvement in business conditions. The predicted recession had "blown itself out," and prophecies of coming market conditions were optimistic. Dearborn concluded a $4 million sale of its products to the government of Israel, which pleased everyone except the Arabs. Concurrently, the agreements with the English and Canadian companies, which in the spring of 1949 had faced numerous obstacles, were now completed. The Ford-US Board of Directors on November 10, 1949 approved the new arrangement with Ford-Canada, and it became effective retroactively on May 1, 1949. Meanwhile in August 1949 Ford, Ltd. and Ford-US reached a final decision for the latter to purchase such shares in the continental Ford companies as were owned by Dagenham's holding unit, the Ford Investment Company Limited, of Guernsey. This put into effect the plan that had been under discussion since November 1947.

The actual purchase of these holdings by the American company took place on January 27, 1950. Using blocked dividends amounting to £4,256,860, Dearborn acquired direct ownership in the Ford companies on the continent of Europe.* The transaction was especially satisfactory to Ford-US because in September 1949 the British government had devalued the pound sterling (from $4.03 to $2.80). At the same time, as noted earlier, the considerable sum of money that Ford, Ltd. received was useful in implementing its plans for postwar expansion.

The acquisition by Ford-US included stock holdings in Ford companies in Egypt (99 per cent), Italy (100 per cent), Belgium (57 per cent), Holland (60 per cent), Denmark (60 per cent), Spain (60 per cent), France (21 per cent), and Germany (6 per cent). As brought out in Chapter 11, Ford-US already controlled much of the French and German stock, and so by this purchase it increased its equity in the French and German Ford units to 55 and 58 per cent, respectively, of the stock outstanding. It also acquired indirect holdings in Ford-Sweden, Ford-Finland, and Ford-Portugal.**

The balance of the shares in the Belgian, Dutch, Danish, Spanish, Finnish, Swedish, French, and German firms continued to be publicly owned, most of it by nationals within these countries. The Ford-US acquisition of the Guernsey company's stock in no way altered the American ownership of the common stock of Ford-England, which con-

---

* Actually, the sale was accomplished as follows: the European and Egyptian companies were controlled by the Ford Investment Company, Guernsey, a wholly owned subsidiary of Ford Ltd. The latter firm made a cash distribution of £4,256,860 to the American Ford company. (Because of British currency restrictions this cash could not be turned into dollars but could be used to purchase holdings in the companies.) Ford Ltd. also capitalized £2,943,140 in favor of the minority stockholders of the English company. This last sum was applied in full payment of 3,678,925 new 4½ per cent redeemable preference shares of 16s., which were then allotted to the minority stockholders. The American company paid the blocked £4,256,860 to the Guernsey investment company in return for the latter's interest in the European and Egyptian subsidiaries. Early in 1951 the Investment Company was liquidated and all its funds transferred back to Ford Ltd.

** Ford-Denmark owned 60 per cent of Ford-Sweden, which in turn owned 60 per cent of Ford-Finland. The Portuguese company was 100 per cent owned by the Spanish Ford company.

tinued to be 59 per cent. Likewise the Irish Ford company, linked with Dagenham, remained a wholly-owned subsidiary of Ford Ltd.[24]

On the very day of the purchase (January 27, 1950), all the European Ford companies revised their agreements with Ford-US, and under these new pacts American Ford cars could enter any foreign market (subject of course to tariffs, quotas, licensing and currency restrictions), and units produced by Ford companies anywhere in the world would be free to compete in markets that had previously been the American company's preserve.

With the purchase and the agreements, Ford entered a new epoch. It was one in which Dearborn would continue to rectify what it considered the blunders of prewar Ford management. By the beginning of 1950, the American company had obtained the majority of voting stock in all of its foreign affiliates, but only in the Egyptian, Italian, the moribund Japanese, and the Mexican companies did it have 99 or 100 per cent of the stock.* The feeling in Dearborn now was that the corporation, like General Motors, should move toward a full ownership of all its foreign activities. Officials felt that overseas operations had got out of hand by being developed abroad and that with 100 per cent ownership could be brought back into the fold. If a foreign company were American-owned in its entirety, nothing could interfere with its being operated in the manner most profitable to the home office. Dividend and expansion policy could be shaped without deference to minority stockholders.[25]

The new approach had been formulated under Howard's aegis, but it was destined to develop without him. He had given a new burst of energy to foreign activities. While he was vice president important changes had taken place in the American company's relationships to its affiliates abroad. But Howard had too many ideas. As a friend put it, he "wanted to move too far, too fast." His daring projects soon began to show a lack of proportion. In some cases flamboyance became a substitute for hard realistic planning. Breech first, then soon Henry Ford II, discovered that Howard tended to venture without sufficient prudence, and that an excess of enthusiasm swept him into undertakings that reason would have rejected. As 1950 began, Howard found himself increasingly isolated from the Dearborn executives. It was a physical

---

* In some cases 99 per cent was held instead of 100 per cent because qualifying shares were required by local law. Most of the Latin American operations were run as branches and thus were fully controlled.

isolation: they in Dearborn, he in New York. But more important, a number of conflicts arose that ranged from matters of policy (Howard, for example, wanted a foreign products sales division to market English Ford cars in the United States, while Breech and others doubted if such a division would be profitable) to matters of personality (Howard neglected to keep Dearborn officials informed concerning his work and irritated them with what they regarded as irresponsible suggestions). His relations with the Canadian company showed no signs of improvement, and in the spring of 1950 an incredible mixup arose with respect to Ford Ltd. dividends. In this case, as in other instances, Howard did not coordinate his actions with the finance staff in Dearborn. The result of these occurrences was that on May 19, 1950, he took a leave of absence from the company and never returned.[26]

Howard had made no small contribution to Ford overseas policy. In the little more than two years he had been with the company (and in the preceding months when he acted as adviser) he had helped mold its character for the next eight or nine years. He and Henry Ford II had built Ford International and put it in operation. Howard's successor, Arthur J. Wieland, was a legacy from the vigor and direction of its first two years. Employed by Howard, trained like him in General Motors, Wieland continued the work his more vital predecessor had begun. Experienced, mild-mannered, cautious, and amenable, he was to conduct an activity that was modest compared with his former master's.

When after considerable delay Wieland on September 12, 1951 became vice president of Ford International,* he took over an operation that had shown dollar sales in 1950 of $713,654,000 with net profits of $48,097,000. Even so, its potential was greater than anyone in the Ford organization realized.[27]

---

* On May 19, 1950 Wieland had become the chief executive of Ford International. However, it was not until September 12, 1951 that he was elevated to the former post that Howard had held, the vice presidency.

18

Manufacturing for World Markets: From Dagenham to Geelong

"For the British Motor Industry, 1954 was another year of tremendous expansion," Sir Rowland Smith, now chairman of the Board, told his Ford Ltd. stockholders in the annual report for that period. "More than a million cars and trucks were produced in this country by the Industry as a whole, and we played a leading part in this achievement." The statement was no exaggeration. Dagenham had sold 297,-768 vehicles in the past twelve months, more than three times its 1939 total. Over half its products (155,496) were being sold abroad, and its domestic production, freed from governmental fetters, was rapidly expanding.

Its dramatic rise was part of a massive movement by the entire automobile industry of Europe. Stimulated by the Marshall Plan, the Western nations had shown dynamic productive strength, in which the automotive output shared. While England was building more than a million units, Germany manufactured more than 700 thousand, France 600 thousand, and Italy 217 thousand.* The sum total of foreign output amounted to less than half the 6.6 million vehicles built by American factories, but it represented a startling upsurge. How had it come about in a world which some prophets had felt was saturated with cars even as early as 1949? [1]

2

There had been no saturation, but rather an ascending curve of production and buying. Ford-England illustrates what had happened.

*Even Sweden produced 54 thousand cars, a record achievement for that country. Canadian production amounted to 357 thousand, Japanese to 61 thousand, that of Australia to 55 thousand, and Russian (mostly commercial vehicles) to 395 thousand.

In 1950 the English government limited the total output of all firms for home consumption to 110,000 cars. Dagenham had "domestic orders for over 250,000 passenger cars on our books," and the estimated banked-up orders for the industry amounted to a million. Steel and other crucial materials were doled out by state officials "according to national needs." Only the export market, as noted, offered a free flight, and there Dagenham spread its wings. In 1950 it dispatched 146,102 vehicles abroad, 78.9 per cent of the company's production of 185,124.

Ford Ltd. had basic advantages over other British automotive companies. Aside from brilliant managerial talent, its chief asset was the Dagenham plant. Designed in 1928 for an annual capacity of 200,000, it had hitherto never approached this maximum; but in 1950, with new car and truck models to be launched, and a large tractor program, its factories showed limitations. Nevertheless they provided the company with facilities no competitor could match. As the London *Times* stated in October 1949: "Dagenham is something of a show-piece among the bigger British motor car factories because it was conceived and built on the present scale, whereas most of them have been developed from small factories started in the early years of the century." [2]

Ford executives were not satisfied with their superior properties. Despite a government curb on new building, the company kept pressing for more factory space. In 1948 it purchased land at Rainham, four miles from Dagenham, where later it established a center for product engineering design. In the same year the government finally leased to Ford Ltd. a former aircraft building at Langley, thirty-five miles away in Buckinghamshire. But permission to extend the main Ford plant, although land on the site was available, was limited to "such measures as will improve working conditions there, notably an improved and extended foundry." Lord Airedale lashed out at such restrictions: "I must place on record my view that the dispersal of some of our activities is a retrograde step, nullifying as it does in part the cost advantages we derive from fully integrated operations at Dagenham." Even with the nullification, Ford in England still had the most complete motor vehicle plant in the country. The power house, blast furnace, coke ovens, and foundry, once "white elephants," now rendered the fullest service.

A second major advantage Ford Ltd. enjoyed over its competitors lay in the location of its works on the Thames, which promoted export activity. The sterling devaluation of 1949, bringing lower prices overseas, had given an impetus to all British export sales. Dagenham not only profited by this but also by the world-wide chain of Ford distribution outlets. Indeed, when in 1950 the British motor industry took first place in world automotive exports, Ford Ltd. easily led all companies in the land in the size of its foreign consignments.[3]

In the late 1940's the English Ford company was obligated to pay Dearborn for its help in designing the new postwar cars, the Consul and the Zephyr. The British government promptly recognized its achievements in helping to provide the country with dollars through its export activity and saw to it that Hennessy got the American money he needed. Similarly, when he and his associates needed dollars to buy machinery not available in England Sir Herbert Britain of the Treasury on October 6, 1949 told Lord Airedale and Hennessy that he "would be prepared to provide up to 4½ million to Fords Dagenham over the next two years, for payment of U.S.A. machinery and equipment."[4] *

While the motor industry was under complete state control, Ford of England prepared its first postwar models: the Consul and the Zephyr. English Ford officials had been thinking of small cars; Dearborn experts suggested increasing their size. The new units were to sell in the medium-price range. Introduced in October 1950 these cars quickly led the industry in styling. They were designed symmetrically, and the press asked: "Are they going front or back?" They were not the first British postwar automobiles to appear, for Standard, Rootes, Austin, and Morris had already presented new models. But they commanded attention by their appearance and construction. Their overhead valve engines, steel-welded bodies, independent front-wheel suspensions, and new hydraulic brakes quickly won the respect of car buyers. The 4-cylinder Consul and the 6-cylinder Zephyr were not inexpensive. The Morris Oxford cost more than the Zephyr, but in the same price class the Standard, Vauxhall, Hillman, and Austin were all cheaper. Yet the Ford cars competed successfully with these rivals and at the same time enhanced Dagenham prestige, for no longer could the company be thought of as a builder of cheap cars only.

Since the British tax laws had been changed in 1947, the levy on automobiles was no longer based on horsepower. This permitted a free-

---

* Sterling devaluation occurred on September 26, 1949.

dom in engine design which the new Ford models had fully utilized. The Consul and the Zephyr (having the same body shell but differing as to engines and front ends) expanded the Ford line of products. The smaller prewar Anglia (8 h.p.) and Prefect (10 h.p.) were retained.[5]

The sale of Dagenham's commercial vehicles also increased. Only in one area had a not unexpected competition developed. For more than fifteen years Ford had held practically a monopoly in the English tractor market. This condition now became one of sharp competition. We have seen that Harry Ferguson during World War II had pressed frantically to substitute the Ford tractor-Ferguson system for the English-designed Fordson. And while as we have noted his relationship with Ford-US had been severed, as early as 1945 Ferguson had arranged with the Standard Motor Company in England to build his tractor. By 1948 this machine (essentially that engineered by Ford-Dearborn) confronted the new Fordson. Lighter and more maneuverable than the latter, it quickly took a commanding position in the market. Nevertheless, in important ways the Fordson was superior and maintained a stiff contest. By 1951 Standard and Ford were producing 80 per cent of the 137,387 tractors made in England, Standard leading. It was a dismal paradox that two tractors designed by the Ford organization should be in competition with one another!

By 1951 the Ford diesel engine which Hennessy had assiduously promoted was at last ready for use. The 4-cylinder motor, "the cheapest diesel of its class in the world," was installed in the tractor and soon found an almost 100 per cent use in English Fordsons and a 90 per cent acceptance abroad. It definitely improved the Ford position with respect to the Ferguson machine, and the sales gap between the two began to narrow. The diesel also aided Ford export activities.[6]

3

In 1951 the Conservative Party again took power in England, and business conditions there became more "normal." Steel and some other industries were denationalized, but important controls were retained, notably the stringent limitation on dollar spending.

By 1951 Ford-Dagenham had adopted some of the financial policies of Dearborn. "We had visits from Mr. Breech and the top people on the financial staffs at Dearborn," Hennessy recalled, "and we were able gradually to acquire their techniques on financial controls where they improved our methods." In January 1948 (before Henry Ford II's first visit) the initial meeting of the Dagenham Policy Committee was held, and this group soon helped to shape the company's chief activities. (Dearborn had had a similar committee with the same name almost from the beginning of the new regime in September 1945.)

Ford-Dagenham had emerged in 1948 as the chief motor manufacturer of England, and had since held that position. But in 1952 it suddenly lost preëminence—not because of diminishing production, but because its two chief rivals, Austin and Morris, merged, becoming the British Motor Corporation. Their combined output was the highest in the land. Ford continued to increase its own production, with 297,788 vehicles in 1954, as earlier noted, and 355,772 in 1955. Two British economists point out, moreover, that from 1953 to 1955 Ford and GM's Vauxhall, utilizing American financial methods, were making higher profits per vehicle than other British manufacturers. "They were followed by BMC, with Rootes and Standard well behind." [7]

Dagenham adopted various Dearborn suggestions, introducing organization charts and some decentralization. It got advice on specific problems, but in the main depended on its own resources. When an English writer asked Dagenham officials if their policy was strongly, partly, or negligibly "controlled by your American associates," he was told that it was "partly controlled."

Typical both of cooperation and the growing independence of Ford Ltd. were the new postwar small cars, the Anglia and the Prefect, offered to the British public in 1953. When work on these models began, Hennessy visited Dearborn and on his return told the Ford Ltd. Policy Committee that Henry Ford II and Breech had informed him that "the development work on this project was a matter for the Dagenham Company's decision." Accordingly the cars were designed in England, although Earle S. MacPherson (vice president in charge of American Ford engineering) made helpful suggestions.

Ford of England had been steadily building up its Engineering Department. Once, as we have seen, the company had depended entirely upon Dearborn for car design; by 1939, although growth toward local responsibility had started, it employed all told only 101 engineers. By 1949 this number had increased to 208, by 1950 to 270, and was still growing. To Hennessy it seemed a "tragic thing" that the company had not an even larger staff to cover the engineering projects that his fertile mind was constantly evolving. He gave the fullest support to the expansion of this activity. But in one respect he was perhaps too conservative. He wanted to "make" experts from within the company, rather than employ university graduates. By 1955 the Dagenham engineers were still unready to attempt long-range experimental work, "recognizing that under present circumstances, it is more economical for us for it to be done by Ford U.S.A." Naturally Ford of England paid Dearborn for the services it rendered.[8]

To the styling of the new cars, Hennessy gave close attention. Oldtimers who had never seen Perry in the drafting room saw Hennessy often. When one employee was asked who was in charge of Dagenham's styling, he replied with a glint of humor, "Sir Patrick is our chief stylist."

In their plans for the new cars, British Ford executives followed three policies. The first recognized that with the low volume of English output (as compared with American) the models would be changed less frequently. Clear, simple design was therefore given preference. The second held that the cars must be easy to service and maintain. "The easy service theme has run through all our planning," recalled Sir Patrick. The third policy stressed reliability.

The postwar Anglia and Prefect, introduced in 1953, showed completely new bodies along classical lines. The Anglia had two doors, the Prefect four. The British press praised the cars both for their styling and their performance. In 1953 also appeared the Ford Popular, the lowest-priced car on the English market. It was a brilliant marketing stroke. "We took the old Anglia," said one engineer, "stripped it of everything and made a few changes, and we called it the Popular." It sold for £275 ($770), which was £50 less than its nearest competitor. Sir Rowland Smith hailed it as "the lowest priced car in the world." The public, eager for basic transportation, purchased it *en masse*.[9]

That year in addition saw a broadening of the English line to include a luxury model, the Zodiac. The sales staff had asked for a de luxe addition to the Consul and Zephyr line with a new name. They argued that there was a demand for a higher-priced unit, just as one existed for a low-priced car. As a result, the de luxe Zephyr was introduced, at first called the Zephyr-Zodiac and then simply the Zodiac. It came in two-tone colors, with attractive trim and decor.

Indeed, Ford of England in 1953 was offering the public a greater range of products than ever before in its history, with an adroitness in styling that was unequaled. In October 1949 the London *Times* had described the ambitions of Sir Rowland Smith, Sir Patrick Hennessy, and Lord Airedale:

> These men believe that Britain should not attempt to copy the vehicles of other countries and that she should develop a new and completely distinctive style of her own. Moreover, they believe that so long as the most economical form of motoring is required (as it always will be in many parts of the world) it is the business of Ford, Dagenham, to supply that need. In its [Ford's] view it is Dagenham's task to set the standard of low price and value for the money. Nevertheless they stipulate that the cars they make must take four people safely and comfortably as well as economically.

With the 1953 passenger cars these careful plans of Dagenham were fulfilled. In addition, in the commercial field the company introduced a new "cost-cutter" gasoline engine, and early in 1954 a "cost-cutter" diesel engine, both of which filled obvious demands.[10]

The way was now open for plant as well as vehicular expansion. Although dollars were still short, the days of steel scarcity had gone, along with government control of other raw materials. Dagenham had not neglected its plant facilities. Throughout the postwar period, from the acquisition of Kelsey-Hayes in 1947 to the leasing of Langley in 1949, the company had steadily increased its factory space. The funds that Ford of England received in 1951 from the sale to the American firm of its holding company's investment in the European and Egyptian associated companies could now be used effectively. Ford-Dagenham officials turned "actively and aggressively [to] seeking out opportunities for equity investment within Britain." Between 1950 and 1953 Ford Ltd. acquired at Dagenham a new two-story manufacturing building, a new battery of forty-eight coke ovens, more powerhouse equipment, and made notable improvements in its foundry. By 1953 the company was ready for much larger action.

Briggs Motor Bodies Ltd., with its main plant on the Dagenham estate, had for years supplied the bodies for Ford of England vehicles. It was a partly-owned subsidiary of the American Briggs company, and had British shareholders as well. Hennessy became convinced that "Chrysler would buy Briggs in America and would then control our body supply." Since the cost of a body was about 40 per cent of that of the entire car, this posed a grave problem. Moreover, other comparable suppliers of bodies were not available in England.

To purchase the English Briggs company was no small undertaking. Briggs had built its plant at Dagenham in 1931 and at first produced only Ford bodies. However, it had no exclusive arrangement with Dagenham and in time accepted other British business: from Daimler, Chrysler, Riley, and Humber. When England began to rearm before World War II, Briggs undertook to make aircraft parts, leasing for this work a "river plant" in Dagenham off Ford property. In September 1939 besides its government work the company was doing about 20 per cent non-Ford business. With war, it devoted both its plants to military production and acquired six additional factories. Some of these it disposed of after the war, but acquired others for peacetime work. By 1953 it owned its main plant, the river plant at Dagenham, four other big factories, works at Doncaster and Southampton, and had two smaller leased properties at Rumford and Croyden. It was still doing government work and handling non-Ford as well as Ford business.

Between 1951 and 1953 Hennessy made a number of attempts to purchase the Briggs properties, but there was "always a wide gap between what our people were prepared to consider and what the Briggs people were prepared to consider." He remembers that "negotiations took place and ultimately [in 1953] on the telephone, I got an option for some weeks and undertook to supply dollars in the belief that there was some way of doing this despite the rigid Government control at that time."

He got the dollars. Ford of England paid £3,202,478 (almost $9 million) for 62 per cent of the shares in the British Briggs company owned by the American Briggs company. Dagenham also purchased the remaining shares held by the public. To effect these arrangements it created *new* ordinary shares in Ford Ltd. and gave Briggs shareholders two of these plus 5 shillings in cash in exchange for each Briggs ordinary share. In this fashion Dagenham acquired full ownership of Briggs Motor Bodies Ltd.[11]

The transaction not only fully protected Ford's supply of bodies (for Chrysler in the United States did buy the American Briggs company), but put under Dagenham control all the Briggs plants in England. Hennessy later spoke of the purchase as one of the most important events in Ford-England's postwar history. It brought with it a bevy of bad labor relations problems, but, more importantly, it gave Ford a new and significant degree of integration.*

* Ford in buying Briggs acted as had its rivals, for Austin in 1946 had acquired the body builders Vanden Plas (London), and six months after Ford's purchase of Briggs, BMC acquired its body supplier, Fisher & Ludlow. (See chapter by George Maxcy in P. L. Cook and Ruth Cohen, *Effects of Mergers*, London, 1958, 376–377.)

An incidental consequence of the Briggs purchase was that with the issue of the new Ford Ltd. shares the American Ford company's holdings in its English firm were diluted and fell from 59 to 54 per cent. This marked the sole instance, since the new management at Dearborn had taken direction of foreign operations, that there had occurred a *reduction* of the American company's stock equity in any of its overseas enterprises. The general trend had rather been toward an increase in the holdings of Ford-US in its various ventures abroad.[12]

Dagenham's expenditures on buildings, plants, and machinery from 1950 through 1953 amounted to £19.45 million (roughly $54.46 million), including the net book value of the Briggs properties. In 1954 the Ford firm was ready to embark upon larger programs. It was now building almost 300,000 cars, trucks, and tractors a year, an output second only to that of the giant British Motor Corporation. Its assets were £55,725,699 (about $156,031,957),* which gave it second rank in size after Jersey Standard among the American industrial firms in Britain. Its impressive achievements had been due to brilliant leadership, to a plant unequaled in Britain, and to American Ford assistance in exporting, financial planning, and engineering. Dagenham had the available cash for further expansion, and a growing market for its products. Hennessy had capitalized on the advantages the firm commanded, and had wisely increased its capacity, providing a range of products styled, engineered, and priced to fill both domestic and export demands. The results were visible in new sales records, in a constantly improving position in the industry, and in excellent financial returns.[13]

4

Elsewhere in the Ford overseas empire the accomplishments were not so great. In Germany, Erhard Vitger, as we have seen, had sought to invest Ford-Werke's cash in fixed assets before a currency reform took place. On June 1, 1948, he had cabled Roberge, "Have possibility purchase factory . . . about 40 km from Cologne." Graeme K. Howard, however, replied: "React unfavorably proposal . . . regard first priority acquisition of adjacent land parcels." On June 12 the military government permitted Ford of Germany to buy 80 acres of land, which the company paid for at once. Eight days later, like a shearing ax-stroke,

---

* The assets of FMC Ltd. *and its subsidiaries* on Dec. 31, 1954, were £62,433,687.

the currency reform smote the Cologne firm. Its cash balance fell at a ratio of 16½ to 1, from RM 22,600,000 to DM 1,650,000. The plans Vitger had made for a foundry and forge, the orders he had placed with suppliers, had to be canceled with the fantastic reduction of available cash. Whether he could have bought the factory he wanted in twenty days' time is doubtful; however, Howard erred in not giving him authority.

With the currency reform, restrictions on the sale of automobiles in the three West German zones were removed. At first business was difficult to transact because of the scarcity of cash; but soon normal trading was resumed, except that East Germany was now lost as a market. In the prewar period this territory had taken 43 per cent of the passenger cars and 40 per cent of the trucks sold in the nation, so the loss was significant.

In June 1948 elections for the Works Council were held in the Ford-Werke factory. "The political change in our plant," Vitger reported to his directors, "is more complete and more revolutionising [*sic*] than in any other of the big industries in our district." The Christian Democrats had triumphed; only one Communist (as compared with twelve in 1947) had been elected to the fourteen-man council. Communism as a problem now disappeared for the Ford-Werke management. In fact, the company's relations with labor were to be marked by a lack of friction and an absence of strikes.[14]

Vitger pushed ahead with the rebuilding of the Cologne plant. He reorganized the dealer network (finding new sales agents in the Western zone for those who had been lost by the cutting off of the East) and discovered suppliers in non-Communist territory to replace those under Russian control.* The Berlin blockade of 1948–1949 may have raised doubts in Dearborn about investing further in a Germany increasingly under the Russian shadow; it also affected Ford-Werke in that it made trade between the East and West less likely. At the same time, the Germans were working hard at rehabilitation, and by the end of 1949 marked progress had been made; the scarcities of raw materials that had previously been so disruptive no longer existed. Ford production could go forward freely.

This year saw the ratification of West Germany's constitution. Elections were held for the Bundestag, which chose Dr. Theodor Heuss

---

* Ford-Werke had 593 dealers in prewar Germany. Of these 178 had been located in what was now the Russian zone and 58 in territory now in Polish hands. In 1948 Ford had 353 dealers in West Germany and was trying to increase the number.

as first president of the Republic. Dr. Konrad Adenauer, former mayor of Cologne, took the position of federal chancellor, the most important office in the realm. Economic recovery showed every sign of marching forward with political independence.[15]

Vitger discovered that the demand for cars was ravenous; the need for increased production facilities fairly shrieked its urgency, for the Cologne plant had been small before the war and was now woefully inadequate. Yet Ford officials in Dearborn and Cologne did little to meet the situation. By the end of 1948 company production had somewhat expanded: Ford-Werke was turning out 3- and 5-ton trucks as well as the prewar Taunus car. But its chief rivals, Volkswagen, Opel, and Daimler-Benz, easily outproduced it.

Not until the end of 1950, when the curve of German recovery was clearly rising, did the German Ford company launch an expansion program. By this time the dealer organization had been restored to prewar size (591 dealers). The time was ripe to increase production and stock Ford showrooms across the land with cars. Dearborn executives had gained confidence in the German economy. Arthur Wieland told a product planning group in Dearborn in February 1950 that "England's experiments in government, and the constant political crises in France, make the German product source a valuable hedge and protection for our international distributing organization." Yet Wieland, remembering that Howard had parted with Dearborn because of over-enthusiasm, did not suggest that the parent company should invest funds in Germany. Rather he cautiously proposed that Ford-Werke should modernize out of its own earnings, with no American capital and not even with outside borrowing. As 1950 closed this project was being pushed.[16]

Because it was absorbed in its own problems, the American company could not and did not think it important enough to send experts in layout, production, or engineering to Cologne. Walter McKee, Dearborn's regional manager for Europe, recognized this fact. When he was in Paris in 1948 a General Motors representative was staying at his hotel. "The GM man," recalls McKee, "had with him a team of 16 Americans who were going to give Opel assistance. We didn't have one guy to send to Germany." The Ford company at Cologne badly needed the assistance that its competitor was receiving.

Ford-Werke really needed help much more than did Ford of England. The German operation was smaller than the British; it was scantly supplied with management personnel (there was no group comparable to Sir Patrick Hennessy, Sir Stanford Cooper, and Sir Rowland Smith, and the further array of Squire, Thacker, Denne, and Page). It had far less factory space, far fewer machines, and a far smaller engineering department. Vitger had been trained in finance and accounting, and his production experience was minimal. Since Dearborn could not spare the men to assist him, his company rapidly lost the lead it had held in 1945. Opel was aided by the GM group from the United States. Volkswagen, which got its postwar start filling orders for British occupation authorities, had a brilliantly engineered product and was under the highly able management of Heinz Nordhoff. Both catapulted ahead.

Decisions for Ford in Germany were made in Dearborn rather than in Cologne, and in 1950 the American Ford executives decided that Ford-Werke should not try to compete with Volkswagen in the lowest-priced market. They concluded the state-owned Volkswagen did not live by profit alone, but that its "taxes, depreciation, amortization, and even operating deficits, could be covered up in government budgets." This situation did not provide fair competition. It seemed that General Motors had decided not to challenge it; the Opel was priced above the Volkswagen. Ford executives decided to compete in the same price range as the Opel.[17] General Motors was their chief competitor at home; it was natural for the Americans to think of it as their rival abroad.

With this as its policy, Ford-Werke in 1950 began to build facilities out of its earnings. Behind its main factory on the Rhine, it erected a new assembly plant to accommodate the body departments and the final assembly lines for the first postwar Taunus passenger cars, which finally appeared in 1952.

The German company expanded—not rapidly, but steadily. After some years of absence, Robert H. Schmidt returned as technical director; his skill and energy were badly needed.* In 1951 the plant acquired new transmission-manufacturing facilities; in 1952 it built a new power plant, a new transformer station, a medical building, a garage, and an apprentice shop. By 1952 these additions had called for the local currency equivalent of $2.5 million, including machinery and tools. As 1953 opened both American and German Ford executives were actually growing optimistic about prospects in Cologne.

---

* Schmidt had a hard time getting back into the company after his removal from employment after the war. "I hammered on them until they asked me back," but when he returned, it was as technical director and not to his former post of manager.

In 1952, with a production of 40,334 vehicles, the company for the first time bettered its 1939 accomplishment. In 1952 it also introduced the new Taunus, designed in America by German and American engineers. The car showed a unitized body, independent front-wheel suspension, and a 4-cylinder engine. It competed in the German market as a medium-sized, medium-priced car.

No parts of the Taunus were interchangeable with those of the new British Ford products, the Consul and the Zephyr, or with the postwar French Vedette. These four European Fords were approximately the same size, all had been at least in part engineered in Dearborn, and all sold in the same price range. Yet all looked different from one another; two were 4-cylinder cars (the Consul and the Taunus), one a 6-cylinder (the Zephyr), and the fourth an 8-cylinder (the Vedette). None of these models had any interchangeability with any automobile built by the American company, for the Dearborn products were all notably larger.

In April 1951 Ford-Werke introduced a new diesel truck. This was a success, for it was inexpensive to operate, and gasoline in Germany was both scarce and high-priced, and their percentage of the commercial vehicle market rose. Ford-Germany never had built and did not now build tractors. Dagenham remained the sole Ford center for producing those vehicles in the Eastern Hemisphere.[18]

The 1950's saw Ford-Werke's output rise dramatically, yet its share of the national automotive output declined. In the passenger car field Volkswagen moved from 82,399 units in 1950 to 202,174 in 1954, in each instance taking about 38 per cent of the national production. Similarly, Opel increased its volume from 59,990 to 148,242, holding almost 28 per cent of the German total. Ford in 1950 built 24,443 units, and in 1954, 42,631; yet it actually dropped from more than 11 per cent of the full German output in 1950 to less than 8 per cent four years later. It did provide sharp competition for Daimler-Benz (1954: 48,816 cars) for third place in the German industry but was far outdistanced by Volkswagen and Opel; its per cent of production was cut down by such smaller carmakers as Auto-Union and Lloyd.*

With the rapid development of German industry, Dearborn officials perceived that a dynamic effort would have to be made to raise Cologne production: the gradual reinvestment of earnings was not enough. The growth of the company had to be rapid and commensurate with the im-

---

* Auto-Union's per cent of passenger car production rose from .7 per cent in 1950 to 6.6 per cent in 1954, Lloyd's from .7 per cent to 5.4 per cent for the same period.

mense possibilities of the market. In June 1954 Henry Ford II visited Germany and noted "the strides which your nation is making toward prosperity and stability." In that year authority came from Dearborn for a mammoth expansion program, startlingly larger than any previously contemplated.[19]

5

Just as the American company had not sent experts to Germany, it failed to send any to France.* It did not know French conditions or French Ford personnel. Accordingly, when the sixty-year old Dollfus suggested in 1948 that François Lehideux should succeed him as managing director, it approved his choice.

Lehideux was a nephew of Renault. His experience in the automobile business had been extensive, and during the German occupation he had exercised control over the entire French motor vehicle industry. Dollfus had worked well with him, and recommended him. But Lehideux was a disastrous choice. He employed a new staff—very much needed—asked Dearborn for additional funds, but scorned American advice, feeling that he himself could run the company alone.[20]

He was mistaken, for he was not qualified for sole command. Renault, Citroën, Simca shot ahead in production and sales, while Ford SAF, despite its advantages, made no progress. The Vedette, introduced in 1948, was an attractive car, but the first models showed numerous defects. Still worse, the average Frenchman could not afford it. Despite Dollfus' scorn for the low-priced car, the volume market and the profits both lay in the small-car field, and in that area Ford of France had no entry.

The American Ford executives were not greatly concerned about the troubles of the French company. The return on their investment in it had been minimal; and except for Henry Ford II all the important Dearborn personnel had absorbed the General Motors philosophy that "you can't do business in France." This attitude was based on the kaleidoscopic governmental changes, the unpredictability of the currency (the franc had steadily fallen for years), and the general inefficiency ("Try to make a telephone call in France!").

Had Lehideux proved unusually able, the feeling in Dearborn

---

* A few men like Frank Cort went over for brief periods, but their visits were not adequate.

would probably have been modified if not totally changed. The Americans were not unprepared for a happy surprise. In 1949 (the first year of his tenure), Ford SAF had issued 6 per cent bonds to the amount of 250 million francs. With this aid Dearborn had hoped that a firm basis for future operations could be established. But the company's percentage of passenger car sales declined (despite a slight rise in output). Moreover, a diesel engine for French trucks, approved in 1945, because of incredible delays did not appear until 1950. By this time other French manufacturers were well entrenched in the diesel market, and Ford SAF found its sales of commercial vehicles actually declining. The postwar accomplishment of Ford in France was diminishing daily.

In addition, the faltering organization became a battleground for intracompany factions and soon was losing money, although the period was one of general French prosperity. By October 1952 so badly had the situation deteriorated that the American Ford Executive Committee learned that unless they were willing to guarantee certain loans made to their French firm, it would go into bankruptcy or receivership. Wieland told the Committee what was obvious, that liquidation of Ford SAF would be most unfortunate. He proposed that Dearborn guarantee the loans and seek to put the company back on a profitable basis. It might then be possible "to negotiate a successful merger with another company, or if . . . it became necessary to liquidate, liquidation could be achieved with substantially better results than under present conditions." [21]

Apparently the seed of the merger idea was firmly planted at this time. The American company agreed to guarantee the loans, amounting to 1.5 billion francs ($.0029 per franc was the current exchange rate). A month later it finally sent an American to join the staff of Ford-France. Its choice was a talented young man named Francis C. ("Jack") Reith, one of the "Whiz Kids," who had joined the Ford Motor Company in 1946. Reith was to see what could be done to save the staggering French Ford company from disaster. He was also to keep the possibility of a merger in mind.

His arrival was awaited at Poissy with almost reverent suspense. The staff there "felt as though they knew God was coming." One former employee recalls that the office force expected sweeping changes in personnel (and were accordingly agitated), but that it also had implicit faith that a new company would arise which would win an imposing role in the country. The Frenchmen were sure that Reith would completely transform the sick Poissy organization.[22]

He did not disappoint these high expectations. On Lehideux's resignation in 1953 he took over the post of general manager, employed efficient assistants, reduced costs, improved the Vedette, and soon had the company operating at a profit. Product plans were made for a new line of Vedette cars to be introduced in 1954. Early in that year Gabriel Panier, who had returned to the company after Reith's arrival and assumed his former post of works manager, presented preliminary designs for "the Cardinal," a small car that would bring Ford into the low-priced field in France. The new Vedette models were exhibited in mid-1954, and their styling promised well for Ford SAF's future. Reith seemed to have resurrected the dying organization as easily as a conjuror produces a radiant young woman from a cabinet where all life had apparently been extinguished by a dozen strokes of a sword.[23]

Then a rumor began to circulate that Ford SAF and the French firm Simca would soon merge.* "At first people couldn't believe it," recalls one Poissy employee of that day. Then they gave it a natural interpretation: "Ford had bought Simca." But Reith, under instructions, had been working toward a different end, and on November 30, 1954, it was announced that Simca would buy Ford SAF—plant, staff, dealer organization. In return the American Ford company was to receive 15.2 per cent of Simca stock, an amount insufficient to exercise control. The son of the French Ford's earliest successful dealer later wrote that he had been sold *"comme le mouton."*

The transaction ended Ford manufacturing in France. Dearborn officials, glad to be free of the often unprofitable and always exasperating investment, sighed with relief. Reith's temporary success had provided an opportunity; they felt that it promised no permanent recovery.

Behind the merger were realistic considerations. The 8-cylinder Vedette was a Buick on the French market. High in price and expensive to operate, it could never achieve sales volume. This could only be realized through a small, 4-cylinder car. But the development of such a

---

* Simca (Société Industrielle de Mécanique et Carrosserie), which had developed from a Fiat dealership many years previously, had taken a modest place in the French industry in the 1930's. In the postwar period, under H. T. Pigozzi, it had gone forward steadily, had one of the best plants in the country, and had risen to fourth place among French motor car makers. (See PEP, *Report Motor Vehicles,* London, 1950, 120.)

vehicle would require from $50 to $100 million (in engineering, tooling, and facilities). What if this formidable program were undertaken? The small car would at once have to battle Renault and Citroën, already dominating the low-priced field; and who could say if such a new model, an American one, could compete with the established French products? Moreover, a small Ford car made in France might create confusion for Dearborn executives, who considered with dread coordinating the export of French, English, German, and American Ford products. Finally, the Dearborn engineering staff was overworked. An additional task of creation would be unwelcome; the new project might interfere with the successful execution of more important work. Thus to take up the project of a small French Ford model seemed both hazardous and burdensome.

To be sure, in theory Dearborn might have bought a French firm with a small car, but no such company existed that wanted to sell.

Two possibilities were thus rejected, and the third, represented by the Simca merger, seemed the only practical solution. Since there were severe restrictions on building in the Paris area, and since the Poissy plant was modern and efficient, it was a prize. Simca offered what the Americans considered a fair price. But the determining factor in the merger was undoubtedly the thoroughly disheartening experience that Dearborn had had in France since 1928. After Breech and Henry II had taken charge of Ford-US they had administered two financial injections to the ailing Ford SAF, and a third had preceded the arrival of Reith. None had brought recovery. Had the prospect for the Common Market been bright at this time, holding out a future of stability and prosperity for France, with all Europe as a market for her products, automobiles among them, the Americans might have been tempted to finance the small car. We do not know that such a prospect was even considered, but in any case in 1954 the hope for European economic unity was a feeble one. No Dearborn Ford executives frowned upon the sale to Simca, although in England Sir Patrick Hennessy opposed the move. Considering Perry's negative attitude toward Ford manufacturing in France, this may seem surprising, but Sir Patrick argued that Ford SAF "could have been successful with good management." His words carried great weight in Dearborn when he dwelt on Ford affairs in England, but the policy-makers in the home office felt no hesitation about ignoring them when they were on topics outside his jurisdiction.[24]

Was the decision a mistake? The Common Market's notable success a few years later made many observers wonder. As to the old Ford employees in France, they considered the merger a disaster. "We had to fight to build this plant," a loyal Ford-France executive told one of the authors at Poissy, "and now it goes away for nothing." And again, in viewing the marvelous Simca complex that soon arose at Poissy: "All this could have been Ford's." That the Ford company which had sold its first car in France in 1905 and had once stood among the three leaders in the country's automobile industry, which had built the Poissy plant and formed a network of more than 350 dealers, should end a long career in such a fashion, seems disheartening. Yet the yardstick for any business is return upon investment, and this had been pitifully small for more than twenty-five years.

Ford did not quit France entirely. It established a new company in Paris to market the products of its American, English, and German plants. With tariffs, taxes, and exchange controls the prices for these imports were at first very high; they have decreased since because of the Common Market's reduction in duties on German cars that enter France; but even so the French Ford company now does only a small business. It has had to start from scratch to build an entirely new dealer organization. The Asnières plant of Ford SAF had been sold in 1941 and is now used by Citroën. In 1958 Dearborn disposed of its 15.2 per cent share in Simca. Its rivals have engulfed what the company had, and today Ford in the French automobile industry is little more than a name and a memory.*

After the Ford-Simca merger, Dearborn executives turned their attention to Germany. The vigorous expansion plans there for 1954 were surpassed by those of the succeeding year. At that time new Taunus cars were introduced, and in 1955 Ford-Werke produced 64,872 passenger cars and 21,924 trucks. West German postwar recovery had become a miracle. The Germans now were well fed and clothed, had jobs and homes, and wanted automobiles. The market seemed bound to expand. For the unfolding future, Ford-Werke needed much greater capacity, and Ford in America was prepared to help extend its plant and equipment and to supply technical aid to supplement what the Germans themselves could offer. Here was a field for funds and talent that promised abundant reward.[25]

* Ford sold its holdings in Simca to Chrysler. In 1963 that corporation purchased enough additional shares so that it now holds a majority interest in the French firm.

6

"The fine showing of 1949 stands as a tribute to every man and woman in our organization," Rhys M. Sale told his Canadian shareholders in April when he first addressed them as president of the company. Douglas B. Greig resigned on December 31, 1949, and Sale took his position. "The company produced last year 112,130 passenger cars and trucks," he pointed out. "That was almost 11,000 more than in 1947, the previous record year." Sale announced that "our ability to sell is limited only by our ability to produce" and promised to increase Ford-Canada facilities. Several weeks later he told the company's management committee that his goal was to "outproduce and outmerchandise" all competitors and win 40 per cent of the Canadian market. But in 1950 Windsor lost first place in Dominion production and did not regain it. The first four years of the 1950's saw its percentage of total Canadian sales hover between 24 and 32 per cent.[26]

The basic cause of its loss of first place was the decline of business abroad. The company had always exported more than its rivals, and with the drop in all Canadian overseas sales, it was the chief sufferer. In the markets to which Windsor had sent its products: Australia, South Africa, India, New Zealand, and Malaya, more small European importations were now sold than the larger North American one. For example, in Australia Ford in 1949 marketed three times as many English-type cars as it did V-8's. Fearful of making an extra investment in tooling for a 4-cylinder car, and ignoring the Ford 6-cylinder type, Ford-Canada manufactured the V-8 exclusively (Ford, Mercury, Meteor, and Monarch). Not until 1956 did the company introduce a 6-cylinder model. It did not make a 4-cylinder car at any time in the 1930's, 1940's, or 1950's.

If competition from the European small car was of crucial importance in the decline of Windsor's sales abroad, the insistence of the Australian and Indian governments that Ford should manufacture locally was an additional factor. As domestic production in Australia increased, Dominion imports diminished. In India, Ford decided not to manufacture and, because of government rulings, could not import. Other import restrictions, including quotas and limitations on foreign exchange, especially the granting of dollars, also acted against the Canadians in overseas markets.[27] *

---

* European cars, in addition to being produced cheaper, had a great advantage in being able to accept sterling, for dollars were scarce and payments in them limited. This was

Because Ford-Canada's domestic sales had steadily increased from 1946 to 1950, the expansion of company facilities seemed to be warranted. Windsor had been the center of Dominion activity since 1904,* but Rhys Sale believed that new ventures should be located in the Toronto area, where the sales potential was highest and where the company could use the contacts the metropolitan character of that city offered. Windsor, with 120,049 inhabitants in 1951 was relatively speaking a village when compared with Toronto, second largest city in Canada, with a population of 674,754.**

Thus in 1951 the company bought a 420-acre tract in the Toronto suburban area of Oakville, some twenty miles west of the city, on which it built a large final assembly plant. The completed factory produced its first vehicle in May 1953. The building was not on a water front, for such a location lacked the value it had had in the days of Henry Ford I. It faced on the Queen Elizabeth Highway, one of the Dominion's best expressways.

One year later, for the third time in nine years, Ford of Canada officials were unable to get access to their offices in Windsor because of a UAW strike. As a result, the company staff moved to the city of Toronto. Here the company's central offices were located until 1961, when they were transferred to a new Central Office Building in Oakville.[28]

This shift from Windsor to the Toronto area by no means signified an end to operations across the river from Detroit. The vacated final assembly building in Windsor became an up-to-date engine plant. Additions and improvements were made in the power house and machine shop. These projects required an investment of $32.5 million. The foundry in Windsor was also enlarged and re-equipped.

Delmar S. Harder, vice president in charge of manufacturing at Dearborn, joined the Board of the Canadian Ford company in 1950 to help expand its facilities. Sale later recalled that Harder and R. S. Bridge, the Dominion company's manufacturing head, were "like two peas in a pod." They bent to the task of developing capacity at Windsor and Oakville. At about the same time appeared Theodore J. Emmert, executive vice president under Sale; the latter hoped that Emmert

particularly true of Commonwealth countries, which had pounds but were short in Canadian or American currency.

* Walkerville was incorporated with Windsor in 1934.

** Greater Toronto had a population of 1,117,470, almost ten times that of Windsor.

would succeed him as head of the company when he retired. In 1953 Ford-Canada's sales rose to a new high with 141,478 vehicles, representing 32.5 per cent of the market.

Following the Dearborn pattern, the Canadian executives tried to train men in leadership, to make organization charts, and to introduce more modern methods of financial planning. When the company's sales in 1954 dropped to 111,701 units on the domestic market, the dip was a reflection of the general financial situation and of an extended Ford strike (October 1954 to January 1955). The general course of the company had been one of expansion, even though Sale's goal of 40 per cent of Dominion automotive business had never been reached.[29]

7

During the early 1950's the youngest of Ford manufacturing ventures took its first sturdy steps. Ford-Canada's wholly-owned subsidiary in Australia responded to the insistence of that federal government on the development of local manufacturing by increasing the Australian-made content of its cars. By the end of July 1950 54 per cent of the V-8, 48 per cent of the Ford truck, and 59 per cent of the English-designed Prefect were built in Australia.

H. C. French, for many years the director of Ford affairs "down under," retired in 1950; he was replaced by Charles A. Smith, who had been trained in the Windsor organization and for a short time had managed Ford–South Africa. Smith in 1950 recommended that the company's Geelong plant extend its manufacturing to include such components as the transmission, engine, front and rear truck axles, and rear passenger car axles. This done, the Ford car and truck would be 93 per cent "made in Australia."

When he made this recommendation, the question arose as to what products the Australian company should manufacture. Smith, supported by Ford-Canada executives, ruled out a special Australian unit, because of the "excessive extra cost" of designing such a car. Instead, he and Ford-Canada decided that the Geelong plant should manufacture *both* the North American and the English Fords. The Canadians felt that both types were needed to meet competition: the increase in small car sales in Australia was important, but there was also a demand for the larger vehicles. After the decision had been made in Windsor, George Jackson (vice president in charge of Canada's overseas activities) and

C. A. Smith were sent to New York "to inform" Ford International.[30]

As a result, in 1951 Ford-Australia announced a £4.6 million ($13.3 million) expansion program, including the manufacture of an overhead valve V-8 engine. But before this activity began Ford sales in Australia started to decline, although small cars increased their proportion of the total marketed. Ford executives began to wonder if it were wise to manufacture a V-8 engine and delayed taking action. Late in 1955 nothing had been accomplished with the manufacturing project.

In 1954 Ford-Australia sold 16,318 North-American type Fords, 21,611 British Fords, and 4,915 tractors, making a total of 42,844 vehicles. Its share in the market was only 18 per cent, compared with 35 per cent for General Motors, which was making the popular Holden car. Ford also had stiff competition in Australia from the British Motor Corporation. In this year BMC set up an Australian subsidiary, which undertook to manufacture complete vehicles. It was to rank with GM and Ford in the Big Three of the motor industry in Australia.[31]

8

The development of Ford manufacturing facilities in Australia, Germany, England, and Canada was amply warranted. The population of these countries could afford cars; in per capita income they stood high among the nations of the world; all four had local steel industries that could supply their automobile makers; all four had secondary manufacturers (Australia was rapidly developing them), from whom the builders of motor vehicles could purchase components. Ford had begun building automobiles in Canada as early as 1908, when the tariff had made Dominion production economically desirable. The first Ford manufacturing started in England in 1912 when freight charges across the Atlantic made the cost of local production cheaper (not until 1915 with the McKenna tariff did customs duties become effective in England). Ford had no choice but to produce in Germany, at first because of the almost prohibitive tariff and after 1933 because intense German nationalism rejected imported goods and foreign exchange was not available for their purchase. Likewise, in Australia in the 1950's under a very different type of government Ford was being "forced" to manufacture. It is of interest that the only foreign country where government action did not, either by tariff or edict, spark Ford production was England.

By the mid-1950's governments all around the world were putting pressure upon foreign builders of cars to manufacture locally. India, for example, wanted its own automotive industry and called upon firms like Ford to help create it. Yet India did not seem to offer good conditions for a private manufacturing enterprise. Low per capita income meant a small market; secondary industries were undeveloped; and the government attitude toward foreign capital was subject to frequent change. When Basil Stevenson asked Indian officials why his company should undertake hazardous and unprofitable activities, he received the reply: "Ah, but this is your opportunity to help us build up an industry!" In May 1954 the Ford Indian company went into voluntary liquidation.*

Dearborn had a similar experience in Spain. The government wanted a national industry, but the Americans felt that the size of the market and various other factors made it impossible. In May 1954 Ford-US sold its partly-owned Spanish company to local interests. It became Motor Ibérica and without financial ties with Dearborn began a manufacturing program.**

In both India and Spain one important consideration deterring Ford from engaging in local production was the insistence of the respective governments that a controlling interest in any joint venture should rest in Indian or Spanish hands. This stipulation was repellent to the Ford management in Dearborn, which felt that even a majority interest in its foreign companies was unsatisfactory and wanted 100 per cent ownership in all of them. They might settle for a controlling interest, but looked coldly on the idea of a minority one, whether in India, Spain, or any other country. (The one-time willingness to hold say a 30 per cent interest in a Ford Japanese company now no longer existed.) In Latin America, as the decade advanced, Ford faced similar pressures to manufacture locally. But more on this later.[32]

9

In 1955 the world production of automobiles reached a total of 13.6 million units, a record for all time. Dearborn's factory sales amounted

* This decision was re-evaluated a number of times in the late 1950's and early 1960's but was not altered.

** In selling its interest in the Spanish company, Ford-US acquired 100 per cent of the stock in the Portuguese Ford operation (a sales company), formerly owned by the Spanish firm.

to 2.6 million vehicles, Ford-England built 306,900, Ford-Canada 165,710 units, Ford-Germany 80,380; the total Ford production was more than 3.2 million cars, trucks, and tractors. Various factors may have contributed to the high production: good credit facilities, the necessity to replace 1946–1948 cars, the prosperity and consequent demand of the public, and the prospect of settled peace.

Yet the peace of 1955 was an uneasy one. Although the Korean war had ended two years earlier, there were numerous troubled areas in widely separated parts of the globe. Southeast Asia was a cauldron of difficulties. In the Near East there were clashes along the Israeli border. The rift between the Communist East and the democratic West daily grew wider, with the United States, Great Britain, France, West Germany, Italy, Canada, and other nations linked tightly in the North Atlantic Treaty Organization, and the Eastern powers joined in a twenty-year treaty of mutual defense, signed in Moscow in May 1955. However, West and East were not at open war and were soon talking at "the summit." In Geneva in July 1955 the first of several famous summit meetings was held.

An agreement signed in Paris in October 1954 had given West Germany full sovereignty and permitted her to enter NATO. The country had fully recovered from the war, and was prepared to assume the responsibilities of a sovereign state.

Arthur Wieland was still in charge of the Ford International Division in New York in 1955. His had been a cautious role. He had concentrated chiefly on consolidating the policies developed by his dynamic predecessor Graeme Howard. Ford of England had performed brilliantly in the preceding five years, due in the main to vigorous guidance given it by Sir Patrick Hennessy and to the work of his able British staff. Wieland had moved slowly in reviving Ford-Germany. During this period Ford International had given aid and advice to Ford companies and branches in Europe and Latin America, and had kept closer watch on their activities than on the business of Ford-Canada and its subsidiaries.[33]

However, the important fact in the mid-1950's was that Henry Ford II was clearly taking a greater and greater interest in the companies overseas. Along with Breech he was on their boards of directors, he had traveled through Europe and become thoroughly aware of the Ford problems there. Moreover, he had begun to take a stand on issues involving America's position in world affairs.

He spoke out strongly in the better spirit of his grandfather:

I believe that this country should step forth boldly and lead the free world toward freer trade. . . . We need competition the world over to keep us on our toes and sharpen our wits. The keener the competition, the better it will be for us. . . . Instead of building up barriers to hinder the free flow of world trade, we should be seeking to tear existing barriers down. People cannot keep on buying from us unless we buy from them, and unless international trade can go on, our business will stagnate here at home.

As a first step Ford called for an end to the American tariff on automobiles. His words won public notice and acclaim.

In the fall of 1953 Henry Ford II became an alternate United States delegate to the United Nations. His experience in the "great world forum," as he was later to call the UN, gave him a new breadth. The work with peoples of all nationalities and points of view contributed to his understanding of international problems. Early in 1954 Ford declared: "What economic development really requires is lots more trade, lots more investment, and a minimum of 'giveaway' aid to oil the gears and do a few essential things which private funds can't do."

More and more Ford became aware that *his* company would do well to extend *its* trade and *its* investments abroad. His lieutenants paid much attention to the company's foreign activities: Breech watched, as did Gossett and R. M. Campbell (concerning legal matters), Alan Gornick (with respect to tax problems), Theodore Yntema,* P. F. A. Prance, and George Malone (on financial policy), Earle S. McPherson (on engineering), and Delmar S. Harder (on manufacturing).** And when foreign activities were discussed at Executive Committee meetings, John S. Bugas, the alert, former FBI man, in charge of Ford's industrial relations, would listen attentively but rarely comment.[34]

In 1955 there was no attempt to impose Dearborn's labor relations policies on overseas Ford companies. In fact, Ford-US made a point of not doing so. Ford-Canada, Ford-England, Ford-Germany all made

---

* Yntema, then vice president of finance, had written his Ph.D. dissertation at the University of Chicago on a mathematical reformulation of the general theory of international trade. His little, highly-specialized volume (118 pp.), was published in 1932 by the University of Chicago Press.

** In 1953–1954, J. R. Davis held the title Vice President—International and Tractor Group (as of Feb. 2, 1953; it was changed on July 15, 1953 to Vice President and Group Executive). Wieland reported to Davis, who in turn reported to Henry Ford II.

contracts with their unions, influenced by local conditions. Their success in dealing with unions varied from Ford-England's poor labor record to Ford-Germany's most adequate handling of its employer-employee relationships. Dearborn officials in the mid-1950's favored greater financial, engineering, sales, and administrative coordination between the overseas ventures and the home company, but independence for their overseas companies in labor policy. In this respect, their approach differed profoundly from that of Henry Ford I, who had preached a world-wide doctrine of high wages and no unions. Bugas as vice president in charge of Industrial Relations recognized that if foreign operations were to be competitive abroad, they must pay rates in accord with existing national practices. He let each local management cope with its own problems. Meanwhile he heard discussions of other aspects of foreign trade, broadening his knowledge and deepening his insight.

Arthur Wieland, vice president in charge of the Ford International Division, was not a member of the American company's Board of Directors, or of its Executive Committee.* The head of Dearborn's overseas domain had no voice in shaping the corporation's highest policies. In contrast Henry Ford II, Breech, Yntema, Harder, and Bugas participated in that activity. As the 1950's advanced, it was significant that all of them recognized increasingly the importance of Ford works abroad. Their interest was a promise for the future. As the foreign enterprises of the company shared with domestic trade the attention and creative thinking of the highest executives in Dearborn, its status in days to come was assured.

---

* The Executive Committee was composed of "inside directors," and handled the most important matters of management.

19

New Times, New Faces, New Policies

It is not hard to imagine a group of high Ford company executives on the twelfth floor of the new Central Office Building on Michigan Avenue in Dearborn discussing the firm's financial returns for 1958. At this meeting Henry Ford II, Ernest Breech, John Bugas, Theodore Yntema (finance), William T. Gossett (general counsel), Robert S. McNamara (car and truck divisions), and John Dykstra (manufacturing) might well have been present. Their downcast expressions would have told any observer the mood of the gathering.

The year had been one of sharp recession; sales had sunk; profits had declined; the company's new car, the Edsel, for which there had been the highest hopes, had failed. Were there any bright spots? Actually, one star did shine, conspicuous in a black sky: the company's performance in international sales. Foreign deliveries and profits had surged to a record level. Moreover, in practically every year since World War II, Ford's dollar sales abroad had mounted, averaging about 12 per cent increase per annum.*

Clearly, the international operations of the company were of crucial importance for sales and profits. In 1956 the offices of Ford International had moved from New York to Dearborn, bringing the staff to the hub of the Ford empire. Ford International vice president Arthur Wieland died in 1957 and was replaced by Tom Lilley, former assistant director of research at the Harvard Graduate School of Business Administration, who had been in Ford finance and international activities for almost a decade. Then in October 1959 John S. Bugas, veteran industrial relations vice president of the company, who had since 1957

---

* During the 1950's, only in 1956 did sales decline slightly, owing to the Suez crisis, which brought gasoline rationing and other restrictions (1955 foreign sales $1,275 million; 1956 foreign sales $1,259 million).

served as vice president for both industrial relations and overseas activities, relinquished his other responsibilities "to devote full time to his duties as Vice President-International Group." This was an event; for with Bugas' appointment, for the first time in the entire history of the company a member of the Board of Directors assumed the leadership of Ford work abroad as his exclusive assignment.

At the end of 1959, Bugas and Lilley, who reported to him, had under their charge a business with a sales volume of $1.6 billion, which was larger than RCA Victor, Reynolds Tobacco, or Republic Steel.

2

The tremendous expansion of Ford's foreign sales and profits was chiefly the result of the development of its affiliated European companies. Exports of American-built units: the Ford cars, Mercury, Thunderbird, Lincoln, trucks, and tractors had shown no rise in the postwar period.* Ford passenger cars had become increasingly expensive; they emphasized comfortable rides, attractive styling, low lines, and luxury items (radios, power steering, power brakes, automatic transmission). The cost of making them mounted annually, and by 1959 the American worker in the automobile industry averaged $2.70 per hour. The inflationary spiral raised the cost of parts from supplier concerns and also the cost of raw materials. The higher prices that followed, and the barriers to trade erected in foreign lands, sharply cut the overseas sales of American Ford products. Other makers of motor vehicles in the United States faced the same difficulty, and, for the first time since 1906, in 1957 the value of car *imports* into this country exceeded the value of exports! The next year, Volkswagens, Renaults, Fiats, Anglias, and other small European-made cars garnered an unprecedented 9.87 per cent of the American market.[1]

Across the Detroit River, for similar reasons, Ford-Canada's exports had declined. By 1962 this company was selling its cars and trucks primarily in Canada, in sharp contrast with its former activities (in the 1930's it had exported between 30 and 61 per cent of its output). The change threw into relief the new state of the Dominion automotive industry; whereas for about three decades Canada had been a net ex-

---

* The 1949 exports were 69,905 units; the 1959 were 63,248 units. There had been higher years in between with exports reaching a peak of 107,252 cars, trucks, and tractors in 1955.

porter of automobiles, in 1953 it became a net importer, and European cars comprised the bulk of the imports.[2]

Toward the end of the 1950's, in England, Germany, France, and Italy, for the first time in automotive history, manufacturers could make motor vehicles of world-wide appeal that sold at prices lower than those built in North America. European labor had always been cheaper than American labor, so this factor was not decisive: however it was now important, when combined with others. Most crucial, European automobile makers had learned and adopted American methods of production. None but a few (Rolls-Royce, for example) still scorned mass production: most achieved volume output and, moreover, for the first time in their histories could find large enough markets to achieve the economies of scale. Another factor in reducing the costs of the foreign vehicles was that the large producers—Volkswagen, British Motor Corporation, Ford Motor Company Ltd., Renault, Opel, and Fiat, for example —did not make annual model changes and could spread the expense of dies, jigs, and engineering over a long term, with a lower cost per unit as the result.

European automobile builders automated extensively, frequently surpassing American industry in employing advanced techniques. A European company, for instance, would erect a new stamping plant, neatly designed with the presses in sequence and manual labor at a minimum. Such a factory could produce stampings far cheaper than comparable plants in the United States built in the 1930's. Yet American businesses were "stuck" with some of these old facilities; they could improve the material handling operations, but unless they began from scratch by erecting new factories they could not meet European costs. The old plants had been expensive, and American companies hesitated to scrap them. The result was higher costs in the United States.*

Likewise, in response to labor shortages, German firms invested in labor-saving equipment which some executives thought uneconomical. But the extra investment served them well. On the other hand, Americans with a surplus of labor at times were discouraged from automating to the fullest extent.[3] **

---

* Ford-US had, for instance, in the 1950's built new stamping plants in Buffalo, Cleveland, and Chicago, but it also had the relatively inefficient Dearborn stamping plant, built in the 1930's. German industry, on the other hand, had no old stamping plants.

** The new depreciation provisions (1962) supported by President Kennedy and just approved may have good effects on changing this situation.

In Europe and elsewhere around the globe people demanded "basic transportation," products that might lack beauty and accessories but were cheap to operate, sturdy, and dependable. A large part of the world now called for what Henry Ford had offered in the Model T and what the American automobile industry (catering to the tastes of its own affluent society) had stopped providing. European industry filled the gap.[4]

When sales of American-type vehicles declined because of European competition, Ford believed that the only way to succeed abroad was to meet its rivals on their own ground. The American company did so by expanding its European installations.

At the middle of the decade, imports of European-built Ford units into the United States had dwindled to a mere 1,636 units. Dearborn's Foreign Products Branch,* which handled these, had a staff of only 11 men in March 1954 and planned to cut this number, since "reports indicate that the market for foreign cars is still very much on the decline." But with the recession late in 1957, a large segment of the American public suddenly wanted a small car and American manufacturers had little to offer. Now came the rapid rise in foreign imports, and Ford-England's and Ford-Germany's exports to the United States surged upward; with them, the Ford organization was able to fill the surprise American demand. Ford could cope with the emergency by offering "17 foreign economy cars . . . the widest range of foreign economy cars available in America." [5]

Selling the English and German Ford cars in quantity in this country was a new experience for American Ford dealers. Dearborn executives in February 1958 put the supervision of these sales under the Mercury-Edsel-Lincoln (M-E-L) Division of Ford-US. The company's International Division handled operations outside the country; but it was thought that a domestic division with its network of American dealers would be better equipped to market the imported cars.

The idea, while good in theory, was not a success in practice, for to distribute the foreign cars required special efforts that the M-E-L (and its successor, the Lincoln-Mercury) Division was not in a position to make. Moreover, as soon as the American company discovered the existence of a market for the small car in the United States, it prepared compact models—the Falcon and the Comet—which were far

---

* Set up in 1950, the Foreign Products Branch was part of Ford International Division.

more appealing to the American public than Ford products from overseas.

With the introduction of the Falcon (1959) and the Comet (1960), the imports of English and German Fords dropped sharply (42,512 English Fords were imported in 1959; only 23,602 in 1960). While the company continued to explore the possibilities of marketing its foreign-built cars in the United States, and of importing components built in its overseas plants for American vehicles, its experience up to the present time has been that from the standpoint of cost and of fulfilling the domestic demand, it is wiser to build for the home market in this country rather than in England or in Germany.*

But if the Ford compact cars (and similar offerings by GM and Chrysler) checked the rise of European imports, they did little to promote this nation's exports. The Falcon and its American rivals were still too expensive when sent abroad. Yet, foreign markets were growing, and if Ford was to share fully in them, it would have to expand its overseas facilities. "If we want to participate in Europe's rich automotive market, we must do so largely from the inside—through investment," declared Henry Ford II. This statement was true for other foreign markets as well.[6]

3

In 1957 Belgium, Holland, Luxembourg, Germany, France, and Italy signed and ratified the Treaty of Rome, best known as the Common Market Treaty. Their aim was to unite their resources and to have a market with a common outside tariff in which there would be eventually free movement of goods, services, and persons. The action of the "inner six" powers came as a surprise to observers. For years European integration had been debated, and the Coal and Steel Community of the early postwar years had presaged closer cooperation. Yet the collapse of the European Defense Community (1954) had seemed to many an omen of disaster for continental integration. Nonetheless,

---

* The Lincoln-Mercury Division announced in October 1960 that Ford-Germany's Taunus would no longer be imported and that while it would continue to sell the English Anglia, other models made by Ford Ltd. would be marketed only on a special order basis. The so-called "Cardinal"—a small car to be built partly in Germany and finished in the United States—was planned for 1962. But the all-German model (the Taunus 12M) was introduced in Germany in 1962 and not in the United States, for the demand did not seem to warrant it. (See note 6.)

the Common Market had come into being January 1, 1958, and exactly one year later tariff reductions were made and the first steps taken to unite the six nations into an economic bloc.

In response, England, Sweden, Denmark, Norway, Austria, Switzerland, and Portugal—the "outer seven"—had banded together with looser ties in a European Free Trade Area. Ford officials in Dearborn, Dagenham, and Cologne watched these developments, and were well aware of the tremendous economic growth of Europe in the postwar period.[7]

Ford-England, under Sir Patrick Hennessy's direction, had shared in European prosperity. It had increased its facilities to meet the urgent needs for transportation in England and overseas. Its profits had been excellent, and it could afford to expand. In the last half of the 1950's building after building jutted up: a new parts depot and engineering center eight miles from Dagenham at Aveley; added manufacturing facilities twenty miles from Dagenham at Basildon; and at the manufacturing center itself, a second foundry, "the most modern in Europe and possibly the most modern in the world," a new press shop, a new assembly building and many other lesser projects. Then Ford-England, forbidden by the British government to expand further in the Dagenham area but encouraged to build where surplus labor existed, in 1959 purchased a 329-acre site at Halewood, near Liverpool, where it began to construct a plant with a capacity of 200,000 cars annually. (This, the reader will recall, was the first planned capacity for Dagenham; and Dagenham in 1960 actually produced 575,417 units.) The new plant would have factories for everything from metal stamping to final assembly, although certain components would be procured from Dagenham and from suppliers.[8]

Ford-England's Engineering Department swelled from 270 men in 1950 to 1,830 men in 1960. The company continued to offer a range of products entirely different from those made by Ford-US, including the Popular, Anglia, Consul, Capri, Zephyr, and Zodiac, as well as a full selection of trucks and the Fordson tractor. In 1960 the sales of the Fordson were almost three times that of the American Ford tractor. Ford-England's Engineering Department described its aims as economy, durability, easy servicing, and top performance in all its products. Its personnel worked closely with the men in Dearborn and came to expect prompt and "off-the-shelf service from any area of their [Ford-US's] vast engineering resources." [9]

Under Hennessy's guidance,* Ford Ltd. had grown into a business that more than fulfilled the original promise of Dagenham. In production, Ford Ltd. ranked second only to the British Motor Corporation. By 1961 the former had assets of £204,080,802 ($571,426,245.60) and a sales volume of £258,950,000 ($725,060,000.00); in this year it had under way an expansion and modernization program estimated to cost about $196,000,000.[10] ** Ford-England was Ford-US's largest foreign subsidiary. Vauxhall, GM's English company, lagged far behind. Even GM's big German plant, Opel AG was outproduced by Ford-England.

Ford's German plant in Cologne was still comparatively small-sized in the mid-1950's. Its 1955 production totaled 80,380 units, while Volkswagen built 329,199 and Opel 185,340 vehicles. But annually, especially after 1958, Dearborn expanded Ford-Werke's capacity: old buildings were extended, a stamping plant was erected, a new final assembly plant, a new engine factory, power plant, forge, and other units. In 1945 Ford-Germany had had one solitary factory and an administration building; by the early 1960's it could count eighteen major and scores of minor buildings at the Cologne site. The Cologne area in 1962 comprised 476 acres (as compared to 123 acres at the start of 1955). Then in 1962 Ford-Werke completed the purchase of 441 acres in Genk, Belgium, on the Albert Canal, and announced that it would enlarge the company's capacity by 50 per cent at a cost of approximately $120,000,000.[11]

Ford activities in Germany in many ways took cognizance of European economic integration. That the German Ford company should buy land in Belgium and plan a factory there that would be dependent on supplies from Cologne was an indication of faith in the Common Market. To get from Cologne to Genk, the road crosses two national frontiers (those of Holland and Belgium) but this did not disturb Ford officials. One remarked after a return from Europe that "people say there may be hydrogen bombs; there may be Russian expansion;

---

* Hennessy was managing director from 1948 to 1956, and on Sir Rowland Smith's retirement in 1956, he became chairman of the Board. Charles Thacker followed Hennessy as managing director (1956–1962), but his activities were somewhat obscured by the far more dynamic Hennessy. J. A. Barke became managing director in 1962.

** To one of the authors, who asked if Ford Ltd. would be satisfied with 35 per cent of the British market, a high Dagenham official replied, "Emphatically NO. The company is going all-out to surpass BMC." That, he added, would be increasingly difficult as new plants could be built by any rival, and new machine tools evolved by Ford could not be kept from general knowledge. However, Ford would seek supremacy through administrative capacity, engineering, and up-to-date methods of production.

there may be war; but *no one* says the Common Market may fail." It was this attitude that encouraged Ford to expand in Germany and Belgium. At Cologne, where labor was short, Ford brought in Italian workmen—acting in accord with the basic idea of the European Economic Community that there should be movement of goods, services, *and labor* from one country to the next according to the needs.[12]

Ford-Germany continued to sell a range of products styled and engineered in a manner different from either Ford-US or Ford-England offerings. The first postwar Taunus (the 12 and the 12M) was marketed for the decade after 1952, when it was followed by another small car. Slightly more expensive were the Taunus 15M (1955–1958) and the Taunus 17M (1957–1960). An entirely new Taunus 17M, a handsome four-seater with advanced styling, appeared in October 1960. Like its predecessors, it had been designed and engineered in Dearborn by American and German engineers. This model proved an immediate triumph both in Europe and in Latin America. In 1962 a new small car, a substitute for the Taunus 12M, was introduced. Ford-Germany also made trucks, but unlike Ford-England and Ford-US it produced no tractors. Its sales for 1961 rose to 262,034 cars and trucks.

By 1960 Ford-England and Ford-Germany were the two largest foreign manufacturing operations of Ford-US. From 1950 to 1960, the first (which began as a grand plant) had quadrupled its production, while the second (which began modestly) had multiplied its output eightfold. Ford-Werke at the start of the 1960's remained in fourth place in the German industry (following Volkswagen, Opel, and Mercedes-Benz), but its production mounted and its rise in sales from 1950 to 1960 was second only to Volkswagen.* Ford-Canada, before 1932 the largest of Ford's foreign ventures, had increased its output steadily from the war's end to 1955; then, with its exports dwindling and its domestic market shared with foreign imports, its sales had declined. In 1958 Ford-Werke surpassed the Ford Motor Company of Canada in production. Two years later the German company was building double the number of vehicles made by Ford-Canada. However, Ford-England still held the position, as it had for three decades, of Ford's largest foreign company. It was the only American-owned automotive firm to rank in the top five (with Volkswagen, British Motor Corporation, Renault, and Fiat) of the European industry.[13]

---

* In this period Volkswagen sales increased 8.7 times compared to Ford-Werke's 8 times.

4

The prospects for sales of automobiles and trucks in Latin America, John S. Bugas declared in 1961, were "generally less developed [than in Europe] but potentially promising."

In the late 1950's, Ford's Executive Committee began to pay close attention to the developments south of the border. Henry Ford II visited Mexico, Brazil, and Argentina in 1959, dined with Presidents Adolfo Lopez Mateos, Juscelino Kubischek, and Arturo Frondizi, and became well versed in problems of inflation, the attitudes toward foreign investment, exchange regulations, the balance of payments situation, and the desire to industrialize in each of the three countries.

Not long after Ford's trip, Dearborn started to erect its first assembly plant in Venezuela and formed its first subsidiary in Colombia. But these were small steps compared with the dynamic efforts in other nations.

> Whether we like it or not [Henry Ford II declared in the spring of 1961] Africa, Asia, Latin America are going all-out into the industrial age. . . . It does no good to tell them this is all very unsound, that they ought not to try to do so much so fast, that they should relax and buy from us a lot cheaper than they can make it. They just won't go along; they are deeply committed to fast industrialization.
>
> If we want to share in those markets, rich and vast as they will some day surely be . . . we are going to have to go in with our capital and tools and know-how and help them get the things they want.[14]

Such a statement especially applied to Ford's position in Brazil and Argentina.

At first, as the 1950's began, Ford officials had not wanted to manufacture in Brazil. Importation and assembly involve no large foreign investment; the poverty of much of the Brazilian population meant restricted automobile sales, no economies of scale, and hence expensive vehicles.* Dearborn executives repeatedly pointed out that Brazilian

---

* One way to get economies of scale would be to use a manufacturing plant in Brazil to export as well as to supply domestic markets. This however for the present was impossible: other countries could buy from Ford-US, Ford-Germany, or Ford-England cheaper than from Ford-Brazil; the channels of trade (transportation, tariffs, exchange procedures, etc.) were not so arranged that Ford-Brazil could supply its neighboring coun-

customers would get imported units cheaper than those locally made (assuming that the government did not impose high tariffs or adjust exchange rates to the disadvantage of the importer).

But just as Dr. Heinrich Albert and Maurice Dollfus had earlier recognized and insisted that Ford must manufacture in Germany and France, so in Brazil assistant manager Humberto Monteiro submitted a presentation to the Brazilian government in March 1951, indicating that Ford understood the "wishes and desires of public opinion in Brazil for local production of motor vehicles." "The Government," he declared, "can count on Ford support." To Dearborn Monteiro reported what he had done and added that Brazilian bank officials were stating that "those companies which refuse to assist in the industrialization of Brazil and insist only on importing to Brazil will not be in business long." [15]

Aviso No. 288 prohibited the importation into Brazil of replacement parts for cars. It was issued on August 19, 1952 and was the first of a series of government moves designed to build a national industry. In the fall of that year Ford began to make extensive purchases from Brazilian suppliers.

The Brazilian Central Bank imposed a complicated system of foreign exchange restrictions which raised the cost of imported vehicles out of all proportion. Slowly in Brazil suppliers began to develop small industries to fill the needs of the automobile assemblers. In Rio de Janeiro in January 1953 the automobile parts manufacturers held their first national show, and the Brazilian press acclaimed its success: "It was the biggest industrial show presented to date in Brazil by one specialized industry sector," reported *Correio da Noite* (Rio de Janeiro). Brazilian President Getulio Vargas attended the show, strongly backing every effort to develop this industry. Although still reluctant, Dearborn officials became aware that Ford "must go along with Government objectives of a gradually developing local vehicle manufacturing program." [16]

Meanwhile, some businesses started to make motor vehicles in that country: Fábrica Nacional de Motores, SA (known as FNM) with a bus (1951) and a truck (1952); then Willys-Overland, which initiated jeep manufacture in February 1954. Government decrees designed to

tries easily, and nationalistic sentiment elsewhere in Latin America meant that other republics would want to manufacture for themselves rather than import from their neighbors.

force all companies to manufacture in Brazil were now drafted. President Vargas' suicide in August of that year put a temporary halt to progress in this direction, but when in 1956 Juscelino Kubischek was elected president, it was clear he would follow the road opened by his predecessor. "Fifty Years Progress in Five" became his motto.

President Kubischek made an outstanding contribution to the development of a national automobile industry. In June 1956 GEIA (Grupo Executivo da Industria Automobilistica, the government automobile industry group*) was created by presidential decree. Then in July another decree specified that all trucks sold in Brazil by July 1, 1960 must by weight be 90 per cent nationally made. Other decrees followed on automobiles (February 1957) and tractors (December 1959).

The net worth of Ford in Brazil as of December 31, 1955, was $14.1 million, an investment that the company was unwilling to abandon. Accordingly, Ford decided to submit a program under the government decree on trucks. On January 30, 1957 the company filed such a program, which was accepted by GEIA on February 8 of that year. Ford-Brazil then proceeded with an impressive expansion program: its new assembly plant (constructed in 1950–1952 and inaugurated in 1953) was supplemented by an engine plant, a foundry, a stamping plant, and a product engineering test facility, all built in 1957–1958.

Its operation was far more integrated than Ford-Werke had been when it had started to manufacture, or than Ford-France, or even for that matter Ford-US in its earliest years. But this integration was essential, for there were no outside foundries to supply Ford-Brazil. Although many local suppliers were starting businesses, Ford still had to make a large number of parts for itself. The creation of an automobile industry is far more expensive and difficult in a country which is just beginning to industrialize than in one whose manufacturing is already well developed.

But it was done, and by mid-1960 Ford trucks were more than 90 per cent of Brazilian content. In fact by June 1960, twelve manufacturers had accepted the challenge of participation in the Brazilian government's car and truck programs. Ford (with three truck models), General Motors (with two trucks), and Mercedes-Benz (with two trucks and a bus) were the three largest builders of commercial vehicles.

---

* GEIA was composed of representatives of the Ministry of Commerce and Public Works, the Ministry of War, the Customs Authority, and the Bank of Brazil.

GEIA also approved passenger car programs presented by Willys, Volkswagen, Vemag, Simca, and Máquinas Agricolas Romi. Willys, which had the headstart, became the largest Brazilian automotive producer (1957–1960), making a jeep, a rural Willys station wagon, an Aero-Willys car, and also the Renault Dauphine. Volkswagen, however, with rapidly mounting sales provided fierce competition and in 1961 overtook and outsold Willys.[17]

Ford and General Motors were not in top positions in the Brazilian industry, for at first they built only trucks. They had not submitted programs under the government passenger car decree, feeling that they could not comply with its requirements without investing sums that they were not prepared to risk. Already they had committed themselves to high investments under the truck program. Later, when Ford and General Motors wanted to make a car, GEIA was reluctant to approve their plans; thus Volkswagen and Willys shot ahead in the passenger car field. Ford and GM dealers had no cars to sell since new tariff and exchange regulations made the cost of imported automobiles prohibitive.

Ford remained in first place in Brazilian truck production from 1957 to 1962, its output reaching 19,037 in 1960. By the end of 1960, under the 1959 government decree, Ford-Brazil began manufacturing tractors. It was the first to enter this field, and while others followed, here too it remained first in volume.

In 1963 it is still too early to assess the net results for the Ford organization of its vast Brazilian expenditure in manufacturing. The company made good profits in Brazil in 1957–1958; 1959 was not a good year; 1960 was ordinary; in 1961 with political disruption and inflation, the company lost money.

There is, however, no question that from the Brazilian standpoint an industrial miracle has been achieved. By exchange regulations, tariffs, and decrees, the Brazilian government has created an automobile industry in less than five years.

Of the twelve participating companies in mid-1960, only the two smallest (Toyota, which made jeeps, and Máquinas Agricolas Romi, SA, which made the Romi-Isetta car) had no foreign capital. The others were financed in the main from abroad, with foreign investment primarily from the United States, Scania Vabis (Swiss) and Volkswagen (German) being the notable exceptions. On June 30, 1960 the foreign investment of Willys was $26.8 million, of Ford $21 million, of General

Motors $20 million, of Mercedes-Benz $18 million, and of Volkswagen DM 51.611 million (at the then rate of exchange about $12.4 million).[18]

When Kubischek left office at the start of 1961, the Brazilian economy was virtually bankrupt, the currency had gone wild, and inflation was uncontrollable. But if he left financial chaos, he also left a firmly founded automobile industry. Ford and the other manufacturers had gone far to train Brazilians in modern industrial methods and teach suppliers how to make machine tools and components. The achievement had been initiated by government decrees, but its direction had been entirely shaped by private enterprise. It was a creation of which the country could be proud—the first automobile industry in Latin America.

5

In all the Southern continent, the Brazilian economy developed the most rapidly in the late 1950's. Argentina, once the leader in South America, had been left behind, owing to the disastrous economic mismanagement of the Perón era (1946–1955).

Like Vargas, Perón had favored a national automobile industry. To some extent he had succeeded in creating one, for Fiat built facilities to manufacture the tractor; Daimler Benz, trucks, and Kaiser-Willys, a passenger car and jeep. Although Dearborn officials contemplated manufacturing tractors in the Argentine as early as 1950, they held back, wary of investing while Perón held sway.[19] The meddling of the Perónists in industry, corruption, and disregard of contractual obligations, made such executives as Henry Ford II and Ernest R. Breech justifiably apprehensive.

Yet the national ambition to manufacture was there. With Perón's overthrow (1955) the trend toward industrialization did not slacken. Under the provisional government a decree covered tractor manufacturing, and Deere and Company submitted a proposal.

With the inauguration of Arturo Frondizi in May 1958 (as with Kubischek in Brazil) the automobile industry finally began to take definite form. Ford shifted its plans from tractor to truck manufacture, and in 1959 formed a new company in the Argentine to undertake such activity. Having made good profits in Brazil in 1957–1958, Dearborn executives entered into the Argentine program with little hesitancy. At Pacheco, on the outskirts of Buenos Aires, Ford-Argentina purchased

244.5 acres of land for an engine plant and other facilities. Early in 1960 under the government decree it began to manufacture trucks *; in 1962 it started to make the Falcon car as well. It made two engines, the V-8 for the truck and the 6-cylinder for the car.

In Argentina as in Brazil, the Ford operations were wholly financed by Ford-US with no local capital participating. By 1961 in the Argentine about twenty companies manufactured cars, trucks, and tractors, and the country produced 134,000 vehicles all told. In that year Ford truck deliveries were 13,027 compared with GM's 13,414.[20]

As the 1960's began and steel industries developed in Latin America, the trend toward automobile manufacture seemed destined to accelerate. Other countries considered it. The Mexican government studied the Argentine and Brazilian programs in deciding on its own. The Mexicans contemplated starting an automobile manufacturing industry, but meanwhile, to safeguard its balance of payments, the government put strict quotas on imports, banned the introduction of high-priced cars, and enforced tight restrictions on assembly operations. It even went into the automobile business itself with a firm called Diesel Nacional, which it strove with the greatest difficulty to make a success. Early in 1963 it assigned production quotas to selected foreign manufacturers—Ford, GM, Chrysler, and Volkswagen among them—who had laid out manufacturing programs in accord with the wishes of the Mexican authorities.

By 1962 Ford was committed to expansion in Latin America. There was full recognition of the risks involved: intense nationalist sentiment (from both right and left), continuance of government intervention in business, political instability in many countries, and inflationary difficulties; but there was also an awareness that the company had large investments in Latin America and that these markets had enormous promise.

When Fidel Castro came to power in January 1959, Ford no longer had a sales branch in Cuba, for it had been closed in 1949 because of diminishing business. A Ford credit company was operating: Créditos y Descuentos Mercantiles, S.A. (known as Credesco). In October 1960, in his expropriation of American businesses, Castro nationalized Credesco. Ford's investment was not substantial.[21] If the action underscored the perils of overseas operations, it had no effect on the company's general policy of Latin American expansion. New American

---

* The decrees were similar to those in Brazil, except that the percentage of local content to be obtained was based on value rather than weight.

government guarantees against expropriation also made the path smoother.

In the early 1960's, Ford went into markets to the south with none of the bravura that had earlier marked the entry of Henry Ford. The latter's comment on Mexico in 1916 that "not a cent will be taken out" would find no echo in Dearborn in 1962.[22]

Yet the effects of the programs of Henry Ford and his grandson have much in common. Both were in fact helping underdeveloped countries at the same time as they aided the domestic company. The capital, machinery, personnel, along with the technical and managerial know-how that Ford-US offered the Latin American republics was comparable to that which English concerns had given the United States in the early years of our industrial development and had immensely aided our growth.

6

"The Australian Motor Vehicle Industry," read an Australian government report in 1959, "during the past 40 years, and particularly after the Second World War, has developed from small beginnings into a major industrial activity. The demand for motor vehicles has grown in Australia as a natural result of the high standard of living, and the necessity to transport persons and goods for considerable distances."

Since 1948 General Motors–Holden, Ford's traditional rival in the Commonwealth, had manufactured 6-cylinder cars in Australia. For a dozen years, car buyers there wondered, "What is Ford going to do about Holden?"

Ford-Australia had considered building the V-8 car, but declining sales of 8-cylinder models checked this plan. Next the company thought of making the 6-cylinder English Ford Zephyr. While Ford officials debated, the Australian-built Holden (priced lower than any Ford product on the market) captured a lion's share of the sales. In 1959 Holden sold a little over 46 per cent of all passenger cars in Australia, but Ford could muster only 13 per cent with its Fairlane, Zephyr, Consul, Prefect, and Anglia. Never had Ford outsold GM-Holden in Australia, yet the 1959 performance was the worst in a succession of defeats.

Meanwhile, preparations went forward in Dearborn on the compact 6-cylinder Falcon. This car, Ford executives realized, would be ideal for the Australian market, and soon the product-problem was solved. In 1957 Ford invested about $28 million in a new Australian assembly plant, which opened in August 1959 and began to assemble the imported Ford Fairlane plus the English Ford products. John Bugas in February 1960 visited Australia to announce that this new plant would soon be used to assemble Australian-made Falcons. Accordingly in 1960 Ford committed itself to spend another $27 million to adapt its manufacturing plant at Geelong, Victoria, for Falcon production. Dearborn engineers, called in by Ford-Australia's parent company (Ford-Canada) aided the Australians in preparing for manufacture. In September 1960 the Falcon was introduced and well received. The *Australian Financial Review* called it "the best value on a £ for horsepower basis both new and on the resale market." The company's sales at once began to rise. The Geelong factory was the third foreign plant (with Canada and Argentina) to manufacture the Falcon.[23]

7

As Ford-US executives took this active interest in the company's overseas enterprises, they drew these into closer coordination with the home office: through sharing skills in management and production, through studies of marketing potentials, through purchasing on an international basis, and through increasing investment and percentage of ownership of the foreign operations.

Ford-US had progressed a long way in the postwar years—from third place in the United States industry, operating in the red, with a weak management corps, a wretchedly small engineering cadre, and only three products (Ford, Mercury, and Lincoln), to a clear second place, good profits, and a management that evoked praise and enthusiasm. Its products in the early 1960's included the Falcon, Comet, Fairlane, Meteor, Galaxie, Monterey, Thunderbird, and Lincoln-Continental, and its research and engineering staff numbered over 10,000.[24]

"There was a change in climate in Dearborn between 1957 and 1960," one Ford international executive has stated; "projects that had met resistance now were approved with little difficulty." The company could afford to aid its overseas affiliates with money and the best of its talent. Its investments abroad increased, and to Brazil it sent 76 Americans to start up that manufacturing program; more than 100 went to Buenos Aires to train Argentines to make cars and trucks, while a team of 24 men from Dearborn had flown to Australia to start the Falcon program there. As we have seen, Ford-US had in the past often sent personnel to aid its foreign enterprises, yet never had the totals approached those sent abroad in the later 1950's and early 1960's.

On the highest level, Dearborn installed American general managers overseas. Gone entirely were the days of the 1930's when the firm believed managers should be native to the country where the plant was located. By 1962 Ford had American general managers in every Latin American Ford company and branch. In Europe, of the twelve Ford sales, assembly, and manufacturing companies there, eight had United States citizens as managers. Ford-Germany since February 1958 had John Andrews, an American, trained in Dearborn, at its head. Of all the big Ford plants, Ford-England remained alone with its two chief executives British-born. Even Ford-Canada, which for more than five decades had been under Canadian managers, had a man from Ford-US at the helm.* With Americans directing these overseas operations the total had a greater unity than had existed when the managers lacked a common nationality. Presumably too, the Americans would have more loyalty to Dearborn than men of differing training and background who rose to managerial posts in their native lands.[25]

Not only in management but in other respects the Ford business became a well-organized international enterprise. Throughout most of the postwar period Ford-Germany, Ford-England, and Ford-US had sold in markets around the world. In the early 1960's, Henry Ford II issued an executive communication which reads:

> In order to further the growth of our world-wide operations, each purchasing activity of the Company or an affiliated company should consider the selection of sources of supply not only in its own company but also sources located in other countries.

Ford had become multi-national in purchasing as well as in sales.[26]

In order to ensure the effectiveness of an American world-wide enterprise, Dearborn executives became convinced that it was wise for the home office to own, when possible, all the stock in Ford companies outside this country. These officials recognized that total ownership

---

* Karl Scott, elected president of FMC-Canada at the Board of Directors meeting in November 1960, was Canadian-born but had moved to the United States as a child. He had been trained in America and was an American citizen.

gave major advantages. Most important was flexibility of operations. If there were no minority shareholders to consider, financial policies could be formed unilaterally; earnings could be applied for business expansion when the home company thought it advantageous; product planning and marketing could be based on international rather than national considerations.* Likewise, if as seemed to be the case, the overseas operations were to continue highly profitable, why not let Dearborn enjoy the full profits from its investments? Another factor was probably American antitrust legislation. The law on antitrust and business abroad is still unclear, but certain decisions in the postwar period indicated that a company might be liable for antitrust action when it made arrangements with an affiliated firm, whereas comparable action affecting a wholly-owned subsidiary would not be vulnerable.[27]

In addition, as one Ford executive put it:

> General Motors has always had 100 per cent ownership of its subsidiary operations as a central policy. This is very sensible. Ford however had had local capital involved. This is nothing but a pipe dream. Outside holdings are unwise. They do not involve the public, as envisaged. They are only an investment to the local man.[28]

As if to prove this, Ford-US conducted a survey in Germany when its holdings in Ford-Werke were 52 per cent and General Motors' holdings in Opel were 100 per cent. The findings showed that most Germans considered Ford-Werke an American enterprise, while they thought of Opel as a German firm. Stock ownership appeared to have no connection with the reputation of a company.[29]

Throughout the 1950's (with one exception **) Ford-US increased its shareholdings in Ford companies outside the United States. By 1962 its ownership in the Canadian Ford company was up to 75 per cent, in the German Ford company 99 per cent, and in the English Ford company 100 per cent. In 1961 it had completed its purchase of Ford-England for the dramatic sum of $368 million. It owned wholly the enterprises in Argentina and Brazil. Of the manufacturing ventures, only Ford-Australia remained an anachronism in the well-organized picture; it continued in its historical position as a fully-owned subsidiary of Ford-Canada.[30]

* One Ford executive noted that minority shareholders have been "used as an umbrella to resist change. Local personnel will point to the minority shareholders when they want to argue against innovation."—Interv. J. Wilner Sundelson, Dearborn, May 11, 1960.

** The results of Ford-England's Briggs purchase. (See Chap. 18.)

By favoring total control, Ford-US went contrary to the trend of many American businesses. In the early 1960's more and more companies considered propositions that involved joint-ventures with foreign firms. Proponents of this course argued:

> Because of the dangers involved in local production arising from nationalism, the insecurity of being foreign, the peril of risking capital in areas where popular and political movements may wipe out investments, joint ventures offer many advantages. They permit a company to become part of the economy of the host country, enjoying the same privileges and protection that national companies obtain from government, labor, and local public.[31]

This statement, published in 1962, could have been written by Ford officials in the 1930's but not in the 1950's or early 1960's. By 1963 Ford management had come to feel that advantages of full ownership far outweighed any merits of joint ventures. The point of view had gone a full circle since the late 1920's.

As the company acted in the eleven years prior to the end of 1961, despite its substantial foreign investments, it contributed approximately $2 billion to the United States balance of payments. The returns on international business far surpassed the outlay.[32]

8

Ford's large investments abroad (they equaled $668.3 million between 1955 and 1962) were part of a general move of American businesses overseas. In 1956 and 1957 private capital outflow from this country into foreign branches and subsidiaries hovered around the $2 billion mark annually; between 1958 and 1960 it averaged $1.4 billion per year.[33] *

Few American businesses which went into foreign nations in these years with their capital, equipment, and know-how, had more experience than the Ford Motor Company. By 1963 Ford had engaged in international business activities for fully six decades. In retrospect, what can be learned from these sixty years?

Clearly, foreign activities entail more risks and difficulties than domestic undertakings. Unfamiliarity is the biggest obstacle: diverse currencies, languages, customs, laws, and government regulations con-

---

* Direct investment, not portfolio investment.

tribute to the perplexities of doing business abroad. Flexibility in adapting to strange conditions became everywhere a prerequisite for success; when rigid conformity with home office patterns was imposed the operation suffered.

Ford's foreign enterprises early forked into two distinct channels. On the one hand, there was the evolution from its first export agent in New York to a vast empire of sales, assembly, and manufacturing enterprises around the world; on the other hand, there was the entirely separate development of Ford-Canada, from a wagon factory to a miniature Ford-US, spawning foreign subsidiaries of its own throughout much of the British Empire.

To follow the first of these forks is to see Lockwood on a commission basis in charge of overseas business; the appointment of dealers in many overseas markets; then in the areas where sufficient volume justified a sales branch, a salaried Ford employee going overseas to start one. Soon the sales branches developed into assembly operations, and when the tax situation required it the branches were transformed into companies. In England Ford manufacturing started on a small basis before World War I. In the 1920's, the number of assembly plants increased, purchasing parts locally when possible. In this decade the English manufacturing, and the other assembly and sales companies and branches were linked to the home office by American managers, and Detroit gave orders; all activities were 100 per cent owned and controlled by American Ford interests.

Then came the policy change. In Europe in the late 1920's and 1930's the important men overseas were Perry, Albert, and Dollfus, all nationals of the countries in which Ford developed full-scale manufacturing enterprises. Dagenham assumed the direction and control of Ford assembly and sales operations on the European continent. Englishmen, Frenchmen, Germans, Belgians, Dutchmen, and Spaniards bought Ford stock in local companies. Conformity to American Ford practices was no longer required. Ford companies introduced distinctive European cars to fill special needs and to compete with national makes. In Europe, Japan, and Latin America (but not in the United States), Ford offered wholesale and retail financing facilities. Local market differences and their requirements were carefully considered in the development of overseas business in this decade.

In the mid-1930's, Dearborn participated in its only joint-venture with a foreign automobile manufacturer. The union with Mathis was

425

successful only in giving Ford SAF temporary French guise; otherwise it was a fiasco, leading to financial difficulties, management quarrels, and litigation.* Ford-US in this decade made its first sizeable investments abroad, in Germany, England, and France in connection with the manufacturing programs there. Other expansion of overseas facilities was in the main financed through the reinvestment of earnings. In Dearborn, Sorensen, Edsel Ford, and occasionally Henry Ford himself gave a personal direction to activities abroad. Overseas managers were free to consult Ford-US specialists in branch operations, engineering, purchasing, manufacturing, as the needs arose. When Edsel Ford died in 1943, and Sorensen left the company in 1944, the company's foreign operations were cut adrift. For several years they received no direction from Dearborn.

The post-World War II management of Ford-US under Henry Ford II inherited the fruits of previous company labors: the vast dealer organization abroad, the plant facilities, some gifted personnel. Yet it became apparent that the administration and control of the international ventures desperately needed reorganization. Moreover, now Ford-Canada for the first time came into the stream of a consolidated Ford-US policy.

The Canadian development represented the second fork in Dearborn's foreign operations. Unlike the first fork, the initiative for Ford-Canada's formation came from the Dominion and not from the United States. All the working capital for the Windsor operation (which was planned as a manufacturing enterprise from the start) was obtained by cash subscriptions, mainly from Canadians.

With the aid of top level advice from Dearborn, Ford-Canada charted its own course. Its managers in the pre-World War II years, first McGregor and then Campbell, had personal friendships with the Fords, and called on Ford-US for engineering, purchasing, manufacturing, product, and sales guidance as the need arose. But otherwise, these managers had full independence. Here was a truly successful joint venture between Canadians and Americans. Ford-Canada grew up as a miniature Ford-US; it set up its own foreign assembly plants in the British Empire. These continued to be wholly owned by Windsor

---

* The merger with Simca in 1954 was a bird of a different feather. Ford got stock in Simca (15.2 per cent), which was not sufficient to exercise control. Ford did not participate in management. The Simca stock was essentially a portfolio investment rather than a joint venture.

(even while the public could buy stock in the European Ford companies). When World War II ended, the 1904 agreement made between the American company and Ford-Canada was in all essentials unaltered.

In the post-World War II years, the Dearborn management has tried for the first time in company history (1) to develop an international division to provide services to and skillful coordination of all foreign operations including Ford-Canada and its subsidiaries; (2) to direct the overseas ventures from the United States, having basic policies stem from the American Ford company; and (3) to install American general managers in Ford companies and branches abroad.

In introducing American world-wide policies and programs, Dearborn found it difficult to fit Ford-Canada and its subsidiaries into an integrated international organization, so strong had been the historical separation of Ford-US and Ford-Canada and so distinct had been their paths.*

Especially since 1959 Dearborn has recognized that it must make large investments abroad to develop overseas projects. Ford officials realized that reinvestments of profits earned (the older method of financing Ford's foreign enterprises) were inadequate for their giant plans. Markets were opening up everywhere, and Ford had to be equipped to fill the tremendous demand for motor cars that seemed inevitable. Moreover foreign markets now grew with amazing rapidity, while the American market seemed pegged to population growth.

Over the sixty years the international activities of both Ford-US and Ford-Canada have followed the principal line of development from selling to assembly to manufacturing in foreign lands. The Ford credit companies overseas were not high-profit enterprises but more a means of increasing automobile sales. Only once did Ford go abroad to produce raw materials—for rubber—and its plantation in Brazil was no success; never did Ford rubber go into the tires of Ford cars. Likewise, Ford only in one instance sent its technicians to aid a foreign government-owned operation. Technicians were sent to Russia to set up a plant there; Ford was to profit through the sale of 72,000 units and the sale of machinery. That the Russians reneged on their part of the contract made this atypical venture a disappointing one.

Ford's greatest achievements abroad were in England and in

---

* Ford-US now furnishes technical and administrative advice and services, on a fee basis, to Ford-Canada's subsidiaries.

Canada, where its companies generally held as prominent a rank as did Dearborn in the American market. In these two countries, Ford found the happy combination of energetic local management, respectful of Dearborn authority and advice, yet with creative suggestions for adaptation to English and Canadian conditions.* In the last few years, the rapid growth of the German Ford company has held out a rich promise for the future.

Actually, Ford's entry into overseas markets has netted a three-fold advantage. It has brought profits to Dearborn, to the United States, and to the host nations abroad. If Henry Ford invested little in other countries, he reinvested a large part of the profits earned overseas in new foreign facilities and in expanding existing ones. By this means Ford-US built the strong international organization that it has today. Since 1956, Ford-US stock has been on the market, and there have been thousands of shareholders in the American company. These have been enriched by the returns from Ford's investments in foreign lands.

With the net inflow (in dividends and cash remittances) far exceeding the outlay, the United States balance of payments has been favorably affected.** But the countries that have been the recipients of Ford investments have also gained important advantages.

As to the nations in which the company has operated, Ford executives have taught men of many nationalities the principles of making automobiles. The founders of today's mass production European automobile industry—William Morris, Herbert Austin, Percival Perry, André Citroën, and Louis Renault, all learned lessons directly from Henry Ford. The government planners in Brazil, Argentina, Mexico, and elsewhere have been able to adapt the experiences of present-day Ford officials.

The first commercially successful automobile firm in Canada was the Ford Motor Company of Canada. In Latin America, Asia, and Africa as well as in Europe and Canada Ford introduced the first as-

---

* In Latin America and in Japan in the period before World War II, Ford's rank in automotive sales was considerably better than in the United States, but then Ford activities in these countries were assembly operations rather than manufacturing. Although highly profitable, they were of comparatively small volume.

** For years, before Ford started extensive manufacturing abroad, its subsidiaries bought American exports, thus adding a favorable item to the balance of payments record. As it has set up manufacturing plants, large shipments of machinery from the United States have been sent to foreign lands, here again favoring the balance of payments situation.

sembly plants. The company gave and continues to give people on these continents training in how to assemble and service vehicles. It also has taught management skills to men of many diverse nationalities. In three decades Ford has given work to literally hundreds of thousands of men in foreign countries. Likewise thousands of independent dealers and their employees from Buenos Aires to Beirut have earned a livelihood by selling Fords, and some of the leaders have become the wealthiest men in their communities.

The company has also purchased from suppliers abroad. From the 1920's, Ford policy has always been to buy parts in the country where it had a plant—if it could get the right price, good quality, reliable delivery, and sufficient quantity. By the late 1950's and early 1960's, Ford extended this approach and began to think of the world as its source of supply for all its overseas and domestic plants and not merely for the nation in which a factory was located. Wherever the company has operated, it has taught suppliers how to manufacture specific parts.

Furthermore, all Ford plants over the years have paid taxes in the various lands where they have operated, taxes which have contributed to the welfare of the nations and communities in which they did business.

But more important than any of these benefits has been that of providing men and women in many countries, the United States included, with their first opportunity to buy a cheap, reliable, sturdy car.

This then has been the balance sheet of accomplishments. They stand out against a background of challenge. International business has always been vulnerable to a many-angled attack: Britishers and Brazilians have joined in protesting the entry and success of American firms in their countries, at the same time as they have been eager to learn from these very corporations. The inflammatory words of "economic imperialism" and "exploitation" have been tossed about by propagandists. In the last three decades in practically every country in the world there have been flare-ups of anti-Americanism.

American business abroad has also posed financial problems for governments and corporations. Recently officials of the United States have watched with anxiety the outflow of American dollars, fearing the effect on the balance of payments. Foreign governments in turn have been alarmed lest the influx of money should cease. Again, American businesses want to see profits coming to their home offices from the

429

countries in which they operate; these countries in turn grudgingly eye the dividends going to America, and would like to keep more of them in their own lands.

International business is fraught with difficulties not evident in domestic activity: risks of revolution, nationalization, major fluctuations in foreign government policies and in the government itself, and war (where the country in which business is done is an enemy and not an ally). Nonetheless, despite the risks, unfamiliarity, and complications, Ford and other American firms have found that in overseas markets the rewards far exceed the risks.

Transportation is the lifeblood of international growth. Raw materials must go from mines to factory; finished products from factories to customers; consumers from home to job or from home to market. In the nineteenth century the railroads made the basic contribution to the development of the industrial countries of the world; the twentieth has seen a great shift to the motor vehicle. Always, the world is in process of change. The space age has brought the jet airliner, the rocket, and the space ship; and the adaptation of atomic power to industry is an immediate possibility. To be sure, the automobile and the gasoline-driven truck have not realized their potentials in many parts of the world. They have served the farmer, the shipper, the consumer (who uses his car for business, vacation, and shopping in an age of supermarkets), and through their services have remade the modern social fabric. Their role is being extended. But the question of motor power may not be fully answered: the turbine or some form of nuclear force may compete with or displace the gasoline engine, and transportation by air may further reduce the role of the paved street and the speedway. At present, however, the motor car is the indispensable unit for all lands that are building economic strength.

9

We have seen, in the early 1960's, to fill its growing needs abroad, Ford promoted three new full manufacturing ventures overseas: in Brazil, Argentina, and Australia, and was developing a fourth in Mexico. These supplemented the company's previous foreign manufacturing centers in Canada, England, and Germany. In thirteen other countries around the world the American and Canadian companies had assembly plants.* The Ford factory in Rhodesia (completed in 1961) was the company's third African assembly plant, adding its capacity to that of Ford-Egypt and Ford-South Africa.

In a large number of areas (from Norway to France to Italy to Uruguay) Ford-US had sales companies. Moreover, in Jersey City, New Jersey, it had an Overseas Distributors and Export Supply Operation, which arranged exports of cars to its foreign subsidiaries and supervised export sales to Ford dealers in ninety-seven countries.** In some of these lands, where the sales volume was small (as in Indonesia, Pakistan, the Philippines, Thailand, and Turkey), the company authorized *dealer* assembly plants.

Throughout the postwar period, because of the cold war, Ford business was confined to half the globe. Ford aid to the Russians ended with the tire plant shipped there in World War II. The nationalization of the Hungarian and Roumanian Ford plants and the termination of Ford activities in the eastern half of Germany when that country was divided into zones of occupation, plus the restrictions of the United States government on trade with the Communist bloc, shut the door to Ford's Eastern European trade. Likewise, with the closing of the Shanghai Ford branch in 1948, sales on the Chinese mainland (Hong Kong of course excepted) had stopped. While American trade with Communist China is illegal, trade with the latter is carried on from England and Canada. But Ford companies in those countries do not as a matter of policy export cars and trucks to Communist China.***

If the division of East and West limited markets, the demand for automotive products in the free world grew to offset by far the loss.

Ford officials looked ahead with confidence in the early 1960's. Of primary importance in creating optimism was the Common Market. Ford officials from the start were alert to Common Market developments and planned to take advantage of them. Ford's expansion in Germany and in England was predicated on the assumption that the economic spurt forward in Europe had just begun.[34]

Ford executives attended conferences at Punta del Este, Uruguay; they considered the effects of President John F. Kennedy's Alliance for

---

* Ireland, Mexico, Chile, Venezuela, New Zealand, Malaya, Southern Rhodesia, Union of South Africa, Egypt, Belgium, Denmark, Holland, and Portugal.

** The Overseas Distributors' unit was moved from Jersey City to Wixom, Michigan, and the export facility was transferred to Newark in 1963.

*** Actually, they can not under the U.S. Trading With the Enemy Act.

Progress on their projects. They participated in government studies. The still embryonic projects for a Latin American Free Trade area, the Central American Customs Union, as well as the trade groupings discussed by various African countries were reviewed in Ford planning. It was the trend toward economic growth and freer trade among non-Communist countries in the early 1960's that gave the company confidence in its enterprises abroad.[35]

The Fords—the grandfather, the son, and the grandson—all thought in international terms. Each contributed to making the Ford worldwide organization a big business. Henry Ford II, no less than his grandfather, held that without the fullest and freest international trade, without competition on world as well as domestic markets, the automobile industry (and industry in general) would stagnate. His plea for "a strong and growing flow of trade, of capital, of technology throughout the free world" would have been endorsed fully by the first Henry Ford.[36]

If the Ford plans to spend over a billion dollars overseas in the early 1960's would have awed the grandfather and his son, to the grandson they represent necessary expenditures to gain the vast rewards of participating in the expanding automotive markets of the world. The future only can test the validity of this viewpoint, but at the present time the prospect for vindication is bright.

Appendices

APPENDIX 1. Heads of Ford's Foreign Activities, 1903–1962.

A. Export heads and foreign department managers.

1903–1910 R. M. Lockwood (on a commission basis)
1910–1911 H. B. Harper
1911–1912 A. C. Vanderpoel
1913   Ellis Hampton
1913–1918 Eber Sherman
1919   R. S. Neely
1920–1946 R. I. Roberge

B. International Division heads.

1946–1948 R. I. Roberge
1948–1950 Graeme K. Howard
1950–1957 Arthur Wieland
1957–1959 Tom Lilley
1959–   John Bugas and
          Tom Lilley (scope of the operations greatly enlarged)

SOURCES: The Nov. 1903 contract of Lockwood's is in Acc. 140, Bx. 5, as are his Nov. 1906 and Dec. 1907 contracts. The Dec. 1907 contract was to last until Dec. 31, 1908. No further contract seems to exist. *Ford Times* III, June 1, 1910, 372, notes the appointment of H. B. Harper to take charge of the foreign department, succeeding R. M. Lockwood. *Ibid.*, V, Feb. 1911, 179, announces A. C. Vanderpoel will follow H. B. Harper. (Payroll records, Ford Archives, show Harper in charge of the foreign office June 1, 1910 to Feb. 1, 1911.) When in Feb. 1913 Roberge joined the company, Ellis Hampton was head of the foreign department (see Roberge, *Reminiscences*). Roberge notes the short duration of Hampton's being head of the department. In the account books in the Archives for the year ending Sept. 30, 1913, Eber Sherman is listed among the branch managers; from the size of his bonus, it is obvious that he had not been in that position long. Liebold to Sorensen, July 30, 1918, #34086 Ferg-M., indicates that Eber Sherman will be handling Latin American distribution of the Fordson tractor from Aug. 1, 1918. In the contract between Ford Motor Company and Charles McEnearney, in files of Charles McEnearney & Co., Trinidad, R. S. Neely signs as Ford-US foreign department manager (Mar. 18, 1919). FMC Personnel Records have Roberge appointed manager of the foreign department, July 1, 1920. Graeme Howard became vice president in charge of international activities, Apr. 15, 1948: announcement in files of Organization Planning Office, Dearborn. On May 19, 1950, Wieland became principal executive in Ford International, and on Sept. 12, 1951 was elevated to the vice presidency. The appointments of Lilley and Bugas are recorded in the Ford *Annual Reports*.

APPENDIX 2. Ford's Automotive Foreign Operations.

Country	Year of Formation of Branch or Incorporation of First Company		Year Ford Assembly Started	Year Ford Manufacture Started	Year of Termination of Activities
Algeria	1941 (Co)		—	—	1954
Argentina	1913 (Br);	1959 (Co)	1916	1961	—
Australia	1909 (Br)		—	—	1918
	1925 (Co)		1925	1925	—
Austria	1945 (Co)		—	—	—

434

APPENDIX 2. (Continued)

Country	Year of Formation of Branch or Incorporation of First Company	Year Ford Assembly Started	Year Ford Manufacture Started	Year of Termination of Activities
Belgium	1922 (Co)	1922	—	—
Belgian Congo	1958 (Co)	—	—	—
Bermuda	1960 (Co)	—	—	—
Brazil	1919 (Br)	1920	1959	—
Canada	1904 (Co)	1905	1908	—
Canal Zone	1927 (Br)	—	—	1949
Chile	1924 (Br)	1924	—	—
China	1928 (Br)	—	—	1948
Columbia	1961 (Co)	—	—	—
Cuba	1922 (Br)	—	—	1949
Denmark	1919 (Co)	1919	—	—
Egypt	1926 (Br); 1932 (Co)	1950	—	—
England	1909 (Br); 1911 (Co)	1911	1912—Manchester 1931—Dagenham	—
Finland	1926 (Co)	1946	—	—
France	1908 (Br); 1916 (Co)	1913—Bordeaux 1926—Asnières 1939—Poissy	1934—Strasbourg 1939—Poissy	—
	1954 (Co)	—	—	1954
Germany	1925 (Co)	1926—Berlin 1931—Cologne	1931—Cologne	—
Greece	1932 (Co)	—	—	1946
Holland	1924 (Co)	1932	—	—
Hungary	1938 (Co)	1941	—	1945
India	1926 (Co)	1926	—	1954
Ireland	1917 (Co)	1919 (tractors) 1923 (cars)	1919 (tractors) 1921 (car parts)	—
Italy	1922 (Co)	1922	—	—
Jamaica	1960 (Co)	—	—	—
Japan	1925 (Co)	1925	—	1940
Malaya	1926 (Co)	1926	—	—
Mexico	1925 (Co)	1925	—	—
New Zealand	1936 (Co)	1936	—	—
Norway	1960 (Co)	—	—	—
Peru	1926 (Br)	—	—	1931
Philippines	1946 (Br)	—	—	1949
Portugal	1932 (Co)	1963	—	—
Puerto Rico	1926 (Br)	—	—	1927
Rhodesia	1960 (Co)	1961	—	—
Roumania	1931 (Co)	1936	—	1946
South Africa	1923 (Co)	1924	—	—
Spain	1919 (Co)	1920	—	1954
Sweden	1924 (Co)	1948	—	—
Switzerland	1958 (Co)	—	—	—
Turkey	1928 (Br)	1929	—	1944
Uruguay	1920 (Br); 1955 (Co)	1920	—	—
Venezuela	1926 (Br)	—	—	1927
	1959 (Co)	1962	—	—

NOTE: In some cases dates relate to assembly of partially-knockdown units in rented plants or to very limited manufacturing. We have not included, however, the Belgian manufacturing program during World War II (which was terminated directly thereafter) nor the small Brazilian manufacture of truck cabs, etc., which was pre-World War II (this did not indicate any commitment to a full manufacturing program).

The date of termination is the date when the company or branch ceased Ford operations. This summary does not include the Brazilian rubber plantation, the credit company operations abroad, nor the holding companies (Liechtenstein, Luxembourg, and Guernsey).

APPENDIX 3. Ford U.S. Production of Cars and Trucks Compared with Ford Production for Foreign Markets, 1903–1962.

Date	U.S. Plants	U.S. Exports	England	France	Germany	Canada
1903	1,708	*	n.m.	n.m.	n.m.	n.p.
1904	1,695	*	n.m.	n.m.	n.m.	n.p.
1905	1,599	n.a.	n.m.	n.m.	n.m.	117
1906	8,729	n.a.	n.m.	n.m.	n.m.	99
1907	14,887	350	n.m.	n.m.	n.m.	327
1908	10,202	n.a.	n.m.	n.m.	n.m.	466
1909	17,771	n.a.	n.m.	n.m.	n.m.	1,280
1910	32,054	n.a.	n.m.	n.m.	n.m.	2,805
1911	69,762	n.a.	n.m.	n.m.	n.m.	6,388
1912	170,068	n.a.	3,187	n.m.	n.m.	11,584
1913	195,954	n.a.	7,310	n.m.	n.m.	15,657
1914	299,797	n.a.	8,352	n.m.	n.m.	18,771
1915	489,202	n.a.	12,291	n.m.	n.m.	32,646
1916	718,397	n.a.	16,204	n.m.	n.m.	50,043
1917	645,309	n.a.	12,767	n.m.	n.m.	46,914
1918	479,166	n.a.	9,293	n.m.	n.m.	39,112
1919	867,826	n.a.	12,175	n.m.	n.m.	55,616
1920	444,581	n.a.	46,362	n.m.	n.m.	15,626
1921	928,750	n.a.	31,955	n.m.	n.m.	42,349
1922	1,237,721	n.a.	27,303	n.m.	n.m.	50,266
1923	1,923,360	n.a.	30,596	n.m.	n.m.	79,115
1924	1,797,331	142,641	27,497	n.m.	n.m.	71,726
1925	1,783,625	164,342	22,271	n.m.	n.m.	79,244
1926	1,457,978	128,625	21,859	n.m.	n.m.	100,611
1927	359,068	38,199	12,558	n.m.	n.m.	37,677
1928	719,885	96,050	6,685	n.m.	n.m.	74,798
1929	1,717,617	182,561	25,756	n.m.	n.m.	87,800
1930	1,270,548	175,339	27,861	n.m.	n.m.	70,253
1931	630,151	108,456	24,152	n.m.	916	30,850
1932	341,813	62,052	25,571	n.m.	1,728	28,221
1933	389,549	49,613	52,561	n.m.	3,956	26,219
1934	689,991	85,898	53,613	n.m.	10,008	47,708
1935	1,120,606	100,938	66,605	9,692	12,768	80,172
1936	972,312	88,564	94,180	9,438	20,843	60,282
1937	1,056,994	135,695	94,165	13,849	31,720	72,796
1938	526,828	103,236	76,705	7,555	36,582	67,919
1939	755,596	87,678	65,387	5,779	35,364	61,015
1940	876,960	54,792	38,008	4,693	16,500	96,457
1941	914,238	70,558	31,362	3,799	14,330	111,384
1942	217,651	44,050	36,987	2,993	14,672	104,740
1943	142,357	0	36,954	1,591	17,202	75,266
1944	153,248	5,269	31,078	n.a.	12,915	62,805
1945	156,064	14,168	28,590	6,000	2,443	46,346
1946	619,343	79,038	65,796	8,422	4,550	80,273
1947	949,535	107,128	79,957	10,470	2,600	101,058

APPENDIX 3. (Continued)

Date	U.S. Plants	U.S. Exports	England	France	Germany	Canada
1948	1,013,995	81,543	102,531	14,947	5,731	97,015
1949	1,323,828	53,700	118,418	18,232	17,357	112,130
1950	1,897,242	62,193	142,849	20,033	29,816	129,026
1951	1,485,992	85,072	134,932	23,059	35,160	118,856
1952	1,238,294	76,810	132,170	20,178	40,397	132,190
1953	1,856,508	73,781	204,049	23,000	44,041	155,626
1954	1,991,179	89,511	252,099	n.a.	58,470	122,581
1955	2,613,195	101,396	306,900	n. m.	80,380	165,710
1956	1,963,857	85,167	279,062	n. m.	82,707	149,482
1957	2,224,205	85,853	293,019	n. m.	90,047	132,692
1958	1,466,802	66,355	361,967	n. m.	125,848	107,484
1959	2,091,106	56,113	406,766	n. m.	154,913	118,047
1960	2,224,859	65,769	474,719	n. m.	209,323	113,213
1961	2,026,319	77,742	433,625	n. m.	262,034	113,931
1962	2,303,850	69,537	445,470	n. m.	305,379	144,857

	Australia	Brazil
1960	14,361	19,037
1961	30,900	14,044
1962	52,775	21,622

*—Under 100 units.
n.a.—Not available.

n.m.—No manufacture.
n.p.—No production.

SOURCES:

1. *US Plant Production*
   1903–1948: World Production Report, Ford Archives.
   1948–1955: FMC-US, *Annual Report 1955* (factory sales).
   1956–1961: FMC-US, *Prospectus,* April 1962, 5 (factory sales).

2. *US Exports*
   1907: Ledger Bk., Acc. 235, Bx. 11.
   1924–1928: Ford International (knockdown and built up exports).
   1929–1948: Ford Assembly Operation, Distribution Control Department (knockdown and built-up exports); note the figures for Ford-US exports for 1946–1948 as given in FMC-US, *Annual Report 1955,* are 74,487, 78,559, 75,181. While quite different from those in the table, the figures indicate the same upward and downward slopes on the curve.
   1949–1958: FMC-US, *Annual Report 1958* (exports cars and trucks).
   1959–1962: Accounting Department, FMC-US.

The World Production Report gives export figures for years when we indicate that they are not available, but these figures are so far from what we know to have been delivered to the dealers that they are excluded. Foreign delivery data given in Appendix 5, Chart 1 should correspond quite closely to export performance. With the exception of those partially manufactured in England after 1912, all the units noted on Chart I were exported from the United States.

The figures included in the category of exports, 1924–1928, may overlap slightly with the English and Canadian production figures, but the duplication is insignificant.

APPENDIX 3. (Continued)

3. *England*
>   1912–1931: FMC-England (factory sales).
>   1932–1955: FMC-England.
>   1956–1961: FMC-US, *Prospectus*, April 1962, 9 (factory sales).

4. *France*
>   1935–1937: Gabriel Panier's production files, Paris.
>   1937–1939: Accounting Department, FMC-US.
>   1940–1944: Folder "Ford SAF Data," FI.
>   1946–1953: Accounting Department, FMC-US; 1953: approximate.
>   1954: Incomplete year for company sold to Simca.

5. *Australia*
>   1960–1961: FMC-US, *Prospectus*, April 1962, 9; cars only in 1960 (factory sales).

6. *Brazil*
>   1960–1961: FMC-US, *Prospectus*, April 1962, 9; only trucks built (factory sales).

7. *Germany*
>   1931–1939: Sales Analysis Department, FMC-US (production).
>   1940–1946: Report of Office of Lord Perry, FI and Ford-Werke, *Business Reports*.
>   1947–1955: Sales Analysis Department, FMC-US (production).
>   1955–1961: FMC-US, *Prospectus*, April 1962, 9 (factory sales).

8. *Canada*
>   1905–1948: FMC-Canada.
>   1949–1955: FMC-US, *Annual Report 1955*.
>   1956–1961: FMC-US, *Prospectus*, April 1962, 9 (factory sales).

Unless otherwise indicated, figures are for production. When production figures were not available the authors used factory sales. (The difference between factory sales and production is negligible for most units produced are sold from the factory.) All 1962 figures, except as noted for exports, are factory sales from FMC-US, *Annual Report 1962*.

APPENDIX 4. Tractor Production—Fordson, Ford-Ferguson System, and Ford——Dearborn–Detroit, Cork, and Dagenham, 1917–1962.*

>   1907 Tractor with Copper Jacket Built at Piquette
>   1915 50 Tractors Built with Model 'T' Worm-Drive
>   1916 First Experimental Fordson Built
>   1917 First Tractor sent to England

Year	U.S.	Accum: Total	Cork	Accum: Total	Dagenham	Accum: Total	Grand Total	Accum: Grand Total ***
1917	254	254					254	254
1918	34,167	34,421					34,167	34,421
1919	56,987	91,408	303	303			57,290	91,711
1920	67,329	158,737	3,626	3,929			70,955	162,666
1921	35,338	194,075	1,433	5,372			36,781	199,447
1922	66,752	260,827	2,233	7,605			68,985	268,432
1923	101,898	362,725					101,898	370,330

APPENDIX 4. (Continued)

Year	U.S.	Accum: Total	Cork	Accum: Total	Dagenham	Accum: Total	Grand Total	Accum: Grand Total ***
1924	83,010	445,735					83,010	453,340
1925	104,168	549,903					104,168	557,508
1926	88,101	638,004					88,101	645,609
1927	93,972	731,976					93,972	739,581
1928	8,001	739,977					8,001	747,582
1929			9,686	17,291			9,686	757,268
1930			15,196	32,487			15,196	772,464
1931			3,501	35,988			3,501	775,965
1932			3,088	39,076			3,088	779,053
1933					2,778	2,778	2,778	781,831
1934					3,582	6,360	3,582	785,413
1935					9,141	15,501	9,141	794,554
1936					12,675	28,176	12,675	807,229
1937					18,698	46,875	18,698	825,927
1938					10,647	57,521	10,647	836,574
1939	10,233	750,210			15,712	73,233	25,945	862,519
1940	35,742	785,952			20,276	93,509	56,018	918,537
1941	42,910	828,862			22,210	115,719	65,120	983,657
1942	16,487	845,349			27,650	143,369	44,137	1,027,794
1943	21,163	866,512			26,300	169,669	47,463	1,075,257
1944	43,444	909,956			23,845	193,514	67,289	1,142,546
1945	28,729	938,685			17,770	211,284	46,499	1,189,045
1946	74,004	1,012,689			25,290	236,574	99,294	1,288,339
1947	85,589	1,098,278			34,915	271,489	120,504	1,408,843
1948	103,462	1,201,740			50,561	322,050	154,023	1,562,866
1949	104,267	1,306,007			33,375	355,425	137,642	1,700,508
1950	97,956	1,403,963			42,275	397,700	140,231	1,840,739
1951	98,442	1,502,405			35,868	433,568	134,310	1,975,049
1952	82,041	1,584,446			30,444	464,012	112,485	2,087,538
1953	72,543	1,656,989			29,575	493,587	102,118	2,189,652
1954	51,490	1,708,479			45,689	539,276	97,179	2,286,831
1955	66,656	1,775,135			48,872	588,148	115,528	2,402,359
1956	39,056	1,814,191			40,991	629,139	80,047	2,482,406
1957	39,685	1,853,876			46,114	675,253	85,799	2,568,205
1958	46,315	1,900,191			58,518	733,771	104,833	2,673,038
1959	47,633	1,947,824			67,238	801,009	114,871	2,787,909
1960	26,806 **	1,964,630			71,455 **	872,464	98,261	2,886,170
1961	24,319 **	1,988,949			70,710 **	953,174	95,029	2,981,199
1962	27,489 **	2,017,438			71,596 **	1,024,770	99,085	3,060,284

* All figures to 1939 are for Fordson: in 1939 began the manufacture of Ford tractor–Ferguson system in the United States. Ford-US ceased in 1946 to manufacture for Ferguson, and produced the Ford tractor. FMC-Eng. continued to manufacture improved Fordsons.
** Factory sales. *** To the final 1962 figure should be added 3,100 tractors made in Brazil.

APPENDIX 5, Chart I.   U.S. Ford Deliveries to Europe, Latin America, and Asia, 1903–1921 (cars and trucks after 1918) *

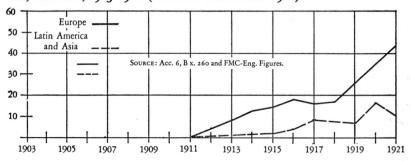

APPENDIX 5, Chart II.   Ford Deliveries to Foreign Dealers *

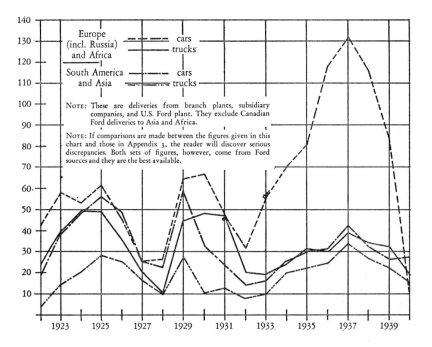

* All figures are in 1000s of units.

APPENDIX 5, Chart III.   U.S.-Type v. European-Type Ford Passenger
Cars Delivered to Foreign Dealers, 1932–1940 *

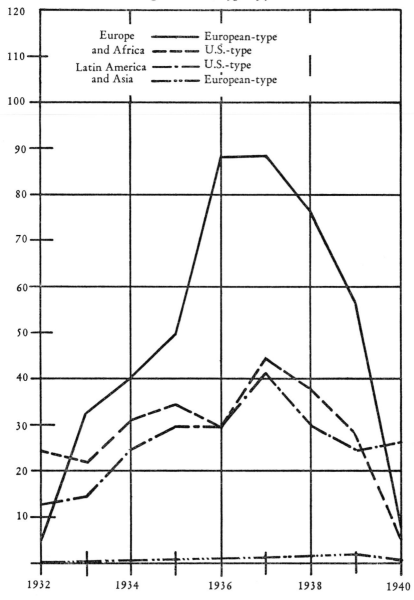

Europe   ————— European-type
and Africa   — — — U.S.-type
Latin America — · — U.S.-type
and Asia   —— ·· — European-type

* All figures are in 1000s of units.

Sales of North American-type vehicles
...alaya, and Ford–New Zealand.

(11) Percentage (10) of (5) %	(12) Total to India	(13) Percentage (12) of (5) %	(14) Total to Malaya	(15) Percentage (14) of (5) %	(16) Total to New Zealand	(17) Percentage (16) of (5) %	(18) Total Sales to Export Dealers (Etc.)	(19) Percentage (18) of (3) %
							26	100.00 *
							86	100.00
							112	100.00
							119	100.00
							483	100.00
							1,089	100.00
							2,677	100.00
							757	100.00
							5,932	100.00
							4,428	100.00
							10,645	100.00
							9,235	100.00
							8,910	100.00
							10,384	100.00
							26,330	100.00
							16,435	100.00
							6,875	100.00
							16,801	100.00
							38,023 *	98.81
							29,617	88.19
79.58							27,019	69.06
83.96 *							20,323	51.43
57.10	1,653	28.32					3,912	40.13
53.97	5,062	17.02	4,658 *	15.68			7,730	20.63
40.07	5,005	20.40	4,392	17.90			10,866	30.69
27.01	6,280 *	39.94 *	2,215	14.09			9,412	37.45
—	2,376	38.05	1,128	18.06			2,862	31.43
49.31	1,011	19.25	313	5.96			6,247	54.33
38.10	2,831	25.78	480	4.37			4,226	27.79
36.29	4,572	22.19	991	4.81			9,127	30.70
30.84	5,347	16.61	1,681	5.22			15,350	32.29
44.02	2,579	9.98	1,656	6.39	2,205	8.53	6,304	19.59
35.02	4,490	13.05	2,922	8.49	5,116	14.87	5,637	14.08
43.32	3,301	9.80	2,213	6.57	5,875 *	17.45 *	3,635	9.75
41.62	5,316	16.38	2,381	7.34	3,784	11.66	1,139	3.39
35.16	2,460	14.45	2,923	17.17	—	—	2,044	10.72
33.18	2,041	13.86	3,156	21.43 *	265	1.80	2,906	16.48
42.95	948	11.71	(20)	(.25)	—	—	875	9.75
—	—	—	—	—	—	—	15	7.58
—	—	—	—	—	—	—	85	100.00 *
—	—	—	—	—	—	—	8,902	88.33
44.30	3,988	14.14	848	3.01	2,279	8.09	14,474	33.92
22.64	5,485	17.49	1,452	4.63	4,411	14.08	9,788	23.79
21.40	4,410	14.03	2,112	6.72	1,222	3.88	3,405	9.77
35.62	1,633	11.24	1,226	8.43	968	6.66	2,882	16.55
68.00	686	4.66	283	1.92	1	.01	969	6.17
52.28	1,241	6.10	1,667	8.20	1,014	4.99	6,215	23.41
56.82	1,506	8.81	752	4.40	68	.40	9,145	34.85
78.71	167	.93	224	1.25	9	.05	367	2.00
66.49	8	.04	193	.97	436	2.19	933	4.49
58.70	12	.04	364	1.26	2,116	7.35	1,235	4.11
56.97	—	—	651	2.77	654	2.78	642	2.66
48.04	—	—	96	.54	441	2.48	1,202	6.34
48.96	—	—	55	.90	160	1.15	1,059	7.10
51.36	—	—	64	.61	291	2.77	1,257	10.68

Parentheses denote red figures.

SOURCE: General Accounting and Financial Analysis Overseas Division, Ford-Canada.

Year #	(1) Total Sales Dom. & Export	(2) Total Dom. Sales	(3) Total Export Sales	(4) Percentage (3) of (1) %	(5) Total Sales to Sub Cos.	(6) Percentage (5) of (1) %	(7) Percentage (5) of (3) %	(8) Total to South Africa	(9) Percentage (8) of (5) %	(10) Total to Australi
1905	117	117								
1906	99	73	26	26.26						
1907	327	241	86	26.30						
1908	324	212	112	34.57						
1909	486	367	119	22.43						
1910	1,280	797	483	37.73						
1911	2,805	1,716	1,059	38.82						
1912	6,388	3,711	2,677	41.91						
1912 x	1,245	488	757	60.80						
1913	12,485	6,556	5,932	47.50						
1914	14,401	9,973	4,428	30.75						
1915	28,855	18,210	10,645	36.89						
1916	33,676	24,441	9,235	27.42						
1917	58,857	49,947	8,910	15.14						
1918	39,638	29,254	10,384	26.20						
1919	49,567	23,237	26,330	53.12						
1920	48,240	31,805	16,435	34.07						
1921	42,349	35,474	6,875	16.23						
1922	50,298	33,497	16,801	33.40						
1923	80,864	42,385	38,479	47.58	456	.56	1.19	456	100.00 *	
1924	71,394	37,812	33,582	47.03	3,965	5.55	11.81	3,965	100.00 *	
1925	79,286	40,162	39,124	49.34	12,105	15.27	30.94	2,472	20.42	9,6
1926	100,668	61,150	39,518	39.26	19,195	19.07	48.57	3,080	16.04	16,1
1927	37,891	28,142	9,749	25.73	5,837	15.40	59.87	851	14.58	3,3
1928	75,292	37,828	37,464	49.76	29,734	39.49	79.37	3,965	13.33	16,0
1929	87,839	52,434	35,405	40.31	24,539	27.94	69.31	5,310	21.64	9,8
1930	70,280	45,144	25,136	35.76	15,724	22.37	62.55	2,982	18.96	4,3
1931	30,750	21,644	9,106	29.61	6,244	20.31	68.57	2,740	43.88	
1932	25,214	13,715	11,499	45.61	5,252	20.83	45.67	1,338	25.48	2,
1933	26,380	11,174	15,206	57.64	10,980	41.62	72.21	3,486	31.75	4,
1934	48,600	18,870	29,730	61.17	20,603	42.39	69.30	7,563	36.71	7,
1935	79,834	32,299	47,535 *	59.54	32,185	40.31	67.71	15,231	47.32	9,
1936	59,789	27,606	32,183	53.83	25,879	43.31	80.41	8,044	31.08	11,
1937	73,716	33,673	40,043	54.32	34,406 *	46.67	85.92	9,829	28.57	12,049
1938	68,373	31,073	37,300	54.55	33,665	49.24	90.25	7,692	22.85	14,584
1939	59,697	26,109	33,588	56.26	32,449	54.36	96.61	7,462	23.00	13,506
1940	46,399	27,326	19,073	41.11	17,029	36.70	89.28	5,658	33.22	5,988
1941	44,207	26,573	17,634	39.90	14,728	33.32	83.52	4,379	29.73	4,887
1942	13,077	4,101	8,976	68.64	8,101	61.95 *	90.25	3,694	45.59	3,479
1943	1,532	1,334	198	12.92	183	1.19	92.42	183	100.00 *	—
1944	3,104	3,019	85	2.74	—	—	—	—	—	—
1945	13,170	3,092	10,078	76.52 *	1,176	8.93	11.67	1,176	100.00 *	—
1946	78,982	36,311	42,671	54.03	28,197	35.70	66.08	8,589	30.46	12,493
1947	101,912	60,771	41,141	40.37	31,353	30.76	76.21	12,905	41.16	7,100
1948	98,800	63,955	34,845	35.27	31,440	31.82	90.23	16,968 *	53.97	6,728
1949	117,140	99,725	17,415	14.87	14,533	12.41	83.45	5,530	38.05	5,176
1950	143,472	127,772	15,700	10.94	14,731	10.27	93.83	3,744	25.41	10,017
1951	129,066	102,522	26,544	19.44	20,329	15.75	76.59	5,780	28.43	10,627
1952	133,508	107,264	26,244	19.66	17,099	12.81	65.15	5.056	29.57	9,717
1953	159,791	141,478 *	18,313	11.46	17,946	11.23	98.00 *	3,420	19.06	14,126
1954	132,498	111,701	20,797	15.70	19,864	14.99	95.51	6,018	30.30	13,209
1955	170,632 *	140,592	30,040	17.61	28,805	16.88	95.89	9,405	32.65	16,908 *
1956	155,709	131,540	24,169	15.52	23,527	15.11	97.34	8,818	37.48	13,404
1957	140,469	121,508	18,961	13.50	17,759	12.64	93.66	8,690	48.94	8,532
1958	119,805	104,893	14,912	12.45	13,853	11.56	92.90	6,856	49.49	6,782
1959	133,972	122,202	11,770	8.79	10,513	7.85	89.32	4,758	45.26	5,400

Fiscal Year ending September 30–1905/1912–Calendar year.
Calendar Year beginning 1913.

x Period October 1, 1912–December 31, 1912.

* Record.

APPENDIX 7. Ford Motor Company International and Total Sales, 1954–1962.

(In millions of dollars)

	International Sales (*Including U.S. Exports*)	*Total World-Wide Sales* (*Including Domestic*)
1954	$1,010	$4,860.3
1955	1,275	6,609.6
1956	1,259	5,655.5
1957	1,330	6,839.3
1958	1,389	5,280.9
1959	1,583	6,648.8
1960	1,806	6,797.6
1961	1,912	6,709.4
1962	2,158	8,089.6

SOURCE:
International Sales: *Annual Reports 1955–1961*.
Total Sales: *Annual Report 1962*.

APPENDIX 8. Ford U.S. Equity in Net Assets of Foreign Subsidiaries and Branches, 1952–1962.

(In millions of dollars)

Year	*Equity*
1952	$138.1
1953	150.8
1954	172.2
1955	199.1
1956	219.3
1957	240.0
1958	271.1
1959	407.6
1960	461.6
1961	629.4
1962	671.1

SOURCE: Controller's office, Ford Motor Company.

APPENDIX 9. Ford Motor Company: Profits of Foreign Operations and Dividends and Profit Received, 1946–1961.
(In millions of dollars)

Year	Total Profits After Taxes	Company Equity in Net Income	Dividends and Profit Received
1946	$ 15.9	$ 11.6	$ 4.6
1947	30.3	15.8	9.8
1948	34.4	14.7	6.9
1949	8.7	(2.7)	2.6
1950	40.3	17.2	17.6
1951	37.7	18.5	8.3
1952	33.6	15.5	7.9
1953	49.4	25.0	11.8
1954	51.9	26.5	11.3
1955	59.6	28.3	11.2
1956	46.8	23.3	12.4
1957	53.2	28.0	16.3
1958	63.2	33.5	13.1
1959	91.0	49.0	16.5
1960	102.3	71.6	27.2
1961	81.3	69.4	49.7

SOURCE: Controller's office, Ford Motor Company.

Bibliographical Essay

The book has extensive footnotes and the reader seeking additional information on matters discussed in the text has only to refer to them. Here however is a more comprehensive presentation of the materials that the authors have found especially valuable. We have not included the endless number of books, magazines, and newspapers used to supply background information, but only indicated the manuscript collections and the books that we have found of key importance (or occasionally to save the reader time and energy, those which by their titles look as though they may offer the most but do not do so!).

I. MANUSCRIPT MATERIALS.

A. *General Location.*

We have relied primarily on basic documents in the possession of the American Ford Motor Company, in the files of Ford companies and branches outside the United States, in the James Couzens Papers at the Library of Congress, in the Couzens Papers in Birmingham, Michigan, and in the Public Records Office, London, England. We have also found interesting reports, circulars, and letters in the private papers of Gabriel Panier, Paris; Oscar Permeke, Antwerp; George Jackson, Grimsby, Ontario; W. W. Townsend, Mexico City; and Kristian Orberg and Humberto Monteiro, both in São Paulo, Brazil.

By far the largest collection of source material consulted lies in the Ford Archives, Dearborn, Michigan. This superb body of documents on Ford history at home and abroad, from 1903 to the present, is arranged by Accessions. As the Archives receives materials from the various departments in the company and from the company's record storage center at Highland Park, members of the staff of the Archives put each set of papers into an Accession. At the time of writing there were 780 Accessions and some of these contain one or two boxes, while others have thousands of boxes. Here are to be found letters and memoranda from Ford's foreign representatives, old corporate records, ledger books on early dealers, dealer contracts, cost accounting data, production and sales information, and so forth. This is the first stop for any historian of the Ford Motor Company.

Also in Dearborn and Detroit, there is information on Ford's foreign activities in the Ford International files (in general covering the period 1938 to the present), in the Secretary's office (from the 1920's to the present), in the Product Planning

Committee files (all post-World War II), in the Highland Park records (very scattered materials, spanning the entire company history), in the Ferguson case materials (1916–1950), and in the possession of particular individuals engaged in the specific activity being studied.

In England, Ford's historical records are at Dagenham in the Permanent file, in the Secretary's office, and in the files of particular executives. There are also records kept in the Regent Street office of the company in London; and at Langley in Windsor there is a notable body of records.

All the French Ford company's historical records (which have been reduced to a bare minimum) are in the possession of Simca, at Poissy. However, the private files of Gabriel Panier, former works manager, contain much information of interest. Actually, there are more documents on the French Ford company in Dearborn than in Paris.

The records of the German Ford company are in Cologne. This firm has an Archives, the files of which do not go back prior to 1933 and have been well weeded; the material we got from them did not compare in value to information that is in Dearborn. At Cologne, as at every Ford plant, the private files of particular departments often contain more relevant information than the general record collection.

Ford-Belgium, Ford-Denmark, and Ford-Holland have historical records on their premises. Since these companies were small, their volume relatively low, their problems specific rather than general, we did not spend much time scrutinizing their files. In Belgium, however, we found data available nowhere else dealing with the early history of Ford in Europe. This information was in the possession of Oscar Permeke (who became a Ford dealer in 1911 and whose records date back to that year). We also got interesting information from the Vandersmissen family (Ghent), dealing with Ford history in the World War I period.

The historical record files of the Canadian Ford company are efficiently organized, but regrettably incomplete. The company's collection of documents on its past are divided between Oakville and Windsor. In Oakville there is a Record Retention File containing basic records, there are the Secretary's office files, and the files of particular departments of the company. In Windsor the personnel files and another general historical record collection are housed. In this last body of documents are such assorted materials as the books and records of the Walkerville Wagon Company, data on war production, on labor relations, etc. But missing from all the Canadian Ford evidence is any run of high executive correspondence. McGregor's and Campbell's files have been destroyed. Letters from other key executives likewise have been disposed of. Only by accident does one find old correspondence or cables—a letter dated 1905 was found in the Customs and Excise Department files; and a cable from South Africa to the home office was found misfiled in the personnel records (had it not been misfiled it would have been thrown out). Among the best sources on Canadian Ford history are the presentations that the Company made in 1920, 1926, 1935, and 1960 to the Tariff Commission in Canada. The first of these is in Dearborn, Acc. 23, Bx. 4; the 1926 presentation is in the possession of the secretary of the chairman of the Board of Ford-Canada; the 1935 presentation is in the Oakville historical files, and the 1960 presentation is in the possession of Mr. J. S. Urie, Customs and Excise Department, Ford-Canada.

In São Paulo, Montevideo, Buenos Aires, Santiago, and Mexico City are some historical records on Ford activities, but they are discouragingly incomplete. In Santiago one of us was present as a large packing case (out-of-doors in the yard) was pried open, and from it tumbled a set of papers covered with dirt, all mixed up, but containing some useful information: this was their archives! In general, however, most locations in Latin America could supply such records as old balance sheets, real estate files, ledger books, personnel records, check books. But very little old executive correspondence has been retained. In the vault of the old plant at Buenos Aires (at La Boca), one of us did find an exceptional collection of B. R. Brown's papers on the building of the Brazilian and Argentine assembly plants at the start of the 1920's. It is from very scattered and disparate letters and ledgers that we have been able to reconstruct the history of Ford in Latin America.

We did not visit the Orient because at the time of preparing this volume, the Japanese Ford company was inactive, the Indian company in a state of voluntary liquidation, and the Chinese operation moribund. On the Asian and Australian activities, we have relied on material in Dearborn and Oakville.

B. *Crucial Records.*

The starting point for any corporate history is the *minutes of the Board of Directors and of stockholders' meetings.* In Ford records these have been filed together. We have consulted the minutes of all the companies dealt with in this volume. The complete minute books of all presently-existing Ford companies (with the exception of Ford-Canada and its subsidiaries) are in the Secretary's office, Dearborn. The minutes of all defunct Ford companies are in the Ford Archives: thus, Ford-France minutes are in Acc. 606 and Acc. 334; Ford-Greece in Acc. 316; Ford-Roumania in Acc. 302, Ford-Spain in Acc. 608, Ford Investment Co., Guernsey, Acc. 604, Ford International Inc., Acc. 312, Société Investissement Ford, Luxembourg, Acc. 313, Ford-US (1903–1919), Acc. 85. Ford-Canada has in *its* Secretary's office, Oakville, Ontario, the minutes of that company's meetings, plus those of all its overseas subsidiaries (Australia, India, New Zealand, Malaya, and South Africa). In general, the minutes will have correspondence connected with the agenda or the contents of the meetings filed with them. This correspondence varies in value to the historian: some of it is excellent, but much of it is routine. When a branch establishment rather than a company operated in a foreign land, there is no set of records comparable to the Board minutes, and the basic history is much more difficult to reconstruct.

For the post-World War II period the *minutes of management, policy, and executive committee meetings* are an important supplement to the Board and shareholders' meeting minutes. Committee meeting minutes for the American, English, and Canadian Ford companies are on file in the Secretary's office of the particular company. We have found them to be replete with details on day-by-day activities and an excellent source. For a short period (post-World War II) a foreign operations committee held meetings in Dearborn, and its minutes (located in the Secretary's office, Dearborn) are useful. Also, the American Product Planning Committee minutes have some interesting information on overseas activities (these are located in the Product Planning office of Ford-US)

An essential source for the post-World War II period are the multitude of *presentations made by Ford International* to the various top executive bodies (Board of Directors, Executive Committee, etc.) of the American Ford Company. Regrettably, these have not been collected. There are some in the Secretary's office, Dearborn; some in what was formerly called the Central Files of Ford International (but now is just a general file run by Miss Charlene Farrell), some exist in the possession of the individuals in Ford International who prepared the presentation, while others are in still unclassified materials in the Archives.

In the Archives, Acc. 78, and Acc. 235 are so-called *general letters*—mimeographed policy letters sent from the home office to the domestic and foreign operations. They are essential for a history of the domestic company and its plans at home and abroad. These cover the years 1915–1948.

Managers' monthly or quarterly letters came from most of the Ford-US-run overseas operations to the home office from 1913 on. These were circulated among various executives and landed sometimes in one file, sometimes in another, and sometimes in the wastepaper basket. There are isolated copies of these valuable reports in the Archives and in Ford International files, but there is no complete set from any one operation. Unfortunately, not one of the Latin American branches or companies, for example, has retained carbons of these letters, which were sent to Dearborn from the time of origin to the present (only the most recent reports are on file in Latin America and of course in Dearborn). Had these sets been kept, they would have been invaluable from what we have seen of those few extant. Ford International has the files on reports for recent years; and in the Secretary's office, Dearborn, there is a run of Ford-England monthly manager's letters in the 1930's.

For the period when Ford-England supervised the European continental operations (1928–1949) that company has splendid records. The *files of the Office of Sir Percival Perry* (and its successors: the Office of Lord Perry and the Office of Sir Stanford Cooper) are very complete. They are stored at Langley, near Windsor, England, in 410 60-pound boxes, which contain a mine of information. Some of the Office of Sir Stanford Cooper records have been microfilmed, and the microfilms are in Ford International files, Dearborn. Comparable files on the way Ford-Canada coordinated its foreign subsidiaries do not exist.

General correspondence with foreign representatives of the Ford company is available in great quantity in the Archives. For specific letters see the footnotes of this book. For overall purposes, the most useful collections are the following:

Sorensen's files (Acc. 38),

Edsel Ford's files (Acc. 6),

Henry Ford's files (Accs. 1, 23, 62, 284, and 285),

Roberge's files (Acc. 507 and 713),

Wibel's files (Acc. 390),

Carnegie's files (Acc. 157), and

Select File (prepared by the researchers for Nevins & Hill's history of the Ford Motor Company, it has many relevant documents).

For the post-World War II period, the International Division has good files; correspondence is of course in the particular departments of the division as well as in the collection formerly called "Central Files."

For the post-World War II period, the so-called "Blue Letters" are a key historical source. These are departmental communications, giving decisions made by high executives in all spheres of company activities, international included. Many officials in the company have sets of such letters, but we have not been able to locate any central file called "Blue Letters." The organization planning office of the Ford company, however, does have a series of all such letters dealing with changes in administration.

Sales and production statistics. For the early period these are hard to obtain and must be assembled from a variety of sources in the United States and overseas. Statistics are often conflicting. Some discrepancies result because figures (loosely referred to as "sales") may be production, imports, registrations, dealer deliveries, etc. We have tried in every case to label accurately all figures used. Appendices to this volume give available information (with sources). Ruth Baker on Ford International staff has been especially helpful in finding figures for us for the years 1922ff. She has all kinds of statistics on foreign sales for the post-World War II period, and earlier.

Dealer organization. The earliest foreign dealer contracts we have been able to locate are in the files of the dealer Oscar Permerke, Antwerp, 1911–1912 and in Acc. 76, 1912–1913. The number of dealers at any time has to be obtained from the local Ford companies and branches, which generally have historical records on their dealer network. The pre-World War II balance sheets of the foreign operations supplied such information.

Production facilities. General data on manufacturing facilities abroad is well organized by operation (in alphabetical order) in Wiesmyer's files, Acc. 106. More current manufacturing information (with historical backgrounds) is available from C. T. Alexander on the Ford manufacturing staff in Dearborn. Highland Park records contain early contracts for building overseas; much of this material is now being transferred to the Archives. Accs. 101 and 104 have old leases, and Acc. 134 has good data on properties. Practically all of the local companies have excellent real estate records. Ford-England can give full data on plant expansion, and Ford-Germany has comparable information for that company's activities after 1931. The Board minutes of many of the companies furnish considerable information on plant expansion activities (the funds appropriated for them, etc.).

Purchasing. The files of the local companies will give data on local suppliers. The Purchasing Department in Dearborn was helpful in furnishing information on company policy in regard to overseas purchasing. Acc. 390, Wibel's files, has data on prewar foreign purchasing policies. There is also material in the files at Highland Park on "international purchasing."

Engineering data up to 1946 is all in Dearborn, because practically all the engineering was done there. After 1946 it is worth investigating Ford-England files on engineering, but most information on overseas engineering is available in the home office.

Organization and administration. Information on the management of the foreign companies and branches must be gotten from "official" records (Board minutes, foreign companies' personnel files, etc.) or from contemporary correspondence. Personnel records at all the overseas locations are quite good, while those in Ford International files that relate to early overseas management are fragmentary. The numbers of persons employed in any location can generally be gotten from the overseas companies. The pre-World War II balance sheets gave this information. Organization charts of Ford International are in the division's files.

Labor relations. Almost all data on labor relations must be obtained from the foreign companies, although scattered letters in the Archives and in Ford International files throw light on such matters.

Finances. For the period before World War II, the financial records relating to Ford's overseas activities are in general appalling. There are of course the balance sheets for each operation. Acc. 713, Bx. 54 has data on profits from Latin American operations (1925–1944). Ford International prepared at one time a summary of the profits (translated into dollars at the current rate of exchange) for most of the European associated companies (1922–1948). This is in the folder "England-Guernsey Ford Investment, Shares 1948 (Jan–Sept)", which was located in what was formerly called Central Files, International Division. Letters in Edsel Ford's files (Acc. 6) and Sorensen's files (Acc. 38) have information on costs of particular undertakings. Acc. 134 has some financial data. For the post-World War II period there is extensive financial information available for internal use within the company, much of which is confidential.

Contracts and agreements. The best source for these is of course the Secretary's office, Dearborn. Old records from the Secretary's office have in many cases been transferred to the Archives. Those accessions which have key contracts and agreements relating to foreign activities are Accs. 95, 140 (very important, for it contains Lockwood's, Perry's, and White's early contracts), and 363 (contains Canadian-Ford US agreement 1904). Ford International Division files also contain copies of certain agreements.

II. Published Company Records.

All of the companies whose stock was publicly held (the Canadian company from its origin; Ford-England, France, Germany, Spain, Denmark, Sweden, Finland, Belgium, and Holland from 1928–1929; Ford-US from 1956) published *Annual Reports.* We have a complete set of the Canadian, English, and American reports. A complete set of the French reports is in the possession of Simca, Poissy, France. A practically complete set of the German business reports can be derived from copies in Select File, Ford Archives, Acc. 38, and Ford International files. As for the other companies, scattered copies are in Acc. 38, and Ford International files, but the best source for a complete set is the local company. These reports are invaluable.

There were for many years printed *Addresses to the Shareholders* made by Campbell and Perry at the annual meetings. We have a complete set of the Canadian addresses; the English ones are scattered in Acc. 38, Acc. 285, and Ford International files. Accurate and quite complete summaries of Perry's speeches were run every year in the *Economist* (London). These addresses give a good appraisal of happenings within the companies in the context of current economic conditions.

When Ford stock was offered the public, printed *Prospectuses* were issued, and these contain valuable information about the companies.

III. Oral History.

A. *General.*

Not only have we used written documents, but we have ourselves interviewed more than one hundred persons involved in the companies' overseas activities. We have also been able to use the reminiscences taken by Owen Bombard in connection with the Ford oral history project and transcripts of interviews made by Norman St. John Stevas in connection with his unpublished history of Ford-England.

Some of the interviews, such as the one Nevins and Hill had with Sorensen in 1954, the one we had with Kanzler in 1960, and the one Dr. Wilkins had with R. I. Roberge in 1961 have covered general Ford overseas activities. We have gotten valuable suggestions on approaches to the history from Messrs. T. Lilley, W. McKee, M. J. O'Neill, and W. J. Sundelson. Among the individuals in Dearborn who have filled us in have been L. Beebe, J. Bennett, N. Bowe, G. E. Braden, E. Callahan, R. M. Campbell, D. Duncan, P. J. Fuller, J. Goodrich, J. Goulden, D. Irwin, J. Mayhew, James A. MacAlarney, and J. R. Robertson. Mr. Bombard's interviews with B. R. Brown, G. J. Crimmins, and Roberge have also been useful.

More specifically, the following interviews have been valuable in dealing with Ford abroad:

B. *England, Ireland, and the European Continent.*

Mr. Hill with Dr. Nevins had the opportunity to meet and interview Lord Perry in 1952 before the idea for this book was conceived. Both Dr. Wilkins and Mr. Hill have talked at length with Sir Patrick Hennessy, Sir Rowland Smith and Sir Stanford Cooper, who have spent their valuable time giving us invaluable information on Ford-England's past. Other Ford-England executives and former employees who have helped us are: W. Batty, T. N. Beckett, L. T. Blakeman, M. J. Buckmaster, J. L. Claridge, F. S. Thornhill Cooper, A. Cox, H. A. Denne, S. J. Elliott, J. P. Higgins, Miss Vera Howard, H. Mortimore, E. Page, M. Ronayne, J. M. A. Smith, and W. J. Squire.

On Irish Ford activities, Sir Patrick Hennessy, John O'Neill, M. J. O'Neill, M. Ronayne, and W. J. Squire were especially helpful.

Dr. Heinrich Albert, J. Andrews, A. Beck, G. Carlson, M. Cola, F. S. Thornhill Cooper, D. De Jonghe, M. Dollfus, V. Falbe-Hansen, J. Gutzeit, C. W. Hauss, B. H. C. Huntelaar, H. C. Møller, G. A. Panier, W. Reiber, G. F. Riedt, E. Sagabiel, H. Schmidt, R. H. Schmidt, W. Schmidt, W. P. Schmidt, M. van Grootel, J. van Luppen, E. Vitger, and E. Wiese gave Dr. Wilkins a wide range of opinions and approaches to European Ford history. She also had the opportunity to visit the dealership of O. Permeke and P. Plasman in Belgium.

Mr. Bombard's interviews with T. Gehle, H. Hanson, and W. Klann have also been informative on the European story.

C. *Canada.*

We were in Canada and had the chance to talk with the following past and present members of the Ford organization there: G. H. Bates, F. G. Batters, J. M. Cochrane, G. Dewar, Miss Grace Falconer, A. S. Harrison, G. Jackson, R. M. Sale, B. Stevenson, and J. S. Urie. Dr. Wilkins saw Don McGregor—brother of the first manager of Ford-Canada—in Windsor, Ont. Earlier Mr. Bombard interviewed production manager G. Dickert, and we have found this *Reminiscence* helpful.

D. *Latin America.*

On Mexican Ford history, M. Acosta, L. Etcharren, M. Carniel (interviewed in Buenos Aires), R. E. Chaplin, M. Carrillo, B. Kopf, E. Molina, E. Rangel, F. Rhuberry, and W. W. Townsend were especially helpful.

In the Caribbean the dealers, W. Smallwood, K. Lancaster (of Hull-Dobbs), R. Gibson (of McEnearney & Co.), and V. Henriques (of Henriques Bros.), have provided useful information. W. W. Townsend, manager of the Cristobal branch from 1928–1941, gave us valuable insights into Ford activity in this territory, which he supervised. Also useful have been comments made by M. Carniel, R. E. Chaplin, and G. T. Rehfeldt.

In South America certain former general managers of Ford operations have had broad experience and were of the greatest assistance: Kristian Orberg (interviewed in São Paulo) on Argentina, Uruguay, and Brazil; Benjamin Kopf (interviewed in Mexico City) on Argentina, Brazil, Uruguay, and Chile; Guillermo Boxer (interviewed in Montevideo) on Argentina and Uruguay; R. P. Monteverde (interviewed in Buenos Aires) on Argentina and Uruguay; and Jorge Matray (interviewed in Santiago) on Argentina and Chile. We have also used Mr. Bombard's taped Reminiscence of Orberg.

More specifically, in Brazil Dr. Wilkins found especially helpful H. Monteire. She also interviewed P. Andersen, F. Salles Cesor, C. Michelitti, S. Nielsen, A. D. Villares, and J. Waegte. Some of her interviews dealt with the rubber plantation as well as Brazilian automotive activities. Those specifically dealing with rubber were with Dr. Sylvio Braga and Sr. Paivia. Both of us interviewed Silvino da Silva in New York. We have also consulted Mr. Bombard's interviews of O. Z. Ide, W. C. Cowling, and Carl La Rue for materials on the plantation. On Ford in Uruguay, R. L. Rice was helpful. W. Bryan, M. Carniel, D. B. Kitterman, F. F. Dover, D. H. Tarakdjian, and P. M. Zinkgräf gave information on Ford-Argentina which supplemented that which we obtained from the general managers mentioned above. J. Nielsen was very helpful on Ford in Chile.

E. *Far East.*

On the early history of Ford-Canada's activities in the Far East (India, Malaya, etc.) we obtained valuable information (1907–1926) from V. A. Dodge, former president of Dodge & Seymour, whom we interviewed several times in New York. On India, especially, Basil Stevenson, H. A. Denne, and Sir Rowland Smith (the first interviewed in Oakville, Ont., and the last two interviewed in England) were helpful. For Ford-US activities in the Far East, V. A. Dodge, B. Kopf, and R. I. Roberge provided much information. We have also consulted *Reminiscences* prepared by Mr. Bombard of Cowling, Roberge, and F. Rieck.

F. *Oceana.*

On New Zealand, G. Jackson (interviewed in Grimsby, Ont.) provided us with much information. On Ford activities in Australia, R. M. Sale, B. Stevenson, and G. H. Bates gave us considerable background information.

G. *Africa.*

On South Africa, E. A. Love and B. Stevenson were helpful; on Egypt, F. S. Thornhill Cooper (interviewed in Rome, Italy) and C. Mataras (interviewed in Detroit) provided much information. J. W. Sundelson gave us interesting material on current developments in Africa.

IV. Ford Periodicals.

A. *Published by Ford-US.*

The *Ford Times, Ford News,* and the *Dearborn Independent.*

B. Published by Ford Enterprises.

The *Ford Times* (Canadian ed.), *Ford Times* (English ed.), *Ford News* (Canadian ed.), *Ford News* (English ed.), *La Revue Ford* (Belgian), *Revista Ford* (Argentina), *O Mundo Ford* (Brazilian). Each foreign operation has and had its own publications that are a good source of information.

V. Printed or Typed Ford Histories.

A. *Books on Ford-US.*

Few books on the domestic company deal, except in passing, with the foreign operations. The best data are in Allan Nevins and Frank Ernest Hill, three-volume history of the Ford Motor Company, New York, I. *Ford: the Times, the Man, the Company,* 1954; II. *Ford: Expansion and Challenge, 1915–1932,* 1957; and III. *Ford: Decline and Rebirth,* 1963 (cited in the notes as Nevins & Hill). Edgar N. Duffield, *Ford Through European Eyes,* Chelmsford, 1947, is perfunctory. Other histories of Henry Ford and the Ford Motor Company: Roger Burlingame, *Henry Ford,* New York, 1956; William C. Richards, *The Last Billionaire,* New York, 1948, and Keith Sward, *The Legend of Henry Ford,* New York, 1948, for example, are *not* helpful on the overseas ventures, but do give a general background of what was going on in the domestic company. C. E. Sorensen, *My Forty Years with Ford,* New York, 1956, gives both background and direct information on foreign operations.

B. *Studies of Ford Overseas Companies.*

There have been a number of detailed local company histories, which we have read but have not relied on heavily. Ford of England has had two historians: Norman St. John Stevas and C. Fawcett, both of whose manuscripts we read in typescript. Neither has been published. The Stevas manuscript is dated 1954 and the Fawcett, 1961.

There have been short pieces on Ford-Canada history prepared by their Public Relations Department. These are in Ford-Canada's Public Relations Department files. The Canadian Ford *Annual Report of 1954* and *Ward's Report of 1954* both contain typical Canadian Ford company histories, written on the occasion of the company's fiftieth anniversary.

Ford-Germany issues a little booklet, *Facts on Ford Germany* that gives basic historical dates. Also a number of the management "trainees" in Ford-Werke have written up short studies of their company. There is a first-rate history of Ford-Denmark, *Ford Motor Company: Gennem 25 Aar,* København, 1944. No history was prepared of Ford-France, but some splendid pictures of the Poissy plant are in a Simca publication, *Poissy*, Paris [1959?].

Practically every one of the overseas operations has in recent years recounted in a few pages the history of the unit in its company or branch publication. These are very brief and at times inaccurate. One of those filled with the most errors is in *Ford Argentina*, No. 20, n.d. [October 1961?], 2–4. It is unnecessary to recount others, for these are based mostly on information informally gathered and undocumented.

On each foreign operation there is a folder entitled "Historical Data" in the Ford International files (in Miss C. Ferrill's files). Generally the folder will contain a chronology of the company or branch in question plus other relevant data. The folders are arranged by geographical location, and their contents are excellent.

VI. Studies of the American Automobile Industry.

The best collection of information on the American automobile industry are the published materials in the Ford Archives; the books, periodicals, and pamphlets in the Detroit Automotive Collection (which is in the Detroit Public Library) and the vast statistical data accumulated in the research library of the Automobile Manufacturers Association. The New York Public Library also has a large collection of material on the automobile industry in its Technology Department files, although it is disconcerting to discover that many of its unique pieces have been lost, mislaid, or stolen.

The books on the American automobile industry's history are mostly old, and out of date. Nevins & Hill, *op. cit.*, has the most recent information, presented as a background for the Ford study. The Federal Trade Commission, *Report on Motor Vehicle Industry*, 76th Cong., 3rd Sess. House Doc. No. 468, Washington, 1939, is invaluable but needs to be brought up to date. Other volumes useful to us have been Ralph C. Epstein, *The Automobile Industry*, New York, 1928; E. D. Kennedy, *The Automobile Industry*, New York, 1941, Arthur Pound, *The Turning Wheel*, Garden City, 1934, which deals with GM and has a good section on GM's overseas operations, and Lawrence Seltzer, *A Financial History of the American Automobile Industry*, New York, 1928. Actually one of the best ways to study recent automobile history is to read the annual *Ward's Reports*, which give the yearly activities of the industry. For a more complete bibliography on the American industry, see Nevins & Hill, Vol. I (*Ford: The Times, the Man, the Company*), 656–664. Most of the studies of the American automobile industry have a small amount on foreign activities of the industry. Such American automobile industry periodicals as *Automotive Industries, Automobile Topics*, etc., have some material on foreign as well as on American industry activity.

VII. The Automobile Business and Foreign Activities.

A. *Statistical Data.*

Statistical information on the automobile industry is available from the United States Department of Commerce, from the American Automobile Association, from the Dominion Bureau of Statistics (Ottawa), from the Society of Motor Manufacturers and Traders (London), and from Chambre Syndicale des Constructeurs (Paris). AMA publishes annually a booklet called *Automobile Facts and Figures*, while the SMMT has an annual volume entitled *The Motor Industry of Great Britain*. This last contains statistics dealing with foreign countries' industries as well as with England's. The Germans published *Tatsachen und Zahlen aus der Kraftfahrzug Industrie*. *Ward's Reports* publish figures on registrations of foreign imports in the United States. The Ford companies in overseas markets have been helpful in furnishing us with much statistical data about automotive activities abroad. For other source material on the diffusion of private automobiles and an excellent summary of this data see W. W. Rostow, *Stages of Economic Growth*, Cambridge 1960, 168–70.

B. *U.S. Department of Commerce Studies.*

Over the years there has been a wide range of Department of Commerce studies of the automotive activities abroad. All are Washington, D.C. The following are typical:

1. *From the Bureau of Foreign and Domestic Commerce:*

American Automotive Products in India, 1923 (Spec. Agents series #223).
Argentine Market for Motor Vehicles, 1917 (Misc. series #62).
Automotive Market in Argentina, 1929 (Trade Promotion series #84).
Automotive Markets in China, British Malaya, and Chosen, 1923 (Spec. Agents series #221)
Development of Motor-Vehicle Trade Abroad, 1913 (Spec. Consular Rpt. #59).
Japan as an Automotive Market, 1922 (Spec. Agents series #217).
Motor Vehicle Regulations and Taxation in Foreign Countries, 1930 (Trade Promotion series #108).
Motor Vehicles in Japan, China, and Hawaii, 1918 (Spec. Agents series #170).

2. *From the Bureau of Manufactures:*

Foreign Market for Motor Vehicles, 1912 (Spec. Consular Rpt. #53).

C. Few books deal with the American automobile business and foreign trade. D. M. Phelps, *Effect of the Foreign Market on the Growth and Stability of the American Automobile Industry*, Ann Arbor, 1931 is an exception.

D. *Publications dealing with foreign automobile industries.*

1. On the English industry the following are especially useful:

Andrews, P. W. S. and Elizabeth Brunner, *The Life of Lord Nuffield*, Oxford, 1955.

Castle, H. G., *Britain's Motor Industry*, London, 1950.

Cook, P. L., in collaboration with Ruth Cohen, *Effects of Mergers*, London, 1958, has chapter on the motor industry by George Maxcy.

Maxcy, George and A. Silberston, *The Motor Industry*, London, 1959, an exceptionally useful study by two economists.

Nixon, St. John G., *The Story of the Society of Motor Manufacturers and Traders 1902–1952*, London, 1952.

PEP, London, *Motor Vehicles*, London, 1950.

Rolt, L. T. C., *Horseless Carriage, The Motor Car in England*, London, 1950.

Talbot, Frederick A., *Motor Cars and Their Story*, London, 1912.

Wyatt, Horace, *The Motor Industry*, London, 1917.

In addition, for a number of years the London *Times* published a "Survey of the British Motor-Car Industry." We have used the issues published in 1948, 1949, 1950 and 1952 to great advantage.

2. There have been two studies of the history of the Canadian automobile industry:

Aikman, C. Howard, *The Automobile Industry of Canada*, Toronto, 1926.

Sun Life Assurance Co. of Canada: Study on behalf of the Royal Commission of Canada's Economic Prospects, *The Canadian Automotive Industry*, Sept., 1956. In addition, the recent Royal Commission on the Automotive Industry, *Report*, Ottawa, Apr. 1961, has some useful historical materials.

3. On the Australian Motor Vehicle industry, see Industries Division, Department of Trade, *The Australian Motor Vehicle Industry*, Melbourne, Mar. 1959.

4. On the German automobile industry there is no history that we would recommend, although there have been a number of studies in German on the development of that industry and specific accounts of the Benz, Daimler, and other German concerns. The U.S. Strategic Bombing Survey, *German Motor Vehicle Industry*, Washington, Nov. 1945, is useful, but we found it to be often inadequate.

5. As for France, Jacques Rousseau, *Histoire Mondiale de l'Automobile*, Paris, 1958 while general in scope devotes a great deal of attention to the national industry. S. Saint-Loup, *Renault de Billancourt*, Paris, 1956 is a readable study. Elvinger (Paris), "Etude de Marché faite pour la Guaranty Trust Company of New York," Feb. 1946, unpublished typescript, has a good summary of the French automotive industry. There is a copy of it in Acc. 713, Bx. 29 of the Ford Archives.

6. Fiat, *"Fiat," A Fifty Year Record*, [Turin?], 1951, has useful data on the Italian industry.

7. F. Schmitto, *Automobilets Historie og Dets Maend,* København 1938, 2 vols. has good information on the industry in general and, specifically, in Denmark.

8. Edgardo Sotelo Ortiz, *Las Plantas Armadores de Automoviles en México,* Mexico 1952 (a thesis prepared at the Universidad Nacional Autónoma de México) has information on assembly plants in that country.

E. *Foreign Automobile Periodicals.*

Anyone dealing with overseas automobile industries will want to consult the foreign automobile periodicals which abound in number. The Detroit Automotive Collection has an excellent sampling of such journals. We have found that for English automotive history, *Autocar, Motor, Car,* and *Motor Trader* are especially helpful; for France, *Voiturette, La Vie Automobile* (1900–1957) and *Omnia* (1906–1936); for Germany, *Motorwagen* (the title of this periodical changed over the years), for Mexico, *El Automovile in México;* for Argentina, *A.C.A.*

VIII. American Business Activities Overseas.

For general background on other American businesses in overseas markets we have used a vast number of sources. Senate and House Committee Hearings have been consulted (see footnotes for specific references). Among the most useful books have been the American Exporter, *Export Trade Directory* (published bi-annually 1912–1922) and Cleona Lewis, *America's Stake in International Investments,* Washington, 1938. Also of interest are P. D. Dickens, *American Direct Investments in Foreign Countries,* Trade Information Bull. #731, Washington, 1930; his *American Direct Investments in Foreign Countries,* U.S. Dept. of Com., Bur. of For. & Dom. Com., Ec. Series #1, Washington, 1938; and U.S. Treasury Dept., *Census of American-Owned Assets in Foreign Countries,* Washington, 1947. We have gotten considerable background from recent publications of Business International, Inc., Southwestern Legal Association, the International Monetary Fund, the United Nations, and the U.S. Department of Commerce, Office of Business Economics.

For American business activities in particular markets, we have found of special interest, John Dunning, *American Investment in British Industry,* London, 1958; Frank Southard, *American Industry in Europe,* Boston, 1931; D. M. Phelps, *Migration of Industry to South America,* New York, 1936 (on Argentina, Brazil, Chile, and Uruguay only); George Wythe, *Industry in Latin America,* New York, 1949; Herbert Marshall, Frank A. Southard, and Kenneth W. Taylor, *Canadian-American Industry,* New Haven, 1936.

IX. General Background Information.

In dealing with international economic problems in this volume, we have referred to any number of histories of the localities about which we have dealt. It is unnecessary to list them all, but we do want to note William Ashworth, *A Short History of International Economy, 1850–1950,* 3rd impression, London, 1959, to which we owe a great debt and which is truly an excellent short summary.

Notes

Location and Company Abbreviations

Acc.____, Bx.____	Accession, Box, Ford Archives, Dearborn, Michigan.
Det. Autov. Col.	The Automotive History Collection, Detroit Public Library, Michigan.
Ferg-M	Ferguson case records on microfilm (in possession of Office of the General Counsel).
FI	Ford International Files, Dearborn.
FMC-Arg.	Ford Motor Argentina SA records; includes records of operation when it was a branch. Specific locations indicated in notes.
FMC-Austl.	Ford Motor Company of Australia Proprietary, Ltd.
Ford Mfg. Co.-Austl.	Ford Manufacturing Company of Australia Proprietary Ltd.
FMC-Belg.	Ford Motor Company (Belgium) S.A., Antwerp, Belgium.
FMC-Brazil	Ford Motor do Brasil SA; also refers to records of this operation when it was a branch of Ford Motor Company, Export, Inc. Specific locations indicated in notes.
FMC-Can.	Ford Motor Company of Canada Ltd., Oakville. Material at Windsor, Ontario is indicated FMC-Can., Windsor.
FMC-Denmark	Ford Motor Company Aktieselskab, Copenhagen, Denmark.
FMC-Eng.	Ford Motor Company Ltd., Dagenham. English materials at locations other than Dagenham is so indicated in the notes.
FMC-Fr.	Automobiles Ford, SA, Ford SAF, and Ford (France), SAF. Specific location of documents is noted.
FMC-Ger.	Ford-Werke, AG. These files are in Cologne and in New York; some of those cited are still in Cologne; most however will go to Ford Archives, Dearborn.
FMC-Italy	Ford Italiana Società per Azioni. Location material as indicated in notes.
FMC-Mex.	Ford Motor Company, SA, Mexico City, Mexico.
FMC-Roumania	Ford Romana, SAR. Location of data is indicated in notes.
FMC-S. Africa	Ford Motor Company of South Africa (Proprietary), Ltd. Location of data indicated in notes.
FMC-Sp.	Ford Motor Iberica, SA. Location of data indicated in notes.
FMC-Urug.	Ford (Uruguay) SA and its predecessor branch of Ford Motor Company. Data in Montevideo, Uruguay.
FMC-US	Ford Motor Company, Dearborn. Files other than those in the Archives, Ferg-M, or Ford International files.
Lib. of Cong.	Library of Congress, Washington, D.C.
OOSPP	Office of Sir Percival Perry records, located at Langley, near Windsor, England.

Notes

prodn. production	stat(s). statistic(s)
pub.rels. public relations	sub. subsidiary
pubn. publication	trs. translated
Pty. Proprietary	univ. universal
rev. revised	*v*. compared with, against
serv. service	vol. volume
standzn. standardization	

CHAPTER 1

1. FMC-US, Mins. Shareholders Mtg., Oct. 15, 1903 and FMC-US, Annual Report, Oct. 1, 1903, Acc. 85, Bx. 1; EMC-US, Ledger Bk., Acc. 85, Bx. 8 (Canada); FMC-US, Mins. Bd. Dirs., Sept. 29, 1903, Acc. 85, Bx. 1 (Lockwood) and Oct. 24, 1903 (Selden Patent suit filed).

2. U.S. Bur. of Census, *Census of Manufactures: 1905, Automobiles and Tricycles,* Wash., 1907, gives the number of firms in 1900 as 57; Theodore McManus and Norman Beasley, *Men, Money, and Motors,* N.Y., 1929, 17–18, name 132 firms as operating in the U.S.; *Evening Union* (Springfield, Mass.), Sept. 22, 1893 (Duryea's first run); Allan Nevins and Frank Ernest Hill, *Ford: the Times, the Man, the Company,* N.Y., 1954, 246, hereafter cited as Nevins & Hill, I (Ford production); Det. *News-Tribune,* Feb. 4, 1900 (horses); Arthur Pound, *Turning Wheel,* Garden City, N.Y., 1934, 54, 104 (Olds, Cadillac prod.).

3. Nevins & Hill, I, 277, 221 (Olds and the Smiths; Olds price); Henry Ford, in collab. with Samuel Crowther, *My Life and Work,* Garden City, N.Y., 1923, 22–25 (Ford's early ideas); Ford Catalog, 1903, Acc. 175, Bx. 1 (Ford price); McManus & Beasley, 42 (Olds).

4. FMC-US, Mins. Shareholders Mtg., Sept. 18, 1903; FMC-US, Mins. Bd. Dirs., Oct. 24, 1903, Acc. 85, Bx. 1; Nevins & Hill, I, Chap. 12. Parker advised the stockholders on Sept. 18 that they could successfully oppose the patent. It was not until Jan. 9, 1911, that the U.S. Appellate Court proved him right. For full account of Selden Patent case see William Greenleaf, *Monopoly on Wheels,* Detroit, 1961.

5. Nevins & Hill, I, Chaps. 7–10; Ford, *My Life and Work,* 22 (Ford on the farm); Pound, 103. The Henry Ford Company after Ford's departure was reorganized as the Cadillac Automobile Company. See *Horseless Age,* X, Nov. 5, 1902, 519. This firm later became the Cadillac Motor Car Company.

6. FMC-US, Ledger Bk., Acc. 85, Bx. 8 (cash payments; Rackham paid in the last $1500 for his stock in 1904); Nevins & Hill, I, Chap. 11; *Motor Age,* Mar. 15, 1900, 1–3; George N. Fuller, *Michigan, A Centennial History of the State,* Chicago, 1939, 148 (on early assembly practices).

7. Nevins & Hill, I, 242–43; Harry Barnard, *Independent Man, the Life of Senator James Couzens,* N.Y., 1958, 19–20; Couzens' 1907 passport, Couzens Papers, Birmingham, Mich.; Nevins & Hill, I, Chap. 12 and p. 646.

8. G. G. Huebner, "The Foreign Trade of the United States Since 1780" in Emory R. Johnson, *History of Domestic and Foreign Commerce of the United States,* Wash., 1915, II, 67–70; U.S. Bur. of Census, *Historical Statistics,* Wash., 1949, 242.

9. *The Growth of American Economy,* ed. Harold F. Williamson, N.Y., 1946, 501; C. W. Moore, *Timing a Century,* Cambridge, 1945, 54; Huebner, 68, 73; Frank Southard, *American Industry in Europe,* Boston, 1931, xiii; John Dunning, *American Investment in British Industry,* London, 1958, 18, 32.

10. William Kilbourn, *The Elements Combined, A History of the Steel Company of Canada,* Toronto, 1960, 35; Herbert Marshall, Frank Southard and Kenneth W. Taylor, *Canadian-American Industry,* New Haven, 1936, 3–19; U.S. Dept. of Com., Bur. of For. & Dom. Com., *American Direct Investment in Foreign Countries,* Wash., 1930, 41–42; W. W. Rostow, *Stages in Economic Growth,* Cambridge, 1960, 37.

11. Cleona Lewis, *America's Stake in International Investments,* Wash., 1938, 578, 599–602 and *passim.;* U.S. Dept. of State, Bur. of For. Com., *Commercial Relations of the United States with Foreign Countries, 1900,* Wash., 1901, I, 170, 688 (S. Amer.); Ralph and Muriel Hidy, *Pioneering in Big Business,* N.Y., 1955, 258 (Standard Oil); George Wythe, *Industry in Latin America,* N.Y., 2nd ed., 1949, 102, 294–95, U.S. Bur. of Census, *Historical Statistics,* 250; *Fortune,* XXXII, Nov. 1945, 132.

12. Theodore Roosevelt, *Presidential Addresses,* N.Y., n.d., I, 302 (Roosevelt's speech on April 4, 1903).

13. It is not clear if French output alone exceeded American in 1903 because statistics are unreliable. The Automobile Manufacturers Association gives US production as 4,192 (1900), 7,000 (1901), 9,000 (1902), and 11,235 (1903). The French equivalent of the AMA gives French production for 1900 as 2,000. No information is available for them for 1901–1903 (ltr. A. Selliers of Chambre Syndicale des Constructeurs d'Automobiles, Paris, to Mira Wilkins, Dec. 15, 1960). In Frances Miltoun's *Automobilist Abroad,* Boston, 1907, 350, French production is given as 2,200 (1899), 4,100 (1900), 6,300 (1901), 7,800 (1902), and 11,500 (1903). Lawrence H. Seltzer, using *Automotive Trade Journal* (n.d.) as a source, says in his *Financial History of the American Automobile Industry,* Boston and N.Y., 1928, 18, that in 1902 the French produced 16,500 vehicles as against American output of 11,000! Seltzer's figures appear out of line with the other data.

14. Pound, 47, 243 (Olds sale); *Horseless Age,* XIV, Aug. 3, 1904, 99; U.S. Dept. of Com. & Labor, Bur. of Stats., *Foreign Commerce and Navigation—1904,* Wash., 1905, 188; U.S. Federal Trade Commission, *Report on Motor Vehicle Industry,* 76th Cong., 3rd Sess., House Doc. No. 468, Wash., 1939, 7, henceforth cited as *FTC Report.* On US cars abroad see *Autocar* (London) 1900–03, *Motorwagen* (Berlin) 1900–03, and Paris Auto Show Catalogs in Det. Autov. Col.

15. *Horseless Age,* XIV, July 20, 1904, 66–67; Harold B. Chase, *Auto-Biography,* N.Y., 1955, 16 (1902 Olds); *Autocar* (London), XIV, Feb. 18, 1905, 234 (on Duryea); F. A. Talbot, *Motor Cars and Their Story,* London, 1912, 108–09 (Brit. opinion of Amer. cars); *Horseless Age,* XII, Nov. 25, 1903, 543. The same journal pointed out, "The defeat of the American team in the Gordon Bennett Cup Race has again created the impression abroad that America is several years behind in the construction of automobiles." It denied this. See *ibid,* XII, July 29, 1903, 1.

16. *Horseless Age,* XII, July 8, 1903 (Mexico); U.S. Dept. of State, Bur. of For. Com., *Vehicle Industry in Europe,* Special Consular Report XXI, pt. 2, Wash., 1900, 340, 327, 372, 375 (Eur. car mfrs.), U.S. Dept. of Com., Bur. of For. & Dom. Com., *Argentine Market for Motor Vehicles,* Wash., 1917, 12; L. T. C. Rolt, *Horseless Carriage,* London, 1950, 28–36, 40, 70–74; Charles Wilson and William Reader, *Men and Machines: A History of D. Napier & Son,* London, 1958, 68–79.

17. Wilson & Reader, 71; *The Growth of American Economy,* 503; G. Maxcy and A. Silberston, *The Motor Industry,* Cambridge, 1959, 12–13; Talbot, 108–109; *Automobile Engineer* I, Oct. 1911, 481; *Det. Journal,* Feb. 3, 1912.

18. Nevins & Hill, I, 211–12; ltr. from D. W. Houghton, Bombay, India, Feb. 19, 1896 in *Horseless Age,* I, Apr. 1896, 21.

19. Floyd Clymer, *Treasury of Early American Automobiles, 1875–1925,* N.Y., 1950, 25 (Ford ad); ltrs. and complaints, chiefly in Acc. 1, Bx. 121.

20. Charles H. Bennett, *Reminiscences;* Lockwood's contract, Nov. 11, 1903, Acc. 140, Bx. 5; FMC-US, Mins. Bd. Dirs., Sept. 29 and Oct. 15, 1903, Acc. 85, Bx. 1. The original domestic prices for Model A, as noted, were $750 in Detroit for the runabout and $100 more for the tonneau. But when Lockwood's contract became effective, the directors had already raised the prices to $800 and $900 respectively. This was to be effective Jan. 1, 1904. See Bd. Mins., Oct. 15, 1903, Acc. 85, Bx. 1, and catalogs in Acc. 175, Bx. 1. The prices for Lockwood seem to have been based on the new figures plus freight to New York.

CHAPTER 2

1. Intervs. Don McGregor, Windsor, Ont., May 17, 1961 and Miss Grace Falconer, Windsor, May 17, 1961; Walkerville Wagon Company, payroll records, Record Retention Ctr., FMC-Can., Windsor.
2. The story that Gordon McGregor talked with many automobile manufacturers in Detroit is frequently told in Windsor: intervs. Miss Falconer, Don McGregor, also interv. Rex McInnes in *Windsor Daily Star,* Aug. 14, 1954. Gordon Dewar of FMC-Can. claims to have seen a letter in the vault of the company ("some 35 years ago") wherein Gordon McGregor recounted his interviews with Ford and Leland. This letter does not appear to be in existence now. There seems no reason to doubt this story, although there is no documentary evidence to substantiate it. Nevins & Hill, I, 649 (dividends).
3. Unsigned Statement, undated, Secty's off., FMC-Can., a typed two-page document. From the context, it was clearly written by Gordon McGregor, probably in late June 1904 (henceforth cited as Plan for Canada–1904). Henry Ford, *My Life and Work,* Garden City, N.Y., 1923, 162; interv. Don McGregor.
4. Plan for Canada–1904; that FMC-US could not fill Canadian wants is confirmed in FMC-US, Mins. Bd. Dirs., Apr. 29, 1904, Acc. 85, Bx. 1, when the directors decided "that in as much as their [the Canadian Cycle and Motor Company's] contract had been filled we not accept . . . any new orders while we had unfilled contracts on our books."
5. Canadian Automobile Chamber of Commerce (220 cars); *The Automobilist,* IX, Oct. 1959, 2, and *Autocar,* London, IV, Oct. 21, 1899, 933 (Canadian makes), and XII, Jan. 23, 1904, 107 (Englishman's statement); Plan for Canada–1904 (HF in Canada).
6. Plan for Canada–1904 (HF and suppliers); Donald Creighton, *The Story of Canada,* Boston, 1960, 189–97; O. D. Skelton, *Life and Letters of Sir Wilfrid Laurier,* N.Y., 1922, II, 44; and Gerald S. Graham, *Canada,* London, 1950, 148 (bkgnd.).
7. *Evening Record,* Windsor, May–July 1904, and esp. July 9, 30, 1904; interv. Miss Falconer ("jug town").
8. Ledger Bk., FMC-Can., Windsor (early stockholders); Walkerville Wagon Company, books and records, Record Retention Ctr., FMC-Can., Windsor; Plan for Canada–1904; Agreement between FMC-US, Gordon McGregor, and HF, Aug. 10, 1904, Acc. 363 (henceforth cited as Canadian Agreement) (facilities of wagon works).
9. FMC-US, Mins. Bd. Dirs., June 15, 20, July 19, 23, 1904, Acc. 85, Bx. 1; First Stockholder List, FMC-Can.; *Evening Record,* Windsor, 1905 *passim,* esp. Feb. 19 (Reaume and his appt. to the Cabinet); Joseph Maw to G. M. McGregor, July 25, 1904, Secty's off., FMC-Can.; intervs. Miss Falconer and F. G. Batters, May 1961 (Miss Falconer knew all the early Canadian stockholders personally and was able to identify them by occupation as could Batters. Some of their occupations are in the Ledger Bk., FMC-Can.); Ledger Bk., FMC-Can. (Michigan stockholders).

10. Canadian Agreement; Records Secty's off., FMC-Can.

11. O. J. McDiarmid, *Commercial Policy in the Canadian Economy*, Cambridge, Mass., 1946, 209.

12. R. C. K. Ensor, *England*, Oxford, 1936, 376 (Chamberlain); *Evening Record*, Windsor, May–Aug. 1904 (Finance Minister W. S. Fielding's pronouncements on preferential tariffs were all reported. The story on South African commercial relations appears on p. 1, July 8, 1904). Later in a presentation made by FMC-Can. to the Tariff Inquiry Commission in Windsor, Nov. 30, 1920, the company declared, "The logic of establishing in Canada might be explained as follows (a) to secure the benefits of any Inter-Colonial preferential tariffs either existing or prospective, (b) to effect a saving to the Canadian purchaser as against the imported cost of manufacturing in Canada. . . ." See brief in Acc. 23, Bx. 4. See also Plan for Canada–1904.

13. See p. 23. (English agent); Canadian Agreement; FMC-Can., Mins. Bd. Dirs., Aug. 29, 1904, Secty's off., FMC-Can. (officers of co.); *Evening Record*, Windsor, July 1, 1904 (devil wagons).

14. Plan for Canada–1904; FMC-Can., Mins. Bd. Dirs., Oct. 14, Nov. 8, 11, 1904, Secty's off., FMC-Can.; Gen. Ledger 1904–07, FMC-Can.; John McDougald, Commissioner of Customs, to G. M. McGregor, Jan. 27, 1905, J. S. Urie off., FMC-Can. (suppliers).

15. Gen. Ledger 1904–97, FMC-Can. (all shipments and staff); the figure 114 comes from the gross sales as given in the first annual report, Aug. 31, 1905; it covers only the six-month period. Interv. Miss Falconer (tap-dancing); interv. Don McGregor (Campbell's link with the family); Plan for Canada–1904 (400 units).

16. Arthur Pound, *The Turning Wheel*, Garden City, N.Y., 1934, 47; *Horseless Age*, I, Mar. 1896, 5 and XIV, Dec. 7, 1904, 582.

17. Acctg. and sales records, FMC-Can. (sales figs.); while no contract between Lockwood and FMC-Can. remains, the Gen. Ledger 1904–07 indicates that after May 1906 FMC-Can. exports were handled by Lockwood; interv. Miss Falconer (McGregor's sales methods); personnel records, FMC-Can. (Dickert); Ford, *My Life and Work*, 45 (quote).

18. Interv. Don McGregor; FMC-Can., Mins. Bd. Dirs., Secty's off., FMC-Can.

19. Catalogs, etc., Ford Archives, Dearborn (cars marketed); acctg. and sales records, FMC-Can. (sales; the 327 fig. is included in the 540 total cited earlier); dividend records, FMC-Can.; also James Couzens to Miss R. V. Couzens, Apr. 12, 1912, Couzens Papers, Bx. 1, Libr. of Cong.; Nevins & Hill, 649 (US dividends).

20. *Automobile Topics*, Jan. 31, 1903, 953 (Olds); *Canadian Motor*, Toronto, XII, Aug. 1906, inside leaf; Herbert Marshall, Frank A. Southard, and Kenneth W. Taylor, *Canadian-American Industry*, New Haven, 1936, 63, 65; C. Howard Aikman, *The Automobile Industry of Canada*, Toronto, 1926; Pound, 235–36; and Dept. of Com. and Labor, Bur. of Mfrs., *Foreign Markets for Motor Vehicles*, Wash., 1912, 8 (McLaughlin).

21. Our story differs sharply from that presented by Nevins & Hill, I, 359–60, because of further research. Defunct Co. Records, Central Motor Car Company, #82600, Public Records Office, London (American Motor Car Agency and Central Motor Car Emporium; Blakiston).

22. Interv. Perry (by Nevins & Hill) Mar. 28, 1952; interv. Perry (by Norman St. John Stevas), Sept. 1952 (an attempt at clarification of the first interview which on this point only adds greater confusion); Defunct Co. Records, Central Motor Car Co. (Blakiston agent in 1904). The rights to sell the Ford in England must have been granted prior to Aug. 1904, the date of the FMC-US–FMC-Can. agree-

ment because of the nature of that agreement. FMC-US, Ledger Bk. 1906–07, Acc. 235, Bx. 11 notes in one place that Perry had the rights until Dec. 1, 1907 and in another place that Perry, Thornton, and Schreiber had the rights until Dec. 1, 1909. The rights must have transferred from one agency to the next. No contract however exists.

23. R. M. Lockwood, "Our Foreign Position," *Ford Times,* III, Jan. 15, 1910, 176. Lockwood met with the Ford Board of Directors after his return and "strongly urged the continuance of the Model A as it was preferred by the majority of foreign buyers." Doubtless what he meant was that the Model A was preferred over more expensive models. At his suggestion, the Board scaled down the export prices. FMC-US, Mins. Bd. Dirs., Oct. 28, 1904, Acc. 85, Bx. 1.

24. Defunct Co. Records, Central Motor Car Company. Perry told St. John Stevas that five people were present at the Albemarle Club: Stourton, Perry, Hasslacher, and two others. Blakiston must have been there. We add the name of Russell, who listed in Defunct Co. Records, Central Motor Car Company, as a director of the new company. Interv. Perry, and *Who's Who* (Perry's bkgnd.); L. T. C. Rolt, *Horseless Carriage,* London, 1950, 70–71 and H. G. Castle, *Britain's Motor Industry,* London, 1950, 33, 39 (Lawson).

25. Defunct Co. Records, Central Motor Car Company; interv. Perry (noisy cars, trip to U.S.).

26. Defunct Co. Records, Central Motor Car Company; Defunct Co. Records, Perry, Thornton and Schreiber, #92163, Public Records Office, London; *Autocar,* London, XII, Nov. 10, 1906, 646; *The Car,* London, XIX, Nov. 21, 1906, 28, and XXII, Sept. 1907, 41; interv. Perry; FMC-US, Ledger Bk. 1906–07, Acc. 235, Bx. 11 (102 units).

27. Frances Miltoun, *Automobilist Abroad,* Boston, 1907, 356–61 (European tariffs; nowhere in Europe were the tariffs as high as the U.S. impost of 45 per cent); FMC-US, Ledger Bk., Acc. 85, Bx. 8 (French shipment Mar. 23, 1904); FMC-US, Ledger Bk., Acc. 235, Bx. 11 (List of agents apptd. by Lockwood, as of Apr. 1907 and sales); *Horseless Age,* XVIII, Dec. 26, 1906, 913–14 (French show) and Sept. 5, 1906, 295 (roads in Spain).

28. FMC-US, Ledger Bk., Acc. 235, Bx. 11; FMC-Can., Gen. Ledger, 1904–07 (for Lockwood's activities on behalf of FMC-Can.); interv. R. I. Roberge, Birmingham, Mich., Aug. 1, 1961. Roberge, who was in foreign trade before he joined Ford Motor Company in 1913, has given us the distinctions on type. These are confirmed by entries in ledger books of FMC-Can. and FMC-US. By 1919 about 70 per cent of US export trade was handled through commission houses which charged from $2\frac{1}{2}$ to 5 per cent. See Norbert Savay, *Principles of Foreign Trade,* N.Y., 1919, 90. The use of the commission house was probably higher in the pre-World War I period.

29. *Ford Times,* IV, Apr. 1911, 228.

30. FMC-US, Ledger Bk., Acc. 235, Bx. 11 (agents as of Apr. 1907 and exports); *Motor Trader,* XIII, Dec. 9, 1908, 697 (the Austrian consul in Milan indicated 62 auto. mfrs. in Italy in 1907); Denis Mack Smith, *Italy,* Ann Arbor, 1959, 249 (estimates 70 in Italy in 1905). On Fiat, the most important, see *Fiat: A Fifty Year Record,* Rome, 1951. Minerva, Pipe and F.N. were among the key Belgian makes of this age. *La Nación,* Buenos Aires, Dec. 1, 1961 (Anasagasti). See W. W. Rostow, *Stages in Economic Growth,* Cambridge, 1960, 7, 36ff. (concept of the "take off" period); Nevins & Hill, I, 644 (total sales, from which we have subtracted exports); Lawrence H. Seltzer, *A Financial History of the American Automobile Industry,* Boston and N.Y., 1928, 79 (US exports autos); Sales figs., FMC-Can. (export ratios).

31. *Horseless Age,* XVIII, Dec. 19, 1906, 887.

32. Postcards to EBF, Acc. 1, Bx. 132; Nevins & Hill, I, 330–32 (HF and Couzens gain control).
33. "Couzen talks about export trade conditions," *Automobile*, XVII, Aug. 29, 1907, 308.
34. James Couzens to White, Dec. 23, 1907, Acc. 140, Bx. 5; *Ford Times*, I, July 1, 1908, 18 (White's bkgnd.); FMC-US, Mins. Bd. Dirs., in between Apr. 30, 1908 and Sept. 22, 1908, Acc. 85, Bx. 1 (agreement with H. B. White); FMC-US, Mins. Bd. Dirs., Sept. 22, 1908, Acc. 85, Bx. 1 (approval of agreement); R. M. Lockwood contracts, Nov. 11, 1906 and Dec. 24, 1907, Acc. 140, Bx. 5; picture in *Ford Times* and interv. Miss Vera Howard, Stock, Essex, England, Aug. 10, 1960; *Ford Times*, I, Dec. 15, 1908, 7 (White's address to English Ford agents).
35. *Motor Trader*, XIV, Nov. 18, 1908, 488; "La Nouvelle Voiturette Légère—Ford 1909," *La Voiturette*, I, Nov. 1908, 271.
36. Branch Acctg. Records, Acc. 260, Bx. 1; Automobile Manufacturers Association figs. (auto production); U.S. Bur. of Census, *Historical Statistics*, Wash., 1949, 187 (steel). Steel output would dip in 1908 to 14.0 million long tons in response to the inventories built up during the Panic, only to rise again, in 1909, to 24 million long tons.

CHAPTER 3

1. Horace L. Arnold and Fay Leone Faurote, *Ford Methods and the Ford Shops*, N.Y., 1919, 23 (purchase of land and start of construction); Ford Stockholders' Tax Suit, p. 84, Acc. 84, Bx. 1 (purchase of land); Henry Ford, *My Life and Work*, Garden City, N.Y., 1923; Nevins & Hill, I, 644 (production figs.), 649 (dividends); AMA statistics (for U.S.A. production), *Chambre Syndicale des Constructeurs* (French), Society of Motor Manufacturers and Traders (English), and *Tatsachen und Zahlen aus der Kraftfahrzug Industrie*, Berlin, 1927 (German).
2. U.S. Federal Trade Commission, *Report on Motor Vehicle Industry*, Wash., 1939, 421 (General Motors Co.), 431 and 634 (cash sales of GM and Ford); Arthur Pound, *The Turning Wheel*, N.Y., 1934, 64, 108, 90, 194, and Chap. 8 (prod. figs., founding and merging of cos. in GM); Theodore McManus & Norman Beasley, *Men, Money, and Motors*, N.Y., 1929, 68–72 (possible Ford sale). Oakland was bought and added to GM early in 1909, and Cadillac merged in July 1909. The GM figures for sales are for the year ending Oct. 1, and Ford figures for that ending Dec. 31, 1909.
3. Ralph C. Epstein, *The Automobile Industry*, Chicago, 1928, 76 (other firms); Arnold & Faurote, 23 (first building at Highland Park); H. Ford, *My Life and Work*, 74 (Ford methods); *Cycle and Automobile Trade Journal*, XIV, Dec. 1, 1909, 127–28 (Ford factory); *Det. Journal*, Feb. 16, 1909 (Ford explains methods).
4. *Ford Times*, 1908–13 (feats, advg. and pics.); interv. Perry, in *ibid.*, Apr. 1914, 293, Phila. *Press*, Dec. 15, 1912 and *Boston Transcript*, Dec. 26, 1912, and Eber Sherman to N. A. Hawkins, Dec. 14, 1916, Acc. 76, Bx. 67 (taxicabs); *Ford Times*, IV, Sept. 1911, 342–44, 347 (Lie, White); pics. in Ford Archives and Fritzell Collection (early Fords).
5. Pics., Fritzell Collection, also camouflaged Fords shown in *Autocar*, 1908–11, *passim*, intervs. V. A. Dodge, N.Y., Nov. 23, 29, 1960 (adaptations); "American Automobile Manufacturers Protest Tariff Reduction," *Horseless Age*, XXIX, Apr. 3, 1912, 623–26 (Couzens letter, attitude of others); Horace Wyatt, *The Motor Industry*, London, 1917, 3 (subsidies); R. M. Lockwood, "Our Foreign Position," *Ford Times*, III, Jan. 15, 1910, 177. Congress attempted to aid the Merchant Marine in 1913, but its rider in the tariff law was voided by the Supreme Court. See J. E. Otterson, *Foreign Trade and Shipping*, N.Y., 1945, 190.

6. FMC-US, Mins. Bd. Dirs., July 28, 1909, Acc. 85, Bx. 1 (Couzens given authority); Nevins & Hill, I, 649–50 (dividends); data in branch acctg. records, Acc. 260, Bx. 1 (White's record); *Ford Times,* I, July 15, 1908, 13 (Sweepstakes and Perry's leaving); Defunct Co. Records, Perry, Thornton and Schreiber, #92103, Public Record Office, London (Schreiber, and also Perry departures); interv. Miss Vera Howard, Stock, Essex, England, Aug. 10, 1960 (Perry and the Thorntons, Perry and HF, Perry with Reo); Perry to HF, Apr. 15, 1909 and reply Apr. 27, 1909, Acc. 2, Bx. 30.

7. Corresp. 1904–14, Perry and Mrs. Perry with HF and Mrs. HF and interv. Miss Howard as cited in note 6 (Perry's regard for Ford and the FMC); payroll records, Acc. 235, Bx. 5 (Perry's salary); Branch Acctg. Records, Acc. 260, Bx. 1 (London and Paris branches—financial status).

8. FMC-Can. Mins. Annl. Mtg., Oct. 5, 1909 and HF to Campbell, Nov. 24, 1909, both in Mins. Bd. Dirs., Secty's off., FMC-Can.; Branch Acctg. Records, Acc. 260, Bx. 1 (Perry's work force).

9. *Ford Times,* III, Oct. 1, 1909 (Melbourne, Durance), III, June 15, 1910, 14 (Australia), and III, Dec. 1, 1909, 88 and George Wythe, *Industry in Latin America,* N.Y., 2nd ed., 1949, 276 (Mexico); Foreign Dealer's Agreement, 1912–13, Acc. 76, Bx. 66; FMC-US, Mins. Bd. Dirs., Feb. 5, 1909, Acc. 85, Bx. 1 (authority to Hawkins); C. H. Bennett, *Reminiscences* (Couzens-Lockwood); *Ford Times,* 1910–12, *passim* (Harper, Vanderpoel); Roberge, *Reminiscences* (Hampton, work of NY office). Roberge recalled that Hampton was heading the foreign department when he (Roberge) joined the FMC in 1913.

10. *Christian Science Monitor,* Oct. 12, 1912; Fin. Records, FMC-Can.; FMC-Can., Bd. Dirs. Min. Bk., Secty's off., FMC-Can. (stock traded at $500 a share Jan.–May 1913); Nevins & Hill, I, 644 (Ford-US sales) and 649–50 (Ford-US dividends); FMC-Can. Brief to the Tariff Commission, Acc. 23, Bx. 4 (Canadian sales).

11. George Dickert, *Reminiscences;* Records of Property Mgt. Dept., FMC-Can. (plant expansion); FMC-Can. Mins. Bd. Dirs. 1908–14, *passim* (plans and progress); *Windsor Daily Star,* Apr. 3, 1954 (Ford City).

12. *Ford Times* (Can.), I, Aug. 1913, 29 (new branches); *ibid.,* (US) VI, May 1913, 348 (Walkerville prod.) and VI, Jan. 1914, 166 (Lawrence quote and FMC-Can. *v.* other Canadian prod.).

13. Personnel Records, FMC-Can. Windsor (Canadian officials); FMC-Can. Annual Mtgs., 1906–09, *passim* (Canadian and American officers of co.). Lawrence had formerly been sales manager of the Motor Wagon Company, Detroit.

14. FMC-Can. Brief to Tariff Commission, Nov. 30, 1920, Acc. 23, Bx. 4 (percentage of exports to total); *Ford Times* (Can.), I, Oct. 1913, 126 (Canadian and USA exports); FMC-US, Mins. Bd. Dirs., Dec. 30, 1910, Acc. 85, Bx. 1 ($2\frac{1}{2}$ per cent paymt.).

15. Intervs. Dodge, Nov. 23, 29, 1960; interv. Sir Rowland Smith, London, Aug. 23, 1960 (Russa Engineering); *Autocar,* XXVIII, Nov. 11, 1911, 978 (the Durbar: Fiats and Rolls-Royces also there); *Ford Times* (Can.), I, May 1914, 485 (H. T. Dodge on Eastern trade); Dept. of Com. and Labor, Bur. of Mfrs., *Foreign Markets for Motor Vehicles,* Wash., 1912, 111 (conds. in East).

16. *Ford Times* (Can.), I, Dec. 1913, 215 (Arkell & Douglas); data on Ford in S. Africa from N. du Preez, Port Elizabeth, June 21, 1961, and Eric Rosenthal, *The Story of Holmes Motor Company,* n.p. [published in S. Africa], n.d. [1957?] (Wessinger and Holmes, etc.).

17. *Ford Times* (Can.), I, July 1914, 548; *ibid.,* (US) III, Feb. 1, 1910, 180 (McGregor

on Australia); interv. R. J. Durance in *S.F. Examiner,* Oct. 13, 1912 (Fords in Australia).

18. *Ford Times,* IV, Sept. 1911, 369 (Manchester plant); "Where Should My Factory Be?" pamphlet by Trafford Park Estates Ltd., n.d. [about 1931] (description of Trafford tract); FMC Ltd. Chronology, FMC-Eng. (start of plant); Perry to HF, Feb. 26, 1913, Acc. 2, Bx. 59 (quote on location).

19. *Glasgow News,* May 29, 1911 (Ben Nevis); *Ford Times,* IV, Sept. 1911, 369 (Manchester plant almost ready); Records in Secty's off., FMC-US (incorporation); Branch Reports, Acc. 26, Bx. 2 (sales FMC-Eng. Ltd 1909–11); F. L. Klingensmith, Detroit, to Commissioner of Interl. Rev., Eng., Sept. 16, 1912, FMC-Eng. (profits).

20. Diaries of Clara Ford and EBF, Acc. 1, Bxes. 21 and 31.

21. Perry to HF, Feb. 26, 1913, Acc. 62, Bx. 59 (freehold *v.* lease); *Ford Times* (Can.), I, Dec. 1913, 240 (capacities of three plants).

22. Perry to HF, as in note 21 (Manchester labor troubles); CES to H. S. Jenkins, Sept. 9, 1926, Acc. 38, Bx. 52 (job security); CES to HF, June 3, 1914, Acc. 62, Bx. 59 (CES's gen. activities); J. M. A. Smith to Moekle, Aug. 15, 1946, Acc. 134, Bx. 37 (in July 1913 outside body plant was acquired).

23. CES to HF, as in note 22 (gen. situation); pics. Model T in *Autocar* XXXI and XXXII (right-hand drive); advertisements in *ibid.* (special bodies); interv. Perry (by Nevins and Hill), Mar. 28, 1952 (modifications of Ford cars by dealers).

24. See for example advertisement by Lookers Ltd., Manchester, in *Autocar,* XXX, July 6, 1912, ix (Austins, Crossleys, Fords); Perry to Hawkins, Aug. 18, 1914, Acc. 62, Bx. 59 (Perry's sales methods).

25. FMC-Eng. (Ford sales); G. Maxcy and A. Silberston, *The Motor Industry,* London, 1959, 12 (output of competition); *Ford Times,* VII, Apr. 1914, 397 (Perry quote); Maxcy & Silberston, 12 (total pass. car prodn.); Report from London correspondent in *Inter-Ocean* (Chicago, Ill.,), Oct. 13, 1912 (British industry's response to American intrusion); F. A. Talbot, *Motor Cars and Their Story,* London, 1912, 109 and Horace Wyatt, *The Motor Industry,* London, 1917, 31 (response of British public); P. W. S. Andrews and Elizabeth Brunner, *The Life of Lord Nuffield,* Oxford, 1955, 59 (Morris-Oxford) and 71 (quote).

26. Arnold & Faurote, 1 (Ford plant), 245 (commutator); Samuel Reznick, "Mass Production Since the War Between the States," in *The Growth of American Economy,* ed. by H. F. Williamson, N.Y., 1946, 513, 515, and throughout Chap. 22.

27. Nevins & Hill, I, 644–47; Pound, Chaps. 8 and 9, and particularly p. 141. General Motors had fallen on evil days because of Durant's over-expansion. In 1913 it was under the control of bankers.

28. Nevins & Hill, I, Chap. 20, and particularly p. 519; FMC-Eng. Ltd., "Notice to Employees," Apr. 17, 1914, Acc. 62, Bx. 60, and CES to HF, June 3, 1914, Acc. 62, Bx. 59 (pay in England); *Ford Times* (Can.), II, May 1915, 387ff; FMC-Can., Mins. Bd. Dirs., Oct. 27, 1913, Secty's off, FMC-Can. (Canadian labor policy).

29. Perry to Klingensmith, Sept. 6, 1917, Acc. 6, Bx. 260 (English cars to continent); *Annuaire Officiel des Abonnés aux Réseaux Téléphoniques de la Région de Paris,* Jan. 1, 1908, 1909, and 1910 issues (*Depasse's* addresses); Acct. Bk., Acc. 208, Bx. 3 (Bordeaux); Financial Statement [Oct. 1914], Couzens Papers, Birmingham, Mich. (Paris sales).

30. Ford-Eng. Ltd., Automobile Sales Record, 1912–13, FMC-Eng. (Sweden); Carl Thalbitzer, *Ford Motor Company: Gennem 25 Aar,* København, 1944, 15 (Denmark); Dept. of Com. & Labor, Bur. of For. and Dom. Com., *Development of Motor Vehicle Trade Abroad,* Wash., 1913, 30 (Spain); Perry to Klingensmith, Sept. 6, 1917, Acc. 6, Bx. 260 (Russia's standing); Ford-Eng. Ltd., Automobile Sales Record, 1912–13,

FMC-Eng. (Russian shipments); *Ford Times* (Can.), I, Nov. 1913, 165–66 (Friede's acct.).

31. *Ford Times* (U.S.), V, Jan. 1912, 116 (like a religion); Dept. of Com. & Labor, Bur. of Mfrs., *Foreign Markets for Motor Vehicles,* Wash., 1912, 68 (American cars in Germany); L. Mainyess, Paris, to Oscar Permeke, June 11, 1912, Permeke Papers, Antwerp (quote is a translation from the French); Dept. of Com. & Labor, *Development of Motor Vehicle Trade Abroad,* Wash., 1913, 12, 34 (Vanderpoel); A. Tuma to E. G. Liebold, Aug. 18, 1920, Acc. 284, Bx. 13 (German branch, Tuma); CES to HF, June 3, 1914, Acc. 62, Bx. 59 (German trip). The government's reference is clearly to Vanderpoel, although neither he nor the FMC was mentioned by name. Interv. Miss Howard (White and Perry); Couzens to H. S. Morgan, Feb. 4, 1913, Couzens Papers, Bx. 1, Lib. of Cong. (dispute between White and Perry); L. C. Griffin, Asst. European Mgr. to Oscar Permeke, July 11, 1913, Permeke Papers, Antwerp (quote).

32. FMC-Can., Annual Report, 1914 (Can. prodn.); Fin. Statement, Couzens Papers, Birmingham, Mich. (Eng. sales); *Commercial and Financial Chronicle,* XCVII, July 19, 1913, 148 (trade with Latin America); *Ford Times,* 1913, *passim* (FMC business); *Foreign Markets for Motor Vehicles,* 46, 48, 40 (Chile, Peru, Venezuela) and 40–43, 49 (Argentina, Brazil, Uruguay); Ellis Hampton to Couzens, Mar. 24, 1917, Couzens Papers, Birmingham, Mich. (Couzens the promoter of South American branch); FMC-US, Mins. Bd. Dirs., Dec. 31, 1913, Acc. 85, Bx. 1, and Pittsburgh *Press,* Oct. 12, 1913 (Hampton assigned Buenos Aires branch).

33. Hampton to Couzens, as in note 32 (conds. in Argentina); George Wythe, *Industry in Latin America,* N.Y., 2nd ed., 1949, 83 (same); Acc. 140, Bx. 5 (lease); Hampton, Buenos Aires, to Couzens, Jan. 22, 1914, Acc. 76, Bx. 66 (Chile); contracts, Acc. 76, Bx. 66 (other agents).

34. Contract, FMC with Markt & Hammacher, Oct. 1, 1913, Acc. 76, Bx. 66. The 1914–15 contract raised the commission to 3 per cent.

35. Klingensmith to Couzens, Mar. 2, 1914 and McGregor to Couzens, Feb. 26, 1914, both in Couzens Papers, Bx. 1, Lib. of Cong. (Canadian prodn.); Perry to HF, Feb. 25, 26, 1913 (Eng. plant, Ireland), CES to HF, June 3, 1914 (Perry's British Empire plans), and Perry to Hawkins, Aug. 18, 1914 (quote on Britain and Empire), all in Acc. 62, Bx. 59.

36. CES to HF, June 3, 1914, Acc. 62, Bx. 59 and Report of H. B. White, June 1, 1914, Acc. 62, Bx. 60 (European plants); Perry to Hawkins, as in note 35 (Perry's idea of European assembly); Perry to Klingensmith, July 23, 1914, Acc. 62, Bx. 56, and paper on option in Lovell and White Records, Permanent Files, FMC-Eng. (extension of option). It was extended to Dec. 30, 1914.

CHAPTER 4

1. Perry to Hawkins, Aug. 18, 1914, Acc. 62, Bx. 99; *Ford Times* (Eng.), III, Oct. 1914, 67 (editorial), 76–77 (first ambulances); "War office" folder with invoices, Permanent File, FMC-Eng.

2. Perry to Hawkins, *loc. cit.*

3. Interv. Perry (by Nevins and Hill), Mar. 28, 1952 (English volunteers); Couzens to R. L. Jobling, Nov. 9, 1914, Couzens Papers, Bx. 1, Lib. of Cong.; "War office" folder, Permanent File, FMC-Eng. (ambulance orders with prices); St. John Stevas, "Ford in the United Kingdom," MS. with English Ford Co. (shells); *Ford Times* (Eng.), III, Oct. 1914, 76–77 and Nov. 1914, 119 (ambulances).

4. Perry-HF Corresp., Acc. 1, Bx. 145.

5. Stevas (enlistments); Perry to Col. Holder of War Office, Apr. 14, 1915 (training proposals), "War Trade Dept." folder (exports), and Perry to Capt. F. H. Browning of War Office, May 7, 1916, Permanent File, FMC-Eng.

6. Shepard Bancroft Clough and Charles Woolsey Cole, *Economic History of Europe,* Boston, 1941, 722 (McKenna duties); Stevas (new facilities).

7. *Det. Free Press,* Aug. 22, 1915 (Ford on war); James Couzens to Milton A. McRae, Nov. 19, 1915, Couzens Papers, Lib. of Cong., Bx. 2. The *Daily Mail* and other English papers were angered by Ford's pacifistic statements.

8. Nevins & Hill, II, 25–39. The Peace Ship cruise was arranged for in a few days, and many prominent Americans could not sail on it. Also, the management of the venture was extremely haphazard.

9. *Daily Mail,* Nov. 18, 20, 24, 1915; *N.Y. Herald,* Dec. 2, 1915 (official's comment).

10. Perry to editor of *Pall Mall Gazette,* Dec. 2, 1915; Perry-Liebold cables and ltrs., Dec. 1915, Acc. 62, Bx. 19; Perry to HF, Dec. 8, 1915, Acc. 1, Bx. 145; Nevins & Hill, II, Chap. 2 (Ford's leaving Peace Ship; subsequent events related to peace work in Europe, etc.).

11. Perry to HF, Feb. 25, 26, 1913, Acc. 62, Bx. 59; FMC-Eng. Ltd., Secty William Barnes to Lovell and White (lawyers), Feb. 23, 1915, Permanent File, FMC-Eng. (purchase Ridgeway); Perry to R. J. White, July 2, 1915, in *ibid.* (Southampton idle); Perry to EBF, Dec. 19, 1918, Acc. 6, Bx. 456 (Sorensen, Milbrook site).

12. L. C. Griffin (White's asst.) to H. B. White, Aug. 26, 1915, Acc. 334, Bx. 1 (tax position, sales, etc.).

13. Perry to Mrs. HF, May 15, 1916, Acc. 1, Bx. 145; FMC-US, Mins. Bd. Dirs., Oct. 31, 1916, Acc. 85, Bx. 1 (White's power in France canceled); Automobiles Ford, Mins. Bd. Dirs., May 25, 1916, Acc. 606, Bx. 1 (formation and stockholders); Gaston Plantiff, Stockholm, to Liebold, July 26, 1916, Acc. 23, Bx. 6; Perry to Liebold, June 20, 1916, Acc. 62, Bx. 20; Perry to Klingensmith, Apr. 10, 1918, Acc. 6, Bx. 240 (gen. cond. in France); Automobiles Ford, Mins. Bd. Dirs., Dec. 17, 1917 (Vandersmissen discharged) Stats. of Cars Delivered to Continental Europe, 1914–17, Acc. 6, Bx. 260; Acc. 284, Bx. 27 (ambulance order).

14. Frank P. Chambers, *The War Behind the War, 1914–1918,* London, 1936, 413, 416.

15. T. H. Middleton, *Food Production in the War,* Oxford, 1923, *passim;* Farkas, *Reminiscences* (final 1916 model, 50 units); *Motor Age,* XXXII, Aug. 23, 1917, 12 (lightning flash).

16. Perry to HF, Feb. 25, 26, 1913, Acc. 62, Bx. 59 (Cork site); interv. Perry (Lloyd George suggests Cork factory, Perry's feelings); *N.Y. World,* Nov. 23, 1916 (Perry's agent in Cork); HF & Son Ltd., Mins. Bd. Dirs., Secty's off., FMC-US (HF & Son orgd.); Perry to EBF, May 8, 1917, Acc. 44, Bx. 14 (act passed by Parliament); FMC-US, Mins. Bd. Dirs., Jan. 28, 1916, Acc. 85, Bx. 1 (settlement); HF & Son, Inc., Arts. of Assn., July 27, 1917, Ford Archives; Cork *Examiner,* Mar. 19, 1917 (map of Cork site, comment); *Times* (London), Mar. 26, 1917 (O'Donnell).

17. Farkas, *Reminiscences* and C. E. Sorensen, *My Forty Years with Ford,* N.Y., 1956, 236 (sending tractors); Perry to HF, Feb. 28, 1917, Doc. no. 150059, Ferg.-M. (arrival tractors); H. A. Bate to CES, Mar. 23, 1917, Doc. no. 15773, Ferg.-M.; Perry to CES, Mar. 28, 1917, Acc. 38, Bx. 44; Perry to EBF, Apr. 7, 1917, Acc. 6, Bx. 260 (proposal to manufacture in England); HF to Perry, Apr. 8, 1917, Acc. 266, Bx. 1 (Ford's reply); Acc. 62, Bx. 26 (ltrs. of introduction for CES and other Ford men).

18. CES to HF, May 17, 18, 1917, Doc. nos. 15780 and 15782, Ferg-M. (arrival; nuts, bolts, etc.); Katie Perry to Mrs. HF, June 4, 1917, Acc. 1, Bx. 145; C. Addison to HF, July 2, 1917, Doc. no. 15793, Ferg-M. (impression of CES and staff, war cabinet decision); Lloyd George to Perry, June 28, 1917, Doc. no. 47240, Ferg-M.; interv. E. C. Kanzler, June 11, 1956 (Northcliffe persuades Ford); *London Weekly Times,* Oct. 26, 1917 (Northcliffe on tractor); Acc. 328, Bx. 1 (for contract and relevant ltrs.).

19. Addison to Perry, June 28, 1917, Doc. no. 47241, Ferg-M.; tractor prodn. stats., FMC-US; Northcliffe to HF, Mar. 1, 1918, Doc. no. 47337, Ferg-M.; HF to Northcliffe, Mar. 10, 1918, Doc. no. 33973, Ferg-M. (improvement in shipments); Northcliffe to HF, Mar. 13, 1918, Doc. no. 47333, Ferg-M. (Lloyd George's role); Sherman to Liebold, Mar. 20, 1918, Doc. no. 34044, Ferg-M. (3,000 kd. and 3,000 bu.).

20. Middleton, 225–226, 232–235, 257; Underdown to HF, Feb. 21, 1919, Acc. 6, Bx. 260; Fordson Sales Facts, Acc. 179, Bx. 3; insert entitled "Distribution of the Ford Tractor," in *Ford News* (Can.), II, Feb. 1918, 1 (defines FMC-Can.'s position).

21. Horace Wyatt, *Motor Transports in the War,* London, 1914, Chap. 2. Wyatt, writing at the beginning of the war (late 1914), was describing what might and ought to be done as much as what had been done but gives a number of valuable pictures of different types of automotive vehicles.

22. *Ford Times* (Can.), III, Nov. 1918, 118 (gasoline); *History of the Ministry of Munitions,* n.p. [London ?], 1922, 8 vols: Vol. II, App. 3, and Vol. VII, 49; Society of Motor Manufacturers and Traders, *Motor Vehicle Industry of Great Britain,* London, 1960, 11 (European prodn.); Sun Life Assurance Co., *Canadian Automotive Industry,* Ottawa, 1956, 6 (Canadian prodn.); Automobile Manufacturers Association, Detroit (American prodn.).

23. Col. A. M. Henniker, *Transportation on the Western Front, 1914–1918,* London, 1937, 147–148 (divisional equipment), 152–153 (Verdun); A. D. Ellis, *The Story of the Fifth Australian Division,* London, n.d. [1920?], 6–7; *The Australian Army Medical Services in the War of 1914–1918,* Melbourne, 1930, 28, 107, 274, 421.

24. *Ford Times* (Eng.), III, Nov. 1914, 118 (quote on Ford); Acc. 44, Bx. 14 (Perry's list of noted persons commenting on car); Perry to EBF, May 31, 1918, Acc. 6, Bx. 260; *Ford Times* (Can.), Special War Issue, June 1915, 9, 30 (quotes from officers, function).

25. *Ford Times* (Eng.), II, Sept. 1914, 51; Brief for Tariff Inquiry Com., Nov. 30, 1920, Acc. 23, Bx. 4 (prodn. figs.); *Ford Times* (Can.), Special War Issue, 195, 251; Charles G. D. Roberts, *Canada in Flanders,* London, 1918, 8; *Ford Times* (Can.), Oct. 1917 and Nov.–Jan. 1917–18.

26. *Ford Times* (Can.), Special War Issue, 4; Clement Hirtzel, "Helping in East Africa," in *ibid.,* 47; ltr. Arkell & Douglas (Port Elizabeth, S. Africa) to FMC-Can., July 22, 1918, in *Ford News* (Can.), III, Oct. 1918, 7 (British East Africa). See Chap. 3 on Arkell & Douglas.

27. Interv. H. A. Denne, June 19, 1961; interv. Sir Rowland Smith, London, June 26, 1961; McGregor address to shareholders, Oct. 27, 1919, Secty's Off., FMC-Can.; W. T. Massey, *Allenby's Final Triumph,* London, 1920, 14, 155–158; B. H. Liddell Hart, *Colonel Lawrence: the Man Behind the Legend,* N.Y., 1934, 212, 235, 263; T. E. Lawrence, *Revolt in the Desert,* N.Y., 1927, *passim;* Gaston Plantiff to E. G. Liebold, Mar. 24, 1919, Acc. 62, Bx. 107 (Lowell Thomas); *A Brief Record of the Advance of the Egyptian Expeditionary Force under the Command of General Sir Edmund Allenby, Compiled from Official Sources,* London, 1919, 97.

28. Nevins & Hill, II, 64–80 (US war contribution); George Dickert, *Reminiscences*

(Eagle boats); McGregor's address to shareholders at FMC-Can. Annual Mtg., Oct. 28, 1918, Secty's off., FMC-Can. (eagle boats, tanks, and quote).

29. Sales Dept., FMC-Can. (exports); Acc. 6, Bx. 260; and FMC-Eng. files.

30. HF & Son Ltd. Mins. Bd. Dirs., Oct. 22, 1918.

31. Perry to Klingensmith, Perry to EBF, both Apr. 10, 1918, Acc. 6, Bx. 260.

32. Perry to EBF, Dec. 19, 1918, Acc. 6, Bx. 456; Klingensmith to EBF, Feb. 3, 5, 1919 and CES to Perry, Feb. 24, 1919, Select File; Knudsen to Klingensmith, Mar. 4, 1919 (sent from Manchester) and Mar. 15, 1919 (poor health), both in Acc. 334, Bx. 1; Perry to CES, Sept. 30, 1919, Acc. 328, Bx. 1 (fainting spells).

33. Knudsen to Klingensmith, Mar. 4, 1919; unsigned memo (in Knudsen's handwriting), entitled "Perry Memorandum," Mar. 4, 1919; and Knudsen to Klingensmith, Mar. 15, 1919, Acc. 334, Bx. 1 (Knudsen's reports); FMC-Eng., Mins. Bd. Dirs., Jan. 14, 1919, Secty's off., FMC-US (details of truck plan); Knudsen to Klingensmith, Aug. 31, 1919, Acc. 334, Bx. 1 (hire purchase and insurance).

34. FMC-Eng. Annual Mtg., Apr. 24, 1919, Secty's off. (postponement); interv. E. C. Kanzler, Jan. 14, 1960 and HF guest book, Apr. 25, 1919, Acc. 285, Bx. 492 (Mobbs's presence); HF guest book, Apr. 29, 1919, Acc. 285, Bx. 492 (Perry mtg.); Perry to EBF, May 30, 1919, Acc. 6, Bx. 270 (EBF's presence at mtg.); Perry to CES, Sept. 30, 1919, Acc. 328, Bx. 1 (HF feels his running of motor business "not . . . altogether successful"); interv. Perry (by Nevins & Hill), Mar. 28, 1952 (Southampton matter); Alfred Lucking to Knudsen, May 11, 1919, Secty's off., FMC-US and FMC-Eng., Mins. Bd. Dirs., Aug. 28, 1919 and Mins. Annual Mtg., Apr. 15, 1920 (HF purchases English-owned shares); Perry to EBF, Sept. 30, 1919, Acc. 328, Bx. 1 (*re:* salaried position with HF & Son, Ltd. offered him at time of his resignation from FMC); Notice to Stockholders, FMC-Eng., May 5, 1919, Acc. 62, Bx. 90 (Perry's resignation); HF & Son, Ltd., Mins. Bd. Dirs., Sept. 29, 1919 and Oct. 20, 1919, Secty's off., FMC-US and Perry to CES, Sept. 30, 1919, Acc. 328, Bx. 1 (Perry leaves HF & Son, Ltd.).

35. Interv. Perry (by Nevins and Hill), Mar. 28, 1952; materials and answered questionnaire by G. A. Mobbs (son of Noel), Nov. 17, 1961; London *Daily Mail*, Apr. 12, 1920. The American vehicles bought in France (also 15,000) also cost £7,000,000, but did not prove profitable because of exposure to the weather. Perry spent, according to G. A. Mobbs, only a few days a month on Slough after 1922. The Estates were later expanded and are an active operation today.

36. Sir Compton Mackenzie to Frank Ernest Hill, Oct. 31, 1961 (Perry's arrival, lease); R. M. Lockley, *The Charm of the Channel Islands,* London, 1950, 58–59 (description of Herm); Catherine and Percival Perry, *The Island of Enchantment,* London, 1926 (description of the island, called "Hame," in both prose and verse); G. A. Mobbs to Frank Ernest Hill (his questionnaire), Nov. 17, 1961 (date of lease).

37. HF to Perry, Oct. 9, 1919, Acc. 1, Bx. 145.

Chapter 5

1. John Maynard Keynes, *Economic Consequences of the Peace,* N.Y., 1920, *passim,* esp. 36, 273, 274; *Dearborn Independent,* XIX, Aug. 16, 1919 and XX, Dec. 6, 1919, 4; W. Ashworth, *Short History of International Economy,* London, 1952, 187–88.

2. In Apr. 1918 Congress had passed the Webb-Pomerene Bill, which allowed exporters to ally with one another without fear of prosecution under antitrust laws. U.S. Bur.

of Census, *Historical Statistics,* Wash., 1949, 244 and 242 (figs. on exports and investments overseas).

3. *Dearborn Independent,* XXIV, Apr. 9, 1921, 4; U.S. Senate, Com. on the Judiciary, Rpt. of Subcom. on Antitrust and Monopoly, *Administered Prices—Automobiles,* Wash., 1958, 5 (Ford era).

4. Nevins & Hill, II, 686 (Ford world sales 1919, 1,047,858), 200ff. (Rouge), 110 (acquisition stock), 111 (quote), 105 (Edsel becomes pres.); FMC-Eng., Finance Staff, Historical Review, Mar. 31, 1959, 1–2 (stock acquisitions; a few dirs'. qualifying shares were of course not held by the family).

5. Intervs. European Ford executives, summer 1960 ("American period"); Nevins & Hill, II, 254 (trucks); Henry Ford, *My Life and Work,* Garden City, N.Y., 1923, 204 (quote).

6. Deptl. com., Knudsen to Hampton, Feb. 10, 1919, Vault, FMC-Arg., La Boca (summary of mtg.); dealer contracts, Acc. 76, Bx. 66; Sales Dept., FMC-Arg. (1915 sales); *Caras y Caretas,* XVII-XVIII, 1914–15, *passim* (competition); interv. Frederick Foss Dover, Buenos Aires, Nov. 22, 1961 (gen. situation 1916); Gen. Ledger, FMC-Arg. (rent paid on Calle Peru 752 from Oct. 1, 1916), salary roll, FMC-Arg. (personnel).

7. Hampton to Couzens, Mar. 24, 1917, Couzens Papers, Birmingham, Mich. (divided factories; gen. situation); interv. William Bryan, Buenos Aires, Nov. 21, 1961 (gen. situation); Hampton to Klingensmith, Apr. 9, 1917, Acc. 140, Bx. 5 (recommends purchase of land); Accts. Receivable Ledger, Aug. 1916–17, FMC-Arg. (dealer contracts); U.S. Dept. of Com. & Labor, Bur. of Mfrs., *Foreign Markets for Motor Vehicles,* Wash., 1912, 46 (Chile); FMC-Arg., Balance Sheet (Dec. 1917 figs. and totals for the year); Perry to EBF, Sept. 6, 1917, Acc. 6, Bx. 260 (FMC-Fr. figs.).

8. Luis P. O'Farrell to Hampton, Apr. 3, 1917 and Hampton to Klingensmith, Apr. 9, 1917, Acc. 140, Bx. 5 (condns. in Argentina); FMC-US, Mins. Bd. Dirs., May 1, 1917, Acc. 85, Bx. 1 (approval of plant); Mrs. Hampton to HF, Sept. 28, 1917 and EBF's penciled notation, "He says nothing doing for the present," in Acc. 62, Bx. 4.

9. FMC-Arg., Balance Sheet (sales figs.); deptl. com. Knudsen to Hampton, Feb. 10, 1919, Vault, FMC-Arg., La Boca; Gen. Ledger and Check Register, FMC-Arg. (locations rented); FMC-US, Mins. Bd. Dirs., Apr. 24, 1919, Acc. 85, Bx. 1 (approval branch in Brazil); Gen. Ledger, FMC-Brazil (expense acct. items indicate founding group, transfer capital); Check Register, FMC-Brazil (E. A. Evans signs as mgr. from start); Gen. Ledger, FMC-Brazil (rentals); W. A. Ryan to Evans, Dec. 15, 1920, Select File (refers to start of assembly). In studying Ford's South American branch operations it is an error (occasionally made in Ford company records) to date any of them from the time a company was incorporated. FMC-Arg. began as a branch of FMC-US, and remained such until 1959, when a corporation came into being. In Brazil the Ford company started to do business in May 1919. Four years later, in 1923, the Ford Motor Company of Brazil—a Delaware corporation—was formed; it was a wholly-owned subsidiary of FMC-US. This subsidiary's title was changed to Ford Motor Company, Exports, Inc. in 1925, and for many years Ford operated in Brazil under this name. (FMC, Exports, Inc. also had branches in Egypt, Turkey, and China.) See Appendix II.

10. Kristian Orberg, Report on Agent in Uruguay, Mr. Juan Shaw, of Montevideo, Dec. 16, 1919, Orberg Papers, São Paulo; Conf. Memo, June 23, 1920, Acc. 6, Bx. 34 (approval of branch in Uruguay); Hampton to Orberg, July 13, 1920, Orberg Papers, São Paulo (cable); interv. Kristian Orberg, São Paulo, Nov. 7, 1961.

11. E. B. Arnold to B. R. Brown, July 3, 1920 (Argentine plant discussed with Hamp-

ton); and deptl. com., Feb. 10, 1919 (Knudsen's agreement), Vault, FMC-Arg., La Boca; Louis Kahn to FMC, Feb. 21, 1919, Acc. 117, Bx. 1 (confirms contract with Albert Kahn); Chambers & Thomas to Hampton, Mar. 24, 1919, Vault, FMC-Arg., La Boca (local architect goes over plans); deed, Feb. 14, 1920, FMC-Arg.; interv. Dover (other side of river); B. R. Brown, corresp., Apr.–Oct. 1920, Vault, FMC-Arg., La Boca (Brown's and Hampton's activities); Conf. Memo, June 23, 1920, Acc. 6, Bx. 34 (approval São Paulo plant); *Autocar,* XLIV, Mar. 13, 1920, 475 (Ford's first place).

12. The first visit was in Mar. 1919: Knudsen to Klingensmith, Mar. 4, 1919, Acc. 334, Bx. 1 (arrived safely); he left for Europe again on May 15, 1919, see William Knudsen, Report Dealing with Establishment of Foreign Branches and Development of Foreign Business, Oct. 1, 1919, Acc. 95, Bx. 1 (hereafter cited as Knudsen Report); (Knudsen's findings in Germany); FMC-US, Mins. Bd. Dirs., June 25, 1919, Acc. 85, Bx. 1 (authorization of German sub.); Sales Dept. FI (R. Baker), FMC-US (sales figs.).

13. G. R. Doyle, *The World's Automobiles, 1880–1955,* London, 2nd ed., 1957, *passim* (40 makes); *A.C.A.* (Buenos Aires), II, Aug. 1919, 20 (gen. bkgnds. European industry); Jacques Rousseau, *Histoire Mondiale de l'Automobile,* Paris (?), 1958, 202–06, 209, 228.

14. Knudsen Report (his plans); *Ford Times,* I, Aug. 1, 1908, 6 ("Fuzzy" Anderson, branch mgr. St. Louis); Conf. Memo June 22, 1920, Acc. 6, Bx. 34 and Grace to CES, Aug. 5, 1920, Acc. 38, Bx. 46 (Anderson has responsibility for all European business); *Automotive Industries,* XLI, Aug. 28, 1919, 446 (new policies); Knudsen Report (views on France); Citroën to CES, June 30, 1919 and reply, July 1, 1919, Acc. 38, Bx. 132; Liebold to Joseph Bailie, Feb. 18, 1922, Acc. 285, Bx. 84 (quote).

15. FMC-US, Mins. Bd. Dirs., May 13, 1919, Acc. 85, Bx. 1 (authority to establish Danish and Spanish cos.); Knudsen Report (gen. findings); Knudsen, Copenhagen, to Klingensmith, July 1, 1919, Secty's off., FMC-US; FMC-Denmark, Min. Bk., Secty's off., FMC-US; *Ford Times,* IX, Nov. 1915, 171 and X, Mar. 1917, 357 (bkgnd. on Harrington); interv. George Carlson, Copenhagen, Aug. 2, 1960 (Carlson's apptmt.; we have not seen the telegram to which Carlson referred); FMC-US, Mins. Bd. Dirs., Dec. 31, 1918, Acc. 85, Bx. 1 (Ryan's appt. as sales mgr.); FMC-Denmark, Mins. Bd. Dirs., Jan. 3, 1920, Secty's off., FMC-US, and Carl Thalbitzer, *Ford Motor Company: Gennem 25 Aar,* København, 1944 (early activities co.); Arthur Beck to Walter McKee, Mar. 31, 1950, FI (prodn. 1919–20).

16. Knudsen Report; Knudsen to Klingensmith, Aug. 4, 1919, Acc. 608, Bx. 3, and FMC-Sp., Mins. Bd. Dirs., Acc. 608, Bx. 2.

17. Craig to Lloyd Davies, Apr. 23, 1921, Acc. 608, Bx. 3 (scolding ltr.); copies of gen. ltrs. in Ford Archives; in Belgium, Dr. Wilkins saw a copy of the "Ford Bible"; elsewhere—in England, Germany, Denmark, Holland—she heard from old Ford employees of its influence on them. W. L. Graham, Treasurer's office, FMC-US, sent a copy of the letter on investment certificates to E. G. Liebold, Dec. 8, 1920, with the information that it had been sent to all foreign companies except HF & Son Ltd. in Ireland; Liebold sent a comparable one to Cork, Acc. 285, Bx. 11.

18. Knudsen Report (instructions to Anderson); *Automobile Topics,* LV, Sept. 20, 1919, 773 ("Ford knifes"); CES & Brubaker to EBF, Dec. 3, 1921, Select File (not cut down that drastically); Perry to CES, Sept. 30, 1919, Acc. 328, Bx. 1 (quote); Easton to HF, Sept. 27, 1919, Select File (dealer complaint); Perry (?) to McGregor, Apr. 28, 1919, Acc. 6, Bx. 260 (right-hand-left-hand drive); *Autocar,* LXV, July 24, 1920, 146 (converters); Knudsen to Klingensmith, Aug. 4, 1919, Acc. 608, Bx. 3 (Spain);

Autocar, passim (England); Conf. Memo Lloyd Davies to Craig, Mar. 12, 1921, Acc. 608, Bx. 3 (Spanish guise); Memo, June 22, 1920, Acc. 6, Bx. 34 (Danish situation).

19. *General Motors World,* XXX, Jan. 1951, 1 (GM overseas sales). Incredible as it may seem, there are no figures for Ford sales overseas in 1920, but Ford sales in Brazil and England together were well over the 30,000 mark, and the Ford was sold around the world. *Automotive Industries,* XLII, Jan. 1, 1920, 41 (new Ford program).

20. HF & Son Ltd. Min. Bk., Secty's off., FMC-US (gen. info.); Memo, Nov. 5, 1919, Acc. 328, Bx. 1 (territory); E. L. Clarke to H. S. Cooper, Aug. 22, 1930, OOSPP, Bx. 18 (first tractor); Dearborn tractor prodn. records, Ford Archives (Cork and US output); CES to Grace, June 25, 1920, Acc. 38, Bx. 42 (funds made available).

21. Typed, unsigned statement, Henry Ford in Mexico, Acc. 62, Bx. 22 (HF's intent); *Tribune,* Aug. 18, 1918 (quoted passage); Liebold to Hon. Pastor Rouaix, Nov. 20, 1918, Acc. 234, Bx. 20 (Oct. trip); M. S. Levussove to Liebold, May 6, 1919, Acc. 62, Bx. 22 (Mexican students' training); interv. Enriques Rangel, Mexico City, Dec. 15, 1961 (a Mexican student); folder of applications from students and Liebold to A. Cominetti, Commissioner of Immigration, Wash., D.C., June 4, 1919 (President Carranza) and Liebold to A. Horcasitas, July 2, 1919 (idea of plant was still alive at this time), all in Acc. 62, Bx. 22; Liebold to E. L. Torres, June 1, 1921, Acc. 285, Bx. 14 (prices on Mexican property too high).

22. Byrnes to CES, Mar. 25, 1920, Acc. 38, Bx. 42 (quote); Federal Trade Commission *Report on Motor Vehicle Industry,* Wash., 1939, 639 (acquisition HF & Son, Inc.); *Revista Ford,* I, Feb. 1921, 2 (Sherman & Sheppard canceled Jan. 1; branches take on business); see for instance FMC-Sp., Mins. Bd. Dirs., Aug. 1, 1920, Acc. 608, Bx. 2 (taking over tractor business).

23. Grace to CES, June 12, 1920, Acc. 38, Bx. 43 (progress); CES to Grace, June 21, 1920 and Grace to CES, May 9, 1921, Acc. 38, Bk. 46 (on decision Europeans would buy from Cork); Grace to CES, Aug. 19, 1920, Acc. 38, Bk. 43 (Model T parts).

24. P. B. Steward to CES, Aug. 13, 1920, Acc. 38, Bx. 43 (armoured cars); cable Grace to CES, Oct. 16, 1920 and ltr. Grace to CES, Oct. 20, 1920, Select File (activities *re:* Lord Mayor's imprisonment); CES to Grace, Nov. 11, 1920, Acc. 38, Bx. 43 (policies); CES to Grace, Dec. 6, 1920, Acc. 38, Bx. 46 (US tractor prodn.); Grace to CES, Nov. 30, 1920, Acc. 38, Bx. 46 (mtg. with Anderson); E. L. Clarke to CES, Nov. 16, 1920, Acc. 38, Bx. 45 (sales chariot); CES to Grace, Nov. 16, 1920, Acc. 38, Bx. 42 (CES's query); Grace to CES, Dec. 4, 1920, Acc. 38, Bx. 43 (his reply). Data in Acc. 106, Bx. 4 on Cork buildings indicate that the power house was never built.

25. Grace to CES, Dec. 17, 1920, Acc. 38, Bx. 46 (martial law); Grace to CES, Apr. 16, 1921, Select File (Grace's request); Grace to CES, May 9, 1921 (Grace's protest) and deptl. com., EBF to CES, June 13, 1921 (EBF and HF's decision), Acc. 38, Bx. 46; CES, Cork, to EBF, Dec. 8, 1921, Select File (instructed Grace to reduce tractor stock to nothing; plans *re:* Germany); CES to Liebold, Dec. 23, 1921 and Jan. 1, 1922, Select File (conds. in Germany); tractor prodn. records, Ford Archives (totals); on Mar. 6, 1922, Grace wrote Sorensen (ltr. in Select File), "It will be necessary for us to build approximately 2,000 tractors from the stock we have here and the commitments outstanding. . . ." The actual total for 1922 came to 2,233.

26. Grace to Lord Mayor of Cork, Aug. 25, 1921, Acc. 38, Bx. 45 (what Cork was doing); *Det. News,* Feb. 27, 1922 (action Cork Council); HF to Grace, Feb. 27, 1922, Acc. 285, Bx. 56; Copy of Deed of Agreement, July 15, 1922, Acc. 328, Bx. 1; Grace to CES, July 19, 1922 ("completed to your satisfaction") and Mar. 7, 1922 (investment in Cork as of Mar. 1, 1922 £1,097,089 or over $5 million), Acc. 38, Bx. 45.

27. *FTC Report,* 640–43 and Nevins & Hill, II, 152–70 (crisis in FMC-US); Liebold to Anderson, Dec. 31, 1920, Anderson to Liebold, Jan. 3, 1921, and reply, Jan. 3, 1921, Acc. 285, Bx. 9 (Anderson's demise); CES to Grace, Feb. 1, 1921, Select File ("things are horribly jammed up" because of Anderson); FMC-Eng., Mins. Bd. Dirs., Jan. 23, 1921, Secty's off., FMC-US (accepts resignation of Anderson as mng. dir. and elects H. A. Bate) and Aug. 29, 1921 (accepts resignation of Bate); Sales Dept., FMC-Eng. (sales figs.); FMC-Eng. Finance Staff, Historical Review, Mar. 31, 1959, FMC-Eng. (financial data).

28. Craig to Harrington, July 27, 1921, Acc. 608, Bx. 3 and FMC-Sp., Mins. Bd. Dirs., Aug. 30, 1921, Acc. 608, Bx. 2 (removal Lloyd Davies); FMC-Fr., Mins. Bd. Dirs., Apr. 5, 1921, Acc. 606, Bx. 1 (L. C. Griffith replaced by Russel Munro); W. E. Davis and Edward Grace Report, June 22, 1921, Select File (situation in France); Thalbitzer, 23 (Denmark).

29. Brubaker to CES, Apr. 7, 1921, Acc. 38, Bx. 133 (arrived Buenos Aires); interv. Benjamin Kopf, Mexico City, Dec. 11, 1961 (tornado); intervs. Dover and Orberg (gen. impressions); interv. Guillermo Boxer, Montevideo, Nov. 18, 1961 (situation in Urug.); Brubaker to CES, May 6, 1921, Select File ("have disposed of garages and retail at Montevideo and Buenos Aires. Body plant at Buenos Aires. . . ."); FMC-Arg., Gen. Ledger (rent paid from Apr. 1920 on Herrera 315 where commercial bodies were made; paid for only a year); FMC-Arg., FMC-Brazil, and FMC-Urug. balance sheets indicate end to retail sales; Brubaker to CES, June 9, 1921, Select File (Buenos Aires assembly started today); FMC-Brazil, balance sheet (decline in employees and sagging sales); Memo, C. T. L[athers], São Paulo, to K. Orberg, July 9, 1921, Acc. 6, Bx. 260 (plant nears completion in Brazil); Brubaker to CES, Apr. 17, 1921 (Hampton thru) and June 19, 1921 (Evans' resignation and appt. of Orberg) both in Select File.

30. Nevins & Hill, II, 685 (US prodn.); Acc. 106, Bx. 23 (overseas prodn.).

31. *General Motors World,* XXX, Jan. 1951, 1 (GM); FMC, Exports, Inc., formed in 1925, was not comparable. GM's export company had its *own* GM vice presidents and was more than a corporate shell. The directors of FMC, Exports, Inc. were Henry Ford, Edsel Ford, and Kanzler, all of whom had their greatest responsibilities in the domestic operations.

32. CES to Grace, Nov. 20, 1922, Acc. 38, Bx. 28; *Autocar,* L, Jan. 12, 1923, 71 (announce change); Sales Dept., FMC-Eng. (sales figs.); FMC-Eng., Mins. Bd. Dirs., Aug. 29, 1921, Secty's off., FMC-US (Gould mng. dir.).

33. Grace to CES, Mar. 6, and 31, 1923 (duties), cable CES to Grace, Mar. 13, 1923 and ltr. of same date, all in Select File (stay out of politics); interv. John O'Neill, London, Sept. 7, 1960 (gen. situation).

34. Rousseau, 202–03, 206, 209, 228; Citroën Press Release, n.d. [1958?], Det. Autov. Col.; S. Saint-Loup, *Renault de Billancourt,* Paris, 1956, 203–04 (influence of Ford on Citroën and Renault); Harrington to EBF, Oct. 17, 1922, Acc. 6, Bx. 260 (Paris show); Nevins & Hill, II 200–16 (Rouge); Davis to CES, Mar. 1923, Acc. 38, Bx. 108 (Southampton).

CHAPTER 6

1. FMC-Can., Mins. Bd. Dirs., Mar. 16, 1922, Secty's off., FMC-Can.; *Border Cities Star,* Mar. 11, 1922.

2. No figures are available on plant capacity in 1922, but in 1917 the directors planned to raise the capacity to 60,000. This seems to have been done, and in 1920 subsequent increases were contemplated; however, the recession intervened. Thus, 60,000 seems

a reasonable estimate. FMC-Can., Mins. Bd. Dirs., May 17, 1917 and July 9, 1920; FMC-Can. *Annual Report* for year ending July 31, 1920; McGregor's address to the shareholders, Oct. 25, 1920 in FMC-Can., Bd. Dirs. Min. Bk.; FMC-Can., *Annual Report* for year ending July 31, 1922 (assets); "The Real Facts About Ford," data presented by FMC-Can. to Tariff Inquiry Com., 1926, in Vault, FMC-Can., Windsor (employment figs.); FMC-Can., Sales Dept. Files (figs. as of Dec. 31, 1922 on Fords and Chevrolets on the Canadian roads); Brief to Tariff Inquiry Com., Nov. 30, 1920, Acc. 23, Bx. 4 (Canadian content).

3. FMC-Can., Financial Records through Mar. 1922; conversation F. G. Batters, Apr. 1961.
4. Stockholder Records, FMC-Can. (HF's holdings); Acc. 284, Bx. 13 (details on sale of this stock); William Greenleaf memo, Nov. 23, 1953 on what Clifford Longley and Kanzler told L. J. Thompson, in our possession. (HF's point of view); FMC-Can., Bd. Dirs. Min. Bk. (attendance); McGregor to EBF, June 7, 1921 and reply June 11, 1921, Acc. 6, Bx. 260.
5. Brief to Tariff Inquiry Com., Nov. 30, 1920, Acc. 23, Bx. 4; personnel records on Lawrence, Windsor (indicate date of his trip).
6. McGregor's address to shareholders, Oct. 25, 1920 in FMC-Can., Bd. Dirs. Min. Bk.; FMC-Can., Mins. Bd. Dirs., Oct. 31, 1919 and July 9, 1920.
7. McGregor's address to shareholders, Oct. 25, 1920; D. W. McKenzie to HF, Dec. 20, 1920 and Walter McGregor to HF, Dec. 20, 1920, Acc. 284, Bx. 13 (McGregor's illness); McGregor's address to shareholders, Oct. 24, 1921, in FMC-Can., Bd. Dirs. Min. Bk.; Nevins & Hill, II, 155–66 (situation in Detroit); FMC-Can., Sales Stats.
8. Personnel Records, Windsor (Lawrence left the co. Aug. 11, 1921); interv. George Bates, Oakville, Ont., Apr. 21, 1961 and personnel records (other changes); interv. Don McGregor, Windsor, Ont., May 17, 1961 (Campbell); FMC-Can., Mins. Bd. Dirs., Mar. 16, 1922 (appts.); interv. Miss Grace Falconer, Windsor, Ont., May 17, 1961 (the pass.; Campbell and McGregor); intervs. V. A. Dodge, New York, Nov. 23, 29, 1960; R. M. Sale, Oakville, Ont., Apr. 26, 1961; F. G. Batters, Oakville, Ont., Apr. 10, 1961, and others (Campbell and McGregor).
9. FMC-Can., *Annual Report* for the year ending July 31, 1922; FMC-Can., Mins. Bd. Dirs., July 12, 1922; Campbell's address to shareholders, Oct. 23, 1922, in FMC-Can., Bd. Dirs. Min. Bk.; Bd. Dirs. Min. Bk., Oct. 22, 1923; FMC-Can., Property Mgt. Dept. (new facilities); price trend, Acc. 6, Bx. 260; *Motor* (N.Y.) May 1926, 30ff. (prices of American Ford touring cars).
10. George Dickert, *Reminiscences;* intervs. Bates, Miss Falconer, and others (mgmt.); S. A. Funk (Canadian Ford dealer in Manitoba) to HF, June 25, 1924, Acc. 285, Bx. 241, intervs. V. A. Dodge, personnel records, Vault, Windsor (gen. data on Pritchard); interv. George Jackson, Grimsby, Ont., Apr. 19, 1961 (quote on Pritchard).
11. Interv. R. M. Sale (quote); Gen. Acctg. & Fin. Analysis Dept., Overseas Divn., FMC-Can. (exports); FMC-Can., Mins. Bd. Dirs., July 12, 1923; Eric Rosenthal, *The Story of Holmes Motor Company,* n.p. [S. Africa?], n.d. [1957?], 18–19 (S. African visitors); Chap. 3 and typed FMC–S. Africa *Annual Report,* July 31, 1924, Secty's off., FMC-Can. (bkgnd. on Arkell & Douglas); Stockelbach to Bd. of Trade and Industry, Apr. 15, 1925, Secty's off., FMC-Can. (high prices); cable Charles Holmes to FMC-Can., Aug. 18, 1923 in salary records of H. S. Pritchard, Vault, FMC-Can., Windsor (marketing other vehicles).
12. FMC–S. Africa, *Annual Report,* 1924, as in note 11 (this will be our source for the first year of FMC–S. Africa activity, unless otherwise noted); Holmes to FMC-Can., Aug. 18, 1923 as in note 11 (await Wessinger).
13. Stockelbach to Bd. of Trade and Industries, Apr. 15, 1925, and Feb. 11, 1925, Secty's

off., FMC-Can.; interv. E. A. Love, Dearborn, May 1961 (white labor); Campbell address to shareholders, Oct. 27, 1924, in FMC-Can. Bd. Dirs. Min. Bk., Secty's off., FMC-Can.; Gen. Acctg. & Fin. Analysis Dept., Overseas Divn., FMC-Can. (stats.); Stockelbach to Bd. of Trade and Industries, Feb. 11, 1925, cited note 11 (quote); Campbell to EBF, Sept. 10, 1924, Acc. 95, Bx. 1 (intentions).

14. Intervs. R. M. Sale, and Basil Stevenson, Oakville, Ont., Apr. 26, 1961 and FMC-Austl. and Ford Mfg. Co.–Austl., Mins. Bd. Dirs., FMC-Can., Secty's off., FMC-Can. (founding group); Campbell to EBF, Sept. 10, 1924, Acc. 95, Bx. 1 (quote); Craig to FMC-Can., Oct. 1, 1924, Acc. 95, Bx. 1 (FMC-US's approval and $3 million line of credit).

15. U.S. Dept. of Com., Bur. of For. and Dom. Com., *The Automotive Market of Australia,* Trade Info. Bull. #611, Wash., 1929, 6–8 (gen. conds.), 38 (Holden's output); Campbell to EBF, *loc. cit.* (distributors; Holden; gen. plans); Arthur Pound, *The Turning Wheel,* Garden City, N.Y., 1934, 252, and Federal Trade Commission, *Report on the Motor Vehicle Industry,* Wash., 1939, 481 (GM buys Holden).

16. Personnel records on H. C. French, Vault, FMC-Can., Windsor; intervs. Sale, and Stevenson (early group); Ford Mfg. Co–Austl. and FMC-Austl., Mins. Bd. Dirs., Secty's off., FMC-Can. (two cos.; their capitalization, execs., etc.); Campbell address to Canadian Ford shareholders, Oct. 26, 1925, in FMC-Can., Bd. Dirs. Min. Bk. (happenings in Austl.; reasons for two cos.).

17. FMC-Austl., Mins. Bd. Dirs., Apr. 15, 1925, Secty's off., FMC-Can. (acquisition of land); interv. Sale (reasons for this locale); *Geelong Advertiser,* Mar. 31, 1925 (Grandjean's statement on why Geelong was chosen; community's reaction).

18. FMC-Austl., Mins. Bd. Dirs., Apr. 15, May 25, July 20, 1925 (Sydney, Brisbane, Adelaide, Fremantle); intervs. Stevenson (quote on new arrivals); and Sale (gen. conds.); FMC-Austl., Mins. Bd. Dirs., Apr. 15, 1924 (lease of wool warehouse of Dalgety & Co., in Geelong).

19. FMC-Austl., Mins. Bd. Dirs., July 20, 1925 (taking over stocks); *Geelong Advertiser,* Mar. 31, 1925 (quote); Dept. of Overseas Trade, *Report on the Economic and Financial Situation in Australia,* Rev. to Oct. 1922, London, 1922, 46 (British complaints and report); Campbell address to Canadian shareholders, Oct. 27, 1924 (20,000 chassis); interv. Sale (his views); L. Powell to E. L. Morris, May 25, 1961, FMC-Austl., Mins. Bd. Dirs., L. R. Leeman to J. Foster, June 15, 1955, and interv. Stevenson (on which distributors remained with Ford); Dept. of Overseas Trade, *Report on the Economic and Commercial Situation of Australia to June 1927,* London, 1927, 76 (big distributors); interv. Stevenson (the bitter comment).

20. Dept. of Overseas Trade, *Report on Australia to June 1927,* 237 (imports; these figs. make it clear Ford was in first place in 1922–23); Gen. Acctg. & Fin. Analysis Dept., Overseas Divn., FMC-Can. (percentage of registration); FMC-Austl., Mins. Bd. Dirs., July 20, 1925 (special equipment); Campbell to EBF, *loc. cit.* (30,000 goal).

21. Intervs. V. A. Dodge, *Export Trade Directory* (date of formation Dodge & Seymour); intervs. H. A. Denne, London, June 18, 1961 (Denne's role) and Stevenson (his role); FMC-India, Mins. Bd. Dirs. and FMC-Malaya, Mins. Bd. Dirs., Secty's off., FMC-Can. (new cos; Milliken; Denne).

22. Intervs. H. A. Denne, FMC-India, Mins. Bd. Dirs. and FMC-Malaya, Mins. Bd. Dirs. (date incorporation; headquarters, and assembly locations); FMC-Can., *Annual Report* 1926; FMC-Can., Mins. Bd. Dirs., July 12, 1923 (the promise).

23. Campbell address to shareholders, Oct. 27, 1924 and Oct. 26, 1925; Rackham to EBF, July 3, 1924 and reply, July 7, 1924, Acc. 6, Bx. 260; Stock Transfer Bks., FMC-Can. (Detroit Trust Co.); Agreement with E. E. MacCrone, Nov. 28, 1924, Select

File (Ford intentions); Stock Transfer Bks., FMC-Can. (Mott transaction and Ford stock holdings).

24. Canadian Automobile Chamber of Commerce (prodn. figs. for industry); C. Howard Aikman, *The Automobile Industry of Canada,* Toronto, 1926, 11 (11 car and truck producers: Ford, Studebaker, Chrysler, Godfredson (trucks and commercial chassis), GM, Willys Overland Sales Co., Durant Motors, Dodge Bros., National Car Co., International Harvester, and Brooks Steam Motors); FMC-Can, *Annual Report* for the year ending Dec. 31, 1926 (FMC-Can., prodn. figs.).

25. In discussing the projected reduction in duty, a debate took place in the Canadian House of Commons (Mar. 29, 1926). Attention was called to Ford-Canada's "abnormally large dividends." It was argued that the company had profited from the tariff by pricing its vehicles not at cost plus a small profit but at Ford-US cost plus the tariff minus a little to make the car cheaper in Canada than a U.S. import. Ford-Canada denied such charges, claiming it aimed at the lowest possible price. See House of Commons Debates, 1926, 2076, Aikman, 37, and FMC-Can. data. Campbell, Brief to Tariff Inquiry Com. at Windsor, Ont., Nov. 30, 1920, Acc. 23, Bx. 4 (his point of view).

26. Quoted in Aikman, 41 (HF's statement); *N.Y. Times,* Aug. 10, 1930 (HF's volteface). *Office Consolidation, Canada Customs Tariff,* 1925; *Handbook of Canadian Customs Tariff and Excise Duties,* Ottawa, 1930; FMC-Can., Presentations to Tariff Com., Oct. 1935 in Record Retention Ctr., FMC-Can.; Records in FMC-Can., Customs and Excise Dept. (J. S. Urie), FMC-Can.; discussions with J. S. Urie and J. M. Cochrane, Oakville, Ont., Apr. 1961 (all on FMC-Can. and tariff).

27. Canadian Automobile Chamber of Commerce (vehicles-in-use figs.); FMC-Can., *Annual Report 1926* (assets, plant investment); FMC-Can., Dealer Development off. (no. of dealers).

CHAPTER 7

1. Chap. 5 (bkgnd. on Cork situation); Memo Grace to EBF and CES, May 15, 1923, Acc. 38, Bx. 108 (the decision); Grace to EBF, July 10, 1923, Select File.

2. J. P. Shawcross, *History of Dagenham,* London, 1904, 2 and *passim;* Grace to EBF, July 10, 1923 and Grace to CES, July 27, 1923, Select File (on the site); Acc. 6, Bx. 47 (Kanzler's trip); interv. Ernest Kanzler, Detroit, Jan. 14, 1960 ("I chose Dagenham"; reasons for choice); interv. Sir Stanford Cooper, Stock, Essex, Aug. 10, 1960 (reasons for choice of Dagenham); Perry to CES, Aug. 24, 1928, Acc. 38, Bx. 1 (what investigators did not consider).

3. Gen. Ltr., Nov. 6, 1923, Select File (the mtg.); Harrington to EBF, Nov. 26, 1923 and reply, Dec. 1, 1923, Acc. 6, Bx. 46 (their responses); Acc. 157, Bx. 267 (opening Havana branch).

4. A. F. Hosmer to Roberge, Statement of Assets—Foreign cos. and branches as of Aug. 31, 1923 (except for Cork figs. which are as of July 31, 1923), Select File; Gen. Ltr., Nov. 6, 1923, Select File (8 per cent) and Sales Dept. FI (R. Baker), FMC-US (more than half); Kanzler to EBF, Oct. 3, 1923 and reply, Oct. 3, 1923 (cables), Acc. 6, Bx. 47 (Citroën).

5. Sales Dept. FI (sales in various markets); "Earnings of Associated Ford companies— at official rates of exchange" in "England Guernsey Ford Investment" folder, FI; FMC-Sp., Mins. Bd. Dirs., Mar. 10, 1923, Acc. 608, Bx. 2 (move from Cadiz to Barcelona).

6. Earnings of Associated cos., and Sales Dept. FI; foundation dates of all cos. are from

the Mins. Bd. Dirs. of each co.; intervs. George Carlson, Copenhagen, Aug. 1, 2, 1960 and Willy Schmidt, Cologne, July 19, 1960 (Posekel); Arthur Pound, *The Turning Wheel,* Garden City, N.Y., 1934, 250 (Opel).

7. Carlson to CES, Nov. 20, 1924, Acc. 38, Bx. 48 (Fordsons); Ryan-Hadas to EBF, Nov. 21, 1924 (their plans), and reply, Nov. 24, 1924 (approves orgn. co.); Carlson to EBF, Nov. 29, 1924 (sent from Berlin); Craig to Carlson, Dec. 23, 1924 (5 million mark capitalizn); FMC-Ger., Mins. Bd. Dirs. (formation co., Jan. 5, 1924), all in Secty's off., FMC-US; interv. Erhard Vitger, Cologne, July 15, 1960 (Danish personnel); interv. W. Schmidt (dealers).

8. Interv. Carlson (discussion with Minister of Labor); Statement by Carlson and EBF, n.d. in FMC-Ger., Bd. Dirs. Min. Bk., presented to Shareholders Mtg. Mar. 15, 1926 and Carlson Report FMC A/G Berlin, Dec. 31, 1926, Secty's off., FMC-US (start of business and facilities); data on GM from that co.

9. Min. Bks. of respective cos. (dates of formation; the branch in Egypt was a branch of the Ford Motor Company, Exports, Inc.—a wholly owned sub. of FMC-US. See fns. 9 and 31, Chap. 5).

10. Acc. 38, Bx. 48 (Danish site); Real Estate Records, FMC-Eng. (Dagenham); Real Estate Records, FMC-Belg. (Hoboken); FMC-Fr., Mins. Bd. Dirs, Feb. 19, and Apr. 2, 1925, Acc. 606, Bx. 1 (approval purchase land Asnières); *Ford News,* V, Jan. 1, 1925, 1 (Nov. 1924 opening of Danish plant); F. Schmitto, *Automobilets Historie og Dets Maend,* København, 1938, I, 234 and Carl Thalbitzer, *Ford Motor Company, Gennem 25 Aar,* København, 1944 (bkgrnd. on FMC-Den.); *N.Y. Herald Tribune,* May 25, 1926 (opening Asnières plant); FMC-Belg., Mins. Shareholders. Mtg., May 10, 1926, Secty's off., FMC-US (move from old plant to Hoboken approved); Real Estate Records, FMC-Eng. (Dagenham site: size and cost; more land would be purchased later); Jenkins' statement to press, July 10, 1924, Clipbook, Ford Archives (capacity of projected Dagenham plant); Acc. 106, Bxs. 21, 18, 19, 23 (capacities of Danish, Belgian, French, and English plants).

11. Interv. Kanzler; Perry to CES, Sept. 30, 1919, Acc. 328, Bx. 1 (quote); T. Gehle, *Reminiscences;* William C. Klann, *Reminiscences;* intervs. H. Mortimore, London, Aug. 29, 1960; Sir Stanford Cooper, Sir Rowland Smith, London, Aug. 23, 1960, Sir Patrick Hennessy, London, Aug. 1960; Roland Philip to CES, Mar. 16, 1923, Select File; W. E. Davis to CES, Apr. 12, 1923, Acc. 38, Bx. 108 (all on Gould's activities); *Motor Trader,* May 9, 1923, 189 ("Sacrificed Again").

12. The Finance Act 1909/10 introduced a graduated h.p. tax based on the h.p. formula. A small car (6 h.p. to 12 h.p.) was taxed at £3.3.0, while the Model T had a tax of £6.6.0. The new act raised the Model T tax to £23. Society of Motor Manufacturers and Traders, *The Motor Industry of Great Britain,* London, 1939, 16 (bkgnd. on the tax); Gehle, *Reminiscences* (quote).

13. Gehle, *Reminiscences;* CES to Gehle & Klann, Nov. 24, 1923, Select File (pleasant journey); Reports from Gehle & Klann, Select File; Klann, *Reminiscences* (trouble seeing Gould); Gehle & Klann to Kanzler, Dec. 22, 1923 (dismissal Davis), Jan. 7, 1924 (orgn. neglected), Feb. 7, 1924 (new car), Select File; *Autocar,* LII, Jan. 25, 1924, 165, and Feb. 8, 1924, 269 (new Model T); FMC-Eng., Mins. Bd. Dirs., Apr. 3, 1924, Secty's off., FMC-US (resignation Gould effective Apr. 15); *Autocar,* LII, Mar. 7, 1924, 426 ("almost entirely of British material"); *Ford Times* (Eng.), I, n.s. Dec. 1924, 19 (reprint of Aug. 1924 statement).

14. EBF to H. S. Jenkins, Mar. 24, 1924, Acc. 6, Bx. 384 (cable); interv. Sir Stanford Cooper, London, July 4, 1961 (a good man); intervs. Sir Rowland Smith, Sir Stanford Cooper, and H. Mortimore, 1960 (Jenkins); Ford Archives (clipbook on

Jenkins' press luncheon); EBF to Jenkins, Sept. 25, 1924, Acc. 6, Bx. 260 (EBF's views); Acc. 106, Bx. 23 (prodn. figs. for Ford plants); P. W. S. Andrews and Elizabeth Brunner, *The Life of Lord Nuffield*, Oxford, 1955, 112 (Morris figs.); *Evening Chronicle*, Aug. 13, 1925 (royalty visit); Sales Dept., FMC-Eng. (Ford sales).

15. Carnegie, Report on Trip to England, June 1925, Acc. 157, Bx. 266; Gehle, *Reminiscences* (his visit with HF probably took place in May 1925: see Acc. 38, Bx. 111 and HF's visitor list, Acc. 285, Bx. 492); EBF to Perini, Dec. 21, 1925, Acc. 6, Bx. 384 (EBF's cable); N.G.I[sitt] to Roberge, July 1, 1925, OOSPP, Bx. 291 and Jenkins to CES, Aug. 13, 1925, Acc. 38, Bx. 52 (obstacles to sales progress).

16. Jenkins to Ryan, Oct. 12, 1925, OOSPP, Bx. 291 (GM marketing procedure); GM Fin. Com. Report, Oct. 1925, quoted in Federal Trade Commission, *Report on the Motor Vehicle Industry*, Wash., 1939, 489 (GM plans for Vauxhall); *The Motor Car Index 1928*, Norwich, 1928, 188 (h.p. of smallest 1925 model Vauxhall); Sales Dept. FMC-Eng. (Ford statistics); N.G.I[sitt] to Ryan, Nov. 6, 1925, OOSPP, Bx. 291 and Herbert Austin to HF, Nov. 10, 1926, Acc. 285, Bx. 44 (competition); Jenkins to Ryan, Dec. 29, 1925, OOSPP, Bx. 291 (Morris propaganda); Sales Dept., FI (Eur. cont. stats.); GM started assembly operations in Europe with plants in London and Copenhagen; in 1925 it bought Vauxhall in Luton, Eng.; by 1926 it had plants in Antwerp and Berlin and warehouses in Malaga and Le Havre—info. from R. Johnson, GM Overseas Operations; Frank Southard, *American Industry in Europe*, Boston, 1931, 1 (Shredded Wheat); Palmolive Company, *Annual Report 1925* (Palmolive); John Dunning, *American Investment in British Manufacturing Industry*, London, 1958, 42 (Liggett).

17. Sales Dept. FI (sales stats.); Hosmer, *loc. cit.* (assets); Acc. 57, Bx. 266 (Uruguay investment); Geo. J. Gariepy, Feb. 4, 1927, Acc. 38, Bx. 52 ("sell service"); FMC-Brazil, Circular ltrs. (esp. July 30, 1925—claim Ford has largest sales orgn. in country), Monteiro Papers, São Paulo (methods of pushing sales); interv. Pedro Zinkgräf, Buenos Aires, Nov. 27, 1961 (teach dealers); interv. Kristian Orberg, São Paulo, Nov. 7, 1961 and Orberg, *Reminiscences* (situation in Brazil); Joseph Grew to FMC, Detroit, Aug. 4, 1924, Acc. 6, Bx. 270 (São Paulo uprising). The Rebels took by force 78 batteries, 3 service trucks, and some parts as well as about 35 automobiles that were loading at the railway stations. Orberg was summoned before General Lopes, who demanded the plant supply the insurgents. Acc. 106, Bx. 23 (prodn. figs.).

18. *Ford News*, V, Dec. 1, 1924, 8 (shipment to Cuenca sub-agent); interv. Benjamin Kopf, Mexico City, Dec. 11, 1961 (Uruguay and Chile); Circular Ltr., K. Orberg to dealers, July 3, 1925, Monteiro Papers (on assembly line in Rio—Aug. 1–16, 1925).

19. *El Automovil en México*, n.v., May 1925, 12 (stats. registration); intervs. Michael Carniel, Buenos Aires, Nov. 22, 1961; Ralph E. Chaplin, Cuernavaca, Dec. 11, 1961; W. W. Townsend, Mexico City, Dec. 22, 1961 (Lajous); files on FMC-Mex., Secty's off., FMC-US (concessions); Lajous to Ryan, May 8, 1925, Secty's off., FMC-US (labor); *Diario Official*, XXXII, Oct. 16, 1925, 658 (tariff concessions for kd. units); FMC-Mex., Balance Sheets (full assembly began Aug. 1926).

20. FMC-Brazil, Circular Ltrs., Monteiro Papers (Recife & Rio branches); Check Bk., FMC-Brazil (Pôrto Alegre branch—first entry June 1926); interv. Jorge Matray, Santiago, Dec. 4, 1961 (Peruvian branch; Arthur S. Odin was the first mgr.); Sales Dept., FI (start Peruvian operations, 1926); R. I. Roberge to To Whom It May Concern, May 15, 1926, Townsend Papers, Mexico City (opening San Juan branch); Acc. 101, Bx. 7 (1926 leases San Juan, Caracas); interv. Townsend (gen. pic.).

21. Sales Dept., FI (dealers); D. M. Phelps, *Migration of Industry to South America*, N.Y., 1936, 325–29.

22. Acc. 713, Bx. 54 (profits); Sales Dept. FI (plant deliveries); FMC-Arg. sold 25,000 units in 1925 and 24,000 in 1926; list of men from foreign Ford cos., Acc. 390, Bx. 50 (frequent visits of foreign execs.).

23. Foreign visitor list, Acc. 285, Bx. 492 (Bailie visit); Liebold to Bailie, Dec. 2, 1921 and reply, Feb. 22, 1922, plus other Bailie ltrs., Acc. 285, Bx. 84 (sites); Liebold to Bailie, Feb. 28, 1923, Acc. 285, Bx. 736 (students); Sun Yat-sen to HF, June 12, 1924, Acc. 285, Bx. 285.

24. R. I. Roberge to EBF, Sept. 7, 1924, Acc. 6, Bx. 267; FMC-Japan, Bd. Dirs. Min. Bk., Secty's off., FMC-US; FMC-US and FMC-Japan agreement, Mar. 7, 1925, Acc. 363, Bx. 1. The Japanese company was wholly owned by American Ford interests; Roberge, *Reminiscences;* interv. Kopf; U.S. Dept. of Com., Bur. of For. & Dom. Com., *Japan as an Automotive Market,* Wash., 1922, 48 (est. market); Acc. 713, Bx. 54 (Ford imports and profits); Roberge, *Reminiscences* (practically nil); U.S. Dept. of Com., Bur. of For. & Dom. Com., *Automotive Markets in China, British Malaya, and Chosen,* Wash., 1923, 51 (est. market China); Acc. 713, Bx. 54 (Ford deliveries).

25. Sales Dept. FI (Ford deliveries); Friedrich v. Gottl-Ottlilienfeld, *Fordismus,* Jena, 1926; Acc. 285, Bx. 252 (corresp. *re:* Japanese translation); H. S. Pritchard to HF, Nov. 14, 1923, Acc. 285, Bx. 174 (Dutch translation); *N.Y. Times,* Jan. 26, 1924 (Lenin's library); the jingle was recited to the authors by a man who had grown up in Barbados; *FTC Report,* 645 (Ford profits).

26. *Ford News,* V, Nov. 1, 1924, 1; Nov. 15, 1924, 1; Jan. 1, 1925, 5; Feb. 15, 1925, 1; June 15, 1925, 1; VI, Feb. 15, 1926, 1; Sept. 1, 1926, 1; VIII, Nov. 15, 1927, 6 (Ford shipping); interv. M. J. O'Neill, Dearborn, 1960.

27. Henry Ford, *My Life and Work,* Garden City, 1923, 242 (quote); *Dearborn Independent, passim* (same theme); Knudsen Report, Roberge, *Reminiscences,* and data in Secty's off., FMC-US (gen. comments).

28. Nevins & Hill, II, 393–94, 416ff.

29. Orberg Reports to EBF, Sept. 25, 1926 and Feb. 8, 1927, Acc. 6, Bx. 446; Acc. 713, Bx. 54 (Ford deliveries); F. F. Griffith Report, Sept. 15, 1926, Acc. 6, Bx. 446; Brubaker to CES, June 22, 1921, Select File (for highly critical appraisal of Ford official, who later became GM mgr. in Buenos Aires). Ford deliveries to Argentina: 1925, 24,913; 1926, 23,590; 1927, 14,127.

30. Nevins & Hill, II, 410 (Kanzler quote); EBF to Jenkins, Mar. 31, 1926, Acc. 6, Bx. 258 (would see Jenkins in Manchester); Jenkins to A. A. Backus, May 1, 1926 and Backus to Jenkins, May 6, 1926, Acc. 6, Bx. 260 (Peugeots and Austins); *N.Y. Herald Tribune,* May 25, 1926 (EBF's denial); Carlson to EBF, May 6, 1926, Acc. 6, Bx. 260 (his report).

31. Austin to HF, Nov. 10, 1926 and Liebold to Austin, Nov. 26, 1926, Acc. 285, Bx. 444; in addition, see cordial exchange of corresp. Austin to HF, Nov. 24, 1927 and Liebold to Austin, Dec. 7, 1927, Acc. 285, Bx. 577; Jenkins to EBF, Sept. 7, 1926 (prestige falling) and Jenkins to Ryan, July 23, 1926 (complaints) both in Acc. 6, Bx. 260; John Evelyn Wrench, *The Spectator,* to HF, Oct. 12, 1926 and Liebold to Wrench, Oct. 30, 1926, Acc. 285, Bx. 552.

32. Nevins & Hill, I, 430 (HF's statements); Jenkins to CES, Aug. 24, 1926 and H. L. Leister to CES, Sept. 10, 1926, Acc. 38, Bx. 52 (cutting down staff—first round); cables to and from Harrington, Brubaker, and Hoffman (who signed themselves "Fordson"), Nov. 15–Dec. 23, 1926, Acc. 38, Bx. 52 (firings etc.); intervs. B. H. C. Huntelaar, Amsterdam, Aug. 4, 1960; W. Schmidt, Cologne, July 19, 1960; H. C. Møller, Copenhagen, Aug. 2, 1960; J. Van Luppen, Brussels, July 29, 1960 and L. E. Briggs, *Reminiscences* (on trip); Fordson to Martin and CES, Dec. 7, 1926,

Acc. 38, Bx. 52 and H. S. Jenkins, Report to EBF on Cork operation, Feb. 22, 1926, Acc. 6, Bx. 446 (Hennessy).

33. Registration statistics furnished by FMC-US (Ford *v.* Chevrolet, 1926–27); *FTC Report*, 27 (GM total sales). The data in *FTC Report* on Ford sales does not coincide with the registration statistics here given. The reason seems to be that cars sold in 1926 (at the end of the year) were registered in 1927.

34. *Ford News*, VIII, Dec. 15, 1927, 1 (appearance Model A); FMC-Austl. (Melbourne showing); *N.Y. Times*, Dec. 3, 1927 (Holland Park Show); Ford Catalog, Acc. 175, Bx. 28 (Ford advertisement).

35. GM plant info. from General Motors; *Japan Advertiser*, Tokyo, Apr. 15, 1928 (new Ford plant); *O Mundo Ford*, I, July 1929, 27 (Japanese plant opening); B. R. Brown, *Reminiscences* (bldg. plant); Acc. 106, Bx. 27 (capacity); FMC, Exports, Inc., Mins. Bd. Dirs., May 26, 1927, Secty's off., FMC-US (Chinese branch); FMC, Exports, Inc., Mins. Bd. Dirs., Oct. 19, 1928 (Turkey); FMC-Can., *Annual Reports* 1927 and 1928 (Canadian expenditures).

36. Jenkins to CES, July 12, Nov. 22, 1927, Acc. 38, Bx. 52; Jenkins to EBF and HF, Dec. 2, 1927, Acc. 285, Bx. 636; E. L. Clarke to CES, Dec. 19, 1927, Acc. 38, Bx. 56; *Autocar*, Dec. 9, 1927, 1228; *N.Y. Times*, Dec. 3, 1927 (English reaction), Jan. 27, 1928 (French reaction; the price was so much higher than the American price because of duties and freight charges), and Dec. 15, 17, 1927 (German tariff).

37. "Model A" folder, Select File (exports and prodn. difficulties); Gen. Acctg. & Fin. Analysis, Overseas Divn., FMC-Can. (Australia registrations); *Ford News*, VIII, Oct. 15, 1928, 219 (by Oct. 1, 1928, all foreign assembly plants which built the Model T were in prodn. of the Model A); Sales Dept., FMC-Eng. (sales of Ford Ltd.); Society of Motor Manufacturers and Traders, *The Motor Industry of Great Britain*, London, 1959, 11 (industry stats.); G. Maxcy and A. Silberston, *The Motor Industry*, London, 1959, 99 (competitive situation in England).

Chapter 8

1. Harvey Firestone to HF, Feb. 17, 1923, Acc. 62, Bx. 2.

2. For Goodyear, see the *National Cyclopedia of American Biography*, N.Y., 1893, III, 86; for Hancock, *Dictionary of National Biography*, Oxford, 1921–22, VIII, 1160; Charles Wagley, *Amazon Town*, N.Y., 1953, 82–89, gives a good picture of the gathering of rubber and the temperament of the *seringalistes* (owners of rubber tracts) and of the collectors, as well as the behavior of planted and wild rubber trees. Hancock was a pioneer in rubber manufacturing and in 1842 saw some specimens of Goodyear's vulcanization. He "investigated," and took out a patent in England for vulcanization in 1843, before Goodyear's first American patent; but never claimed to have invented the process.

3. H. A. Wickham, *On the Plantation, Cultivation and Curing of Para Indian Rubber (Hevea brasiliensis)*, London, 1908, *passim*. Wickham was knighted for his exploit of procuring the *Hevea* seeds.

4. E. G. Holt, *Marketing of Crude Rubber*, Trade Promotion Series, Dept. of Com. Bull. No. 55, Wash., 1927.

5. John F. Melby, *Rubber River: An Account of the Rise and Collapse of the Amazon Boom*, Chicago, 1942 (part of a Ph.D. dissertation published in *Hispanic American Historical Review*, XXII, Aug., 1942).

6. Alfred Lief, *The Firestone Story*, New York, 1951, Chap. X.

7. *Ibid.*

8. *Ibid.* (Philippines, Liberia, rubber prices), 145, 152–54, 163; Nevins & Hill, II, 20, 485–88 (vacations); Lief, 132 (Ford as customer), 159 (Edison); Acc. 62, Bx. 2 (Hines, Ford, Liebold, April 1923); J. C. A. de Lima to HF, Apr. 9, 1923, Acc. 285, Bx. 139; Edison to HF, Sept. 14, 1923, Accs. 104 and 358, Bx. 1.

9. Norman Beasley, "Henry Ford Says," *Motor* (N.Y.), XLI, Jan. 1924, 70–71; Henry Ford, in collaboration with Samuel Crowther, *Today and Tomorrow,* Garden City, N.Y., 1926, 41; Nevins & Hill, II, Chaps. 8, 9; de Lima to HF, July 8, 1925, W. L. Schurz to HF, July 21, 1925 and Liebold to Bentes, Aug. 26, 1925, in "History of the Companhia Ford Industrial do Brasil," n.d. [1929], unsigned typescript, Acc. 38, Bx. 61, hereafter cited as "History."

10. J. L. McCloud, C. La Rue, O. Z. Ide, in their *Reminiscences;* Liebold and Zahnow, corresp. touching on Edison's work, Acc. 285, Bxs. 214, 479; P. W. Barker, *Rubber: History, Production, and Manufacture,* Dept. of Com., Wash., 1940, 23–25; "History" (Blakeley expedition). Edison selected a type of goldenrod as holding out the best hope for an American product. But the rubber produced was poor and would probably cost $2 a pound. Acc. 285, Bx. 956.

11. *N.Y. Times,* Oct. 27, 1927 (Edsel); Lief, 167–69; Ide, *Reminiscences;* "History"; interv. Humberto Monteiro, São Paulo, Nov. 6, 1961; J. C. Younkins, Report, June 7, 1933, Acc. 390, Bx. 26 (price); Companhia Ford Industrial do Brasil, Min. Bk., Acc. 301, Bx. 1.

12. *Ford News,* VIII, Aug. 1, 1928, 159 and Aug. 15, 1; *N.Y. Times,* July 27, 1928. Pictures of the two ships are seen. The *Lake Farge* was 253.6 ft. long, 43.6 ft. wide, and had a "capacity of about 3800 net tons."

13. Ide, *Reminiscences* (seedlings); *Det. News:* three arts. by A. M. Smith, Nov. 4, 5, and 8, 1928 (description of site); interv. Orberg, São Paulo, Nov. 7, 1961; Orberg, *Reminiscences;* Companhia, Min. Bk., May 18, 1928 (Blakeley apptd.), Sept. 9, 1928 (Orberg, Oxholm); *Det. News,* Mar. 25, 1930 (Oxholm quote).

14. Douglas O. Naylor, "Now the Amazon Jungle is Stirred by Henry Ford," *N.Y. Times,* Jan. 13, 1929; Wagley, I, 10–13; interv. Silvino da Silva, N.Y., Sept. 18, 1961. Da Silva for a time had charge of employment at Boa Vista.

15. Companhia Ford Industrial do Brasil, Report of Directorate, Sept. 12, 1928, Acc. 301, Bx. 1; "History."

16. Kennedy to Gerald A. Drew (vice consul), "History"; Kennedy to Carnegie, Mar. 15, 1929, Acc. 38, Bx. 61.

17. Cowling, *Reminiscences;* CES to Braunstein, to Kennedy, and to Oxholm, "History." Before sending Cowling, Sorensen had tried through Braunstein (manager at Rio) and Kennedy to get the export duties lifted. He also enlisted the support of the U.S. State Dept. See Cowling to CES, Oct. 3, 1929, Acc. 38, Bx. 61 (Cowling and Rio officials).

18. Interv. Da Silva (workers); Oxholm to CES and Kennedy to CES, "History"; invoice, Mar. 13, 1930 from Albert Kahn, Inc., Acc. 33, Bx. 65 (cost of hospital).

19. Interv. Da Silva, Carnegie-CES, cables and letters, CES-Oxholm corresp., all in "History."

20. Carnegie Report, Acc. 38, Bx. 68; James R. Weir, "A Pathological Survey of the Para Rubber Tree (*Hevea brasiliensis*) in the Amazon Valley," Wash., 1926.

21. "History and Facts of Companhia Ford Industrial do Brasil," [n.d., but stamped rec'd, Oct. 16, 1933] typescript, Acc. 390, Bx. 86 (riot and aftermath); Johnston report and Johnston-CES corresp., Acc. 38, Bx. 68.

22. Johnston to Braunstein, Dec. 10, 1931 (lots of heart), Braunstein to Carnegie, Dec. 31, 1931 (Collor and Barata visit), Braunstein to Johnston, Feb. 4, 1932 (desire

decree), Feb. 5 (Aranha), Feb. 16 (Collor), and Johnston to Braunstein, Feb. 24 (waning enthusiasm), all in Humberto Monteiro Papers, São Paulo.

23. Johnston and Roberge, Memo to EBF, Apr. 24, 1933, Acc. 6, Bx. 316 (Roberge points out claims for duty cancelled: "the Brazilian Government had claims against us amounting to over $2,000,000 covering duties on this material"; also recommends cessation lumber export); Johnston to Wibel, July 5, 1932, Acc. 390, Bx. 86; interv. R. I. Roberge, Birmingham, Mich., Aug. 1, 1961 (lumber export); A. M. Wibel to H. Firestone, July 11, 1932 and H. Firestone to Wibel, July 16, 1932 (clones), R. E. Sheahan (U.S. Rubber Co.) to Wibel, July 18, 1932 (approves bud-grafting), all in Acc. 390, Bx. 86.

24. Wibel to Johnston, Mar. 13, 1933 (employing Weir), Acc. 390, Bx. 86; FMC-US Personnel Records (date of first work); Reports by Weir, Mar. 31 and May 15, 1933 (rubber culture), Wibel to Johnston, Oct. 27, 1933 (Weir's Far Eastern trip) and July 17, 1934 ("will make a go of it"), all in Acc. 390, Bx. 86, EBF to Weir, May 10, 1933, Acc. 6, Bx. 316; Report by George S. Armstrong & Co., Industrial Engineers, acting for the Estate of Edsel Ford—June 16, 1947 (Weir's find in Far East; British, Dutch, and French colonies' action, and 1934 stats.). Weir's pamphlet, cited in note 20, gives the positions he had occupied.

25. As early as 1929 Henry Ford had declared his company in Brazil would be manufacturing tires and other articles made of rubber. See *O Mundo Ford,* I, May 1929, 20. The revival of this idea is in Memo Wibel to Roberge, Oct. 2, 1934, Acc. 390, Bx. 86.

26. Companhia Ford Industrial do Brasil, Reports to Shareholders, Feb. 20, 1935, Mar. 4, 1936, and Mar. 1, 1937, Acc. 301, Bx. 1 (Belterra and Fordlandia).

27. Johnston-Braunstein corresp., Monteiro Papers, São Paulo (foreign doctors and radio licenses); interv. Monteiro, São Paulo, Nov. 6, 1961 (wrong foot) and for similar sentiment interv. Orberg, São Paulo, Nov. 7, 1961; Weir Report, Apr. 20, 1936 and Weir to Johnston, Sept. 23, 1936, Acc. 390, Bx. 86 (modification of sentiment); Companhia Ford Industrial do Brasil, Report to Shareholders, Mar. 1, 1937, Acc. 301, Bx. 1 (progress and quote).

28. David R. Moore, *A History of Latin America,* N.Y., rev. ed., 1942, 618 (Vargas and Amazon concessions); Braunstein to EBF, Oct. 17, 1940, Acc. 6, Bx. 376 (9-p. ltr. on Vargas visit); interv. Monteiro (the contest); Report on Plantation, Oct. 1940, Acc. 6, Bx. 376 (Manaos speech).

29. R. D. Rand, "Hevea Rubber Culture in Latin America," *India Rubber World,* CVI, June 1942, 3, 7.

30. George S. Armstrong & Co., Report (Belterra yield); Report on Plantation, Oct. 1940, Acc. 6, Bx. 376 (trees, Fordlandia); Johnston Report, Nov. 6, 1942, Acc. 6, Bx. 376 (Fordlandia 1941 yield and gen. situation); Lief, 170, 208, 253, 327 (Firestone's activities in Liberia) and 248–49, 251–53, 272–82 (synthetic rubber). Firestone had been working on synthetic rubber research since the early 1930's, and the Fords knew this. Their awareness of the possible competitive significance of synthetic rubber was given expression in the Companhia Ford Industrial do Brasil, Report to Shareholders, Mar. 4, 1936, Acc. 301, Bx. 1.

31. Johnston, Memo of Telephone Conversation with Mr. Thomas, Nov. 20, 1942 and deptl. com. Johnston to EBF, Nov. 24, 1942 with EBF's notation, Acc. 6, Bx. 376; interv. Orberg; FMC-US, Mins. Bd. Dirs., Sept. 21, 1945, Secty's off., FMC-US (HF II pres.); FMC-US, Mins. Gen. Plang. Com., Nov. 5, 1945, Secty's off., FMC-US (decision to sell); Acc. 134, Bx. 4 (fin. data). Note that the loss was calculated at exchange rate of Cr. $20.475. Actually the loss was greater because US dollars

were invested at varying rates of exchange, some for example at Cr. $12.000. The deed of sale was signed Dec. 28, 1945, Acc. 301, Bx. 1.

32. Dr. Felisberto Cardoso de Camargo, Appraisal Companhia Ford Properties on Rio Tapajos, Nov. 30, 1944, Acc. 134, Bx. 4 (quote); visit to Belterra by Dr. Wilkins, Nov. 1961; and her conversation with Dr. Sylvio Braga, Belterra, Nov. 1, 1961.

CHAPTER 9

1. *N.Y. Times*, Mar. 31, Apr. 7, 8, 11, 12, 16, 27, 29, May 3, 6, 9, 1928; *Ford Times* (Eng.), June 1928, 112; Diary of Clara Ford, Acc. 1, Bx. 21 (two days only); *London Economist*, Apr. 14, 1928, and clippings in Acc. 292, Bx. 22; interv. Sir Stanford Cooper, London, July 4, 1961 (Detroit in Europe). See Chaps. 4 and 7 for Ford's attitude toward Southampton.

2. *N.Y. Times*, Apr. 11, 1928 (tariff); William T. Cosgrove to HF, Nov. 19, 1928, Acc. 38, Bx. 56 (Dulanty conference); Sir William Letts to HF, Nov. 9, 1927 and other corresp., Acc. 285, Bx. 274; Sir Herbert Austin to HF, July 9, 1920, Acc. 284, Bx. 2 (failure of GM negotiations, approach to HF); Isitt to Ryan, Nov. 6, 1925, OOSPP, Bx. 291 (GM-Austin-Vauxhall); Austin to HF, Nov. 10, 1926, Acc. 285, Bx. 444 (second Austin proposal).

3. Perry-CES corresp. Nov. 11, 1922—July 20, 1926, Acc. 38, Bx. 138 and Select File; CES to Perry, July 24, 1923, Acc. 38, Bx. 138 (Ford's attitude); also Feb. 7, 1923, Select File (Perry's devotion to FMC); Lady Perry to Clara Ford, Apr. 21, 1928, Acc. 292, Bx. 22.

4. Interv. Miss Vera Howard, Stock, Essex, Aug. 10, 1960 ("bolt from blue"); EBF to Perry, May 23, 1928, Acc. 6, Bx. 104 (establishes the mtg.); interv. CES (by Nevins & Hill), June 29, 1954 (CES' feeling about Perry's return); interv. Sir Stanford Cooper, Stock, Essex, Aug. 10, 1960 (Longley's version of HF and papers as given to Sir Stanford).

5. EBF to Perry as cited in note 4; interv. CES; telegram, CES to Perry June 30, 1928, Acc. 38, Bx. 113 ("Pleasant Voyage"); Perry to EBF, Aug. 8, 1928, Acc. 6, Bx. 283 (on continental cos.).

6. T. Goldsmith to Frank Campsall, Aug. 17, 1928, Acc. 285, Bx. 796 (Jenkins leaving England); Perry to CES, July 31, 1928 (on engaging Smith, Jenkins' recommendation) and reply, Aug. 18, 1928, Acc. 38, Bx. 113 (approves); intervs. Sir Rowland Smith, London, Aug. 23, 1960 (Jenkins compared with Perry, Perry and Smith's meeting) and J. M. A. Smith, Dagenham, Aug. 30, 1960 (other personnel); Perry to CES, Oct. 14, 1929, Select File (H. S. and F. S. Thornhill Cooper).

7. Interv. Sir Stanford Cooper, London, July 4, 1961.

8. CES to Perry, Sept. 19, 1928, Acc. 38, Bx. 113 (plans for Perry's second trip); Nevins & Hill, II, 460, 466 (US daily production Model A); *FTC Report* (as cited Chap. 7, note 16), 480–81 (GM activities); U.S. Bur. of Census, *Historical Statistics,* Wash., 1949, 242 (US private investment abroad); James Harvey Rogers, "Foreign Markets and Foreign Credits," in *Recent Economic Changes,* II, N.Y., 1929, 750 (quote); Frank A. Southard, *American Industry in Europe,* Boston, 1931, xiv (1,300 cos.).

9. *Prospectus* for stock flotation Dec. 7, 1928, Secty's off., FMC-US; Henry Ford & Son Ltd. Mins. Bd. Dirs. July 7, 1927 and interv. Sir Stanford Cooper, Aug. 10, 1960 (Irish co.). It was FMC practice at this time to have "exclusive sales agreements," a procedure recommended by the Department of Commerce. Writing in 1927 Julius Klein, Director of the Bureau of Foreign and Domestic Commerce, had

declared in an official publication: "One of the most prominent causes of grievance and of misunderstanding is inadequate control of the distribution of goods. . . . It has been found that little or no control is exercised in foreign countries over the execution or operation of exclusive agency arrangements. Such arrangements, while in fact restraining commerce to a certain extent, are recognized as sound commercial practices." Such a statement clearly indicates that there was no intention in the closing years of the 1920's of invoking U.S. antitrust laws in connection with exclusive agreements. See Dept. of Com., Bur. of For. and Dom. Com., *Exclusive Sales Agreements in Foreign Trade,* Wash., 1927, v. 13.

10. *Prospectus;* CES to Perry, Oct. 5, 1929, Select File (quote).

11. *Prospectus;* interv. Sir Stanford Cooper, Aug. 10, 1960; FMC-Eng. *Annual Report 1929;* dossiers on dirs., Acc. 6, Bx. 292. Current press reports describe the reception of the issues. The Italian company was never reorganized because obstacles blocked its development. However, in late 1929 Perry still thought that its reconstruction would take place. See Perry to EBF, Feb. 10, 1930, Film No. 12, Item 6, OOSSC-M. In the reorganization of the Swedish company, 60 per cent of its shares were held by the Danish company instead of by Ford-Eng.; likewise 60 per cent of the shares of the Finnish company were held by the Swedish company. The remaining Finnish shares were not offered to the public but allotted to the directors. See H. S. Cooper to Lovell, White & King (lawyers), Dec. 4, 1929, Permanent File, FMC-Eng. Acc. 282, Bxs. 1 and 2, contain basic data on reorganization.

12. Corresp. in Acc. 38, Bx. 6, explains the formation of the office; its files are in storage at Langley, Eng. For Liechtenstein, see Perry to EBF, July 10, 1930, Acc. 313, Bx. 1; for Société d'Investissements Ford, Acc. 313, Bx. 1; also FMC-Eng., Mins. Shareholders Mtgs., Acc. 38, Bx. 40, and Perry to EBF, Mar. 4, 1936, Acc. 38, Bx. 34.

13. EBF wrote A. R. Lajous, Jan. 27, 1928, Acc. 6, Bx. 274, "The tractor assembly line has been shut down. . . . We are starting on designs for a new type tractor. . . ." Cosgrave to HF, Nov. 19, 1928, Acc. 38, Bx. 56 (refers to "new tractor"); "Darragh Memorandum Concerning Henry Ford and Ford Motor Company Tractor Development," n.d., Legal Files, FMC-US (end tractor Rouge); Perry to CES, July 30, 1928 (report on tractors) and CES to Perry, Aug. 10, 1928 ("agree to plan of making Cork tractor plant"), Acc. 38, Bx. 113; R. I. Roberge, testimony, U.S. Sen. Com. on Fin., *Tariff Act of 1929,* Hearings, 71st Cong., 1st Sess., Wash., 1929, 843 (tractor costs); *Evening Echo* (Cork), Nov. 8, 1928 (arrival first shipment); Clarke to CES, Jan. 19, 1929 (shipments service parts) and Squire to CES, Mar. 12, 1929 (service shipments), Select File; intervs. Sir Patrick Hennessy, London, Aug. 1960 (machines without roofs) and Squire, Dagenham, Sept. 5, 1960 (working in rain); Clarke to CES, Apr. 18, 1929, Select File (first tractors), stats. on tractor prodn., FMC-Eng.; data on countries receiving tractors, Select File.

14. Intervs. Sir Rowland Smith, Aug. 23, 1960 and June 26, 1961; Harry Hanson, *Reminiscences;* and Select File (for other Americans at Dagenham).

15. Perry to CES, Aug. 7, 24, 1928 (size of task, foundations); *Facts About Ford Works,* London, n.d. [1960?], 4 (number, character of piles); *N.Y. Times,* May 17, 1929 (Edsel); interv. Sir Rowland Smith, Aug. 23, 1960; interv. Miss V. Howard, (Perry and his guests); Perry, Report to Second Ordinary Gen. Mtg., Mar. 18, 1931 (difficulties at Dagenham); interv. Squire (on work there).

16. Perry to EBF and Perry to CES, both Aug. 30, 1929, Acc. 38, Bx. 1 (Perry-CES trip); CES to EBF, Aug. 16, 1929, Acc. 6, Bx. 15 ("great reputation").

17. Ford-Can., Mins. Bd. Dirs., Mar. 15, 1929 and ltr. to shareholders, same date; "Public Offering of Stock—Canadian Issue," Mar. 27, 1929 (in Bd. Mins.); Ford-

Can., Mins. Bd. Dirs., Mar. 26, 1929, all in Secty's off., FMC-Can. W. R. Campbell named as president in the March 1929 mins.

18. Interv. F. G. Batters, Apr. 1961; Campbell to E. G. Liebold, June 21, 1929, Acc. 285, Bx. 970. Campbell wrote EBF, July 10, 1930, Acc. 6, Bx. 29, that he had been "rounding up a majority of the voting stock of this Company" on EBF's behalf. At the time Ford holdings were 32,724 B shares, whereas 35,000 were required for control. Campbell advised against getting more than 50 per cent because of new tax laws. Ford holdings in August rose to 32,803 B shares, Acc. 6, Bx. 29 (transaction *re* EBF's increased holdings).

19. Sales Dept. stats. (R. Baker) and Sales Dept. Ford-Arg. (sales stats.); U.S. Dept. of Com., Bur. of For. and Dom. Com., *The Automotive Market in Argentina*, Wash., 1929, 1 (quote).

20. No series of manager's monthly letters from Latin American branches has been found, but interviews with R. I. Roberge, Aug. 1, 1961; Jorge Matray, Dec. 4, 1961; Kristian Orberg, Nov. 7, 1961, Guillermo Boxer, Nov. 18, 1961, and Frederick Foss Dover, Nov. 22, 1961 indicate such reports were made. Isolated copies are in Ford Archives. For plant approvals, see CES to Griffith, Nov. 13, 1929, Acc. 38, Bx. 1; Humberto Monteiro Memo, July 31, 1936, FMC-Brazil vault; and Russell Gnau's cables to CES June 17, 18, 24, 1930, Acc. 38, Bx. 63. For GM *v.* Ford stats., Acc. 38, Bx. 38; data on Cowling's trip in Acc. 689, and Cowling's *Reminiscences*.

21. Arthur M. Schlesinger, Jr., *The Crisis of the Old Order, 1919–1933,* Cambridge, 1957, 162–63 (quotes Charles M. Schwab, Bethlehem, Geo. E. Roberts, Natl. City Bank, and John E. Edgerton, NAM, as well as Ford); Henry Ford, *Moving Forward,* Garden City, N.Y., 1931, 7; Real Estate Records, FMC-Eng. (acreage at Dagenham); Perry to CES, Nov. 1, 1929, OOSPP, Bx. 1 (Slough Estate considered); booklet on Ford Estate at Dagenham, Select File; FMC-Eng., Mins. Bd. Dirs., May 25, Sept. 23, Oct. 19, 1931, Secty's off., FMC-US (leases). As to acreage, between 1934 and 1936 85.7 more acres were purchased, making the Dagenham site 586.7 acres. However, between 1931 and 1941 some 24.4 acres were sold. The site area after 1941 was therefore 562.3 acres.

22. Acc. 38, Bx. 1 and Select File (Italy, Holland, Sweden); Mayor Konrad Adenauer to E. C. Heine, Oct. 18, 1929 and cable Heine to Perry, same date, OOSPP, Bx. 1; Press Data, Oct. 29, 1929, Select File (acreage); AMA statistics on US prodn.; R. L. Polk & Co., stats. on American sales; *FTC Report,* 36 (US percentage of world prodn.); Sales Dept., FI (foreign sales).

23. Clarke to CES, Mar. 8, 1930, Select File (Mar. prodn.); L. Pearce to G. S. Hibberson, Feb. 28, 1930, OOSPP, Bx. 18 (Cork employees 6,924); Perry, Report to Annual Mtg., Mar. 18, 1931 ("This time last year we were employing almost 7000 men at Cork"); Industrial Relations Dept., FMC-Eng. (Manchester employees); R. I. Roberge, testimony, as cited in note 13, 840ff. (Ford's view on the tariff); *N.Y. Times,* July 3, 1929 and Oct. 6, 1930 (Ford on Smoot-Hawley); Acc. 390, Bx. 40 (attitude Ford personnel); cables, OOSPP, Bx. 8 (date of Ford arrival); Clara Ford's diary; Acc. 1, Bx. 24 (Ford goes to Dagenham); Perry to Wibel, Oct. 10, 1930, OOSPP, Bx. 9 (Ford to contractors); *N.Y. Times,* Oct. 3, 1930 (laying cornerstone German plant); stats. from GM (Opel).

24. Interv. B. H. C. Huntelaar, Amsterdam, Aug. 4, 1960 (Ford at Rotterdam); *De Maasbode,* Oct. 4, 1930, and *Nieuwe Rotterdamsche Courant,* Oct. 5, 1930 (Rotterdam); R. L. Polk, Registration figs., 1930. Ford gave permission for the Dutch company to complete the Rotterdam building on condition that it never use it! (After all, one couldn't sell the foundations of the building. The structure was rented for some years, then sold after World War II.)

CHAPTER 10

1. V. I. Meshlauk to EBF, May 6, 1929, Acc. 199, Bx. 1A; Copy of Agreement, May 31, 1929 between FMC, the Supreme Council of National Economy, and Amtorg, Acc. 199, Bx. 1A (henceforth cited as Russian Agreement).

2. Chap. 3 (early history).

3. Gaston Plantiff to E. G. Liebold, July 26, 1916, Acc. 23, Bx. 6; FMC-Ltd., "Automobile Record," FMC-Eng.

4. *N.Y. Herald,* June 27, 1919 and *N.Y. Times,* June 27, 1919 (Lusk); Contract with Ivan Stacheeff & Co., Mar. 14, 1919, EBF to R. S. Neely, Mar. 31, 1919, and W. A. Ryan to Roberge, Mar. 17, 1921 (results contract), all in Acc. 49, Bx. 1.

5. EBF to R. S. Neely, Mar. 31, 1919, Acc. 49, Bx. 1 (agreement confidential); *Dearborn Independent,* XIX, "Some Explanations of Conditions in Russia" and "The Framework of Affairs in Russia," both by J.L., Feb. 8, p. 7 and Feb. 15, p. 2; "Mr. Ford's Own Page," Mar. 8, 1919, 3; Lt. Boris Brasol, "The Bolshevik Menace to Russia," Apr. 12, 1919, 12; W. W. Shurupoff, "Russian Trade and Industrial Opportunities," Apr. 26, 1919, 2; L. A. Martens in *N.Y. Times,* June 27, 1919 (Russian conversations with Liebold).

6. *Dearborn Independent,* XXVI, Apr. 4, 1926, 9 (here) and XXVII, Sept. 27, 1927, 10 (new era).

7. W. A. Ryan to Roberge, Mar. 17, 1921, Acc. 49, Bx. 1 (end contract); corresp. Allied American Corporation with R. I. Roberge, Mar. 30, 1923, Ford Archives; Sales Stats., Russia, 1921–26, Ford Archives.

8. *Ford News,* IV, Aug. 15, 1924, 1 (quote), 1924–25 *passim,* and III, Oct. 15, 1923, 1, 4 (iron horse); Julius Hammer to Roberge, June 3, 1923, Acc. 38, Bx. 47 (2 to 1); *Ford News,* VII, Feb. 15, 1927 (Fordson distribution ctrs., repair depots, schools).

9. Report of the Ford delegation to Russia and the USSR, Apr.–Aug. 1926, Ford Archives. The five men who composed the group were H. D. Luedtke (Fordson plant), W. S. Ostendorf (Service Dept.), W. R. Tuban (Los Angeles branch), Bredo H. Berghoff (Fordson plant), and W. G. Collins (Italian Ford company). Joseph V. Stalin, *Leninism,* Eden and Cedar Paul, trs., N.Y., 1932, I, 389 (quote in starred fn.).

10. Report of Ford delegation; *Ford News,* VI, Mar. 15, 1926, 1 and June 1, 1926, 2 (students), and VII, Feb. 15, 1927, 1 (order for Fordsons); Maurice Hindus, "Henry Ford Conquers Russia," *Outlook,* June 29, 1927, 280–83; *N.Y. Times,* Nov. 13, 1926 and Sept. 14, 1927 (HF's reputation in Russia).

11. Bredo H. Berghoff, *Reminiscences;* Report of Ford delegation (credit); Chap. 9 (move to Cork); E. G. Liebold, *Reminiscences;* CES to Perry, May 6, 1929, and reply, May 14, 1929, Acc. 38, Bx. 115.

12. Frank A. Southard, *American Industry in Europe,* Boston, 1931, 203–06 (lists 51 Russian-American contracts as of Jan. 1931); Russian Agreement.

13. Report of Ford delegation; Joseph V. Stalin, *Problems of Leninism,* Moscow, 1933, II, 373 (quote); Russian Agreement (Meshlauk's role); CES, *My Forty Years with Ford,* N.Y., 1956, 195–204 (on his trip to Russia, which was after the final agreement had been signed and not before, as he mistakenly asserts); Perry to EBF, Aug. 30, 1929, Acc. 38, Bx. 1 and CES to EBF, Aug. 16, 1929, Select File (on trip, McGregor).

14. Russell Gnau to CES, Aug. 23, 1929, Acc. 38, Bx. 60 (activity in Dearborn); *Economic Review of the Soviet Union,* V, Apr. 1, 1930, 131 (Austin Co.); H. E. Fitzgerald to C. A. Malychevitch, Nov. 11, 1929, Acc. 199, Bx. 1 (Russian

engineers); Harry Bennett, *We Never Called Him Henry*, N.Y., 1951, 91 (1932 episode).

15. Frank Bennett, *Reminiscences*.

16. Report of P. McGregor, Sept. 16, 1929, Acc. Bx. 61; McGregor to CES, Oct. 3, 1929, Acc. 38, Bx. 1.

17. Bennett, *Reminiscences*; E. J. Driscoll to H. C. Bills, Nov. 1, 1932 (dates assembly started at Nizhni Novgorod and Moscow) and Dillingham to J. Crawford, July 16, 1930 (Russian performance first year of contract) both in Acc. 199, Bx. 1A; *Economic Review of the Soviet Union*, VI, Jan. 15, 1931, 42 (Kahn's statement); H. L. Moekle, Memo., Apr. 3, 1931 (equipment); G. I. Konevez (of Amtorg) to Roberge, Aug. 15, 1930 and reply, Aug. 26, 1930 (credit) and gen. data on fulfilment of contract, all in Acc. 199, Bx. 1A.

18. Benjamin Kopf to Roberge, Oct. 16, 1931, Acc. 38, Bx. 7.

19. E. J. Driscoll to H. C. Bills, Nov. 1, 1932, Acc. 199, Bx. 1A and *Economic Review of the Soviet Union*, VII, Feb. 15, 1932, 18 give start of Nizhni Novgorod plant as Jan. 25 and Jan. 29, 1932, respectively. Kopf to Roberge, *loc. cit.* (Kopf's opinion).

20. CES to Perry, June 6, 1932, Select File.

21. Squire to CES, Mar. 12, 1929, Select File (Cork starts service parts shipments to Russia); E. L. Clarke to Perry, May 14, 20, June 3, 1930, OOSPP, Bx. 18 (Russian orders and credit); CES to Perry, July 13, 1931, Acc. 38, Bx. 53 (quote); *Economic Review of the Soviet Union*, V, Dec. 1, 1930, 735 (Putilov tractor plant output 1929–30); IX, May 1934, 122 (date Stalingrad plant started production); V, Sept. 1, 1930, 357 (80 US cos.) and VI, May 1, 1931, 472 (Kharkov and Cheliabinsk plant).

22. Data in Acc. 199, Bx. 1A (fin. info.); Roberge to P. A. Bogdanov (Amtorg), June 15, 1933 and Oct. 31, 1933, Acc. 199, Bx. 1A (on fulfilment of contract). Roberge had written Bogdanov earlier that the arrangement Amtorg and Sorensen had made in Detroit to reduce temporarily the volume of purchases under the contract was only a short-term measure. The Russians would be expected to comply in the long term. See Roberge to Bogdanov, May 17, 1933, Acc. 199, Bx. 1A. CES to Wibel, Apr. 18, 1935, Acc. 199, Bx. 1A (cancellation of the contract, and notes he has asked the Russian engineers to leave the Rouge offices).

23. HF, "Why I am Helping Russian Industry," *Nation's Business*, June 1930, 20–23 (quote); *Digest of the Soviet Press*, XIII, Feb. 22, 1961, 3 (Russian prodn.); *The Motor Industry of Great Britain 1960*, London, 1960, 12. Tractors are not included in either the Russian or the British figures which are for 1959. The British total: 1,560,427.

24. Figs. furnished Nevins & Hill by the Treasurer's off., FMC-US, Dec. 9, 1954; Moekle Memo, Apr. 3, 1931, Acc. 199, Bx. 1A; Craig to Amtorg, June 28, 1935, Acc. 199, Bx. 1A (billing price as in starred fn., and also indication of desire to keep doing business with the Russians).

CHAPTER 11

1. Clarke to Perry, May 14, 20, June 3, 1930 and Hennessy to Buckmaster, Aug. 11, 1930, OOSPP, Bx. 18 (Irish conds.); William Ashworth, *A Short History of the International Economy 1850–1950*, London, 1959, 196–97.

2. Perry to CES, Oct. 14, 1929, Select File; intervs. Maurice Buckmaster, London, Sept. 6, 1960 and J. M. A. Smith, London, July 13, 1961.

3. Perry to EBF, Feb. 10, 1930, Apr. 2, 1931, OOSSC-M and Acc. 38, Bx. 2 (Livorno purchase) and Bx. 7 (decree); Perry, in FMC-Eng., *Report of Second Ord. Gen.*

Mtg., Mar. 18, 1931 (gen. situation in Italy); interv. F. S. Thornhill Cooper, Rome, June 27, 1960; Perry to EBF, July 15, 1932, Acc. 6, Bx. 310 (Italian duty); Acc. 38, Bx. 68 (registrations). In July 1932 the Italian duty on Model B (an improved model A) was $898, or one and one half times the retail price in the U.S.A. On the V-8 it was $2,145 (nearly 45,000 lira).

4. *N.Y. Times*, Aug. 2, 6, 1930; FMC-Eng. to Prodn. Dept., Dearborn, Sept. 18, 1930 and Jenkins to N.Y., Oct. 31, 1930, OOSPP, Bx. 9; Perry to CES, Dec. 1, 1931, Acc. 38, Bx. 6 (situation 1931). Ford of course had been opposed to the tariff but was not given credit in Europe for his attitude.

5. Interv. Maurice Dollfus, Paris, Sept. 6, 1960; Ford SAF, Report of Bd. Dirs., year ending Dec. 31, 1930, Acc. 606, Bx. 4; Perry to CES, Jan. 9, 1930 (ltr. and cable of that date), CES to Perry Jan. 10, 1930 and Perry to CES, Jan. 10, 1930, Acc. 38, Bx. 3 (shipments before tariff imposition); interv. Dollfus, and Perry to EBF, May 15, 1929, Acc. 606, Bx. 4 (tax saving); Perry to CES, Apr. 1, 1932, OOSPP, Bx. 44 (review of French co.'s history); Ford SAF Mins. Bd. Dirs. Nov. 14, 1930, Acc. 606, Bx. 1 (appt. Dollfus and suggestions, *re:* mfg. in France); CES to Perry, July 17, 1931, Select File (Perry's approach); "Earnings of Associated Ford Companies— at official rates of exchange" in "England Guernsey Ford Investment," folder, FI.

6. Perry to CES, July 16, 1930 and CES to Heine, July 30, 1930, Select File (mfg. in Germany); E. Vitger to H. S. Cooper, Dec. 22, 1931, OOSPP, Bx. 33 (officers); in-tervs. Vitger and Schmidt, Cologne, July 1960 (Albert, Heine, and co. in gen.); E. C. Heine to Perry, Apr. 20, June 22, 1931, OOSPP, Bx. 33 (situation in spring and opening of plant); FMC-Ger., *Annual Report 1930* (description of plant).

7. Perry-Heine corresp., in OOSPP, Bx. 33; Ashworth, 204–06 (Austria, Germany, Hoover); Heine to CES, May 4, 1931 (prodn.), Perry to CES, July 24, 1931, and Heine, Report to Dirs. for July 1931, Aug. 14, 1931, all in Acc. 38, Bx. 6.

8. Perry-Heine-Vitger-Riorden corresp., Oct.–Dec. 1931, Thornhill Cooper to A. R. Smith, June 24, 1931, all in OOSPP, Bx. 33.

9. Acc. 38, Bx. 10 (car registrations); Earnings of Associated Cos.

10. G. F. Wilkinson, "The Wonder Workers of Dagenham," *Ford Times* (Eng.), VIII, Jan. 1931, 84; W. J. Politzer, "Double or Lose Seen as Ford's Answer in Europe," *Automotive Industries*, LXVI, Jan. 30, 1932, 145; Report on Progress at Dagenham, June 1932, Acc. 572, Bx. 18; cable, A. R. Smith to CES, Oct. 1, 1931. Acc. 38, Bx. 9; FMC-Eng., *Annual Report*, 1932; employment figs., 1931–45, FMC-Eng.

11. Interv. W. J. Squire, Dagenham, June 20, 1961; List of British Plants, and Dates when Acquired and Vacated, J. M. A. Smith to Moekle, Aug. 15, 1946, Acc. 134, Bx. 37; FMC-Eng., Mins. Bd. Dirs., Feb. 25, 1931, Secty's off., FMC-US (increase in capital); Perry in FMC-Eng. *Report of Third Ord. Gen. Mtg.,* Apr. 8, 1932 (Man-chester). Perry wanted to raise the capitalization to £12,000,000, which would have eased the company's operations in the future, but Dearborn would not approve. See FMC-Eng. Mins. Bd. Dirs., Feb. 25, 1931, Secty's off., FMC-US. Much general cor-respondence in this period reveals the conditions that caused the abandonment of Manchester.

12. FMC-Eng. *Report of Second Ord. Gen. Mtg.,* Mar. 18, 1931; Perry to CES, Aug. 21, 1931 (Cork) and Apr. 22, 1932 (Clarke), Perry to EBF, Apr. 15, 1932, all in Acc. 572, Bx. 18; W. J. S. McCurdy, "The New Industrial Fordson Makes Its Bow," *Ford Times* (Eng.), IX, Jan. 1932, 108ff.; *Ford Times* (Eng.), IX, Oct. 1932, 611ff. In the October issue a picture of "the latest development of the Fordson Industrial Tractor" is shown, which, reads the copy, has been "notably improved"; interv. Michael Ronayne, Aveley Eng. Ctr., June 22, 1961.

13. Prodn. stats., FMC-Eng.; interv. Sir Rowland Smith, London, June 26, 1961 (cars); Chap. 7 (Jenkins' attitude); Perry to EBF, July 31, 1931, Acc. 6, Bx. 301 (Perry's attitude); Perry to Liebold, Oct. 20, 1930, OOSPP, Bx. 8 (car shipments).

14. FMC-Eng., *Annual Reports,* 1929–31; A. R. Smith to Dirs., Report for Oct. 1931, Acc. 38, Bx. 5; data on A. R. Smith's trip in Acc. 38, Bx. 5; Sheldrick, *Reminiscences;* Memo, Sheldrick to Dunton (purchasing), Dec. 3, 1931, Acc. 38, Bx. 119 (allotment of engineering work); A. R. Smith to CES, Feb. 2, 1932, Acc. 38, Bx. 71 (changes in Model Y); interv. Sir Rowland Smith, London, Aug. 23, 1960.

15. Perry to EBF, Mar. 27, 1931, Acc. 23, Bx. 6; Perry to G.T.T., Both, May 9, 1932 in Holland-Amsterdam Ford AF Mtgs. Divs., FI; Perry to EBF, July 5, 1932, OOSPP, Bx. 41; interv. Squire, June 20, 1961.

16. Memo, CES to Ford execs., July 6, 1932, Acc. 38, Bx. 71 (Model Y); deptl. com., Sheldrick to execs. and engrs., Dec. 3, 1931, Acc. 38, Bx. 19 (assignments of engs. in Model Y project); Perry to CES, Mar. 18, 1932, and cable A. R. Smith to CES, Feb. 23–24, 1932, both in Acc. 38, Bx. 71 (reception of Model Y); A. M. Wibel to Roland Philips, Dec. 1, 1931, Acc. 390, Bx. 84 (orders for 14 bodies); FMC-Eng., Mins. Bd. Dirs. Mar. 18, 1932, Secty's off. FMC-US; interv. Sir Patrick Hennessy, Aug. 1960; FMC-Eng. *Annual Report, 1932* (loss); gen. stats., FMC-Eng.

17. FMC-Can. *Annual Reports,* 1929–32; sales figs., FMC-Can.

18. Australian Ford Figs. from Overseas Divn., FMC-Can., Oakville (which include stats. for other Canadian-supervised cos. and agencies); L. R. Leeman to J. Foster, June 15, 1955, FMC-Austl.; description of Australian co. plants, Sept. 20, 1933, Acc. 1, Bx. 115.

19. Sales data, Acc. 38, Bx. 68 (Japan 1930); telegrams in Acc. 38, Bx. 7 and Ashworth, 209 (gold standard); Cowling, *Reminiscences* and Scrapbook, Acc. 689; Acc. 38, Bx. 4 and Wiesmyer and Riecks, *Reminiscences* (their reports and opinions); J. V. Crowe to Cowling, May 16, 1932, Acc. 38, Bx. 6 and Soong to HF, Sept. 12, 1932, Select File (China); EBF to Soong, Nov. 11, 1932, Select File; Acc. 713, Bx. 54 (Ford deliveries, which were 1387 for 1931, 1321 for 1932, and 1640 for 1933); V. A. Dodge and Roberge give info. about China in their intervs.

20. Hubert Herring, *A History of Latin America,* N.Y., 1961, *passim.*

21. Gnau to CES, June 16, 1930, Acc. 38, Bx. 63; interv. Francisco Salles Cesár, São Paulo, Nov. 10, 1961 (Pôrto Alegre branch and Vargas); corresp. in vault FMC-Brazil, 1930–31; interv. Povl Anderson, São Paulo, Nov. 13, 1961; Griffith to CES, Jan. 24, 1931, Acc. 38, Bx. 2.

22. Orberg, *Reminiscences* (Brazil); interv. W. W. Townsend, Mexico City, Dec. 21, 1961 (credit); Craig to Natl. City Bank, Jan. 22, 1931, Acc. 49, Bx. 9; Credit Dept., Ford-Arg., also Acc. 49, Bx. 8; records Crédito Centrale, S.A. Acc. 303 (data on Mexican credit operations).

23. Albert Kahn records, Acc. 33, Bx. 66; Griffith corresp. in Acc. 38, Bxs. 1, 2, and 8 and corresp. in Pacheco Vault, FMC-Arg. (difficulties finding site in Argentina); Griffith to CES, Oct. 29, 1934, Acc. 38, Bx. 26 (purchase land); Gnau to CES, June 23, 1930, Acc. 38, Bx. 63 and Roberge, deptl. com., Jan. 6, 1933, Acc. 106, Bx. 24 (closing Brazilian branches); FMC-Chile, balance sheets, 1932 (stoppage assembly); Odin to EBF, Sept. 3, 1931, Acc. 6, Bx. 300 (Peru); Sales Dept., FI (R. Baker), FMC-US (closing Peruvian branch); FMC-Urug., balance sheets; Scrapbook of Carlos Ramirez, FMC-Mex. (clippings on the new Mexican plant); Mfg. Staff (C. T. Alexander off.), FMC-US (Mexican plant facilities); Sales Dept., FI (Latin American sales).

24. FMC-Arg., balance sheet (Apr. 1933 sales); *O Mundo Ford,* IV, Mar. 1933, 11; FMC-Brazil, sales figs., 1933–37; Sales Dept., FI (Latin American sales for 1933).

25. FMC-Eng., Mins. Bd. Dirs., Sept. 28, Nov. 23, 1932, Secty's off., FMC-US; FMC-Eng., *Annual Report 1932* (loss).

26. FMC-Eng., Mins. Bd. Dirs., Feb. 27, Apr. 11, 1933 and June 11, 1934 (blast furnace); intervs. Sir Patrick Hennessy, London, Aug. 1960 and June 19, 1961; Mins. of Extraordinary Mtgs. of Stockholders for European countries, Dec. 15–30, 1933, FI; FMC-Eng., *Annual Report 1933;* Data from Prodn. Plang. Dept., FMC-Eng.; G. Maxcy and A. Silberston, *The Motor Industry,* London, 1959, 100, 107 (percentages and changes in type of cars preferred).

27. Heine to A. R. Smith, Sept. 12, 1932, OOSPP, Bx. 50; Dollfus to CES, Feb. 26, 1932, Acc. 38, Bx. 9 (order for 10,000 Model Y's); Perry to EBF, Aug. 2, 1932, Acc. 572, Bx. 18; CES to Perry, Oct. 4, 1932, and replies, Oct. 5–6 (both ltr. and cable), Mgrs. Report to Dirs., Oct. 1932, all in Acc. 38, Bx. 10 (mfr. in Germany). Perry had not entirely opposed manufacture in Germany, but he had advocated sending the car from England for a time to test public reaction. Heine and CES agreed, but soon this was an impossible approach.

28. Heine to Thornhill Cooper, Mar. 24, 1933, corresp. files, FMC-Ger.

29. Data in Select File covers the fin. reorgan.: see esp. FMC-Ger., *Business Report and Balance Sheet for 1933* (pub. Sept. 1934); the percentage calculations are ours based on balance sheet and Perry to Craig, Aug. 1, 1934, Select File.

30. Dollfus to CES, May 20, 1931, Acc. 38, Bx. 6 (price of Model A); Perry to EBF, Oct. 10, 1933 (V-8 price), Perry to EBF, Mar. 20, 1933, Select File (price of Model Y); Sales Dept., FI (Model Y sales 1932 and 1933 in France); interv. Buckmaster; Earnings of Associated Cos. (profit and loss figs. for all European Ford companies, in dollars); Perry to CES, Dec. 19, 1933 and Dollfus to Perry, Dec. 22, 1933, Select File.

31. CES to Perry, Dec. 5, 1933 (Dollfus and Mathis have been here ten days); Dollfus to Perry, Dec. 22, 1933 (Dollfus' quote) both in Select File; CES to Perry, Mar. 29, 1934, Acc. 507, Bx. 63 (plans); H. C. Kellogg to CES, Apr. 27, 1934, Acc. 38, Bx. 22 (Mathis plant); CES's trip, Acc. 38, Bx. 74; interv. CES (by Nevins & Hill), June 29, 1954 (reaction to Strasbourg plant); Perry to CES, Jan. 12, 1934, Select File (mfg. supervision); Lybrand, Ross Bros. & Montgomery, to W. T. Gossett, Jan. 7, 1948, in Earnings of Associated Cos. (purchase of shares; price and evaluation of price); Acc. 606, Bx. 6 (per cent Ford-US interests owned); Acc. 507, Bx. 63 (final documents on Matford); Acc. 334, Bx. 1 (Matford Statutes etc.). The Ford-group directors of Matford were M. Dollfus, J. C. Charpentier, and Edsel Ford (all directors of Ford SAF as well). The Mathis group was represented by E. E. C. Mathis and M. Boyer (brother-in-law of Mathis); Dollfus to HF and EBF, Oct. 9, 1934, Acc. 6, Bx. 324 (no. of dealers); Mathis to EBF, July 6, 1934 and reply, Sept. 26, 1934, Acc. 507, Bx. 63.

32. W. R. Loughran, Percentage of Cost per Tudor Represented by American and Local Expenditures, June 28, 1932, Select File. Prodn. figs. from FMC-Eng.

33. Interv. Dollfus (Dollfus quote); Earnings of Associated Cos. and FMC-Eng., *Annual Reports* 1929–33.

34. Perry to CES, Dec. 19, 1933, Select File (quote); Society of Motor Manufacturers and Traders, *The Motor Industry in Great Britain 1952,* London, n.d., 21, 28–30 (historical world automobile prodn. figs.); Ashworth, 209 (gold standard); Donald Bailey Marsh, *World Trade and Investment,* N.Y., 1951, 10 (world trade).

493

CHAPTER 12

1. Kopf to Riecks and Hesser, Mar. 28, 1935 and Riecks to Hanson, Feb. 15, 23, 1935, Acc. 390, Bx. 85.
2. Nathaniel Peffer, *The Far East,* Ann Arbor, Mich., 1958, 354–60.
3. Mitsubishi Economic Research Bureau, *Japanese Trade and Industry,* London, 1936, 306 (stats.); *Japan Advertiser,* May 8, 1937; Peffer, 362 (rail and highway mileage); A. M. Wibel to A. Johnston, Apr. 3, 1935, Acc. 390, Bx. 86.
4. Ford corresp. and memos, Feb. 1935 to July 1936 (mostly Kopf-Crawford), Acc. 390, Bx. 85; interv. Kopf, Mexico City, Dec. 11, 1961; *Japan Advertiser,* May 28, 1937; *N. Y. Times,* July 19, 1936 (motor car law).
5. Corresp. Kopf-Crawford, Sept. 1936—Jan. 24, 1940, and particularly Kopf to Crawford, Sept. 22, 1936 (appraisal of situation) Acc. 390, Bx. 85; Frank Riecks, *Reminiscences;* Sales Dept., FI (R. Baker), FMC-US.
6. Hubert Herring, *A History of Latin America,* 2nd ed., N.Y., 1961, 670, 673, and *passim.*
7. Frank A. Waring, "Economic Problems of the Latin-American Republics," in Seymour Harris, ed., *Economic Problems of Latin America,* N.Y., 1944, 54; George Wythe, *Industry in Latin America,* N.Y., 1945, *passim;* Sales Dept., FI (sales figs.); U.S. Senate, Com. on For. Relations, *United States–Latin American Relations,* 86th Cong., 2nd Sess., Sen. Doc. No. 125, Wash., 1960, 566–67.
8. Interv. Pedro Zinkgräf, Buenos Aires, Nov. 27, 1961 (competition with GM), FMC-Brazil (sales figs.)
9. Intervs. Humberto Monteiro and others, São Paulo, Nov. 16, 1961 (trucks), Sales Dept., FMC-Brazil (truck deliveries); data in Vault, FMC-Brazil (truck body business).
10. Herring, 376, 383 (Cardenas); *N.Y. Times,* May 10, 1938 (Ford strike); interv. Ralph Chaplin, Cuernavaca, Dec. 18, 1961 (Lajous, CES, Bennett); *N.Y. Times,* May 20, 1938 (Ford attitude and end of strike).
11. *Ford News,* XVIII, Feb. 1938, 40–41, 43.
12. Report by George S. Armstrong & Co., Inc., June 16, 1947, Arjay Miller office, FMC-US (FMC-US loss); Comparative Sales, Profits, etc., So. Amer. and Asiatic Plants, Acc. 713, Bx. 54 (L.A. profits). For 1930–39 earnings of European companies including England came to about $32,000,000, but owing to the ownership pattern under the 1928 plan, little of this came to Dearborn. See "Earnings of Associated Ford Companies—at official rates of exchange" in "England-Guernsey Ford Investment" folder, FI.
13. Earnings of Associated Cos.; FMC-Egypt, Mins. Shareholders Mtg., Dec. 1935, FI (list of territories); conversation, Christopher Mataras, Asst. Mgr. FMC-Egypt, Detroit, Apr. 20, 1960.
14. *Ibid.;* FMC-Egypt Mgr.'s Report to Dirs., June 30, Sept. 30, 1935, Acc. 38, Bx. 29; Sales Dept., FI (sales figs.).
15. *N.Y. Times,* Oct. 18 (Ford shipments) and Dec. 16, 1935 (Graziani quote); Earnings of Associated Cos.; conversation Mataras. Mataras thought Dearborn and even Henry Ford knew where the trucks were going; in view of Ford's record on war, it seems unlikely that he was informed before the appearance of the *Times* article of Oct. 18, 1935.
16. Perry to Craig, June 8, 1936, Acc. 38, Bx. 34 and other materials there (situation in Italy); Earnings of Associated Cos. (losses); interv. Roberge, Aug. 1, 1961 (appraisal);

"Memo on Discussion with Mr. H. S. Cooper" (unsigned, probably H. L. Moekle), in folder "Istanbul," FI; Ford Romana, SAR, Mins. Bd. Dirs., Acc. 320, Bx. 1; Sales Dept., FI (sales Ford-Romana); Perry to EBF, Jan. 2, 1941, Acc. 320, Bx. 1 (financing Ford-Romana).

17. Earnings of Associated Cos.; Perry to EBF, Feb. 17, 1936, Acc. 608, Bx. 2 (percentage business in Spain); EBF to Jenkins, Apr. 9, 1936, Acc. 6, Bx. 335; "Memo to be submitted to the Nationalist Government," attached to FMC-Sp., Mins. Bd. Dirs., Mar. 16, 1939, FI (plans for plant in 1936, war).

18. Perry to CES, July 24, 1936 (Jenkins' message) and July 27, 1936 (unions take charge), both in Acc. 38, Bx. 34; *N.Y. Herald Tribune,* July 29, 1936 (same); Perry to CES, July 31, 1936, Acc. 38, Bx. 34 (Jenkins' flight); Ubach, "Memo," Aug. 6, 1936 and ltr. to Perry, Aug. 8, both in Acc. 6, Bx. 335 (relations with workers); *N.Y. Times,* Aug. 30, 1936 and Ford Iberica to Hon. Secty of Economy of Govt. of Catalonia, Oct. 26, 1936, Acc. 6, Bx. 335 (prodn. for Loyalists).

19. G. Nadal to Ford dealers in Spain, Sept. 29, 1936, Acc. 38, Bx. 34 (Jenkins' order to sell to insurgents); Perry to Associated Cos., Sept. 29, 1936, Acc. 38, Bx. 34 (no sales to either party in Spain); Perry to Jenkins, Oct. 7 (rebuking him) and reply, Nov. 20, 1936 (case for Franco), and further corresp. Perry-Jenkins, Nov.–Dec. 1936, all in Acc. 38, Bx. 34; Earnings of Associated Cos.; intervs. Georges Lesto, Paris, June 9, 1960, and Marcel Cola, Grenvilliers, July 11, 1960 (FMC-Fr. and Spanish Civil War); FMC-Sp., Mins. Bd. Dirs., Mar. 13, 1939, FI (deliveries to insurgents).

20. Dollfus to CES, Sept. 13, 1934, Acc. 6, Bx. 324 (Mathis problems); interv. G. A. Panier, Poissy, France, Sept. 12, 1960 (Strasbourg plant); Dollfus to CES, Apr. 2, 1936, Acc. 38, Bx. 32 (French govt.); interv. Jules Gutzeit, Cologne, July 20, 1960 (Americans at Strasbourg). Among the experts from Dearborn were Lester Mix, Frank Cort, Claude Stevens, Stanley Hill, Fred Farrell, and Harry Ford. See list in Acc. 38, Bx. 22. First group under Mix sailed on Aug. 25, 1934, and others followed on Sept. 1, Oct. 13, and Jan. 3, 1935.

21. Intervs. Maurice Dollfus, Paris, Sept. 13, 1960 and Panier (cars, engines); Ford-SAF, Mins. Bd. Dirs., Oct. 26, 1937, Acc. 606, Bx. 2 (summary Ford-Mathis relations); CES cable, Aug. 1934, record of Panier conversation with CES, Aug. 1935, and Panier to Dollfus, Aug. 24, 1935, all in Panier's personal files.

22. Interv. Panier (mfg. at Strasbourg; stats. from his personal files); Dollfus to EBF, May 1, 1935, Acc. 38, Bx. 27 and *La Vie Automobile,* XXXI, Sept. 25, 1935, 430 (*Normandie* trip and Charles Faroux comments); Ford-SAF, Mins. Shareholders. Mtg., June 28, 1935, Acc. 606, Bx. 2 (quote about prod.); Dollfus to CES, July 17, 1935, Acc. 38, Bx. 27 (Mathis demands; Dollfus objection.); Dollfus to EBF, Sept. 26, 1935, Acc. 6, Bx. 309 (name of car); protesting ltrs. from Mathis, Acc. 38, Bx. 27.

23. Interv. Panier (design of chassis). A copy of a cable, CES to Dollfus, about the Model 62 chassis is in Panier's personal files.

24. Earnings of Associated Cos.; prodn. figs., Panier's files; Ford-SAF, Mins. Bd. Dirs., Oct. 26, 1937, Acc. 606, Bx. 2, and Dollfus Memo, June 1, 1938, Acc. 6, Bx. 346 (Mathis' cars a loss); interv. Dollfus (cruelly underlined); intervs. Panier and Gutzeit (Mathis' methods); corresp. Acc. 38, Bx. 32 (Ford contribution, Mathis obstruction); Dollfus to CES, June 15, 1936, Acc. 38, Bx. 32 (quote).

25. Mix to CES, June 3, 13, 23, 25, 1936 (Europe and situation, Strasbourg), CES to Gnau, Mar. 10, 1936 (Gnau to send cable, all in Acc. 38, Bx. 32; CES in Florida).

26. Dollfus to CES, June 3, 13, 23, 25, 1936, Acc. 38, Bx. 32.

27. Corresp. in Acc. 38, Bx. 37 (on Mathis relationship); Ford-SAF, Mins. Bd. Dirs., June 28, 1938, Acc. 38, Bx. 40 (Mathis demands); Dollfus to EBF, July 12, 1938, Acc. 6, Bx. 346 (Mathis accepts Ford offer); Ford-SAF, Mins. Bd. Dirs., Feb. 18, 1942, Acc. 606 (Ford paid Mathis 5.5 million francs more).

28. Ford-SAF, Mins. Bd. Dirs., Oct. 26, 1937, Acc. 38, Bx. 37 (Mathis deal off, Dollfus to find new site); Dollfus to CES, July 28, 1937 (no capital in France); Dollfus to CES, Jan. 6, 1938, Acc. 38, Bx. 40 (Poissy site—informing French govt.).

29. Dollfus to CES, Nov. 10, 1937 (small car; scribbled on ltr. by CES: "The German small car is what I believe he needs"), CES to Dollfus, Dec. 3, 1937 (suggests German car), Dollfus to CES, Dec. 21, 1937 (must be French, needs extra million), all in Acc. 38, Bx. 40; interv. Roberge, Birmingham, Mich., Aug. 1, 1961 (Dollfus and Ford money); CES to Dollfus, Jan. 14, 1938 (second thoughts) and Dollfus to EBF, Jan. 28, 1938 (defense of small car), both in Acc. 507, Bx. 67; Dollfus to CES, Jan. 14, 1938, Acc. 38, Bx. 40 (market for small car); Ford-SAF, Mins. Bd. Dirs., May 2, 1938, Acc. 38, Bx. 40 (approval Poissy plant and financing). The Bd. Mins. read $40 million for cost of plant, but from other data this appears to be a typographical error. See Dollfus to Craig, Aug. 8, 1939, Acc. 334, Bx. 2, who estimates cost at $3,825,000.

30. Earnings of Associated Cos. (Matford profit 1937); F. C. Riecks to CES, Oct. 7, 1938, Acc. 38, Bx. 40 (troubles, progress with plant); Dollfus to EBF, Dec. 19, 1938, Acc. 6, Bx. 354 (prophecy of loss); Ford-SAF, Mins. Bd. Dirs., Dec. 14, 1938 (govt. request) and Dollfus to CES, June 14, 1938 (aircraft motors a possibility), Acc. 38, Bx. 40; Guy La Chambre to Dollfus, Jan. 31, 1939, Acc. 6, Bx. 354 (appeal to participate in defense); data on Dollfus visit, Acc. 38, Bx. 128 and Acc. 6, Bx. 354; intervs Dollfus and Panier (their visit to Eng.); Dollfus to EBF, May 9, 15, 1939, Acc. 6, Bx. 354 (Rolls-Royce plans for France and American technicians); Report on Financial Condition Ford-SAF, Dec. 31, 1945, Acc. 415, Bx. 1 and Dollfus to EBF, June 21, 1939, Acc. 6, Bx. 354 (Ford air); Ford-SAF, Mins. Bd. Dirs., July 20, 1939, Acc. 507, Bx. 67 (purchase Bordeaux plant); Dollfus to EBF, May 23, 1939 and reply, May 24, 1939, Acc. 6, Bx. 354 (small car); Dollfus to EBF, Aug. 1, 1939, Acc. 606, Bx. 6 (agrees to take post chairman Ford-SAF); materials in Acc. 507, Bx. 17, and interv. Gutzeit (plans for small car, tools and dies prepared for shipment, etc.).

CHAPTER 13

1. *Voelkischer Beobachter*, Feb. 13, 1933 (Hitler Exposition speech); Prince Louis Ferdinand, *The Rebel Prince*, Chicago, 1952, 240–41 ("You can tell Herr Ford"); Mgr.'s Report, Mar. 1933, FMC-Ger. files (status of Ford cars and trucks).

2. Interv. Dollfus, Paris, Sept. 13, 1960 (comment on Albert); Perry to CES, Dec. 19, 1933, Select File (on retaining Heine). FMC-Ger. files and corresp. deal with Vitger and Schmidt, and Perry's role is indicated in corresp. with him, A. R. Smith, Thornhill Cooper, and Roland Philip in FMC-Ger. Files, 1933–34. For Sorensen's increasing role see CES-Perry corresp., Select File.

3. Heine-Philip-Thornhill Cooper corresp. and other material in FMC-Ger. Files, particularly Heine to T. Cooper, Aug. 25, 1933 (causes of low sales) and July 31, 1933 (National Socialist Party and Ford car). Heine claimed to stand well with the Party, and attributed his poor record to the slanders of the German manufacturers. Perry to CES, Jan. 10, 1934, Select File (opposition of the Society of Automotive Manufacturers.)

4. *Voelkischer Beobachter*, Mar. 9, 1934 (Hitler's 1934 speech); Albert to CES, Aug. 16, 1934, FMC-Ger. Files (standzn.).

5. Perry to CES, Mar. 13, 1934, Select File (Bosch, Albert, and political situation); Albert to Heine, June 21, 1934 (proposing to use "Volkswagen" or "Volksford" as name for Ford car) and German Assn. of Automobile Industry to Heine, June 22, 1934, both in FMC-Ger. Files (forbidding use of "Volkswagen").

6. FMC-Ger. Files, *passim* (character of Cologne plant); T. F. Gehle-Wibel corresp. (items Ford-Cologne had to get from suppliers); Mgrs. Reports, FMC-Ger., 1933–34 and comment from England such as W. R. Nieland, OOSPP, to Heine, July 6, 1934 (Ford and Chevrolet prices), and Heine-Philip-Thornhill Cooper corresp. on trade condns., cancellation of orders, pleas for help from England, etc. (confusion and difficulties of the Germans).

7. CES to Perry, Jan. 30, 1934 ("kicked to pieces"), Prince Louis Ferdinand to CES, Apr. 26, June 26, 1934 (Ford AG and German govt.), and reply, July 12, 1934 (fin., German govt.), Select File.

8. Albert Memo, June 14, 1934, Select File; Wibel to Perry, Mar. 8, 1934 (disapproving German purchasing), and Wibel to Albert, July 23, 1934 (quote), FMC-Ger. Files.

9. Gehle to Wibel, Aug. 23, 1934, FMC-Ger. Files (letter-report); V. Y. Tallberg, *Reminiscences;* Albert to Perry, Sept. 1, 1934 (Prince LF, Hamburg plant idea, relations with German officials); CES to Perry, Aug. 22, 1934, Select File (Prince LF, Dr. Albert); Perry to Albert, Sept. 4, 1934 (reassuring him) and Albert to CES, Dec. 14, 1934, both in Select File (account of Wibel's visit).

10. Sorensen, conversation (with Nevins & Hill) June 29, 1954 (Heine's discharge); Gehle to Wibel, Jan. 31 (Heine sailing to USA) and Feb. 14, 1935 (Diestel introduced), FMC-Ger. Files; *Rhein-Weste Zeitung,* Jan. 24, 1937, *Nachtausgabe* (Berlin), Jan. 3, 1937, and *Deutsche Bergwerke Zeitung,* Jan. 24, 1937 (Diestel's qualifications); Tallberg, *Reminiscences;* A. L. Byrns to Moekle, May 24, 1935, Acc. 6, Bx. 415; FMC-Ger., Mins. Bd. Dirs., May 28, 1935, Acc. 38, Bx. 33 (Diestel's election).

11. Mgr.'s Reports, 1st, 2nd, and 3rd quarters (Eifel, trucks, V-8, percentages of market), and Gehle-Wibel corresp., 1934–37 (American experts) FMC-Ger. Files; Byrns Report, Acc. 6, Bx. 415, and R. I. Roberge, "Memoranda with Reference to European Organizations," June 20, 1935, Acc. 507, Bx. 95 (gen. condns.). Byrns and Roberge dealt mostly with the difficulties of FMC-Ger.

12. Diestel and Albert to Minister of National Economy, Jan. 13, 1936, and Albert to CES, Jan. 20, 1936, Acc. 38, Bx. 33 (merger, Prince LF); Albert, "Memorandum," Mar. 9, 1936, Acc. 6, Bx. 335 (discrimination *v.* Ford); FMC-Ger., Mins. Bd. Dirs., May 13, 1936, and Albert to CES, May 13, 1936, Acc. 38, Bx. 33 (govt. and merger); Byrns to Moekle, May 10, 1935 and his report, May 24, 1935, Acc. 415, Bx. 1; Perry to CES, Dec. 13, 1935, Acc. 38, Bx. 33 (exports-Spain).

13. Diestel to CES, Mar. 2, 1936, Acc. 38, Bx. 33 (Hitler pics., sales); Albert Memo, Mar. 9, 1936, Acc. 6, Bx. 335, and Albert to CES, Feb. 3, 1936 (advantages Stoewer merger), Dearborn Instructions to Albert, Apr. 6, 1936 (tentative agreement), CES to Albert and to Perry, June 18, 1936 (Diestel's Jewish ancestry, Hoyler coming to Dearborn), Perry to CES, July 14, 1936 (loan, Stoewer exposed), and Albert to CES, July 20, 1936 (break with Stoewer), all in Acc. 38, Bx. 33.

14. FMC-Ger., Mins. Bd. Dirs., Aug. 10, 1936 (sales), Diestel to CES, Sept. 28, 1936, Moss to CES, Aug. 5, 18, 1938, all in Acc. 38, Bx. 33 and Gehle to Wibel, Apr. 20, 1936, FMC-Ger. Files (all factory improvements); Albert Memo, Mar. 9 (German cloak) and Aug. 17, 1936 (latent antagonism, program, standzn.), Acc. 6, Bx. 335; Albert to CES, Dec. 17, 1935 (exports and standzn.), Acc. 38, Bx. 33.

15. Perry to CES, Sept. 11, 1936, Acc. 38, Bx. 33 (exports); Report to FMC-Ger. Bd. Dirs., May 13, 1936, FMC-Ger. Files (progress in exports); Export Passenger Cars and Trucks, 1936, FMC-Ger. Files (totals for year).

16. Perry to CES, July 14, 1936 (Diestel dismissal) and reply, July 29, 1936 (opposes) Acc. 38, Bx. 33; Albert Memo, Aug. 17, 1936, Acc. 6, Bx. 335.

17. Cable Albert and Vitger to Dearborn, Aug. 30, 1936 and Diestel to CES, Sept. 10, 1936 (hopeful), E. Vitger, "Memorandum Concerning Rubber Transaction," Sept. 28, 1936 (Dearborn confs., arrangements), unsigned "Memorandum Concerning Raw Materials," Dec. 10, 1936 (further details), all in Acc. 38, Bx. 33.

18. CES to Perry, Nov. 20, 1936, Acc. 38, Bx. 33 (urging sacrifice); Perry to CES, Dec. 9, 1936 (reservations) and Roberge to CES, "Memorandum," Jan. 4, 1937, Acc. 38, Bx. 38; Exports of cars and trucks, FMC-Ger. Files (figs. for 1937).

19. Details of financing and trade in Interl. Purchasing Records, Bxes. 4 & 8, Highland Park; FMC-Ger., Mins. Bd. Dirs., Feb. 16, 1937 (expectations) and agenda for FMC-Ger. Bd. Mtg., Cologne, Apr. 20, 1938 (prodn., sales, 1937), both in Acc. 38, Bx. 40.

20. FMC-Ger., Business Report and Balance Sheet, 1937, Select File; Diestel to CES, Mar. 3, 1937, Acc. 38, Bx. 38; Roberge "Memorandum," July 21, 1937, Acc. 507, Bx. 95.

21. Cables Albert to CES and reply, Dec. 1, 1937 (govt. orders) and Albert-Wibel corresp., Dec. 1937, Acc. 38, Bx. 37; cable CES to Albert, Jan. 17 (approving in principle), and reply, Jan. 20, 1938, Acc. 38, Bx. 40; FMC-Ger., Mins. Bd. Dirs., Apr. 20, 1938, Acc. 38, Bx. 40 (Berlin plant).

22. Albert to CES, June 17, 1938 (truck order), Diestel to CES, July 11, 1938 (new orders), and Albert to CES, Aug. 26, 1938 (1939 prodn.), all Acc. 38, Bx. 40; Tallberg, *Reminiscences* (Taunus); R. H. Schmidt, "Memorandum on Production Program for Cologne Anticipated for 1939," Sept. 28, 1938, Acc. 6, Bx. 346 (1939 cars trucks).

23. Diestel, "Memorandum," Nov. 25, and Albert to CES, Dec. 15, 1938, both Acc. 38, Bx. 40.

24. Albert to CES, Dec. 15, 1938 (Diestel's resignation) and Vitger to H. L. Moekle, June 13, 1939 (stats. FMC-Ger. progress, prodn. prospects 1939) both in Acc. 38, Bx. 40; "Earnings of Associated Ford Companies—at official rates of exchange" in "England-Guernsey Ford Investment" folder, FI (dollar profits 1934 and 1938); Tallberg, *Reminiscences* (Berlin plant); Albert to EBF, Feb. 12, 1940, Acc. 6, Bx. 361 (1939 profits).

CHAPTER 14

1. *Ford Times* (Eng.), IX, Apr. 1932, 253 (dealer's quote); intervs. Sir Rowland Smith, London, June 26, 1961 and W. J. Squire, Dagenham, June 21, 1921 (quotes FMC-Eng. execs.); FMC-Eng. balance sheets and sales records (sales performance); H. S. Cooper to H. L. Moekle, Aug. 16, 1932, Acc. 38, Bx. 9 (arrangement with Canada).

2. Royal Commission on Auto Industry, *Report,* Ottawa, 1961, 8 (1932 duty-free entry for motor vehicles imported from U.K.); *Ford Times* (Eng.), II, Jan. 1934, 67 (Gloucester trial) and July 1934, 11 (Royal Scottish); FMC-Eng., Mins. Bd. Dirs., Nov. 28, 1934 Secty's off., FMC-US; Prod. Plang. Records, FMC-Eng. (V-8 prodn.); FMC-Eng., Mins. Bd. Dirs., June 24, 1936 (Lincoln co., June 22, 1936).

3. Society of Motor Mfrs. and Traders (SMMT) stats. on car and truck prodn.; G. Maxcy and A. Silberston, *The Motor Industry,* London, 1959, 102 (54 per cent); FMC-Eng., *Annual Report 1934* (profits); FMC-Eng., *Report of Sixth Ord. Gen. Mtg.,* Apr. 17, 1935 (Dagenham assets—£7, 956,653 at current rate of exchange); interv. Sir Patrick Hennessy, London, Aug. 1961 (white elephants).

4. FMC-Eng., *Annual Report 1935* (mfg. efficiencies); Wibel to Perry, June 28, 1935,

Acc. 507, Bx. 84 (help with purchasing); interv. Hennessy (his role); Sir Stanford Cooper to editors, *Ford Bulletin,* June 5, 1961 (combined effort); interv. F. S. Thornhill Cooper, Rome, June 27, 1960 (his claim); A. Hall to dealers, June 27, 1932, Dec. 31, 1934, and Payne to dealers, Sept. 25, 1935, Permanent File, FMC-Eng. (price reductions); Young to dealers, Oct. 17, 1935, *ibid.* and *Ford Times* (Eng.), XII, Nov. 1935, 685 (Perry's announcement); A. Hardcastle, asst. wholesale mgr., to dealers, Nov. 4, 1935, Permanent File, FMC-Eng. (first quote); *Ford Times* (Eng.), XII, Dec. 1935, 749 ("complete misconception"); *Motor* (Eng.), LXVIII, Oct. 29, 1935, 9 (prices cheapest Austin 7 and Morris 8).

5. FMC-Eng., Mins. Bd. Dirs., Dec. 24, 1936 ("entirely British"); Perry to Roberge, Nov. 30, 1936, Acc. 38, Bx. 31 (details sales orgn.); interv. Sir Rowland Smith, London, June 26, 1961 (quote).
6. Intervs. Sir Patrick Hennessy, Aug. 1960 and June 19, 1961.
7. FMC-Eng. & FMC-Can. (prodn. figs.); A. W. L'Estrange Fawcett, *Wheels of Fortune,* unpublished history of FMC-Eng. (Mar. 1932 strike); T. S. Rowntree, "Ford Motor Co. Ltd. and Their Work People," *Ford Times,* XIV, Aug. 1937, 505ff. (Dagenham's cleanliness and good working conds.); Cresswell Curtiss, *The Survival of the Slickest,* London, 1939, 162 (novel about Dagenham). Correspondence, labor data, and testimony about the drive for economy, already cited, cover Perry's general attitude and conditions at the Dagenham plant.
8. Employment figs., FMC-Eng. (1935 work force); H. S. Cooper to Craig, Feb. 16, 1937, Acc. 38, Bx. 36 (employee benefits); FMC-Eng. *Annual Report 1937* (pension and benefits expenditures); Craig to Perry, May 3, 1937, Acc. 38, Bx. 36 ("heavy handicap"); FMC-Eng., Mins. Bd. Dirs., July 27, 1938 (approval holidays with pay).
9. This sharing of top executive responsibility is indicated in interviews and in correspondence of Perry with Sorensen and others in Dearborn.
10. Export Dept., FMC-Eng. (stats.); Sales Dept., FI (R. Baker) FMC-US (sales of small car and V-8 by affiliated cos.); Perry in FMC-Eng. *Report of Sixth Ord. Gen. Mtg.,* Apr. 17, 1935 (small English cars unpopular abroad); A. N. Gentes, Asst. Mgr. For. Dept., Guaranty Trust Co. of N.Y., "Foreign Exchange Restrictions," Dec. 21, 1934, Acc. 507, Bx. 94; interv. H. A. Denne, London, June 18, 1961 (start of Export Dept., progress). Data on early exports, countries, percentages, figs., furnished by Mr. Denne's office.
11. Perry in FMC-Eng. *Report of Tenth Ord. Gen. Mtg.,* May 9, 1939 ("tragic degeneration"); FMC-Eng., *Annual Reports* for the 1930's; "Earnings of Associated Ford Companies—at official rates of exchange" in "England-Guernsey Ford Investment" folder, FI (profit and loss); Perry to CES, Sept. 23, 1936, and CES to Perry, Oct. 15, 1936, Acc. 38, Bx. 34 (procedures, quote).
12. Camille Gutt to EBF, Dec. 7, 1938, and Perry to EBF, Dec. 12, 1938, Acc. 38, Bx. 39; FMC-Belg., Mins. Bd. Dirs., Secty's off., FMC-US. The Europeans felt more at home in dealing with Dagenham than with Dearborn. As to buying Dagenham products, that was a matter of values and prices.
13. FMC-Can., *Annual Report 1934* (assets, profits); W. R. Campbell, *Address to Shareholders of FMC-Can.,* Apr. 27, 1936 (no. of shareholders); FMC-Can. Personnel Records (nationality).
14. Interv. R.M. Sale, Oakville, Ont., May 1, 1961 (policies, Campbell in Dearborn); CES to Perry, May 18, 1932, Acc. 38, Bx. 9 (Campbell, cooperation); FMC-Can. Mins. Bd. Dirs. (attendance); Campbell, *Address* (new foundry).
15. W. R. Campbell, Speech to Canadian Ch. of Commerce, Sept. 11, 1934, FMC-Can.; FMC-Can., Mins. Bd. Dirs., Apr. 30, 1934 and Apr. 27, 1936 (decisions on wages);

interv. G. Dewar, Oakville, Ont., Apr. 24, 25, 1961 (no labor problems).

16. Biographical Sketch, Gregory G. Kew, Pub. Rels. Divn., FMC-Can., Sept. 21, 1954 and Press Release, Apr. 29, 1946, FMC-Can. (Kew's overseas trips); "History of Ford Motor Company of South Africa (Pty.), Ltd.," typescript, 1961, lists three Canadian visitors in the pre-World War II period; intervs. Basil Stevenson, Oakville, Ont., Apr. 1961 (overseas cos., visits of their officials to Canada); Mins. Bd. Dirs. of all overseas cos., Secty's off., FMC-Can.

17. Corresp. M. Visvesvaraya—CES, June 28, 1939; P. B. Advani to CES, Aug. 10, 1939, draft of proposals, Aug. 25 and Sept. 19, 1939, Campbell to EBF, Sept. 25, 1939, and P. B. Advani to HF, Oct. 11, 1939, all in Acc. 38, Bx. 41.

18. Data from FMC-Austl. (gen. activities); Gen. Acctg. & Fin. Analysis, Overseas Divn., FMC-Can. (stats.); FMC-Can., *Annual Reports;* Gen. Acctg. & Fin. Analysis Overseas Divn., FMC-Can. (percentage exports); Campbell to Shareholders Mtg., Apr. 27, 1936 (1935 data); Commonwealth of Australia, Industries Divn., Dept. of Trade, *The Australian Motor Vehicle Industry,* Melbourne, 1959, 37 (Holden). It was noted in Chap. 6 that in 1922 30 per cent of the cars imported into Australia were Model T's, but this was before Windsor had a subsidiary in the Commonwealth. Australia is exceptional in that Ford had a larger percentage of the market when the car was handled by distributors than when a Windsor subsidiary operated.

19. New car registrations, FMC-Can. (Ford sales); interv. R. M. Sale, Oakville, Ont., Apr. 26, 1961 (quote); FMC-Can., *Annual Reports,* 1930–39 (the operating loss is calculated by adding the operating profit before income tax and the loss over the 10-yr. period for Canadian factories and branches); Campbell's addresses to shareholders at annual mtgs. (plant expansion).

20. Maxcy & Silberston, 102, 107 (Ford share small car market); FMC-Eng., Mins. Bd. Dirs., Sept. 23, 1936 (dealer protests); FMC-Eng. Prodn. Figs. 1937; CES to Perry, Nov. 20, 1936, Acc. 38, Bx. 36 (CES's viewpoint); Facsimile Ltrs., Permanent File, FMC-Eng. (F. S. Thornhill Cooper's new position).

21. Facsimile Ltrs., Permanent File, FMC-Eng. (new models); intervs. Hennessy.

22. FMC-Eng., Mins. Bd. Dirs., June 23, Sept. 22, 1937 (abandonment £100 car, new prices); Thornhill Cooper to dealers, Sept. 15, 1937 (retail prices, discounts increased), Payne to dealers, Oct. 25, 1938 (features of new Ford units), Thornhill Cooper to dealers, Oct. 4, 1938 (Prefect to be shown Oct. 12), A. Hall to dealers, Dec. 21, 1939 (Anglia), all in Facsimile File; Perry to EBF, Dec. 3, 1937 and Mar. 18, 1938, Acc. 507, Bx. 99 (losses); Sales Dept., FI (R. Baker), FMC-US (small cars *v.* V-8); Maxcy and Silberston, 107 (Ford percentages); Hennessy to Wibel, Oct. 19, 1938, Acc. 507, Bx. 61 (gen. situation and competition).

23. Unsigned memo, June 21, 1937, Acc. 285, Bx. 2025 (trucks); Thornhill Cooper, Memo, May 11, 1938, Acc. 507, Bx. 99 (truck situation); FMC-Eng., Mins. Bd. Dirs., Sept. 23, 1936 (dealer complaints); Thornhill Cooper to dealers, Sept. 1937, Facsimile File (reintroduction 4-cyl. engine); interv. W. J. Squire, Dagenham, Sept. 5, 1960 (Ger. BB engine); Prodn. Plang. Records, FMC-Eng. (4-cyl. prodn.).

24. Tractor prodn. figs., FMC-Eng.; Society of Motor Mfrs. & Traders (industry figs.); interv. Sir Rowland Smith, London, Aug. 23, 1960 (Perry and political circles); Hennessy to Wibel, Oct. 19, 1938, Acc. 507, Bx. 61; FMC-Eng., Mins. Bd. Dirs., Nov. 30, 1938 (appts., including Hennessy's, effective Jan. 1, 1939); Perry to dealers, May 7, 1941, Facsimile File (mng. dirs.).

25. Hennessy to CES, May 26, 1939, #45378 Ferg-M (outlining final scheme); Perry to CES, May 11, 1939, #17511 Ferg-M (Dorman-Smith's concern); Nevins & Hill,

III, Chap. 5 (Ferguson tractor story); CES to Perry, May 21, 1943, in Ferg. Dep., Ferg. *v.* Ford, 9209 (gentlemen's agreement); *Det. News,* June 29, 1939 (debut); Perry to CES, May 11, 1939, #17511, Ferg-M (Perry's report to Minister); *Hansard,* May 18, 1939; Hennessy to CES, May 26, 1939, #45378, Ferg-M.

26. FMC-Eng., Mins. Bd. Dirs., Sept. 6, 1939 (June 30, 1939 contract); J. M. A. Smith to CES, Jan. 3, 1939, Acc. 38, Bx. 40 (air raid precautions); Ford Investment Co., Mins. Bd. Dirs., Acc. 604, Bx. 1 (incorporation of Guernsey co.); Perry to CES, June 27, 1939, Acc. 606, Bx. 6 (annual dinner); FMC-Eng., Mins. Bd. Dirs., June 28, 1939 (govt. contracts).

27. Deptl. comm. Moekle to EBF, July 5, 1939, Acc. 58, Bx. 2 (Moekle and Roberge); Roberge to EBF, June 13, 1939, Acc. 608, Bx. 2 (Roberge in Spain); interv. Roberge, Birmingham, Mich., Aug. 1, 1961 (his view on possible war); Acc. 38 (CES corresp.); Harry Bennett, *We Never Called Him Henry,* N.Y., 1951, 122; Nevins & Hill, III, Chaps. 5, 7, 8 (HF's aging); Chap. 12 above (Dearborn's knowledge).

CHAPTER 15

1. Raymond Gram Swing, *Preview of History,* N.Y., 1943, 11 (Gamelin quote); Louis L. Snyder, *The War: A Concise History,* N.Y., 1960, 128 (U-boat attacks); Hiliary St. George Saunders, *Ford at War,* n.d., 10 (camouflage of plant), 52–59 (tractor prodn. and use, 1939–45). England and France declared war on Germany Sept. 3, 1939, Canada on the 10th, and other Dominions followed. Saunders, 14 (German war map).

2. *Ford Bulletin,* V, Apr. 26, 1957, 1 (early tractor prodn.); D. H. E. Harkness, *War and British Agriculture,* Westminster, 1941, 55 (ploughed area, 1914–39); Bela Gold, *Wartime Planning in Agriculture,* N.Y., 1939, 34 (increase in acreage); FMC-Eng. *Report of Eleventh Ord. Gen. Mtg.,* May 16, 1940, Acc. 285, Bx. 2286 (Dagenham prodn. Fordsons); *British War Production* (1939–45), comp. London *Times,* London, 1945, 140 (£2 per acre); cable, CES to Perry, Sept. 8, 12, and Oct. 24, 1939, #45385, #45387, and #45446; Perry to CES, Sept. 28, 1939, #45392; Perry to Ferguson, Nov. 21, 1939, #17520; Ferguson to Sherman, Oct. 24, 1939, #45444; Lord Illingworth to Perry, n.d., #17574; EBF to Lord Illingworth, Apr. 19, 1940, #17590; and Perry to EBF, May 1, 1940, #17591. (All numbered references in Ferg-M.) As to manufacture of the Ford Tractor-Ferguson System, Ford Ltd. was on record (see *Report of Eleventh Ord. Gen. Mtg.,* above) as being willing to undertake this task when conditions permitted it to procure the necessary machine tools and raw materials, which would be after the war.

3. Saunders, 11 (V-8's trucks, Balloon Command); *Ford Times* (Eng.), XVI, Nov. 1939, 637, 639 (ambulances); Arthur L'Estrange Fawcett, *Wheels of Fortune,* ms. bk. 1960, Chap. 6 (Perry Food Adviser); interv. Sir Rowland Smith, London, June 26, 1961 (Merlin project—initial stages); interv. William J. Squire, London, June 20, 1961 (plang. for factory, layout, methods); "Models Produced by Ford Motor Co. Ltd.," May, 1941 (chart). FMC-Eng. Files (Anglia); intervs. Sir Patrick Hennessy, London, Aug. 1960; Olive Moore, "Man of the Month, Sir Rowland Smith," *Scope,* Oct. 1948, 62–78, and Saunders, 19, 59ff (Merlin factory).

4. L. F. Ellis, *The War in France and Flanders,* London, 1953, Chaps. 12–16, and esp. p. 247 (men evacuated); Snyder, 93–94 (no. vessels used, effect on public).

5. Ellis, 327 (equipment lost).

6. Hennessy to Wibel, May 10, 1940, Acc. 507, Bx. 61 (Dagenham and govt. orders); Saunders, 18, 20–21.

7. Intervs. Sir Patrick Hennessy, Aug. 1960, June 1961; David Farrer, *Beaverbrook, "A Difficult Fellow,"* London, 1945, 5–17; Peter Fleming, *Invasion, 1940,* London, 1957, Chaps. 1–13.

8. C. E. Sorensen, *My Forty Years with Ford,* N.Y., 1956, 273–76 (Rolls-Royce contract); *Det. News, N.Y. Times,* June 19, 1940 (Beaverbrook's announcement); *N.Y. Times,* June 20, 1940 (Ford's refusal); Folder, "Airplane Motors for England," Acc. 6, Bx. 359 (American protests); *N.Y. Post,* June 27, 1940 (Canadian fury); cable, E. G. Liebold to editor London *Daily Mail,* June 26, 1940 (Ford's final statement); interv. Sir Patrick Hennessy, June 19, 1961 (supply of aircraft maintained, attitude of English workers); Tom Driberg, *Beaverbrook: a Study in Power and Frustration,* London, 1956, 260 (nos. of English aircraft in Aug. and late Sept.); Fleming, *Invasion, 1940,* Chap. 19 (end of Operation Sea Lion); *Ford Times* (Eng.), XIX, Sept.–Oct. 1942, 131 (food vans). Farrer, 31, gives the total no. of aircraft available to the RAF as 2,700 in May 1940, and 6,400 in Sept. This includes bombers and other types as well as fighters.

9. Dollfus to CES, Sept. 9, 1939, Jan. 23, 1940 (gen. plans, Panier), and Panier to CES, Feb. 16, 1940, Acc. 606, Bx. 6; Dollfus to EBF, Dec. 8, 1939, Acc. 507, Bx. 67 (Hispano-Suiza, Poissy, difficulties); Dollfus to EBF, Mar. 4, 1940, Acc. 6, Bx. 361 (Bordeaux producing trucks); Gnau to EBF, Mar. 10 (?), 1939, Acc. 38, Bx. 127 (Spain); Albert to EBF, Feb. 12, 1940, Acc. 6, Bx. 361.

10. H. C. Møller, "Memorandum," Dec. 11, 1944 in FMC-Denmark, Mins. Bd. Dirs., FI (invasion, types of work, etc.); FMC-Holland, Mins. Bd. Dirs., 1940–43, FI (Army orders, Stenger approved, Schmidt's actions); Historical Data, Ford-Werke, FI (Schmidt apptd. dir. Ford-Belg.); James Van Luppen, Report on Ford Motor Co. (Belgium), Sept. 18, 1944, OOSSC-M (history of co. during occupation); cable Albert and Schmidt to EBF and CES, n.d. (June 28, 1940?), Acc. 6, Bx. 361.

11. Cables Albert and Schmidt to EBF and CES, June 28, July 9, 1940, Acc. 6, Bx. 361 (European plants, including France); interv. Dollfus, Paris, Sept. 13, 1960 (Schmidt, Berlin trip, mfr. trucks); Roberge to Perry, July 12, 1940, Acc. 46, Bx. 3 (no. European plants, Roumanian order, Petsamo, Alexandria); Dollfus to EBF, Oct. 11, 1940, and numerous other ltrs., particularly that of Aug. 21, 1941, Acc. 6, Bxs. 361, 369, 376 (mfg. in France); Tallberg, *Reminiscences;* Office of Lord Perry, "Report on German Company," Sept. 19, 1946 (typescript) in folder "Germany Cologne Ford-Werke AG," Historical Data, FI (German stats.); interv. R. H. Schmidt, Cologne, July 22, 1960 (occupied territories and Germany).

12. Interv. Arthur Beck, Copenhagen, Aug. 3, 1960 (Sweden, Finland, Denmark). Beck brings out anti-German feeling in Denmark, and pro-German feeling in Sweden and Finland (because of Russia chiefly).

13. *Canada at War,* No. 3, June 1, 1941, issued by the Dir. of Public Info., Ottawa, 5 (Army, Air Force); *Canada Carries On:* Review of the War Effort of the Dominion as Discussed in the House of Commons, July 25–30, 1940, published by the Dir. of Public Info., Ottawa, 7–25 (Army, Air Force, Navy); William Yandell Elliott and H. Duncan Hall, eds., *The British Commonwealth at War,* N.Y., 1943, Chaps. 6, 7, 8 (gen.) and particularly p. 295 (Canadian troops in France); Peter J. Field, *Canada's Wings,* London, 1942, 27–45, and *passim* (Canadian flyers in Britain); also L. E. Charlton, *The Royal Air Force from December 1939 to December 1940,* London, 1941, 259 (American Squadron); and Arkady Fiedler, *Squadron 303: the Story of the Polish Fighter Squadron with the R.A.F.,* N.Y., 1943.

14. Elliott and Hall, 287 (coordination with the U.S.); *Ford Times* (Can.) Special War

Ed., June 1941 (equipment overseas divns.); interv. George H. Bates, Oakville, Apr. 21, 1961 (Campbell's role in Ottawa, war-minded); interv. Rhys M. Sale, Oakville, May 1, 1961 (Campbell at Ottawa, C. D. Howe); Elliott and Hall, 337 (Howe apptd. Minister in Apr. 1940); W. R. Campbell, *Address to Shareholders FMC-Can.,* Apr. 29, 1940 (arrangement for developing war vehicles with Dept. Natl. Def., prodn. stats.; empire at war) and Apr. 28, 1941 (equipment overseas divns.); interv. Bates (chief men in FMC-Can. at outbreak of war, Engineering Dept.); George Dickert, *Reminiscences* (Engineering Dept.).

15. Campbell, *Address to Shareholders FMC-Can.,* Apr. 28, 1941 (quote, doubling capacity, expenditures, prodn. 1940, and tractors); *Canada Carries On* (Ford assembling univ. carrier, special factory); *Ford Times* (Can.), Mar. 1945 (order for 600); FMC-Can. prodn. figs. (defense output); Elliott and Hall, 348–49 (agric. prods.).

16. *Ford Times* (Can.), Special War Ed., June 1941 (Campbell quote) and Apr. 1944 (Canadian trucks in Africa); FMC-Can. prodn. figs. (So. African, Indian assembly); Elliott and Hall, 459 (Indian troops in Egypt); *Canada Carries On,* 30 (Howe quote); Saunders, 35–36 (quality Eng. prodn., Rommel's orders quoted); Charles Graves, *Drive for Freedom,* London, 1945, 39 (Rommel orders). The Canadian and British Ford vehicles were in most cases practically identical.

17. FMC-Can. prodn. figs. (India, Australia, Canada); Campbell to Shareholders, Apr. 29, 1940 (Austl. to manufacture); "Strong Grows the Future," FMC-Austl. pubn., n.d. [1950?] (Austl. prodn. during the war); Dickert, *Reminiscences,* and interv. Sale (Dickert's retirement and Porter); interv. Bates (Millmun); Memo J. E. Thompson, to Gordon C. Garbutt, Dir. Pub. Rels., FMC-Can., FMC-Can. (account of labor difficulties); intervs. G. G. Dewar, Oakville, Apr. 24–25, 1961 (view of union); Elliott and Hall, 346–47 (govt. supervision of labor). The J. E. Thompson memo, which is the source for most of the company-labor attitudes and episodes, was actually a compilation by four men that cites many newspaper and other non-Ford sources. For the American labor troubles and settlement, see Nevins & Hill, III, Chap. 6. Elliott and Hall bring out that the National War Labor Board took over supervision of all war-work employees chiefly under Orders of Council Oct. 18, 1941, and Mar. 24, 1942.

18. Air Raid Precaution Facts & Figures, 1939–45, typed material in FMC-Eng. files (early bombings, etc.); Saunders, 17–18, 22–24, 30 (ARP orgd., its work, shelters, noise); *Danger Over Dagenham* (anonymous), Dagenham, 1947, 14 (noise etc.).

19. Saunders, 21, 84 (women), 35 (vehicles), 41–42, 49 (Bren carrier, Leamington), 49–50 (V-8's), 90 (1945 employment); FMC-Eng. *Annual Report,* Dec. 1944 (men in service); FMC-Eng. files (figs. prodn. vehicles by type).

20. Intervs. Sir Rowland Smith, London, June 26, 1961 (Squire, Denne, gen.); H. A. Denne, London, Aug. 1, 1960, and July 4, 1961 (his role, three factories, "trouble shooting"); W. J. Squire, Dagenham, Sept. 5, 1960 (work at Rolls-Royce, Derby; Phillips mgr.) and June 20, 1961 (character of job, Ford and Rolls-Royce methods); A. R. Smith to Sorensen, Nov. 28, 1941, Acc. 390, Bx. 84 (status at that time); Saunders, 59–70 (size of site, factory; gauges, gen.). Various statements have been made as to when the factory began quantity production, which is usually dated from the summer to autumn of 1941. Smith's letter to CES shows that it had not begun on Nov. 28, and probably commenced in Jan. or Feb., 1942.

21. Nevins & Hill, III, Chaps. 7, 8.

22. Resolutions of Superior Court, May 15, 1942, in FMC-Ger., Mins. Bd. Dirs. FI (Schmidt in charge Cologne); interv. R.H. Schmidt (his statement Ford mgrs., Dr. Albert's troubles); FMC-Fr., FMC-Belg., FMC-Holland, Mins. Bd. Dirs., 1940–45 (character of prodn.); Møller, "Memorandum," *loc. cit.* (Denmark); Dollfus to

EBF, Jan. 28, 1942, Acc. 6, Bx. 84 (mfg. trucks); Hennessy to Wibel, July 13, 1942, Acc. 390, Bx. 84 (comment on Dollfus); Ford-SAF, Mins. Bd. Dirs., Apr. 1942—Nov. 1943, Acc. 606, Bx. 2 (Poissy, Bordeaux bombings, dispersal; Albert, Tannen, Beckers in charge; French protests etc.); Wibel to Hennessy, June 2, 1942, Acc. 390, Bx. 84 ("good hammering"); Breckinridge Long (State Dept.) to EBF, June 3, 1942, Acc. 6, Bx. 377 (cond. of Poissy); Dollfus to EBF, Aug. 15, 1942, Acc. 6, Bx. 376 (dispersal effected); Carl R. Wiskott to Beckers, Oct. 12, 1943 in "Ford-SAF France, Poissy Historical Data 1940–1948," FI; Postwar Reports of Cologne Plant Damages, "Germany Cologne Ford-Werke AG—Decontrol, 1945–1947," FI (Cologne plant not damaged); Walter L. McKee, "Memo," July 12, 1949, in "Hungary Historical Data," FI; General Motors Overseas Operations, *The War Effort of the Overseas Division,* N.Y., 1944.

23. Statement by Perry, FMC-Eng. *Annual Report 1940* (assisting employees in service); Saunders, 72 (labor agreement signed); interv. H. A. Denne, London, Aug. 31, 1960 (unions at Merlin plant); interv. Sir Patrick Hennessy, London, Aug. 1960 (operation agreement); Saunders, 72 (agreement signed at Dagenham); interv. L. T. Blakeman, London, Sept. 2, 1960 (agreement, atmosphere "bad").

24. A. Hall to dealers, June 27, 1940 (end pass. car prodn.), Harold Mortimore to dealers, Nov. 1, 1940 (assembly imported vehicles), and W. R. Nieland to dealers, June 16, 1941 (govt. to use dealer facilities) all in Permanent File, FMC-Eng.; Saunders, 44, 54, 86 (dealers, Wigan, Cramlington, Barking, Lincoln depot, spare parts, servicing tractors); FMC-Eng. *Annual Report 1942,* and *Annual Reports 1941, 1944, and 1945* (work of dealers).

25. EBF to Perry, Mar. 12, 1941, in "England Dagenham Shares-Dividend, 1938–1946," FI (donation for food vans); *Ford Times* (Eng.), XIX, Sept.–Oct. 1942, 131 (other contributions, first year's work); Saunders, 48 (food vans, no. meals), 86 (meals served at Dagenham).

26. FMC-Eng. and FMC-Can., *Annual Reports, 1939–45* (their earnings); "Earnings of Associated Ford Companies—at official rates of exchange" in "England-Guernsey Ford Investment" folder, FI (European cos.); in folder, FMC-Eng. *Annual Report 1944* (foreign investments not settled).

27. Intervs. in Nov. and Dec. 1961 with Ford officials Argentina, Brazil, Mexico (gen. conds. during war, dealers); Balance Sheets, FMC-Mex., Mexico City, 1939–45 (annual profits).

28. FMC-Eng., FI, and "Vehicle Production at Dagenham During Second World War," FMC-Eng. (stats. vehicles and autov. engs.); *Scope* (no vol.), Oct. 1948, 62–73 and PEP, *Motor Vehicles,* London, 1950, 39 (Merlin prodn.); FMC-Can., stats. (military vehicles and univ. carriers); W. R. Campbell to Shareholders, Apr. 24, 1944 (tractors); FMC-Can., *Annual Report 1946* (quote on Canadian prodn., and value of); FMC-Can., stats., defense sales, 1939–46; *Canada at War* (no. air crew graduates); Saunders, 59–70 (Merlin) and *passim* (assembly, overhaul, etc.). Saunders gives the Merlin total prodn. as 34,000; other sources 30,000 and 30,008.

29. FMC-Can. (stats. on sales of vehicles by country, 1939–45); FMC-Austl. (war data); Saunders, 94–95 (N. Zeal. prodn. of all types).

CHAPTER 16

1. FMC-US, Mins. Prod. Plang. Com., 1945–46, Prod. Plang. off., FMC-US; FMC-Eng. *Annual Report 1946* (quotes on English conds.); FMC-Can. *Annual Report 1946* (Can. conds.); Detroit press, 1945–46 (comments industrial execs.).

2. FMC-US, Mins. Bd. Dirs., Sept. 21, 1945, Secty's off., FMC-US (resignation, HF II's election); Nevins & Hill, III, Chap. 12 (HF II's problems).

3. Deposition HF II, *Ferg. v. Ford,* Nov. 1949, 1451–55 and HF II to Ford SAF, May 21, 1945, Acc. 713, Bx. 30 (Roberge's first apptmt.); HF II, deptl. comm., Sept. 18, 1946, Acc. 536, Bx. 44 (apptd. head Interl. Divn.). HF II acted upon the advice of Moekle and Craig in selecting Roberge to handle foreign affairs.

4. *Business Week,* Mar. 16, 1946 and "Henry Ford Speaks Out—A Conversation with Tom Lilley," *Atlantic,* CLXXX, Dec. 1947, 28 (Ford fleet). For details concerning rubber plantation, see Chap. 8.

5. FMC-Eng. *Annual Report 1947;* Prodn. Plang. Dept., FMC-Eng. (stats.).

6. Perry's statement to Shareholders, May 15, 1946; G. Maxcy and A. Silberston, *The Motor Industry,* London, 1959, 112 (labor conds.; unauthorized strike); Labor Agreements, 1944 and 1946, FMC-Eng. files; *N.Y. Times,* Mar. 10–16, 1946; interv. L. T. Blakeman, Dagenham, Sept. 2, 1960 (conds. in 1946).

7. Sir Rowland Smith to Roberge, Feb. 11, 1947 in "Roberge Gen.—Exec. Corr.," FI; FMC-Eng. *Annual Report 1947;* Prodn. Plang. Dept., FMC-Eng. (stats.).

8. Sir Stanford Cooper to Roberge, Sept. 26, 1945, on Film No. 12, Item No. 13, OOSSC-M; "Observations of Mr. Frank Cort on his Visit to Ford Motor Co., France," n.d., Acc. 507, Bx. 18.

9. P. North to Cort, Sept. 21, 1945, Acc. 507, Bx. 27 (tank engines produced by Ford-SAF); Cort, Memo, July 2, 1945, Acc. 507, Bx. 18 (truck prodn. Poissy); Dollfus, Memo, Dec. 14, 1944, Acc. 713, Bx. 30 (his appraisal situation); also other materials in Accs. 507 and 713; Roberge, Memo on June–July 1945 trip, Acc. 713, Bx. 30 and Roberge Memo Mar. 12, 1946, Acc. 507, Bx. 3 (talks with Dollfus, small car); Cort, Memo, *loc. cit.* (early plans for Vedette); Acc. 507, Bx. 1 (more on same); Dollfus to FMC, Dec. 7, 1945, Acc. 507, Bx. 17 (scrapping machinery small car). Dearborn engineers thought the small car would be obsolete because it was a prewar model: see Frank Harding to H. C. Kellogg, Nov. 10, 1942, Acc. 507, Bx. 17.

10. Elvinger, Étude de Marché faite pour la Guaranty Trust Co. of N.Y., Feb. 1946, Acc. 713, Bx. 29 (govt. plan, prodn. of three cos.); HF II and Graeme K. Howard, Report on European Trip, Feb.–Mar. 1948, Acc. 536, Bx. 46; FMC-Fr., Mins. Bd. Dirs., Sept. 6, 1945, Acc. 606, Bx. 2 (Ford-SAF work).

11. Perry and Sir Stanford Cooper to Roberge, Nov. 7, 1945, Film No. 12, Item 13, OOSSC-M; Dollfus to HF II, Sept. 22, 1945, Acc. 713, Bx. 30; Acc. 507, Bxs. 70–71, esp. Roberge, Memo of Telephone Conversation with Dollfus, May 8, 1946, Acc. 507, Bx. 71 (Dollfus wants funds); Acc. 713, Bx. 31 (more data finances FMC-Fr. and recapitalization); HF II–Howard Report (Dollfus beguiled HF II); deposition E. R. Breech, *Ferg. v. Ford,* Feb. 1950, 21 (FMC-Fr. in gen. and recapitalization). Accs. 507 and 713 contain additional data.

12. Cort, Report, n.d. [1945?], Acc. 507, Bx. 17; interv. Jules Gutzeit, Cologne, July 20, 1960; Thacker to Sir Stanford, Dec. 8, 1947, Acc. 713, Bx. 20; Office of Lord Perry, Report on German Company, Sept. 19, 1946, in Ford-Werke AG Historical Data (A), FI (gen. bkgnd.); interv. Erhard Vitger, Cologne, July 15, 1960 (his quote), FMC-Ger., *Business Report for Years 1944, 1945, 1946,* Nov. 1947 (truck prodn. figs.); *Verband der Automobilindustrie* (Ger. figs.).

13. Report on German Company, *loc. cit.;* folder on Schmidt, Acc. 713, Bx. 20; interv. Vitger; C. B. Lonsdale, Cologne Plant—General Review, Jan. 1946—Sept. 1947, Acc. 713, Bx. 20 (cond. plant, workers, fire).

14. Lonsdale, *loc. cit.* (work of Ger. co.); Hennessy to Roberge, June 18, 1946, Acc. 713, Bx. 19 (headstart, Volkswagen); FMC-Ger. *Business Report for Years 1944, 1945,*

1946 (Ford prodn. figs.); *Verband der Automobilindustrie* (W. Ger. figs.); Lonsdale *loc. cit.* (1946 success, causes).

15. Lonsdale *loc. cit.* and prodn. figs. from *Verband der Automobilindustrie;* FMC-Ger., Mgr.'s report to dirs., July 16, 1948, and Mgr.'s Monthly Ltrs., 1938–48, FI (Works Council); Vitger to Roberge, Jan. 19, 1948 in Mgr.'s Monthly Ltrs., FI (factory conds., workers, hot meals).

16. FMC-US, Mins. For. Operations Com., July 1, 1947, Acc. 713, Bx. 20, and Vitger to Roberge, Aug. 22, 1947 "Ford-Werke AG Decontrol 1945–47," FI (bypassing Albert); Vitger to P. R. Whitney, Feb. 13, 1948, *ibid.* (Berlin office closed); deptl. com., Vitger to Roberge, Sept. 26, 1945, Acc. 713, Bx. 19 (his ideas, Roberge's cable).

17. Sir Stanford Cooper to Roberge, Sept. 26, 1945, Film No. 12, Item 13, OOSSC-M (charges *v.* Dutch); C. Thacker to G. S. Hibberson, Oct. 7, 1946, FMC-Belg. files; interv. Desire De Jonghe, Antwerp, Aug. 5, 1960; Sales and Market Analysis Dept. FMC-Belg. (prodn. sheets).

18. Vitger to Roberge, June 26, 1947, Acc. 713, Bx. 19 (Hungary); S. J. Elliott to L. E. Briggs, Dec. 17, 1945, Film No. 12, Item 13, OOSSC-M; Reports on Confs. in London, Sept. 13, Nov. 15, 1948, Film No. 10, Item 3, OOSSC-M; conversation Christopher Mataras (Asst. Mgr. FMC-Egypt), Detroit, Apr. 20, 1960; FMC-Roumania, Mins. Shareholders Mtg., June 30, 1947, Acc. 320, Bx. 1; "Greece-Athens FMC A/S Liquidation" folder, FI.

19. J. B. Fabregas to F. J. Cort, June 12, 1947, Acc. 507, Bx. 47 (Spain); Film No. 2, Item 17, OOSSC-M (Span. govt. proposals); OOSSC-M (data on all three assembly operations); H. Nakashidze to R. E. Curry, Oct. 16, 1946, Acc. 507, Bx. 27 (preliminary work on Egyptian plant).

20. FMC-Can., Mins. Bd. Dirs., Aug. 14, 1945, and FMC-S. Afr., Mins. Bd. Dirs., Jan. 18, 1946, Secty's off., FMC-Can.; FMC-S. Afr., History of the Ford Motor Company of South Africa (Pty.) Ltd., 1961 (typescript prepared by staff of FMC-S. Afr.).

21. Mgrs. Monthly Ltrs. from F. J. Dover, Apr. 25, 1946 and from F. F. Griffith, July 18, 1946, FI (quotes); C. L. Holm, Memo, Feb. 18, 1947, Acc. 712, Bx. 37 (new plant plans, including Mexico); Orberg, Report, Feb. 4, 1946, FI.

22. Richards, Manila, to Roberge, Nov. 2, 1945, and other letters, Acc. 713, Bx. 27 (his arrival and activities); Lt. Col. J. L. Farmer, Jr. to FMC, Sept. 15, 1945 and Roberge to Farmer, Oct. 9, 1945, Acc. 713, Bx. 28 (Japan); B. J. Jamieson to Rhys Sale, May 17, 1961, in our files (Singapore plant); Abbot Low Moffat, Chief Divn. of SE Asia Affairs, U.S. State Dept., to FMC, Oct. 4, 1945, Acc. 711, Bx. 4 ("good condition"); FMC-Can., Mins. Mgt. Mtg., Jan. 31, 1946, Secty's off., FMC-Can. (mgr. in Malaya).

23. Overseas Divn., FMC-Can. (stats.); interv. Basil Stevenson, Oakville, Apr. 26, 1961 (postwar activities).

24. Campbell, Report to FMC-Can. Bd. Dirs., Feb. 14, 1945; French, Report to Ford Mfg. Co. Bd. Dirs., Apr. 4, 1945; Milliken, Reports to FMC-Can. Mgt. Com., Jan. 29 and 30, 1946; Milliken, Presentation to FMC-Can. Mgt. Com.: Proposal to Manufacture Chassis in Austl., June 29, 1946; FMC-Can., Mins. Bd. Dirs., Dec. 18, 1946; Report on Austl. Com. in FMC-Can., Mins. Mgt. Com., Dec. 4, 1950, all in Secty's off., FMC-Can.; Acc. 507, Bx. 27 (Austl. foundry); Dept. of Trade, Melbourne, *The Australian Motor Vehicle Industry,* Melbourne, 1959, 20.

25. FMC-Can., *Annual Report 1945* (assets); Windsor *Star,* Sept. 12–Dec. 20, 1945 (running acct. of strike); G. G. Kew to Shareholders, Oct. 30, 1945, Acc. 1, Bx. 115 (FMC-Can. mgt. view); FMC-Can. files (Feb. 15, 1946 union contract).

26. FMC-Can., Mins. Bd. Dirs., Apr. 29, 1946 (Greig pres., Campbell given honorary

title chm. of Bd.); interv. George H. Bates, Oakville, Apr. 21, 1961 (quotes); interv. Sale (dual-line plan); FMC-Can., Mins. Mgt. Mtg., Jan. 19, 1946 (same).

27. Interv. Sale (his career); Personnel Records, FMC-Can. (more facts); FMC-Can., Mins. Bd. Dirs., Apr. 29, 1946 (Sale V-P) and FMC-Can., Mins. Mgt. Com., June 28, 1946, both in Secty's off., FMC-Can. (Greig yields to Sale); *Ward's Report 1946* (strikes); FMC-Can., Mins. Mgt. Com., Feb. 12, Mar. 1, 1946 (interference with prodn.); William Kilburn, *The Elements Combined,* Toronto, 1960, 189 (gen. situation in Canada); Mins. Mgt. Com., June 28, 1946 (Greig's statement); FMC-Can., *Annual Report 1946* (final loss).

28. Prodn. figs. and percentages, FMC-Can.; interv. Sale (expansion plans, Bridge).

29. Henry Ford, *My Life and Work,* N.Y. 1923, 187 (quote).

30. *N.Y. Times,* Jan. 15, 1928 (editorial); FMC-US, Mins. Gen. Plang. Com., Apr.–Sept. 1946 (Light Car Divn.); Nevins & Hill, III, Chap. 12 (J. R. Davis quote on public taste).

31. Acc. 507, Bx. 1 (Vedette in France); interv. Sir Patrick Hennessy, Aug. 1960 (Eng. cars and policy).

32. FMC-US, *Annual Report 1955* (Ford-US figs.); FMC-Can., Mins. Mgt. Mtg., Oct. 1, 1947 (Canadian concern); Acc. 507, Bx. 37 (licensing requirements, exchange controls, etc. facing U.S. trade in 1947); L. J. Marcoux, deptl. com., Aug. 11 and Oct. 3, 1947, Acc. 507, Bx. 37 (Chinese situation); *Diario Oficial* (Mexico), July 11, 1947 (decree of July 9 temporarily prohibiting importation of automobiles); FMC-Mex., "A Study of Automobile Manufacturing in Mexico," Apr. 1960, FMC-Mex. files (1947 actions); FMC-Brazil, Mgr.'s Report for 3rd Quarter 1947, Dec. 31, 1947, unclassified, Ford Archives, Dearborn (Brazilian situation); Roberge, deptl. com. "Argentine Exchange Regulations Effective Jan. 20, 1947," Acc. 713, Bx. 12, and translation Circular #637 of Banco Central, Jan. 20, 1947, Acc. 713, Bx. 13 (Argentina rulings); K. E. McCleary, deptl. com., July 11, 1947, Acc. 507, Bx. 37 (rulings, situation Buenos Aires); Griffith to Roberge, Jan. 23, 1948 (spare parts) and Jan. 16, 1948 (shutdown), Acc. 713, Bx. 12; FMC-Arg., Mgr.'s Report for 4th Quarter 1947 and Mgr.'s ltr., Jan. 14, 1949, FI (gen. situation); Sir Rowland Smith to Roberge, Feb. 28 and Mar. 20, 1947, "Roberge Gen.—Exec. Corr.," FI; FMC-Eng. *Annual Report 1946* and *Annual Report 1947* (English export data); FI (R. Baker), FMC-US (exports).

33. FMC-Brazil, Mgr.'s Report 3rd Quarter 1947, Dec. 31, 1947, unclassified material, Ford Archives (French exports); FMC-US, For. Operations Com. Mtg., July 1, 1947, Secty's off., FMC-US (German possibilities); Lord Perry to Sir Stanford Cooper, Nov. 25, 1947, in "England-Guernsey Ford Investment Shares 1946–47," FI; A. R. Smith for Lord Perry to Sir Stanford Cooper, Nov. 25, 1947, in "Roberge Gen.—Exec. Corr.," FI; deposition HF II in *Ferg. v. Ford,* Nov. 1949, 5431, Acc. 375, Bx. 3.

34. FMC-US, *Annual Report 1955* (U.S. exports, German, English, Canadian car prodn.); Sales Dept., FI (French prodn.).

CHAPTER 17

1. HF II's address to Interl. Mgt. Mtg., Dearborn, June–July 1948, unclassified materials, Ford Archives (quote); Nevins & Hill, III, Chaps. 12, 13 (transformation of co.); FMC-US, *Annual Report 1955* (for 1946, 1947 figs.).

2. Cleona Lewis, *United States and Foreign Investment Problems,* Wash., 1948, 213–15 (Gen. Marshall quote); "Denmark Copenhagen, FMC a/s—Historical Data," and "Sweden Stockholm FMC A/B—Historical Data," both n.d. [1950?], FI. France,

Germany, Spain, Italy, and other countries as well as England, made a variety of laws and decrees affecting the automotive business.

3. HF II and Graeme Howard, Report on European Trip, Acc. 536, Bx. 46; interv. Walter McKee, Dearborn, Apr. 28, 1960 (description of Howard, quote); *Who's Who in America, 1958–59* (Howard record).

4. *The Times*, London, *Review of the British Motor Industry, 1948*, Dec. 1948, *passim;* G. Maxcy in P. L. Cook and R. Cohen, *The Effects of Mergers*, London, 1958, 365.

5. *The Times, op. cit.,* 19; HF II and Howard, Report (Eng. execs.).

6. FMC-Eng., Mins. Policy Com., Apr. 30, 1948, Secty's off., FMC-Eng. (Smith's report); Hennessy Address to Interl. Mgt. Mtg., Dearborn, June–July 1948, in unclassified materials, Ford Archives.

7. HF II and Howard, Report (Eng. plang., HF II and Eng. imports); *The Times, op. cit.,* 5; Ministry of Supply, Natl. Advisory Council for Motor Mfg. Industry, *Proceedings*, London, 1947; PEP, *Motor Vehicles*, London, 1950; *Bristol Evening Post*, Feb. 11, 1948 (Ford and Prefect). In the prewar period only 11 British Ford cars had been exported to the US, probably as demonstration models (export figs. from H. A. Denne, Dagenham).

8. Chap. 9 (Perry's 1928 ideas); HF II and Howard, Report; interv. Sir Patrick Hennessy, June 19, 1961 (quote from HF II); ltr. Sir Patrick Hennessy to M. Wilkins, Sept. 1960 (quote on HF II); *U.S.* v. *National Lead Co.*, 63F Supp. 531 (SD NY 1945), aff'd 332 U.S. 319 (1947). Timken Roller Bearing, incidentally, was a supplier of FMC; its case was scheduled for April 1948. When a change was finally made by FMC in its agreements with affiliates, Ford Ltd. informed its stockholders that the existing agreement, "although enforceable under English law, may not be so under American law." See ltr. to Stockholders, printed in deposition of HF II, *Ferg.* v. *Ford*, 5476. In March 1949 Timken was convicted of the cartel charge (*N.Y. Times*, Mar. 3, 1949). On the general anti-trust situation see Kingman Brewster, *Antitrust and American Business Abroad*, N.Y., 1958, 28–30.

9. HF II and Howard, Report; FMC-US, Report of Mgt. Mtg., Jan. 1949, Acc. 422, Bx. 1. At the management meeting in January, Breech introduced Howard. He remarked: "I thought he could speak every language, but when we got to France I found out that he couldn't speak French." This, a small fact, emphasizes Howard's unfamiliarity with that country.

10. HF II and Howard, Report (German conds., prodn., Gen. Clay, Volkswagen); FMC-Ger., Mins. Bd. Dirs., Mar. 2, 3, 1948 (small cars); R. I. Roberge to Breech, Jan. 21, 1948, Acc. 713, Bx. 20 (Prohibition of land purchases). Volkswagen was a risky investment. Thousands of Germans had paid deposits on Volkswagens in the prewar period and had never received their cars; Volkswagen's debt to these depositors might be upheld in the courts, potentially a big liability. Likewise, the ownership of the company was highly complicated and might involve the purchaser in protracted litigation. It is said (we have not been able to confirm this) that Chrysler also had the opportunity to buy Volkswagen and rejected it as an uncertain investment.

11. HF II and Howard, Report.

12. *Ibid.* (recognition of diesel's importance); interv. Sir Patrick Hennessy, London, Aug. 1960 (his full story); interv. E. Page, Dagenham, Aug. 18, 1960 (engineering); Prodn. Plang. Records, FMC-Eng. (prodn. of tractors and trucks). Page first assured Sir Patrick that the engine he envisaged was practicable, and made a rough design to show how it could be built.

13. HF II and Howard, Report (Ford potentialities); Appt. Announcement in files of Orgn. Plang. off., Dearborn (Howard's appt.).

14. Transcript Interl. Mgt. Mtg., unclassified materials in Ford Archives (details about personnel, routines, etc.).
15. HF II Address to Interl. Mgt. Mtg., *ibid.;* for 1923 mtg., see Chap. 7.
16. Graeme K. Howard, "Report on International Division," Dec. 9, 1948, unclassified materials, Ford Archives. In practically the same form this report was presented to the Ford managers on Jan. 25, 1949 and is in Acc. 422, Bx. 1. In general the first version is used; the dollar sales however are taken from the second, since it included year-end figures.
17. FMC-US, Mins. Policy Com., Dec. 15, 1948 (Howard's proposals accepted); HF II to Sir Stanford Cooper, Apr. 25, 1949 in "England Dagenham FMC Ltd. Shares Dividend 1948–1949," FI; draft of Howard talk to University Club, Feb. 24, 1950, FI (no. of staff); S. African plant began operations Oct. 1948, FMC-Can. files; FMC-US, Mins. For. Ops. Com., July 15, 1948, Secty's off., FMC-US (approval Brazilian plant operation); Ford News Bureau Press Release, Apr. 20, 1949, Acc. 227, Bx. 3 (Mexican plans); interv. Hennessy, 1960 (his quote). Other plants are referred to earlier in the chapter. Fraine B. Rhuberry replaced Kopf. See Howard to Griffith, Apr. 1, 1949, Acc. 713, Bx. 12 for quote.
18. Crimmins, *Reminiscences* (English cars); intervs. H. A. Denne and Harold Mortimore, 1960 and 1961; interv. Nelson Bowe, Dearborn, May 11, 1960; import figs. from files, Export Dept. FMC-Eng.; Breech to Sir Rowland Smith, Dec. 29, 1948 in folder "Howard to Breech, Feb. 2, 1950," FI.
19. Lord Airedale to FMC-Eng. Stockholders, May 9, 1950 (figs. Eng. exports 1948, 1949); FMC-US *Annual Reports,* 1948–50 (American figs.); FMC-Can. export figs. (Canadian exports).
20. Howard to University Club (some of the problems); intervs. with FI personnel.
21. T. G. Eybye to Latin America mgrs., Dec. 28, 1949, FMC-Chile files, Santiago, Chile (gen. situation L.A.).
22. FMC-US, Mins. Bd. Dirs., Jan. 30, 1948, Secty's off., FMC-US (seeking larger control FMC-Can.); Bogdan to Howard, Aug. 26, 1948, unclassified data, Ford Archives (American control effected). In conversations with the authors, Canadian officials in 1961 referred to the "ripe plum," and their own attitude toward Howard's plans.
23. Howard to University Club (gen. and cut in personnel); Ford Interl., Mins. Bd. Dirs., July 15, 1949, Acc. 312, Bx. 12 (liquidation of Ford Interl.).
24. *Interford,* I, Oct. 1949, 2 (Israel); FMC-US, Mins. Bd. Dirs., Nov. 10, 1949 and FMC-Can., Mins. Bd. Dirs., Nov. 9, 1949 (pact of May 1 with FMC-Canada ratified); copy of agreement with FMC-Eng. about sale of continental Ford cos., in folder, "England-Guernsey Ford International Shares, 1949 (Apr. Dec.)," FI; FMC-US, *Annual Report 1949,* 24 (interests acquired by FMC-US); deptl. com. R. M. Campbell to A. W. Wedemyer, Apr. 10, 1950, in "Ford International, Agreements Relationships, 1948–1956," FI (same).
25. *Ibid.* (new agreements); FMC-Fr., Mins. Bd. Dirs., Oct. 18, 1949, Acc. 606, Bx. 3 (discussion of same).
26. N. A. Bogdan, "Dagenham Dividend—Schedule of Events," May 17, 1950, in folder, "England-Dagenham, FMC Ltd. Shares-Dividends, 1950," FI (Howard's difficulties); orgn. plang. data: on Sept 20, 1950, the Bd. of Dirs. accepted Howard's resignation, effective Jan. 1, 1951.
27. FMC-US, *Annual Report 1951* (1950 and 1951 foreign sales and profits); orgn. plang. off. files (Wieland's appt.).

CHAPTER 18

1. FMC-Eng., *Annual Report 1954* (Smith); FMC-Eng. prodn. figs. (Dagenham prodn.); *Motor Industry of Great Britain,* London, 1960, *passim* (world prodn.).

2. Intervs. Sir Patrick Hennessy, Aug. 1960 (quote); Lord Airedale to FMC-Eng. stockholders, May 1950 (taxation, quotas, banked-up orders); FMC-Eng. export figs.; *The Times* (London), *Survey of the British Motor Industry,* Oct. 1949, 19 (quote).

3. Lord Perry to stockholders, FMC-Eng. *Annual Report 1947* (lack of space); *The Times* (London), *Survey of the British Motor Car Industry,* Oct. 1950 (review of motor industry); Political and Economic Planning, *Motor Vehicles,* London, 1950, 63 (gen. restrictions); FMC-Eng. Mins. Policy Com., Feb. 6, 1951, FMC-Eng. (cond. of factory); Plant Data Bk., FMC-Eng. files (Langley, Rainham); Lord Airedale to FMC-Eng. stockholders, Apr. 27, 1949; FMC-Eng., *Annual Report 1951* and Sir Rowland Smith to stockholders, Mar. 28, 1951 (prodn. exports); Ford Ltd., Prospectus 1928 (character, location of plant).

4. FMC-Eng., Mins. Policy Com., Sept. 9, 1948, Oct. 24, 1949 (aid from govt.); Sir Patrick Hennessy to Dr. Wilkins, Sept. 1960 (comment on aid).

5. Interv. Sir Patrick Hennessy, 1960 (Consul and Zephyr); *The Times* (London), annual supplements on motor industry, postwar period, and G. Maxcy and A. Silberston, *The Motor Industry,* London, 1959, 114, 117 (other cars, prices); interv. T. N. Beckett, Sept. 7, 1960, *Motor* and *Autocar, passim,* and *The Times* (as in note 3 above, p. 19 (all on Consul and Zephyr); PEP, *Motor Vehicles,* 65 (taxes). The tax (previously explained) was changed in 1947 to one based on cylinder capacity, and in 1948 to a flat rate of £10 per car.

6. Intervs. J. P. Higgins, Sept. 1960 and W. Batty, July 12, 1961 (tractors); FMC-Eng. figs. on tractor prodn.; interv. Hennessy, 1960 (diesel engine). See also Chaps. 14 and 16 for Ford-Ferg. tractor, and for a detailed account of the American company's relations with Ferguson, Nevins & Hill, III, Chap. 14.

7. Sir Patrick Hennessy to Wilkins, Sept. 1960 (help from Dearborn officials); FMC-Eng., Mins. Policy Com. (first meeting Jan. 5, 1948); Maxcy & Silberston, 19–20 (formation of BMC) and 142–43 (Ford and Vauxhall profits); FMC-Eng. prodn. figs.

8. Interv. Sir Patrick Hennessy, 1960 and Hennessy to Wilkins, Sept. 1960 (relations with Dearborn); John H. Dunning, *American Investment in British Manufacturing Industry,* London, 1958, 107, 111 (influence Dearborn); FMC-Eng., Mins. Policy Com., July 20, 1950 (Hennessy's report); intervs. Beckett, Ronayne, Hennessy, and data FMC-Eng. Engineering Dept. (expansion Ford Ltd. engineering); FMC-Eng., Mins. Policy Com., Mar. 29, 1955 (long-range experimentation).

9. Interv. Beckett ("chief stylist," Anglia and Prefect; the Popular); FMC-Eng. *Annual Report 1953* (Popular, Smith quote).

10. *The Times* as in note 2 above (quote); FMC-Eng., *Annual Reports, 1953* and *1954* (Zodiac, engines).

11. Plant Data Bk., Mfg. office, FMC-Eng. (details of plant acquisition); N. I. Bogdan to Wieland, Feb. 17, 1951 in folder, "England-Dagenham, FMC Ltd" FI (quote on FMC-Eng. investments); interv. Hennessy, 1960, and Hennessy to Wilkins, Sept. 1960 (Briggs purchase); FMC-Eng., Mins. Extraordinary Shareholders Mtg., May 15, 1953 (approval of purchase).

12. Interv. Hennessy, 1960; FMC-Eng., Mins. Extraordinary Shareholders Mtg., May 15, 1953. Shortly before the Briggs purchase FMC-Eng. increased its capitalization from £9 million to £18 million to approximate its actual assets, providing for this by

the capitalization of certain reserves. This did not affect the proportion of shares held by the American company. But when new shares were issued to Briggs stockholders the capitalization was raised to £20 million, and the proportion was altered.

13. FMC-Eng., *Annual Report 1953* (expenditures); FMC-Eng., *Annual Report 1954* (assets); Dunning, 103 (rank of American firms).

14. Chap. 15, Section 5 (Vitger's earlier plans); Vitger to Roberge, June 1, 1948 and Howard to Vitger, June 4, 1948, Acc. 713, Bx. 20; Mgrs. Report to Dirs., July 16, 1948 in "Ger. Col. Mgrs. Monthly Ltrs., 1938–1948," FI; FMC-Ger., *Business Report 1948*, FI.

15. *Ibid.;* information from Ford-Werke, Cologne, Market Research off.

16. Wieland, Presentation to Prod. Plang. Com., Feb. 27, 1950, Prod. Plang. Com. Files, FMC-US.

17. Interv. Walter McKee, Apr. 28, 1960; German Co. files (Vitger's training); Wieland, Presentation and Mins. Prod. Plang. Com., Feb. 27, 1950 (Volkswagen and German situation generally).

18. Ford-Ger., *Business Reports, 1952, 1953.*

19. Ford-Ger., *Annual Report 1954* (comparative prodn. of firms); HF II, Speech at Cologne, June 25, 1954, Ed. Serv. Files, FMC-US (quote).

20. Interv. Maurice Dollfus, Sept. 13, 1960 (Lehideux); intervs. G. A. Panier, Marcel Cola, G. Lesto, June 1960; Acc. 6, Bx. 292 (Dollfus' age).

21. FMC-Fr. fin. records in files of Simca, Poissy; intervs. J. Gutzeit, Panier, Lesto, June 1960 (condns. in co.); FMC-US, Mins. Exec. Com., Oct. 15, 1952, Secty's off., FMC-US (Ford-US and loans).

22. Nevins & Hill, III, Chap. 12 (Whiz Kids); interv. Lesto (attitude toward Reith). Reith was thirty-eight when he came to FMC-Fr.

23. Intervs. Lesto, Panier, FMC-Fr., *Annual Reports 1953, 1954.* Dr. Wilkins saw the sketches for the Cardinal in the papers of G. A. Panier.

24. Intervs. Panier, Cola; FMC-US, Mins. Exec. Com., June 30, 1954 (approval of agreement); Orgn. Plang. off. Records, FMC-US (announcement of merger); François Depasse to Dr. Wilkins, Dec. 1960 (*"comme le mouton"*); conversations with various Ford execs. about the merger; Gunnar K. Myrdal, *An International Economy,* N.Y., 1956 (bkgnd. on European unity); interv. Sir Patrick Hennessy, Aug. 1960.

25. Interv. Lesto (on merger); FMC-US, Mins. Exec. Com., Oct. 21, 1954 (forming of "Ford (France) SA," approved); FMC-US, *Annual Report 1958* (sale of Simca holdings); Ford-Ger., *Annual Reports 1954, 1955* and intervs. in Cologne in 1960 (German prodn., conds., plans). After taxes, Ford gained $9 million from the sale of its Simca interest.

26. FMC-Can., *Annual Report 1950* (Sale to shareholders); Sale, Report to Mgt. Com., May 4, 1950, Secty's off., FMC-Can. ("outproduce and outmerchandise"); FMC-Can. sales figs. (percentage of total market).

27. Interv. Rhys M. Sale, May 1, 1961; FMC-Can., *Annual Reports.*

28. FMC-Can., sales figs. 1946–50; FMC-Can.; *Annual Reports* and Mins. Bd. Dirs.

29. FMC-Can. *Annual Reports 1951, 1952, 1954;* Sale interv.

30. Dept. of Trade, Melbourne, *The Australian Motor Vehicle Industry,* Melbourne, 1959, 20 (bkgnd.); FMC-Can., Mins. Mgt. Com., Dec. 4, 1950, Secty's off., FMC-Can. (covers Austl.).

31. *Austra-Ford Gazette,* mid-Oct. 1951, 2; FMC-Can., Mins. Bd. Dirs., Jan. 29, 1951 (outline of program) and Dec. 4, 1955 (on plans); Ford-Austl. stats., Overseas Divn., FMC-Can. (sales figs.); FMC-Can., *Annual Reports 1953, 1954,* interv. Sale, and FMC-Can., Mins. Bd. Dirs., Oct. 26, 1953; data in Orgn. Plang. off., FMC-US.

32. Intervs. Sale, May 1961 and Basil O. Stevenson, Apr. 26, 1961 (quote); data, Orgn. Plang. off., FMC-US (Spanish sale). The Ford postwar goal of full or controlling interest in foreign Ford companies is shown in Ford International correspondence during these years.

33. AMA, *Facts and Figures, 1956* (world prodn.); Ford-US, *Annual Report 1955* (FMC-Eng., FMC-Can., and Ford-Ger. figs.); FMC-Can., sales figs. (Ford-Austl.); Ford Interl. corresp. 1951–55, FI (Wieland).

34. HF II, Address to Inland Daily Press Assn., Feb. 17, 1953, Ed. Serv. Files, FMC-US (quote); HF II, Speech to Poor Richard Club, Jan. 16, 1954, *ibid.* (more trade, etc.).

CHAPTER 19

1. FMC-US, *Annual Reports 1956, 1960* (export stats.); Dept. of Com. & Labor, Bur. of Stats., *Foreign Commerce and Navigation,* Wash., 1907, II, 953, 507 (1906 imports and exports); subsequent vols. for comparative figs.; Automobile Manufacturers Association, *Automobile Facts and Figures* (avg. hourly wage; recent import/export figs.); *Ward's Report 1960* (1959 precentage market).

2. FMC-US, Prospectus on Ford Stock Offering, Apr. 1962, 10 (FMC-Can.'s market); Overseas Divn., FMC-Can. (percentages exported in 1930's); Royal Commission on Automotive Industry, *Report,* Ottawa, 1961, 11–12 (gen. conds. in Canada).

3. Generalizations are based on innumerable interviews with executives in the automobile industry in the United States, Canada, and Europe.

4. See Emile Benoit, *Europe at Sixes and Sevens,* N.Y., 1961, 227–28 for a perceptive comment on U.S. firms' "upgrading" their products for the domestic market and making them no longer competitive abroad. This was true in automobiles as well as refrigerators.

5. Programming Dept. (Miss Hartman), FMC-US (1954 Ford imports); James J. Welker to J. R. Davis, Mar. 30, 1954, "For. Prods. Br." FI (quote and staff branch); FMC-US, *Annual Report 1958* (17 cars). Ford offered 11 English Ford line models and 6 Taunus models.

6. R. S. McNamara, Exec. Com., Feb. 26, 1958, "FI-Exec. Coms. Jan.–June 1958," FI (MEL Divn. role); Programming Dept., FMC-US (Eng. imports); *Ward's Report 1961,* 167 (impact of compacts; L-M Divn. announcement); in 1962 the company had planned to introduce a small car in the United States (the Cardinal) with a German-Ford-built engine; but on careful consideration this vehicle was dropped from the 1963 U.S. Ford line; HF II, Speech on Foreign Competition, Apr. 15, 1961 (quote from HF II).

7. Benoît, *passim.* American interest in the Common Market and the European Free Trade Area is indicated by a FMC-US presentation in May 1959, "European Integration to Date," FI.

8. FMC-Eng., *Annual Reports 1955–1961;* Plant Data Book, Mfg. off., FMC-Eng.; FMC-Eng. prodn. figs.

9. Eng. Staff Presentation, Jan. 1960, Eng. off., FMC-Eng.

10. FMC-Eng., *Annual Report 1961;* FMC-US, *Annual Report 1961.*

11. Prodn. Stats., FMC-Ger.; Plant Tour 1960; FMC-Ger., *Business Reports 1955* ff.; Plant Eng. Dept., FMC-US (plant facilities and land at Genk); FMC-US, *Annual Report 1961* (capacity increase and cost).

12. Conversation J. Wilner Sundelson, Dearborn, May 22, 1962.

13. John S. Bugas, Presentation at Greenbriar, Jan. 12, 1961, FI; Prodn. figs., FMC-US; FMC-US, *Annual Report 1961* (German prodn.).

14. Bugas, Presentation (quote); Data in Mexico, Argentina, and Brazil (HF II's 1959 trip); in May 1959 FMC (Venezuela) S.A. was formed and also a subsidiary of it. Ford purchased land at Valencia and began construction of an assembly plant. See FMC-US, *Annual Reports 1959, 1961.* FMC-US, *Annual Report 1961* (chart shows new Colombian co.); HF II, Speech on Foreign Competition, Apr. 5, 1961 (quote).

15. H. Monteiro to Guilhermo Arinos, Mar. 16, 1951, Monteiro Papers, São Paulo; FMC-Brazil, Mgrs. Monthly Report, Apr. 19, 1951, FI.

16. "Brazil São Paulo, FM do S.A., Org. & Mgmt. Location Review" folder, FI; *Correio da Noite,* Feb. 9, 1953 (quote); *A Noite* (Rio de Janeiro), Jan. 30, 1953 and *Fôlha da Manha,* Jan. 7, 1953 (natl. show); FI Presentation to FMC-US, Bd. Dirs., Jan. 30, 1953, Secty's off., FMC-US (Dearborn attitude).

17. Sindicato da Industria de Tratores, Caminhoes, Automoveis, e Veículos Similares no Estado de São Paulo, *Industria Automobilistica Brasileira,* São Paulo, June 1960 (best overall description of the Brazilian automobile industry—its participants, its products, and its vital stats.); Proposals to FMC-US, Exec. Com., Oct. 10, 1956 and Jan. 16, 1957, FI (investment and Ford plans); H. Monteiro, Presentation to the Executive Group of the Automobile Industry, Jan. 31, 1957, "Local Manufacturing Trucks" folder, FI; Mfg. Staff (C. T. Alexander), FMC-US (plant data); FI stats. (Volkswagen *v.* Willys).

18. Intervs. J. Goulden, Dearborn, May 16, 1962 and Walter McKee, Dearborn, May 29, 1962; FI (rank in industry); FMC-US, *Annual Report 1960* (tractor program); *Industria Automobilistica Brasileira* (investments).

19. "Local Manufacturing" folders, FI (1950 discussions); FMC-US, Mins. Exec. Com., Nov. 4, 1953, Secty's off., FMC-US (*re:* tractor mfg. in Argentina); Exec. Com., Lilley and Bugas to FMC-US, Bd. Dirs., Apr. 8, 1959, FMC-Mex. files (gen. situation in Argentina); conversation, J. Wilner Sundelson, Dearborn, May 22, 1962 (US execs. reluctance).

20. Exec. Com., *op. cit.;* Mfg. Staff (C. T. Alexander), FMC-US (facilities); prodn. stats., FI.

21. FMC-US, *Annual Report 1960* (Credesco).

22. See Chapter 5. Actually, Henry Ford never kept faith with such utterances; many dollars were taken out of Latin America. In 1962, however, no Dearborn official would think of making comparable comments.

23. Commonwealth of Australia, Industries Divn., Dept. of Trade, *The Australian Motor Vehicle Industry,* Melbourne, 1959, 1 (quote); *Melbourne Herald,* Feb. 29, 1960, and *Wheels Motor Magazine,* Apr. 1960 (the public questions); Overseas Divn., FMC-Can. (percentages); FMC-Can., *Annual Reports 1959, 1960* (plant opening); FMC-US, *Annual Report 1960* (introduction of Austl. Falcon). *Australian Financial Review,* Mar. 31, 1960.

24. Nevins & Hill, III, *passim.*

25. Personnel data from Industrial Relations Dept., FI (the Brazilian and Argentine figs. are the peak numbers of Americans sent to the locales at any one time); intervs. Sundelson, McKee, Coulden, Lilley, 1960–62.

26. Exec. Com. HF II, Feb. 9, 1961; also speeches by HF II, Apr. 21, 1961 and Jan. 17, 1962.

27. Southwestern Legal Foundation, *Proceedings of the 1959 Institute on Private Investments Abroad,* N.Y., 1959, 265, 278, 571, and *Proceedings of the 1961 Institute,* N.Y., 1961, 154ff; Kingman Brewster, *Antitrust and American Business Abroad,* N.Y., 1958 (all on antitrust implications).

28. Interv. H. A. Denne, London, Aug. 31, 1960; interv. Sundelson, May 11, 1960.

29. Interv. Sundelson.

30. FMC-US *Annual Reports*. In 1959 FMC-US increased its holdings of the outstanding capital stock in FMC-Can. from 27.5 per cent to 75 per cent at a cost of approximately $149 million. To finance its expansion, FMC-Ger. increased its outstanding stock during 1955, as it had during 1954. By subscribing to shares not taken up by other stockholders, FMC-US during 1955 increased its stock holdings in the German company from 78 per cent to 84.1 per cent. In August 1957 the U.S. Ford company agreed to purchase bonds of the German unit, which would give Ford-Werke the capital needed for its expansion and integration. The U.S. company then offered to exchange these bonds for the publicly-owned German company stock. The offer was widely accepted, and the home company's holdings in Ford-Werke rose to 99 per cent.

31. Thomas Aitken, Jr., *A Foreign Policy for American Business*, N.Y., 1962, 105; Roy Blough, "Joint International Business Ventures in Less Developed Countries," in Southwestern Legal Foundation, *Proceedings of the 1960 Institute on Private Investments Abroad*, N.Y., 1960, 535.

32. HF II Speech, Jan. 17, 1962.

33. Acctg. Dept. FI (Ford investment); Dept. of Com. stats.

34. J. Wilner Sundelson, "Planning for the New Wave of Overseas Automotive Investment," not pub., n.d. [1962], FMC-US, *Annual Reports* 1958ff.; info. from FI.

35. FMC-US, *Annual Reports* 1958ff.

36. HF II, Speech on Foreign Competition, Apr. 5, 1961 (quote).

Index

Index

517

The manuscript was edited by Alexander Brede. The book was designed by Edgar Frank. The typeface for the text is Linotype Granjon designed by Claude Garamond and redesigned under the supervision of George W. Jones, 1928–31. The display face is Weiss Roman designed by Prof. E. R. Weiss and cut by Baur in 1926.

The book is printed on S. D. Warren's Olde Style Antique paper and bound in Columbia Mills' Riverside cloth. Manufactured in the United States of America.